1969

A STUDY OF
HISTORY

A STUDY OF HISTORY

BY

ARNOLD J. TOYNBEE

HON. D.LITT. OXON. AND BIRMINGHAM
HON. LL.D. PRINCETON, F.B.A.

*Director of Studies in the Royal Institute
of International Affairs
Research Professor of International History
in the University of London
(both on the Sir Daniel Stevenson Foundation)*

'Work . . . while it is day . . .'
JOHN IX. 4

'Nox ruit, Aenea . . .'
AENEID VI. 539

'Thought shall be the harder,
Heart the keener,
Mood shall be the more,
As our might lessens.'
THE LAY OF THE BATTLE OF MALDON

VOLUME III

*Issued under the auspices of the Royal Institute
of International Affairs*

OXFORD   UNIVERSITY   PRESS
LONDON   NEW YORK   TORONTO

Oxford University Press, Amen House, London E.C. 4

EDINBURGH GLASGOW NEW YORK TORONTO MELBOURNE
WELLINGTON BOMBAY CALCUTTA MADRAS CAPE TOWN

Geoffrey Cumberlege, Publisher to the University

FIRST EDITION	1934
SECOND EDITION	1935
SECOND IMPRESSION	1939
THIRD IMPRESSION	1945
FOURTH IMPRESSION	1948

CONTENTS
VOLUME III

III

THE GROWTHS OF CIVILIZATIONS

A. THE PROBLEM OF THE GROWTHS OF CIVILIZATIONS

The Arrested Civilizations

IN giving this chapter its title, are we not begging a question? And, if the question is raised, can we really maintain that the growths of civilizations present a problem at all? The problem of the geneses of civilizations is another matter. That problem is genuine beyond all doubt; and our attempts to solve it have exercised our minds severely. But if we may venture to suppose that these efforts have had any substantial measure of success, do we need to seek further? For does not any solution of the problem of birth dispose of the problem of growth *a priori*? When birth is once achieved, does not growth follow of itself? This is a question which has to be answered if our title is to stand. Let us turn, for an answer, to the empirical method of inquiry which has often stood us in good stead.

If we take a survey of civilizations that have duly come to birth—in contrast to those embryonic civilizations that have miscarried—do we find, as a matter of fact, that they have invariably grown thereafter in wisdom and in stature? Frequently—perhaps usually—they have gone on growing, no doubt. Our twenty-one specimens of this species of societies are cases in point. For although, in our day, all but seven of the twenty-one are extinct, and although the majority of these seven are now unmistakably in decay, it is evident, on the other hand, that even the shortest-lived and least successful of these twenty-one societies did achieve at least some measure of growth after it had come to birth. But the twenty-one developed civilizations[1] and the four abortive civilizations[2] are not the only examples of civilizations that an empirical survey reveals to us. If we now look further, we shall come across specimens of yet a third class. We shall find examples of civilizations which have not been abortive yet have not developed either, but have been arrested after birth. It is the existence of these arrested civilizations that justifies the title of the present chapter by presenting the problem which we have now set ourselves to solve. The first step

---

[1] See the list in vol. i, on p. 133, above.
[2] The Abortive Far Western Christian, Abortive Far Eastern Christian, Abortive Scandinavian, and Abortive Syriac. (See II. D (vii), vol. ii, pp. 322–94, above.)

towards solving it will be to collect as many specimens of arrested civilizations as we can.

We can readily lay hands on half a dozen specimens of the kind. Among the civilizations that have come to birth in response to physical challenges, there are the Polynesians and the Esquimaux and the Nomads. And, among the civilizations that have come to birth in response to human challenges, there are certain peculiar communities, like the 'Osmanlis in the Orthodox Christian World or the Spartans in the Hellenic World, which have been called into existence by local accentuations of the prevalent human challenges when these have been keyed up, through peculiar circumstances, to pitches of unusual severity. These are all of them examples of arrested civilizations; and we can see at once that they all present a picture of the same general predicament.

All these arrested civilizations alike have been immobilized in consequence of having attempted, and achieved, a *tour de force*. They are responses to challenges of an order of severity on the very borderline between a degree that still affords some stimulus and a degree that brings into operation the law of diminishing returns.[1]

In the imagery of our fable of the climbers' pitch,[2] the representatives of the arrested civilizations are like climbers who happen to have started to scale the precipice in places where they are brought up short, at an early stage, against beetling projections on the face of the cliff. In these circumstances, a timid or a clumsy climber might have lost his hold and fallen, while a more prudent or a less obstinate climber might have redescended to the ledge from which he had just taken off, in order to try his fortune again at another point, or else to rest, unambitiously, from his labours. These actual climbers, however, have been neither defeated, nor daunted, nor inspired with that wisdom which is the better part of valour, by the unexpected and formidable obstacles that they have encountered. They have accepted their challenge as they have found it, grasped the projecting rock, and levered themselves over it, outwards and upwards, with a movement of magnificent audacity and vigour and skill. But though the gesture is magnificent, it is not good climbing; for it entails a consequence which the expert climber is ever on the look out to foresee and to avoid. The expert climber is on his guard against making any move that will preclude him from moving on; and our over-audacious climbers cannot break this rule with impunity. They grapple with the jutting crag, only to find them-

---

[1] In concrete terms, they are responses to challenges of an intermediate degree of severity between the challenge that stimulated the Achaeans to create the Hellenic Civilization and the challenges which were just too severe to allow the Irish and the Norsemen to bring the Abortive Far Western Christian and the Abortive Scandinavian Civilization to birth.

[2] See II. B, vol. i, pp. 192–5, above.

selves, the next moment, clinging to the crag's projecting face in a rigid posture from which they dare not budge. Their superabundant skill and vigour and boldness is now all absorbed in a supreme effort to save themselves from falling, and they have no purchase, and no margin of energy, for climbing on until they have rounded the formidable projection and reached a normal surface again. Their motto—and eventual epitaph—is 'J'y suis, j'y reste'. They are performing an astonishing acrobatic feat, but a feat in the realm of Statics and not in the realm of Dynamics. In fact, these arrested civilizations, unlike the primitive societies, are real instances of 'peoples that have no history'.[1] Immobility is their unalterable posture, so long as they are what they are. They become what they are by grappling with the projecting crag; they remain what they are by gripping the crag so close that their once free and supple bodies mould themselves stiffly into all the contours of the rock; and they cease to be what they are when they either turn to stone and merge into the crag to which they have clung, or else drop, like a stone, from exhaustion.

This common posture of perilous immobility at high tension may be observed, in the several examples that we have cited, under the widest variety of conditions.

The Polynesians, for instance, ventured upon the *tour de force* of Oceanic voyaging. Their skill was to perform these stupendous voyages in frail open canoes. Their penalty has been to remain in an exact equilibrium with the Pacific—just able to cross its vast empty spaces, but never able to cross them with any margin of security or ease—until the intolerable tension has found its own relief by going slack, with the consequence that these former peers of the Minoans and the Vikings have degenerated into incarnations of the Lotus-Eaters[2] and the Doasyoulikes:[3] loosing their grip upon the Ocean and resigning themselves to be marooned, each in his own insular paradise, until the Western mariner comes at last from the ends of the Earth to exterminate them as he exterminates the Arctic hunters' seals or the prairie hunters' bison.[4] We need not dwell here upon the Polynesians' latter end, since we have touched upon it already apropos of Easter Island.[5]

[1] For the unrecorded, but not unenacted, history of the primitive societies, in the Yang-activity which must have preceded their present Yin-state, see I. C (iii) (e), vol. i, pp. 179–80, above.
[2] See II. D (i), vol. ii, pp. 22–3, above.
[3] See II. D (i), vol. ii, pp. 25–31, above.
[4] The decimation of the Polynesians by the Western 'beach-combers' has not, of course, been deliberate; yet the bullet and the harpoon which have done such execution among the non-human fauna of North America are not so deadly to Primitive Man as the germs of contagious diseases which the Westerner involuntarily brings—not to speak of the profound devitalizing influence which the Westerner's very spiritual presence exerts upon the Primitive who suddenly comes into social contact with him.
[5] See II. D (i), vol. ii, pp. 12–15, above.

The Esquimaux

As for the Esquimaux, 'the Palaeeskimo Culture was an original North Indian form of culture, the winter side of which had become specially and strongly developed by adaptation to the winter ice of the Arctic Ocean.[1] . . . The essential impulse to the development of the Eskimo Culture did not come until the Eskimo accustomed themselves to stay at or on the sea ice in the winter and hunt seals.'[2] This was the Esquimaux's *tour de force*; and the stimulus which excited them to achieve it seems, on the whole, more likely to have been the attraction of economic advantage than the pressure of human aggressors.

'It might be asked whether the pre-Eskimo advance towards the north, to the Tundra and the Archipelago, took place voluntarily or was due to pressure from southern neighbours. One will probably never be able to decide the question. But . . . it is to be strongly emphasized that life at the Arctic sea-coast, far from indicating a step backwards, in reality indicated a step forwards as regards economy, inasmuch as, in addition to the hunting of terrestrial mammals and summer fishing in the fresh waters, which was already known, the practice of hunting aquatic mammals was acquired as compensation for the ice fishing on lakes and streams. The contrast between this fishing on the ice of lakes, which was only resorted to in times of need, and the sea ice hunting of seals, gives a kind of standard of progress. One can then very well imagine that no pressure has been necessary, but that the pre-Eskimo have been tempted on to the coasts of the Arctic Ocean by natural conditions.'[3]

Whatever the historical incentive may have been, it is evident that, at some point in their history, the forefathers of the Esquimaux grappled audaciously with the Arctic environment and adapted their life to its exigencies with consummate skill.

'It is [the] natural conditions in the [Arctic] Archipelago, or, to put it more exactly, in the coast and sea regions between the mainland and the islands, which have been able to force a slow hunting people such as the ancient Eskimo must have been to undertake so thorough a cultural change as that which the modification of the Eskimo Culture must necessarily have required.'[4]

The skill evoked in the Esquimaux by this formidable problem of adaptation is justly celebrated. 'As regards certain dexterities, they really furnish an example of the utmost effort of human ability';[5] and, to prove the point, it is only necessary to recite the catalogue

---

[1] Steensby, H. P.: *An Anthropological Study of the Origin of the Eskimo Culture = Saertryk af Meddelelser om Grønland Liii* (Copenhagen 1916, Lunos), p. 186.
[2] Steensby, op. cit., p. 205. [3] Steensby, op. cit., p. 206.
[4] Steensby, op. cit., p. 168. For the evolution of the Esquimaux's most characteristic piece of technical apparatus, the kayak or sealskin canoe, from the North American Indian birch-bark canoe, see auct. cit., op. cit., p. 162.
[5] Steensby, op. cit., p. 41.

of the material appliances which the Esquimaux have elaborated or invented: 'kayak, umiak (women's boat), harpoon, and bird-dart with throwing board, the three-pronged salmon spear, the compound bow, strengthened by a backing of sinews, the dog sledge, the snow shoe, the winter house and snow house with the lamps for burning blubber oil, and the platform, the summer tent, and lastly the skin garments.'[1]

These are the outward and visible signs of an amazing feat of wit and will; yet

'in certain directions, for instance as regards social organization, the Eskimo display somewhat inferior development. But it is a question whether this inferior social differentiation is due to primitiveness, or whether it is not rather a result of the natural conditions under which the Eskimo have lived from time immemorial. No deep knowledge of the Eskimo Culture is needed to see that it is a culture which has been obliged to employ an immensely large part of its force simply to develop the means wherewith to gain a livelihood.'[2]

The penalty which the Esquimaux have had to pay for their audacity in grappling with the Arctic environment and compelling it to yield up its latent economic riches, has been the rigid conformation of their life to the annual cycle of the Arctic climate. 'All the bread-winners of the tribe are obliged to carry on different occupations at the different seasons of the year';[3] and the tyranny of Arctic Nature imposes almost as exacting a time-table upon the Arctic hunter as is imposed on any factory worker of the temperate zone by the human tyranny of 'scientific management'.[4] A distinguished student of the Eskimo Culture has made out this time-table, in two local variants, as follows:[5]

Arctic Eskimo Culture.

Season.	Place of Abode.	Occupation.	Principal Implements.	Dwelling.
Winter	In the beginning of winter, the coast land; later in the winter, the sea ice.	Hunting on the sea ice.	Dog sledge, Harpoon.	In the beginning of winter, earth house; later in the winter, snow house.
Summer	Inland.	Hunting on land and fishing in rivers.	Kayak, Lance, Bow and Arrow, Salmon Spear.	Tent.

[1] Steensby, op. cit., p. 43. For a systematic and detailed survey of the ingenuities by which the Esquimaux have adapted their life to their physical environment, see Weyer Jr., E. M.: *The Eskimos: Their Environment and Folkways* (New Haven 1932, Yale University Press), ch. iv.
[2] Steensby, op. cit., p. 42.   [3] Steensby, op. cit., p. 156.
[4] 'There is hardly another people in the world whose self-maintenance *mores* are so strictly regulated by the changes in the seasons.' Weyer, op. cit., p. 79.
[5] Steensby, op. cit., pp. 157–8. Compare the more elaborate chart in Weyer, op. cit., on pp. 80–2 (fig. 11), which illustrates the author's account of the 'Seasonal Life-Cycle of Eskimos' in ch. v, § 1.

Sub-Arctic Eskimo Culture.

Season.	Place of Abode.	Occupation.	Principal Implements.	Dwelling.
Winter	The coast.	Hunting in Ka-yaks.	Kayak, Harpoon, Umiak.	Earth house.
Summer	Inland (otherwise the coast).	Inland hunting, fishing in rivers.	Kayak, Lance, Salmon Spear, Bow and Arrow.	Tent.

Another Western anthropologist, who has lived through this Arctic annual cycle himself by sharing the life of the Esquimaux of Coronation Gulf, has described the sharp transition from one seasonal rhythm to another as he encountered it in his own personal experience.

'A fortnight's fishing exhausted the bay and compelled us to make another move. It mattered little which way we turned, for every ridge bounded a lake that contained both trout and salmon. But since the total catch would be greater if we scattered our forces and settled on different lakes, the families separated. . . .

'This dispersal of the individual families completed one-half of the strange cycle through which the Eskimos passed year after year. They reacted to the seasons, to their constantly changing environment, more than most of the inhabitants of our globe. The problem of obtaining life's basic needs—food, clothing, and shelter—left little time for other thoughts; and the seals and caribou, that furnished them with food, furnished also the materials for clothing and tents. In winter, when the land lay bare and silent beneath the snow, when the caribou had migrated south, when the twilight hours were brief and the nights long, the natives had banded together into tribes, and tribe combined with tribe to wrest a precarious livelihood from the frozen sea by united effort. Food had been common to all, and their snow-houses had adjoined each other so closely that the families seemed absorbed in the group. With the returning sun and lengthening days, Nature had recalled its life;[1] the seals had appeared on top of the ice, the caribou had come northward again, and the tribes of Eskimos had broken up into little bands. For a time they had lingered on the ice to hunt more seals; then, turning landward, they had pursued the caribou over the snow-covered hills and plains. Now the snow was vanishing, the caribou had scattered, and fish alone provided a sure livelihood until midsummer. So my party, like many another throughout the country, was dividing into its constituent households, each of which now toiled for itself alone. The tribe no longer existed; Society had dissolved into its first element, the family.'[2]

As we ponder over the scene which is here so vividly depicted,

[1] Weyer points out, in op. cit., on pp. 20 and 28–9, that in the Esquimaux's habitat the transition from winter to summer is abrupt, while the transition from summer to winter is relatively gradual.—A.J.T.

[2] Jenness, D.: *The People of the Twilight* (New York 1928, Macmillan Company), pp. 136–7.

we may be inclined to ask ourselves whether the Esquimaux are the Masters of Arctic Nature or her slaves. We shall meet with an equivalent question, and find it equally difficult to answer, when we come to examine the lives of the Spartans and the 'Osmanlis. Meanwhile, we have still to consider the fate of another arrested civilization which has been evoked by a physical challenge, before we pass on to examine those which human challenges have brought to birth.

The Nomads

The *tour de force* of the Esquimaux has been to take up the challenge of the Ice and the *tour de force* of the Polynesians to take up the challenge of the Ocean. The Nomad, who has taken up the challenge of the Steppe, has had the audacity to grapple with an equally intractable element; and indeed, from the social (as distinct from the physiographical) point of view, the Steppe, with its surface of grass and gravel, actually bears a greater resemblance to 'the unharvested sea'[1] than it bears to terra firma that is amenable to hoe or plough. Steppe-surface and water-surface have this in common, that they are both accessible to Man only as a pilgrim and a sojourner. Neither offers him anywhere on its broad expanse (apart from the islands and oases) a place where he can rest the sole of his foot and settle down to a sedentary existence. Both provide strikingly greater facilities for travel and transport than those parts of the Earth's surface upon which human communities are accustomed to live in permanence;[2] but both exact (as the penalty for trespassing upon them) the necessity of constantly 'moving on', or else 'moving off' their surface altogether and finding some standing ground upon terra firma somewhere beyond the coasts which respectively surround them. Thus there is a real similarity between the Nomadic horde which annually follows the same orbit of summer and winter pasture-ranges, and the fishing-fleet which cruises from bank to bank according to the season; between the convoy of merchantmen which exchanges the products of the opposite shores of the sea, and the camel-caravan by which the opposite shores of the Steppe are linked with one another; between the water pirate and the desert raider; and between those explosive movements of population which impel Norsemen or Minoans or Crusaders to take to their ships and to break like tidal waves upon the coasts of Europe or the Levant, and those other movements which impel Imoshagh or Arabs or Scyths or Turks or Mongols to

[1] 'Unharvested' (ἀτρύγετος) is one of the stock epithets of the sea in the Homeric Epic:
[2] For the light thrown upon this question of relative 'conductivity' by a study of the geographical distribution of languages, see III. A, Annex I, below.

swing out of their annual orbit on the Steppe and to break, with
equal violence and equal suddenness, upon the settled lands of
Egypt or 'Irāq or Russia or India or China.

It will be seen that the Nomads', like the Polynesians' and the
Esquimaux's, response to the challenge of Physical Nature is a *tour
de force*; and in the case of the Nomads the historical incentive to
this *tour de force* is not, as in the case of the Esquimaux, altogether
a matter of conjecture. We are entitled to infer that Nomadism
was evoked by the same challenge that evoked the Egyptiac and
the Sumeric civilizations and that drove the forefathers of the
Shilluk and the Dinka into Equatoria and the forefathers of the
Norsemen into Scandinavia. Nomadism, likewise, may be conceived
as having arisen in response to the searching challenge of desiccation; and we have touched upon its possible origins already incidentally, in inquiring into the origins of the fluvial cultures.[1] The
origins of the Nomadic Civilization, as well as those of the sedentary
civilizations which have arisen in the same arid zone, are illuminated
by the discoveries of modern Western Archaeology;[2] and the clearest light which we have upon Nomadism, up to date, has been
thrown by the researches of the Pumpelly Expedition in the Transcaspian oasis of Anau:[3] a site in the extreme south-western corner
of the Eurasian Steppe, at the foot of the north-eastern escarpment
of the Iranian Plateau.

In the Transcaspian oases, as in the river-valleys of the Lower
Tigris and Euphrates and the Lower Nile,[4] we find the challenge of
desiccation, in its first incidence, stimulating certain communities
which had formerly lived entirely by hunting to eke out their livelihood under less favourable conditions by taking to a rudimentary
form of agriculture.

'With the gradual shrinking in dimensions of habitable areas and the
disappearance of herds of wild animals, Man, concentrating on the oases
and forced to conquer new means of support, began to utilize the native
plants; and from among these he learned to use seeds of different grasses
growing on the dry land and in marshes at the mouths of larger streams

---

[1] See II. C (ii) (b) 2, vol. i, pp. 304–5, above.

[2] On this point, a cautionary note has been communicated to the writer of this Study
by Mr. G. F. Hudson: 'Nomadism has to be carefully distinguished from the keeping
of domestic animals by sedentary folk, and the archaeological evidence only refers to the
latter. I think it is very probable that both intensive agriculture and animal-domestica-
tion began in oases as a result of a process of desiccation, namely the drying-up of North
Africa, Arabia, and Iran when the climatic belts shifted north at the end of the Ice Age—
though even this is rather conjectural. Nomadism, on the other hand, was a development about which we have not, and cannot have, satisfactory archaeological evidence.'

[3] Pumpelly, R.: *Explorations in Turkestan: Expedition of 1903* = Carnegie Institution
Publication No. 26 (Washington, D.C., 1905, Carnegie Institution); auctor idem:
Explorations in Turkestan: Expedition of 1904: Prehistoric Civilizations of Anau =
Carnegie Institution Publication No. 73 (Washington, D.C., 1908, Carnegie Institution,
2 vols.).

[4] See II. C (ii) (b) 2, vol. i, pp. 305–18, above.

on the desert. With the increase of population and its necessities, he learned to plant the seeds, thus making, by conscious or unconscious selection, the first step in the evolution of the whole series of cereals.'[1]

Whether agriculture in Transcaspia was an independent invention or a loan from the Indus Valley or from Sumeria is not apparent. Archaeology simply reveals that, at Anau North Kurgan, 'they cultivated cereals from the beginning'[2] and that agriculture was already the mainstay of the earliest inhabitants that have left their mark on the local archaeological record,[3] though 'at first, besides cultivating the soil, they' still 'hunted wild animals'.[4]

Thus, in Transcaspia, agriculture supervened directly upon hunting, and thereafter these two methods of obtaining a subsistence were practised there simultaneously side by side. The most significant fact, however, which archaeological research at Anau had brought to light is the fact that 'the agricultural stage preceded domestication and [thus preceded] the Nomadic shepherd stage of civilization'.[5]

'At the time when the lowest layers of the North Kurgan at Anau were formed, Man lived in this region entirely without domestic animals. The mighty wild ox (*Bos namadicus* Falconer and Cautley) and the small wild horse—possibly in the form that Wilckens thought he discovered among the finds of Maragha in Persia, or in that of *Equus przewalskii*—roamed on the steppes and the oases of the Kara Kum desert and sought shelter in the forest which probably then occupied the valleys and slopes of the Kopet Dagh. There lived, too, the large-horned wild sheep (*Ovis vignei arkal* Lyddeker) and the gazelle (*Gazella subgutturosa* Gueldenstedt). From the absence of all stone weapons in the oldest period, we may conclude that Man lived on a friendly footing with these animals and that he could gain possession of them only by depriving the wolves of their prey or by the use of fire-hardened wooden weapons. . . . It would be guess-work to attempt to picture the method of domestication and to assume . . . that the wild horse, the wild sheep, and the wild ox voluntarily (or compelled by the necessity of food from outside the oasis) approached human dwellings in order to graze on the weeds and other plants, and so were gradually brought into companionship with Man, who then assumed the care of their nourishment. We know only that after the accumulation of the lowest ten feet of the strata in the North Kurgan this same ox occurs in an almost equally large, but certainly a domesticated form, becoming more and more frequent in the higher

[1] Pumpelly, op. cit., *Expedition of 1904*, vol. i, pp. 65–6.
[2] Pumpelly, op. cit., *Expedition of 1904*, vol. i, p. 38; cp. p. 67.
[3] Pumpelly, op. cit., *Expedition of 1904*, vol. i, p. 39.
[4] 'While the bones of these, as well as those of the animals which they domesticated later, show that they ate the flesh of these, including the pig and probably also the fox and the wolf, these bones are not sufficiently abundant to prove that meat formed by any means the chief part of their diet.' (Op. cit., loc. cit.)
[5] Pumpelly, op. cit., *Expedition of 1904*, vol. i, p. xxviii.

strata, when the horse and the sheep also pass over into the domesticated condition.'[1]

Thus the first turn of the climatic screw in Eurasia not only stimulated a society which had formerly lived by hunting to take to agriculture. It also had another—indirect but not less important—effect upon the social history of these *ci-devant* hunters who had made this first successful response to its challenge. By stimulating them to turn to agriculture instead of hunting as their staple source of food-supply, it gave them the opportunity to enter into a wholly new relation towards wild animals. For the art of domesticating wild animals, which the hunter, by the very nature of his occupation, is unable to develop beyond narrow limits, has vastly greater potentialities in the hands of the agriculturist. The hunter may conceivably domesticate the wolf or jackal with whom he disputes or shares his prey by turning the wild beast into a partner in the hunter's own human predatory activities. But it is virtually inconceivable that the hunter should succeed in domesticating the game which is his quarry and his victim. It is not the hunter with his hound but the *ci-devant* hunter, transformed into an agriculturist with his watch-dog, who has it in his power to accomplish the further transformation which brings into existence the shepherd with his sheep-dog. The agriculturist enjoys a double advantage for this purpose. Unlike the hunter, he is not preying upon the wild animals and therefore is not inspiring them with a deadly fear of his presence; and, unlike the hunter again, he possesses food-supplies which are attractive to ruminants like the ox and the sheep, which 'would not, like dogs, be attracted by meat or other products of a hunting or fishing life'.[2]

Archaeological research at Anau indicates that this further step in social evolution had been accomplished in Transcaspia by the time when Physical Nature gave her screw its second turn. The first spasm of desiccation had found Eurasian Man a hunter and nothing else; the second spasm found him a sedentary cultivator and stock-breeder, with his hunting reduced to a subsidiary means of livelihood. In these circumstances, the challenge of desiccation, when it was now redelivered with greater insistence than before, evoked two new and diverse human reactions. By achieving the domestication of ruminants, Eurasian Man had potentially recovered the mobility which he had forfeited in his previous metamorphosis from a hunter into a cultivator; and, in response to the fresh incidence of the old challenge, he made use of his new-found mobility in two quite different ways.

[1] Duerst, J. U., in Pumpelly, op. cit., *Expedition of 1904*, vol. ii, p. 435.
[2] Duerst in Pumpelly, op. cit., *Expedition of 1904*, vol. ii, p. 437.

Some of the Transcaspian oasis-cultivators simply used their mobility in order to emigrate progressively—moving ever further on as the climatic trend towards desiccation increased in severity at the heart of the Steppe and in range on the periphery—so as always to keep abreast of a physical environment in which they could continue to practise their existing way of life without being constrained to revolutionize it once again.

'The establishment of the first domestic breeds of pigs, long-horned cattle, large sheep, and horses was followed by a deteriorating climate which changed these to smaller breeds. The climatic deterioration, by diminishing the productivity of the fully-peopled oases, caused unrest and migrations of agriculturists. . . . Dr. Duerst identifies the second breed of sheep [at Anau] with the turbary sheep (Torfschaf) and the pig with the turbary pig (Torfschwein), which appear towards the end of the Neolithic period in the Swiss lake-dwellings and other Neolithic stations of Europe, already as domestic animals and unaccompanied by any transitional forms that might indicate local origins. These animals must therefore have been descendants of those domesticated on the oases of the Anau district. The turbary breed was established not later than towards the end of the oldest settlement of the North Kurgan. . . . It was formed during the part of the climatic cycle in which prevailed those conditions, unfavourable to nutrition, to which the breed owed its stunted character. Its characteristic features became firmly fixed during the subsequent existence of many generations after transference to a Nomadic life on the arid plains during the dry extreme of the cycle. And the firm establishment of the characteristics of the breed is proved by the persistence down to the present time; for it still exists at one point in the high Alps of the Grisons in Switzerland, and in Wales.'[1]

This was one reaction to the recurring challenge of desiccation in Eurasia. But these cultivators and stock-breeders who trekked away across the withering Steppes with their seed-corn and their cattle, in order to find new homes where they could sow and reap and breed and pasture under the old conditions, had brethren who parted company with them at this point in order to respond to the same challenge in a more audacious fashion. These other Eurasians likewise abandoned the now untenable oases and launched them-

[1] Pumpelly, op. cit., *Expedition of 1904*, vol. i, pp. 67–8. Mr. G. F. Hudson comments as follows: 'In this passage it seems to be suggested that the pig of Neolithic stations in Europe (turbary pig) was brought by emigrants from the Anau district via the desiccated Steppe. But swine-breeding is absolutely unknown to Steppe-Nomadism, for pigs cannot be kept on the Steppe at all unless they are specially fed. Swine-breeding has in historical times been characteristic of forest regions at both ends of the Eurasian Steppe (in Europe and in China and Manchuria), but not at all of the Steppe itself. Thus if, as Duerst holds, the Anau pig is the turbary pig, it must have come from the Anau district by way of Northern Iran and Asia Minor—which is otherwise probable in view of the southern affinities of the early "Danubian" culture.' [For this highland route of migration, see II. C (ii) (b) 2, vol. i, pp. 324–7, above.—A.J.T.] 'Or it may be that both the Anau and the Swiss breed were derived originally from a culture-centre west of Anau; so very little of Asia Minor and Transcaucasia has as yet been explored archaeologically. Anyway, I protest against the pig being brought across the Steppes!'

selves and their families and their flocks and their herds upon the
inhospitable surface of the Steppe. But these other men did not
embark upon the Steppe as timid fugitives seeking to reach and
pass its boundaries and so escape from its clutches. They abandoned their former staple occupation of agriculture, as their agricultural forefathers had once abandoned their former staple occupation
of hunting, and staked their existence upon their latest-acquired
economic art, which, this time, was the art of stock-breeding. They
flung themselves upon the Steppe not in order to escape beyond its
bounds, but to make themselves at home upon it *en permanence* and
to wrest a livelihood from it under physical conditions which were
more inimical to life than any which had yet prevailed on the Steppe
since Man had first set foot on it. 'Through the accomplished
domestication of ruminants, men obtained freedom of motion for
travelling with cattle after good pasture, and commenced a Nomadic
life. This must be the real explanation of the origin of the wandering peoples.'[1]

It will be seen that the Nomad's response to the challenge of
recurring and increasing desiccation is a *tour de force* indeed. At
the first onset of desiccation, the Nomad's pre-agricultural forefathers had abandoned their hunting-grounds on the Steppe and
had retreated to the oases, where they took to agriculture as their
staple source of food supply and looked to their former hunting
grounds for no more than a subsidiary supply from that time
onwards. And now, when the rhythmic process of desiccation, in
its next onset, has made life still more difficult in the oases, and
more difficult on the Steppe *a fortiori*, the patriarchs of the Nomadic
Civilization audaciously return to the Steppe in order to wring out
of it, now, no mere subsidiary supply but their entire livelihood—
and this under climatic conditions under which the hunter and the

---

[1] Duerst, in Pumpelly, op. cit., *Expedition of 1904*, vol. ii, p. 437. Duerst also notes, in
loc. cit., that 'among the Turkomans of to-day occur also cultivators of soil and breeders
of cattle designated as Chomru and Chorva who intermarry and whose children choose
either the life of Nomads or of farmers'. In a communication to the writer of this
Study, Mr. G. F. Hudson questions whether the hypothesis of a second turn of the
climatic screw (see p. 10, above) is necessary to account for the transformation of the
sedentary stock-breeders who had come into existence in the oases into the Nomadic
stock-breeders on the Steppes. 'We have no date, even approximate, established for the
beginning of Nomadism, and we do not know of any period of desiccation which would
be adequate thus to displace the oasis-dwellers *after* the winding-up of the Ice Age—
unless it be the so-called Sub-Boreal period; and this is too late, as the Steppe seems
already to be full of Nomads at this time. The facts can surely be explained just as well
by supposing an analogy with the case of the Esquimaux, which you have put convincingly. The Esquimaux launched themselves on the Arctic ice, not because there
was a spread of the ice (which would correspond to the desiccation hypothesis for
Nomadism), but because they found a way of living off the ice which had previously been
uninhabitable. In the same way, when animals had once been domesticated (the original
domestication having been probably due to the desiccation, as you suggest), the herdsmen would sooner or later have found that by migrating so as to use seasonal pasture
they could live off the Steppe, which had previously been either uninhabited or thinly
peopled by roaming hunters. Thus no *second* desiccation is necessary for the theory.'

cultivator alike would find life on the Steppe quite impossible. The Nomad grapples with the arid Steppe in the strength of his new-found pastoral art; but, in order to practise this art success-fully under these exceedingly exacting conditions, he has to develop a special skill; and, in order to exercise this skill, he has also to develop special moral and intellectual powers.

When we compare the civilization of the Nomad who has aban-doned agriculture and has held his ground on the Steppes with the civilizations of his brethren who have preserved their agricultural heritage by changing their habitat, we shall observe that Nomadism displays a superiority over Agriculture in several ways.

In the first place, the domestication of animals is manifestly a higher art than the domestication of plants, inasmuch as it is a triumph of human wit and will over a less tractable material. The power of physical locomotion and the direction of this power by volition are the two main points in which Fauna differs from Flora; and these two characteristics, which Man's fellow-animals share with Man himself, evidently make the Animal Kingdom a less easy realm than the Vegetable Kingdom for Man to conquer. In other words, the shepherd is a greater virtuoso than the husbandman, and this truth has been expressed in a famous passage of Syriac mythology.

'Adam knew Eve his wife; and she conceived, and bare Cain. . . . And she again bare his brother Abel. And Abel was a keeper of sheep, but Cain was a tiller of the ground. And in process of time it came to pass that Cain brought of the fruit of the ground an offering unto the Lord. And Abel, he also brought of the firstlings of his flock and of the fat thereof. And the Lord had respect unto Abel and to his offering; but unto Cain and to his offering he had not respect.'[1]

In fact, the art practised by Abel, the afterborn, is not only posterior in the time of its invention to the art of Cain, the elder brother; and it is not only an art of greater skill and greater difficulty. Nomadism is also superior to Agriculture economically; and from this technical standpoint it is comparable not so much with Agri-culture itself as with Industrialism: another newfangled economic system which, like Nomadism, has differentiated itself out of a rudimentary agricultural economy in course of time and in response to a novel challenge. Whereas the cultivator produces raw materials which he can consume directly, the Nomad, like the Industrialist, makes his living out of raw materials which are of no utility to Man until they have been deliberately transformed. The cultivator lives off artificial grasses which he eats himself. The Nomad manages to live off natural grasses which he cannot eat himself—the coarse

[1] Gen. iv. 1–5.

and scanty herbage of the Steppe—by causing these non-human
foodstuffs to be eaten by his tame animals and then feeding himself on these animals' milk and flesh, and clothing himself in their
wool and hides.

And this indirect utilization of the vegetation of the Steppe
through an animal medium makes demands on human wit and will
which go far beyond the bare knowledge of the domesticator's art.
If a shepherd or herdsman who had grown up in a sedentary
society were suddenly put in charge of the Nomad's flocks and
herds in the Nomad's environment, he would find himself almost
as helpless as a vine-dresser or a ploughman; for the shepherd of
the Steppes has no meadows to yield him hay for winter fodder, and
no brother-husbandman to provide him with cattle-food by artificial cultivation, and no brother-industrialist to transform an unwieldy truss of soya-beans into handily portable oil-cake. In season
and out of season, the Nomad must find subsistence for his cattle
from the natural vegetation of the barren and parsimonious Steppe;
and he can only find it by adapting his life and his movements
meticulously to the vagaries of a severe and unfriendly physical
environment. He must manœuvre himself and his family and
his flocks and his herds over the vast spaces of the Steppe from
winter-pasture to summer-pasture and from summer-pasture back
to winter-pasture again in conformity with the climatic and vegetational year-cycle; and the Nomad patriarch cannot wrest victory
out of this annual economic campaign without exercising—and
exacting from the human beings and animals under his patriarchal
authority—those virtues of forethought and self-control and physical and moral endurance which a military commander exercises, and
exacts from his troops, when Man is at war with Man and not with
Physical Nature.

Thus the material *tour de force* of Nomadism demands, from
those who take the responsibility on their shoulders, a rigorously
high standard of character and behaviour. They must combine the
pastoral with the military virtues. They must know, by sure intuition, when to be benevolent and when to be severe; when to be
prudent and when to be prompt in action. It is no wonder that the
Christian Church has found in the everyday life of the Nomadic
Civilization a symbol for the highest Christian ideal: the image of
'the Good Shepherd'.[1] It is also no wonder that the very achievement of so great a *tour de force* should have doomed the society that

---

[1] For the Nomadic origin of this image, see II. D (vii), vol. ii, p. 317, footnote 1,
above. It is found alike in the Semitic languages of the Afrasian Nomads (e.g. the Arabic
راعٍ) and in the Indo-European languages of the Eurasian Nomads (e.g. the Greek
ποιμένα λαῶν).

has accomplished it to atone for its audacity by paying a penalty of equivalent magnitude.

The Nomads' penalty is in essence the same as the Esquimaux's. The formidable physical environment which they have succeeded in conquering has insidiously enslaved them in ostensibly accepting them as its masters. The Nomads, like the Esquimaux, have become the perpetual prisoners of an annual climatic and vegetational cycle;[1] and in acquiring the initiative on the Steppe they have forfeited the initiative in the World at large. The Nomads have not indeed passed across the stage of the histories of civilizations without making their mark. From time to time they have broken out of their own domain into the domains of neighbouring sedentary civilizations, and on some of these occasions they have momentarily carried all before them and have turned their sedentary neighbours' lives upside down; but these outbreaks have never been spontaneous. When the Nomad has issued out of his Steppes and has trespassed upon the cultivator's garden, he has not been moved by a deliberate intention to depart from his customary cyclic annual manœuvres. The violence of his occasional aberrations is not the expression of a demonic will-power, but the effect of powerful external forces which the Nomad is obeying mechanically. There are two such external forces to which he is subject: one force which pushes, and another force which pulls. The Nomad is occasionally pushed off the Steppe by a fresh turn of the climatic screw which intensifies the pressure to a degree which even the trained and hardened steppe-dweller cannot endure; and again he is occasionally pulled out of the Steppe by the suction of a social vacuum which has arisen in the domain of some adjacent sedentary society through the operation of historic processes, such as the breakdown and disintegration of a sedentary civilization, which are quite extraneous to the Nomad's own experiences. A survey of the great historic interventions of the Nomads in the histories of the sedentary civilizations seems to show that these interventions can all be traced to one or other of these two mechanical causes, and that they are not attributable to any active and positive responses, on the Nomads' part, to challenges arising out of any inner evolution in their own Nomadic life.[2]

Thus, in spite of these occasional eruptions out of the Steppe and

---

[1] In one sense, the Nomads are freer than the Esquimaux; for, 'unlike pastoral peoples, who lead their domesticated animals in quest of grazing grounds and water, the Eskimos are themselves led hither and thither by the animals, which follow their natural instincts'. (Weyer, op. cit., p. 99.) 'It cannot be maintained, however, simply from the failure of the Eskimo to domesticate the caribou, for instance, that he is culturally inferior to all pastoral peoples. His indirect mastery over the animals in their wild condition displays a more highly developed cultural adaptation than do the simple adjustments of some herding peoples.'

[2] A survey of this kind is attempted below in Part III. A, Annex II.

incursions into the field of historical events, Nomadism is essentially a society without a history. Once launched on its annual orbit, the Nomadic horde revolves thereafter round the same identic track and might continue to revolve *in saecula saeculorum* if an external force against which Nomadism is ultimately defenceless did not eventually bring the horde's movement to a standstill and its life to an end. This force is the pressure of the sedentary civilizations round about; for although the Lord may have respect for Abel and his offering and not for Cain and his, no power can save Abel from being slain by Cain in revenge.[1]

There is, indeed, a primordial antipathy and misunderstanding between the cultivator and the Nomad which has been observed in the life by a recent Western investigator in Manchuria:

'Within Manchuria, . . . while the Manchus have amalgamated themselves with the Chinese, there persists a profound cleavage between the Manchu-Chinese amalgamation and the still practically intact Mongol mass. What emerges from this is a realization of the profound power of culture—the way of life—in comparison with the factors of Race and Environment. . . . There is little difference, in physical racial type, between the majority of Northern Chinese and the majority of Mongols. . . . It is often possible to mistake a Chinese in Mongol costume for a Mongol, or a Mongol in Chinese costume for a Chinese. On the other hand, when it is possible to tell them apart, . . . it is only possible because of differences in stance, movement, expression, manner, which are intangible in the material sense but unmistakable. They are not differences of the physique itself, but of the life within the physical structure. Yet these intangibles, which belong to outlook, culture, feeling, and the way of life, establish a cleavage.'[2]

The causes of this social and moral cleavage can be laid bare by analysis, which makes it apparent that the relation between the cultivator and the Nomad is not unlike the relation between the landsman and the seaman.

'The Nomad moves in an annual orbit, and drives his herds each season over the ground on which he has pastured them at the same season the year before. His perpetual motion is not a symptom of waywardness and perversity. It is as scientific as the agriculturist's rotation of crops or performance of different operations in different fields at different times of year. Both are perpetually shifting the scene of their activities in order not to exhaust a particular parcel of ground. There is only a quantitative difference in the range of their oscillation, conditioned by the difference between their media of productivity. The Nomad, ranging widely in order to convert grasses into human food through chemical transformations in the bodies of tame animals, regards

[1] Gen. iv. 6–8.
[2] Lattimore, O.: *Manchuria Cradle of Conflict* (New York 1932, Macmillan), pp. 70–1 and 299–300.

the agriculturist as a stick-in-the-mud. The agriculturist, raising edible seeds and roots in sufficient quantities out of a much smaller area of land, regards the Nomad as a vagabond.

'There would be nothing more in this than the commonplace mutual contempt of different trades, if the frontiers between Nomad's land and Peasant's land were stable. On his own ground, each of them is following that mode of life which the experience of generations has shown to be economically the most productive. He is in equilibrium with his environment and therefore more or less harmless and amiable. In fact, the Nomad who visits the Peasant or the Peasant who visits the Nomad at home is generally agreeably surprised at the courtesy of his reception.[1] ... The traditional bitterness between Peasant and Nomad arises from a physical cause for which neither is to blame. Their respective environments and the frontiers between them are subject to periodic change.

'Recent meteorological research indicates that there is a rhythmic alternation, possibly of world-wide incidence, between periods of relative desiccation and humidity,[2] which causes alternate intrusions of Peasants and Nomads into one another's spheres. When desiccation reaches a degree at which the Steppe can no longer provide pasture for the quantity of cattle with which the Nomads have stocked it, the herdsmen swerve from their beaten track of annual migration and invade the surrounding cultivated countries in search of food for their animals and themselves. On the other hand, when the climatic pendulum swings back and the next phase of humidity attains a point at which the Steppe becomes capable of bearing cultivated roots and cereals, the Peasant makes his

[1] The sedentary observer usually paints the Nomad in dark colours because he usually comes across him in a hostile relation: either as an aggressor to be anathematized or else as a victim of aggression who has to be given a bad name in order that the wrong which is being committed against him may be justified. (On this, see further the footnote on p. 18, below.) There are, however, a number of descriptions of the Nomad at home which, although they come from the hands of sedentary observers, are nevertheless surprisingly different from the usual picture of the 'Tartarean' Tatar or the hideous Hun; and since the authors of these descriptions are not only describing the Nomad in his native environment, but are themselves the children of several different sedentary civilizations and have written their accounts quite independently of one another, at wide intervals of space and time, there is a strong presumption that, in so far as these pictures of the Nomad agree with one another, they are likely to be more faithful portraits than the usual caricature.

The following references are offered as samples: Homer, *Iliad*, xiii, ll. 5–6: 'Those splendid horse-dairy-farmers the Abioi, who live on a milk diet and are the justest of Mankind'; Hippocrates: *De Aeribus, Aquis, et Locis*, ch. xviii; Herodotus, Bk. IV, ch. xlvi; de Rubruquis, Frater Willielmus: *Itinerarium Anno Gratiae 1253 ad Partes Orientales*, ch. iii; Marco Polo, ch. lii; Huc, l'Abbé: *Souvenirs d'un Voyage dans la Tartarie, le Thibet et la Chine pendant les années 1844, 1845, et 1846* (Paris 1850, Le Clere, 2 vols); Atkinson, T. W.: *Oriental and Western Siberia: A Narrative of Seven Years' Explorations and Adventures in Siberia, Mongolia, the Khirgiz Steppes, Chinese Tartary and Part of Central Asia* (London 1858, Hurst and Blackett). The aforementioned works are all descriptive of the Nomads of the Eurasian Steppe. For their Afrasian fellow Nomads who range the North Arabian Steppe, see the Pentateuch, *passim*, and, among modern Western observers, above all Doughty, C. M.: *Travels in Arabia Deserta*, 2nd ed. (London 1931, Cape, 2 vols.) and the abridgement entitled *Wanderings in Arabia* (London 1908, Duckworth, 2 vols.). For the Afrasian Nomads who range the Sahara, see Rodd, F. R.: *The People of the Veil: The Wandering Tuareg Tribes* (London 1926, Macmillan).

[2] See Dr. Ellsworth Huntington's works, *passim*, but especially *The Pulse of Asia* (Boston and New York 1907, Houghton Mifflin) and *The Climatic Factor as illustrated in Arid America* (Washington, D.C., 1914, Carnegie Institution). In this 'Study of History', the phenomenon of climatic periodicity is discussed further in Part III. A, Annex II, below.

counter-offensive upon the pastures of the Nomad. Their respective
methods of aggression are very dissimilar. The Nomad's outbreak is as
sudden as a cavalry charge, and shatters sedentary societies like the
bursting of some high explosive. The Peasant's is an infantry advance.
At each step he digs himself in with mattock or steam plough, and
secures his communications by building roads or railways. The most
striking recorded examples of Nomad explosion are the intrusions of the
Turks and Mongols, which occurred in what was probably the last dry
period but one. An imposing instance of Peasant encroachment is the
subsequent eastward expansion of Russia. Both types of movement are
abnormal, and each is extremely unpleasant for the party at whose
expense it is made. But they are alike in being due to a single uncon-
trollable physical cause.[1]

'The relentless pressure of the Cultivator is probably more painful in
the long run, if one happens to be the victim of it, than the Nomad's
savage onslaught. The Mongol raids were over in two or three generations; but the Russian colonization, which has been the reprisal for them,
has been going on for more than four hundred years—first behind the
Cossack lines, which encircled and narrowed down the pasture-lands
from the north, and then along the Transcaspian Railway, which
stretched its tentacles round their southern border. From the Nomad's
point of view, a Peasant Power like Russia resembles those rolling and
crushing machines with which Western Industrialism shapes hot steel
according to its pleasure. In its grip, the Nomad is either crushed out of
existence or racked into the sedentary mould, and the process of penetration is not always peaceful. The path was cleared for the Transcaspian Railway by the slaughter of Türkmens at Göktepé.[2] But the
Nomad's death-cry is seldom heard. During the European War, while
people in England were raking up the Ottoman Turks' Nomadic ancestry
in order to account for their murder of 600,000 Armenians, 500,000
Turkish-speaking Central Asian Nomads of the Kirghiz Qāzāq Confederacy were being exterminated—also under superior orders—by that
"justest of mankind" the Russian muzhik. Men, women, and children
were shot down, or were put to death in a more horrible way by being
robbed of their animals and equipment and then being driven forth in

---

[1] 'It is as erroneous to attribute [the] workings [of this physical cause] to human
wickedness in the one case as in the other. Yet while the intrusive Nomad has been
stigmatized as an ogre, the intrusive Peasant has either escaped observation or has been
commended as an apostle of civilization. The reasons for this partiality are clear. One
is that the Nomad's tactics are more dramatic than the Peasant's and make a corre-
spondingly greater impression on the imagination. The other is that history is written
for and by the sedentary populations, which are much the most numerous and sophisticated portion of Mankind, while the Nomad usually suffers and pines away and
disappears without telling his tale. Yet, if he did put it on record, he might paint us as
monsters.' One of the oldest and most famous of the extant literary presentations of this
secular conflict is, in fact, written from the Nomad's standpoint; and here, in the fourth
chapter of the Book of Genesis, our own prototype Cain—the first tiller of the ground
and the first builder of a city—is branded for all time with the mark of his blood-
guiltiness for the slaying of his pastoral brother. But if Abel's advocate has had the first
word, Cain's advocates have held the floor ever after. In the Iranian epic of the struggle
between Iran and Turan, the sympathy has already been transferred to Cain's side.
This revised version of the story has prevailed down to this day. And it is usually the
last word that carries weight in the minds of the jury.   [2] In 1881,

winter-time to perish in mountain or desert. A lucky few escaped across the Chinese frontier.[1] These atrocities were courageously exposed and denounced by Mr. Kerensky in the Duma before the first Russian Revolution; but who listened or cared? Not the Czar's Government, nor the great public in the West.'[2]

The epitaph of Nomadism has been written, in a famous work of literature, by a son of the sedentary civilization which has given the Nomad the *coup de grâce*.[3] In Eurasia, Nomadism was doomed from that moment in the seventeenth century of the Christian Era when two sedentary empires, the Muscovite and the Manchu, stretched their tentacles round the Eurasian Steppe from opposite quarters until they interlaced with one another. From that moment onwards, it was merely a question of how long it would take for this living noose to strangle the Eurasian Nomad who was caught fast in its toils. In the Manchu Empire, a horde of non-Nomadic barbarian conquerors were serving the purposes of the Far Eastern Society, whose domain they had overrun and whose culture they had adopted, by helping to extirpate, on the adjoining steppe-land, the alien Nomadic way of life.[4] In the Muscovite Empire, a first infusion of Western Civilization was inspiring an Orthodox-Christian body politic with fresh energy and arming it with newfangled weapons. In our own 'post-war' generation, our Western Civilization, which has now spread its tentacles over the entire surface of the planet, is completing the extirpation of Nomadism not only in Eurasia, but in all its other ancient domains.

In the Eurasian domain, the powerful solvent of Russian Communism is now being applied to disintegrate the Nomadic way of life over a vast range of territories stretching from Transcaspia to Outer Mongolia, while in Inner Mongolia and Manchuria the last of the Nomad conquerors of China have been almost extinguished on their own ancestral pasture lands by the peaceful penetration of the conquered Chinese peasantry.[5] In Kenya, the pasture-lands of

[1] For details see Czaplicka, M. A.: *The Turks of Central Asia in History and at the Present Day* (Oxford 1918, Clarendon Press), p. 17. The respective estimates of the total numbers of murdered Qāzāqs and Armenians are both conjectural.

[2] Toynbee, A. J.: *The Western Question in Greece and Turkey*, 2nd ed. (London 1923, Constable), pp. 339–42.

[3] de Quincey, Thomas: *Revolt of the Tartars: Or, Flight of the Kalmuck Khan and his People from the Russian Territories to the Frontiers of China* [in A.D. 1771], reprinted in *The Collected Writings of Thomas de Quincey*, ed. by Masson, D.: vol. vii (London 1897, Black), pp. 368–426.

[4] See Courant, M.: *L'Asie Centrale aux xviie et xviiie siècles: Empire Kalmouk ou Empire Mantchou?* (Paris 1912, Picard).

[5] See Toynbee, A. J.: *Survey of International Affairs: 1920–3*, p. 433; *1925*, vol. ii, pp. 350–1; *1928*, pp. 434–5. See further an article by Young, C. W., in *Current History*, New York, July 1928. In *Manchuria Cradle of Conflict* (New York 1932, Macmillan), on pp. 125–32, Mr. Owen Lattimore describes in detail the process by which the Mongol Nomad is being replaced by the Chinese peasant in Inner Mongolia and Manchuria. For the contrast between the antipathy of the Mongol and the sympathy of the Manchu towards the Far Eastern culture, see further op. cit., pp. 73–4 and 131–2.

the Masai have been cut up and cut down to make room for intrusive European farmers who aspire to sow and reap on the Equator. In the Sahara, the Imoshagh are seeing their hitherto impenetrable desert fastnesses invaded by the aeroplane and by the eight-wheeled automobile. In Libya, where the Afrasian Nomadism has been organized to resist the European onset by the Islamic religious order of the Sanūsīyah, the resistance collapsed when, in January 1931, a column of Italian troops occupied the Sanūsī fastness in the reputedly impregnable oasis of Kufarā. Even in Arabia—the classic home of the Afrasian Nomadism and the most impervious of all the continents to penetration by Western pioneers—the Badu are being forcibly converted, in this age, into fallāhīn, and this by no alien Power, but by the deliberate policy of an Arab of Arabs, ʿAbd-al-ʿAzīz Āl-Saʿūd, the King of the Najd and the Hijāz, and the temporal head of the Wahhābī community of puritanical Muslim zealots.[1] When a Wahhābī potentate in the heart of Arabia is fortifying his political authority with the weapon of armoured cars and solving his economic problems by means of petrol pumps and artesian wells, it is evident that the spirit of the Western Civilization is prevailing in the Nomadic Civilization's innermost citadel, and that the last hour of Nomadism has struck.

Thus Abel has been slain by Cain; and, of all the sedentary civilizations which the Nomadic Civilization has encountered in the course of some five thousand years of contact between these two varieties of the same social species, it is our own Western Civilization that has consummated the fratricidal act. This Western Civilization has swept Nomadism off the face of the Earth, almost without noticing what it has been doing, as one incident in the titanic social revolution by which, within the last hundred and fifty years, all the habitable lands and navigable seas on the face of the planet, and the entire living generation of Mankind, have been linked together, by a Western-made mechanism, into a single world-wide economic order. Western enterprise has built up this new world order by burying its own fields under mushroom cities and putting the virgin grasslands of all the continents under the plough in order to feed these mushroom cities' pullulating industrial populations. In this oecumenical society, with its dynamic economy, there is no place for the arrested civilization and the static economy of the Nomadic

1 For Ibn Saʿūd's policy of converting the tribesmen of Central Arabia from Nomadism to agriculture on a large scale by planting them in organized settlements, and for his triumph over the recalcitrants, see Toynbee, A. J.: *Survey of International Affairs: 1925,* vol. i, p. 281; *1928,* p. 290; *1930,* pp. 177–82. For details of Ibn Saʿūd's agricultural settlements (*hijrahs*), see Philby, H. St. J. B.: *The Heart of Arabia* (London 1922, Constable), vol. i, pp. 299–300; Amīn-ar-Rihānī: *Tarīkh Najd al-Hadīth* (Cairo 1928), pp. 412–14, and *Ibn Sa'oud of Arabia* (London 1928, Constable), pp. 191–9; Philby, H. St. J. B.: *Arabia* (London 1930, Benn), pp. 225 seqq.

horde revolving perpetually round its closed annual cycle.[1] Abel is indubitably dead, and we are left to inquire whether the curse of Cain is duly descending upon his slayer.

'And now art thou cursed from the Earth, which hath opened her mouth to receive thy brother's blood from thy hand; when thou tillest the ground, it shall not henceforth yield unto thee her strength; a fugitive and a vagabond shalt thou be in the Earth.'[2]

This first clause of Cain's curse has manifestly proved ineffective; for though the oasis-cultivator has certainly found himself unable to raise crops from the desiccated steppe-land, his migrations have carried him, several thousand years ago, into regions round about in which the climatic conditions have not proved insuperably adverse; and thence, in the fullness of time, he has returned, as we have seen, with the new driving force of Industrialism behind him, to claim the grasslands for the plough and to make the desert blossom[3] by the latter-day arts of artesian-boring and dry-farming. It is rather in building the city from which these new arts and this new driving-power derive that Cain has given hostages to Fortune. The emergence of Industrialism and the extinction of Nomadism are two outstanding events in the history of the last 150 years; and, as we have seen, these two events are not merely contemporary but

---

[1] The impossibility of finding a place for Nomadism in the economy of an industrialized world is proved not only by the recent revolution on the grasslands of the Old World, from which an old-established Nomadism has been evicted by the Russian and the Chinese peasant's plough. It is demonstrated still more cogently by what has happened on the grasslands of South and North America, where the pioneers of European colonization found only hunting peoples in previous occupation. (See II. C (ii) (a) 2, vol. i, p. 255, above.) The immediate effect of the European pioneers' advent was to turn these former hunting-grounds not into fields and cities but into cattle-ranches; and the 'cow-boys' have been more ephemeral than the 'Indians' whom they have exterminated. They have been merely the foam frothing on the crest of the oncoming wave; and, within less than two generations, they have been supplanted in their turn by the ploughman and the mechanic, who all the time were following hard at their heels in irresistible force. To-day, the Middle Western prairies are being covered by a network of fields and cities, no less than the Central Asian Steppes. Yet our urban imaginations have been rightly captivated (see II. C (ii) (a) 2, vol. i, p. 255, above) by the 'cow-boy's' wild ride across our prosaic social stage. For his brief appearance has been a repetition—performed in the full light of history—of the evolution (sketched above) through which the Nomads of the Old World were begotten by earlier sedentary societies. The latter-day Nomadism which has been begotten in the New World by our Western Society has, it is true, been abortive. But let us imagine, for a moment, that, after the occupation of the prairies by the 'cow-boys' in the middle of the nineteenth century, these grasslands had been rendered unfit for the production of cereals (even by 'dry farming') through an access of aridity; or let us imagine that plantation-slavery or civil war or some other social disaster had blighted, in North America, the growth of the sedentary civilization from whose bosom the 'cow-boys' had emerged: then, in either of these eventualities, we can readily picture the 'cow-boys' making the prairies their own not merely for two brief generations, but perhaps for centuries or even for thousands of years. In that event, the history of Nomadism in the Old World would have repeated itself in the New. For this abortive Nomadism of the North American Prairies, see French, the Hon. W.: *Some Recollections of a Western Ranchman, New Mexico, 1883–1899* (London 1927, Macmillan); James, W.: *Lone Cowboy: My Life Story* (London 1930, Scribners); Love, C. M.: 'The History of the Cattle Industry in the South West' (in *The South-Western Quarterly*, vol. xix); Paxson, F.L.: 'The Cow Country' (in *The American Historical Review*, vol. xxii); Rollins, P. A.: *The Cowboy* (New York and London 1922, Scribners).

[2] Gen. iv. 11–12.   [3] Isaiah xxxv. 1–2.

are also interconnected. In this year 1935, when the new economic world order is threatened with break-down and dissolution, it seems not impossible that Abel may be avenged, after all, upon his fratricide brother; and that *Homo Nomas*, *in articulo mortis*, may yet linger on to see his slayer, *Homo Faber*, go down, distraught, to Sheol.

The 'Osmanlis

So much for the civilizations that have suffered arrest as a penalty for a *tour de force* in response to some physical challenge. In order to complete our survey, we must now consider the two parallel cases—the predicament of the 'Osmanlis and the predicament of the Spartans—in which the superlative challenge that has evoked the *tour de force* has been not physical but human.

The superlative challenge to which the Ottoman system was a response was the geographical transference of a Nomadic community from its native environment on the Steppe, where it had been at grips with Physical Nature, to an alien environment in which it found itself free from the physical pressure of desiccation but was confronted, in exchange, with the novel problem of exercising dominion over alien communities of human beings. We have already taken note[1] of these occasional aberrations of Nomad hordes out of their regular annual orbits on the Steppe into the domains of neighbouring sedentary civilizations in mechanical obedience to physical pushes or to human pulls. We have also had occasion to observe incidentally, apropos of a particular instance of this phenomenon, the first reaction which this new challenge is apt to evoke. We have seen how the Avar Nomads, when they found themselves expatriated from their cattle-ranges on the Steppe and stranded, *in partibus agricolarum*, in the derelict provinces of the Roman Empire in the sixth century of the Christian Era, sought to deal with the sedentary population which they had conquered as though it were a human flock, and attempted to transform themselves from shepherds of sheep into shepherds of men.[2]

This Avar experiment has been tried by other *ci-devant* Nomads who have found themselves from time to time in similar situations, and it is indeed a logical application of an obvious analogy. In their native environment on the Steppe, the Nomads live off the local vegetation at second hand by subjecting it to a preliminary transformation through the agency of certain fellow members of the Animal Kingdom whom the Nomads have at their command. In the alien environment of fields and cities, an intrusive horde of *ci-devant* Nomads almost inevitably expects to make its living in an

[1] On p. 15, above. [2] II. D (vii), vol. ii, pp. 317–19, above.

analogous way. Instead of living off the wild herbage of the Steppe through the transforming medium of tame animals, the *émigrés* now propose to live off the cultivated crops of the ploughland and the manufactured goods of the workshop and the profits of the counting-house through the transforming medium of subject human beings: a servile peasantry and a servile bourgeoisie. The analogy is tempting to apply, and it works out in practice up to a point; but the empirical test discovers in it one almost fatal flaw.

On the Steppe, the composite society constituted by the Nomads and their non-human cattle is the most effective social instrument of economic utilization which can be devised for dealing with that kind of physical environment at that degree of aridity. While the Nomad would not, of course, be able to keep alive on the Steppe at all without his flocks and herds, he is not a parasite upon his non-human partners in the pastoral business, since it would be just as impossible for these sheep and cattle and dogs and horses and camels to keep alive on the Steppe, in anything like their actual numbers, under the actual climatic conditions, without the assistance of their human overseers. At this degree of aridity, neither the human nor the non-human denizens of the Steppe could continue to live there in any considerable numbers except in association with one another,[1] and *a fortiori* they could not survive there in the anti-social relation of hunter and hunted, in which their predecessors once stood to one another in the Pluvial Age, before the challenge of desiccation was presented to both alike. On the other hand, in an environment of fields and cities, a composite society constituted of expatriated Nomads and indigenous 'human cattle' is economically unsound; since in these alien circumstances the 'shepherds of men' are always economically—though not always politically—superfluous and therefore parasitic. From the economic

[1] In this connexion it is significant that the one-humped Camel of the Afrasian Steppe is one of the rare species of animals that are now represented only by domesticated breeds, without any wild specimens having survived. Mr. G. F. Hudson points out, however, that wild specimens of the Eurasian two-humped camel (i.e. the Mongolian Wild Camel) are still to be found in Tsaidam and round the Lob Nor; and that specimens of the Afrasian one-humped camel which had reverted to a wild state were to be found—at any rate until the close of the nineteenth century of the Christian Era—in the arid fens of the Guadalquivir in Spain. (These were the descendants of camels which had been brought in from Africa, after the Muslim conquest of the Iberian Peninsula, by the Arabs and Moors.) Moreover, there are not only wild camels but wild horses and wild asses still extant in Mongolia and in the Tarim Basin. An account of these rare animals will be found (as Mr. Huds n has brought to the attention of the writer of this Study) in Sir Henry Howorth: *A History of the Mongols*, vol. iv (London 1928, Longmans), pp. 19–23. Apropos of Mongolia, Howorth observes that 'the most interesting district in many ways in regard to its fauna is the most barren and unattractive wild part, where the absence of water and fodder make it practically uninhabitable by Man.... This kind of country is chiefly found in Alashan and the Steppes of the Ordus and in the land about Lob Nor and parts of Dzungaria.' This is evidently the limiting case; but for the major part of the Steppe, which lies climatically between the extreme of aridity and the degree of humidity that is required for cultivation, the thesis put forward here in this Study probably holds good.

standpoint they have ceased to be shepherds keeping their flocks and have turned into drones exploiting the worker-bees. They have become a non-productive ruling-class maintained by the labour of a productive subject-population which receives from them no economic contribution in exchange for an uneconomic tax, and which could therefore utilize its fields and cities to much better economic effect if this human incubus were absent.

For this reason, the empires established by Nomad conquerors of sedentary populations have usually suffered the fate of the seeds in the parable which 'fell upon stony places where they had not much earth; and forthwith they sprung up, because they had no deepness of earth; and when the Sun was up they were scorched; and because they had no root they withered away'.[1] The usual career of such empires is to begin with an imposing display of power, but to belie their first promise by a rapid decadence and a premature extinction. The great Maghribī historian Ibn Khaldūn (*vivebat* A.D. 1332–1406) was thinking in terms of Nomad empires —the prevalent type of empires in Ibn Khaldūn's time and place— when he assessed the average duration of empires in general at not more than three generations or 120 years.[2] Nomad empires are apt to be powerful at the outset because the moral virtues of self-control and endurance and the intellectual aptitudes for forethought and organization, which are developed in the Nomad by his proper profession of pasturing his flocks and herds on the Steppe, are also potent for the military conquest of sedentary human populations. At the same time, these Nomad empires are apt to be ephemeral because the special qualities of the Nomad, being the outcome of his response to the challenge of his native environment, inevitably tend to atrophy in a new environment which fails to provide the requisite stimulus. Thus Nomad empire-builders usually degenerate, while on the other hand their sedentary subjects, after having been first stunned by the shock of the conquest (which is often a brutal business) and having then been hypnotized into acquiescing in the unnatural status of 'human cattle', usually begin to recover their *moral* at about the time when their *ci-devant* Nomad masters begin to lose theirs—and this for the inverse reason. If the ex-Nomad 'shepherd of men' degenerates because he has passed out of his own element and has become economically superfluous, his 'human cattle' recuperate because they have remained on their own

[1] Matt. xiii. 5–6.
[2] Ibn Khaldūn: *Muqaddamāt*: French translation by de Slane, Baron McG. (Paris 1863–8, Imprimerie Impériale, 3 vols.), vol. i, pp. 342–59, especially p. 347. Compare the passage in the same volume, p. 286, in which the author lays down that nobility lasts for four generations on the average and that corruption is of the essence of the Universe. (These passages from Ibn Khaldūn have been cited already in the present Study in vol. ii, on p. 212, above.)

ground and have not ceased to be economically productive—even under the adverse social conditions of political subjection.

In these circumstances, the false social analogy breaks down, and the 'human cattle' reassert their manhood by either expelling their shepherd-kings or assimilating them. The dominion of the Avars over the Slavs lasted, in all probability, for less than fifty years;[1] and while the transitory Avar ascendency was the making of the Slavs, the enslavement of the Slavs proved to be the undoing of the Avars. While the Slavs proceeded to make their mark on both Orthodox Christian and Western history, the Avars simply lingered on, in the outlying Hungarian enclave of the Eurasian Steppe, until they were exterminated, after the lapse of two centuries, by Charlemagne. Some Nomad empires have had still shorter lives than this. For example, the empire of the Western Huns, who passed out of Eurasia into the Hungarian Alföld about a century and a half before the Avars, lasted no longer than the life-span of a single individual: Attila.[2] The empire of the Mongol Il-Khans over Iran and 'Irāq lasted less than eighty years (circa A.D. 1258–1335),[3] and the empire of the Great Khans themselves over Southern China had an equally short duration (circa A.D. 1280–1354).[4] The empires of the Chaghatāy Mongols over Transoxania[5] and of the Hyksos over Egypt[6] each lasted a bare century. The Magyars, who were the next Nomad occupants of the Hungarian Alföld after the Avars, were absorbed, by conversion, into the body social of Western Christendom within little more than a hundred years after their arrival. The span of more than two centuries (circa A.D. 1142–1368) during which the Mongols and their immediate local predecessors the Kin ruled continuously over Northern China,[7] and the longer span of over three centuries and a half (circa 140 B.C.–A.D. 226/232) during which the Parthians were masters of 'Irāq as well as Iran, were distinctly exceptional.[8]

[1] See Peisker, T.: The Expansion of the Slavs (= The Cambridge Medieval History, vol. ii (Cambridge 1912, University Press), ch. xiv), cited already in II. D (vii), vol. ii, p. 318, above.
[2] Similarly, the dominion of the Eastern Huns (the White Huns or Ephthalites) was limited to the life-span of a single individual, Mihiragula, in India. In the Oxus-Jaxartes Basin, on the other hand, the Ephthalites succeeded in maintaining their ascendancy for a period—extending from the early part of the fifth century of the Christian Era to A.D. 567—which approximated to Ibn Khaldūn's figure of 120 years.
[3] See vol. ii, p. 144, above.   [4] See vol. ii, p. 121, above.
[5] See vol. ii, pp. 144–6, above.
[6] See vol. i, pp. 104–5, 137–9, and 144, and vol. ii, pp. 113, footnote 3, and 388–91, above.
[7] See vol. ii, p. 121, above.
[8] The average period of the ascendancies which have been exercised from time to time over a sedentary population in the Russian forest-belt by Nomads in occupation of the western arm of the Eurasian Steppe, which skirts the north coast of the Black Sea, appears to have been decidedly longer than Ibn Khaldūn's average of 120 years. The Scythians held their 'human cattle' in subjection (Herodotus, Bk. IV, ch. 3), and extracted from them a surplus of cereals for export to the Aegean, throughout the fifth and fourth centuries B.C. The Khazars drew tribute from the Russian Slavs from the

By these standards of comparison, the duration of the Ottoman Empire over the Orthodox Christian World was unique. If we date its definitive establishment from the Ottoman conquest of Macedonia in A.D. 1371–2, and the beginning of its end from the peace-treaty of Küchük Qaynarjy, which terminated the most disastrous of the Russo-Turkish Wars in A.D. 1774, we shall be assigning to the zenith of the Ottoman régime a period of fully four centuries without reckoning in the time which it took, before that, to rise and, after that, to fall. What is the explanation of this relative durability of the Ottoman Nomad empire-builders' work?

A partial explanation is, no doubt, to be found in the course of Orthodox Christian history, in which the Ottoman régime was an episode. For although on the economic plane the 'Osmanlis were not less parasitic than any other *ci-devant* Nomads who had been carried by conquest on to a sedentary society's ground, they were fortunate in finding on the political plane an unusually positive and constructive function to fulfil. Ejected from the Eurasian Steppe by the explosion of the Mongols (a social convulsion produced by one of the periodical turns of the Eurasian climatic screw), the fathers of the 'Osmanlis were driven deep into the Orthodox Christian World, and were lodged there by chance in a position of exceptional strategic advantage,[1] at a turning-point in Orthodox Christian history. This little band of Eurasian Nomad refugees happened to arrive at the north-western edge of the Anatolian Plateau, overlooking the Sea of Marmara, just after the Orthodox Christian 'Time of Troubles' had reached and passed its nadir. The break-down of the Orthodox Christian Civilization may be dated by its most prominent outward symptom: the Great Bulgaro-Roman War of A.D. 977–1019.[2] The landmarks in the subsequent disintegration of Orthodox Christendom were the military *débâcle* of the East Roman Power at Manzikert in A.D. 1071, which left the interior of Anatolia at the mercy of the Saljūqs; the successful insurrection of the Bulgars against the East Roman domination in A.D. 1186; and—crowning catastrophe—the capture and sack of

latter part of the sixth century of the Christian Era until the Norsemen filched their Slav tributaries from them in the ninth century. The Mongols of Qipchāq exercised dominion over Russia, off and on, from the first half of the thirteenth century of the Christian Era until the latter half of the fifteenth. This longer Russian average, however, may be regarded as the exception which proves Ibn Khaldūn's rule, for the relations between the sedentary peoples in Russia and their Nomad overlords on the Black Sea Steppe were not quite of the usual kind. The Nomads did not here transfer their own habitat from the Steppe to the forest. They remained on the Steppe—on their own ground—and exercised their suzerainty over the forest-dwellers from a distance.

[1] For the settlement of Ertoghrul and his fellow refugees in Sultan Önü in the latter part of the thirteenth century of the Christian Era, see II. D (v), vol. ii, pp. 150–3, above.

[2] For the cause of this destructive internecine warfare in the Orthodox Christian World, see II. D (vii), vol. ii, pp. 368–9, above, and Part IV, below.

the East Roman capital, Constantinople, itself in A.D. 1204 by the Western military and commercial adventurers who were seeking their fortunes on the so-called Fourth Crusade. The tide turned when an Anatolian Greek successor-state of the East Roman Empire, the Principality of Nicaea—starting from a base of operations at the foot of that very section of the plateau-rim on which the fathers of the 'Osmanlis were in the act of pitching their tents—actually anticipated, and conceivably inspired, the subsequent exploits of the 'Osmanlis themselves by crossing the Dardanelles, conquering Adrianople, and enveloping Constantinople on the landward side in A.D. 1235, annexing Macedonia in A.D. 1246, and finally recapturing the Imperial City from the Western usurpers in A.D. 1261. To play the historic role of being the empire-builders of an Orthodox Christian universal state was not the Nicene Greeks' destiny. Yet their passage of the Dardanelles in A.D. 1235 marked a transition, in the Orthodox Christian 'Time of Troubles', from the process of disintegration to a process of reconstruction; and the work of consolidation and pacification, which these Nicene Greeks had initiated and which was the crying need of the Orthodox Christian Society in that age, was duly accomplished in the fullness of time by the 'Osmanlis. Treading on their Nicene forerunners' heels, the 'Osmanlis made their passage of the Dardanelles in A.D. 1355 and their conquest of Adrianople in 1360 and their conquest of Macedonia in 1371–2; and they crowned their construction of a universal state, embracing the whole of the main body of Orthodox Christendom, by their capture of Constantinople in A.D. 1453.

It will be seen that the *Pax Ottomanica* fulfilled a long-unsatisfied and urgent requirement of the Orthodox Christian Society; and this partly explains the duration of an empire which was able to perform for its subjects this vitally important service. Yet this explanation is incomplete; for, from the Orthodox Christian standpoint, the Ottoman Empire was always an alien and an odious Power whose heavy yoke was only worn under sheer compulsion and whose genuine social services were recognized grudgingly, if at all. Moreover, this Ottoman Power was not exempt from the economic weakness, analysed above,[1] which is inherent in all Nomad dominions over sedentary populations. The relative durability of the Ottoman Empire, by comparison with other Nomad dominions of the same general type, only becomes fully intelligible when we view it in the light of the special Ottoman adaptation of the common Nomad institutions in response to an extraordinary challenge.[2]

[1] See pp. 23–5, above.
[2] For the stimulus which was administered to the 'Osmanlis by the challenge of Orthodox Christendom, see II. D (v), vol. ii, pp. 150–4, above, where the history of the 'Osmanlis is contrasted with that of the Qaramanlis.

We have seen that the Avars and their like, when they have trespassed from the Desert on to the Sown, have attempted—and failed—to deal with their new situation by turning themselves from shepherds of sheep into shepherds of men. Their failure seems the less surprising when we consider that these unsuccessful Nomad empire-builders *in partibus agricolarum* have not attempted to find any sedentary human equivalent for one of the essential partners in the composite society of the Steppe. For this Steppe Society does not consist simply of the human shepherd and his flock. In addition to the domesticated animals which he keeps alive in order to live off their products, the Nomad keeps other animals—the dog, the camel, the horse—whose function is not to provide him, as his sheep and cattle provide him, with food and clothing, but to assist him, as non-human auxiliaries, in his pastoral task.[1] These auxiliary animals are the *chef d'œuvre* of the Nomadic Civilization and the key to its success. Without their aid, the Nomad's *tour de force* would pass the bounds of human capacity; yet this aid can only be enlisted by a miracle of human ingenuity. The sheep or the cow has merely to be tamed (though that is difficult enough) in order to be of service to Man. The dog and camel and horse cannot perform their more sophisticated services until they have been tamed and trained into the bargain. The training of his non-human auxiliaries is the Nomad's crowning achievement; and it is the adaptation of this higher Nomad art to sedentary conditions, over and above the adaptation of the comparatively commonplace art of taming sheep and cattle, that distinguishes the Ottoman Empire from the Avar Empire and accounts for its vastly greater strength and durability. The Ottoman Pādishāhs maintained their empire by training slaves as human auxiliaries to assist them in keeping order among their 'human cattle'.

This remarkable institution of making soldiers and administrators out of slaves—an idea which is so congenial to the Nomad genius and so alien from ours—was not an Ottoman invention. We find it in other Nomad empires over sedentary peoples—and this precisely in those which have had the longest duration next to the Ottoman Empire itself.

We catch glimpses of military slavery in the Parthian Empire in the last century B.C. One of the Parthian armies that frustrated

---

[1] The division between these two categories of animals is not, of course, completely clear-cut. The horse, for example, belongs to both classes, since it provides its Nomad master with milk and meat, besides providing him with a mount of greater mobility than the cattle which the Nomad herdsman has to round up. The primary animal in the auxiliary class appears to be the dog, who was also perhaps the first animal ever to be domesticated by Man. The transformation of the hound into the sheep-dog must have been accomplished through the middle term of the watch-dog; and this must have happened during the agricultural stage which intervened between hunting and Nomadism. (See p. 10, above.)

Mark Antony's ambition to emulate Alexander the Great was reported to have borne only 400 free men on its strength out of a total
of 50,000 effectives;[1] and the Surēn who commanded the earlier
Parthian army which annihilated the Roman army of Crassus was
reported to have brought into the field no less than 10,000 slaves
and clients of his own.[2] In the same region a thousand years later,
the 'Abbasid Caliphs maintained—and forfeited—their authority
in the ninth and tenth centuries of the Christian Era by purchasing
Turkish slaves off the Eurasian Steppe and training them at Baghdad for the calling of soldiers and administrators.[3] This 'Abbasid
institution was adopted, and perhaps elaborated, in the principality
of the Sāmānidae (regnabant A.D. 819–999),[4] which was the successor-state of the 'Abbasid Caliphate on its north-eastern marches,
over against the Eurasian Steppe. These Sāmānid princes, who
ruled at Balkh and Bokhārā, were closer than the Caliphs at Baghdad to the source from which the raw material for a Turkish slave-
staff was derived, and at the same time they had a proportionately
stronger incentive to train a pack of 'human watch-dogs' in order to
protect their perilously exposed dominions from the depredations
of their domesticated Turks' wild kinsmen. The Sāmānids' Turkish
slaves were put through a long and minutely graduated probation
which, for individuals who showed merit, became a *cursus honorum*
culminating in an appointment to some responsible administrative
office at, but not before, the age of thirty-five.[5] This Turkish
slave household was a factor both in the long preservation of
the Sāmānid régime and in its ultimate extinction; for, while
the greater part of the Sāmānid dominions was eventually overrun by the wild Turkish Nomads from the Steppe—the Saljūq
Khān's horde on the left bank of the Oxus and the Ilek Khān's
horde on the right bank—the House of Sāmān itself actually

[1] Mommsen, Th.: *A History of Rome: the Provinces from Caesar to Diocletian*:
English translation (London 1886, Bentley, 2 vols.), vol. ii, p. 7.
[2] Plutarch: *Life of Crassus*, ch. xxi.
[3] The 'Abbasids' Turkish bodyguard at Baghdad had its counterpart, at the court
of the 'Abbasids' Umayyad contemporaries and rivals at Cordova, in a bodyguard of
European barbarians who were purchased by the Spanish Caliphs from their Frankish
neighbours. The Franks supplied the Cordovan slave-markets by making slave-raids
across the opposite frontier of the Frankish dominions. The barbarians who were thus
captured by the Franks in order to be sold to the Spanish Umayyads happened to be
Slavs; and this is the origin of the word 'slave' in the English language.
[4] See II. D (v), vol. ii, p. 142, above.
[5] The Sāmānids' slave-system is sketched by the Nizām-al-Mulk Abu 'Alī Hasan in
the 'Siasset Namèh' = Siyāset-Nāmeh (French translation by Schéfer, Ch. (Paris 1893,
Leroux), p. 139, cited by Lybyer, A. H.: *The Government of the Ottoman Empire in the
Time of Suleiman the Magnificent* (Cambridge, Mass. 1913, Harvard University Press),
pp. 22–3. Sāmānid institutions are a subject on which the Nizām-al-Mulk may be
accepted as an authority, since he was himself an administrator in the service of the
Saljūqs: the Turkish intruders from the Eurasian Steppe who were the Sāmānids'
successors in Khurāsān. Moreover, the Nizām-al-Mulk and the House of Sāmān had a
common cultural background as fellow Iranians and as joint heirs of the Syriac
Civilization.

received its *coup de grâce* from one of its own slave administrators: Sebuktegin.[1]

In the interregnum which followed the extinction of the successor-states of the ʿAbbasid Caliphate, we find slave-soldiers and slave-administrators not only repeating Sebuktegin's individual exploit of supplanting the dynasties in whose service they had been trained, but actually replacing these by slave-dynasties, in which the dominion passed from slave to slave instead of passing from father to son. In the thirteenth century of the Christian Era, the new domain in Hindustan which had been conquered for the nascent Iranic Civilization by a series of Turkish soldiers of fortune, beginning with Sebuktegin, was ruled from Delhi by a sequence of 'Slave-Kings' (*regnabant* A.D. 1206–87). A more celebrated instance of the same remarkable phenomenon was the Mamlūk régime in Egypt. These Egyptian Mamlūks, as their name implies,[2] were originally the slaves of others. Their makers and masters were Saladin and the heirs of his body, the dynasty of the Ayyūbidae; but in A.D. 1250, at a critical moment in the life-and-death struggle of the nascent Arabic Civilization against the Crusaders, the Ayyūbids' Mamlūks brushed the Ayyūbids themselves aside and took the Ayyūbid slave-system over on their own account as their own slaves and own masters—perpetuating themselves, as before, by the purchase of fresh relays of slaves from abroad,[3] without resuming the normal human method of procreation.

Behind the façade of a puppet Caliphate—invested in a line of latter-day ʿAbbasids, to whom the Mamlūks gave asylum in Cairo after the Mongol sack of Baghdad, on the understanding that these august refugees should reign but should not govern[4]—the self-owned slave-household of the extinct Ayyūbids ruled Egypt and Syria, and held the redoubtable Mongols in check at the line of the Euphrates, from A.D. 1250 to A.D. 1516–17, when they met more than their match in the slave-household of the ʿOsmanlis. Yet the Ottoman conquest was not the end of the Mamlūks; for although the strong slave armed had been overcome by a stronger than he, and had been constrained to submit to a division of his spoils,[5] the

---

[1] For details see Barthold, W.: *Turkestan down to the Mongol Invasion*, 2nd ed., translated into English and revised by the author with the assistance of H. A. R. Gibb (London 1928, Luzac), pp. 261–4.

[2] Mamlūk is the past participle passive of the Arabic verb *malaka*, which denotes the ownership of property.

[3] The Egyptian Mamlūks made sure of their source of supply by maintaining a political entente with the Mongol khanate of Qipchāq and with the maritime power of Venice. The Khans of Qipchāq made slave raids upon the Caucasian highlanders and the Russian forest-dwellers and the Eurasian Nomads beyond the pale of the Khan's own horde. The Venetians were the middlemen who conveyed the newly captured slaves from Tana to Damietta. This slave-trade was one of the most lucrative lines of Venetian business.

[4] For these Cairene ʿAbbasidae, see I. C (i) (*b*), vol. i, p. 67, footnote 2, and pp. 70–1, above, and Part X, below. [5] Luke xi. 21–2.

'Osmanli forbore to take from the Mamlūk the armour wherein he trusted. Under the Ottoman régime in Egypt, the Mamlūk corps was permitted to perpetuate itself, as before, by the same method of training and from the same sources of recruitment; and, as the Ottoman power declined, the Mamlūk power reasserted itself. In the eighteenth century of the Christian Era, the Ottoman Pasha of Egypt came to be virtually a state prisoner of the Mamlūks; and he reigned as the Pādishāh's viceroy without having much more share in the government of Egypt than the Cairene 'Abbasids had been allowed in their day. At the turn of the eighteenth and nineteenth centuries, it seemed an open question whether the Ottoman heritage in Egypt would revert to the Mamlūks or fall to some Western Power; and although both these alternatives were overruled, in the event, by the genius of Mehmed 'Alī, this great Ottoman statesman had more ado to settle accounts with the Mamlūks than to keep the British at arm's length or to step into the shoes of the French. It needed all Mehmed 'Alī's ability and energy and ruthlessness to exterminate this self-perpetuating slave-corps after it had kept itself alive on the alien soil of Egypt, by constant drafts of Eurasian and Caucasian man-power, for more than five hundred years; and even then the Mamlūks died hard. The last stand which was made, after the massacre of A.D. 1811, by a handful of survivors in the unexplored African hinterland of Egypt on the Upper Nile, was not the least impressive demonstration of the singular vitality which this extraordinary institution displayed from the beginning to the end.

In discipline and organization, however, the Mamlūk slave-household which had supplanted the Ayyūbid Dynasty in the dominion over Egypt, was far surpassed by the somewhat younger slave-household which the Ottoman Dynasty created as an instrument for the establishment and maintenance of its dominion over the Orthodox Christian World. To exercise dominion over the entire body social of an alien civilization was evidently the hardest task which a Nomad conqueror could set himself; and this audacious enterprise called out, in 'Osmān and his successors down to Suleymān the Magnificent, a supreme display of the Nomad's social capacities. The Ottoman slave-household is the finest recorded specimen of the species and on that account the most illuminating example for our purpose.[1]

---

[1] The universal state which was imposed upon the Orthodox Christian World by the 'Osmanlis has, of course, its historical counterpart in the universal state which was imposed upon the Hindu World, some two centuries later, by the Timurid 'Mughals' who, like the 'Osmanlis, were Turks of Nomadic antecedents with a veneer of Iranic culture; but here an equivalent challenge evoked no more than the rudiments of an equivalent response. We have seen that the Egyptian Mamlūks had their counterparts, in the thirteenth century of the Christian Era, in the Delhi 'Slave-Kings'; and in the following century certain contemporaries, in Hindustan, of the early Ottoman empire-builders

Its general character is conveyed in the following passage from a brilliant study by an American scholar:[1]

'The Ottoman Ruling Institution included the Sultan and his family, the officers of his household, the executive officers of the Government, the standing army of cavalry and infantry, and a large body of young men who were being educated for service in the standing army, the court, and the Government. These men wielded the sword, the pen, and the sceptre. They conducted the whole of the government except the mere rendering of justice in matters that were controlled by the Sacred Law, and those limited functions that were left in the hands of subject and foreign groups of non-Muslims. The most vital and characteristic features of this institution were, first, that its personnel consisted, with few exceptions, of men born of Christian parents[2] or of the sons of such; and, second, that almost every member of the Institution came into it as the Sultan's slave, and remained the Sultan's slave throughout life—no matter to what height of wealth, power, and greatness he might attain. . . .

appear to have laid the foundations of something like the Ottoman system. For example 'Alā-ad-Dīn (*regnabat* A.D. 1296–1316) is recorded to have possessed 50,000 slaves, and Fīrūz (*regnabat* A.D. 1351–88) 180,000; and these Turkish slave-households in Hindustan were elaborately trained and organized (see Lane-Poole, S.: *Mediaeval India* (London 1903, Fisher Unwin), pp. 147–8). Thereafter, however, in Hindustan, the slave-system receded into the background; and in the institutions of the Timurid 'Mughals', who actually established the universal state of Hindu history, the slave-household was not at all prominent. Indeed, the principal evidence for the existence of this institution at the Mughal Court is indirect. It is an unverified inference from the established fact that, in the eighteenth century of the Christian Era, an ex-feudatory of the Mughals, the Nawwāb of Farrukhābād, Muhammad Khān Bangash, is known to have 'maintained what was practically a replica in miniature of the Ottoman system. Hindu boys between the ages of seven and thirteen, some of them sons of Rājputs and Brahmans, were seized, bought, or accepted as *chelas* or slaves to the number of one or two hundred a year. They were taught to read and write, and were specially rewarded when the task was completed. Five hundred *chelas* from eighteen to twenty years of age were trained as a regiment of musketeers. From among the older *chelas* were chosen the officers of the household, generals of the army, and deputy governors of provinces'. (Lybyer, A. H.: *The Government of the Ottoman Empire in the Time of Suleiman the Magnificent* (Cambridge, Mass. 1913, Harvard University Press), p. 282, following Irvine, W.: 'The Bangash Nawabs of Farrukhabad', in the *Journal of the Royal Asiatic Society of Bengal*, 1878, pp. 340 seqq.)

We seem to catch a glimpse of the same institution in the universal state which, in the seventeenth century of the Christian Era, was imposed upon the main body of the Far Eastern Society by the Manchus: a barbarian people who (it is true) were not Nomads themselves, but who were in geographical contact with the easternmost hordes of the Mongol Nomads and were certainly responsive to Mongol cultural influences, as is shown by the Manchu adoption and adaptation of the Mongol version of the Syriac Alphabet. At the Manchu Court in Peking, 'it is curious and interesting that the Chinese officials referred to themselves, when received by the Emperor, as *ch'en* (an official); it was the Manchu officials who used the term *nu* (a slave)—thus emphasizing that they were regarded as the Emperor's personal or "party" followers'. (Lattimore, O.: *Manchuria Cradle of Conflict* (New York 1932, Macmillan), p. 72.)

[1] Lybyer, A. H.: *The Government of the Ottoman Empire in the Time of Suleiman the Magnificent* (Cambridge, Mass. 1913, Harvard University Press). See also Miller, B.: *Beyond the Sublime Porte: The Grand Seraglio of Stambul* (New Haven 1931, Yale University Press), ch. iii, and an article by the same author on 'The Curriculum of the Palace School of the Turkish Sultan' in *Macdonald Presentation Volume* (Princeton 1933, University Press), chap. xxi.

[2] The Egyptian Mamlūks, in their latter days, were likewise recruited mainly from the children of Christian parents who were sold into slavery or were carried away captive in their childhood. The Orthodox Christian peasantry of Transcaucasia, which was the principal source of supply for the latter-day Egyptian Mamlūks, was also one of the recruiting grounds of the Ottoman slave-household.—A.J.T.

'The royal family . . . may rightly be included in the slave-family [because] the mothers of the Sultan's children were slaves; the Sultan himself was the son of a slave; and his daughters were married to men who, though they might be called vizier and pasha, wore these titles at the Sultan's pleasure, whereas they bore indelibly the title of *qūl* or slave. The Sultan's sons, though they might sit upon the throne, would be the consorts of none but slaves. Long before Suleymān's time, the Sultans had practically ceased either to obtain brides of royal rank or to give the title of wife to the mothers of their children. . . .[1]

'Perhaps no more daring experiment has been tried on a large scale upon the face of the Earth than that embodied in the Ottoman Ruling Institution. Its nearest ideal analogue is found in the Republic of Plato,[2] its nearest actual parallel in the Mamlūk system of Egypt; but it was not restrained within the aristocratic Hellenic limitations of the first, and it subdued and outlived the second. In the United States of America men have risen from the rude work of the backwoods to the Presidential chair, but they have done so by their own effort and not through the gradations of a system carefully organized to push them forward. The Roman Catholic Church can still train a peasant to become a pope, but it has never begun by choosing its candidates almost exclusively from families which profess a hostile religion. The Ottoman system deliberately took slaves and made them ministers of state. It took boys from the sheep-run and the plough-tail and made them courtiers and the husbands of princesses; it took young men whose ancestors had borne the Christian name for centuries, and made them rulers in the greatest of

[1] In fact, the Ottoman Pādishāhs bred their children from picked and chosen female slaves as their Nomad forbears on the Steppe had bred pedigree cattle from selected stock, and their attitude towards their own human progeny resembled their attitude towards the younglings of their flocks and herds. Sultan Mehmed II the Conqueror obtained a fetvā from the 'ulemā of his day in which it was declared lawful—'in order to secure the peace of the World'—for the Sultan's successors on the Ottoman throne to have all their brothers put to death. Sultan Mehmed issued an Imperial qānūn in which he made this precept jussive instead of merely permissive, and his successors duly carried out his instructions. Sultan Mehmed's condemnation of the majority of his own male descendants to a premature death by violence for the sole crime of being superfluous has become famous in our Western World as a hyperbole of inhuman barbarity; but we must suppose that the great Ottoman statesman felt no more compunction in condemning his own superfluous offspring to be strangled than a twentieth-century Western bourgeoise feels when she condemns her pet cat's superfluous kittens to be drowned.—A.J.T.

[2] 'Plato would have been delighted with the training of the Sultan's great family, though his nature would have revolted from its lowliness of birth. He would have approved of the life-long education, the equally careful training of body and mind, the separation into soldiers and rulers (even though it was not complete), the relative freedom from family ties, the system's rigid control of the individual, and, above all, of the government by the wise. Whether the founders of the Ottoman system were acquainted with Plato will probably never be known, but they seem to have come as near to his plan as it is possible to come in a workable scheme. In some practical ways they even improved upon Plato—as by avoiding the uncertainties of heredity, by supplying a personal directing power, by insuring permanence through a balance of forces, and by making their system capable of vast imperial rule.' (Lybyer, op. cit., p. 71.)
    The Ottoman system was also Platonic in picking out and training women as well as men. 'The Imperial haram partook of the characteristics of the schools of pages' (Lybyer, op. cit., p. 78); but, while the male and female departments of the household were trained, *mutatis mutandis*, on parallel lines, they were kept rigidly separate. 'Before the middle of the reign of Suleymān, no woman resided in the entire vast palace where the Sultan spent most of his time' (Lybyer, op. cit., p. 121).—A.J.T.

Muhammadan states, and soldiers and generals in invincible armies whose chief joy was to beat down the Cross and elevate the Crescent. It never asked its novices "Who was your father?" or "What do you know?" or even "Can you speak our tongue?"; but it studied their faces and their frames and said: "*You* shall be a soldier and, if you show yourself worthy, a general", or "*You* shall be a scholar and a gentleman and, if the ability lies in you, a governor and a prime minister". Grandly disregarding that fabric of fundamental customs which is called "human nature", and those religious and social prejudices which are thought to be almost as deep as life itself, the Ottoman system took children for ever from parents, discouraged family cares among its members through their most active years, allowed them no certain hold on property, gave them no definite promise that their sons and daughters would profit by their success and sacrifice, raised and lowered them with no regard for ancestry or previous distinction, taught them a strange law, ethics, and religion, and ever kept them conscious of a sword raised above their heads which might put an end at any moment to a brilliant career along a matchless path of human glory.'[1]

It will be seen that the essence of the Ottoman system was the picking and training of 'human watch-dogs' to keep the Pādishāh's 'human cattle' in order and his human neighbours at bay. To become an Ottoman public slave of the highest order was the most arduous and dangerous and important and magnificent profession that could be followed by any subject of the Ottoman Pādishāh. Yet an essential, as well as an astonishing, rule of Ottoman statecraft was that this profession should be reserved almost exclusively for persons who were infidel-born[2]—without its mattering whether their infidel parents happened to be the Pādishāh's subjects or not—whereas the Pādishāh's own Muslim co-religionists were ineligible *ex officio religionis*, even if they happened to be the sons of the Ottoman feudal landed gentry who were the Pādishāh's equals in the sight of God and his companions in arms and even in some sense his social peers. This provision is astonishing because it is an extreme denial of natural expectations to disqualify the members of a conquering community from bearing rule;[3] but, given the ability to enforce this disqualification, as it actually was enforced during at least two centuries of Ottoman history (*circa* A.D. 1365–

[1] Lybyer, op. cit., pp. 36, 57–8, and 45–6.

[2] The only regular exceptions were the sons of members of the slave-household who had risen to one of the two highest classes—the class of administrative officials or the class of troopers in the household cavalry. These young men were Muslims, Muslim-born, in spite of the fact that their fathers must have been infidel-born *ex hypothesi*, since conversion to Islam, as well as infidel birth, was required of a slave as one of the necessary conditions for enrolment in the regular army or for appointment to an administrative office. Nevertheless, the sons of public slaves of either of the two highest classes were allowed, by special privilege, to follow in their fathers' footsteps. This privilege, however, did not extend to the next generation. The grandsons of pashas and sipāhīs, and the sons of public slaves of lower rank, were disqualified for admission into the Pādishāh's slave household by being enfeofed among the free Muslim landed gentry.

[3] The point is put forcibly by Lybyer in op. cit., p. 117.

1565), its utility is manifest. The Ottoman system of training a 'human watch-dog' made such severe demands upon human nature that only an individual who had been torn out of his own hereditary social environment, and had been introduced into the system as an isolated human atom, could be expected to submit to it. Now of all the human materials at the Ottoman Pādishāh's disposal, the least tractable were the children of his free Muslim feudatories with their pride of race and religion, their local connexions, and their family solidarity. The Ottoman Pādishāhs realized that, if once they were to admit this free-born and free-minded element into their household, an acute conflict would arise between the personnel and the system and that, in this trial of strength, it would not be the system that would prevail. Hence the ban upon the admission of free Muslims; and this drastic policy was justified by the sequel; for, when the free Muslims did at last force an entry into the household, the system did break down.

Until the time of that revolutionary and disastrous innovation, which began in the last years of Suleymān's reign,[1] the Sultan's slave-household was recruited—with the exceptions already mentioned—from infidel sources of supply. Recruits from beyond the Ottoman frontiers were obtained either by capture in war[2] or by purchase in the slave-market[3] or by gift of previous owners[4] or by voluntary enlistment.[5] Recruits within the frontiers were obtained by the periodical levy of children by conscription. Through which-

[1] Lybyer, op. cit., p. 69, note 3.
[2] We have works from the pens of two Western prisoners of war who were passed through the Ottoman system and who afterwards escaped to put their experiences on record. One of these is the German, Johann Schiltberger, who was taken prisoner in A.D. 1396 at the Battle of Nicopolis at the age of sixteen, spent six years as a slave in the service of Sultan Bāyezīd I, was taken prisoner a second time, together with his Ottoman royal master, by Timur Lenk at Angora in A.D. 1402, spent twenty-five years more as a slave in the service of Timur, and finally succeeded in making his escape and finding his way back to Western Christendom. (German text of Schiltberger's narrative: Tübingen 1885, Literarischer Verein in Stuttgart; English translation by Telfer, J. B.: London 1879, Hakluyt Society). The second Western prisoner who has left a record of his experiences is Giovanni Antonio Menavino, a Genoese who was captured by the Barbary Corsairs at the age of twelve, about the year 1505. He was presented by his captors to Bāyezīd II, was placed in the school of pages, and made his escape in 1514 during Selīm I's expedition against Ismāʿīl Shāh Safawī. (Menavino, G. A.: *Trattato deʾ Costumi e Vita deʾ Turchi* (Florence 1548).)
[3] The Ottoman slave-market was kept supplied by two sets of professional slave-raiders: the Barbary Corsairs (Ottoman colonists in Tunis and Algiers), who raided the sea-coasts of Western Europe by ship; and the Krim Tatars (a remnant of the Mongol horde of Qipchāq, which had survived under an Ottoman protectorate), who raided the steppe-coasts of Muscovy and Poland on horseback. Rycaut (in op. cit. *infra*, p. 81) estimates the average annual import of slaves from Krim Tatary to Constantinople at 20,000 head. The Tatars and the Algerines ought to be classed by our anthropologists among 'the higher hunters'.
[4] e.g. by gift of the Barbary Corsairs (Rycaut, op. cit. *infra*, p. 25). This was how Menavino was acquired by Bāyezīd II. (See footnote 2, above.)
[5] The fourth of the four regiments of Ottoman household cavalry, i.e. the Ghurebā ('the Westerners'), was recruited entirely from non-Ottomans, both Muslim and Christian. The career of a renegade in the Ottoman service remained attractive to Western Christians until as late as the turn of the eighteenth and nineteenth centuries of the Christian Era.

ever of these channels the recruit made his entry into the Pādishāh's
slave-household, and whatever the age at which he was received, he
was put through a long and elaborate and strenuous course of training before he was gazetted to a post in the Ottoman public service.[1]
The leading features of this Ottoman public educational system
were a minute and constant supervision by the responsible officers;[2]
a perpetual selection and specialization at every stage;[3] and a stimu-
lation of the candidates by the administration of the strongest
possible incentives, both negative and positive. The discipline was
meticulous and the punishments, though not unregulated, were
savage,[4] while on the other hand there was a deliberate and unceasing appeal to ambition. Every boy who entered the Ottoman
Pādishāh's slave-household was—and was no doubt aware that he
was—a potential Grand Vizier; and his prospects depended on his
prowess, in competition with his contemporaries, in the course of
his training.[5] At each stage, he had the possibility of qualifying for
a higher category of service; and success meant an immediate
increase of pay (for these Ottoman slave-apprentices were paid
from the outset),[6] as well as a greater chance, in the future, of
climbing to the top of the tree.

The method and spirit of the Ottoman educational system in its
heyday are vividly portrayed in the following appreciation by
a first-hand observer, the Flemish scholar and diplomat Ogier Ghiselin de Busbecq, who was resident in the Ottoman Empire, as
ambassador to Suleymān the Magnificent from the Hapsburg Court
at Vienna, during the years 1555–1562:[7]

'Every year the Turkish sovereign sends commissioners into different

[1] The usual age for passing out of the educational system and being appointed to a
military or administrative post seems to have been 25 in all grades.

[2] Rycaut, op. cit. *infra*, p. 25; Lybyer, op. cit., pp. 71–2.   [3] Lybyer, op. cit., p. 83.

[4] See the quotations from original authorities in Lybyer, op. cit., pp. 108–9, as well
as the references on pp. 77–8. See also Rycaut, op. cit. *infra*, pp. 2 and 26, and d'Ohsson,
op. cit. *infra*, p. 205.   [5] Lybyer, op. cit., p. 83.

[6] Lybyer, op. cit., pp. 76–7 and 82–3. See further the table of 'Differential Allowances
of Pages of Palace School' in Miller, 'The Curriculum of the Palace School', opposite
p. 310.

[7] Busbecq's observations on Ottoman affairs are contained in four letters written home,
during his diplomatic mission in the Near East, to a friend in Western Christendom,
Nicholas Michault, and in a subsequent pamphlet entitled *Exclamatio, sive de Re Militari
contra Turcam instituenda Consilium*. These five papers are all printed in *A. Gislenii
Busbequii Omnia quae Extant* (Leyden 1633, Elzevir). Busbecq observed the Ottoman
System just before it passed its zenith. A century later, when the system was still
outwardly intact but was verging towards its fall, it was observed again by another
Western diplomatist of equal acumen, the Englishman Sir Paul Rycaut, who served in
the Levant first as English Consul at Smyrna and afterwards as Secretary of the English
Embassy at Constantinople. His observations are recorded in *The Present State of the
Ottoman Empire* (London 1668, Starkey and Brome). He states (p. 42) that his information
has been taken 'from the mouth of one who had spent nineteen years in the schools of
the Seraglio', and in another passage (p. 132) he cites 'one Albertus Bobovius, a Polonian
by nation, but educated in the Seraglio and instructed in all the learning of the Turkish
literature (from whom I freely confess to have received many of my observations)'. Thus
Rycaut had good informants, apart from what he saw himself. Finally, the Ottoman
system was observed, when it lay in ruins, but before the rubble had been removed to

provinces who levy one in every three or four of the boys of Christian parentage.[1]

'These boys are brought in droves to Constantinople; and there those of more gentlemanly appearance, and those who show signs of greater innate ability, are allocated to the domestic service of the sovereign himself or the pashas or other high officials.[2]

'The rest are taken to a place where a great crowd of men of every condition, especially countryfolk, is gathered in waiting; and these apply to the official in charge for any boys who strike their fancy. The official hands over the boy to the applicant on payment of a gold piece, after entering in the public records the boy's name, birthplace, social status, and age, as well as any permanent physical marks of identity. Upon fulfilment of these formalities, the recipient of the boy—be he countryman or townsman—is at liberty to take the boy away with him across the sea to Asia or wherever he likes, according to his place of domicile, in order to break him in there as a slave by steady hard labour. The boy receives rations of bread and water, with an occasional seasoning of porridge or fruit or vegetables, and he is supplied with sufficient clothing to protect him against the inclemency of the weather. He is also instructed in the practice and the tenets of the Muhammadan religion. Thus the boy grows up a stranger to luxury, and with no parents to spoil him, until he becomes a strong man capable of standing any exertion.[3]

'Then, when the Government requires the young man's services, it demands him back from the private master who has had him on deposit, and transfers him to the military service; and this is the seminary from

clear the ground for a new social structure, by Ignatius Mouradgea d'Ohsson, a Levantine born and brought up in Turkey. His survey of the civil institutions of the Ottoman Empire in his day will be found in the seventh volume of his *Tableau Général de l'Empire Ottoman* (Paris 1788–1824, 7 vols.). See further the admirable descriptive bibliography in Lybyer, op. cit., pp. 305–30. The text of a treatise on the Seraglio School from the hand of Bobovius himself has been discovered by Miss Miller (see Miller, *The Grand Seraglio*, p. 48).

[1] Actually, this levy (called *devrishmé* or 'rotation') was made once in every four or five years (or at shorter intervals when the Pādishāh's slave-household was depleted by heavy military casualties). Out of a total determined on each occasion by the Central Government, a quota was levied on each district. The commissioners who picked the children reviewed the boys of between 12 and 20 years of age, as shown on the parish priests' baptismal registers (Lybyer, op. cit., pp. 51–2). Contemporary Christian evidence shows that parents were not always unwilling to see their children taken; and there were instances of Muslim parents evading the disqualification to which their own children were subject by bribing their Christian neighbours to exchange children surreptitiously (op. cit., pp. 53–5). The use of violence was rare; and the forcible conversion of the Christian conscript children, though it did occur, was not countenanced by the Ottoman authorities (d'Ohsson, op. cit., pp. 326–7). Forcible conversion was, indeed, usually superfluous, for the combined effect of segregation, education, and ambition would lead almost all Christian boys who entered the system to embrace Islam voluntarily before their time arrived for passing out and entering the public service. (See Lybyer, op. cit., pp. 66–8.)—A.J.T.

[2] The further education of this *crême de la crême*, which was thus skimmed off and set apart at the outset, is described below (see the present quotation, seventh paragraph on pp. 39–40).—A.J.T.

[3] The common run of conscript children, who were put out to be brought up by foster-masters in this way, were called '*Ajem-oghlans* ('alien boys'). For their training see further Lybyer, op. cit., pp. 79–82, and Rycaut, op. cit., Bk. I, ch. x. The rural fosterfathers seem to have been usually members of the free Muslim feudal landed gentry and not simple peasants (as Busbecq's description seems rather to imply that they were).—A.J.T.

which drafts are taken to make good the wastage in the ranks of the Janissaries.[1]

'Upon enrolment in the Janissaries, the cadet's pay starts at about a ducat and a half *per mensem*—a remuneration which is considered quite enough for a soldier who has yet to learn his trade. But, to insure that he is properly fed, he receives rations *gratis* from the mess of the platoon to which he is posted, on condition that he re-pays the platoon in scullion's-work and other fatigue duty. In return, the best master of arms in the platoon gives the cadet military instruction and teaches him, by daily practice, the science of handling his weapons. Thus the cadet acquires physical strength and endurance and professional skill; but he is still his messmates' inferior in rank and pay; and his sole hope of attaining equality with them lies in his own prowess: that is to say, if, in his first experience of active service, he gives a sufficiently good account of himself to be discharged from his probation and to be put on a par with the full-blown Janissaries in rank and pay. The hope of this reward stimulates many cadets to perform numerous feats of distinguished valour and to vie with the veterans in giving proof of their courage; and so they win the higher pay, which rises, for Janissaries, to a maximum of eight ducats *per mensem*.[2] If, however, a Janissary qualifies, through

[1] Busbecq here skips over an intermediate stage which is recorded in Rycaut, op. cit., ch. x, and in Lybyer, op. cit., pp. 79–82. The drafting of the '*Ajem-oghlans* into the Janissary Corps did not follow immediately upon their recall to Constantinople. The cream of them were thereupon selected for service, *en permanence*, in the Pādishāh's household as gardeners and in other menial non-military capacities (with a possibility of rising thereafter, by merit, to the lesser administrative posts in the Palace). The remainder were either drafted temporarily into the Navy or were hired out by the Government to private contractors to perform hard urban labour (as described by Busbecq in his next paragraph). It was from these two latter sub-categories of '*Ajem-oghlans* that the recruits for the Janissaries were eventually taken. In this last probationary stage, the '*Ajem-oghlans* were organized in companies (*odalar* or 'chambers'); and in each company facilities were provided for teaching any member, who wished to learn, to read and write (d'Ohsson, op. cit., p. 327).—A.J.T.

[2] The Janissaries were a professional paid standing corps of 12,000 regular infantry—disciplined, drilled, uniformed (in uniforms of blue cloth, without armour), and equipped with muskets. In other words, they resembled the infantry of Western Christendom as it came to be in the eighteenth century; but they were so different from, and in every way so superior to, the Western infantry of the sixteenth century that they moved an intelligent Western observer of that age, such as Busbecq was, to astonishment and envy. The whole purpose of Busbecq's *Exclamatio*, from which the passage here quoted is taken, was to induce the sovereigns of Western Christendom to save themselves and their peoples from the Ottoman peril by raising troops of their own on this Ottoman model. The unfamiliarity of uniformed troops to sixteenth-century Western eyes comes out in Busbecq's description of Suleymān defiling through the streets of Constantinople at the head of his troops in A.D. 1559 (in Letter III: Elzevir edition, p. 246): 'The cavalry were followed by a long column of Janissaries, few of whom carried any weapons except muskets, which are their regular arm. They were dressed in uniforms of practically identical cut and colour, which marked them out as the slave-force, or slave-household, of a single master. There was no extravagance or exaggeration in their dress, no slashings or perforations. They say their clothes wear out quite fast enough, even without deliberately tearing them!'

As in the Roman standing army of the Imperial period, marriage was discountenanced, though in the case of the Janissaries it was not actually disallowed (Lybyer, op. cit., p. 70). The unmarried Janissaries lived in barracks. They were organized in messes of ten members each ('For their living expenses each contributes so much a day; and they have a steward and a cook, who provide their necessary living': Ramberti, B.: *The Second Book of the Affairs of the Turks*, written in A.D. 1534, and translated from the Italian by Lybyer, in op. cit., p. 249). Ten messes constituted an *orta* or company. A schoolmaster was attached to each *orta* to teach any Janissary, who wished for instruction, to read and write (d'Ohsson, op. cit., p. 327).

good conduct and distinguished service, for promotion, he is either given an officer's commission in his own corps or is enrolled in the household cavalry called Sipāhīs.[1]

'The residue of the boys above-mentioned are kept in Constantinople and are employed in labour of various kinds. For instance, you may often see a couple of hundred or three hundred of them clearing a site, removing rubble, and transporting stones or timber or other heavy weights. None is allowed to live in idleness, and none receives his subsistence *gratis*. These likewise, upon reaching maturity, are transferred into the land or naval forces.[2]

'As for those who are selected[3] for the personal service of the sovereign at court, these generally end up as men of mark, and are appointed to the highest posts of public responsibility, according to their individual fortunes or characters.[4] From these are chosen the senior officers of

The corps was privileged in many ways. The Pādishāh himself, from Suleymān's time onwards, was enrolled in a Janissary *orta* and drew Janissary's pay (d'Ohsson, op. cit., p. 354. Compare the similar practice of modern Western sovereigns, who likewise flatter their troops by wearing their own uniforms and holding honorary rank in their own service). If a Janissary were condemned to suffer capital punishment, the sentence could not be executed until the culprit had been expelled from the corps, and this could not be done without the corps' consent. (Compare the similar privilege of the Macedonian citizen army in the time of Alexander the Great.) When a Colonel-in-Chief of the Janissaries (Yenicheri Aghasy) died, his property escheated, not (like the property of all other high officials) to the Crown, but to the regimental chest (Ryçaut, op. cit., p. 193). By Rycaut's time, the Corps had acquired corporate estates in Anatolia; and *'Ajem-oghlans* destined for enrolment in the Janissaries were sent to these estates for the first stage of their training (Rycaut, op. cit., p. 192), instead of being put out to service with private foster-masters, as they were in Busbecq's day.—A.J.T.

[1] These 'Sipāhīs of the Porte' (as distinct from the ordinary Sipāhīs, who were a territorial mounted militia of free feudal land-holders) were the Pādishāh's professional paid household cavalry. Of the four regiments of which this regular cavalry force was composed, the fourth, called the Ghurebā or 'Westerners' (see footnote 5 on p. 35, above), was a foreign legion. The rest were recruited partly from Janissaries who had earned promotion and partly from Imperial Pages (see below). Troopers recruited from the latter source were men of literary education (Rycaut, op. cit., p. 184).—A.J.T.

[2] As noted above (in footnote 1, on p. 38), this was a stage which all *'Ajem-oghlans*—including those eventually drafted into the Janissaries—had to pass through upon their recall to Constantinople from the Interior of Anatolia, with the sole exception of those who were appointed at this stage to menial non-military posts in the Palace service.—A. J. T.

[3] i.e. selected at the outset, upon the first arrival of the conscript children at Constantinople, when the remainder were put out into private service with foster-masters in the Anatolian countryside to be brought up as *'Ajem-oghlans*.—A.J.T.

[4] These boys, who were selected from the outset to be Imperial Pages, were called *Ich-oghlans* ('Interior Boys', i.e. boys admitted to the Pādishāh's privy service) in distinction from the *'Ajem-oghlans* ('Alien Boys'). They were an *élite*—numbering not more than 2,000 in all at any given moment, while there were perhaps as many as 20,000 *'Ajem-oghlans*. It was on the quality of the *Ich-oghlans* that the performance of the Ottoman *tour de force* ultimately depended, and these Imperial Pages were given a special education throughout. When the *'Ajem-oghlans* were drafted off to their foster-masters in Anatolia, the *Ich-oghlans* were placed in one or other of three residential schools (one in Stamboul, one in Galata, and one in Adrianople), which were the first rung in an educational ladder of four grades. The three higher grades were represented by six halls, culminating in the Hall of the Imperial Bedchamber (*Khās Oda*), which were all situate within the precincts of the Seraglio; and here the *Ich-oghlans* received an education which was both liberal and professional and both intensive and many-sided. They were first educated in Arabic and Persian literature, and afterwards in athletic and military accomplishments. They also had to learn some handicraft—an element in all Ottoman higher education, including that of the Pādishāh himself (Suleymān the Magnificent, anticipating the precepts of Mr. Gandhi, is reported to have devoted a certain time every day to working at his handicraft: Lybyer, op. cit., p. 76; cp. Withers, R.: *Description of the Grand Signor's Court* (London 1650, Martin and Ridley), p. 78; and Miller, *The Grand Seraglio*, pp. 68-9, and 'The Curriculum of the Palace School', pp. 307-8). The Arabic

the Janissaries, the admirals of the fleet, the beylerbeys and—at the top of the tree—the Vizier Pashas.[1] To these, again, the sovereign's own daughters are given in marriage.

'I think I have now sufficiently elucidated the origin, selection, discipline and education of this Turkish soldiery which has made itself so greatly feared the whole World over. At the same time, I will not deny that there are other avenues of entry into the Turkish military service, though the system which I have described is the most usual way. For the Turks do occasionally also make recruits of the boys or young men whom they take prisoners in raids or in regular warfare against Western Christendom.

and Persian literary education corresponded to the contemporary Western education in the Greek and Latin humanities.

Rycaut, however, notes (in op. cit., p. 32) that the *Ich-oghlans'* curriculum included no mathematics or physical science or geography. Moreover, printing was still rigorously forbidden in Turkey in Rycaut's day—an ominous symptom of mental rigidity.

Geography was certainly a science of which the statesmen and admirals of the Ottoman Empire remained abysmally ignorant. There is a legend of an Ottoman admiral who was sent out with orders to capture Malta and who returned to Constantinople, after cruising round the Mediterranean for many weeks, to report *'Malta yoq'* ('There is no Malta'). Again, in the great Russo-Turkish War of 1768–74, when the Ottoman Government received intelligence from friendly Powers in Western Europe that the Russians were fitting out a fleet in the Baltic for service in the Mediterranean, they are said to have ignored the warning in the belief that the Baltic and the Mediterranean were not connected with each other by any through-waterway!—A. J. T.

[1] Instances of *Ich-oghlans* who eventually distinguished themselves by rising to the highest offices of state are noted in Jorga, N.: *Geschichte der Türkei* (Gotha 1908–13, Perthes, 5 vols.), especially in volume ii, pp. 199 seqq. For example, Mahmūd Pasha, who was Grand Vizier in A.D. 1453–67, and again in 1472–3, was the son of a Greek father and a Serbian mother. He had been captured by 'Osmanli raiders in childhood (Jorga, op. cit., vol. ii, p. 200). Mawlā Khosrev, who rose to the highest Ottoman posts in the Islamic legal career as qādi of Constantinople and Grand Mufti in the reign of Sultan Mehmed II the Conqueror, was of Greek parentage (op. cit., vol. ii, p. 202). Khurrem (called by Franks 'La Rossa' and by Frankish pedants 'Roxalana'), who was Suleymān's favourite slave-concubine and who so won the Pādishāh's heart that he broke the long-established rule of the dynasty by making her his legally wedded wife, was a Russian girl who had been captured on a slave-raid by the Tatars of Krim, sold to the Porte, and educated in the female section of the Pādishāh's slave-household (op. cit., vol. ii, p. 345). Ibrāhīm of Parga, who was Grand Vizier in A.D. 1523–36, was the son of an Albanian peasant (on whom he afterwards conferred a *sanjāq* or provincial governorship). Ibrāhīm had been enslaved at the capture of Santa Maura, selected for an *Ich-oghlan*, and brought up at Mānysa until Suleymān before the latter came to the throne (op. cit., vol. ii, pp. 347–9). Mustafā of Cattaro, who was second vizier under Ibrāhīm and who was also Sultan Suleymān's brother-in-law, was a Serb who had been bórn a Venetian subject (op. cit., vol. ii, pp. 249–50). Ayas of Khimarra, who was third vizier under Ibrāhīm, was the son of a Christian peasant-woman. While he had become a vizier at Constantinople, his mother had become a nun at Avlona, and Ayas used to remit an annuity to her there (op. cit., vol. ii, p. 350). Rustem, who was Ibrāhīm's successor in the Grand Vizierate and who received in marriage Mihrmah, Suleymān's daughter by Khurrem, was a Serb (op. cit., vol. ii, p. 350); and Mehmed Sököllü (Sokolovic), who was Grand Vizier at the close of Suleymān's reign and the opening of Selim II's reign for fifteen years without a break, had started life as an acolyte in a Serbian church. One of Mehmed's acts as Grand Vizier was to restore the 'autocephaly' of the Serbian Orthodox Church and to instal one of his own relatives called Makarios, who had remained an Orthodox ecclesiastic, in the resuscitated Serbian Patriarchate of Ipek (Peč) (op. cit., vol. iii, p. 167; and Temperley, H. W. V.: *History of Serbia* (London 1917, Bell), pp. 123–4. The date of Sököllü's restoration of the 'autocephalous' Serbian Patriarchate at Ipek was A.D. 1557). Counting in Mehmed Pasha Sököllü, who was still in office when Suleymān died, and Mehmed Pasha Piri, whom Suleymān had found in office at his accession, the Grand Vizierate was occupied by nine different persons in Suleymān's reign, with terms of office which amounted in the aggregate to sixty-two years. All nine, with the sole exception of Mehmed Piri, were men of infidel birth who had passed through the slave-household (Lybyer, op. cit., p. 167). For the Dalmatian Slav 'Alī, who was Grand Vizier in A.D. 1561–5, between the Grand Vizierates of his fellow-Serbs Rustem and Mehmed Sököllü, see Busbecq's *Turkish Letters, passim.*—A.J.T.

'These prisoners are immured for years on end in the cloister-like palaces which they call *serays*. When, in this confinement, they are judged to have lost all memory of, and all feeling for, their Western homeland and civilization, and to have made sufficient progress in the practice of Arabic letters and Turkish arms under eunuch instructors, they are eventually let out of their prison-house by their Ottoman masters, and are appointed to the branches of the military service for which they appear best fitted. Recruits are also taken from among the slaves acquired—in war or otherwise—by the Pashas and other Imperial Grandees. At the same time, no prospective recruit from any of these categories is ever accepted without definite scrutiny and consideration. In every single case there is a preliminary investigation into the candidate's physique and character, to make sure of his being equal to the position assigned to him.

'In this connexion, I have found myself again and again struck with wonder at the sheer power of the Turkish system of discipline and education, when I have seen men who in our world had been despised and rejected making such progress in a few years in the Turkish environment that they were not only able to acquit themselves uncommonly well as common soldiers but were considered worthy, in the unanimous opinion of the Turks, of being entrusted with the duty of serving as military instructors to others.

'It has sometimes happened that, when I have been sitting, for recreation, at my window and looking out upon the public thoroughfare, Turks, sitting at my elbow, have pointed out to me passers-by who (they have told me) have been put in charge of the training of recruits on account of their own expertness in arms. I have then asked what these men's nationality was—imagining to myself that champions who enjoyed such a reputation as masters of arms among the 'Osmanlis must be Khurāsānīs or Balkhīs or Uzbegs or something of the kind (*nescio quos Parthos aut Bactrianos aut Massagetas*). Then I have been told that this one was a Hungarian, that one a Croat, the third a German. At this I have been much surprised; but I have imagined to myself that this outstanding proficiency in arms must have been the consequence of previous practice in the use of Western arms at home, and that these men must have been of noble birth and have received a liberal education and have seen military service [before their capture]. So I have proceeded to inquire from my Turkish informants whether they knew what station in life these men had occupied at home and what career they had followed. My Turkish friends have then searched their memories and told me that now they remembered: this one (they have said) would tell you that he had been, may be, a cook's son, the second a novice in a monastery, the third a publican's bar-tender. They had been captured in war-time or in time of truce, had been brought to Constantinople with other prize of war, and had thus entered the household of this or that Pasha.

'At this point, I have become more surprised than ever, and have asked how on earth it could happen that they should turn into such doughty warriors. Then my Turkish friends have explained that the

masters into whose possession these prisoners had passed retained in
their palaces distinguished men who were masters of arms and who were
equipped with a profound experience and knowledge of the military
art. To these masters the prisoners were handed over for instruction
(if the masters judged, by their intuition of the prisoners' physique and
character, that they were worth the trouble); and, under this tutelage,
the men had made such rapid progress that they had outstripped all
their contemporaries and had given good earnest of their own future
prowess. There had followed campaigns in which they had done yeoman service and had brought back a reputation for distinguished valour
on the unanimous testimony of their comrades in arms. Hence the
positions of high authority to which they had attained.

'When I have heard this explanation, I have been cut to the heart by
the thought of the great gulf that lies between this Turkish practice and
our Western way of doing things. And I have envied the Turks this
system of theirs. It is always the way of the Turks, whenever they come
into possession of a man of uncommonly good parts, to rejoice and be
exceeding glad, as though they had found a pearl of great price. And,
in bringing out all that there is in him, they leave nothing undone that
labour and thought can do—especially where they recognize military
aptitude. Our Western way is different indeed! In the West, if we come
into possession of a good dog or hawk or horse, we are delighted, and
we spare nothing in our efforts to bring the creature to the highest perfection of which its kind is capable. In the case of a man, however—
supposing that we happen to come upon a man of signal endowments—
we do not take anything like the same pains, and we do not consider that
his education is particularly our business. So we Westerners obtain
many sorts of pleasure and service from a well-broken-in horse, dog and
hawk, while the Turks obtain from a man whose character has been
cultivated by education (*ex homine bonis moribus informato*) the vastly
greater return that is afforded by the vast superiority and pre-eminence
of Human Nature over the rest of the Animal Kingdom.'[1]

The fine fruits which were the product of this wonderful system
of human cultivation are depicted by Busbecq himself in a passage
in the first of his four Turkish Letters, in which he is describing his
visit to Sultan Suleymān's camp at Amasīyeh in A.D. 1555:

'The Sultan's head-quarters were crowded by numerous attendants,
including many high officials. All the Cavalry of the Guard were there
—the Sipāhīs, the Ghurebā, the Ulufajīs—and a large number of Janissaries. In all that great assembly, no single man owed his dignity to
anything but his personal merits and bravery; no one is distinguished
from the rest by his birth; and honour is paid to each man according to
the nature of the duty and offices which he discharges. Thus there is
no struggle for precedence, every man having his place assigned to him
in virtue of the function which he performs. The Sultan himself assigns

[1] Busbecq, O. G.: 'Exclamatio, sive de Re Militari contra Turcam instituenda Consilium', in *A. Gislenii Busbequii Omnia quae Extant* (Leyden 1633, Elzevir), pp. 432–9.

to all their duties and offices, and in doing so pays no attention to wealth or the empty claims of rank, and takes no account of any influence or popularity which a candidate may possess; he only considers merit, and scrutinizes the character, natural ability, and disposition of each. Thus each man is rewarded according to his deserts, and offices are filled by men capable of performing them. In Turkey every man has it in his power to make what he will of the position into which he is born and of his fortune in life. Those who hold the highest posts under the Sultan are very often the sons of shepherds and herdsmen, and, so far from being ashamed of their birth, they make it a subject of boasting, and the less they owe to their forefathers and to the accident of birth the greater is the pride which they feel. They do not consider that good qualities can be conferred by birth or handed down by inheritance, but regard them partly as the gift of Heaven and partly as the product of good training and constant toil and zeal. Just as they consider that an apti-tude for the arts, such as music or mathematics or geometry, is not transmitted to a son and heir, so they hold that character is not here-ditary, and that a son does not necessarily resemble his father, but [that] his qualities are divinely infused into his bodily frame. Thus, among the Turks, dignities, offices, and administrative posts are the rewards of ability and merit; those who are dishonest, lazy and slothful never attain to distinction, but remain in obscurity and contempt. This is why the Turks succeed in all that they attempt and are a dominating race and daily extend the bounds of their rule. Our method is very different; there is no room for merit, but everything depends on birth, considera-tions of which alone open the way to high official position. On this subject I shall perhaps say more in another place, and you must regard these remarks as intended for your ears only.

'Now come with me and cast your eye over the immense crowd of turbaned heads. . . . What struck me as particularly praiseworthy in that great multitude was the silence and good discipline. There were none of the cries and murmurs which usually proceed from a motley con-course, and there was no crowding. Each man kept his appointed place in the quietest manner possible. The officers . . . were seated; the common soldiers stood up. The most remarkable body of men were several thousand Janissaries, who stood in a long line apart from the rest and so motionless that, as they were at some distance from me, I was for a while doubtful whether they were living men or statues, until, being advised to follow the usual custom of saluting them, I saw them all bow their heads in answer to my salutation.'[1]

Such were the 'human watch-dogs' that were bred by the Otto-man 'shepherds of men' in order to perform the *tour de force* of keeping the whole of Orthodox Christendom in subjection and holding the whole of Western Christendom at bay. The twentieth-century Western student of history, who can no longer see the

[1] Original Latin text in *A. Gislenii Busbequii Omnia quae Extant* (Leyden 1633, Elzevir), pp. 99–102; English translation, here quoted, by Forster, E. S.: *The Turkish Letters of Ogier Ghiselin de Busbecq* (Oxford 1927, Clarendon Press), pp. 59–62.

Ottoman slave-household with a Busbecq's, or even with a Rycaut's, living eye, can still conjure up a vivid image of this long since defunct institution's former power by paying a visit to a building on the outskirts of the Seraglio grounds in Stamboul which was once the Orthodox Christian church of St. Irene before it became the Ottoman military museum. As the visitor's eye falls upon the apse, piled high with 'breasts' and 'backs', gorgets and cuisses, helmets and morions, and all the elaborate apparatus of sixteenth-century and seventeenth-century Western armour, lying in profusion, disregarded, just where the pieces happened to be thrown down when they were first brought in as spoils of war, perhaps three centuries or four centuries ago,[1] it is borne in upon the visitor's mind how easily the 'Osmanlis performed their stupendous *tour de force* so long as they kept themselves in training. 'The weapons of war' are 'perished'; but, by the same token, 'How are the mighty fallen'.[2]

The Ottoman system fell because of its 'grand disregard for human nature';[3] but it was not the inhuman—or superhuman—severity of the training and discipline that brought this extraordinary institution to the ground. The Pādishāh's slave-household did not perish for lack of man-power, through failure to compel flesh and blood to continue to undergo its rigours. It perished by suffering the violence of the violent who took it by force, because every man pressed in to share its privileges.[4] The evil that ruined it was not depletion but dilution. The 'fundamental customs' which the Pādishāh's will-power proved unable permanently to set at naught were the pretensions of birth and heredity; and the first breach was made by men who, having known what it was to be the Pādishāh's slaves themselves, were determined to secure the same boon for their sons. A concession had always been made to the principle of heredity in the privilege of enrolling their sons (though not their grandsons) among the Pādishāh's slave-boys which was already accorded to the Sipāhīs of the Porte.[5] On this analogy, Suleymān, towards the close of his reign, began to tolerate the enrolment of Janissaries' sons among the *'Ajem-oghlans*; and his successor Selīm II celebrated his advent to the throne by formally extending to the Janissaries the Sipāhīs' privilege.[6] This concession

---

[1] The 'Osmanlis themselves despised armour—perhaps on account of their own proficiency in the use of long-range missile weapons. (They inherited an aptitude for archery from their Nomad ancestors, and they took kindly to fire-arms.) The Janissaries wore no armour at all, and the Sipāhīs seldom bothered to take any with them when they started on a campaign, since they counted upon being able to capture all that they wanted from the enemy. When they did wear armour acquired in this way, the Sipāhīs made a point of choosing pieces that did not fit, in order to show that they were hermit-crabs.
[2] 2 Samuel i. 27.
[3] See the passage quoted from Lybyer on pp. 33–4, above.
[4] Matt. xi. 12; Luke xvi. 16.
[5] See p. 34, footnote 2, above.   [6] Lybyer, op. cit., pp. 120 and 69.

opened the floodgates; for, when once the Janissaries had thus pressed in, it became a psychological impossibility to keep the free Muslim feudal gentry out any longer.

In fact, between 1574 and 1595, admission to the Janissary Corps was made open to all free Muslims except Negroes;[1] and the sequel shows that inflation produces the same results, with the same rapidity, in a human as in a monetary currency. Down to Suleymān's death, the strength of the Janissary Corps was little more than 12,000, and the total strength of the whole slave-household, on the widest reckoning, was only about 80,000.[2] By A.D. 1598 there were 101,600 Janissaries, alone, on the pay-rolls—not to speak of 150,000 'supernumeraries' who were enrolled though unpaid, and an unknown quantity of honorary 'aspirants'.[3] The 'supernumeraries' earned their living by engaging in trade, and there was a tendency for each *orta* to specialize in a particular craft.[4] The consequence was a collapse of Ottoman military discipline and efficiency.

In psychological 'compensation' for the severity of their upbringing and the sobriety of their normal régime, the Janissaries, even in their best days, had always been prone, in peace-time, to

[1] d'Ohsson, op. cit., p. 328. There appears to have been some attempt, even at this stage, to reserve the higher posts in the civil administration for infidel-born graduates from the Schools of Pages. In A.D. 1582 a free Muslim-born 'Osmanli was refused the Grand Vizierthere on the ground of his birth. (Finlay, George: *A History of Greece from its Conquest by the Romans to the Present Time* (Oxford 1877, Clarendon Press, 7 vols.), vol. v, p. 40, footnote 2.)

[2] Before inflation, the Ottoman Pādishāh's slave-household appears to have been constituted approximately as follows:

1. Boys in process of education:

Ich-oghlans	2,000	
'Ajem-oghlans	20,000	
		22,000
2. Ex-'ajem-oghlans in non-military service:		
Palace Gardeners	2,000	
Other Palace menials	500	
On hire to private employers	5,500	
		8,000
3. Ex-'ajem-oghlans in temporary naval service		2,000
4. Regular Army:		
Sipāhīs of the Porte	12,000—	
Janissaries	12,000+	
		24,000
5. Slave troopers maintained by the Sipāhīs of the three senior regiments of household cavalry at their own charges		30,000

On this showing, the Sultan's slave-household mustered 56,000 head excluding, and 86,000 head including, the slaves of slaves, while that part of the household which constituted the Regular Army mustered only 26,000 on the former reckoning and 56,000 on the latter. (Figures in Lybyer, op. cit., pp. 49, 80, 98, and 130.) The feudal cavalry, including the men-at-arms whom the fief-holders brought into the field with them, totalled something between 80,000 and 100,000 (Lybyer, op. cit., p. 104); but considerations of distance and expense made it impossible for the whole feudal force ever to be mobilized *in toto* for any given campaign. Thus the largest army which the Ottoman Power, at its zenith, was able to put into the field can hardly have reached six figures.

[3] d'Ohsson, op. cit., pp. 330–2. In Rycaut's time there were 100,000 Janissaries on the rolls, of whom only 20,000 were effectives. (Rycaut, op. cit., pp. 171 and 191.)

[4] d'Ohsson, op. cit., p. 332.

sudden outbreaks of temper and turbulence which contrasted oddly with their customary good behaviour; and on active service their contumacy compelled Selīm I to halt at Tabrīz[1] and Suleymān to halt before Vienna,[2] as Alexander had been brought to a halt by his Macedonians on the west bank of the Ganges. Yet, in Busbecq's day, the discipline of the Janissaries was still so exemplary on the whole that they were employed as a military police to protect the Pādishāh's non-Muslim 'human cattle' against molestation from the free Muslim population of the Empire.[3] By Rycaut's time, hardly more than a century later, these 'human watch-dogs' had 'returned to Nature' by reverting into wolves, who harried the Pādishāh's 'human cattle' instead of looking after them and keeping them in order. The Orthodox Christian subject population was now cheated of the *Pax Ottomanica* which had originally reconciled it to bearing the Ottoman yoke. The Pādishāh's *ra'īyeh* were being plundered and enslaved by the Pādishāh's own troops as though they were the inhabitants of enemy countries;[4] and in A.D. 1683, when the Anatolian feudal cavalry were marching to join the Ottoman Army for the second—and last—Ottoman siege of Vienna, the villagers in the Rumelian provinces on the line of march burnt their houses and fled to the mountains rather than await their oppressors' passage.[5] In Rycaut's time, the pristine Ottoman discipline still survived on active service, as Rycaut himself testifies from his own personal observation of the Ottoman Army which was operating against the Danubian Hapsburg Monarchy in A.D. 1665.[6] But in the great war of A.D. 1682–99 between the Ottoman Empire

[1] See I. C (i) (b), Annex I, vol. i, p. 386, above.
[2] Lybyer, op. cit., pp. 92–3.
[3] The Janissaries 'are scattered through almost every part of the Empire, either to garrison the fortifications against the enemy, or to protect the Christians and Jews from the violence of the mob. There is no district which is at all populous, and no city or town, that has not a detachment of Janissaries to protect the Christians and Jews and other helpless people from criminal assault'.—Busbecq, Letter I, Elzevir edition, p. 24.
[4] Rycaut, op. cit., pp. 170–1. See the passage quoted above in II. D (vii), vol. ii, on p. 265 in footnote 2.
[5] Finlay, George: *A History of Greece from its Conquest by the Romans to the Present Time* (Oxford 1877, Clarendon Press, 7 vols.), vol. v, p. 159.
[6] 'In the Turkish camp, no brawls, quarrels, nor clamours are heard; no abuses are committed on the people by the march of their Army, all is bought and paid with money, as by travellers that are guests at an inn; there are no complaints by mothers of the rape of their virgin-daughters, no violences or robberies offered on the inhabitants' (Rycaut, op. cit., p. 205). In the seventeenth-century English observer's opinion, 'this regulation . . . proceeds from nothing more than the strict prohibition of wine upon pain of death'. A twentieth-century observer, the writer of this Study, was equally struck by the exemplary behaviour of a Turkish force which reoccupied the Anatolian town of Ismid, in provocative circumstances, after its evacuation by the Greek Army in A.D. 1921. Though the Greek troops, before their departure, had massacred the Turkish civilian population, plundered their property, burnt their houses, and slaughtered pigs in their mosques, the victorious incoming Turkish troops refrained from making any reprisals upon the persons or property or churches of the Greek civilian population, which had been left at their mercy by the withdrawal of the Greek Army. In A.D. 1921, as in A.D. 1665, the penalty in the Turkish Army for drinking alcohol on active service was death.

and the Powers of Western Christendom—a war which began with
the second Ottoman siege of Vienna and ended with the first of
a series of Ottoman territorial losses that continued thereafter
until A.D. 1922—the superiority in discipline and efficiency passed
definitively from the Ottoman to the Western camp; and in the
eighteenth century of the Christian Era, when Western armies rose
to the level at which the Ottoman Army had stood two centuries
earlier, the Ottoman Army itself degenerated into the kind of
rabble that had done duty for a Western army in Busbecq's day.

The sequel to this decay of the Ottoman slave-household has
brought to light the insuperable rigidity which was the fatal defect
of its otherwise extraordinary qualities. For the 'Osmanlis have not
found it possible to respond to the tremendous challenge from the
West, to which the failure of their own indigenous institutions has
exposed them, by reconditioning the peculiar social system which
they had invented to meet their own special needs and which had
served them so well, for a season, by carrying them to a dizzy height
of military and political greatness. Once thrown out of gear, the
Ottoman system has proved wholly incapable of being either re-
paired or remodelled; and since the close of the seventeenth century
of the Christian Era, at latest, its wreckage has been nothing but an
incubus. Ever since they were first thrown on the defensive, the
'Osmanlis have been forced to seek salvation in a wholly different
quarter and through wholly different measures. They have been
compelled to take *Fas est et ab hoste doceri* for their motto, and to
borrow for their own defence the alien arms and armour with which
they have latterly been worsted by the once despised and long
thereafter hated peoples of the West. This has been the inevitable
path which all Ottoman reformers, for the past two and a half
centuries, have had to follow, whether they have trodden the road
of Westernization with personal repugnance or with personal
enthusiasm.[1]

As soon as the turn in the tide of war, which came in the latter
part of the seventeenth century of the Christian Era, had rendered
the art of diplomacy at least as important as the art of war itself
for the welfare of the Ottoman Empire in its intercourse with the
West, the Pādishāh found himself constrained to create new official
posts of great responsibility and power to be occupied by Orthodox

---

[1] The psychological history of Ottoman 'Westernization', which has been touched
upon in II. D (v), vol. ii, pp. 186–8, above, is a classic illustration of a famous Stoic text:

$$\text{"}Aγου \ δέ \ μ', \ ὦ \ Zεῦ, \ καὶ \ σύ \ γ', \ ἡ \ πεπρωμένη,$$
$$ὅποι \ ποθ' \ ὑμῖν \ εἰμὶ \ διατεταγμένος,$$
$$ὡς \ ἕψομαί \ γ' \ ἄοκνος· \ ἢν \ δέ \ γε \ μὴ \ θέλω,$$
$$κακὸς \ γενόμενος, \ οὐδὲν \ ἧττον \ ἕψομαι.$$

(Cleanthes in J. von Arnim's *Stoicorum Veterum Fragmenta*, vol. i (Berlin and Leipzig
1905, Teubner), p. 118.)

Christian subjects of his who had not been transformed from 'human cattle' into 'human watch-dogs' through being conscripted and educated as pages in the Pādishāh's own palace. The imperious reason which dictated this revolutionary inversion of the established practice was that the traditional curriculum of the Ottoman schools for pages would leave a Greek boy-conscript destitute of the now precious knowledge of Western languages and Western ways, while this same knowledge would be acquired almost as a matter of course by the conscript-boy's rejected brother who had been allowed to be brought up at home and to follow a commercial career in his Greek father's footsteps.[1]

The 'Osmanlis experienced their next great humiliation in the Russo-Turkish War of A.D. 1768–74, when they suffered a signal defeat at the hands of the Muscovites—'poor relations' of the 'Osmanlis' own Orthodox Christian ra'īyeh who had stolen a march upon the 'Osmanlis themselves by their greater promptitude in borrowing the new Western military technique. The shock administered to the Pādishāh's self-esteem and sense of security by the peace-terms to which his Government was compelled to subscribe in A.D. 1774 at Küchük Qaynarjy, stimulated Sultan Selīm III (imperabat A.D. 1789–1807) to drill a contingent of the free Muslim citizens of his Empire into the nucleus of a new model army on Western lines;[2] and this first essay in the 'Westernization' of the Ottoman military establishment was the thin end of a wedge which has since penetrated to the heart of Ottoman life until the process has been completed, on every plane and in every sphere, by President Mustafā Kemāl in our day.

The metamorphosis of the Ottoman body-social which Selīm began and which Mustafā Kemāl has carried to its logical conclusion is as wonderful a tour de force, in its way, as the creation of the Pādishāh's slave-household by an earlier line of great Ottoman statesmen. Yet a comparison of the respective results of these two performances brings out the relative triviality of the second. The makers of the Ottoman slave-household forged an instrument which enabled a tiny band of Nomads, who had been ejected from their native Steppe and cast away in an alien environment, not merely to survive and hold their own in this strange world, but to impose

---

[1] For the success with which the Phanariots qualified themselves, under the stimulus of penalization, for making the most of this opportunity, see II. D (vi), vol. ii, pp. 223–5, above. The social adaptability of these Ottoman ra'īyeh throws the social rigidity of the 'Osmanlis themselves into strong relief. In A.D. 1793, Sultan Selīm III, as part of his 'Westernization' programme (see below), established Ottoman diplomatic missions in Paris, Vienna, London, and Berlin and appointed Turks as ambassadors; but his Turks proved so incompetent in this unfamiliar environment that they had to be replaced by Greek chargés d'affaires (d'Ohsson, op. cit., p. 573).

[2] Selim's bombardier corps was organized for him by Western renegades (d'Ohsson, op. cit., p. 369).

peace and order upon a great Christian society which had gone into disintegration, and to threaten the life of a yet greater Christian society which has since cast its shadow over the whole of the rest of Mankind. Our latter-day Turkish statesmen have simply filled part of the vacuum which has been left in the Near East through the disappearance of the incomparable structure of the old Ottoman Empire by erecting on the desolate site a ready-made 'go-down' of a standard Western pattern in the shape of a Turkish national state. And in this commonplace 'villa-residence' the Turkish legatees of the arrested Ottoman Civilization are to-day content—like the Zionist legatees of a fossilized Syriac Civilization[1] next door and the Irish legatees of an abortive Far Western Christian Civilization[2] across the street—to live henceforth in comfortable nonentity as a welcome escape from the no longer tolerable status of being 'a peculiar people'.

The grateful acquiescence in this *pis aller*, which is the prevalent state of mind among Ottoman Turks of the present generation, gives some measure of the failure to which the old Ottoman institutions have been condemned in the long run by their intractable rigidity, in spite of their amazing efficacy to fulfil the precise functions for which they were originally designed. The denouement is almost ridiculous, yet it has only been achieved through long and painful travail. Selīm III's pioneer effort to supplant the long since useless Janissaries cost the bold reformer his throne and his life; and his cousin Mahmūd II, who shared Selīm's outlook and cherished his policy, had to keep his own counsel[3] and watch for his opportunity for eighteen long years[4] before he was able to emulate the

---

[1] See II. D (vi), vol. ii, pp. 252–4, above.

[2] See II. D (vii), Annex III, vol. ii, pp. 425–6, above.

[3] Mahmūd ascended the throne at the age of 25 in succession to his brother Mustafā IV, who had been deposed and murdered after a reign of only a few months when he had served the Janissaries' turn as a pretext for deposing and murdering Selīm.

[4] In girding himself for the task of clearing away the debris of the slave-household, Sultan Mahmūd II did not have to start *ab initio*; for some of the dead wood had already been cut out by his predecessors. According to Finlay (in op. cit., vol. v, pp. 35–7), the *devrishmé* or rotational conscription of Ottoman Christian children fell into disuse during the reign of Sultan Mehmed IV (*imperabat* A.D. 1649–87); and Rycaut (in op. cit., first published in A.D. 1668) speaks of this institution as obsolete in several passages (on pp. 80, 191, and 197). In another passage, however (on pp. 40–1), Rycaut states that about 2,000 boy-conscripts for the '*Ajem-oghlans* were still being recruited annually, chiefly from the Morea and Albania. Possibly he is here following some informant in the Seraglio who was describing things as they had been one or two decades back. That the *devrishmé* had actually been abandoned before the end of Mehmed IV's reign is indicated—though this is only presumptive evidence—by the fact that two out of the three extramural preparatory schools for *Ich-oghlans* were closed by Ibrāhīm I and the two lowest of the six halls inside the Seraglio by Mehmed IV thereafter. In d'Ohsson's day, none but the Galata Seray remained; and the Sultans, who had once spent their lives in their pages' company, now only visited the school once in every two or three years. Vestiges of the original discipline and curriculum survived; and the school still provided pages for the Pādishāh's personal domestic service; but the promotion of pages to be high officials, or even lifeguardsmen, had long since been abandoned (d'Ohsson, op. cit., pp. 47–53). Thus Sultan Mahmūd II found part of his work already done for him; and even the idea of deliberately destroying the Janissaries was not new. Rycaut declares his

greatest of his subjects by extirpating the Janissaries in 1826 as the Mamlūks had been extirpated in 1811 by Mehmed 'Alī.[1]

The Spartans

If it is possible that the Ottoman slave-household, at its zenith, came as near as might be to realizing the social ideal of Plato[2]—and this on the Hellenic philosopher's own native soil—it is certain that Plato himself, when he conceived his Utopia, was inspired by the actual institutions of the Spartan city-state: a Hellenic community which was the greatest among the Great Powers of the Hellenic World in Plato's day. A direct comparison between the Spartan and the Ottoman system reveals a striking similarity; and this is assuredly attributable, not to any mimesis of the society which happened to be prior by the society which happened to be posterior in the accidental sequence of chronology, but rather to a natural conformity between the responses which were made to a virtually identic challenge by two different communities acting independently of, and unbeknown to, one another.[3] On the point of similarity, there is, of course, a superficial contrast between the Spartan and the Ottoman achievement in mere material scale. The Spartans succeeded, by means of their 'peculiar institution', in making themselves masters of about two-fifths of the Peloponnese, whereas the entire Morea constituted no more than a fraction of the single Ottoman province of Rumili. Yet, when all the relevant factors, human as well as physical, are taken into account, the Spartan achievement would appear to have been at least as great a *tour de force* as the Ottoman. At any rate, the Spartans were hated quite as intensely as the 'Osmanlis were by their 'human cattle', while

belief that, in his time, the Janissaries were being 'studiously destroyed, . . . so as to be able to lay a foundation of a new discipline', by the policy of the Viziers of the House of Köprülü; and that the War of Candia (A.D. 1645–69) had been prolonged, and the Austrian War of A.D. 1663–4 precipitated, with this purpose in view (Rycaut, op. cit., Bk. III, ch. viii, pp. 197–9).

[1] For Mehmed 'Ali's massacre of the Mamlūks, see p. 31, above. Mehmed 'Alī enticed his victims into the Citadel of Cairo and had them shot down there. Mahmūd's destruction of the sole Ottoman regular forces, such as they were, in 1826, when the Greek Revolutionary War was at its height and a new Russo-Turkish War was in the offing, was a courageous act which was justified by results. For the Ottoman Empire managed to survive the Russo-Turkish War of 1828–9; and thereafter, with the incubus of the old slave-household removed at last, Sultan Mahmūd was able with impunity to call in a Prussian military mission (in which Hellmuth von Moltke won his spurs; see his *Briefe über Zustände und Begebenheiten in der Türkei* (Berlin 1841, Mittler)). By 1843, the Turkish Army had been reorganized on nineteenth-century Western lines. The bombardment of the Janissaries and the shooting-down of the Mamlūks were as brutal as Peter the Great's suppression of the Streltzy. Yet it would be false sentiment to waste pity on these military victims of 'Westernization'. If a watch-dog who is clearly past his work goes mad into the bargain, there is no doubt that he has to be shot, however faithful and efficient he may have been in his day.

[2] See the passage quoted from Lybyer on p. 33, above.

[3] The nature of the Spartan response has been indicated, by anticipation, in vol. i, on p. 24, and vol. ii, p. 48, above.

the numerical ratio of 'human cattle' to 'human watch-dogs' appears to have been as high in Laconia as it was in the Ottoman Empire.[1]

When we look into the origins of the Spartan system, we find that the Spartans, like the 'Osmanlis, were confronted with the necessity of performing their *tour de force*, and equipping themselves for the task with their 'peculiar institution', because, at an earlier stage in the course of their history, they had taken a peculiar turning. We have seen that the 'Osmanlis were derived from a band of Nomads which had parted company from the common run of Nomad hordes on the Steppe and had been cast up into the exotic environment of a sedentary society. In a similar fashion, the Spartans parted company, at a certain point in their history, from the common run of Hellenic city-state communities.

The Spartans made a peculiar response to the common challenge which was presented to all Hellenic communities in the eighth century B.C., when, in consequence of the immediately antecedent course of Hellenic social development,[2] the extension of the area under cultivation in the homelands of the Hellenic Society in Peninsular Greece and in the Archipelago had begun to bring in diminishing returns while the population of Hellas was rapidly increasing in numbers. The 'normal' solution which was found for this common problem of eighth-century Hellenic life was the further extension of the total arable area in Hellenic hands by the discovery and conquest of new territories overseas; and this solution proved satisfactory for two reasons. In the first place, the new lands could be conquered—and held—without an excessive military effort from barbarian 'Natives' who were less efficient than the Hellenic intruders in the art of war; and, in the second place, the lands thus conquered could be made to yield a higher economic return to Hellenic cultivators than they had yielded to their previous occupants because the superiority of the colonists over the 'Natives' in arms was only one manifestation of a superiority all round which extended to other branches of social activity, including agriculture. Even where the 'Natives' were not exterminated by the Hellenic conquerors but were assimilated—partly by force and partly by the attraction of a higher civilization—into the new-comers' body social, there would be room in these new Hellenic colonies overseas, under Hellenic husbandry, for an aggregate increase of population without any lowering of the existing standards of living of the diverse elements from which the population was recruited. This

[1] For an estimate of this ratio in the Ottoman Empire and in Laconia, see Annex III, below.
[2] The chain of cause and effect which can be detected here is examined further in III. B, on pp. 120–1, below.

was how the borders of the Hellenic World were gradually enlarged, from the eighth to the sixth century B.C., by the creation of new Chalcidian countrysides overseas in the territories of Chalcidian colonies like Leontini or Tauromenium in Sicily or like Methone or Torone in Thrace,[1] or a new Corinthian countryside in the territory of Syracuse, or a new Megarian countryside in the territory of Calchedon.[2] In the galaxy of new Hellenic city-states that came into existence as a result of this general movement of overseas expansion, there was one foundation, Tarentum, which claimed a Spartan origin; but even if this claim was in accordance with historical fact, the case of Tarentum was unique. Tarentum was the only Hellenic city overseas which even purported to be a Spartan colony; and this Tarentine tradition merely points the truth that, in the main, the Spartans sought to solve the common eighth-century Hellenic population-problem, not along the common lines of overseas colonization, but in their own peculiar way.

When the Spartans found even their broad and fertile plough-lands in the vale of the Eurotas[3] too narrow for a growing population, they did not turn their eyes to the sea, like the Chalcidians or Corinthians or Megarians. The sea is not visible either from Sparta city or from any point on the Spartan plain or even from the heights that immediately surround it.[4] The natural feature which dominates the Spartan landscape is the towering mountain-range of Taygetus, which rises so sheer from the western edge of the plain that its face seems almost perpendicular, while its line is so straight and so continuous that it gives the impression of a wall. This wall-like aspect of Taygetus attracts the eye to the Langádha: a gorge which cleaves the range at right angles as though the titanic architect of plain and mountain had expressly designed this one apparent break in an otherwise uniformly impassable barrier in order to provide his people with a sally-port. When the Spartans began,

[1] For the agricultural colonization overseas which was carried out by the people of Chalcis, and which was typical of a movement in which many other city-states of the Hellenic homeland took part, see I. B (ii), vol. i, p. 24, and II. D (ii), vol. ii, pp. 42–3, above.

[2] For the relative agricultural value of the Calchedonian and Byzantine territories and the consequent diversity of Calchedonian and Byzantine fortunes, see II. D (ii), vol. ii, pp. 43–8, above.

[3] Sparta, which means etymologically 'the sown land', was perhaps the name of the plain which is dominated from the west by the heights of Frankish and Ottoman Mistrà, and from the east by the heights of Minoan Therapne, before the term was confined to denoting the unwalled Hellenic city-state in the midst of the plain which made the name of Sparta famous after Therapne was forgotten and before Mistrà was heard of. (See Toynbee, A. J., in *The Journal of Hellenic Studies*, vol. xxxiii (London 1913, Macmillan), p. 246.) Similarly, Argos meant the arable land dominated by the Minoan fortresses of Mycenae and Midea and Tiryns before it became the name of a Hellenic city-state.

[4] Between the plain of Sparta and the sea-coast, the River Eurotas has to wind its way through a tangle of hills; and in the panorama of the plain, as seen from the crown of the citadel of Mistrà, it is impossible to detect either the point where the river enters the plain or the point where it leaves it. The plain is shut in by hills in every quarter, as far as the eye can see.

in the eighth century B.C., to feel the pinch of population-pressure, they lifted up their eyes unto the hills[1] and beheld the Langádha and sought their help in the pass through the mountains, as their neighbours, under the same spur of Necessity, were seeking theirs in the passage over the sea. At this first parting of the ways, help did come to the Spartans from the lord[2] Apollo of Amyclae and the lady Athana of the Brazen House. The first Messeno-Spartan War (*circa* 736–720 B.C.), which was contemporary with the first Hellenic settlements on the Thracian and Sicilian coasts, left the Spartan victors in possession of broader conquered lands in Hellas than the Chalcidian colonists won overseas at Leontini or the Spartans' own reputed colonists at Tarentum. But the Presiding Genius of Sparta, who led her and who did 'not suffer' her 'foot to be moved'[3] when once she had reached her Messenian goal, did not thereby 'preserve' her 'from all evil'.[4] On the contrary, the superhuman—or inhuman—fixity of Sparta's subsequent posture, like the mythical doom of Lot's wife, was manifestly a curse and not a blessing.

The Spartans' peculiar troubles began as soon as the First Messeno-Spartan War had ended in a Spartan victory; for to conquer the Messenians in war was a less difficult task for the Spartans than to hold them down in peace-time. These conquered Messenians were no barbarous Thracians or Sikels, but Hellenes of like culture, and like passions, with the Spartans themselves: all but their equals in war and perhaps more than their equals in numbers. The First Messeno-Spartan War (*circa* 736–720 B.C.) was child's-play compared to the Second (*circa* 650–620 B.C.), in which the subject Messenians—tempered by adversity and filled with shame and rage at having submitted to a fate by which no other Hellenes had allowed themselves to be overtaken—now rose in arms against their Spartan rulers and fought far harder and longer, in this second bout, to recover their freedom than they had fought in the first bout to preserve it. Their tardy heroism failed, in the end, to avert a second Spartan victory; and, after this unprecedentedly stubborn and exhausting war, the victors treated the vanquished with unprecedented severity. Yet, in the long view of the Gods, the Messenian insurgents had secured their revenge on Sparta, in the sense in which Hannibal was to have his revenge on Rome. The Second Messeno-Spartan War changed the whole rhythm of Spartan life and deflected the whole course of Spartan history. It was one of those wars in which the iron enters into the survivors' souls. It was so terrible an experience that it left Spartan life fast bound in misery and iron, and it 'side-tracked' Spartan evolution into a

---

[1] Psalm lxxi. 1.   [2] Psalm lxxi. 2.
[3] Psalm lxxi. 3.   [4] Psalm lxxi. 7.

blind alley. And since the Spartans were never able to forget what
they had gone through, they were never able to relax, and therefore
never able to extricate themselves from the impasse of their post-
war reaction.

The relations of the Spartans with their human environment in
Messenia passed through the same ironic vicissitudes as the relations of the Esquimaux with their physical environment in the
Arctic Zone. In either case we have the spectacle of a community
which ventures to grapple with an environment that daunts this
community's neighbours, in order to wring from this excessively
formidable enterprise an exceptionally rich reward. In the first
phase, this act of audacity seems to be justified by results. The
Esquimaux find better hunting on the Arctic ice than their less
adventurous Indian cousins can find on the North American
prairies;[1] the Spartans, in the First Messeno-Spartan War, win
richer lands from their fellow-Hellenes across the mountains than
the contemporary Chalcidian colonists can win from barbarians
across the sea. But in the next phase the original—and irrevocable
—act of audacity brings its ineluctable penalty. The conquered
environment now takes its audacious conqueror captive. The
Esquimaux become prisoners of the Arctic climate and have to
shape their lives according to its exacting dictates down to the
smallest detail.[2] The Spartans, having conquered Messenia in
the First War in order to live unto themselves, are constrained, in
the Second War and ever after, to give up their lives to the task of
keeping Messenia. They live as the obedient humble servants of their
own dominion over Messenia from this time forth for evermore;
and this servitude of the Spartiate 'Peers' ($\delta\mu o\iota o\iota$) is as rigorous a
bondage as that of the Ottoman Pādishāh's slave-household (*qūllar*).

The Spartans equipped themselves for performing their *tour de
force* by the same method as the 'Osmanlis. They adapted existing
institutions to fulfil new needs. But whereas the 'Osmanlis were
able to draw upon the rich social heritage of Nomadism, 'the [latter-
day] Spartan institutions are actually built up upon primeval and
altogether primitive foundations, which have been adapted with
amazing dexterity to the [peculiar] requirements of the Spartan
conqueror-state.'[3]

The Spartans were descended from Greek-speaking barbarians
belonging to the so-called 'Dorian' stratum of the external proletariat of the vanished Minoan World: a stratum which had descended
upon the shores of the Aegean, out of the European hinterland, in

---

[1] See the passage quoted from Steensby on p. 4, above.
[2] See pp. 5–7, above.
[3] Nilsson, M. P.: 'Die Grundlagen des spartanischen Lebens', in *Klio* vol. xii
(Leipzig 1912, Dieterich), p. 308.

a kind of human avalanche, at the climax of the post-Minoan and pre-Hellenic Völkerwanderung, about the turn of the thirteenth and the twelfth centuries B.C.[1] The primeval institutions which the forefathers of the Spartans had brought with them were the com mon social heritage of all these 'Dorian' interlopers from the back of beyond; and there were other Hellenic communities of 'Dorian' origin besides the Spartans—e.g. the 'Dorian' conquerors of the heart of the Minoan World in Crete—who retained these primitive institutions down to a late date in Hellenic history. The Cretan 'Dorians', however, seem to have remained socially primitive mainly out of inertia, and to have done little to adapt their inherited social tradition to the conditions of the new social environment in which their conquest of the Minoans had placed them.[2] On the other hand, the primitive 'Dorian' heritage was sloughed off altogether at an early date by those 'Dorians' who had established themselves on the Isthmus of Corinth and in the Argolid and on the islands and peninsulas off the south-west corner of Anatolia and in other regions which, instead of remaining, like Crete, untouched by the main currents of Hellenic history, became focuses for the develop- ment of the new Hellenic Civilization.[3] When 'Dorian' Corinth or Sicyon or Rhodes first come into the light of Hellenic history, they display no more trace of primitiveness than contemporary 'Ionic' communities like Athens or Miletus. 'Dorian' Sparta, however, dealt with her primitive heritage in a different manner from either 'Dorian' Crete or 'Dorian' Rhodes.[4]

'The way . . . in which those primitive institutions, which other- wise vanished in all Greek communities before the face of the rising [Hellenic] culture, were made to serve as the corner-stones of the Spartan organism, is something which exacts from us the deepest admiration.[5]

'In this adaptation, one cannot refuse to discern something which is more than the mere result of an automatic development. The methodical and purposeful way in which everything has been made to lead towards one single goal forces us to see here the intervention of a consciously shaping hand. . . . The existence of one man, or of several men working in the same direction, who have remodelled the primitive institutions into the *Agôgê* and the *Kosmos*, is a necessary hypothesis.'[6]

---

[1] See I. C (ii) (b), vol. i, pp. 92–3 and 100–1, above.

[2] For some account of the primitive 'Dorian' institutions as they lingered on in Crete, see Aristotle, *Politics*, Bk. II, ch. vii, 1271 B–1272 B, and Strabo (following Ephorus) Bk. X, pp. 480–4. Compare the survival of Nomadic institutions among the Egyptian Mamlūks. (See pp. 30–1, above.)

[3] Compare the disappearance of the original Nomadic institutions of the Magyars after their settlement in Hungary and their subsequent absorption into the body social of Western Christendom.

[4] For the differentiation in the fortunes of the various Hellenic city-states of 'Dorian' origin in the course of Hellenic history, see II. D (iii), Annex, vol. ii, pp. 395–9, above.

[5] Nilsson, op. cit., p. 340.   [6] Nilsson, op. cit., loc. cit.

Hellenic tradition attributed not only the reconstruction of the Lacedaemonian Society after the Second Messeno-Spartan War—a reconstruction which made Sparta what she was and what she remained ever after until she collapsed—but also all the antecedent and less abnormal events in Spartan social and political history to 'Lycurgus'. But 'Lycurgus' was a god;[1] and modern Western scholars, in search for a human author of the 'Lycurgean' system, have been inclined to find their man in Chilon, a Spartan Overseer (ἔφορος) who left a reputation as a sage and who appears to have held office about 550 B.C.[2] Perhaps we shall not go far wrong if we regard the 'Lycurgean' system as the cumulative work of a series of Spartan statesmen during something like a century, dating from the outbreak of the Second Messeno-Spartan War, on the analogy of the genesis of the Ottoman system, which we know to have been the work of a series of statesmen that began, perhaps, with Sultan 'Osmān himself and ended with Sultan Mehmed the Conqueror.

In the Spartan system, as in the Ottoman, the outstanding feature—the feature which accounts alike for the system's astonishing efficiency and for its fatal rigidity and for its consequent breakdown—was its 'grand disregard for human nature';[3] and, when we compare the two systems from this standpoint, we find that while in some respects the 'Lycurgean' *agôgê* set human nature at defiance rather less truculently than the Ottoman slave-household, in other ways it challenged it still more provocatively.

The *agôgê* did not go so far as the slave-household in ignoring the customary claims of birth and heredity; and the free citizen landholders of Sparta were in exactly the opposite situation from the free Muslim landed gentry of the Ottoman Empire. Whereas the Ottoman Muslims were excluded from any share in the government of the Empire by rule, and the descendants of the Pādishāh's slaves were debarred from inheriting their fathers' or grandfathers' positions by the practice of conferring upon them the doubtful

---

[1] 'The famous name of Lycurgus has attracted to itself the whole series of developments that make up Spartan history: συνοικισμός, ephorate, rhetra, γῆς ἀναδασμός. The Greeks always imagined Athene springing adult out of the head of Zeus: the idea of growth they had not grasped. Accordingly, we find the [Spartan] νομοθέτης ascribed to the most varied epochs (which was easy, since he never lived in any generation of men). The ninth century B.C. was the favourite estimate, for this put him well at the back of Spartan history, and it is easier to antedate than to postdate political inventions. But each author connects him with the development that loomed largest in his own mind; and Aristotle, at least (*Politics*, 1270 A, 1–5), dates him after the close of the Messenian Wars.' All the time, 'Lycurgus was a god, or at least the epithet of one. We are surely bound to follow the opinion of the Pythia, even though cautiously expressed (Herodotus, Bk. I, ch. 65). The fact that in Sparta he had a *naos*, not a ἡρῷον, clinches the matter: Λακεδαιμόνιοι δὲ καὶ Λυκούργῳ τῷ θεμένῳ τοὺς νόμους οἷα δὴ θεῷ πεποιήκασι καὶ τούτῳ ἱερόν. (Pausanias, *Descriptio Graeciae*, Bk. III, ch. 16, § 6).' Toynbee, op. cit., footnotes on pp. 259 and 256.
[2] For Chilon, see Guy Dickins in *The Journal of Hellenic Studies*, vol. xxxii (London 1912, Macmillan).   [3] See pp. 34 and 44, above.

honour of manumission and enfeoffment, virtually the whole burden
of maintaining the Spartan dominion over Messenia was imposed
on the free-born children of free-born Spartiates. At the same
time, within the Spartiate citizen-body itself, the principle of
equality was not only well-established but was carried to great
lengths.

Though there was not an equalization of wealth, every Spartiate
'Peer' held from the State one of the fiefs or allotments (κλῆροι) of
equal magnitude—or equal productivity—into which the arable
land of Messenia had been divided up after the Second Messeno-
Spartan War; and each of these allotments, which was cultivated
by the labour of Messenians bound to the soil as serfs (εἵλωτες),
was calculated to support a Spartiate 'Peer' and his family, on a
'spartanly' frugal standard of living, without their having to labour
with their own hands.[1] Accordingly, every Spartiate 'Peer', however poor, was economically in a position to devote his whole time
and energy to the art of war; and since permanent and perpetual
military training and service were also incumbent upon every Spartiate 'Peer', however rich he might be, the residual inequality of
wealth[2] was not, at Sparta, reflected in any substantial difference
between the rich man's and the poor man's way of life.

In the matter of hereditary rank, the Spartan nobility appear to
have retained no political privilege denied to commoners except
eligibility to the Council of State (γερουσία). For the rest, they were
absorbed into the rank and file of the 'Peers'; and, in particular, the
three hundred knights (ἱππεῖς) of Sparta were no longer, under the
'Lycurgean' system, either a club of nobles or a mounted force.
They had become a *corps d'élite* of heavy infantrymen which was
recruited by merit from all the 'Peers', who competed eagerly for
admission.[3] The most striking manifestation of the equalitarian
spirit of the 'Lycurgean' system was the status to which it reduced
the Kings.[4] Though the Kings continued to succeed to the throne
by hereditary right, the one substantial power which they retained

[1] The average number of Helot families per Spartiate allotment seems to have been
seven (see Herodotus, Bk. IX, ch. 28, § 2). For the amount of the annual rent in kind
(that is, in barley, wine, and oil) which a Spartiate 'Peer' was supposed to draw from
his allotment, see Plutarch, *Life of Lycurgus*, ch. viii.

[2] There was a residual inequality of wealth, as between one Spartiate 'Peer' and
another, in spite of the equality of the public allotments, because there was private
property in land in the older territories of Sparta which had belonged to her before her
acquisition of Messenia; and the distribution of this freehold land among Spartan
citizens naturally was and remained unequal—in spite of a customary prejudice against
the buying and selling even of freehold land, which seems to have grown up by analogy
with the non-negotiability of the public allotments (see Heraclides Ponticus, ii. 7, in
Müller's *Fragmenta Historicorum Graecorum*, vol. ii, p. 211).

[3] See Xenophon, *Respublica Lacedaemoniorum*, ch. iv, and the passage from Plutarch's
Apophthegmata Laconica which is quoted on p. 65, in footnote 2, below.

[4] There was a double kingship at Sparta, which was hereditary in two separate
dynasties, each of which had to be represented in the person of one of the two kings
reigning simultaneously at any given moment.

was the military command on active service. Otherwise, apart from certain ceremonial duties and privileges which were less important than picturesque, the reigning Kings, as well as all other members of the two royal families, had to submit to the same exacting and life-long discipline as ordinary 'Peers'. As heirs apparent, they received the same education; and their succession to the throne brought them no exemption.

Thus, within the fraternity of the Spartiate 'Peers', differences of birth and of hereditary privilege counted, under the 'Lycurgean' system, for little or nothing; and, although one normal qualification for admission into this fraternity was free Spartiate birth, no candidates for admission would ever have dreamt of saying—even within themselves, let alone in public—the Spartan equivalent of 'We have Abraham to our father';[1] for Spartiate birth was no guarantee of promotion to the coveted though onerous status of a 'Peer'. Indeed, Spartiate birth, though normally required, was not a *sine qua non*. Spartiate birth simply condemned a child (if it were not reprieved by being rejected as a weakling after birth and put out to die of exposure)[2] to undergo the ordeal of a Spartan education; and this ordeal merely entitled a boy to compete for a place in the fraternity of the 'Peers' when he came of age. A child's response to this ordeal of education counted for more than his birth in the last resort. There were Spartiates born who failed to give satisfaction under the educational test and who were therefore eventually refused admission to the fraternity of 'Peers' and were left to weep and gnash their teeth in outer darkness in the unenviable status of 'Inferiors'. Conversely, there were cases—though these were evidently rare—in which non-Spartiate boys were allowed to undergo the Spartan education; and if these 'Alien Boys' (μόθακες) acquitted themselves well, they appear to have been no less eligible for enrolment among the 'Peers' than their Spartiate class-mates.[3]

To this extent the Spartan system, like the Ottoman, ignored the claims of birth and heredity; and there were also points, as has been mentioned by anticipation, in which the God Lycurgus went still farther than the Sultan 'Osmān in defiance of 'human nature'. Whereas, for example, the Ottoman social reformer was content to conscript children who had been born in wedlock in the ordinary way, the Spartan ventured to interfere with marriage itself in the

---

[1] Matt. iii. 9.

[2] The new-born child's fate was decided not by its father, as in most Hellenic communities, but by the public authorities (Plutarch, *Life of Lycurgus*, ch. xvi).

[3] For these so-called μόθακες, see Phylarchus apud Athenaeum, vi. 271, E; Plutarch, *Instituta Laconica*, 22; Aelian, *Variae Historiae*, xii. 43. The μόθακες were apparently recruited both from non-Spartan Lacedaemonians (Helots or Perioeci) and from non-Lacedaemonian foreigners. It will be seen that they corresponded in nature as well as in name to the Ottoman *'Ajem-oghlans.*

interests of eugenics, and sought—with greater audacity but also with greater logic—to do what he could to obtain the kind of human material that he wanted, by breeding, before the time came for selection. In the second place, the Spartan conscription, for the class that was subject to it (that is to say, for all free-born Spartiates who had not been exposed after birth), was universal, whereas the 'Osmanlis only conscripted a portion of the offspring of their 'human cattle' to be trained as 'human watch-dogs', and this every fourth year and in different provinces in rotation. In the third place, the Spartans took the children from their homes and put them into the educational mill at the age of seven; the 'Osmanlis not until the age of twelve and upwards. Finally, the Spartans not only anticipated the 'Osmanlis in conscripting and training girls as well as boys, but they went far farther towards an identical treatment of both sexes. For Spartan girls, as well as for Spartan boys, conscription was universal; and the Spartan girls were not trained in special female accomplishments, nor kept in seclusion from the men, like the girls in the female section of the Ottoman Pādishāh's slave-household. Spartan girls, like Spartan boys, were trained on a competitive system in athletics; and girls, like boys, competed naked in public before a male audience.[1]

In the matter of breeding human stock, the Spartan system[2] pursued two distinct aims simultaneously. It aimed both at quantity and at quality. It secured quantity (proportionately to the miniature scale on which the Spartan Society was built) by addressing itself to the individual male adult Spartiate and seeking to influence his behaviour through inducements and through penalties. The deliberate and confirmed bachelor was penalized by the State and was insulted by his juniors for his shameful lack of public spirit. On the other hand, the father of three sons was exempt from mobilization, and the father of four from all obligations towards the State.[3] At the same time, quality was secured by keeping alive, with

[1] This spectacle, which would have routed the most redoubtable Janissary and have given him a lasting moral shock, was really, of course, a demonstration of the remarkable degree of sexual self-control to which, under the 'Lycurgean' system, it was possible for the Spartan Society to attain. In this matter, our twentieth-century Western Society is still far from having reached the Spartan level; but that level has been attained, and perhaps surpassed, by the Japanese.

[2] See Xenophon, *Respublica Lacedaemoniorum*, ch. i; Plutarch, *Life of Lycurgus*, ch. xv; Nilsson, op. cit., pp. 325-35.

[3] Aristotle, *Politics*, 1270 B, 1-5. Aristotle points out, in loc. cit., that where, as in Lacedaemon, the number of allotments is limited, large families entail a surplus of pauper male population; but this, of course, was just what the Spartan State required. To meet the incalculable losses of war, Sparta needed a standing reserve of military unemployed. In the Spartiate citizen-body the superfluous souls which, in other Hellenic states, would have been absorbed into industry or commerce, or would have been drawn off by emigration, were first unfitted for either agriculture or any other gainful occupation by being compelled to go through the Spartan military education, and were then retained at home to starve. On the Spartan system, the maintenance of the 'Peers' (ὅμοιοι) entailed the existence of 'Inferiors' (ὑπομείονες). The Ottoman system showed

a conscious and definite eugenic purpose, certain primitive social customs governing sexual intercourse which appear to have been relics of a sex-group system of social organization antecedent to the system represented by marriage and the family. A Spartiate husband won popular approval, instead of exposing himself to public condemnation, if he took pains to improve the quality of his wife's progeny by arranging that her children should be gotten upon her by a sire who was a better man—or human animal—than her husband himself. And it even appears that a Spartiate wife could arrange this on her own account with impunity if her husband would not take the initiative in providing her with a substitute for himself when he was manifestly below par. The spirit in which the Spartans practised their eugenics is conveyed by Plutarch in a passage[1] which finds its echo in Busbecq's observations, quoted above,[2] on the social philosophy of the 'Osmanlis. According to Plutarch, the Spartan social reformer

'saw nothing but vulgarity and vanity in the sexual conventions of the rest of Mankind, who take care to serve their bitches and their mares with the best sires that they can manage to borrow or hire, yet lock their women up and keep them under watch and ward in order to make sure that they shall bear children exclusively to their husbands—as though this were a husband's sacred right even if he happens to be feeble-minded or senile or diseased. This convention ignores the two obvious truths that bad parents produce bad children and good parents good children, and that the first people to feel the difference will be those who possess the children and who have to bring them up.'

In the matter of educating[3] the Spartiate children which had been bred in this way, with the ultimate object of selecting the best of them for enrolment among the 'Peers' and endowment with public allotments, the Spartan system again availed itself of the relics of a pre-familial system of social organization in which the child who no longer needed his mother's personal care was educated, not by learning his father's business in a patriarchal household, but by successive membership in a series of 'human packs', in which he consorted, at each stage, with the other children of the tribe who were of his own age and sex. The 'Lycurgean' reform adopted this

itself more statesmanlike, as well as more humane, in taking care that every child which passed through it should learn a trade besides receiving the literary and athletic education required for making administrators and soldiers, and further in arranging thereafter that the adult 'Ajem-oghlans, who were on the waiting-list for admission to the Janissary Corps and who had to be kept in waiting in order to maintain the necessary military reserve, should be enabled meanwhile to earn their livings in some public or private employment.

[1] Plutarch, *Life of Lycurgus*, ch. xv.
[2] See p. 42 above.
[3] For the Spartan education, see Xenophon, *Respublica Lacedaemoniorum*, chs. ii and iv; Plutarch, *Life of Lycurgus*, chs. xvi and xvii; Nilsson, op. cit., pp. 309-25 ('Altersklassen und Syskenien'); Toynbee, op. cit., pp. 261-2.

'age-class' system and at the same time adapted it to its own educational purpose by introducing a cross-division in which children of all ages were brought together in one group, so that the elder children might assist in training the younger.[1] These juvenile 'droves' (ἀγέλαι) were reproductions of, and preparations for, the adult 'messes' (φιδίτια), which were associations of 'Peers' belonging to different 'age-classes', from the highest to the lowest, among the forty 'year-classes' (from the twenty-first to the sixtieth year inclusive) that were subject to military service.[2] The climax of a Spartan boy's thirteen years of education in a 'drove' was his candidature, at the end of his twentieth year, for entry into one of the 'messes', which was the sole avenue of admission into the fraternity of the 'Peers'. Entry into a 'mess' could only be secured by co-option; and a single 'black ball' entailed the rejection of the candidate.[3] A successful candidate, once co-opted, remained an active member of his 'mess' for forty years unless he either failed to make his prescribed contribution, in victuals and money, towards the

[1] For this cross-division (a Spartan innovation upon the primitive 'Dorian' institutions, as is indicated by the fact that there is no trace of it in 'Dorian' Crete), see Nilsson, op. cit., pp. 323–4. The 'age-classes' at Sparta were called 'herds' (βοῦαι), the cross-divisions 'droves' (ἀγέλαι) and 'hordes' (ἴλαι). These vertical cross-divisions, which included boys of all ages, evidently played a more important part than the 'age-classes' in the life and education of a Spartiate boy. In the 'drove' the junior boys were under the authority of one of the senior boys who was appointed 'horde-leader' (ἴλαρχος) and who had much the same duties of exercising discipline and rights of exacting 'fagging' from his juniors as a 'prefect' in an English 'public school'. (The 'prefect system' also existed in the Ottoman chambers of 'Ajem-Oghlans: see Withers, R.: Description of the Grand Signor's Court (London 1650, Martin and Ridley), pp. 65–7.) To supervise the education of the 'fags' by the 'prefects' in the 'droves' and 'hordes' was the informal business of every Spartiate 'Peer' and the official business of the Director of Public Education (παιδονόμος)—an office which, at Sparta, was a step to the highest political career (Xenophon, Respublica Lacedaemoniorum, ch. ii). Though Spartan boys, like Ottoman 'Ajem-oghlans, were taught to read and write (Plutarch, Life of Lycurgus, ch. xvi), their education was otherwise almost exclusively moral and physical. There was no counterpart, in the Spartan system, to the literary education that was given to the Ottoman Ich-oghlans, in spite of the fact that Sparta lay in the midst of a Hellenic World whose posthumous fame rests to-day upon the higher intellectual education which it evolved. In this most un-Hellenic trait, Sparta showed that, in accepting the 'Lycurgean' system, she had sold her birthright. Thenceforward, Sparta was in Hellas but not of it.

[2] For this institution, see Xenophon, Respublica Lacedaemoniorum, ch. v. The Spartan name for a 'mess' was φιδίτιον and for mess-mates σύσκηνοι ('occupants of the same tent'). In popular Greek parlance, the Spartiate mess was called a συσσίτιον: a word which bears its meaning on its face. The 'mess' was the basis, but not the unit, of the military formation. The smallest Spartan military unit, which was called the 'company of sworn comrades' (ἐνωμοτία = Eidgenossenschaft), was apparently a body of 40 men representing the 40 'year-classes' subject to service; and each of these 'companies' seems to have been made up of 2 'messes'. After the reorganization of the Lacedaemonian Army in the fifth century B.C. (see Annex III, below), when the proportion of Spartiates to Perioeci was reduced from 5:5 to 4:6, the 2 Spartiate 'messes' in each Spartiate 'company' appear to have contained no more than 16 men each, the complement of 8 additional men, which was needed to bring the 'company' up to its full strength of 40, being now provided by the Perioeci. Under this organization, the 40 adult 'year-classes' were presumably consolidated into 8 blocks of 5 'year-classes' each, so that, in every 5 years, each of the 2 'messes' in a 'company' would liberate 2 time-expired men and replace them by 2 recruits, while there would be 1 replacement among the supplementary Perioeci. (See Toynbee, op. cit., pp. 261, 264, and 267.)

[3] Plutarch, Life of Lycurgus, ch. xii.

upkeep of the common table or were convicted of the unpardonable offence of cowardice in war.[1]

The leading features in the Spartan system were the same as in the Ottoman[2]—namely: supervision, selection, and specialization; a competitive spirit;[3] and the simultaneous use of the negative stimulus of punishment and the positive stimulus of reward. And in the Spartiate fraternity of 'Peers', as in the Ottoman slave-household, these features were not confined to the educational stage. They continued to dominate the Spartiate's adult life as they had dominated his boyhood; and from the moment when he was taken away from his mother upon the completion of his seventh year he was continuously subject to discipline until the completion of his sixtieth year brought him his release from military service. The outward and visible sign of this discipline was the regulation which prescribed fifty-three years 'service with the colours'; for the Spartiate who had been transferred as a child from his parents' home to a juvenile 'drove' did not find himself at liberty to live in a home of his own when he had been co-opted into a 'mess' and had been endowed with a public allotment and had performed his social duty of taking a wife in marriage. Whereas the Janissaries, who were discouraged from marrying, were allowed to live in married quarters if they did marry nevertheless, the Spartiate 'Peers' were both compelled to marry and forbidden to lead a 'home life'.[4] The Spartiate bridegroom was required to spend even his wedding-night in barracks; and though the ban upon sleeping at home was gradually relaxed as he advanced in years, the ban upon dining at home was absolute and permanent.

'Lycurgus took care that the Spartiates should not be at liberty to take a preliminary dinner at home and so come to mess on full stomachs. If a Spartiate showed no appetite at mess, he was "told off" by his messmates as a glutton who was too soft to stand the common fare; and if he was actually convicted he was fined. There was a famous occasion when King Agis had returned from the wars after a long absence (at the end of his victorious war of attrition against Athens). The King wanted to dine, just once, with his wife, and sent to the mess for his portion; but the Army Council (οἱ πολέμαρχοι) would not allow it to be

---

[1] See Herodotus, Bk. VII, ch. 231; Xenophon, *Respublica Lacedaemoniorum*, ch. ix. There is a similarity in organization and in atmosphere between a Spartan 'mess' and a Janissary 'mess' (as described above in the passage quoted from Busbecq on pp. 38–9). The Janissaries, like the Spartiates, were even famous—or notorious—for their soup; and the senior member of a Janissary 'mess' was called the *chorbaji* ('soup-maker'). The recognized method by which the Janissaries expressed dissatisfaction was to upset their soup-kettles—a gesture which was taken as a danger-signal by any wise Pādishāh. At Sparta, though the soup was no more palatable, such insubordination was unheard of!
[2] See p. 36, above.
[3] See Xenophon, *Respublica Lacedaemoniorum*, chs. iv and x.
[4] Compare the attitude of Oxford colleges, with their monastic tradition, towards married 'fellows'.

sent, and when the incident came to the notice of the Board of Overseers (τοῖς ἐφόροις) next day, they made the King pay a fine.'[1]

Manifestly, a system which set 'human nature' at defiance so truculently as this could not have been enforced without some over-whelming external sanction; and at Sparta this sanction was applied by public opinion, which knew how to chastise an offender against the Spartan social code with scorpions that stung far more cruelly than the Overseers' whips. The point is brought out by an Athenian observer[2] who studied the Spartan system in its eleventh hour, on the eve of its collapse.

'One of the remarkable achievements of Lycurgus is that he has made it preferable, in Sparta, to die a noble death rather than remain alive in disgrace. As a matter of fact, investigation reveals that there are actually fewer deaths in battle among the Spartans than in armies which give way to their fear and prefer to leave the field; so that in reality courage turns out to be a more effective survival-factor than cowardice. The path of courage is easier and more agreeable and smoother and more secure. . . . And I ought not to omit to explain how Lycurgus made sure that this path should be followed by his Spartans. He made sure of that by ensuring inevitable happiness for the brave and inevitable unhappiness for the cowardly. In other communities, a coward's only penalty is to be branded with the epithet. For the rest, he is free to work and play cheek by jowl with men of valour if he chooses. In Sparta, on the other hand, everybody would be ashamed to take a coward for his messmate or to take him for his partner in athletics. And it will often happen that when they are picking up ball-teams the coward finds himself left out, and that in choirs he is pushed out into the least honourable positions, and that he has to yield precedence to everybody in the street and at table and to make way for his juniors and to keep his womenfolk indoors and to bear their reproaches for his lack of manhood and to resign himself to having no housewife in his house and to pay a fine on that account into the bargain, and never to show himself out of doors with his skin oiled, and in fact to do nothing what-soever that is done by Spartans who have no stain on their reputations —under pain of receiving bodily chastisement from his betters. For my part, I am not at all surprised that, in a community in which cowardice is visited with this terrific penalization, death is preferable to a life of such reproach and such dishonour.'[3]

[1] Plutarch: *Apophthegmata Laconica: Lycurgus*, No 6.
[2] Xenophon, *Respublica Lacedaemoniorum*, ch. ix.
[3] These penetrating general observations on the potency of public opinion in keep-ing the Spartan system in force are borne out by a particular case in point which is recorded by Herodotus (Bk. VII, chs. 229–31 and Bk. IX, ch. 71) as a foil to the story of Leonidas and his Three Hundred at Thermopylae in 480 B.C. Two of the Three Hundred, Eurytus and Aristodâmus, were in hospital with acute ophthalmia at a village a few miles behind the front, when they received the news that Leonidas' flank had been turned and that their comrades' duty of holding the pass had become a forlorn hope. At this news, Eurytus groped his way back to the front and fell in action with the two hundred and ninety eight, whereas Aristodâmus went home.
  'The fact . . . that one of them had actually met his death, while the other, who had

Yet penalization alone, however merciless, could never have created the Spartan êthos or have inspired the superhuman heroism which that êthos made possible. The sanction which made the Spartans what they were was internal as well as external; for these implacable souls, whose corporate public opinion made life intolerable for any one of their number who had failed to live up to their common standard of behaviour, were merciless in such cases just because they were single-hearted in exacting the same standard individually from themselves. This 'categorical imperative', in the soul of every true Spartiate 'Peer', was the ultimate driving force which made the 'Lycurgean' system work—in sheer defiance of 'human nature'—for more than two hundred years. And its essence is laid bare in the no doubt imaginary but none the less illuminating conversation which Herodotus[1] puts into the mouths of the Achaemenian Pādishāh Xerxes and the exiled Spartan King Dâmarâtus, who was serving on Xerxes' staff, when Xerxes' army was marching upon Thermopylae from the Dardanelles. Xerxes has asked Dâmarâtus whether he is to expect any resistance; and Dâmarâtus has answered him that, whatever the other Hellenes may do, he can guarantee in regard to his own Spartan countrymen (though he personally has no cause to love them) that they will turn out to

the same excuse (neither better nor worse) to cling to, had not made up his mind to lose his life, compelled the Spartans to be implacable in visiting their resentment upon Aristodâmus. . . . After returning to Lacedaemon, Aristodâmus was received with insult and contumely. The contumely took the practical form that no Spartan would give him a light for his fire or speak to him, while he was insulted with the nickname of "Runaway Aristodâmus" (Ἀριστόδημος ὁ τρέσας). At the Battle of Plataea, however, he made good all the imputations upon his character. . . . At the Battle of Plataea, Aristodâmus . . . was the Spartan who showed by far the greatest gallantry in my judgement. Next to him, the Spartans Poseidonius, Philocyon, and Amompharĕtos distinguished themselves most conspicuously. On the other hand, in a discussion as to which of them had shown the greatest gallantry, the Spartans present came to the conclusion that the prodigies of valour performed by Aristodâmus, who behaved like a man possessed and would not keep his place in the ranks, were inspired by his unconcealed wish to die on account of the imputation under which he laboured, while Poseidonius had fought like a hero without any desire to lose his life—a factor which, in their judgement, gave the measure of his superiority. This pronouncement might conceivably have been dictated by envy; but the fact remains that all the individuals whom I have mentioned who fell in this battle, with the exception of Aristodâmus, were awarded honours, while Aristodâmus, who wished to die on account of the imputation aforementioned, received none.'

Herodotus also mentions (in Bk. VII, ch. 232) another case which, if true, was even more inhuman than the treatment of Aristodâmus:

'There is also said to have been another survivor of the Three Hundred named Pantîtâs, who had been sent with dispatches to Thessaly and who returned to Sparta, was treated with contumely and committed suicide.'

This militant and merciless pressure of Spartiate public opinion, to which the individual Spartiate was subject, was perhaps the most odious feature of Spartan life in Athenian eyes, and it is tacitly stigmatized, by implication, in the following passage from the funeral oration delivered by Pericles on the Athenians who fell in the first campaign of the Atheno-Peloponnesian War of 431–404 B.C., as reported by Thucydides (Bk. II, chs. 34–46):

'We [Athenians] lead a life of freedom not only in our politics but in our mutual tolerance of private conduct. We do not resent our neighbour doing what he pleases, nor subject him to those marks of disapproval which poison pleasure though they may inflict no formal injury.'   [1] Herodotus, Bk. VII, chs. 101–5.

fight without taking any account of the disparity of numbers. When Xerxes refuses to entertain the idea that troops who are free agents, as the Spartans are *ex hypothesi*, would voluntarily face an ordeal into which Xerxes' own troops could only be driven by dread of their commander and by compulsion of the lash, Dâmarâtus replies that,

'free though the Spartans are, they are not free altogether. They too serve a master in the shape of Law, whom they dread far more intensely than your servants dread you. They show this by doing whatever their master orders, and his orders are always the same: "In action it is forbidden to retire in the face of enemy forces of whatever strength. Troops are to keep their formation and to conquer or die."'

This was the spirit that inspired the Spartans' achievements; and those achievements have stamped the Spartan name with the meaning which it still bears in every living language to-day. The deeds are so famous that there is no need in this place to retell familiar tales. The story of Leonidas and the Three Hundred at Thermopylae: is it not written in the Seventh Book of Herodotus? And the story of the Boy and the Fox: is it not written in Plutarch's *Life of Lycurgus*?[1] And do not these two stories, between them, convey the whole *tour de force* of Spartan boyhood and Spartan manhood?[2] And if we cannot take our eyes off the Spartans—as, in candour, we cannot—without first looking also at the other side of the Spartan shield, we have simply to remind ourselves that the last two years of a Spartan boy's education before his coming of age—the crucial years upon which, more than any others, his prospects of co-option on to a 'mess' depended—were probably spent in the Secret Service (κρυπτεία), and that this was nothing else than an official 'murder gang' which patrolled the Laconian countryside surreptitiously—taking cover by day and stalking abroad, like a veritable *negotium perambulans in tenebris*,[3] by night—for the purpose of making away with any Helots who had shown symptoms of restiveness or perhaps

[1] It was part of the education of Spartan boys that they were ordered to steal and were punished if caught. 'And to show what earnestness the boys put into their stealing I will cite the story of the boy who, once upon a time, had stolen a fox and was hiding it under his shirt; and although the creature was tearing the boy's belly with its teeth and claws the boy bore the torture, rather than be found out, until he fell down dead.' (Plutarch, *Life of Lycurgus*, ch. xviii).

[2] If one other touch is still needed in order to complete this bright side of the picture, it will be given by the following rather less well-known anecdote, which illustrates the triumph of public spirit over personal ambition (though ambition was deliberately fostered by the competitive spirit of the 'Lycurgean' system):

'The Spartiate Paedarâtus went off in high spirits, with a smile on his face, after having been passed over as a candidate for enrolment in the Three Hundred (the highest distinction attainable at Sparta). The Overseers (οἱ ἔφοροι) called him back and asked him why he was laughing. "I am laughing", he said, "because I am so delighted at Sparta's good fortune in having three hundred citizens who are better men than I am."' (Plutarch: *Apophthegmata Laconica*, Paedarâtus, No. 3 (cf. *Lycurgi Vitam*, ch. xxv).)

[3] Psalm xci. 6.

merely vestiges of character and ability.[1] While Sparta demanded, and duly evoked, the manly heroism of a Leonidas and his Three Hundred in order to cover the Spartan name with incomparable military glory, she equally demanded—and did not fail to evoke—the juvenile criminality of her Secret Service in order that the tiny minority of Spartiate 'Peers' might keep their feet on the necks of a numerically overwhelming majority of 'Inferiors' and 'Dependants' and 'New Members' and 'Serfs' who would have been delighted, if ever they had the chance, 'to eat' their handful of masters 'alive'.[2] If, under the 'Lycurgean' system, the Spartans rose to some of the sublimest heights of human conduct, they also sounded some of the darkest depths.

Every feature in the 'Lycurgean' system—material or spiritual, evil or good—was directed towards one single aim; and this definite aim was exactly achieved. Under the 'Lycurgean' system, the Lacedaemonian heavy infantry were the best heavy infantry in the Hellenic World. They were as far superior to any other Hellenic troops of the same arm as the Janissaries were superior to the infantry of Western Christendom in Busbecq's day. For nearly two centuries the armies of other Hellenic Powers dreaded to meet the Lacedaemonian Army in pitched battle. In drill and in *moral* alike, the Lacedaemonians were inimitable. But, just because of this, there was no room, in 'Lycurgean' Sparta, for more than one kind of professionalism.

The 'single-track' genius of the 'Lycurgean' *agôgê* leaps to the eye of any visitor to the present-day Sparta Museum. For this museum is totally unlike any other modern collection of extant Hellenic

---

[1] This Spartan Secret Service may be compared with the patrols which used to terrorize the Negro population in the Southern States of the North American Union before the abolition of slavery. The *chef d'œuvre* among the recorded villainies of the Spartan Secret Service was the assassination of the Helots who had responded to a call for volunteers which the Spartan Government had made in the Great Atheno-Peloponnesian War of 431–404 B.C. The story is recorded by a witness of enemy nationality; but since this witness happens to be Thucydides, we can accept the anecdote, nevertheless, without a very heavy discount.

'The whole policy of the Spartans towards the Helots is governed by considerations of security; and one of the acts into which they were led by their fear of the rising generation's spirit and numbers was the following. They proclaimed that all Helots who could show a distinguished war record should present themselves for selection to receive their freedom. This was simply a trap—the calculation being that those Helots who considered that they had the best claim to liberation would be just the Helots who would have the spirit to take the initiative in falling upon their masters. So they selected two thousand of them; and these two thousand gave thanksgiving for their manumission by crowning themselves with garlands and visiting the shrines of the Gods in procession. But the Spartans were not long in making away with them—and this with such secrecy that nobody ever knew how each of the victims had met his end.' (Thucydides, Bk. IV, ch. 80.)

The extermination of the 2,000 does not seem to have been complete (see Toynbee, op. cit., footnote on p. 266); but, even so, the story is black enough. For the general treatment of the Helots, see Plutarch's *Life of Lycurgus*, ch. xxviii. For the policy of compelling the Helots to make buffoons of themselves, see II. D (vi), vol. ii, p. 233, footnote 4, above.

[2] See Annex III, below.

works of art, either in Greece or elsewhere. In other such collections the visitor's eye seeks out and finds and dwells upon the works of 'the Classical Age', which approximately coincides with the fifth and fourth centuries B.C. In the Sparta Museum, however, this 'Classical' Hellenic art is conspicuous by its absence. The visitor's eye is here caught first, and fascinated, by the 'pre-classical' exhibits: delicate ivory-carving and striking polychrome pottery painted by artists who had a gift for line as well as colour. Fragmentary though they are, these relics of early Spartan art bear unmistakable marks of originality and individuality; and the visitor who has made the discovery of them here for the first time looks expectantly to find the sequel—only to look in vain, since this early blossoming of Spartan art remains a promise without a fulfilment. In the place which should contain the monuments of a Spartan version of 'Classical' art there is a great hiatus; and the Sparta Museum contains little more except a superfluity of uninspired and standardized works of minor sculpture dating from the late Hellenistic and early Imperial period. Between the two sets of exhibits in the Sparta Museum a great chronological gulf is fixed; and this gulf is explained by the dates. The date at which the early Spartan art breaks off is approximately that of the Overseership of Chilon in the middle of the sixth century B.C. The almost equally abrupt resumption of 'artistic production' in the age of decadence is posterior to 189–8 B.C.: the date at which the 'Lycurgean' system is known to have been abolished at Sparta by the deliberate policy of a foreign conqueror after Sparta had been forcibly incorporated into the Achaean League.[1] Art was impossible at Sparta so long as Spartan life was confined, by this cast-iron system, to the single track of militarism.

The paralysis which descended, with the *agôgê*, upon Spartan pictorial and glyptic art was equally fatal to the art of music,[2] in which the Spartans had likewise shown early promise. The Spartan authorities even discouraged their nationals from cultivating an art which is so near akin to the soldier's that, in our modern Western World, it is regarded as the best preparation for a military training. The Spartans were prohibited from competing in the

---

[1] For the conquest and incorporation of Sparta into the Achaean League in 189 B.C. and the deliberate eradication of the 'Lycurgean' system by the Achaean authorities, see Polybius, Bk. XXII, ch. 11, 5–12, *fin.*; and Livy, Bk. XXXVIII, ch. 34.

[2] 'At Sparta, any departure from the primitive canons of music was censored. Terpander himself, who was a primitive of primitives and the best harpist of his day and a eulogist of heroism, was fined, all the same, by the Overseers (ἔφοροι), and had his harp permanently confiscated by them, because he had added just one extra string in order to increase the instrument's range. The Overseers only approved of simple melodies. Again, when Timotheus was competing at the festival of the Carnea, one of the Overseers snatched up a knife and asked the performer on which side of his instrument he (the Overseer) was to cut the necessary number of strings in order to bring the total down to the permitted number of seven.' (Plutarch: *Instituta Laconica*, No. 17.)

great Pan-Hellenic athletic sports,[1] on the ground that professionalism in running and jumping and putting the weight was one thing and professionalism in wielding the spear and the shield and performing the evolutions of the parade-ground was something quite different, from which the Spartiate's heart and mind must not be distracted on any account.[2]

Thus Sparta paid the penalty for having taken her own headstrong and hazardous course at the parting of the ways in the eighth century B.C. by condemning herself, in the sixth century, to standing still—with arms presented like a soldier on parade—at a moment when other Hellenes were just moving forward once again on one of the most signal moves in the whole course of Hellenic history.

It requires an effort of imagination to remind ourselves that the fraternity of Spartiate 'Peers' was the earliest Hellenic democracy, and that the redivision of the arable land of Messenia among the members of this Spartiate dêmos in equal allotments became the watchword—γῆς ἀναδασμός—of the revolution that convulsed Athens in the next generation. In Sparta the new movement which had declared itself precociously in the 'Lycurgean' reform was doomed to be arrested prematurely at a rudimentary stage because the 'Lycurgean' system changed the face of Spartan life, only to petrify it for ever after. It was not in Sparta, and not in response to the peculiar challenge that had been presented to the Spartans in the Second Messeno-Spartan War, that these new tendencies in Hellenic life were destined to work themselves out in fresh acts of creation. The creative act of the sixth century B.C. was evoked by a challenge of a different kind; and this challenge was presented in the first instance to those Hellenic communities which had responded to the previous challenge of the eighth century, not on the Spartan lines of conquering a next-door neighbour in Hellas, but on the Chalcidian and Megarian lines of overseas colonization.

After the Malthusian problem had been solved—or shelved—in Hellas at large by this method for a period of some two centuries, it was raised again, and this time more acutely than before, by the simultaneous stoppage of the territorial expansion of the Hellenic World in every quarter.[3] Eastward, Hellenic expansion was checked in the sixth century B.C. by the rise of new Great Powers—the Saite Power in Egypt and the Lydian in Anatolia and the far

[1] This prohibition did not apply to Spartan women—if they were wealthy enough to compete vicariously by entering a chariot for the chariot-races.

[2] Compare the official discouragement, and even prohibition, of golf and tennis, in the supposed interests of cricket, in certain English 'public schools' at the present day; and contrast the *mot*, attributed to the Duke of Wellington, that 'the Battle of Waterloo was won on the playing-fields of Eton'.

[3] For this stoppage, see further III. B, pp. 121–2; III. C (i) (a), pp. 139–40; and III. C (i) (d), pp. 197–8, below.

mightier Achaemenian Empire that first overshadowed and then absorbed them both. During the same century, Hellenic expansion was brought to a halt in the Western Mediterranean by a rally among the rival Levantine colonial peoples—Phoenicians and Etruscans—who now discovered in political co-operation a make-weight for their inferiority to the Greeks in vitality and in numbers. At the same time the indigenous barbarians of the West were beginning to learn how to hold their own against all the Levantine intruders alike by fighting them with their own weapons. In these various ways the expansion of Hellas was cut short all round; and this challenge stimulated the Hellenes to solve their recurrent social problem by substituting, for the mere extensive growth which was no longer open to them, an intensive growth, of a higher social order, which was still within their capacity. They passed from 'subsistence farming' to 'cash-crop farming' and manufactures; from a régime of local self-sufficiency to a régime of international trade; from a natural economy to a money economy; and from a polity based on birth to a polity based on property. And the lead in making this victorious response was taken by Athens: a 'dark horse' who had not taken part in the earlier movement of overseas colonization, but who at the same time had not followed Sparta into her Messenian blind-alley.

The nature of the Athenian response has been examined already in this Study elsewhere in another connexion.[1] In this place it has only to be mentioned in order to point the contrast between Hellenic progress under Athenian leadership and Sparta's un-Hellenic immobility; and this contrast is aptly symbolized in the difference between the Attic and the Spartan money-coinage. The new invention of coined money had found its way into Sparta before the 'Lycurgean' system set hard; and even thereafter it continued to play a not unimportant part in the internal life of the fraternity of Spartiate 'Peers', since a 'Peer's' contribution to his 'mess', which he had to keep up under pain of forfeiting his membership, was payable partly in money as well as in kind. Yet although the sixth-century Spartan reformers could not, or would not, banish coin from Laconia altogether, they succeeded in adapting this institution to their purpose like all the other institutions which they found in the field. They allowed their countrymen to retain a token-currency of iron which was too heavy and bulky for ordinary convenience and was chemically treated in such a way as to make it too poor in quality to have any intrinsic commercial value even in bulk.[2] Thus

---

[1] See I. B (ii), vol. i, pp. 24–5, and II. D (ii), vol. ii, pp. 39–42, above.
[2] Plutarch, *Life of Lysander*, ch. xvii. Plutarch goes on to point out that the Spartan Government was merely preserving, at Sparta, the primitive type of coinage that had once been prevalent everywhere.

Laconia was excluded from the international continuum of financial relations, just as effectively as if she had possessed no coinage at all, by being given a coinage which could have no currency beyond the Laconian frontiers. Meanwhile 'the owls of Athene' became the current coin of the entire Mediterranean World, and the occasional arrival of a flock of these migratory birds in Sparta itself created still greater consternation among the Spartan authorities than the importation of a musical instrument with more than seven strings.[1] The Spartiate Gylippus himself, who had done perhaps as much as any other single man to bring Athens to the ground in the Great War of 431–404 B.C. by foiling the Athenian attempt to conquer Sicily, was forced to go into exile on the morrow of the peace when his servant laid information that there was 'a bevy of owls in the tilery'.[2]

Thus the 'Lycurgean' system, which the Spartans established in order to defend their dominion over the Helots at home, had the effect of throwing them on the defensive against the whole Hellenic World into the bargain. And the greatest irony in Sparta's situation was the fact that, when she had sacrificed everything that made life worth living to the single object of forging an irresistible military instrument, she found that she dared not make use of her dearly bought power because her social equilibrium under the 'Lycurgean' system was so exact, and her social tension so high, that the slightest disturbance of the *status quo* might have disastrous repercussions; and this disaster might be brought on by a victory which would increase the permanent demands on Sparta's man-power almost as readily as by a defeat which would open the way for an invasion of Sparta's home-territories. In the event, the fatal victory of 404 B.C. and the consequent fatal defeat of the year 371 duly brought upon the Spartans the disaster which they had never ceased to dread since they had succeeded in making themselves into the most formidable military power in their world. Yet Spartan statesmanship managed to postpone the evil day for nearly two centuries, dating from the completion of the 'Lycurgean' reforms, by declining to accept for Sparta the greatness which circumstances incessantly sought to thrust upon her.

In this frame of mind the Spartans evaded, time and again, the challenge to assume the leadership of Hellas which the Achaemenian peril presented to them. They forbore to send help to the Anatolian Greek insurgents in 499 B.C.; they arrived too late to fight at Marathon in 490; and after covering themselves with glory, under protest, at Thermopylae and Plataea, they abdicated from

---

[1] See the passage quoted from Plutarch on p. 67, footnote 2, above.
[2] Plutarch, *Life of Lysander*, ch. xvi.

the high command of the forces of liberation in 479–478. Rather than incur the risks which greatness involved for Sparta, they deliberately left their own repudiated greatness lying derelict for Athens to appropriate; and yet, even at this bitter price, they were ultimately unable to elude their tragic destiny. For the Spartans' great refusal to accept the challenge of 499–479 B.C. did not, and could not, purchase for Sparta more than a brief immunity from her peculiar dilemma. In preferring, to the risks of acceptance, the lesser immediate evil of giving the Athenians their opportunity, the Spartans were opening the door for the menace to Hellenic liberties to recur in the shape of an Athenian peril; and this time the Spartans found themselves confronted with a challenge which it was impossible for them to ignore. In the opinion of Thucydides, 'the fundamental . . . cause of the Atheno-Peloponnesian War was the fear inspired in the Lacedaemonians by the rise of Athens to greatness; and this fear compelled them to take up arms'[1] —under threat of seeing the 'sanitary cordon' of their Peloponnesian alliance dissolve and their Athenian enemy from beyond the Isthmus join hands, to their undoing, with their Messenian enemy within their gates.

In 431 B.C. Corinthian diplomacy succeeded in compelling Spartan statesmanship to assume the leadership of Hellas at last; and, in the Great War of 431–404, the Spartan military machine —now tested for the first time to the uttermost—performed all that its makers had intended, and all that Sparta's neighbours hoped or feared. The Spartan nightmare of an *union sacrée* between Athens and the Helots did not come true—not even when the Athenian strategist Demosthenes made his brilliant stroke of establishing a fortified post at Pylos, on the Messenian coast of Laconia, in 425 B.C. On the other hand, the overland expedition of the Spartan commander Brasidas to the Thracian seaboard, and the exhaustion of Athenian strength in Nicias' naval expedition to Sicily, did bring to pass the Athenian nightmare that the Peloponnesians might succeed in joining hands with the Hellenic subjects of Athens on the other side of the Aegean, and might overpower Athens on her own element with a fleet manned by Ionian seamen and financed by Achaemenian gold. When this first stage in the self-inflicted attrition of the Hellenic Society came to an end in the year 404 B.C., it was Athens and not Sparta that lay prostrate. Yet the Spartan King Agis' prophecy—uttered at the moment when the die was cast—that 'this day' would prove to 'be the beginning of great evils for Hellas'[2] came true in respect of the victors no less than the vanquished; for the greatness which Sparta now tardily and

---

[1] Thucydides, Bk. I, ch. 23.   [2] Ibid., Bk. II, ch. 13.

involuntarily retrieved from her prostrated rival proved to be a veritable Shirt of Nessus.

The Spartans were placed in the same predicament by their victorious war of 431–404 B.C. as the 'Osmanlis by their disastrous war of A.D. 1682–99. A people trained consummately but exclusively for warlike contact with its neighbours found itself suddenly compelled, by the outcome of one particular war, to enter into non-military relations for which they were not only unprepared but were positively unfitted by their own peculiar institutions and habits and êthos. These peculiarities which the Spartans, like the 'Osmanlis, had developed in order to grapple with a previous problem, and which had given them superhuman strength within the limits of the narrow environment within which their lines had previously been cast, now took their revenge upon this peculiar people by making them inhumanly or infra-humanly incompetent to live in the wider world into which the fortunes of war had eventually carried them. The very exactness of their adaptation to their previous environment made any readaptation to a new environment so difficult for them as to be virtually impossible; and the very qualities which had been the secret of their success in the one situation became their worst enemies when they found themselves in the other. For these selfsame reasons the 'Osmanlis came to grief when, in consequence of a military defeat, they had to negotiate diplomatically with the Powers of Western Christendom instead of simply imposing their will upon them;[1] and the Spartans came to grief when, in consequence of a military victory, they had to take upon their own shoulders the imperial responsibilities of Athens instead of merely holding the naval and military power of Athens at bay.

The contrast between the Spartan at home and the Spartan abroad was a by-word in Hellas; for whereas, on his own ground, the Spartan admittedly rose above the ordinary Hellenic standards of personal discipline and disinterestedness, he fell below those same standards in at least equal measure as soon as he found himself out of his own element.[2] The spectacular demoralization of

---

[1] In A.D. 1793, under the stimulus of the shock which had been administered by the disastrous outcome of the Russo-Turkish War of 1768–74, the Westernizing Sultan Selīm III took the new departure of establishing permanent Ottoman diplomatic missions in Paris, Vienna, London, and Berlin. It proved impossible, however, to find competent 'Osmanlis to play the Western-style ambassadorial role, and the original appointees, who were naturally Turkish Muslims recruited from the Ottoman dominant minority, had to be replaced by Greek Christian *chargés d'affaires* recruited from the *ra'īyeh* (d'Ohsson, I. M.: *Tableau Général de l'Empire Ottoman*, vol. vii (Paris 1824), p. 573, cited on p. 48, footnote 1, above).

[2] Similarly, Weyer (in op. cit., on p. 7) dwells upon 'the utter inability of the Eskimo culture to fit life-conditions outside of the arctic and sub-arctic regions'. In this connexion, it is to be noticed that, while 'the Eskimos are among the most widely distributed of primitive peoples' (op. cit., p. 3), the physical features of their thirty-four-hundred-mile-long habitat are singularly uniform (at least in so far as they are of concern to Man),

the Spartan Regent Pausanias, when circumstances placed him in command of a Pan-Hellenic force on Achaemenian territory, had been an awful warning which had counted for much in the Spartan Government's decision to abdicate from the leadership of Hellas in 479–478 B.C. And this decision was almost justified in retrospect when, in and after the second and conclusive round of the Great War of 431–404 B.C., Sparta was forced to send abroad Pausaniases by the dozen. 'We have done those things which we ought not to have done and we have left undone those things which we ought to have done, and there is no health in us' must have been the reflection that forced itself, on the morrow of Leuctra, upon the mind of a Spartan statesman like King Agesilaus who was old enough to remember the *ancien régime*.

In that year 371 B.C. the majority of the Spartiate 'Peers' were serving, outside the frontiers of Laconia, on garrison duty in other Hellenic states which had once been Sparta's voluntary allies, but which could no longer be held to their allegiance except by naked military force; and the pick of them had been seconded from their military duties in order to occupy political and administrative posts in which they were making themselves as notorious, on a petty scale, as Pausanias himself, for their Spartan tactlessness and tyranny and corruption, until the respectable title of 'moderators' ($\dot{\alpha}\rho\mu o\sigma\tau\alpha\dot{\iota}$), by which these Spartan martinets abroad were called, had come to sound odious in Hellenic ears. These very Spartiate 'Peers', who were making the Spartan name stink as fish out of water, would no doubt have manifested the traditional Spartan virtues if Fate had allowed them to fulfil the expectations in which they had grown up by leaving them to live their camp-life on the banks of the Eurotas until the Lacedaemonian Army was mobilized for the Leuctra campaign. Unfortunately for their own reputation and their country's, all these men were absent at that grave hour, and, in the Lacedaemonian contingent of the army under King Cleombrotus's command which was so signally defeated by the Thebans at Leuctra in 371 B.C., there were only 400 Spartiates in action apart from the 300 'knights' who always formed a Spartan King's personal bodyguard on active service. This figure seems to mean that, in the Lacedaemonian infantry of the line, on this critical occasion, only one man was a Spartiate in every ten, instead of the four Spartiates in every ten Lacedaemonians which was the regulation quota.[1]

and that this uniformity of the Esquimaux' physical environment is reflected in the cultural uniformity (op. cit., pp. 3–4) of their social life.

[1] The regulation quota (see Annex III, below) appears to have been four Spartiates in every ten Lacedaemonians, the other six being citizens of the autonomous Laconian cities ($\pi\epsilon\rho\dot{\iota}o\iota\kappa o\iota$). At Leuctra, it may be conjectured that the places of the three Spartiates out of the four in every ten Lacedaemonians, who were now missing, were filled by Helots who had been enfranchised, in consideration of volunteering for heavy

If the Spartiate quota had not been thus cut down, at Leuctra, to a quarter of its normal strength, we may doubt whether even the valour of the Theban infantryman and the tactical genius of the Theban commander Epaminondas, who knew how to turn his troops' fighting-power to the best account, would have been able to achieve their historic success of breaking that record of Lacedaemonian invincibility which had remained unbroken, down to that date, for at least two centuries and a half.

Moreover, the Spartan victory over Athens in the Great War of 431–404 B.C. ruined Sparta in other and subtler ways, besides the compulsion which it put upon her to second her 'Peers' from military service, from which they could not safely be spared, to non-military duties with which they could not safely be entrusted. It ruined her, for example, by exposing her belatedly, and therefore disastrously, to the subversive social effects of a money economy from which her people had so long been artificially sheltered. 'The date at which Lacedaemon was first attacked by social disease and corruption practically coincides with the moment at which she overthrew the Athenian Empire and gorged herself with the precious metals.'[1] And the introduction of a money economy brought in its train an equally subversive revolution in the Spartan attitude towards personal property. Spartan conservatism could not, indeed, bring itself to go the length of allowing real estate to be bought and sold in the market; but at some date unknown in the fourth century B.C. the Spartan Assembly passed into law 'a bill making it legal for the holder of a family property or an allotment to give it away during his lifetime, or to bequeath it by will, to anybody whom he chose'.[2] The effect of this piece of legislation in reducing the numbers of the Spartiate 'Peers' must have been much greater than the effect of the relatively light Spartiate casualties at Leuctra, and possibly as great as the effect of the loss of Messenia, which was the political penalty of Sparta's military defeat. When Aristotle was writing his *Politics*, this unfortunate law was already producing noticeably untoward results.[3] By the time of King Agis the Martyr, who came to the throne early in the latter half of the third century B.C., 'not more than 700 Spartiates survived, and of these perhaps 100 may have owned land and an allotment, while the remainder were a destitute and disfranchised mob'.[4]

infantry service, under the name of 'New Members' (νεοδαμώδεις). For these figures see Toynbee, op. cit., pp. 271–2.

[1] Plutarch's *Life of Agis*, ch. v, *ad init*. The whole account of the state of Sparta in the middle of the third century B.C., which is given in chs. v–ix, deserves study.

[2] Plutarch, op. cit., loc. cit. The dates *post quem* and *ante quem* of the 'rhetra' of Epitadeus are the termination of the Atheno-Peloponnesian War in 404 B.C. and the publication, *circa* 325 B.C., of Aristotle's *Politics*. (Toynbee, op. cit., p. 272, footnote.)

[3] Aristotle, *Politics*, 1270 A 15–39.   [4] Plutarch, op. cit., loc. cit.

Another conspicuous social phenomenon in the Spartan, as well as in the Ottoman, decadence was 'the monstrous regiment of women' (γυναικοκρατία). Like the maldistribution of property, this maldistribution of influence and authority as between the two sexes was already noticeable at Sparta in Aristotle's time;[1] and in the legend of the Saviour Kings, Agis and Cleomenes, who reigned at Sparta a century later, the part assigned to the noble women who inspire and encourage and console and mourn the heroes is as prominent as it is in the New Testament.[2] This legend suggests that, notwithstanding Aristotle's strictures on the behaviour of the Spartan women during Epaminondas' invasion of the Eurotas Valley in the winter of 370–369 B.C.,[3] it was really through their virtues that, in the age of Spartan decadence, the Spartan women established their moral ascendancy over their husbands and their sons; and, if this is the truth, it throws some light upon the failure of the 'Lycurgean' system. For although the system had been applied to women as well as to men, the Spartan girls and Spartan married women had not been subjected to its pressure in the same degree as their brothers and their husbands; and if we are right in our belief that the moral breakdown of Spartan manhood was the penalty of a moral rigidity which had been produced by the excessive severity of the 'Lycurgean' temper, then we may conjecture that it was the relative immunity of the women from this unnatural strain that left them with the moral elasticity to bend and rebound in reaction to an ordeal which broke the spirit of the Spartan men outright.[4]

[1] For the ascendancy of the Spartan women over the Spartan men in Aristotle's time, see his *Politics*, 1269 B 12–1270 A 31. No doubt the women had certain unfair advantages. For example, the habit of transferring landed property from one Spartiate family to another in the form of large dowries worked together with the effect of the heavy casualties among male Spartiates in war to create and maintain a class of Spartan heiresses, who doubtless understood how to turn their money-power to account. Aristotle also suggests that the Spartan women were excessively spoilt in psychological 'compensation' (to use our modern Western terminology) for the excessive severity of the discipline that was imposed upon the men. These fortuitous advantages may have given some Spartan women a social 'pull', but this does not really explain the ascendancy of the women at Sparta in the age of decadence, since this ascendancy was manifestly moral and not material in its essence.

[2] The literary relation between the legend of the Spartan Royal Martyrs and the story of the New Testament is discussed in Part V, below.

[3] Aristotle, *Politics*, loc. cit.

[4] In general terms we may say that the women of Sparta were less highly specialized than the men, and were therefore not so much at a loss to adapt themselves when the particular circumstances for which the 'Lycurgean' system had been expressly designed were replaced by new circumstances which called for a readjustment of the Spartan outlook and the Spartan attitude. What was true of 'Lycurgean' Sparta has probably been true in some measure of most societies in most ages. Whatever form of specialism a society may cultivate, the women are apt to go less far in specialization than the men; and whenever a society suffers a breakdown or disaster or reverse, the women, again, are apt to show greater elasticity and greater adaptability than the men in face of the new situation that arises. We may observe that the great Hellenic disaster of the Atheno-Peloponnesian War—a shock which caused the breakdown of the Hellenic Civilization —was accompanied by a rise in the prestige of women not only at Sparta but at Athens, as is attested by the war-plays of Aristophanes and by the role assigned to women in the

The epitaph of the 'Lycurgean' system has been written by Aristotle[1] in the form of a general proposition:

'Peoples ought not to train themselves in the art of war with an eye to subjugating neighbours who do not deserve to be subjugated. . . . The paramount aim of any social system should be to frame military institutions, like all its other institutions, with an eye to the circumstances of peace-time, when the soldier is off duty; and this proposition is borne out by the facts of experience. For militaristic states are apt to survive only so long as they remain at war, while they go to ruin as soon as they have finished making their conquests. Peace causes their metal to lose its temper; and the fault lies with a social system which does not teach its soldiers what to make of their lives when they are off duty.'

Thus the 'Lycurgean' system ultimately and inevitably destroyed itself; yet, even in committing suicide, the system died hard. Although it had been brought into existence for the precise purpose of enabling Sparta to maintain possession of Messenia, the 'Lycurgean' *agôgê* actually continued to be practised at Sparta, out of sheer conservatism, for nearly two centuries after Messenia had been irrevocably lost.[2] And although King Cleomenes the Martyr tardily replaced the 4,000 lost Spartiate allotments in Messenia by redividing the territory that remained to Sparta east of Taygetus, in the Eurotas Valley, into new allotments of an equal number,[3] the royal revolutionary did not take this opportunity to liberate his country from the ancient curse of helotage. Since the 700 surviving Spartiates, all told, could not take up as much as 20 per cent. of the 4,000 allotments into which the estates of the 100 surviving Spartiate 'Peers' were now broken up, Cleomenes presumably gave the Spartan franchise to more than 3,000 Helots and Perioeci in order to fill up the numbers of his new Spartan citizen-body; but these were only a minority of the surviving Helots; for Cleomenes freed 6,000 more of them, at so much a head in ready money, and enrolled 2,000 of these freedmen in his army, on the eve of the Battle of Sellasia, when his Macedonian adversary Antigonus Dôsôn had reached Tegea.[4] And when the Romans invaded Laconia in

Ecclesiazusae, in anticipation of the *Republic* of Plato. The writer of this Study has noticed, from personal observation, the superiority of the women's *moral* over the men's among the *ci-devant* aristocracy in the Southern States of the North American Union under the abiding shock of the Southern defeat in the Civil War, and the same phenomenon among the intelligentzia in China under the long strain of Westernization. The qualities which this ordeal of Westernization has called out among the women of Russia are a matter of common knowledge.   [1] Aristotle, *Politics*, 1333 B–1334 A.
[2] Messenia was liberated from Sparta by Epaminondas in 370/369 B.C.; the 'Lycurgean' *agôgê* was abolished at Sparta by Philopoemen in 189 B.C.
[3] See Plutarch's *Life of Cleomenes*, ch. xi, and *Life of Agis*, ch. viii. The territory which Cleomenes redivided into his 4,000 new Spartiate allotments was only the territory of the Spartan city-state, and did not include the territories of the dependent but autonomous Laconian city-states which were inhabited by the περίοικοι. Cleomenes' forerunner Agis had intended to redivide this perioecic territory into 15,000 allotments and the Spartiate territory into 4,500.   [4] Plutarch, *Life of Cleomenes*, ch. xxiii.

195 B.C., they found Helots still living on there in their traditional status.[1]

The most remarkable feat of Spartan 'Diehardism' was the attempt of the Royal Martyrs, Agis and Cleomenes, to reclothe the dry bones of the 'Lycurgean' system in flesh, and to breathe the breath of new life into the corpse, a full century and a half after the great Spartan victory over Athens had sealed the 'Lycurgean' system's fate. In this last desperate *tour de force* the derelict wheel of Spartan life was turned, by a supreme conservative effort, so very far back that it actually made a revolution; and this violent movement finally wrecked the long-dislocated mechanism. Cleomenes' surgery effectively killed a body social which it could not possibly cure. The bruised reed was broken by the hand that sought to straighten it; and the smoking flax was quenched for ever by the breath which was intended to rekindle a flame.[2]

Thereafter Sparta lived wholly in her dreams of the past and distinguished herself—if it be a distinction—in nothing but the peculiar zest with which she threw herself into the academic game of archaism that was in fashion throughout the Hellenic World during the first two centuries of the Roman Empire.[3] The Spartans of the Imperial age delighted, like all their contemporaries, in composing honorary inscriptions in a caricature of their obsolete local dialect; but at Sparta these harmless archaistic pedantries were accompanied by at least one archaistic morbidity of a gruesome nature. A primitive fertility-rite of scourging boys at the altar of Artemis Orthia, which had been converted by the 'Lycurgean' system, for its own grim but still utilitarian purposes, into a competition in the endurance of pain, was exaggerated, in Plutarch's day, into a sadistic atrocity, in which boys were keyed up to a pitch of hysteria at which they submitted to be flogged to death. 'This would not be incredible of the Spartan youth of the present day', Plutarch writes in recounting the famous legendary story of the Spartan boy and the stolen fox,[4] 'since I myself have seen numbers of them die under the flogging at Orthia's altar.'[5] The essence of this scene, in which a superhuman—or inhuman—feat of endurance is performed without flinching, yet to no effect, is characteristic of the Spartan êthos and emblematic of Sparta's fate. For if any Spartiate ever prayed, for the peace of his soul, that *tantus labor non sit cassus*, that prayer was assuredly breathed by Spartan lips in vain.

[1] Livy, Bk. XXXIV, ch. 27. [2] Isaiah xliii. 3.
[3] For Spartan archaism in the Imperial age, see Pauly-Wissowa, *Realencyclopädie der Classischen Altertumswissenschaft*, Zweite Reihe [R-Z], Dritter Band (Stuttgart 1929, Metzler), s.v. 'Sparta', pp. 1450-2.
[4] For this story see p. 65, above.
[5] Plutarch's *Life of Lycurgus*, ch. xviii, *ad init.*

The vanity of Spartan wishes is exposed in the outcome of an otherwise unimportant arbitral transaction which the Roman historian Tacitus records—apparently without realizing its historic significance—in his annals of the Roman Empire in the year 25 of the Christian Era:

'A hearing was given to delegations from the Lacedaemonian and Messenian Governments in the matter of the juridical status of the temple of Diana [i.e. Artemis] Limnâtis. The Lacedaemonians maintained that the temple had been founded by their own Lacedaemonian forefathers on Lacedaemonian territory, and they supported their claim by an appeal to literary evidence, both historical and poetic. They declared that the temple had been taken from them forcibly, in war, by Philip of Macedon, and had afterwards been restored to them on the strength of a legal opinion which had been rendered by Gaius Caesar and Marcus Antonius. The Messenians, on their side, brought up the ancient division of the Peloponnese among the descendants of Hercules [i.e Hêraklês], and maintained that the territory of Denthelîátis, in which the temple was situated, had been part of the portion assigned to their king. They declared that there were actual records of the transaction still extant, engraved on stone and on archaic bronze; and they added that, if there was to be an appeal to literary evidence, they could also beat the Lacedaemonians in the amount and in the fullness of the testimony of this kind which they were in a position to cite. As for King Philip's decision, they argued that it had not been an act of arbitrary power, but had been based upon the facts and had been confirmed by identic judgements of the Macedonian king Antigonus and the Roman general Mummius; by an arbitral decision of the Milesian Government; and most recently by the decision of Atidius Geminus, the Governor of the Roman Province of Achaea. On this showing, judgement was now given in the Messenian Government's favour.'[1]

Thus, in the first century of the Christian Era, the Spartans were still contending—and this last time without success—over the debatable territory in the mountainous borderland between the Eurotas Valley and Messenia which their forefathers had originally contended for, and conquered, in the eighth century B.C. A dispute over the Denthelîátis was the traditional cause of the First Messeno-Spartan War; and now, after the passage of at least eight centuries, the same dispute between the same two parties over the same insignificant piece of territory was at issue before the arbitral tribunal of the Roman Emperor Tiberius. Assuredly no further proof is needed that the Spartans were veritably a people without a history. And if the reader of this passage from Tacitus happens, like the writer of this Study, to have traversed the Denthelîátis in person, en route through the Langádha defile from Sparta to Kala-

[1] Tacitus: *Annals*, Bk. IV, ch. 43 (*imperante Tiberio Caesare, Anno Christi* 25).

máta, he must have marvelled to think that such a stupendous *tour de force* as the 'Lycurgean' *agôgê* should have been evoked by a desire to possess this patch of highland, with its bare screes and scraggy pine-woods and rare flecks of jejune upland pasture. As the traveller wends his weary way over one rocky ridge after another, he will find himself repeating Oxenstierna's aphorism[1] before he arrives at his Messenian journey's end.

The Reversion to Animalism.

The Spartan body social is the last of the arrested civilizations that we have set ourselves to review; and, now that we have concluded our survey, we may perhaps find ourselves able to lay our finger upon certain common characteristics of this particular class of the species of society which is the object of our study. The two characteristics, common to all these arrested civilizations, that stand out prominently are caste and specialization; and both these phenomena can be embraced in a single formula: The individual living creatures which each of these societies embraces are not all of one single homogeneous type, but are distributed among two or three different categories which differ from one another markedly.

It is of the essence of these arrested civilizations that they are socially composite or polymorphous. In the Eskimo Society, for example, there are two castes: the human hunters and their canine auxiliaries who assist them in two capacities: partly as hunting-dogs and partly as sledge-dogs. In the sub-arctic branch of the Nomadic Society, on the Eurasian Tundra, there are three castes: the human herdsmen; the reindeer used as mounts and beasts of burden; and the same reindeer in their other capacity as cattle tended for the sake of their milk and flesh. In the other branches of the Nomadic Society, on the Eurasian and Afrasian Steppes, there are likewise three castes, but with a greater range of variety in the types. Among these Nomads, there are first the herdsmen or shepherds; second, their animal auxiliaries (dogs, horses, and camels); and, third, their cattle (kine, sheep, and goats). In the Ottoman body social we find the equivalents of the three castes of the Nomadic Society with the substitution of human beings for animals. Whereas the polymorphic body social of Nomadism is constituted by the assemblage, into a single society, of human beings and animals who would none of them be capable of making a livelihood on the Steppes in dissociation from their partners, the polymorphic Ottoman body social is constituted by the exactly opposite process of artificially differentiating a naturally homogeneous Humanity into human castes which are treated, by an

[1] See Part I. C (iii) (*e*), Annex, vol. i, p. 463, footnote 2, above.

inhuman social fiction, as though they differed from one another in nature as widely as human beings actually differ from domesticated animals and as domesticated animals differ among themselves.

This point of unlikeness in the constitutions of those arrested civilizations which are at grips respectively with a physical and with a human environment has been touched upon above;[1] but for our present purpose we may ignore it, since it is a difference of genesis and not a difference of ultimate form. For our present purpose we have simply to take note of the Ottoman castes and of their correspondence to the Nomadic castes. The Ottoman Pādishāh himself is a shepherd of men; his trained human slaves (*qūllar*) correspond to his Nomadic forefathers' auxiliary animals; while the function of the rest of the Pādishāh's subjects in the Ottoman social system is plainly indicated by their official designation as human cattle (*ra'īyeh*). In the 'Lycurgean' system at Sparta we rediscover the same three castes again (though the Spartan community was not of Nomadic origin). In Laconia the Helots are the human cattle, the Spartiate 'Peers' are the human equivalents of the Nomad's trained animal auxiliaries, while the place of the shepherd of sheep or the shepherd of men is occupied at Sparta by an impersonal but not less mighty power: the Law 'whose service is' the 'perfect freedom'[2] of the Spartiate 'Peers', although—or perhaps because—they stand in just as much awe of it as the slaves of a Xerxes or a Suleymān stand in awe of the Pādishāh.[3]

This caste system tends to produce some kind of metamorphosis in the various living creatures that become parties to it. The Eskimo's dog and the Nomad's horse and camel are half humanized by their partnership with Man in hunting or tending other animals. On the other hand, the Ottoman *ra'īyeh* and the Laconian Helots are half dehumanized through being treated as human cattle. Other human partners in these associations are transformed into superhuman or inhuman monsters and *Mischwesen*. The perfect Spartiate is a Martian, the perfect Janissary a monk, the perfect Nomad a centaur, the perfect Eskimo a merman.

The Spartiate stands self-convicted of being the perfect Martian in the following anecdote:

'Hearing on one occasion that the allies of Sparta were chafing at the perpetual campaigns in which they had to follow the Lacedaemonians' lead when the Lacedaemonians were so inferior to them in numbers, Agesilaus determined to put this question of numbers to the test. So

[1] See pp. 22-3, above.
[2] The Second Collect, for Peace, in the Order for Morning Prayer of the Book of Common Prayer of the Church of England.
[3] For the formula 'Spartan Law: Spartiate Peer = Xerxes: Persian Immortal' see the apocryphal conversation between Xerxes and Dâmarâtus which has been cited on pp. 64-5, above.

he ordered all the allies to parade together in one company and the Lacedaemonians to parade separately by themselves. Then he ordered all potters, first, to step out of the ranks; and, when these had stepped out, he next gave the same order to the smiths, and then, in succession, to the carpenters and to the builders until he had run through all the trades. By the end, practically every man of the allies had stepped out, but not a single Lacedaemonian,[1] since the Lacedaemonians were debarred from learning or following any vulgar trade by their constitution. Then Agesilaus laughed and said: "You see, gentlemen, how many more *soldiers* Sparta sends on active service than *you* send." '[2]

The intention of this anecdote is, of course, to glorify the Spartiates at the other Peloponnesians' expense; but, on a more penetrating view, the missile hurled by Agesilaus at his allies' heads looks very like a boomerang. The military superiority of the Spartiates over the non-Spartiates, which is impressive so long as we do not look beyond their respective performances on the battlefield, loses half its glamour as soon as it is brought home to us that the Spartiates are whole-time professionals while their non-Spartiate comrades-in-arms are part-time amateurs. When we give due weight to this crucial point of difference between them, we become inclined to consider the Spartiates' actual superiority less remarkable, in the circumstances, than the fact that the non-Spartiate Peloponnesian amateurs have been able, in their spare time, to turn themselves into good enough soldiers to be able to serve in the same ranks at all with professionals who have had such a vastly greater opportunity of making themselves masters of the military craft. Though the non-Spartiate Peloponnesians naturally cannot emulate the Spartiates in the profession to which the Spartiates have devoted their lives, it is open to them, in compensation, to apply to themselves, in a modest degree, the Athenian boast in which the Athenians took especial pleasure just because it conveyed an implicit criticism of their Spartan rivals' way of life:

'We . . . differ in our military institutions from our opponents. . . . We leave it to them to cultivate manliness by a laborious training from their tender years upwards, while we, with our undisciplined life, are as ready as they to face every reasonable danger. . . . The fact that we preserve a military spirit by a life of ease instead of deliberate hardship and by a natural rather than an artificial courage gives us a double advantage. We are not compelled to anticipate the rigours of war; yet we face them,

---

[1] This is not strictly accurate, since the citizens of the autonomous cities of Laconia, who served shoulder to shoulder with the Spartiates in the Lacedaemonian Army, were not full-time professional soldiers, but a militia of citizens who normally practised some civilian trade, just like the troops furnished by Sparta's non-Laconian allies. To give the story its proper point, the word 'Spartiate' should be substituted for the word 'Lacedaemonian' throughout the passage.—A. J. T.

[2] Plutarch: *Apophthegmata Laconica, Agesilaus*, No. 72, and *Life of Agesilaus*, ch. xxvi.

when they come, as courageously as those who are in perpetual training.
. . . Besides all this, we cultivate the arts without extravagance and the
intellect without effeminacy. . . . Our politicians do not neglect their
private affairs, and the rest of us devote ourselves to business without
losing touch with politics. . . . In short, I maintain that the Commonwealth of Athens is the School of Hellas, and that the individual Athenian
will never meet his equal for self-reliance, versatility, and gallantry, in
whatever situation he may find himself.'[1]

Thus the Athenian glorified his own Attic humanism by pointing
the contrast with the Martian inhumanity in which the Spartiate
took pride. And, if the Spartiate struck his neighbours, and fancied
himself, as a Martian 'robot', the Janissary, who was the Ottoman
equivalent of a Spartiate 'Peer', made a monkish impression, on
first view, upon the mind of the Flemish observer Busbecq:

'In the citadel of Buda there is a permanent garrison of Janissaries . . .
and a pair of these Janissaries used generally to wait upon me. When
they were shown into the dining-room, they would salute me with
bowed heads; and then they would approach me—at a pace which was
almost a run—and touch my coat or my hand, as though they were
going to kiss it; offer me a bunch of hyacinths or narcissi; and forthwith
retire almost as rapidly as they had advanced—this time walking backwards, in order to avoid turning their backs on me (which would be a
breach of courtesy in their code of manners). At the door they would
stand in silence and with the utmost decorum—their hands folded on
their breasts and their eyes downcast—so that they reminded one of our
Western monks rather than of our Western soldiers. . . . In fact, if I
had not been told beforehand that these were Janissaries, I might easily
have mistaken them for some order of Turkish monks, or for the fellows
of some kind of college. Yet these are the notorious Janissaries who
spread terror wherever they go.'[2]

As for the Nomad centaur, his portrait is painted in the following
passage from the pen of one of the most gifted Western observers
of Nomadic life on the Eurasian Steppe:

[1] From the funeral oration delivered by Pericles over the Athenians who had fallen
in the first campaign of the Atheno-Peloponnesian War of 431–404 B.C., as reported by
Thucydides, Bk. II, chs. 34–46. Compare the passage already quoted from the same
speech on p. 64, above.

[2] A. *Gislenii Busbequii Omnia quae Extant* (Leyden 1633, Elzevir), pp. 24–5. The same
comparison suggested itself to the mind of an English observer more than a century later:
'He who hath run through the several schools, orders, and degrees of the Seraglio must
needs be an extraordinary mortified man, patient of all labours, services, and injunctions,
which are imposed on him with a strictness beyond the discipline that religious novices
are acquainted with in monasteries, or the severity of Capuchins or holy votaries.'
(Rycaut, op. cit., Bk. I, ch. v.)
We may take note, in passing, of another important characteristic, besides the virtues
of modesty and austerity and self-control, which the Janissaries of Busbecq's day
possessed in common with the monastic orders of Western Christendom. The Janissaries
resembled the monks, and differed from the Spartiates, in their admirable rule of
tempering their professionalism by learning and practising manual trades. For the
prominence given to handicrafts in the education of the Ottoman Pādishāh's slave-
household, see p. 39, footnote 4, and p. 59, footnote 3, above.

'L'éducation des jeunes Mongols . . . consiste à s'exercer dès l'enfance au maniement de l'arc et du fusil à mèche; l'équitation surtout les absorbe presque entièrement. Aussitôt qu'un enfant est sevré, et que ses forces se sont suffisament développées, on l'exerce à aller à cheval: on le fait monter en croupe, puis on commence une course au galop, pendant laquelle le jeune cavalier se cramponne de ses deux mains à la robe de son maître. Les Tartares s'accoutument ainsi de bonne heure au mouvement du cheval; et bientôt, à force d'habitude, ils finissent par s'identifier, en quelque sorte, avec leur monture. . . .

'Le Mongol est tellement accoutumé à aller à cheval, qu'il se trouve tout-à-fait désorienté et comme jeté hors de sa sphère, aussitôt qu'il a mis pied à terre. Sa démarche est pesante et lourde; la forme arquée de ses jambes, son buste toujours penché en avant, ses regards qu'il promène incessamment autour de lui, tout annonce un cavalier, un homme qui passe la plus grande partie de ses jours sur un cheval ou sur un chameau.

'Quand les Tartares se trouvent en route pendant la nuit, il arrive souvent qu'ils ne se donnent pas même la peine de descendre de leurs animaux pour prendre leur sommeil. Si on demande aux voyageurs qu'on rencontre où ils ont passé la nuit. . . . *Temen dero* (sur le chameau) répondent-ils, d'une voix mélancolique. C'est un singulier spectacle, que de voir les caravanes faire halte en plein midi, lors qu'elles ont trouvé un gras pâturage. Les chameaux se dispersent de côté et d'autre, broutant les grandes herbes de la prairie, tandis que les Tartares, à califourchon entre les deux bosses de l'animal, dorment d'un sommeil aussi profond que s'ils étaient étendus dans un bon lit.'[1]

Here we are shown the picture of a rider who is so completely at home astride his mount that the twain—man and beast—have virtually become one flesh. And one of our foremost modern Western anthropologists has gone so far as to suggest, in a brilliant imaginative reconstruction of a lost chapter of pre-Nomadic history, that the intimate association of Man and Horse on the Steppe has actually produced far-reaching and permanent modifications in the physical type of the human participants in the partnership.

'It is not necessary to suppose that within the great plateaus of Central Asia there was perennial snow, or a wholly uninhabitable region [during the Ice Age]. Rather the vast accumulations of loess, the deposit of countless dust storms, suggest a "continental" climate with wide variations, and the possibility of at least seasonal occupation by fleet grazing-animals, such as the horse. It is indeed to an intimate parasitic connexion with such an animal "host", in some such circumstances, that we have probably to ascribe the highly specialized type of Man characteristic of this region now. The yellow skin-colour of Mongoloid Man gives him protective camouflage in sandy desert and dry-grass steppe; the structure of his straight wiry hair, and its rarity except on the scalp, suggest adaptation to a continental climate; while its extreme length in

[1] Huc, l'Abbé: *Souvenirs d'un Voyage dans la Tartarie, le Thibet et la Chine pendant les années 1844, 1845, et 1846* (Paris 1850, Le Clere, 2 vols.), vol. i, pp. 93-5.

both sexes serves to disguise the characteristic profile of the human head and neck, and approximate it to that of a quadruped seen from behind. From the rather prominent jaw combined with globular brain-case may be inferred long habituation to some food which minimized the pull of the jaw-muscles on the side-walls of the skull; and the only food which fulfils this condition is milk and its products, on which Nomad Tartars still live almost exclusively: the absence of face-hair, the short concave nose with spread nostrils, the peculiar infantile lips, the wide flat face and obliquely set eyes, are adaptations we should expect if for ages this milk was absorbed direct from the udder; and the short legs of some Mongoloids, and poor development of the calf-muscles in all, suggest that, like Tartar infants nowadays, the parasitic proto-Mongol sat tight upon his host between meals, and shared its wanderings. On the Steppes of glacial Europe, Man hunted and ate the horse; if we suppose that in Central Asia, during the same and perhaps in long earlier periods, he made friends with him and lived upon his friendship, we seem to have a clue to the paradox of the emergence of a highly specialized breed of Man from a region which had been for a very long time so little suited, except on these terms, to sustain him at all.'[1]

This Mongol centaur of the Eurasian Steppe has his counterpart in the Eskimo merman of the American arctic waters. While the Nomad has become of one flesh with his domesticated animal mount, the Eskimo—reacting to an equally severe physical environment by performing an equally exacting, and exact, *tour de force*— has become, so to speak, of one skin with his man-made inanimate water-craft. The Eskimo kayak is an adaptation, for sea-faring, of the canoe in which the Esquimaux's North American Indian cousins navigate their inland waters. In kayak and canoe the structural element is identical. Both types of craft are built round a wooden framework. But whereas the Indian canoe is an open boat with a hull of birch bark, the Eskimo kayak, which has to face heavier weather, is covered with seal-skin and is decked over, as well, with the same material.

'As a rule, each hunter makes his kayak for himself, and it is fitted to the man's size just like a garment. . . .

'In the middle of the kayak's deck there is a hole just large enough to enable a man to get his legs through it and to sit down; his thighs almost entirely fill the aperture. Thus it takes a good deal of practice before one can slip into or out of the kayak with any sort of ease. The hole is surrounded by the kayak-ring, which consists of a hoop of wood. It stands a little more than an inch (3 or $3\frac{1}{2}$ centimetres) above the kayak's deck, and the waterproof jacket . . . is drawn over it.

[1] Myres, J. L.: 'Primitive Man in Geological Time', in *The Cambridge Ancient History*, vol. i, 2nd ed. (Cambridge 1924, University Press), p. 22. These fascinating speculations are an admirable mythological expression of the truth about the Nomad's relation to his environment, even though they may be beyond the range of scientific verification.

'In fair weather the kayak-man uses the so-called half-jacket (*akui-lisak*). This is made of water-tight skin with the hair removed, and is sewn with sinews. Round its lower margin runs a draw-string, or rather a draw-thong, by means of which the edge of the jacket can be made to fit so closely to the kayak-ring that it can only be pressed and drawn down over it with some little trouble. This done, the half-jacket forms, as it were, a water-tight extension of the kayak. The upper margin of the jacket comes close up to the armpits of the kayak-man, and is supported by braces or straps, which pass over the shoulders and can be lengthened or shortened by means of handy runners or buckles of bone, so simple and yet so ingenious that we, with all our metal buckles and so forth, cannot equal them. . . . This half-jacket is enough to keep out the smaller waves which wash over the kayak. In a heavier sea, on the other hand, the whole-jacket (*tuilik*) is used. This is made in the same way as the half-jacket and, like it, fits close to the kayak-ring, but is longer above, has sleeves attached to it, and a hood which comes right over the head. It is laced right round the face and wrists, so that, with it on, the kayak-man can go right through the breakers and can capsize and right himself again, without getting wet and without letting a drop of water into the kayak.

'It will readily be understood that it is not easy to sit in a vessel like the kayak without capsizing, and that it needs a good deal of practice to master its peculiarities. . . . But when one has acquired by practice a mastery of the kayak and of the two-bladed paddle, one can get through the water in all sorts of weather at an astonishing speed. The kayak is beyond comparison the best boat for a single oarsman ever invented.

'In order to become an accomplished kayak-man, one ought to begin early. The Greenland boys often begin to practise in their father's kayak at from six to eight years old, and when they are ten or twelve the provident Greenlander gives his sons kayaks of their own. . . . From this age onwards, the young Greenlander remains a toiler of the sea. . . .

'You cannot rank as an expert kayak-man until you have mastered the art of righting yourself after capsizing. . . . An Eskimo told me of another who was so extraordinarily skilful at righting himself that he could do it in every possible way: with or without an oar, with or without a throwing-stick, or with his clenched hand. The only thing he could not right himself with was—his tongue! . . .

'A kayak-man who has entirely mastered the art of righting himself can defy almost any weather. If he is capsized, he is on even keel again in a moment, and can play like a sea-bird with the waves, and cut right through them. . . . The prettiest feat of seamanship I have ever heard of is that to which some fishers, I am told, have recourse among overwhelming rollers. As the sea curls down over them they voluntarily capsize, receive it on the bottom of the kayak, and when it has passed right themselves again.'[1]

This perfect unison between the Eskimo and his kayak or be-

[1] Nansen, F.: *Eskimo Life* (London 1893, Longmans, Green & Co.), pp. 46–54. The whole relevant passage, from p. 44 to p. 77 inclusive, is worth studying.

tween the Nomad and his mount is a marvellous *tour de force*; and, when we contemplate it, our first impression is that we are viewing one of the highest flights of human achievement. This impression is not false so far as it goes; but there is another aspect of the picture which comes to light after further consideration. In either case, the essence of the achievement is the mastery, by a human being, of some non-human animal's prowess.[1] The Nomad centaur acquires the prowess of a horse, the Eskimo merman the prowess of a seal; and for human beings these accomplishments are extraordinarily difficult. The difficulty, however, lies just in this, that an animal is enabled to perform its specific prodigies thanks to the organic— and therefore one-sided and rigid and unalterable—adaptation of its physique to just these particular functions and to these functions only. The animal solves its problem by developing a special permanent organ or a special permanent instinct for the purpose, whereas the man who seeks to emulate the animal's feat has been endowed by Nature with no physical equipment except the human eye and human hand, and with the mental equipment of an errant amateur reason in place of an infallible professional instinct.[2] The *tour de force* is manifestly so very difficult indeed that we ask ourselves how it is possible for human beings to perform it at all; and then, upon further examination, we observe that they actually perform it by a device which is so obvious that we ought to have detected it *a priori*.[3]

[1] 'An ingenious hunting device can take the place of fleetness of foot or sharpness of tooth or talon.' (Weyer, op. cit., p. 65.)

[2] 'La vie est un certain effort pour obtenir certaines choses de la matière brute, et . . . instinct et intelligence, pris à l'état achevé, sont deux moyens d'utiliser à cet effet un outil: dans le premier cas, l'outil fait parti de l'être vivant; dans l'autre, c'est un instrument inorganique, qu'il a fallu inventer, fabriquer, apprendre à manier.' Bergson, H.: *Les Deux Sources de la Morale et de la Religion* (Paris 1932, Alcan), p. 122. The same point is put very clearly by Ibn Khaldūn: 'To every animal, God has given an organ specially designed for repelling its enemies. But to Man He has given, instead, the human intelligence and the human hand. The hand, under the control of the intelligence, is always ready to work at the arts; and the arts furnish Man with the instruments that replace, for him, the organs that have been assigned to the other animals for their defence. Thus lances take the place of horns, swords the place of claws, shields the place of tough thick hides.' (*Muqaddamāt*, translated by de Slane, Baron McG. (Paris 1863–8, Imprimerie Impériale, 3 vols.), vol. i, p. 87.)

[3] The extremeness of the *tour de force* which is performed by the Eskimo is forcibly represented by Weyer in op. cit. on p. 65. Weyer points out that 'physically the Eskimo is in all essential characteristics like other men. Strip him of his clothing, deprive him of his tools and implements, his dwellings, and his ability to create these things essential to life, and he would be scarcely more fit to survive in his northern environment than a savage from the tropical jungle'. *A fortiori*, the Eskimo is at a physical disadvantage, in the struggle for existence in this environment, by comparison with the non-human fauna which he has found in the field and at whose expense he makes his livelihood. Weyer points out that 'what' the Eskimo 'lacks as a physical organism he acquires through ingenuity and invention', and that 'in this manner Man's culture takes the place of physical adaptations among the lower animals'. Weyer, however, does not go on to point out in this connexion that, while 'the Eskimo cannot compete with the animals as an animal' and 'is not compelled to', it is also true that he has assimilated himself to the non-human fauna of his physical environment in a subtler way by sacrificing the adaptability, which is the distinctive quality of his distinctive mental powers, and forcing his mobile human spirit, as far as it can be forced, into the rigid posture of animal automatism —as is suggested in the present Study in the paragraphs that here follow.

These Esquimaux and Nomads and 'Osmanlis and Spartiates achieve what they achieve by putting off their human nature as far as possible, and assuming an animal nature instead. If, being human, they cannot really live and act by instinct, they can still train reason to simulate instinct by imprisoning their thought within the confines of a 'single-track mind'. And if they cannot grow the flippers and tails and waterproof skins of seals to make them at home in the sea, or the legs of horses to make them at home on the Steppe, or the fangs of wolves to give them dominion over human cattle, they can at least extend the limited capacities of their human limbs by devising instruments—animate or inanimate—with which they teach their own arms and legs to enter into such an exquisitely harmonious co-operation that the effect is almost as though they had succeeded in adding a cubit to their stature. The Eskimo acquires an artificial seal's body in the shape of his kayak and an artificial pair of flippers in the shape of his double-bladed paddle. The Nomad acquires an artificial horse's or camel's body in the shape of his mount. The Spartiate acquires an artificial fang in the shape of his spear-head and an artificial carapace in the shape of his shield.[1]

These are, indeed, miracles of human will-power and human ingenuity; but the faculty of working miracles has to be bought at a price, and in this case the price turns out to be so high that those human beings who have consented to pay it might have done better to reject it as prohibitive. The price paid has been nothing less than the determined and systematic repudiation of those very qualities of the human hand and the human eye and the human reason which are distinctive of human nature. The distinctive quality of the human mind is its adaptability. With its manifold analytic and synthetic and mimetic mental faculties, and its versatile physical informants and executants the human eye and the human hand, the mind of Man is capable of unlimited achievement on the one condition that it faithfully follows the bent of its own genius.[2]

---

[1] In the song of Hybrias (the uncouth Cretan cousin of Spartan Brasidas and Leonidas and Agesilaus), the spear and shield and sword are recognized, with conscious cynicism, as being the artificial organs through which a human parasite contrives to live upon the labours of an unwilling human 'host':

I have great riches, spear and sword
And raw-hide fluttering at my breast;
My land is ploughed, my harvest stored,
My sweet wine from the vintage pressed,
The Mnoan trash hath learnt its Lord,
By spear and sword.

And all who dare not walk with spear
And sword and raw-hide fluttering,
They needs must kiss my knees, and cling,
And hail me, cowering in their fear,
Lord and Great King!

(Translation by Gilbert Murray.)

[2] As Weyer expresses it (in op. cit., on p. 66), 'men can modify their culture, whereas

In forcing their human minds into the similitude of animal psychology, and their human legs and arms into the similitude of animal morphology, the Esquimaux and the Nomads and the 'Osmanlis and the Spartans have betrayed their own humanity. They have set their feet on the path of retrogression from humanity towards the animalism out of which Humanity evolved itself once upon a time by one of the greatest creative acts that have yet been achieved in the life-history of the Universe. They have committed the unpardonable sin of Lot's Wife, and in committing it they have duly brought upon themselves the Biblical penalty. Like pillars of salt, they stand bewitched and arrested for ever at the very outset of their life's journey, as an awful warning to other civilizations that are in the act of making their own transition from genesis to exodus.

'The necessity for effort—the "struggle for existence" in the most general sense—has from age to age raised the average level of independence, the measure of individuality's perfection in living beings. In spite of this general rise of level, there has been in every age a falling away, a decline in perfection of individuality in certain species. This decreased independence reveals itself not only as structural degeneration but also in degeneration's opposite, structural specialization. There is, however, a common cause beneath these opposed effects, and that is over-close adaptation, adaptation to very narrow conditions.

'It is self-evident that all organisms must be more or less adapted to their surroundings; in other words they must be more or less dependent upon their environment. Failure to exist in any but a very limited environment is obviously a weakness, a lack of independence, and it seems to be a fact that adaptation to any such limited environment makes it impossible or very difficult for an animal to exist in any other environment. The very success of the adaptation decreases the creature's adaptability.'[1]

Insect Societies and Human Utopias

If we wish for corroborative evidence in support of our conclusion that the turn taken, at the outset, by the Spartan and the 'Osmanli and the Eskimo and the Nomadic Civilization was a blind alley, we shall find what we seek by comparing the social structure of these four actual arrested human societies with that of the imaginary human societies called Utopias, or again with that of the

animals cannot modify their bodily organisms appreciably'. And he goes on to maintain that the application of 'this interpretation of cultural evolution' to the Esquimaux 'is uncommonly striking'. This is, of course, manifestly true if we confine our attention to the first chapter in the Esquimaux's cultural history—the chapter, that is to say, which covers their original feat of adapting their life to the Arctic physical environment. On the other hand, in the ensuing chapter the Esquimaux have hardened into a cultural immobility which is the very antithesis of the characteristic human habitus and which is, *pace* Weyer, very strongly reminiscent of the comparative fixity of the animals.

[1] Huxley, J. S.: *The Individual in the Animal Kingdom* (Cambridge 1912, University Press), pp. 131–2.

social insects. If we enter into the comparison, we shall discern in an ant-heap and in a bee-hive, as well as in Plato's *Republic* or in Mr. Aldous Huxley's *Brave New World* or in Mr. H. G. Wells's fantasy of a lunar society, the same outstanding features that we have now learnt to recognize in all the arrested civilizations which we have been studying. The two phenomena of caste and specialization, and the fatally perfect adaptation of the society to its particular environment which these two phenomena bring about between them, are just as characteristic of the Utopian and the Insect World as they are of the four actual human societies, just examined, which have suffered arrest. And these resemblances are significant, since the insect societies and the Utopias are both patently in a state of arrested development likewise.

The social insects rose to their present social heights, and came to a permanent standstill at those altitudes, many millions of years before *Homo Sapiens* began to emerge above the mean level of the rank and file of the Vertebrate Order.[1] And as for the Utopias, they are static not only as a matter of fact but *ex hypothesi*. For these fictitious descriptions of imaginary human societies that have never existed are really programmes of action masquerading in the disguise of descriptive sociology; and the action which they are intended to evoke is the 'pegging', at a certain social level, of an actual society which has broken down and has entered upon a decline that must end in a fall unless the downward movement can be artificially arrested. To arrest a downward movement is the utmost to which a Utopia can aspire, since Utopias seldom begin to be written in any society until after its members have lost the expectation and ambition of making further progress and have been cowed by adversity into being content if they can succeed in holding the ground which has been won for them by their fathers. Hence, in almost all Utopias—with the noteworthy exception of that work of English genius which has given this whole genre of literature its modern Western name[2]—an invincibly stable equilibrium is the

[1] Wheeler, W. M.: *Social Life among the Insects* (London, no date, Constable), pp. 6–9.

[2] In More's *Utopia* there are indeed traces of those elements, copied or caricatured from the living reality of the 'Lycurgean' system of Sparta, which we shall have occasion to notice below in glancing at the Athenian Utopias of the age immediately posterior to the breakdown of the Hellenic Civilization in the Great War of 431–404 B.C. For example, More's Utopians entertain and display a supreme contempt for the precious metals (ch. vi), and in the communal messes the menial domestic service is performed by bondsmen. Yet, considering More's great knowledge of, and deep regard for, the Greek and Latin classics, and the high prestige of Hellenic Antiquity in the Western World of More's day, it is really surprising that the traces of Plato's and Aristotle's influence in More's *Utopia* are not more prominent than they are. And it is still more remarkable to find More parting company with his Hellenic ensamples in matters which are clearly of fundamental importance. For example, the contempt for the precious metals is offset by the importance which is assigned, in the same chapter, to overseas trade (ch. vi). Again, the employment of bondsmen in menial domestic service is reduced

supreme social aim to which all other social values are subordinated
and, if need be, sacrificed.

This is true of the Hellenic Utopias which were conceived at
Athens in the schools of philosophy that arose there, or established
themselves there, in the age immediately following the catastrophe
of 431–404 B.C., in which the Hellenic Civilization had broken
down.[1] It is also true of certain modern Western Utopias which
have been conceived in England either shortly after or shortly
before the catastrophe of A.D. 1914–18: a great war which may or
may not prove to have been the undoing of our own Western
Civilization.[2]

The Utopias which were published in Athens in the fourth
century B.C. bear the marks of their time and their place. Their
negative inspiration is a profound hostility to Athenian democracy.
For, after the death of Pericles, Athenian democracy had dissolved
its brilliant partnership with Athenian culture under the stress of
the Great War; it had developed a crazy and virulent militarism
that brought devastation upon the world in which Athenian culture

to its true proportions when we find (in ch. viii, *ad init.*) that the institution of bondage
is maintained in Utopia not—as in 'Lycurgean' Sparta or in the imaginary commonwealths of Plato and Aristotle—for the purpose of liberating a privileged caste of citizens
from ordinary economic employments and preoccupations, but simply as a humane
substitute for the death penalty. There is no question of the free citizens of Utopia being
a parasitic dominant class; for they all do an honest day's work with their own hands
(ch. vi). Nor is More obsessed, as Plato and Aristotle are, by Malthusian anxieties.
In Utopia, there is no artificial postponement of marriage. The marriageable age is 18
for women and 22 for men (ch. viii), and an occasional surplus of population is looked
upon as a normal phenomenon which is all in the day's work. When the problem of over-
population arises in Utopia, it is solved by colonization overseas in under-populated
territories where Utopian settlers can find new homes for themselves without having to
evict the previous inhabitants (ch. v, *ad init.*).

It will be seen that More's Utopia differs from its Hellenic predecessors and from
its modern Western successors alike in being almost wholly free from those elements of
caste and specialization and static social rigidity which are the outstanding characteristics
of Utopias as a class. This is really extraordinary when we bear in mind that while Sir
Thomas More welcomed the renaissance of Hellenic culture in the Western Society of
his age, he deplored the simultaneous transition of the Western Society out of its
'medieval' into its 'modern' phase. A social metamorphosis which, in our perspective,
can be seen to have been no more than the passage from one chapter to the next chapter
in the same Western story, must have seemed to More, living in the midst of it, very like
an irreparable breakdown of the Western Civilization itself in the form in which he knew
it and loved it. In these circumstances, we should have expected More to write a *Utopia*
of a thoroughly Platonic and Aristotelian flavour; and the fact that he actually makes his
own the opposite ideal of elasticity and growth is an enigma which has to be explained.
Perhaps the true explanation may be that More was sub-consciously aware of being a
member of a lustily growing society all the time, notwithstanding his conscious conviction that the world in which he had grown up was falling to pieces.

[1] Bergson finds the same bent in the metaphysical as well as in the social speculations
of the Platonic and Aristotelian philosophy. See the critique in *Les Deux Sources de la
Morale et de la Religion* (Paris 1932, Alcan), pp. 257–61. The 'post-war' French philosopher arraigns the 'post-war' Athenian philosophers for trying to 'peg' the flux of
the Universe, as mirrored in human experience, upon the rigid scheme of the human
thinking-apparatus.

[2] The generation now alive will not live to know whether the wound dealt to our
Western Society in 1914–18 has been mortal or not, though the truth—whatever it may
be—will doubtless be manifest, several centuries hence, to our descendants. On this
question, see further Part XII, below.

had found its air and light and nourishment; and it had capped its great sin of omission—the failure to win the War—with a sin of commission—the judicial murder of Socrates—which was certainly more wanton and was naturally more heinous in the philosophers' eyes.

The first concern of the Athenian post-war philosophers was to repudiate everything that, for two centuries past, had made Athens economically and politically great. This comes out almost startlingly in a passage in Plato's *Laws*, in which the fictitious 'Athenian Stranger' makes his first observations upon an imaginary project for the establishment of a new city-state on a depopulated area in Crete.

ATHENIAN STRANGER. 'If the city were going to be built at the seaside and were going to find itself well-supplied with natural harbours but ill-supplied with many of the necessities of life instead of being endowed with a soil that produced something of everything, then it would have needed a mighty saviour and divinely inspired legislators if it was to escape the moral heterogeneity and the moral corruption which are the penalty of this type of physical environment. . . . For the sea is an insidious neighbour which makes itself agreeable to a country in the daily intercourse of the two elements but is intrinsically salt and bitter, in as much as it fills the country with tradesmen's business and the souls of the country's inhabitants with tortuousness and deceit and the body politic itself with distrust and disaffection both in its internal life and in its foreign relations. These social evils are to some extent counteracted if the soil produces something of everything; and, if it is also a rough highland country, it is evident that it will not produce this something of everything, that it does produce, in lavish quantities. If it did do that, it would provide a large export surplus and would attract to itself an equivalent import of gold and silver currency—and that is the greatest conceivable disaster, from the moral standpoint, by which a community can be overtaken. . . .'[1]

[As for sea power], 'it would have profited the Athenians to lose seventy times seven children a year [by having to send them as tribute to the legendary Cretan sea-lord Minos] before turning themselves [in self-defence] into seamen instead of heavy infantry and so losing the habit of standing fast, and acquiring in its place the habit of perpetually jumping ashore and then retreating to their ships again at a run, hardly a moment after they have made their landing. This method of warfare extinguishes any sense of shame at being too cowardly to risk one's life by standing one's ground and receiving the enemy's attack and suggests facile and plausible excuses for leaving one's arms in the enemy's hands and taking to one's heels—never, of course, "in disorder" but invariably "according to plan". . . . There is nothing so demoralizing for infantry in action as a hospitable fleet riding at anchor in their rear. Why, even

[1] Compare with the foregoing paragraph Aristotle, *Politics*, 1326 B-1327 A.—A. J. T.

lions, if they took to tactics of that sort, would take to running away from deer.[1]

'Moreover, sea power practises a kind of inverse selection upon the manhood of a country by awarding political office as well as immunity from being killed in action to the least desirable elements. Sea power depends upon the warrant officers and petty officers and able bodied seamen; these naval ratings are a miscellaneous and not a very reputable body of men; and in such circumstances it is impossible for office to be conferred upon those who are worthy of it. Now, when once it ceases to be possible in politics to put the right man in the right place, how can a country's political life possibly remain healthy?'

CLINIAS OF CRETE. 'How indeed? Yet, all the same, Sir—Well, what about the battle of Salamis? That, after all, was a naval battle in which the Hellenes beat the barbarians; and it is our belief in Crete that this naval victory was the salvation of Hellas.'

ATHENIAN STRANGER. 'I know that is the general view both in Hellas and in the Orient. But in our belief, Sir—and by "us" I mean myself and my Lacedaemonian friend, here, Megillus—it was the land-battles at Marathon and Plataea that were the day-spring of the salvation of Hellas and the crowning mercy. And we also believe that these land victories left the Hellenes better men than they found them, but that the effect of the naval victories was in the contrary sense.'[2]

The unavowed but unmistakable thesis of the Platonic and Aristotelian Utopia is that Hellas could, and should, be saved by a fraternization between the discredited Athenian democracy's two arch-enemies: Athenian philosophy and the 'Lycurgean' system of social life which was the secret of the greatness of Sparta. If Athenian democracy had broken faith with Athenian culture, Athenian culture might still avenge its own wrongs, and save the Hellenic Civilization into the bargain, by contracting a new alliance with the rival social system which (to all appearance) had just proved its superiority over the Athenian democracy in the ordeal of battle. The Platonic and Aristotelian programme is to 'peg' the Hellenic Society at the social level of a 'Lycurgean' system which is to be improved in two ways: first, through being worked out to logical extremes, and, secondly, through being supplemented by the imposition of a sovereign intellectual caste, in the likeness of the

---

[1] Contrast the following passage in Pericles' Funeral Speech as reported by Thucydides in Book II, chs. 35–46:

'The Lacedaemonians never invade our country alone, but with the combined forces of their confederacy, whereas, when we attack our neighbours, we seldom find difficulty in defeating them, though we are the invaders and they are defending their homes. Again, our united forces have never yet been faced by any opponent, because we are continually dispersing them on expeditions by land, in addition to the requirements of our fleet. Yet, whenever they encounter a fraction of our forces and defeat them, they boast that they have been victorious against our total strength, while, if they are worsted, they maintain that it has taken our total strength to secure the victory.'

[2] Plato, Leges, Bk. IV, ad init., 704 A–707 C. The whole passage reads almost like a deliberate rejoinder, point for point, to the eulogy of Athens in Pericles' Funeral Speech as reported by Thucydides in Bk. II, chs. 35–46.

Athenian philosophers themselves, upon a military caste which is
to be created in the image of the Spartiate 'Peers', but is to be
taught, in the Utopian orchestra, to play second fiddle.[1]

In Plato's mind, the enthronement of the philosophers in the
seats of the mighty is the great thing.

'Unless . . . either the philosophers receive royal authority in the states
of Hellas or the present so-called kings and sovereigns take to philosophy, and take to it genuinely and thoroughly; and unless there is a
personal union between these two things, political power and philosophy;
and unless the majority of the personalities which at present enter upon
the one career and upon the other are forcibly excluded from entry:
unless these conditions are fulfilled there cannot possibly be any cessation of evils . . . for the states of Hellas, nor indeed, in my opinion, any
for the Human Race.'[2]

Yet even in Plato's *Republic*, and *a fortiori* in Plato's *Laws* and in
the last two books of Aristotle's *Politics*, the dry bones of 'Lycurgean' Sparta stick out gauntly through the tender Athenian philosophic skin. In their condonation of caste, in their penchant
towards specialization, and in their passion for establishing an invincible equilibrium at any price, the Athenian philosophers of the
fourth century B.C. show themselves docile pupils of the Spartan
statesmen of the sixth.

In the matter of caste, the thought of Plato and Aristotle is
tainted with that Racialism[3] which has been one of the besetting
sins of our own Western Society in its modern age, but which is
something alien from the Hellenic genius. Plato's conceit of 'the
Noble Lie'[4] is a delicate device for suggesting the notion that,
between one human being and another, there may be physical and
psychic differences of such degree and such importance as to constitute a diversity of morphological type of the same order as the
diversity between human beings and animals or between different
animals of diverse species. This notion is worked out in more
prosaic and therefore more brutal terms in Aristotle's discussion of
the moral basis of the institution of Slavery.

'When any human beings . . . differ in nature from their fellows by as
wide a remove as bodies from souls and animals from humanity (and
this is the case with human beings whose utility lies in bodily labour
exclusively, and that is the best that can be got out of them), then such
individuals may be identified as natural-born slaves ($\phi\acute{v}\sigma\epsilon\iota$ $\delta o\hat{v}\lambda o\iota$). . . .

---

[1] The second of these two improvements was first worked out 'in real life' by the
'Osmanlis, who certainly knew nothing at all about the social institutions of Sparta and
probably very little about the social theories of Plato. (See pp. 33 and 50, above.)

[2] Plato, *Republic*, Bk. V, 473 C–D.

[3] For Racialism see Part II. C (ii) (a) 1, vol. i, above.

[4] Plato, *Republic*, Bk. III, 414 B–D. The passage will be found in translation in
II. C (ii) (a) 1, vol. i, on pp. 247–8, above.

The natural-born slave is . . . a human being who participates in the rational faculty to the extent of being responsive to it without being capable of exercising it. The other animals are not even responsive to reason but are governed by their sensations. However, this makes little difference from the utilitarian standpoint. For bodily contributions towards the performance of elementary social service are what we obtain from both alike—from human slaves and from domestic animals. It is the intention of Nature to establish a morphological difference between the bodily types of freemen and slaves, corresponding to the differentiation between their functions. . . . But in actual fact the opposite frequently occurs, and one finds slaves with freemen's bodies and even slaves with freemen's souls. [These exceptions to the rule obscure the truth]; for it is manifest that if even the merely bodily diversity were of the same order as the diversity between the statues of the Gods and the physique of mortals, then the enslavement of the physically inferior type to the physically superior type would be universally approved by public opinion. And if this is true in the case of bodily diversity, the same distinction could be drawn with far more justice if the diversity were spiritual. But of course it is not so easy to discern spiritual as it is to discern physical beauty. . . .'[1]

Aristotle goes on to expound the arguments of the anti-slavery party in the Hellenic World of his day, and notes their refusal to admit that any human beings should be called slaves except barbarians. But, in recording this exception, he not unfairly comments that it is tantamount to accepting the hypothesis of 'the natural-born slave' which Aristotle himself has put forward.

On the strength of this social theory, the Athenian social reformers prescribe a caste-system which reproduces or caricatures almost all the 'Lycurgean' idiosyncrasies. Plato's 'human watch-dogs'[2] are reproductions of the Spartiate 'Peers' and anticipations of the Ottoman Pādishāh's slave-household, while Aristotle's prescription is indistinguishable from the Laconian reality.

'Tillers of the soil and artisans and all the other elements of a labour force are indispensable necessities in commonwealths, but the only true members of the body politic are the military and the statesmen. The division between these three castes is absolute as between the labour force and the other two, but not impassable as between these other two vis-à-vis one another.'[3]

In the philosophers' precepts on specialization, their 'Lycurgean' inspiration obtrudes itself, if possible, still more clearly. 'Human

---

[1] Aristotle, *Politics*, Bk. I, 1254 B.

[2] For a sketch of these 'human watch-dogs', see *Republic*, Bk. II, 375 A–376 B; and Bk. III, 416 A–C.

[3] Aristotle, *Politics*, 1329 A 35–9. Aristotle rejects Plato's prescription of an intellectual governing caste which is to be segregated from the military caste *ab initio* and to exercise authority over it at all times (an idea which Plato rightly believed to be the most important contribution in the *Republic* to Hellenic social philosophy). Aristotle is content to recruit his senate from time-expired soldiers.

watch-dogs' are to be bred by compulsory selective mating, just
like literal dogs and horses and poultry and other domestic animals;[1]
and in the *Republic* Plato goes so far as to abolish outright the institutions of marriage and the family,[2] which 'Lycurgus' had been
content to leave in existence at Sparta when once he had ensured
that they should not interfere with the efficient working of his
system. Children, both male and female, are to be kept in communal crèches from the outset—even before they are weaned—[3]
instead of being allowed to grow up at home as Spartan boys were
allowed until the end of their seventh year and Spartan girls more
or less until they were given in marriage.[4] Private property is to be
abolished:[5] a great leap in the dark beyond the rudimentary col-
lectivism of 'Lycurgean' Sparta, where, as we have seen, private
property was jealously preserved and was distributed ever more
unequally in spite of the socialistic endowment of every Spartiate
'Peer' with a state-owned allotment of real property, and in spite
of the custom by which the 'Peers' made free with one another's
hounds and horses, as well as with the stores in their hunting-
lodges out in the country (in the same spirit in which English
'public-school' boys 'borrow' one another's bicycles and cricket-
bats).[6] The soldier who is to be the finished product of this social
system is to be as professional in his soldiering as an artisan is in
his trade.[7] The 'human watch-dog' cannot and will not be happy;
but his personal happiness is of no account; for the individual
human being exists, not for his own sake, but in order to promote
the welfare of the commonwealth of which he is a member.[8] His
function is to be a part of a corporate social whole; and the metaphor of the 'body politic' is to be translated, as far as may be, into
a reality. The human cells of Leviathan are to be subordinated, on
theory, to the social pseudo-organism as the protoplasmic cells of
a human body are subordinated in fact to the genuine organism in
which they cohere. 'A commonwealth approaches constitutional

[1] Plato, *Republic*, Bk. V, 459 A–460 B; cp. Aristotle, *Politics*, 1334 B–1336 A.
[2] Plato, *Republic*, Bk. V, 457 C–D.
[3] Plato, *Republic*, Bk. V, 460 B–D. For Aristotle's precepts on the rearing of children,
see *Politics*, 1336 A–1337 A.
[4] It is, of course, only logical that, in the *Republic*, the upbringing of girls is to be
socialized as thoroughly as that of boys; for (as we have noted already by anticipation)
women are to be just as eligible for becoming 'watch-dogs' as men; and since they are to
have the same duties, they must obviously have the same education to prepare them for
this. For this complete abolition of the social inequality between the sexes, which of
course goes far beyond the status accorded to women at Sparta, see Plato, *Republic*,
Bk. V, 451 D–457 B, and the burlesque anticipation of this Platonic theme in Aristophanes' *Ecclesiazusae*.
[5] Plato, *Republic*, Bk. III, 416 D–417 B.
[6] For this custom among the Spartiate 'Peers', see Xenophon, *Lacedaemoniorum
Respublica*, ch. vi, and Aristotle, *Politics*, 1263 A, 35–7.
[7] Plato, *Republic*, Bk. II, 374 B–D.
[8] Plato, *Republic*, Bk. IV, 419 A–421 C.

perfection in so far as it approximates to the constitution of a single human being.'[1]

Not happiness and not progress, but stability, is the Alpha and Omega of the Athenian philosopher's social creed. Aristotle, in his matter-of-fact way, envisages this much-desired social stability statistically. There is an optimum size both for the population of a commonwealth[2] and for its territory;[3] and, in his anxiety to keep his population stable at the optimum figure, Aristotle allows his train of thought to carry him so far out of range of practical possibilities that he actually prescribes a difference of nearly twenty years between the respective statutory marriageable ages for women and for men. His women are to marry at 18 and his men at about 37, in order that the son (who is presumably to be an only son in every case) may not approach the statutory marriageable age in his turn until his father is conveniently ready to die off and make room for an heir to step into possession of the family allotment![4]

In this fantastic prescription, Aristotle is consciously departing from the practice of 'Lycurgus'; for in 'Lycurgean' Sparta there was no regulation of the Spartiate population on economic considerations. When Spartiate male infants were destroyed, they were destroyed solely on eugenic grounds; and, as we have seen,[5] the 'Lycurgean' State—like the Fascist State in our own society— deliberately encouraged Spartiate fathers to rear as many sons as they could, so long as the boys were physically fit. In commenting on the 'Lycurgean' social policy, Aristotle points out[6] that the breeding of the largest attainable number of adult Spartiate males in a commonwealth which only disposed of a rigidly limited number of land-allotments for the endowment of Spartiate 'Peers' was bound to produce a pauper surplus of Spartiate male population. This residue of disinherited citizens, who had been disappointed of their natural expectations, and had been condemned to live in poverty and idleness through no personal fault of their own, would evidently be prone to revolution; and, as a grave and standing menace to the stability of the 'Lycurgean' constitution, their existence at Sparta strikes Aristotle as a palpable flaw in the 'Lycurgean' system. Accordingly, when he comes to offer his own prescription for a stable society, he makes a heroic effort to prevent this particular flaw from arising. He does not realize that, even if his scheme for keeping his population at one absolutely constant figure were feasible, his very success in carrying the pursuit of stability to this

---

[1] Plato, *Republic*, Bk. V, 462 c. For a critique of this conception of the relation between individual human beings and human societies, see III. C (ii) (a), below.
[2] Aristotle, *Politics*, 1325 B–1326 B; cp. Plato, *Republic*, 423 B.
[3] Aristotle, *Politics*, 1326 B–1327 A.   [4] Aristotle, *Politics*, 1334 B–1335 A.
[5] On p. 59, above.   [6] Aristotle, *Politics*, Bk. II, 1270 B.

extreme would remorselessly defeat its own object by extinguishing the last spark of his imaginary commonwealth's vitality. The Spartan statesmen who had created the 'Lycurgean' system some two centuries earlier had been wiser in their generation. They can scarcely have been unaware of the gravity of the menace to which the 'Lycurgean' constitution was, and always would be, exposed on account of the Spartiate 'Inferiors' ' inevitable revolutionary proclivities; but we may conjecture that they called this disinherited caste into existence with their eyes open. They realized that, if Sparta was to live at all, she must have a reservoir of man-power; that if this was an absolute social necessity, it could not be purchased at too high a social price; and that an element of pressure and elasticity might be not merely a necessary evil, but even perhaps an indispensable good in a social system that was otherwise altogether rigid and static.

So much for Aristotle's pursuit of social stability through statistical ingenuities. And as for Plato, who follows his own bent by pursuing this same Utopian aim on the plane of intellect and imagination, he involves himself in proclaiming a ban upon poets which might have issued from the mouth of a Spartan Overseer, and in establishing a general censorship over 'dangerous thought' which has its analogues, in the Westernized World of to-day, in the obscurantist regulations of Communist Russia and National-Socialist Germany and Fascist Italy and Militarist Japan.[1]

The Utopian programme of the fourth-century Athenian philosophers was a forlorn hope, for the 'Lycurgean' system, in which they put their trust, was visibly crumbling at the very time when they were seeking to arrest the incipient decline of the Hellenic Civilization by 'pegging' it to the Spartan rock. The philosophers' failure was proved in a general way retrospectively by the continuance of the decline, which persisted, with alternate rallies and relapses, until, some eight centuries after 'the beginning of evils' in 431 B.C., it ended in an irretrievable fall.[2] But the inadequacy of this kind of Utopia for the salvation of Hellas was also demon-

---

[1] For the Platonic censorship of Literature, see *Republic*, Bk. III, 306 A–398 B; and Bk. X, 595 A–608 B; *Laws*, 663 D–664 D. The touches of whimsical Platonic humour with which the heaviness of the passages in the *Republic* is skilfully relieved should not be interpreted as implying that the policy here set forth is not intended by Plato to be taken seriously by his readers. For the Platonic censorship on the expression of private opinion in matters of morality and theology, see *Laws* 662 B–663 A and 907 A–910 E. In the last of the passages here cited, the atheist who preaches his atheism without malice aforethought is condemned to confinement in a reformatory for a minimum period of five years, with death as the penalty for invincible ignorance. The wilful propagandist of atheism is condemned to solitary confinement for life. For the restriction upon travel and migration, see *Laws* 949 E–953 E. On the whole subject of Plato's authoritarianism and obscurantism, see Livingstone, R. W.: *The Greek Genius and its Meaning to Us* (Oxford 1912, Clarendon Press), pp. 186–90.

[2] For the rhythm of declines and falls, see Parts V and XI, below.

strated experimentally, before Hellenic history had run its course, by the mass-production of artificially manufactured commonwealths in which the main Utopian precepts were duly translated into practice. The single commonwealth laid out on a patch of waste land in Crete, which is postulated in Plato's Laws, was actually magnified tenfold and multiplied a thousandfold in the city-states which were founded by Alexander and the Seleucidae in partibus Orientalium and by the Romans in partibus Barbarorum during the next three or four centuries. In these 'Utopias in real life', which were systematically planted, by Hellenically enlightened rulers, over a zone extending from Transoxania and the Panjab at one end to Gaul and the Maghrib at the other, the social order was founded on the dogma, first ventilated by Aristotle, that all non-Hellenes were 'natural-born slaves'. Accordingly, the little bands of Greeks and Macedonians and Italici who were fortunate enough to be enrolled as colonists were liberated for their high cultural task of making the light of Hellenism shine in the outer darkness by having assigned to them an ample labour-force of 'Native' fallāhīn to do the dirty work of providing their new Hellenic masters with the necessary means of material livelihood. In accordance with the Aristotelian precept,[1] these hewers of wood and drawers of water were 'in' but not 'of' the commonwealths to which they were high-handedly 'attributed' and whose existence their labours rendered possible. The 'attributions' were sometimes made on what was—from the standpoint of the privileged citizen-body—a princely scale. A Roman colony in Gaul might be endowed with the entire territory and population of a barbarian tribe or canton; a Seleucid colony in Anatolia with a score of villages which had previously supported the priesthood of a temple-state.[2]

---

[1] There is no evidence to show how far the Hellenic colonization policy of the Alexandrine and post-Alexandrine age was consciously influenced by the precepts of the fourth-century Athenian philosophers. The Seleucid and the Roman foundations had precedents, in the enserfment of the Sikels and the Mariandyni to the older Hellenic colonies of Syracuse and Heraclea Pontica, which are likely to have been more prominent in the minds of the Roman and Seleucid statesmen, when they were working out their policy, than either 'Lycurgean' Sparta or the Athenian Utopias.

[2] For example, the city-state of Nemausus (Nîmes), which was organized by the Roman authorities in the territory of the Volcae Arecomici in the Roman Province of Gallia Narbonensis, received 'the Latin franchise' (an intermediate status between subjection and the Roman citizenship) and at the same time had twenty-four native Arecomican villages 'attributed' to it. (Strabo, Bk. IV, pp. 186–7.) Again, 'Antioch-towards-Pisidia . . . was probably carved out of the once vast estate of [the Anatolian divinity] Mên Askainos' by the Seleucidae (Tarn, W. W.: Hellenistic Civilisation (London 1927, Arnold), p. 116). In general, see Tarn, op. cit., ch. 4, passim; Beloch, K. J.: Griechische Geschichte, 2nd ed., vol. iv, part (i) (Berlin and Leipzig 1925, de Gruyter), ch. 7: 'Die Hellenisierung des Ostens'; Reid, J. S.: The Municipalities of the Roman Empire (Cambridge 1913, University Press). Interesting light is thrown upon the relations between 'attributed' tribes and Roman municipalities by the accident which has preserved for us the text of an edict, promulgated in A.D. 46 by the Emperor Claudius, De Civitate Anaunorum (translation and commentary in Hardy, E. G.: Roman Laws and Charters (Oxford 1912, Clarendon Press)). Compare the present relation between European immigrants and native Africans in the British territory of Kenya Colony.

A broad servile foundation was certainly needed; for the Hellenic city-state of the decadence, with its fine public buildings and its handsome public 'dole' in kind (free bread and free entertainments), was a costly affair—especially when it was arbitrarily and suddenly imposed as a superstructure upon an alien system of society which was already complete in itself. The calculation was that this costly Hellenic superstructure would ultimately pay its way by raising the whole standard of life—economic, as well as political and cultural —of the entire population throughout the vast area over which these seeds of Hellenism were being sown. But this calculation left out of account the blighting effect of the parasitism which was inherent in the Roman and Seleucid performance, as it was in the Platonic and Aristotelian programme. This fatal vice prevented the great experiment from producing the results which its authors had expected of it.[1] The weight of the parasitic Hellenic super-structure merely depressed the level of 'Native' life without pene-trating beneath the surface and loosing the great deeps; and there was therefore no release of new social forces that was in any way comparable to the emergence of the titanic forces of Democracy and Industrialism from the depths of our own modern Western Society towards the close of the eighteenth century of the Christian Era.

In the second century of the same era—when the Hellenic World was enjoying an Indian Summer which contemporaries, and even posterity, long mistook for a Golden Age—it looked superficially as though Plato's most audacious hopes had at last been fulfilled and transcended. From the accession of Nerva in A.D. 96 to the death of Marcus Aurelius in A.D. 180, a series of philosopher-kings sat, in unbroken succession, upon a throne which dominated not merely this or that single Hellenic city-state but the entire Hellenic World of that age. A thousand city-states were living side by side, in peace and concord, under this philosophic Imperial aegis; yet the cessation of evils was only a pause, for all was not well beneath the surface. An impalpable censorship—inspired by the atmosphere of the social environment more effectively than it could ever have been imposed by Imperial fiat—was now eliminating intellectual and artistic originality with a vengeance which would have devastated Plato if he could have returned to see his whimsical precepts so literally realized. And the uninspired respectable prosperity of the second century was followed by the chaotic passionate misery of the third, when the fallāhīn turned and rent their masters.[2] By the

---

[1] Contrast the social effect of the previous Greek maritime colonization in the Mediterranean and the Black Sea (eighth to sixth centuries B.C.), which has been touched upon on pp. 51–2, above.

[2] See Rostovtzeff, M.: *The Social and Economic History of the Roman Empire* (Oxford 1926, Clarendon Press), *passim*.

fourth century the tables had been completely turned; for the once privileged ruling class of the Roman municipalities, so far as it survived at all, was now everywhere in chains. Chained to their kennels, and with their tails between their legs, the municipal decurions of the Roman Empire *in extremis* could hardly be recognized as the ideological descendants of Plato's magnificent 'human watch-dogs!'

The same pursuit of stability and the same achievement of sterility reappear in the *Brave New World* which has been conceived, in a satirical vein, by Mr. Aldous Huxley.[1]

Like the Hellenic Utopias which we have just been surveying, this modern Western Anti-Utopia bears the marks of its place and its time. Written in England and published in the fourteenth year after the Armistice of the 11th November, 1918, it carries the scars of the Great War of 1914–18 and the Great Economic Depression which had begun in 1929. The author portrays an imaginary future generation of our Western Society which is content to sacrifice originality and progress if it can save itself from being destroyed by the terrific new forces of Industrialism and Democracy from which the War and the Depression have emanated.

'The Nine Years' War, the great Economic Collapse. There was a choice between World Control and destruction; between stability and . . .[2]

' "Stability," said the Controller, "stability. No civilisation without social stability. No social stability without individual stability." His voice was a trumpet. Listening, they felt larger, warmer.

'The machine turns, turns and must keep on turning—for ever. It is death if it stands still. A thousand millions scrabbled the dust of the Earth. The wheels began to turn. In a hundred and fifty years there were two thousand millions. Stop all the wheels. In a hundred and fifty weeks there are once more only a thousand millions; a thousand thousand thousand men and women have starved to death.

'Wheels must turn steadily, but cannot turn untended. There must be men to tend them, men as steady as the wheels upon their axles, sane men, obedient men, stable in contentment.

'Crying: My baby, my mother, my only, only love; groaning: My sin, my terrible God; screaming with pain, muttering with fever, bemoaning old age and poverty—how can they tend the wheels? And if they cannot tend the wheels. . . . The corpses of a thousand thousand thousand men and women would be hard to bury or burn.'[3]

The programme of *Brave New World* (a programme which is displayed by the author in order to repel and not in order to attract) is to 'peg' our 'post-war' Western Society at the level of the Industrial System, which is to be improved, like the 'Lycurgean'

---

[1] Huxley, Aldous: *Brave New World* (London 1932, Chatto and Windus).
[2] Huxley, op. cit., p. 56. [3] Huxley, op. cit., p. 48.

system in the Athenian Utopias, and this again in two ways. In *Brave New World*, the application of our Western Physical Science to practical life is to be carried to extremes; and at the same time the vast increase in the material 'drive' behind all our actions is to be counteracted and rendered innocuous by converting the spiritual voltage of Human Nature from high to low tension. In the imaginary extensions of Applied Science—'Ectogenesis'[1] and 'Hypnopaedia'[2]—we are given the same sensation of superhuman skill and ingenuity that we experience in real life when we contemplate the *tours de force* of the Esquimaux and the Nomads and the Spartans and the 'Osmanlis. In the relaxation of the nervous system of *Homo Industrialis* from the *furor Americanus* to the lotus-eaters' tempo,[3] we are reminded of the latter end of the Polynesians.

The difficult scientific enterprise of obtaining and maintaining a low degree of spiritual tension is executed in *Brave New World* by an ingenious variety of means. In the synthetic drug called 'soma', which has the same opiate effect as the legendary lotus fruit, the aid of Applied Physical Science is enlisted;[4] but for the most part the desired psychic effect is induced by psychological methods. The pre-Utopian social heritage of our Western Civilization is consigned to oblivion by a Burning of the Books.[5] The possibility of fresh spiritual creation is ruled out by the elimination of challenges[6] and of all the higher forms of spiritual activity and experience.[7] The personality of the individual is subordinated to the corporate life of the body social to a degree that would satisfy Plato himself.[8] And the majority of individuals are so cultivated[9] that they perform the function for which they have been designed without any discomfort or any repining or even any consciousness that human life has other potentialities than those which they find within their own reach.

---

[1] Huxley, op. cit., ch. i. [2] Huxley, op. cit., pp. 27–32.
[3] For the fable of the lotus-eaters, see II. D (i), vol. ii, pp. 22–3, above.
[4] For 'soma', see Huxley, op. cit., p. 63.
[5] This idea is taken, of course, from the legendary act of the Emperor Ts'in She Hwangti, the founder of the Sinic universal state; but it may be noted that, in the author's own generation, a similar act of vandalism had been performed for a similar purpose by a living dictator. The desire to make a breach with the Ottoman cultural past was one of the motives in the mind of President Mustafā Kemāl when he substituted the Latin for the Arabic Alphabet in Turkey in A.D. 1928. Since the publication of Mr. Huxley's fantasia, there has been an actual Burning of the Books in Germany, to celebrate Herr Hitler's advent to power.
[6] ' "Consider your own lives", said Mustafa Mond: "Has any of you ever encountered an insurmountable obstacle?" The question was answered by a negative silence.' (Huxley, op. cit., p. 51.)
[7] 'You can't make tragedies without social instability' (op. cit., pp. 259–60). The price of happiness is the renunciation of Art and Science and Religion (p. 271).
[8] The official motto of the World State is 'Community, Identity, Stability' (op. cit., p. 1). Its slogans are 'Everyone belongs to everyone else' (p. 45) and 'When the individual feels, the community reels' (p. 109).
[9] 'Cultivated' is the right word; for when life is reproduced by 'Ectogenesis' and birth is replaced by 'decanting', the distinction between the two successive processes of breeding and rearing fades out.

The method of operation by which the inhabitants of the Brave New World are brought into perfect equilibrium with their environment is the deliberate differentiation of Society into a number of separate castes with different social functions; and this is triumphantly achieved by the application of Physical and Psychological Science.

'Of course they did not content themselves with merely hatching out embryos: any cow could do that. "We also predestine and condition. We decant our babies as socialised human beings, as Alphas or Epsilons, as future sewage workers or future. . . ."[1]

' "I suppose Epsilons don't really mind being Epsilons." . . .

' "Of course they don't. How can they? They don't know what it's like being anything else. We'd mind, of course. But then we've been differently conditioned. Besides, we start with a different heredity."

' "I'm glad I'm not an Epsilon," said Lenina, with conviction.

' "And if you were an Epsilon," said Henry, "your conditioning would have made you no less thankful that you weren't a Beta or an Alpha.". . .

' "I was wondering", said the Savage, "why you had them at all—seeing that you can get whatever you want out of those bottles. Why don't you make everybody an Alpha Double Plus while you're about it?"

'Mustafa Mond laughed. "Because we have no wish to have our throats cut," he answered. "We believe in happiness and stability. A society of Alphas couldn't fail to be unstable and miserable. Imagine a factory staffed by Alphas—that is to say by separate and unrelated individuals of good heredity and conditioned so as to be capable (within limits) of making a free choice and assuming responsibilities. Imagine it!" he repeated.

'The Savage tried to imagine it, not very successfully.

' "It's an absurdity. An Alpha-decanted, Alpha-conditioned man would go mad if he had to do Epsilon Semi-Moron work—go mad, or start smashing things up.[2] Alphas can be completely socialised—but only on condition that you make them do Alpha work.[3] Only an Epsilon

---

[1] Huxley, op. cit., p. 14.

[2] This, of course, was the state of mind of the Spartiate 'Inferiors' (ὑπομείονες). The Directors of the World State in *Brave New World* are saved from this Spartan problem by their superior command of Physical Science; for there is no need to maintain a reserve-force when any number of individuals required in any given caste can be cultivated artificially according to plan, and when no provision has to be made against unforeseen casualties through either war or disease.—A. J. T.

[3] The spiritual 'make-up' of Alphas is the crux of the social system. 'Alphas are so conditioned that they do not *have* to be infantile in their emotional behaviour, but that is all the more reason for their making a special effort to conform. It is their duty to be infantile, even against their inclination' (p. 114). On one occasion a very high official, who is an Alpha *ex hypothesi*, confesses in an unguarded moment that 'Happiness is a hard master—particularly other people's happiness. A much harder master, if one isn't conditioned to accept it unquestioningly, than truth' (p. 268). In this Alpha mentality we detect the inevitable residual element of instability which defies elimination in *Brave New World* as in every other Utopia. The Alphas are as indispensable to Mr. Huxley's imaginary commonwealth as the servile labour force is to Aristotle's. And it can be foreseen that, sooner or later, they too will turn and rend the system that is exploiting them. —A. J. T.

can be expected to make Epsilon sacrifices, for the good reason that for him they aren't sacrifices; they're the line of least resistance. His conditioning has laid down rails along which he's got to run. He can't help himself; he's foredoomed. Even after decanting, he's still inside a bottle —an invisible bottle of infantile and embryonic fixations. . . ."

'The Savage sighed profoundly.

' "The optimum population," said Mustafa Mond, "is modelled on the iceberg—eight-ninths below the water line, one-ninth above."

' "And they're happy below the water line?"

' "Happier than above it. . . ."

' "In spite of that awful work?"

' "Awful? They don't find it so. On the contrary, they like it. It's light, it's childishly simple. No strain on the mind or the muscles. Seven and a half hours of mild, unexhausting labour, and then the *soma* ration and games and unrestricted copulation and the feelies. What more can they ask for?" '[1]

What more indeed? And the ingeniously contrived result is an imaginary Western universal state in the likeness of the historic Roman Empire in the age of the Philosopher-Kings after the Augustan failure of nerve, or in the likeness of the Sinic Empire under the Prior Han after Ts'in She Hwangti had delivered 'the knock-out blow' in the internecine warfare of the Contending States. In *Brave New World*, likewise, an unnerved society is bidding for stability by consenting to the sacrifice of everything that makes stability worth having. It has accepted the verdict that 'Civilisation is sterilisation';[2] but the historical parallels indicate that no amount of self-mutilation will avail to placate the Envy of the Gods who hold the keys of immortality. 'For whosoever will save his life shall lose it.'[3]

While Mr. Aldous Huxley's *Brave New World* is a satirical exercise of wisdom after the event, the genius of Mr. H. G. Wells has contrived, in *The First Men in the Moon*,[4] to write a 'post-war' Utopia thirteen years before the outbreak of the War of 1914–18. Without waiting to be enlightened by this portentous catastrophe, Mr. Wells appears to have divined by intuition that our Western Civilization was rushing down a steep place into the sea. He perceives that the social climate of Industrialism is threatening to become as inimical to Life as the physical climate of the Moon; and he presents a programme for 'pegging' our terrestrial society at a habitable level in the adverse environment of a thoroughly industrialized world in the guise of an imaginary description of actual lunar conditions.

---

[1] Huxley, op. cit., pp. 87, 262, 264.   [2] Huxley, op. cit., p. 127.
[3] Matt. xvi. 25. The illusion of immortality, which is one of the regular psychological idiosyncrasies of universal states, is examined further in Part VI, below.
[4] Wells, H. G.: *The First Men in the Moon* (1st ed.: London 1901, George Newnes).

The physical climate of the Moon has become so adverse to Life that the star's surface has ceased to be habitable except intermittently. Mr. Wells portrays his Selenites as being content if they can 'peg' their Selenite Society a point or two above the death-line. And, in the genuine Utopian vein, he imagines them seeking survival through stability, stability through differentiation of social functions, and differentiation through physical and psychic polymorphy.

'In the Moon, every citizen knows his place. He is born to that place, and the elaborate discipline of training and education and surgery he undergoes fits him at last so completely to it that he has neither ideas nor organs for any purpose beyond it. . . . If, for example, a Selenite is destined to be a mathematician, his teachers and trainers set out at once to that end. They check any incipient disposition to other pursuits, they encourage his mathematical bias with a perfect psychological skill. His brain grows, or at least the mathematical faculties of his brain grow, and the rest of him only so much as is necessary to sustain this essential part of him. At last, save for rest and food, his one delight lies in the exercise and display of his faculty, his one interest in its application, his sole society with other specialists in his own line. His brain grows continually larger, at least so far as the portions engaging in mathematics are concerned; they bulge ever larger and seem to suck all life and vigour from the rest of his frame. His limbs shrivel, his heart and digestive organs diminish, his insect face is hidden under its bulging contours. His voice becomes a mere stridulation for the stating of formulae; he seems deaf to all but properly enunciated problems. The faculty of laughter, save for the sudden discovery of some paradox, is lost to him; his deepest emotion is the evolution of a novel computation. And so he attains his end.

'Or, again, a Selenite appointed to be a minder of mooncalves is from his earliest years induced to think and live mooncalf, to find his pleasure in mooncalf lore, his exercise in their tending and pursuit. He is trained to become wiry and active; his eye is indurated to the tight wrappings, the angular contours, that constitute a "smart mooncalfishness". He takes at last no interest in the deeper part of the Moon; he regards all Selenites not equally versed in mooncalves with indifference, derision or hostility. His thoughts are of mooncalf pastures, and his dialect an accomplished mooncalf technique. So also he loves his work, and discharges in perfect happiness the duty that justifies his being. And so it is with all sorts and conditions of Selenites—each is a perfect unit in a world machine. . . .'[1]

The imaginary human investigator of Selenite affairs draws an eerie picture of what the Selenites have come to look like as a result of their adaptation to this lunar social régime:

' "It was an incredible crowd. Suddenly and violently there was

[1] Wells, op. cit., ch. xxiv: 'The Natural History of the Selenites.'

forced upon my attention the vast amount of difference there is amongst these beings of the Moon.

' "Indeed, there seemed not two alike in all that jostling multitude. They differed in shape, they differed in size, they rang all the horrible changes on the theme of Selenite form! Some bulged and overhung, some ran about among the feet of their fellows. All of them had a grotesque and disquieting suggestion of an insect that has somehow contrived to mock humanity; but all seemed to present an incredible exaggeration of some particular feature: one had a vast right fore-limb, an enormous antennal arm, as it were; one seemed all leg, poised, as it were, on stilts; another protruded the edge of his face-mask into a nose-like organ that made him startlingly human until one saw his expression-less gaping mouth. The strange and (except for the want of mandibles and palps) most insect-like head of the mooncalf-minders underwent, indeed, the most incredible transformations: here it was broad and low, here its leathery brow was drawn out into horns and strange features; here it was whiskered and divided, and there with a grotesquely human profile. One distortion was particularly conspicuous. There were several brain-cases distended like bladders to a huge size, with the face-mask reduced to quite small proportions. . . ."

'He does not mention the ant, but throughout his allusions the ant is continually being brought before my mind, in its sleepless activity, in its intelligence and social organization, in its structure, and more particu-larly in the fact that it displays, in addition to the two forms—the male and female form—that almost all other animals possess, a number of other, sexless, creatures—workers, soldiers and the like—differing from one another in structure, character, power and use, and yet all members of the same species. For these Selenites, also, have a great variety of forms . . . differing in size, differing in the relative size of part to part, differing in power and appearance, and yet not different species of creatures, but only different forms of one species, and retaining through all their variations a certain common likeness that marks their specific unity. The Moon is, indeed, a sort of vast ant-hill; only, instead of there being only four or five sorts of ant, there are many hundred different sorts of Selenite, and almost every gradation between one sort and another.'[1]

In this brilliant fantasy, Mr. Wells brings his gift of concrete imagination into play in order to conjure up before our mental vision a society which has actually achieved that morphological differentiation between different social castes which Aristotle—for once allowing his wish to be father to his thought—would have us believe that Nature herself has intended to establish.[2] It is significant that, in staging this fantasy, Mr. Wells finds it con-venient to picture the creatures of which his imaginary Selenite Society is composed as belonging to a fabulous race which is a

[1] Wells, op. cit., ch. xxiv: 'The Natural History of the Selenites'.
[2] See the passage quoted on pp. 93–4, above.

kind of 'missing link' between human beings and insects. By this artifice he diminishes the demand upon the imaginative faculty of his readers; for the conception of a definite and rigid correlation between social function and physical or mental structure is familiar to human minds apropos of the World of Insects; and therefore, if once the readers of Mr. Wells's *Utopia* can be induced to accept his suggestion of kinship between insects and human beings, they may be led on through this association of ideas to entertain, as possibly not inapplicable to their own human kind, a conception which would be not merely unfamiliar but violently repugnant if it were crudely suggested in an uncompromisingly human context.

In the life of the social insects, the morphological diversity of the social castes is, of course, the outstanding fact that strikes the mind of human observers, inasmuch as in the Human Race, Nature—*pace Aristotelis*[1]—has not attempted to go further in morphological differentiation than to diversify the two sexes. In the Insect Kingdom, Nature has given freer play to her plastic faculty. In the social honey bee (*Apis*), she has taken one step beyond mere sexual dualism by differentiating the female sex into workers and queens with different forms corresponding to their different functions.[2] In the ants (*Formicidae*) she has gone further still; for in these insects the three primary morphological castes—workers, queens, and males—not only differ from one another in form more radically than the corresponding castes among the bees, but are further differentiated, in some genera of ants, into sub-castes which each have their own precise social functions.[3] In the Carebara ant, 'the queen is several thousand times as large as the worker'.[4] Finally, in the termites, the number of morphologically diverse castes, which in the ants is four at the highest—males, queens, workers, and soldiers—is normally five and rises in some genera of termites to as many as eight, each of which is represented by both males and females.[5]

In all these social insects, this physical phenomenon of morpho-

---

[1] Aristotle's thesis of a psychic dimorphism in the Human Race between a breed of natural-born masters and another breed of natural-born slaves has received a certain measure of support from a great Western philosopher in our own 'post-war' age:

'Dirons-nous . . . que dans les sociétés humaines il y a "dimorphisme", non plus physique et psychique à la fois, comme chez l'insecte, mais psychique seulement? Nous le croyons, à condition toutefois qu'il soit entendu que ce dimorphisme ne sépare pas les hommes en deux catégories irréductibles, les uns naissant chefs et les autres sujets. . . . La vérité est que le dimorphisme fait le plus souvent de chacun de nous, en même temps, un chef qui a l'instinct de commander et un sujet qui est prêt à obéir.' (Bergson, Henri: *Les Deux Sources de la Morale et de la Religion* (Paris 1932, Alcan), p. 300.)

[2] See Wheeler, W. M.: *Social Life among the Insects* (London, no date, Constable), p. 132.

[3] Wheeler, op. cit., pp. 152 and 158-9.

[4] Wheeler, op. cit., loc. cit.

[5] Wheeler, op. cit., pp. 248-58.

logical diversity between different social castes is associated with a
psychic vein of ruthlessness which is strongly reminiscent of the
êthos of some of our arrested human societies: for example, the
Nomads (who have instituted a polymorphic society by domesticating animals and taking them into partnership) or again the 'Osmanlis and the Spartans (who have done their best to introduce the
equivalent of polymorphy into a society composed throughout of
human beings by the Aristotelian device of treating some human
beings as though they were 'human watch-dogs' and others as
though they were 'human cattle'). Classic illustrations of the insects' ruthlessness are the annual massacre of the drones, in cold
blood, by the worker-bees, as soon as the drones have fulfilled their
social function of fertilizing the queen; the self-mutilation of the
ants of both sexes, when they deliberately break off their own wings,
after a solitary nuptial flight, in order to lead, for the rest of their
lives, a terrene existence of laborious social service; and the self-
sacrifice of the soldier-ants, who rise, on occasion, to the same
heights of selflessness as Spartan Leonidas and his Three Hundred
human warriors.

The ants' discarding of their wings is a symbolic act which
typifies the genius of these arrested societies, both insect and
human: the miracles which they are capable of achieving, and their
still more astonishing limitations.

In the matter of achievement, the ants have risen socially, like
human societies, from the economic phase of hunting to the higher
economic levels of agriculture and pastoralism.[1] The ants have even
acquired an inkling of the technique of Industrialism; for 'there are
species of ants that use their larvae as shuttles in weaving the silken
walls of their nests'.[2] In the bees, we admire the elegance with
which they have solved the geometrical problems involved in the
structure of the honeycomb. In the termites, we are impressed by
the titanic scale of an architecture which, in its largest known
buildings, surpasses, scale for scale, the Empire State Building at New York in height and the Great Pyramid at Gīzah in
massiveness.[3]

Therewithal, some social insects also resemble our arrested
human civilizations in the further point of preserving a certain
measure of adaptability. The ants are decidedly adaptable in their
nesting and feeding habits;[4] the bees in their feeding habits and in
their power of accommodating themselves to a wide range of

---

[1] See Wheeler, op. cit., pp. 176–7, 177–9, and 181–94. For the practice of agriculture
by the termites, see op. cit., pp. 267–71.
[2] Wheeler, op. cit., p. 17.
[3] For the termites' 'sky-scrapers', see Wheeler, op. cit., pp. 262–5.
[4] Wheeler, op. cit., pp. 152–4.

variety in climate.[1] On the other hand, the termites have allowed themselves to be lulled into physical inefficiency by their very success in mastering the technique of architecture.

'With greater elaboration and solidity of nest architecture the termite colonies shut themselves off more and more from the outside world, and all the castes, except the winged males and females, lost their eyes and the tough consistency of their integument. They thus came to resemble the molluscs, crustaceans, and certain fishes and reptiles which have withdrawn within a heavy protective armour and have given up participating in the free competitive and co-operative life of their environment.'[2]

The distinguished student of social life among insects who wrote these lines goes on[3] to compare the termites with the human inhabitants of China and Korea, in the age when these shut themselves off from the rest of Mankind and lived as 'hermit kingdoms'.[4]

Moreover, when we turn our attention from the physical to the psychic plane, we find evidence of a rigidity—induced, apparently, by a too exquisitely exact mental equilibrium—not only in the termites, but in the ants and bees as well.

The amazingly precise and delicate mental tool of instinct, with which the insects perform their wonderful feats, is believed, by at least one close observer of insect behaviour, to be a product of reason in a state of arrest. He suggests

'that instinct began in a reasoned act. That this act, through being continually repeated, tended to lose the reasoning element and to become more and more unconscious. As this process continued through generations, the mental machinery through which it worked got more indelibly engraven in the mind. And in the end it became automatic—in other words, it became instinctive.'[5]

The same observer finds, in insect instinct, the qualities of perfection and wisdom combined with the characteristic of inflexibility.

'Speaking in a broad and general sense, instinct is a force of amazing perfection. It performs acts of such precision that they sometimes seem to surpass intelligence. What can be more perfect than the spider's net with its equal angles, its uniform spirals, its nicely parallel threads? Or see the perfection in the comb of the hive-bee. Why, these creatures have solved a recondite problem. It is only a student of the higher mathematics who could determine after detailed calculations that this

[1] Wheeler, op. cit., p. 132.
[2] Wheeler, op. cit., p. 282.   [3] Wheeler, op. cit., loc. cit.
[4] For this social phenomenon of 'petrifaction' see further Part I. C (ii), vol. i, above, and Parts V, VI, and X, below.
[5] Hingston, R. W. G.: *Problems of Instinct and Intelligence* (London 1928, Arnold), p. 268. This question has been touched upon already in the present Study in II. C (i), vol. i, on pp. 205–7, above.

exquisite system of waxen chambers, with their pyramids and rhombs and particular angles, was the one and only system possible to effect the greatest economy of wax. . . .

'Then, again, instinct is wise in its purpose. We [see] this particularly in the hunting-wasps. How amazingly wise it seems that a wasp can get the end of its sting into the one anatomical point that will bring about a paralysis of its prey.'[1]

At the same time,

'we have seen that instinct is inflexible. It battles against every obstacle in order to fulfil its particular end. We saw how locusts marched out upon a river and allowed themselves to be drowned in millions rather than change their instinctive course. We saw butterflies lost on the Himalayan snow-line in obedience to that unswerving instinct which impelled them across the range. We saw spiders allowing themselves to be cut to pieces rather than change their instinctive device of sitting absolutely still.'[2]

From such inflexibility it is a short step to folly.

'Instinct, when it operates in the normal course, when it fulfils the particular purpose for which that particular instinct exists, acts with admirable wisdom and perfection. But divert that instinct from its normal course; try to turn it in some other channel; endeavour to make it do something which it was not originally intended to do, and the result is a course of action which astonishes us by its utter folly. . . .

'An insect may select the wrong species to mate with, another may lay on the wrong kind of food-plant, another may construct the wrong type of cocoon. These are errors that run through the perfection, and their result is disaster and death. . . .

'What folly, we exclaim, in all these actions! Why can't the creatures just think a little and not fall into these stupid traps? They can't do so, for the instinct that impels their actions demands fulfilment, whatever the cost. . . . Their instincts, so amazingly exact and deliberate, have been given them only for one definite end. When applied to that end they are astonishingly perfect. They act with foresight, with unerring logic, with results which seem even to surpass our reason. The wasp must keep parasites out of her cell. What does she do? Smear the cell outside with glue. The caterpillars have to keep in a procession. What do they do? Cling to a thread. The trap-door spider wants to hide its door. What does it do? Cover it with moss. How foreseeing, how logical, how wise it is! Our reason could do no better. Perhaps it could not do as well. But divert the same instinct. Alter its course. Try to make it do something else. Give the wasp an enemy other than a parasite; make the caterpillar's thread into an endless circle; take away the mossy environment of the spider. We have seen the result. Instinct goes on oblivious of such changes. Darkness takes the place of light.'[3]

[1] Hingston, op. cit., pp. 280–1.   [2] Hingston, op. cit., p. 281.
[3] Hingston, op. cit., p. 285.

What is the bearing of these phenomena of insect life upon the history of Man? The observer here quoted expresses the opinion that 'we are not justified in making barriers between insect and human mentality' and that 'the minds of these humble creatures operate in the same way as the mind of Man in their main essential characteristics'.[1]

'Every animal, Man included, possesses two sets of mental activity: the one instinctive, automatic, innate; the other intelligent, plastic, and acquired. These two activities are always blended. They may differ immensely in degrees of development, but they never completely separate from each other.

'The insect mind and the human mind differ mainly in the development of these two factors. Instinct predominates in the insect mind: intelligence in the mind of Man. Nevertheless, in both the Insect and Man these two factors definitely exist. But their minds have evolved along different channels. They have marched, so to speak, along diverging paths, the one developing the force of instinct, the other the force of reason. And each has brought its own type of development to an amazingly perfect degree.

'Yet the Insect, though predominantly instinctive, possesses also glimmerings of reason. Exactly the same is true of Man. Though his life is so filled with rational judgement, yet underneath are those primitive instincts. . . .'[2]

If our observer is right in this view of insect and human mentality and of the relation between the two, then his analysis projects a ray of light upon the problem of our arrested human civilizations. The cause of their strange and tragic arrest, at a moment when they have already issued, quick-born, from the womb of Time and are standing, alive with youthful energy, on the threshold of their life-course, may be explained, on this showing, in psychological terms as a mental reversion from the human towards the insect type of mental rhythm: from the blundering but progressive mobility of reason to the infallible but inflexible rigidity of instinct. In the life of these arrested human civilizations one prominent feature is, as we have seen, the degree to which their human members have become the slaves of habit; and the well-known process by which human habits are formed through some originally deliberate and conscious action becoming automatic as a result of repetition is manifestly analogous to the hypothetical process by which insect instincts may have arisen out of automatized acts of intelligence.[3]

[1] Hingston, op. cit., p. 285.
[2] Hingston, op. cit., pp. 287–8. Cp. Bergson, H.: *Les Deux Sources de la Morale et de la Religion* (Paris 1932, Alcan), pp. 122–3. For the conventional view, which represents human societies as being founded on reason and insect societies as being founded on instinct, see Ibn Khaldūn: *Muqaddamāt*, translated by de Slane, Baron McG. (Paris 1863–8, Imprimerie Impériale, 3 vols.), vol. i, p. 84.
[3] This analogy is suggested, in this context, by Hingston, op. cit., pp. 266–8.

The existence of the five arrested human civilizations shows that the problem of the growth of civilizations is a genuine problem. The analogy between the human and the insect soul gives us an inkling of the nature of this growth as it is manifested in the histories of our twenty-one civilizations which have not suffered arrest but have duly gone on growing after birth.

B. THE NATURE OF THE GROWTHS OF CIVILIZATIONS

HAVING satisfied ourselves that the growths of civilizations present a problem, and having set ourselves the task of solving this problem by inquiring what the nature of these growths may be, let us start our inquiry by invoking a power which has already proved itself a very present help at another critical point in this Study. Let us call in once again the aid of Mythology.

The myth of the Book of Job and of Goethe's *Faust* has given us an insight into the nature of the geneses of civilizations.[1] We may find that equal light is thrown upon the nature of their growths by the myth of Aeschylus's Promethean Trilogy.

This line of approach to our new problem seems promising because the general structure of the two myths is the same. In both, the theme is a conflict between two superhuman powers: a conflict between Zeus and Prometheus in this case, and a conflict between God and Satan or Mephistopheles in the other. In both myths, again, the field of this superhuman conflict is a human being or human society which is also the stake for which the superhuman combatants are contending. The role of Faust or Job is played in the Aeschylean myth by the Hellenic Society, which expands, in the poet's transcendent imagination, into Mankind at large. And, lastly, in both myths, the relative importance of the human and superhuman actors, as it appears in the mythological fantasy, has to be reversed when we come to the psychological interpretation. From this introverted angle of vision, the human field of conflict or prize of victory takes substance as the sole figure on the stage, while the superhuman combatants resolve themselves into conflicting impulses in this human actor's soul.

To this extent the two myths are analogous. The difference between them lies in the relation of the two superhuman combatants —or two conflicting human impulses—with one another. In the myth of Faust and Job, it is God—the receiver of the challenge—who wins the victory through finding an opportunity, in the challenge presented by Satan or by Mephistopheles, for performing a new creative act from which God would otherwise have been inhibited by his own perfection. In this myth, the challenger—Mephistopheles or Satan—is permitted by God to persecute a human victim, in order that the persecutor may suffer discomfiture and defeat. On the other hand, in the Aeschylean myth, the re-

[1] For an analysis of this myth, see II. C (ii) (*b*) 1, vol. i, above.

ceiver of the challenge, who in this myth is Zeus, is the loser of the battle. For Zeus, so far from yearning to perform a creative act, is anxious to stay as he is and to keep the Universe around him at a standstill; the challenge presented to Zeus by Prometheus, which calls the temper and policy of Zeus in question, moves Zeus to inflict a vindictive persecution upon his challenger; and in this act, which overthrows his cherished equilibrium, Zeus brings about his own defeat, while Prometheus, through suffering, wins his way to victory.

When the superhuman and universal imagery of the Aeschylean drama is translated into terms of human time and place, the issue presents itself as the question whether or not the infant Hellenic Civilization is to grow. The crisis is specifically a crisis of social infancy.

'We have before us something pre-classical. We have the daring of an age that has not yet been frightened. If Euripides had said of Zeus the things that Aeschylus says there would probably have been trouble. By his time people were afraid of the solvent and destructive effects of free speculation; in the time of Aeschylus they were still looking to the powers of the human intellect, to reason and free inquiry, as the great emancipators.'[1]

Aeschylus sees Zeus as he is, and therefore he sees that Zeus has to be saved, in spite of himself, by the Promethean challenge.

This Aeschylean Zeus is the primeval Zeus: a superhuman counterpart of the Achaean barbarian war-lord, with the Olympian Pantheon for his turbulent war-band.[2] The historical feat of the Achaeans in overrunning the domain of the outworn Minoan Civilization and making themselves masters of its debris has its mythical reflection in the legendary feat of Zeus in overthrowing his divine predecessor Cronos.[3] Having accomplished this *tour de force* and mounted the throne of Olympus, Zeus has no other idea except to keep himself enthroned there, in solitary, motionless, tyrannical state, with his foot on the neck of a prostrate Universe, as the human barbarians, deposited in Crete by the 'Dorian' Völkerwanderung, actually sat upon the enserfed Minoans,[4] and as the Nomadic invaders from the Steppes have sat upon the sedentary populations whom they have conquered in various times and places. Zeus, however, has not conquered Cronos by his own unaided

[1] Murray, Gilbert: *Prometheus Bound translated into English Rhyming Verse* (London 1931, Allen & Unwin), Introduction, pp. 8–9.
[2] For this aspect of Zeus, see I. C (i) (b), vol. i, p. 96, above.
[3] The overthrow of Cronos by Zeus is duplicated, in the Hellenic Mythology, in the previous overthrow of Uranus by Cronos. Both Cronos and Uranus are conceived in the image of Zeus, and not in that of the Minoan godhead. (See vol. i, p. 96, above.)
[4] See the Song of Hybrias the Cretan, quoted in Part III. A on p. 87 in footnote 1,

powers. He has conquered him with the help of Prometheus; and, after their joint victory, he has to reckon with his Titanic ally. But Prometheus works—and works indefatigably—for everything in life that Zeus now wishes to rule out. For Prometheus is an insatiable creator, a kindler of fire, a probing progressive mind. Prometheus is a mythical personification of the continuity of the growth-process, the Bergsonian *élan vital*. He knows that, unless Zeus keeps on the move, the new ruler of Olympus will inevitably be overthrown in his turn, like Cronos before him; and therefore he gives Zeus no peace.

In every situation, Prometheus always ranges himself on the side of thought against force, of progress against arrest.

When the Titans stand for force and Zeus for thought, Prometheus takes sides with Zeus against his fellow-Titans.

> When first the immortals learned the taste of wrath,
> And strife arose and between them wound its path,
> Many would cast out Cronos from his throne,
> That Zeus forsooth might reign, but many an one
> Swore that no Zeus should e'er be lord of heaven.
> Wise was I, but no force to me was given
> To move the brood Titanic, born of Earth
> And Sky. All crooked plans they turned to mirth
> In their great hearts, and thought full easily
> By strength to master all. But much to me
> And ofttimes had my mystic mother told—
> Themis and Gaia, titles manifold
> Of one eternal form—what end must fall:
> That in this warfare not by strength at all,
> Only by thought, the conquerors should prevail.
> I spoke, I showed my brethren all the tale,
> But they nor heard my words nor looked at me.
> Best then I deemed it, if such things must be,
> That I with Zeus, led by my mother's light,
> Should stand, will linked with will, in armèd fight;
> And by my counsels now the deep and cold
> Abyss of darkness covereth Cronos old. . . .[1]

Thereafter, when Zeus seeks to make his newly won dominion secure by turning the universe into a desert and calling it peace, Prometheus remains true to his own role and thereby falls out with his late ally.

> When first he mounted on his father's throne
> Straightway he called the Gods, and gave each one
> His place and honours. So he wrought his plan
> Of empire. But of Man, unhappy Man,

[1] Aeschylus: *Prometheus Vinctus*, ll. 201–22, Gilbert Murray's translation.

> He had no care: he counselled the whole race
> To uproot, and plant a strange brood in its place.
> And none took stand against that evil mind
> Save me. I rose. I would not see Mankind
> By him stamped out and cast to nothingness. . . .[1]

In this fresh crisis in the cosmic drama, Prometheus fails to convince Zeus by sheer reason, as he had previously failed to convince the Titans.

> In every tyrant's heart there springs in the end
> This poison, that he cannot trust a friend.[2]

Thereupon, Prometheus sets the will of Zeus at defiance, and leads Mankind onward and upward out of the darkness of the post-Minoan interregnum into the light of the Hellenic Civilization as it had come to shine at Athens in Aeschylus's own day.

> All that of art Man has, Prometheus gave.[3]

And he gave it by inspiring his human protégé and pupil with his own Promethean spirit:

> A thing of no avail
> He was, until a living mind I wrought
> Within him, and new mastery of thought.[4]

For this thwarting of his will, Zeus takes his revenge upon Prometheus by turning against him the whole battery of his super-human force.

> Mercy I had for Man; and therefore I
> Must meet no mercy, but hang crucified
> In witness of God's cruelty and pride.[5]

Therewith, Zeus reveals himself as a tyrant and a blight; and the cosmic forces—Io and Oceanus and the Chorus of the Oceanides—which had been in sympathy with Zeus in his struggle with the Titans now turn against him. But these sympathies, which are inhibited by timidity from issuing in action, are of little avail to Prometheus in his contest of wills with his Olympian antagonist.

In this contest, Prometheus is physically at Zeus' mercy. Yet the victory is in Prometheus' hands; for no torture that Zeus can inflict is able to overcome Prometheus' will-power; and this will-power guards a secret that Zeus fain would know.[6] The secret is that, if Zeus persists in his static, tyrannical posture, he is dooming himself to be overthrown, like his predecessors, by the brute force

---

[1] Op. cit., ll. 230-8.   [2] Op. cit., ll. 226-7.
[3] Op. cit., l. 506. See the whole passage, ll. 436-506, in which Prometheus reviews his labour of love for Man in retrospect.
[4] Op. cit., ll. 443-4.
[5] Op. cit., ll. 241-3.   [6] Op. cit., ll. 511-25 and 907-40.

which he has deliberately enthroned in place of thought.[1] This secret is the key of Zeus' own destiny, and in the *Prometheus Vinctus* —the first, and the sole surviving, play of the Aeschylean Trilogy— we are shown Zeus trying, and failing, to wrest Prometheus' secret from him—first by the mental pressure of a threatening message delivered by Hermes and finally, at the end of the play, by the brute force of the thunderbolt.

'The other two plays of the Trilogy, *Prometheus Released* and *Prometheus the Torchbearer*, are no longer extant, but there is enough evidence to show that the end was reconciliation. Prometheus endured for the sake of Man and the oppressed Elder Gods all the pains that Zeus could inflict; also Zeus himself "learnt by suffering"[2] the lesson of forgiveness. He set free his old enemies, the Titans; he spared Mankind; he invented the right of the suppliant. These two elements are enough in themselves to make possible a reconciliation, but it seems certain that Aeschylus also brought in a third element. From the very beginning, Zeus was not quite what he seemed. . . .'[3]

How was Prometheus' moral victory over Zeus attained? Was it that he stole a march on Zeus by bringing down the divine fire to Man concealed in a fire-stick or in a hollow reed? Or was it that he placed Zeus in the tactical dilemma of having to see his policy of immobility flouted or else depart from it himself in the act of taking up arms to defend it? But moral victories are not won by mental chicane; and the cause of Zeus' surrender to Prometheus assuredly lies deeper. Zeus was 'not quite what he seemed' because there was an element of his ally-adversary's spirit in him—a glimmer of Promethean light in the soul of Zeus which Zeus himself was unable wholly to extinguish. It was this that gave Zeus his inkling that Prometheus possessed a secret which was big with the tyrant's own fate, even though he could not divine what this secret was and could think of no better way of learning it than to extort it by force—until he found by trial that, for this purpose, force was unavailing. The reconciliation between Zeus and Prometheus was achieved because their conflict kindled into a flame the Promethean spark which was latent all the time in Zeus' soul.

This is perhaps another way of expressing an aspect of the relation between these two powers which we have noticed, by anticipation, above.[4] Zeus and Prometheus, who on the plane of Mythology appear as separate superhuman personalities, are seen, in a psychological analysis, to be two impulses in a single human

---

[1] Murray, op. cit., Introduction, pp. 13–14.
[2] For this Aeschylean doctrine of πάθει μάθος see *Agamemnon*, ll. 177–8, quoted in I. C (iii) (b), vol. i, p. 169, footnote 1, above.
[3] Murray, op. cit., Introduction, p. 11.   [4] See p. 112, above.

soul which interpenetrate one another, however vehement their conflict, because it is the same soul that feels them both.

If we apply this analysis to the souls of the men and women who were the constituents of the Hellenic Society in the days of its infancy, we may give the Aeschylean myth the following historical interpretation. Supposing that, in Hellas at large, the lethargy of the Achaean or 'Dorian' barbarians, who had squatted among the debris of the derelict Minoan World, had never been stirred by a current of Promethean mental energy, then all Hellas would have vegetated in perpetuity like 'Dorian' Crete. Or let us suppose that the Promethean challenge had been duly presented to the infant Hellenic soul, but had been answered everywhere as it was answered at Sparta. Then the Hellenic Civilization would have been arrested on the threshold of growth, in static high tension, in the Spartan vein; and Sparta, not Athens, would have been *Hellados Hellas*. If the Hellenic Society at large actually avoided both the Cretan and the Spartan fate, this was because, in a majority of Hellenic souls, during the centuries that intervened between the post-Minoan interregnum and the generation of Aeschylus (*vivebat circa* 525–456 B.C.), the humane progressive civilizing êthos of the mythical Prometheus prevailed over the violent 'die-hard' barbarian êthos of the mythical Zeus. 'Zeus was not quite what he seemed.' He seemed a mere barbarian interloper; yet he must have been something more than that; or the historical fact that the Hellenic Civilization actually grew out of an Achaean barbarian root would be an inexplicable miracle.[1]

The Promethean *élan* in the infant Hellenic Society carried it forward from genesis into growth and did not allow it to stand motionless, like a creature turned to stone, on the threshold of life until its place on the open road should be taken by another. In the Hellenic Mythology the son who is greater than his father is born by Thetis not to Zeus (the power who, when reconciled to Prometheus, stands, like God in Goethe's *Faust*, for the divine whole). Achilles is born to Peleus (who, like Faust or Job, is no more than the human part).[2] And thus Hellenic destiny works itself out as a process of growth within the bosom of the Hellenic Society, and not as a catastrophe in which the forces immobilized in the bosom of an arrested civilization are eventually released by the destruction of the social fabric within which they have been imprisoned, in order to clear the ground for a new attempt at construction from the foundations upwards.

---

[1] For the relation of the Hellenic Civilization to the Minoan Civilization through the Achaean 'external proletariat' of the Minoan Civilization, see I. C (i) (*b*), vol. i, pp. 95–100, and II. D (vii), vol. ii, pp. 315–16, above.

[2] Murray, op. cit., Introduction, pp. 13–14.

The Promethean *élan* of the human intellect, which has been portrayed in mythological imagery by the Athenian poet, has been described in the corresponding terms of his own language by a modern French philosopher.

'Although we have to act only upon the objects around us, and although this was the original function of the intellect, the fact that the mechanical structure of the whole Universe is present in each of its parts has made it inevitable that Man should be born with an intellect virtually capable of embracing the whole material world. It is the same with the intellect as with the sense of sight. The eye, likewise, has been made only for the purpose of revealing to us the objects upon which we are in a position to act; but, just as Nature has not been able to obtain the desired degree of visual power except by constructing an apparatus with an efficiency in excess of its object (in as much as we see the stars, although we are incapable of exerting action on them), in the same way she has given us, of necessity, along with the faculty of understanding the matter which we manipulate, a virtual knowledge of the rest and a power—likewise virtual—to make practical use of it.'[1]

The same Western philosopher has retold the Aeschylean tale of the conflict between Prometheus and Zeus.

'Man, as he issued from the hands of Nature, was a being who was both intelligent and social, with a sociality which was calculated to reach its term in diminutive societies and with an intellect which was destined to serve both the individual life and the group life. But the intellect, dilating by its own efforts, has entered upon an unexpected development. It has liberated human beings from servitudes to which they had been condemned by the limitations of their nature. Under these conditions it has proved not impossible for certain human beings, with particularly rich [psychic] endowments, to re-open that which had been closed, and to perform, at least for themselves, that which it would have been impossible for Nature to perform for Humanity at large. Their example has eventually carried away the rest of Mankind, at least in imagination. The will has its genius, as well as the intellect, and genius defies all prognostication. Through the medium of these wills inspired by genius, the *élan* of Life that traverses Matter obtains from Matter, for the future of the Human Species, promises of which there could not even have been any question at the time when the species first took shape. . . . One might say—to employ Spinoza's terms in a

---

[1] Bergson, Henri: *Les Deux Sources de la Morale et de la Religion* (Paris 1932, Alcan), pp. 180–1. The prologue to the Bergsonian epic of the human intellect is given in the following passage from the work of a contemporary English biologist:
'Throughout life, effort always seems to bring in its train advantages unforeseen and unconnected with the effort's immediate object. To give an extreme example, the eyes and ears and other sense organs of animals were developed chiefly for the capture of prey and the avoidance of enemies; but, once formed, they were the starting-point for the life of consciousness that has culminated in ourselves.' (Huxley, J. S.: *The Individual in the Animal Kingdom* (Cambridge 1912, University Press), pp. 130–1.)
Compare the fable of Solomon's Choice in the First Book of Kings, iii. 5–13 (already cited in this Study in II. D (ii), vol. ii, on p. 55, above), and the histories of Venice and Holland (cited in II. D (vii), vol. ii, on pp. 260–1, above).

new meaning—that it is in order to return to *Natura Naturans* that we detach ourselves from *Natura Naturata*.'[1]

In Bergson's philosophy, as in the poetry of Aeschylus, the personality of Prometheus—the genius of the Human Intellect—is drawn for us with a masterly touch. Can we translate this Promethean image into terms of our own concept of Challenge-and-Response? We have found, by empirical observation, that the most stimulating challenge is a challenge of mean degree between an excess of severity and a deficiency of it.[2] Perhaps we can now gain deeper insight into this apparent 'law' by applying the myth of Prometheus to it. The characteristic of Prometheus is his *élan*, which carries him past the dead point at which Zeus would have stuck if Prometheus had not been there to carry Zeus away with him. And, in terms of Challenge-and-Response, the Promethean *élan* suggests a consideration which has not engaged our attention in this context so far. So far, we have simply noted the truths, or truisms, that a deficient challenge may fail to stimulate the challenged party at all, while an excessive challenge may break his spirit. But what about the challenge with which he is just capable of coping? On a short view, this is the most stimulating challenge imaginable; and, in the concrete instances of the Polynesians and the Esquimaux and the Nomads and the 'Osmanlis and the Spartans, we have observed empirically that such challenges are in fact apt to evoke *tours de force*. We have also observed, however, that in the next chapter of the story these *tours de force* exact, from those who have performed them, a fatal penalty in the shape of an arrest in their development. And, therefore, on a longer view, we must pronounce that the evocation of the greatest immediate response is not the ultimate test of whether any given challenge is the optimum from the standpoint of evoking the greatest response on the whole and in the end. The real optimum challenge is rather one which not only stimulates the challenged party to achieve a single successful response but also stimulates him to acquire a momentum that carries him on a step farther: from achievement to a fresh struggle, from the solution of one problem to the presentation of another, from momentary rest to reiterated movement, from Yin to Yang again. The single, finite movement from a disturbance to a restoration of equilibrium is not enough, if genesis is to be followed by growth. And, to convert the movement into a repetitive, recurrent rhythm, there must be an *élan* which carries the challenged party through equilibrium into an overbalance which exposes him to a fresh challenge and thereby inspires him to make a fresh response in the form of a further equilibrium ending in a further overbalance

[1] Bergson, op. cit., p. 55.   See Part II. D in vol. ii, above.

—and so on in a progression which is potentially infinite. In earthly language:

> So tauml' ich von Begierde zu Genuss
> Und im Genuss verschmacht' ich nach Begierde.[1]

In heavenly language:

> Komm! Hebe dich zu höheren Sphären!
> Wenn er dich ahnet, folgt er nach.[2]

This *élan*, working through a series of overbalances, can be detected in the course of Hellenic history from the genesis of the Hellenic Civilization down to Aeschylus's day.[3]

The first challenge presented to the new-born Hellenic Civilization was the challenge of chaos and ancient night. The disintegration of the 'apparented' Minoan Society had left a welter of social debris—marooned Minoans and stranded Achaeans and 'Dorians' —in the defunct society's derelict domain; and the first question was whether a new order would assert itself in this void and formless world. Would the sediment of an old civilization be buried under the shingle which the new torrent of barbarism had brought down in spate? Would the rare patches of lowland in the Aegean landscape be dominated by the wilderness of highlands which ringed them round? Would the peaceful cultivators of the plains be at the mercy of the shepherds and the brigands of the mountains?

This first challenge to the life of the infant Hellenic Civilization was victoriously met. As Hêraklês, in his cradle, strangled the two serpents that had been sent to take his life, so the people of the lowlands of Hellas solved their problem of self-defence by establishing their mastery over their aggressive highlander neighbours; and their victory decided that Hellas should be a world of cities and not of villages, of agriculture and not of pasturage, of order and not of anarchy. Yet the very success of their response to this first challenge exposed the victors to a second. For a victory which ensured the peaceful pursuit of agriculture in the lowlands gave a momentum to the growth of population; and this momentum did not come to a standstill when the population reached the maximum density which agriculture in the Hellenic homeland could support. This limit was inelastic; for, in the Aegean World, the arable lowlands amount to only a small fraction of the total area of the country; and the line at which the bare limestone skeleton of the land breaks out, as a barren mountain-side, above the level sediment of soil in

---

[1] *Faust*, ll. 3249–50.
[2] *Mater Gloriosa* (Mary) to *Una Poenitentium* (Gretchen), speaking of *Doctor Marianus* (Faust), in *Faust*, ll. 12094–5.
[3] These chapters of Hellenic history have been dealt with, by anticipation, in I. B (i), vol. i, on pp. 24–6 and in II. D (ii), vol. ii, on pp. 36–49, above, and are examined further in III. C (i) (*a*) on pp. 139–40 and in III. C (i) (*d*) on pp. 197–8, below.

the valley bottoms is so sharp that the wayfarer passes from loam to rock, from field to wilderness, at a single step.[1] Thus the very success of the response which the Hellenic Society had made to the first challenge exposed it to a second; and it responded to this Malthusian challenge as successfully as it had responded to the Herculean.

The Hellenic response to the challenge of over-population took the form of a series of alternative experiments. The easiest and most obvious method of solving the problem was adopted first and was applied until it began to bring in diminishing returns. Thereupon, a less obvious and more difficult alternative method was adopted and applied, in place of the first, until, this time, a solution of the problem was achieved.

The first method was to employ the techniques and institutions which the lowlanders of Hellas had created in the process of imposing their wills upon their highlander neighbours at home in order to conquer new domains for Hellenism overseas. With the military instrument of the hoplite phalanx and the political instrument of the city-state, a swarm of Hellenic pioneers established a Magna Graecia in the toe of Italy at the expense of barbarian Itali and Chônes, and a new Peloponnese in Sicily at the expense of barbarian Sikels, and a Hellenic pentapolis in the Cyrenaica at the expense of barbarian Libyans, and a Chalcidicê on the north coast of the Aegean at the expense of barbarian Thracians.[2] Yet, once again, the very success of the response brought down a new challenge upon the victors. For the expansion of Hellas from the coasts of the Aegean far and wide around the coasts of the Mediterranean was itself a challenge to the other Mediterranean peoples—the barbarian victims and the Phoenician and Etruscan rivals of the Hellenic pioneers—whose vital interests were being jeopardized by these Hellenic successes; and eventually the non-Hellenes were stimulated by the Hellenic pressure upon them to bring the expansion of Hellas to a standstill: partly by resisting Hellenic aggression with borrowed Hellenic arts and arms, and partly by co-ordinating their own forces on a greater scale than the Hellenes themselves were able to achieve.[3] Through the increasingly effective resistance of

[1] A modern Western observer cannot fail to be struck by the resemblance between the physiography of Greece and that of Japan; and the situation of the agricultural population of the Hellenic homeland in the first half of the eighth century B.C. must have been not unlike that of the agricultural population of Japan in the first half of the twentieth century of the Christian Era.

[2] See I. B (ii), vol. i, p. 24, and II. D (ii), vol. ii, pp. 42-3, above. For the wrong turning taken on this occasion by the Spartans, when they tried to solve the Malthusian problem by conquering their own Hellenic neighbours and peers in Messenia, see I. B (ii), vol. i, p. 24, and III. A, pp. 52-3, above.

[3] It is one of the laws of the Balance of Power that it is more difficult to achieve political consolidation in the heart and centre of an expanding society than on the periphery. This law is analysed in III. C (ii) (b), on pp. 301-6, below.

these opposing forces, the Hellenic expansion over the Mediterranean, which had begun in the course of the eighth century B.C.,
was brought to a standstill in the course of the sixth century after
having lasted for some two hundred years. Meanwhile, the Hellenic Society was still confronted by the challenge of over-population, by which its expansion had originally been set in motion; and
now that one method of solving the problem had been followed out
to the point of diminishing returns, some alternative method had
to be discovered.

In this new crisis in Hellenic history, the required discovery was
made by Athens, who became 'the education of Hellas' through
learning, and teaching, how to transmute the expansion of the Hellenic Society from an extensive into an intensive process.[1] This
Athenian response to the Malthusian challenge has been described
already in this Study,[2] and the description need not be repeated
here. It need only be pointed out that this Athenian response was
demanded because the pre-Athenian response to the same challenge had carried the balance of forces between the Greeks and
their Mediterranean neighbours beyond the dead point of equilibrium until it had eventually overbalanced into a situation in
which the non-Hellenic resistance to Hellenic expansion made it
necessary for the Hellenic Society to pursue the solution of the
Malthusian problem by other means.

It was in the full *élan* of the Athenian response[3] that the Athenian
poet Aeschylus wrote his Promethean Trilogy, in which the rhythm
of overbalance is captured and immortalized in a myth.

This rhythm, which thus appears in the poetry of Aeschylus as
well as in the pre-Aeschylean chapters of Hellenic history, has been
apprehended, in a far distant time and place, by a modern North
American poet.

[1] The phenomenon of 'etherialization', of which this transmutation is an example, is
examined in III. C (i) (*c*), below.
[2] In vol. i, pp. 24-5, and vol. ii, pp. 39-42, above. Compare the similar policy for
solving the same Malthusian problem which was pursued by the Japanese Government
from the time of the Washington Conference of A.D. 1921-2 down to the 18th-19th
September, 1931. (See Toynbee, A. J.: *Survey of International Affairs, 1931* (London
1932, Milford), pp. 400-3.)
[3] This time, again, the success of the response to one challenge exposed the successful
society to a new challenge. The Athenians had discovered how to solve the Hellenic
problem of over-population by an intensification of economic productivity through
specialized production for export; and through this Athenian discovery an economic
problem received a complete economic solution. But this economic solution of an
economic problem at once created a political problem which could only be solved on
political lines. For the economic change from a system of local autonomy to a system of
intercourse and interdependence demanded a corresponding change on the political
plane. An inter-city-state economy could not be carried on effectively without the provision of some kind of political framework in the shape of an inter-city-state régime of
law and order. The Athenians failed to respond successfully to this political challenge
which arose out of their successful response to the foregoing economic challenge, and
this failure resulted in the breakdown and disintegration of the Hellenic Civilization.
(See further IV. C (iii) (*b*) 10, vol. iv, pp. 206-14, below.)

'It is provided in the essence of things that from any fruition of success, no matter what, shall come forth something to make a greater struggle necessary.'[1]

This intuition of an American man of letters of the nineteenth century has been taken as a text by a twentieth-century English biologist.

'Life can never be in equilibrium. Given the two well-established facts that living substance can vary and that living things, if left to themselves, would multiply in rapid geometrical ratio, then change in the *status quo* is inevitable. A state of equilibrium may for a time exist, but every balanced organism is as it were pressing against every other, and a change in one means a rearrangement of them all. . . .

'If one species happens to vary in the direction of greater independence, the inter-related equilibrium is upset and cannot be restored until a number of competing species have either given way to the increased pressure and become extinct, or else have answered pressure with pressure and kept the first species in its place by themselves too discovering means of adding to their independence. While the balance of power lasts, variation no doubt takes place, but there is no strong necessity to guide it. Once let a large favourable variation take place in a species, however, so giving it a handicap, and then for its competitors natural selection is at once made more active—they must perish or else adjust themselves by a variation, generally in a similar direction. So it comes to pass that the continuous change which is passing through the organic world appears as a succession of phases of equilibrium, each one on a higher average plane of independence than the one before, and each inevitably calling up and giving place to one still higher. . . .'[2]

The same rhythm has been detected, in both the organic and the inorganic realm of the material world, by a South African statesman (often quoted in this Study) who is at the same time a philosopher and a student of Physical Science.

'A . . . peculiar feature about the change in equilibrium in a physico-chemical structure is that it is never such as to produce a perfect new equilibrium; the new is merely approximate, just as the old equilibrium was. We may say that the change is from too little to too much. A structure remains unchanged in spite of a small change in its inner equilibrium; hence the inner instability must pass certain limits before the readjustment in equilibrium takes place. The instance of a super-saturated solution is a case in point, where the solidification or crystallization lags behind the conditions which bring it about. When the change does come, it again proceeds too far; it swings beyond the necessities of the case; it passes the limits of perfect equilibrium on to the other side, so to say. From too little adjustment it passes to too much adjustment, and again there is a condition of instability which has to be

---

[1] Walt Whitman, quoted by Huxley, J. S., in *The Individual in the Animal Kingdom* (Cambridge 1912, University Press), p. 114.   [2] Huxley, op. cit., pp. 114–16.

righted by a swing back in due course.[1] Thence arises the rhythmic character of natural change, which links it on to the rhythm of the life-processes, and shows that they spring from the same source in the inner nature of things. Hence probably arise also the definite quantitative increments of change which the New Physics reveals. . . .

'We may represent an organism as a moving developing equilibrium, which is never perfectly adjusted because it has a persistent slight over-balance in the direction of development. Complete equilibrium is never attained and would be fatal if it were attained, as it would mean stagnation, atrophy, and death.'[2]

This philosophic and scientific intuition of the rhythm of progress is confirmed by the keen eye of the horse-breeder, which finds the same points in the build of a thoroughbred.

'The more unstable, in a forward direction, is the equilibrium of a horse's body during each step at any particular pace, the greater will be the speed that can be developed at that pace; because, the more unstable the equilibrium, the more easily can the centre of gravity be brought forward. This fact needs no mathematical investigation, for we all know that, if a person is bending forward, it is much easier to push him to the front than if he was leaning back. . . . It is evident that the chief advantage which is gained from the "crouching jockey's seat", as regards speed, is due to the fact that the forward position of the rider increases the instability of the equilibrium of the horse. . . . During continued movement, any addition to speed obtained by increased instability of equilibrium necessitates increased muscular effort in maintaining the centre of gravity of the body at a suitable height.'[3]

This homely illustration from the lore of horseflesh raises a question of general interest and of profound importance; for the horse, who is constrained by the instability of his equilibrium to repeat, and to go on repeating, an identic movement of his legs, is carried by this repetitive physical rhythm in a certain direction—'a forward direction'—which is constant.[4] Whatever the directive may be—whether it be the horse's own impulse to outstrip his competitors or the external stimulus of rein and whip and spur—its effect is to make the horse run, from start to finish, the race that is set before him.[5] Is this element of direction an essential feature in the process of growth?

In encountering this question we shall be wise to remind ourselves that the idea of 'direction' can have no literal application

[1] Compare the *loi de double frénésie* which is enunciated, as one of the characteristic phenomena of human social progress, by Monsieur Bergson in op. cit., pp. 318–22.—A. J. T.
[2] Smuts, J. C.: *Holism and Evolution*, 2nd ed. (London 1927, Macmillan), pp. 181 and 223.
[3] Hayes, Captain M. H.: *Points of the Horse*, 5th ed. (London 1930, Hurst and Blackett), pp. 53–4.
[4] For an analysis of the repetitive and the non-repetitive factors in the phenomenon of Rhythm, see IV. C (i), vol. iv, pp. 34–8, below.   [5] Hebrews xii. 1.

except in the physical world, and that we must be on our guard against going astray when we apply the same idea metaphorically in the psychic field. The movement of the Psychê is not 'directed', either by a deterministic push or by a teleological pull; and in the Promethean rhythm of challenge and response and recurrent challenge—or differentiation passing over through integration into differentiation again—the thread of continuity which the repetitive character of the process reveals requires a different metaphor to describe it.

'The essential [notion in] the idea of an *élan vital* [is] the impossibility of foreseeing the forms that Life creates—complete in every detail —by discontinuous leaps along the course of her evolution. If one takes his stand on the doctrine of pure mechanism or on that of pure teleology, on both hypotheses alike the creations of Life are pre-determined, since on the one hypothesis the future can be deduced from the present by a calculation, while on the other it is delineated in the present in the form of an idea—with the consequence, in either case, that Time is of no effect. Pure experience suggests nothing of the kind. "Neither impulsion nor attraction," it seems to say. . . .

'[The goal of human endeavours], which, at long intervals, has been the dream of the elect, realizes something of itself each time in acts of creation—each of which makes it possible, by a more or less profound transformation of Human Nature, to surmount difficulties that have been insurmountable up to that point. . . . Are these steps in progress all taken in one single direction? It goes without saying that the direction is the same as soon as we have agreed upon calling these movements steps in progress. Each movement will in fact then have to be defined as a step forward. But this is merely a metaphor; and if there were really a pre-existing direction along which Mankind had been content to advance, moral revivals would be predictable: the need of a creative effort for each of them would not be there. The truth is that one can always take the latest of them, define it by a concept, and say that the others contained a greater or lesser quantity of what the concept includes, and that consequently all of them were stations on the road to this. But things only take this form in retrospect. In reality, the changes were qualitative and not quantitative, and they therefore defied prediction. There was, however, one side on which they presented in themselves, and not merely in their conceptual transcripts, a factor common to them all. They were all of them attempts to open what was closed. . . . To push our analysis farther, we must add that these successive efforts were not exactly the progressive realization of an ideal, because no idea that had been forged in anticipation would be able to represent a sum of acquisitions each of which, in creating itself, would be creating a special idea of its own. Yet, all the same, this diversity of efforts might well sum itself up in something unique: an *élan*.'[1]

---

[1] Bergson, Henri: *Les Deux Sources de la Morale et de la Religion* (Paris 1932, Alcan), pp. 119–20 and 288–9.

The continuity here is not spatial but summative. As far as direction goes, the line of movement plotted out by the succession of responses may be exceedingly erratic; and, whatever shape this line may take, it has little or no symbolic significance, because the continuous progress that is achieved by the Promethean *élan*, as its response to one challenge exposes it to another challenge *und so weiter*, cannot be registered at all in the form of a curve. This progress has rather to be conceived in terms of control and organization, as a progressive and cumulative increase both in outward mastery over the environment and in inward self-determination or self-articulation on the part of the individual or the society that is in process of growth. A teleological formula may be adequate to express any single term in the progression; but it may become misleading when it is applied to the summation of the whole series; and in attempting to express this whole—in which the essence of growth consists—we shall find the concepts of mastery and articulation more illuminating than any others.

A teleological formulation of the transit from one integration to the next differentiation into which it overbalances is given in the following passages from a 'post-war' English *Anti-Utopia* from which several quotations have been made in this Study already.

'"Don't you wish you were free, Lenina?"

'"I don't know what you mean. I am free. Free to have the most wonderful time. Everybody's happy nowadays."

'He laughed. "Yes, *Everybody's happy nowadays*. We begin giving the children that at five. But wouldn't you like to be free to be happy in some other way, Lenina? In your own way, for example; not in everybody else's way."

'"I don't know what you mean", she repeated. . . .

'Once you began admitting explanations in terms of purpose—well, you didn't know what the result might be. It was the sort of idea that might easily de-condition the more unsettled minds among the higher castes—make them lose their faith in happiness as the Sovereign Good and take to believing, instead, that the goal was somewhere beyond, somewhere outside the present human sphere; that the purpose of life was not the maintenance of well-being, but some intensification and refining of consciousness, some enlargement of knowledge.'[1]

When 'purpose' is interpreted in this somewhat esoteric sense of an *élan* which transcends not only the individual situation and the individual act but also the individual personality or social group, then it becomes virtually identical in meaning with the concepts of progressive mastery of the environment and progressive self-determination; and this identification is explicitly made in the following

[1] Huxley, Aldous: *Brave New World* (London 1932, Chatto and Windus), pp. 106 and 209.

passage from the pen of the South African philosopher-statesman whom we have so often quoted.

'Evolution is a fact of observation and experience, and it shows a persistent trend: from Matter to Life; from Life to more Life and to higher Life; from higher Life to Mind; from Mind to more and higher Mind and to Spirit [*sic*] in its highest creative manifestations. . . . The trend of slight overbalance is towards . . . a structural character which will ever more approximate towards wholeness. . . . The nature of the Universe points to something deeper, to something beyond itself. The persistent direction on the whole shows that it is not self-sufficing. It has a trend; it has a list. It has an immanent Telos. It belongs to or is making for some greater whole. And the pull of this greater whole is enregistered in its inmost structures.'[1]

Perhaps this is as far as we can penetrate into the nature of the growths of civilizations. The process by which they grow makes the next demand upon our attention.

[1] Smuts, J. C.: *Holism and Evolution*, 2nd ed. (London 1927, Macmillan), pp. 185–7.

C. THE PROCESS OF THE GROWTHS OF CIVILIZATIONS

I. THE CRITERION OF GROWTH

(a) INCREASING COMMAND OVER THE HUMAN ENVIRONMENT

WE have seen that the growths of civilizations are in their nature progressive movements. Civilizations grow through an *élan* that carries them from challenge through response to further challenge and from differentiation through integration to differentiation again. We have also seen that this kind of progress cannot properly be described in the spatial metaphor of 'direction'. For the progress which we call growth is a cumulative progress, and its cumulative character is apparent in both its outward and its inward aspect. In the Macrocosm, growth reveals itself as a progressive and cumulative mastery over an external environment; in the Microcosm, as a progressive and cumulative inward self-determination or self-articulation. In either of these two manifestations of growth—the external or the internal—we have a possible criterion of the progress of the *élan* itself. Let us examine each manifestation in turn from this standpoint. In considering, first, the progressive conquest of the external environment, we shall find it convenient to subdivide the external environment into the physical environment, constituted by non-human Nature, and the human environment—which, for any given human society at any given moment, consists of all the other human societies with which it finds itself in contact. Let us begin our examination with the human environment, interpreted in this sense.

The progress made by any growing civilization in the conquest of its human environment may be measured, for practical purposes, in terms of geographical expansion. For, seeing that the greater part of the habitable world may be presumed to have been occupied already, in some fashion and to some degree, by primitive human societies before ever any human society entered on the path of civilization, the geographical expansion of any society in process of civilization can seldom or never have taken place except at some other society's expense.[1] On this showing, the geographical expansion of a civilization can be taken as a fair index of its progress in conquering its human environment; and this index is not only fair

---

[1] The society that is the victim of an alien society's expansion in any given case may, of course, either be still on the primitive level or else have entered on the path of civilization on its own account. The respective effects of the impact of an expanding civilization in these two different cases are dealt with in Parts VIII and IX, below.

but convenient, since expansion is a process which is easy to observe and measure. We have now to ask ourselves whether expansion is an equally good criterion of a civilization's growth—in the comprehensive sense which includes growth in wisdom as well as in stature. If we are to answer our question in the affirmative, we cannot be content with merely showing that geographical expansion is a possible and occasional concomitant of growth in its wider and deeper sense. We must demonstrate that it invariably accompanies growth and that it also invariably comes to a standstill if a civilization suffers abortion or arrest or breakdown and disintegration. More than that, we must demonstrate that the correlation of geographical expansion with growth is as definite as its correlation with the conquest of the human environment: that such expansion keeps pace, in its rapidity and its extent, with the *élan* of the growth of which it is assumed to be the criterion; and that, conversely, it not only comes to a halt when growth is arrested, but gives place to contraction when a civilization disintegrates and is finally reduced to vanishing point when disintegration ends in extinction. If we amplify our original question in these terms and seek to answer it by applying our well-tried empirical method, we find that on every count the answer proves to be in the negative.

In the matter of sheer geographical range, an empirical survey reveals the widest diversity in the actual expansion of different civilizations whose respective achievements in this field are fairly comparable, without revealing any corresponding difference in the degrees of growth attained by the several civilizations which are in question in each instance.

For example, there was an age-long competition between the Egyptiac, Sumeric, and Minoan civilizations for expansion into the no-man's-land of Syria which lay between them; and in this competition the Egyptiac Civilization was decidedly less successful than either of its rivals. At an early date in the history of this generation of civilizations, the Egyptiac culture pushed up the coast of Syria as far as Byblos at the northern end of the Lebanon. Yet although it was the first in the field, and notwithstanding its success in making its way along the forbidding Phoenician section of the coast (where the Lebanon range falls steeply into the sea, with no coastal plain between),[1] the Egyptiac culture failed to penetrate into the interior of Syria before the far more distant Sumeric Society had succeeded in annexing this part of Syria to its own domain.[2] Finally, the original field of Egyptiac expansion

---

[1] For the geographical character of Phoenicia, see II. D (ii), vol. ii, pp. 51–2, above.
[2] For the line of demarcation between the Sumeric and the Egyptiac sphere in Syria in the pre-Hyksos age, see II. D (vii), vol. ii, pp. 388–9, above.

along the Syrian coast was captured from the Egyptiac Society, after the Egyptiac cultural ascendancy here had prevailed for some two thousand years, by the Minoan Society, which, in the Völkerwanderungen of the fourteenth to twelfth centuries B.C., succeeded in establishing itself not only in Cyprus (a natural field of expansion for a maritime power from the Aegean), but even on the Syrian mainland, and this on the southernmost section of the Syrian coast on the very threshold of Egypt itself.[1] In other directions, likewise, the Egyptiac Society shows to equal disadvantage, in terms of geographical expansion, by comparison with its two neighbours. The percolation of the Egyptiac Civilization up the Nile exhibits neither the range nor the drive of the maritime expansion of the Minoan Civilization into the Mediterranean or the overland expansion of the Sumeric Civilization over South-Western Asia and out beyond into Europe and into India. Yet manifestly this marked inferiority of the Egyptiac Civilization in expansive power cannot be taken as a token of any corresponding deficiency in the *élan* of its growth; for an intuitive view of the histories of the three civilizations here in question gives the impression that the Egyptiac Civilization grew at least as fast and as far as either of the two others.

Or let us compare the expansion of the Hellenic and Syriac civilizations with that of their seniors in their own generation—the Indic and the Sinic. The two Mediterranean civilizations display the same expansive power as the older Minoan Civilization, to which they are both related. They not only expand overseas, from the Levant and the Aegean down the whole length of the Mediterranean and out through the Straits of Gibraltar into the Atlantic. They show an equal capacity to expand thereafter overland, in the opposite direction, into the interior of Asia; and here they reach and impinge upon the Indic and the Sinic worlds before ever the Indic and the Sinic societies have crossed their own thresholds in order to go out to encounter them. Just as the Minoan Civilization had once deposited its Philistine pioneers—or refugees—on the threshold of Egypt, so the two Mediterranean civilizations deposit on the thresholds of India and China their exotic styles of art and their exotic scripts.

In India, the Kharoshti script is certainly derived from the Aramaic alphabet and the Brahmi script possibly derived from the Phoenician;[2] while in the Far East the scripts employed in modern times by the Manchus and the Mongols to convey their own

---

[1] For the establishment of the Philistines in the Shephelah, see I. C (i) (*b*), vol. i, pp. 100–2, above. For the affiliation of the subsequent Syriac Civilization to the Minoan Civilization, see I. C (i) (*b*), vol. i, pp. 102–3, and II. D (vii), vol. ii, pp. 386–7, above.

[2] See Jensen, H.: *Geschichte der Schrift* (Hanover 1925, Lefaire), especially pp. 116–17, 146–7, and 199–216.

languages are likewise derived from the Syriac Alphabet and not from the Sinic characters—an extraordinary testimony to the superiority of the Syriac over the Sinic Civilization in expansive power, considering that Manchuria and Mongolia lie close up against the Great Wall, in immediate proximity to the homeland of the Sinic culture, whereas both countries are separated by the whole breadth of Asia from the Syrian birthplace of the scripts which they have actually adopted.[1]

As for styles of art, the modification of the Hellenic Style which was worked out in North-Western India, after the intrusion of Hellenism upon the Indic World, between the second century B.C. and the second century of the Christian Era, was afterwards carried, by Mahayanian Buddhist missionary enterprise, through the Oxus-Jaxartes Basin and the Tarim Basin into North-Western China, to become the germ of the Far Eastern art which has superseded the pre-Helleno-Buddhist style of the ancient Sinic Society.

Thus the expansive power of the Syriac and Hellenic civilizations has been vastly greater than that of the Indic or the Sinic. Yet, who will venture to affirm dogmatically that the Syriac and Hellenic civilizations have surpassed the other two in their general and genuine growth?

The inadequacy of the geographical criterion in the case in point is exposed by the fact that the Indic Civilization, which had waited on its own ground for Hellenism to bring a new style of art to its door, thereafter assumed the expansive role on its own account and became the carrier by which the Hellenic style was conveyed, over the last long stage of its immense journey, from the Indus to the Tarim and from the Tarim to the Yellow River. For (as has just been mentioned) Hellenic art reached the Far East as the instrument of Mahayanian Buddhist propaganda, and the Mahayana, of course, was a creation of Indic souls. This extraordinary difference in the degree of the expansive power which the Indic Civilization has put forth in this or that geographical direction has struck, and baffled, the mind of a great modern Western authority on Indic religion, who finds himself reduced to an arbitrary explanation which is really no explanation at all.

'Ideas, like empires and races, have their natural frontiers. Thus Europe may be said to be non-Muhammadan. . . . Similarly, in the

---

[1] The existence of the Mongol Alphabet may have inspired the invention of the Korean Alphabet; for the invention was made at a time (*regnante* Hsien Wang, A.D. 1419–50) when the Koreans had recently been in contact with the Mongols during the Mongol political domination which had extended over Korea and China alike. On the other hand, the forms of the new Korean alphabetic characters seem to have been borrowed from some Indic script in which the Koreans had received the original texts of the Buddhist Scriptures. (See Jensen, op. cit., p. 152; Carter, T. F.: *The Invention of Printing in China and its Spread Westward*, revised ed. (New York 1931, Columbia University Press), pp. 174–5.)

regions west of India,[1] Indian religion is sporadic and exotic. . . . But in Eastern Asia the influence of India has been notable in extent, strength, and duration.'[2]

If we glance next at the pair of civilizations 'affiliated' to the Syriac Civilization, we find no difficulty in deciding that the Iranic Civilization, which swallowed up the Arabic in the third century after the simultaneous birth of both,[3] has grown further than the sister-civilization which has been its victim. Yet, if geographical expansion be the index of growth, it can only be said that, in this instance, the index is singularly uninformative; for, in terms of expansion, the discomfited Arabic Civilization makes just as good a showing as the triumphant Iranic. The expansion achieved by the Iranic Civilization in the fourteenth and fifteenth centuries of the Christian Era is impressive enough, whether we follow its course into South-Eastern Europe or into the Deccan or on to the Eurasian Steppe; but it is no more impressive than the contemporary and subsequent expansion of the Arabic Civilization up the Nile and across the Sahara into Tropical Africa and over the Indian Ocean into Indonesia. In this instance, at any rate, the attempt to use geographical expansion as a criterion of growth is a conspicuous failure.

Or let us compare the growths of the two sister-civilizations—the Babylonic and the Hittite—which are both related to the Sumeric. On an intuitive view, the Hittite Civilization, in the course of a shorter life, would appear to have gone farther in its growth than its Babylonic sister. Yet the geographical expansion which the Hittite Civilization achieved in the sixteenth to thirteenth centuries B.C. through the militarism of the Khatti Power was not so wide as the expansion of the Babylonic Civilization in the ninth to seventh centuries B.C. through the militarism of the Assyrians.

We find the same absence of correlation between geographical expansion and genuine growth if we extend our survey from the Old World to the New. In the first generation of indigenous American civilizations, the Mayan culture appears to have shown greater expansive power than the Andean. At any rate, at the dawn of Andean history there is some shadow of archaeological evidence for Mayan influence along the stretch of South-American coastline on which the Andean Civilization then emerged,[4] while there appears to be no trace of any counterflow of Andean cultural influence from South America into Central America until the time

---

[1] 'The frontier seems to be about long. 65° E.'
[2] Eliot, Sir Charles: *Hinduism and Buddhism* (London 1921, Arnold, 3 vols.), vol. i, pp. xii–xiii.
[3] See I. C (i) (b), vol. i, pp. 69–70, with Annex I.
[4] See Means, P.A.: *Ancient Civilizations of the Andes* (New York 1931, Scribner), pp. 40–1 and 71–2.

of the interregnum between the disappearance of the Mayan Civilization and the emergence of the related Yucatec and Mexic
civilizations[1]—an epoch which, in Central America, marks the
transition from the first generation of civilizations to the second.
Yet it would be arbitrary to assert that the Mayan Civilization went
farther than the Andean in its growth. And when we come to make
a comparison between the two American civilizations of a younger
generation—the Mexic and the Yucatec—which are both 'affiliated'
to the Mayan Civilization, we find not merely an absence of correlation between expansion and growth, but an actual contrariety.
While the Yucatec culture kept within the bounds of its own Central
American peninsula, its Mexic neighbour not only occupied the
Mexican Plateau but radiated northwards into North America as
far as the Great Lakes.[2] Yet there can be little doubt that the
Yucatec Civilization had achieved a greater measure of growth than
the Mexic by the time when it suffered at Mexic hands the same
fate that, in the Old World, was to be suffered by the Arabic
Civilization at the hands of the Iranic.

In our own World in our own day we have the most imposing
spectacle of expansion of any that are on record. For the first time
in human history, so far as we know, one single human society has
now succeeded in expanding until it has come to embrace within
its system all the habitable lands and navigable seas on the face of
the planet. There could hardly be a greater difference in degree of
expansive power than the difference which has appeared in recent
times between the world-wide expansion of our own Western
Civilization and the relative immobility of the other surviving
civilizations. Every one of these other civilizations has been content to remain within its own bounds while the ever expanding
Civilization of the West has washed round its coasts, encircled its
frontiers, knocked at its gates, broken through its defences, and
forced an entrance into its inmost citadel. Yet at this very moment,
when the 'Westernization' of the non-Western civilizations is making
headway at an unprecedented rate and is being carried to unforeseen
lengths, *Homo Occidentalis* has been overtaken by a mistrust of his
own *élan* and an uncertainty about his own future which (to judge
by the precedents) are ominous symptoms.[3]

These Western misgivings in the heyday of our Western ex-

[1] For the introduction of the technique of metallurgy into Central America during the
post-Mayan interregnum—in all probability from the Andean World—see pp. 161–2,
below. In other departments of material culture besides the metallurgical, Andean
influence is discernible in the Zapotec province of the Mexic culture, in the district of
Oaxaca (see Joyce, T. A.: *Mexican Archaeology* (London 1914, Lee Warner), pp. 192 and
369–70).　　　　　[2] See II. C (ii) (a) 2, vol. i, pp. 264–5, above.
[3] For a survey and analysis of the psychological symptoms of social disintegration,
see Part V, below. For a diagnosis, from this standpoint, of the Western êthos in our own
day, see the present chapter, section (d), pp. 210–12, and Part XII, below.

pansion will not appear fantastic in the light that is thrown upon the present situation of our Western Society by the histories of the abortive and the arrested civilizations. For three out of the four abortive civilizations[1] and four out of the five arrested civilizations[2] went uncommonly far in their geographical expansion; yet in all these cases any correlation between expansion and growth is ruled out *a priori*, since the abortive civilizations ceased to grow before coming to birth and the arrested civilizations in their infancy.

Thus the empirical test plainly shows that, while the progressive and cumulative conquest of the human environment may perhaps be measured fairly in terms of geographical expansion, this geographical index is not a criterion of growth. And indeed the only social 'law', apropos of geographical expansion, which it is possible to discern appears to operate in a contrary sense; for the correlation which this law suggests is not between geographical expansion and social growth, but between geographical expansion and social retardation.

There seems to be some warrant for the formula that, as a rule, the social effect of geographical expansion in an outward direction from the geographical centre of a civilization towards the periphery is equivalent to a retardation of social progress in the Time-dimension: a retardation which, in acute cases, may pass over into an arrest and in extreme cases into an actual retrogression.

A good example of this phenomenon is the history of our modern Western 'Renaissance'.[3] In Northern and Central Italy, where this intellectual movement originally came to birth, it emerged as early as the fourteenth century of the Christian Era and attained its highest point of intensity in the fifteenth. On the other hand, in England the equivalent centuries were the sixteenth and seventeenth, in France the seventeenth and eighteenth, in Germany the eighteenth and nineteenth; so that the German *Aufklärung* of the age of Goethe corresponded in character to the phase through which the Renaissance had been passing in Italy some four centuries earlier. In fact, this modern Western Renaissance was a kind of social wave, first generated in Italy, which took an appreciable time to travel outwards from its centre of dispersion to other parts of the original homeland of the Western Civilization in Western Europe.

The operation of our law becomes more strikingly apparent when

---

[1] The Far Eastern Christian, the Far Western Christian, and the Scandinavian, by contrast with the abortive Syriac. (For a comparison between the Scandinavian and the Ottoman expansion, see II. D (vii), Annex VII, vol. ii, above.)

[2] The Polynesian, the Eskimo, the Nomadic, and the Ottoman, by contrast with the Spartan. (For the failure of the 'Osmanlis, in their expansion, to occupy just those key points which it would have been really profitable for them to occupy, see II. D (vii), Annex VII, vol. ii, above.)

[3] For renaissances in general as outcomes of the contacts between civilizations in the Time-dimension, see Part X, below.

we examine the social effects of the propagation of our Western
Civilization from its homeland in Western Europe into the new
domains which it has acquired by colonization overseas. For the
popular notion that the overseas êthos is essentially radical, if not
progressive, turns out to be illusory on a closer view. It is true that,
in the technological field, the challenge of having to wrestle, short-
handed, with an untamed Physical Nature has sometimes stimulated the Western overseas pioneers who have been exposed to this
ordeal to make remarkable mechanical inventions; and it is also
true, as we have seen in another connexion,[1] that the very process of
transmarine migration has a disintegrating effect upon the migrants'
social heritage which offers an opportunity for new social creation.
This opportunity was taken, with brilliant results, by the Scandinavian settlers in Iceland and the Hellenic settlers in Ionia; but it is
an opportunity and no more, which the overseas settler is at liberty
to take or leave as he chooses. It is equally in his power to justify
the proverb that *caelum, non animum, mutant qui trans mare currunt*.[2]
Transmarine migration is merely a possible stimulus and not an
automatic and infallible forcing-process of mental growth; and, if
this stimulus evokes no response, there is little virtue in the stimulus to mechanical invention which overseas settlement in an un-
developed country likewise administers; for the field of mechanical
invention—however great the pioneer's progress in this field may
be—lies, after all, on an extremely superficial plane of social life.
So that, in neglect of manifest opportunities and in spite of superficial appearances, the colonial êthos may prove, in any given
historical instance, to be mentally old-fashioned. And such old-
fashionedness is undoubtedly the hall-mark of our modern Western
Overseas World.

At an earlier point in this Study,[3] we had occasion to glance at
the living museum of the Egyptiac Society in the predynastic age
which is provided, down to this day, by the Dinka and the Shilluk
barbarians on the upper reaches of the White Nile. Within the
compass of a far shorter Time-span, we can observe, in modern
America and Antipodea, a number of living exhibits of Western
social conditions which are no longer extant in Europe. In our
twentieth-century Quebec and Appalachia and Charleston and
Transvaal and Peru and Macao, we have living museums of a seventeenth-century or sixteenth-century Normandy and Ulster and
England and Holland and Castile and Portugal.[4] And, even in the

[1] In II. D (iii), vol. ii, on pp. 84–100.   [2] Horace, *Epistles*, Bk. I, ep. xi, l. 27.
[3] In Part II. C (ii) (*b*) 2, vol. i, pp. 312–15.
[4] Compare the living museum of a Hellenic city-state which survived down to the
ninth century of the Christian Era at Cherson in the Crimea, at the uttermost extremity
of the colonial domain of the defunct Hellenic Society. (See II. D (vi), Annex, vol. ii,
p. 404, footnote 2, above.)

technological field, the overseas settler is not invariably an inno-
vator. As an offset to those 'Yankee Notions' which we are inclined
to regard as characteristic of the modern Western Overseas World
as a whole, we may remind ourselves that, down to the first half of
the nineteenth century, the descendants of the Spanish settlers in
New Mexico and Texas still rode forth to war equipped with lance
and shield—an equipment which, in Spain itself, was already
ludicrously obsolete by the time when Cervantes was writing *Don
Quixote*! The quaintness of these latter-day Don Quixotes of the
New World made a vivid impression upon the minds of the English-
descended American pioneers who encountered and discomfited
the Spanish-descended Texans and New Mexicans in the early
decades of the nineteenth century. Yet our transmarine Don Quixote,
if he had 'had his eyes skinned', might have turned the laugh
against Uncle Sam; for while the Spaniard of New Spain had clung
to the European military equipment of the early seventeenth century,[1] the New Englander, on his side, had preserved a vestige of
the civilian costume of the same period in the shape of the steeple-
crowned hat.[2] And Don Quixote might also have noted that the
wave of the Italian Renaissance, which had swept over Spain in the

[1] For a description of the shields which were still part of the regular equipment of the
Spanish cavalry in New Spain in the first decade of the nineteenth century, see Pike,
Z. M.: 'Observations on New Spain', in *The Expeditions of Zebulon Montgomery Pike*,
edited by Coues, E. (New York 1895, Harper, 3 vols.), vol. ii, p. 794. See further Gregg,
J.: *Commerce of the Prairies, or The Journal of a Santa Fé Trader* (New York 1844,
Langley, 2 vols.), vol. i, ch. xi, p. 221:
'A great portion of the military are obliged to use the clumsy old-fashioned *escopeta* or
firelock of the sixteenth century; while others have nothing but the bow and arrow, and
sometimes the lance, which is in fact a weapon very much in use throughout the country.'
Sclopetus is actually the word used for 'firelock' in the sixteenth-century Latinity of
Ogier Ghiselin de Busbecq.
For the old-fashioned life of New Spain in the early nineteenth century, see Pike and
Gregg, opp. citt., *passim*: e.g. Gregg's description of the riding-dress of the contemporary
New Mexican Caballero in *Commerce of the Prairies*, vol. i, pp. 211–14.
[2] This antique style of headgear re-emerged from its Transatlantic 'living museum'
on the heads of the envoys from the ex-English colonies in North America who came to
Paris during and after the American Revolutionary War. The unexpected resurrection
of the *chapeau Henri Quatre* caught the French eye and tickled the French fancy and inspired French hands to fashion the embryo of the nineteenth-century top hat! 'The top
hat (Zylinderhut) was . . . known already in the eighteenth century. It originated in
England as the Puritan and Quaker hat and migrated to America in order to find its way
back thence to Europe. It was the European enthusiasm for North America when she
was in the throes of her war of liberation that brought this headgear into fashion on the
Continent—where it had attracted no attention until then—in Liberal circles. The
sympathies . . . which this struggle evoked in the steadily growing Liberal camp were
extended to the American hat as well as to the American cause; and thus our top hat—
which was the form into which the Quaker hat had blossomed out—came to Europe as a
symbol of Liberal ideas.' (Timidior, O.: *Der Hut und Seine Geschichte* (Vienna and
Leipzig 1914, Hartleben), p. 58.) For the political significance of the top hat when it
made its appearance—or rather its reappearance—in Europe, see further op. cit., pp.
80–1, and Rosenberg, A.: *Geschichte des Kostums* (Berlin 1906, Wasmuth), vol. iii, p. 267.)
It is amusing that this revolutionary cachet should have been associated with a type of
hat which was actually more antique than the discomfited *tricorne* of the *Ancien Régime*.
It is also amusing to find that, between 1797 and 1848, the new bourgeois headgear ran
through the whole gamut of symbolism from ultra-revolutionariness to ultra-respecta-
bility. (See Timidior, op. cit., pp. 80–1.)

generation of Cervantes and over Germany in the generation of Goethe, only irrigated New England in the generation in which Texas was conquered from its Spanish-descended occupants by Sam Houston and his fellow-filibusters. Moreover, the intellectual renaissance of Houston's respectable fellow-citizens and contemporaries in New England—an Emerson and a Longfellow and a Thoreau and a Hawthorne—passed over as swiftly and as abruptly as an Indian Summer.[1]

When the landscape of the Catskill Mountains inspired Washington Irving to conceive the myth of Rip van Winkle, an overseas genius was really expressing in mythological imagery the essence of the overseas experience; and, at bottom, this experience is common to the whole Overseas World. It has overtaken the hustling New Yorker and the sharp-witted New Englander, as well as the citizen of Charleston or Cuzco, or the Appalachian mountaineer, or the Afrikander farmer, in whose outward bearing its effects are more manifestly apparent.

The phenomenon is conspicuously manifest in the field of religion. The most old-fashioned form of Protestantism that is a living faith to-day is the 'Fundamentalism' of the Mississippi Basin; the most old-fashioned living Catholicism is the Catholicism of Quebec, or the faith of Mexican Guadalajara with its militant 'Cristeros', who wage a chronic guerrilla war against the modernism of the Mexican Revolution with all the zeal that used to animate their Crusading forefathers when they fought against Islam in medieval Spain. In Russian Orthodox Christendom, again, we find 'the Old Believers' surviving on the periphery of the Russian Empire, in Siberia and the Caucasus and on the Eurasian Steppe.[2] And on the peripheries of the *ci-devant* Syriac and Indic worlds we find the most primitive extant survivals of Syriac and Indic religion. The most primitive forms of Judaism survive, as we have seen, in the peripheral fastnesses of the Caucasus and the Crimea and Abyssinia and the Yaman; and Abyssinia is also the home of a Monophysitism which is the most primitive living specimen of any form of Christianity.[3] In a similar pattern, we find the Hinayana surviving on the southern periphery of the ancient Indic World in Ceylon and Burma and Siam, and the Tantric form of the Mahayana on the northern periphery in the fastness of Tibet.[4]

Our law that geographical expansion produces social retardation may also be illustrated from the philological field. In Appalachia, forms of English speech are still alive that have become extinct in

---

[1] See Mumford, L.: *The Golden Day* (Oxford 1927, University Press).
[2] See II. D (vi), vol. ii, p. 222, above.
[3] See II. D (vi), Annex: 'Jews in Fastnesses', in vol. ii.
[4] See II. D (vi), Annex, vol. ii, p. 405, footnote 1.

the British Isles, and folk-songs are still sung that have been forgotten in their European homeland. Again, the most old-fashioned
living dialect of the Castilian language is to be found to-day, not in
the Peninsula, but among the Castilian-speaking Jews in the Near
East who are descended from Jews expelled from the Peninsula in
the fifteenth century.[1] We find the same phenomena in the Far
East. The most old-fashioned living dialects of Chinese are those
which are spoken in the provinces of the Southern Seaboard from
Kiangsu to Kwangsi inclusive; and these provinces were colonized
by Chinese settlers from the North as lately as the time of the T'ang
Dynasty.[2] Similarly, in the ancient Syriac World, we find the
Canaanite language surviving as a living language in the colonial
domain of the Syriac Society in North-West Africa at least six
centuries after it had been superseded in its Phoenician and
Palestinian homelands by the intrusive Aramaic.[3]

The evidence of Archaeology accords with that of Philology.
We have noticed already[4] how in 'pre-historic' Scandinavia, on the
periphery of the Old World, the successive techniques that had
arisen in the central regions and had gradually radiated outwards
each continued to be practised by Scandinavian craftsmen for many
centuries after they had been superseded by technical innovations
in Sumer and Egypt and Crete.[5] Similarly, we find that the Minoan
style of technique and art survived in Sicily[6] and Cyprus, at the
western and eastern extremities of the Minoan World, after it had
become extinct in the Cretan homeland of the Minoan culture;[7]

[1] For this expulsion, see II. D (vi), vol. ii, pp. 243–4, above.
[2] See I. C (i) (b), vol. i, p. 90, and II. D (iii), vol. ii, pp. 83–4, above.
[3] Aramaic began to become the lingua franca of all the Semitic-speaking peoples in
the Babylonic and Syriac worlds during the eighth and seventh centuries B.C. The process was assisted by the violent redistribution of populations under the impact of
Assyrian militarism, and it was completed by 'peaceful penetration' under the Achaemenian and Seleucid Empires (see I. C (i) (b), vol. i, pp. 80–1, above). By the second
century B.C., the Canaanite language had probably been replaced almost completely as a
spoken language in Phoenicia and Palestine by either Aramaic or Greek. On the other
hand, in North-West Africa, the old Canaanite speech of the original Phoenician
colonists continued to be spoken right down to the time of St. Augustine (decessit A.D.
430) as the vernacular of the peasantry, who then still talked of themselves as 'Canaanites';
and there are even indications that the language lingered on in this region, here and there,
until after the Arab conquest in the seventh century of the Christian Era. (See Mommsen, Th.: The History of Rome: The Provinces from Caesar to Diocletian, Part II, English
translation (London 1886, Bentley), pp. 326–9; see further Gautier, E. F.: Les Siècles
Obscurs du Maghreb (Paris 1927, Payot), Part II, ch. i: 'La Survivance de Carthage.')
As a dead language, Canaanite has, of course, survived down to this day in the Hebrew
scriptures and liturgy of the Jews; and, by an unprecedented tour de force, this dead
Hebrew has been brought to life again during the nineteenth century, in 'the Pale', as
a literary vehicle for the conveyance of modern Western ideas, and in the twentieth
century, in Palestine itself, as the mother-tongue of the Palestinian-born children in the
Zionist colonies.   [4] In II. D (vii), vol. ii, on p. 342, footnote 3, above.
[5] In this connexion, we may also notice that in modern times the conceit of writing
Latin verses, which had been initiated by the Italian Renaissance, continued to be practised in Sweden, as in England, after it had fallen out of fashion in Italy.
[6] See Glotz, G.: La Civilisation Egéenne (Paris 1923, Renaissance du Livre), p. 258.
[7] In Cyprus, a version of the Minoan script also survived down to the fifth century
B.C., in the form of a syllabary which was used for conveying the Cypriot dialect of Greek.

while the Hittite style and technique and pictographic script likewise survived in Northern Syria, at the south-eastern extremity of
the Hittite World, after their extinction in the homeland of the
Hittite culture on the Anatolian Plateau.

So much for the direct effects of geographical expansion upon
social growth. Returning now to our inquest, we may next observe
that, on an empirical test, a good case can be made out for a correlation of geographical expansion, not with social growth, but, on the
contrary, with social disintegration.

Let us take, for example, the history of the Hellenic Civilization.
We have noticed, above,[1] that, at one stage of its history, the Hellenic Society met the challenge of over-population by geographical
expansion on the grand scale; that, after some two centuries, this
expansion was brought to a halt by the successful resistance of
certain non-Hellenic forces; and that Hellenism responded to this
new challenge by changing over from the extensive to the intensive
method of economic development as a new way of dealing with the
persistent problem of over-population under the new conditions
which the stoppage of expansion had imposed. To Hellenic observers, looking back at short range upon this particular crisis of
Hellenic history, the period of readaptation, when the Hellenic
Society was transforming the *élan* of its growth from an extensive to
an intensive rhythm, had all the appearance of a time of tribulation.
As Thucydides saw it, from the age of Cyrus and Darius 'Hellas
was repressed from all sides over a long period of time, with the
consequence that, in this period, she neither performed any great
co-operative achievement nor showed any enterprise in the parochial
life of the individual city-state communities'.[2] As Herodotus saw
it, 'the three successive generations covered by the reigns of Darius
Hystaspes-son and Xerxes Darius-son and Artaxerxes Xerxes-son
saw Hellas overwhelmed by more troubles than she had had to
suffer from first to last during the twenty generations preceding
Darius's accession'.[3] The modern reader finds it difficult to realize
that, in these melancholy sentences, the two greatest of all Greek
historians are describing the age which, in the sight of posterity,
stands out in retrospect as the acme of the Hellenic Civilization:
the age in which the Hellenic genius performed those great acts of
creation, in every field of social life, which have made Hellenism
immortal. Herodotus and Thucydides felt as they did about this
creative age because it was an age in which, in contrast to the age
before it, the geographical expansion of the Hellenic World was
being held in check by the pressure of more potent external forces.

[1] See I. B (i), vol. i, pp. 24–5; II. D (ii), vol. ii, pp. 39–49; and Part III. B,
pp. 120–2, above.
[2] Thucydides, Bk. I, ch. 17.   [3] Herodotus, Bk. VI, ch. 98.

Yet there can be no question but that, during this century between the accession of Darius and the outbreak of the Peloponnesian War, the *élan* of the growth of the Hellenic Civilization was greater than it had been during the two immediately preceding centuries, when the maritime expansion of Hellenism over the Mediterranean was in flood-tide. And if a Herodotus or a Thucydides could have been endowed with superhuman longevity to enable him to observe the sequel, he would have marvelled to find that the breakdown of the Hellenic Civilization in the Peloponnesian War (a catastrophe which Thucydides lived to record) was followed by a fresh outburst of geographical expansion—the expansion of Hellenism overland, inaugurated by Alexander—which not only equalled but far surpassed the earlier maritime expansion of Hellas in material scale. During the two centuries that followed Alexander's passage of the Hellespont, Hellenism expanded in Asia at the expense of all the other civilizations—the Syriac and the Egyptiac and the Babylonic and the Indic—which it encountered on its path. And, for some two centuries after that, it continued to expand, under the Roman aegis, in the barbarian hinterlands of the Hellenic World in Europe. Yet these were centuries during which the Hellenic Civilization was palpably in process of disintegration!

Thus, in Hellenic history, we observe that the *élan* of growth was at its maximum in an age when geographical expansion was at a standstill; that this age of geographical stagnation, which was the great age of spiritual activity, was a relatively short interval which was followed, as well as preceded, by a considerably longer period in which geographical expansion was going forward vigorously; and that in the second of these two periods, when the Hellenic Civilization was already in process of disintegration, the drive of the geographical expansion was even more vigorous than it had been in the earlier period when the Hellenic Civilization had been still in process of growth. This Hellenic illustration suggests that, if expansion has any correlation with growth at all, the ratio is inverse; or, in other words, that geographical expansion is a symptom not of social growth but of social disintegration.

This inference from the Hellenic case is fortified by a similar survey of the histories of other civilizations.

An inspection of Syriac history, for example, reveals a pattern comparable to that which we have just detected in Hellenic history. The great creative period of Syriac history—the age of the Prophets of Israel—was a period in which a previous Syriac expansion from the Levant into the Western Mediterranean had been brought to a standstill and even driven into retreat by the competitive maritime expansion of the rival Hellenic Civilization in the eighth to sixth centuries B.C. Simultaneously, the Syriac Society was being harried from the opposite quarter by a violently aggressive movement on the part of the Babylonic Society in the guise of Assyrian militarism. In the latter part of the sixth century B.C., the Syriac World secured relief from these external pressures. In the maritime zone of conflict, the transmarine Syriac communities of Phoenician origin succeeded in checking the Hellenic advance by allowing one of their own number, the city-state of Carthage, to unite and organize their forces under her hegemony. In the continental zone, the Aramaeans and Israelites who had been transplanted, by the ruthless policy of Assyrian militarism, from their homes in the interior of Syria to the western rim of the Iranian Plateau, succeeded in turning the tables against their Babylonic oppressors by imparting their own Syriac culture to their Median and Persian fellow-victims,[1] with the eventual result that the Empire of the Medes and Persians, which entered into the Assyrians' heritage, came to perform the functions of a Syriac universal state. Thus, from the latter part of the sixth century B.C. onwards, the Syriac Civilization was holding its own again in the Western Mediterranean and was entering upon a new career of expansion on the Asiatic mainland. Yet this time of regained mastery over the human environment and of renewed material prosperity, as measured by geographical expansion, was not a period of spiritual growth. In the spiritual history of the Syriac Society, the interval between the sixth century B.C. and the second presents itself as a time of relative stagnation. After the turn of the political tide in the generation of Cyrus, Syriac souls were not again stimulated to fresh spiritual endeavours until the time when Hellenism renewed its attack on the Syriac World by attempting, under the leadership of Alexander and his successors, to capture its entire continental Asiatic domain and by succeeding, under the leadership of the Romans, in overthrowing the Carthaginian Power in the Western Mediterranean. These latter days, in which the Syriac World was no longer expanding territorially but was standing once again on the defensive, were the days in which the Syriac genius created the Psalms and the New Testament and the Confessions of Saint Augustine. It will be seen that, in Syriac as in Hellenic history, geographical expansion and spiritual growth appear to vary inversely to one another.

As for the Babylonic Society, it displayed singularly little expansive power at any stage of its history. After its emergence from the post-Sumeric interregnum (*circa* 1875–1575 B.C.), it never expanded at all until the rise of Assyrian militarism, which was itself a symptom of Babylonic disintegration; and this militant Assyrian

---

[1] See I. C (i) (*b*), vol. i, pp. 79–82, and II. D (v), vol. ii, pp. 137–8, above.

form of Babylonic expansion was more apt to evoke cultural antipathy than to prepare the way for cultural conquests. The exception which proves the rule is the case of Urartu (Ararat): a
barbarian principality in the highlands of Armenia which bore the
full brunt of Assyrian aggression, and at the same time adopted the
Babylonic culture, in the course of the ninth and eighth centuries
B.C.[1]—apparently on the principle of keeping an enemy at bay by
fighting him with his own weapons.

In Egyptiac history it is much the same story. The incorporation
of the Upper Nile Valley into the domain of the Egyptiac culture—
the only substantial and permanent enlargement of this domain that
was ever achieved after the close of the pre-dynastic age—was not
accomplished until after the Egyptiac Civilization had broken down
and had passed through its 'Time of Troubles' and had entered
into its universal state. Nubia was annexed to Egypt politically
under 'the Middle Empire'; but it was not until after this original
Egyptiac universal state had broken down and had then been
restored in the shape of 'the New Empire' that Nubia was assimilated culturally to the homeland of Egyptiac culture down-stream
from the First Cataract.[2] In Syria, again, it was not until the time
of 'the New Empire' that the ancient Egyptiac sphere of influence
in this quarter was extended from the coast to the interior: from
Byblos to Naharayn.

In Sumeric history, similarly, the first known intrusion of the
Sumeric culture into Syria from its homeland in Shinar was the
raid of the Sumerian militarist Lugalzaggizi, who carried his arms
from the basin of the Tigris and Euphrates to the shores of the
Mediterranean; and Lugalzaggizi's career of military conquest was
one of the outward symptoms of the breakdown of the Sumeric
Civilization.[3] The ensuing Sumeric 'Time of Troubles' saw the
expansion of the Sumeric Civilization in another direction: across
Anti-Taurus and Taurus on to the Anatolian Plateau.[4] And the
radius of Sumeric influence had never before been so wide as it
finally came to be in the time of the Sumeric universal state: the
Empire of Sumer and Akkad and its continuation in the Amorite
Empire of Hammurabi.

Again, the Minoan culture attained its widest range of radiation
in the phase which our modern Western archaeologists have
labelled 'Late Minoan III'; and this phase did not begin until after
the sack of Cnossos *circa* 1425 B.C.: that is to say, not until after the

---

[1] See II. D (v), vol. ii, p. 135, above.
[2] For the connexion between these relations of Nubia with Egypt and the role played
in Egyptiac history by the Thebaid, see II. D (v), vol. ii, pp. 114–15.
[3] For the place of Lugalzaggizi in Sumeric history, see I. C (i) (*b*), vol. i, p. 109, above.
[4] See I. C (i) (*b*), vol. i, pp. 110–11, above.

catastrophe in which the Minoan universal state—'the Thalasso-cracy of Minos'—had broken up and given place to the interregnum in which the Minoan Society went into liquidation. The hall-mark of decadence is stamped upon all the material products of Minoan culture dating from this third phase of the 'Late Minoan' period which our archaeological discoveries have brought to light. The handiwork of 'Late Minoan III' falls below that of the preceding phases of Minoan culture in standard of workmanship and in artistic power as conspicuously as it outranges all previous Minoan handiwork in its geographical distribution. In this Minoan instance, it looks almost as if a deterioration in the quality of craftsmanship was the price which had to be paid for an expansion of 'output'; and the moment at which this apparent sacrifice of quality to quantity was made seems to be coincident with the beginning of the end of the Minoan Civilization.

In Sinic history it is much the same again. During the age of growth, the domain of the Sinic Civilization does not extend beyond the Basin of the Yellow River. It is during the Sinic 'Time of Troubles'—'the Period of Contending States'—that the Sinic World incorporates into itself the Yangtse Basin on the south and the plains beyond the Pei-ho, in what is now the province of Chihli, on the opposite quarter. Ts'in She Hwangti, the founder of the Sinic universal state, carries the political frontiers of the Sinic World up to a line which is still delimited by the Great Wall; the Han Dynasty, which enters into the Ts'in Emperor's labours, pushes forward the Sinic frontiers still farther until they come to embrace the whole of the southern seaboard of China and the whole of the Tarim Basin. Thus, in Sinic history, the periods of geographical expansion and of social disintegration are contemporaneous.

So they are, likewise, in the history of the younger Far Eastern Society to which the Sinic Society is 'apparented'. In the main body of the Far Eastern World, on the Asiatic mainland, it is again the 'Time of Troubles' that is the period of expansion. The intrusion of the Eurasian Nomad barbarians, Khitan and Kin, on to the Far Eastern Society's domain in the role of conquerors—a trespass which convicted the invaded society of decadence on the political plane—provided a social channel along which the Far Eastern culture radiated out into the homelands of the barbarian invaders. The Mongol invaders, who brought the Far Eastern 'Time of Troubles' to a close by establishing a Far Eastern universal state, served the Far Eastern culture as carriers through whom it propagated itself round the western as well as the eastern coasts of the Eurasian Steppe and out beyond into the domains of remote and alien civiliza-tions. Through the instrumentality of the Mongol empire-builders

—short-lived though the Mongol Empire was—the art of the disintegrating civilization of the Far East gave an inspiration to the art of the infant civilization of Iran; and it is possible and even probable, though still non-proven, that the Far Eastern invention of printing was introduced through the same agency into Western Europe.[1] This role of the Mongols was afterwards taken over by the last of the barbarian invaders, the Manchus, who reconstituted the Far Eastern universal state which the Mongols had founded, but which the Mongol Power had been unable to maintain against the indigenous reaction led by the Ming.[2] The Manchu Empire has been the vehicle through which the Far Eastern Society—'taking its savage conquerors captive' once again—has expanded in these latter days by incorporating Manchuria: a territory approximately equal in area to the combined areas of France and Germany as delimited in the peace-settlement of 1919–20.

This correlation between expansion and disintegration is characteristic of Far Eastern history not only in the main body of the Far Eastern World on the Continent, but also in the offshoot of the Far Eastern Society in the Japanese Archipelago. In the Japanese variant of Far Eastern history, as we have already had occasion to notice at an earlier point in this Study,[3] geographical expansion and social disintegration stand to one another in a manifest relation of cause and effect. In Japan, the Far Eastern Civilization broke down and entered on its 'Time of Troubles' in the last quarter of the twelfth century of the Christian Era, when the barbarized—or re-barbarized—Japanese feudal nobility in the Kwanto asserted themselves at the expense of the unmilitary Imperial Court in Yamato: the Japanese province in which the exotic Far Eastern culture had found a second home after its first introduction into the Japanese Archipelago from Korea. This transfer of power from the cultivated men of peace to the uncouth and unruly men of war dealt the Far Eastern Civilization in Japan a blow from which it never recovered. And when we inquire who these usurping Japanese war-lords were and what was the basis of their ascendancy, we find that they were the backwoodsmen who, for several centuries past, had been extending the bounds of the Far Eastern Civilization on the Main Island of Japan at the expense of the barbarian Ainu. Through this long-continuing and ever-victorious border warfare, the backwoodsmen had developed the prowess in arms and acquired the

---

[1] On the question whether the art of printing in the Western World is a derivative from the more anciently established and certainly indigenous practice of the same art in the Far East, or whether our Western printing has been a separate and independent invention, see Carter, T. F.: *The Invention of Printing in China and its Spread Westward*, revised ed. (New York 1931, Columbia University Press).
[2] See II. D (v), vol. ii, pp. 121–5, above.
[3] See II. D (v), vol. ii, pp. 158–9, above.

wealth in land which eventually gave them their ascendancy over the Imperial Court; but, in the self-same process, the backwoodsmen had been losing their own grip over the culture which it was their mission to propagate; and accordingly, when these Japanese backwoodsmen supplanted the Japanese courtiers, who had performed the *tour de force* of conserving the exotic Far Eastern culture in an alien social climate, the political revolution brought with it a cultural set-back, since the re-barbarization of the backwoodsmen now began to react upon the entire Japanese body social. In this instance, again, quality was sacrificed to quantity. A geographical expansion was purchased at the price of a social relapse.

The offshoot of the Orthodox Christian Society in Russia had much the same history, in this respect, as the offshoot of the Far Eastern Society in Japan. In this case—as we have also noticed already in another connexion[1]—there was a transfer of power from the second home which the exotic Orthodox Christian culture had made for itself in the Upper Dniepr Basin at Kiev to the new domain which was conquered by the Russian backwoodsmen from the barbarian Finns in the Upper Volga Basin; and this shift of the social centre of gravity of Orthodox Christian Russia from the Dniepr to the Volga—from Kiev to Vladímir—was duly followed by a social breakdown for the same reasons that account for the parallel course of events in the history of Japan. Social relapse was the price of geographical expansion here again; and this expansion did not cease during the ensuing 'Time of Troubles' (*circa* A.D. 1075–1475), when the Russian city-state of Novgorod succeeded in spreading the Russian version of the Orthodox Christian culture from the Baltic to the White Sea and the Arctic Ocean. Thereafter, when the Muscovite Power brought this 'Time of Troubles' to a close by uniting all the Russian principalities under its own dominion in a Russian universal state,[2] the expansion of the Russian Orthodox Christendom proceeded at an unprecedented rate and on an unprecedented scale. It took the Muscovites less than a century to spread their dominion and their culture across the whole breadth of Northern Asia. In A.D. 1552, the eastern frontier of the Russian World still stood at a point on the River Volga west of Qāzān. By A.D. 1638, the frontier had been carried forward to the shores of the Sea of Okhotsk. In this case, again, geographical expansion was a concomitant, not of social growth, but of social decadence.

This correlation still holds good when we extend our survey from the Old World to the New. In Andean history, for example, Chile was brought within the ambit of the Andean culture for the

---

[1] See II. D (v), vol. ii, p. 154, above.
[2] A convenient conventional date for the establishment of this Russian Universal State is A.D. 1478: the year in which Muscovy absorbed Novgorod.

first time by the military conquests of the later Incas; and the Inca
Power was the Andean universal state: the penultimate stage in the
decline and fall of the Andean Civilization. In Mayan history, the
expansion of the Mayan culture on to the Mexican Plateau and into
the peninsula of Yucatan seems to have occurred at a time when
the Mayan Civilization was approaching its mysterious end.[1] In
Mexic history, the radiation of the Mexic culture over North
America as far as the Great Lakes was contemporary with the
Mexic 'Time of Troubles', when the Aztecs were warring down the
other states-members of the Mexic World and were thrusting their
way forward towards the establishment of a Mexic universal state.[2]

There remains a certain residue of doubtful or exceptional cases.
The Yucatec Civilization, for example, appears—in sharp contrast
to its sister-civilization, the Mexic—to have never expanded at all
beyond its original homeland in the Yucatan Peninsula down to the
time when its absorption into the Mexic body social cut its history
short. The Hittite Civilization, which likewise came to a sudden
violent end through the impact of an alien body, did previously
expand in one direction—from the Anatolian Plateau into Northern
Syria—and it may be questioned whether this expansion occurred
in a time of growth or in a time of decadence. The question cannot
be answered with any assurance, since the premature ending of
Hittite history makes its life-line difficult to read. Yet we may
reasonably conjecture that the collapse of the Hittite Society under
the impact of the post-Minoan Völkerwanderung, in the early years
of the twelfth century B.C., was the nemesis of the militarism in
which the Khatti Power had been indulging for some two centuries
past. In other words, we may interpret Khatti militarism as a
symptom of Hittite social disintegration; and since the propagation
of the Hittite culture in Northern Syria was a direct result of the
conquest of that region by Khatti arms, it seems to follow, on this
line of reasoning, that the correlation of geographical expansion
with social disintegration is borne out by the course of Hittite
history as far as we can make it out.

We have also to consider certain cases in which a civilization
appears to have had an outburst of geographical expansion in its
infancy without suffering any immediate arrest in its growth. Cases
in point are the maritime expansion of the Hindu Civilization into
Indonesia and Indo-China in the latter part of the first millennium
of the Christian Era; the expansion of the Arabic Civilization from
the Lower into the Upper Nile Basin in the fourteenth century of
the Christian Era; and the contemporaneous expansion of the

[1] Spinden, H. J.: *The Ancient Civilizations of Mexico and Central America* (New York 1922, American Museum of Natural History), p. 137.
[2] See I. C (i) (*b*), vol. i, p. 124, and II. D (v), vol. ii, pp. 206–8.

Iranic Civilization in three different directions: into South-Eastern Europe and on to the Eurasian Steppe and into the Deccan. On closer inspection, however, we observe that all these three civilizations belong to the 'related' class; and that their infantile expansions are explicable as a 'carry-over' from previous movements of expansion, in the same directions, in which the antecedent civilizations had been engaged in the last days of their senile decay. Thus the expansion of the Iranic Civilization into South-Eastern Europe through the agency of the 'Osmanlis continues the previous expansion of the antecedent Syriac Civilization into Anatolia which had taken place through the agency of the Saljūqs during the post-Syriac and pre-Iranic interregnum. The expansion of Islam into the Deccan similarly follows on from its previous expansion into Hindustan. And on the Eurasian Steppe Timur Lenk treads in the footprints that had been left on the sand by the Ilek Khans and the Khwārizm Shāhs.[1] In the same way, the early Arabic expansion into Tropical Africa and the early Hindu expansion into Indonesia are simply the continuations of movements which had already been under way during the interregna in which the senile Syriac and Indic civilizations had disappeared and from which their infant successors had emerged. In all the cases here in question, the movement of expansion is traceable, not to some new impulse, but merely to the vestige of an old momentum.

So far, then, our survey appears to have revealed to us only two clear cases—namely, the maritime expansions of the Syriac and the Hellenic Civilization into the Western Mediterranean in the earlier half of the last millennium B.C.—in which a geographical expansion has been the concomitant, not of social disintegration, but of social growth. We may add to these examples the overland expansion of the main body of Orthodox Christendom into the Caucasus on the one hand and into South-Eastern Europe on the other;[2] for this expansion took place before the outbreak of the great Romano-Bulgarian War of A.D. 977–1019, in which the Orthodox Christian Civilization suffered its breakdown. Finally, we may enlarge this list of clear exceptions to our apparent law of the correlation between expansion and disintegration by citing certain obvious cases from our own Western history: for example, the expansion which the Western World achieved in its infancy when it absorbed into its own body social the abortive Far Western Christian and the abortive Scandinavian Civilization on its Atlantic fringes;[3] its contemporary expansion on the European Continent from the Rhine to the Vistula at the expense of the North European barbarism, and from the Alps

---

[1] See II. D (v), vol. ii, pp. 142 and 144–8, above.
[2] See I. C (i) (b), vol. i, pp. 64–5, above.
[3] See II. D (vii), vol. ii, pp. 322–60, above.

to the Carpathians at the expense of the Hungarian advance-guard of Eurasian Nomadism;[1] and its subsequent maritime expansion into every corner of the Mediterranean Basin, from the Straits of Gibraltar to the mouths of the Nile and the Don, in the widespread though ephemeral movement of conquest and commerce for which the most convenient short title is 'the Crusades'.[2]

In these three instances in our Western history, we have clear cases of geographical expansion being neither accompanied nor followed by any arrest in the expanding civilization's growth. But we cannot cite these incidents from our own past experience without evoking in our minds a question concerning our present situation and our future prospects—a question which is of the deepest interest to us in our generation, though, just because we stand *in mediis rebus*, we are reduced to mere guesswork in seeking for the answer. The question arises out of the fact that the whole geographical expansion of our Western Society in all the earlier chapters of its history has been utterly dwarfed in scale by the modern Western tide of world-wide 'Westernization' which set in towards the close of the fifteenth century of the Christian Era and is flowing in full flood in our day. As we contemplate this titanic movement— a movement which is sweeping over all the habitable lands and navigable seas on the face of the planet and which is undoubtedly the most important social phenomenon of recent times—we find ourselves speculating whether this is a concomitant of growth, like the three earlier bouts of Western expansion which we have already cited, or a symptom of disintegration, like the majority of the examples from the histories of other civilizations which we have encountered in the course of the foregoing survey.

Our only clue to the solution of this riddle of the future, in which our own destinies are involved, is the dim and perhaps deceptive light which may be obtained by analogy from the history of some other civilization which has already run its course from start to finish, so that the whole story is known.

If we seek such light from the history of the Hellenic Civilization which is 'apparented' to ours, we perceive first that the earlier instances of expansion in our own history—those Western expansions which unquestionably occurred in an age when our civilization was still in process of growth—are the analogues of the early expansion of Hellas over the Mediterranean. Indeed, this early maritime expansion of the Hellenic Society, which was in progress from about 725 to 525 B.C. and which thus occupied approximately the fifth and sixth centuries of Hellenic history (dating from the

---

[1] See II. D (v), vol. ii, pp. 166–71, above.
[2] See I. B (iv), vol. i, p. 38, above.

emergence of the Hellenic Civilization out of the post-Minoan interregnum), corresponds chronologically as well as morphologically with the early maritime expansion of our own civilization in the same quarter which is covered by the name of the Crusades; for the 200 years between A.D. 1095 and A.D. 1291, which are the two conventional termini of the Crusading period, are approximately equivalent, in our Western horoscope, to the fifth and sixth centuries of Western history (dating from the emergence of our Western Civilization out of the interregnum which followed the dissolution of the 'apparented' Hellenic Society). Pursuing our analogy, we perceive in the next place that, between the end of the Crusades and the beginning of our modern Western expansion, there is an interval during which the tendency of our Western Society to expand is held in check by the pressure of external forces. This period of geographical constriction, which runs from about A.D. 1275 to A.D. 1475, may be taken as the analogue of the period of similar geographical constriction which runs in Hellenic history from the rise of the Carthaginian and Achaemenian Empires to the generation of Alexander the Great. We have observed already that these two centuries of Hellenic history saw the Hellenic genius come to its finest flower. We may now observe that the two analogous centuries of our Western history witnessed the Italian Renaissance.

Up to this point, then, the analogy works out effectively; and we have now to consider whether we are to carry it through to its bitter end. Are we to find a Hellenic analogy to our modern Western expansion in the latter-day dissemination of Hellenism, along furrows ploughed by Macedonian and Roman arms, as far as India in one direction and Britain in the other? This analogy, likewise, works out, if we choose to apply it, both in the matter of date and in the matter of scale; and if we do apply it, we shall be giving an answer—and a melancholy answer—to the question of the significance of our modern Western expansion in the horoscope of our Western Civilization. In Hellenic history, the denouement of the plot makes it clear that this latter-day expansion, which began with Alexander's passage of the Hellespont and closed with Agricola's conclusion of the Roman conquest of Britain, was not merely a concomitant of social disintegration but was actually a symptom of the malady. Shall we follow the argument whither it is leading us, and nerve ourselves to pass the same judgement upon the modern expansion of our Western Society which began with the triumphant voyages of da Gama and Columbus and which now seems to be carrying us, their successors, into seas that run so high that Leviathan himself can scarcely breast the waves? Or shall we refuse to believe, on the strength of mere analogy, in a prospect which cannot be confirmed by observation, and insist, since this prospect happens to be unpleasant, upon giving ourselves the benefit of the doubt?

In whichever of these alternative mental directions our personal temperaments may incline us to turn, our mental reaction to this Western case in point is likely to be highly subjective; but, for our present purpose in this Study, we can afford to leave the interpretation of our modern Western expansion in suspense; for our survey has really demonstrated already that the correlation between geographical expansion and social disintegration holds good at any rate on the whole.

How are we to account for this apparent social law? One obvious explanation is offered by the phenomenon of Militarism; for Militarism—as we shall see at a later point in this Study[1]—has been by far the commonest cause of the breakdowns of civilizations during the four or five millennia which have witnessed the score or so of breakdowns that are on record up to the present date. Militarism breaks a civilization down by causing the local states into which the society is articulated to collide with one another in destructive internecine conflicts. In this suicidal process, the entire social fabric becomes fuel to feed the devouring flame in the brazen bosom of Molech.[2] The single art of war makes progress at the expense of all the arts of peace;[3] and, before this deadly ritual has completed the destruction of its votaries, they may have become so expert in the use of their implements of slaughter that, if they happen for a moment to pause in their orgy of mutual destruction and to turn their weapons for a season against the breasts of strangers, they are apt to carry all before them.

A case in point is the latter-day expansion of Hellenism to India and to Britain between the fourth century B.C. and the first century of the Christian Era; for the roads which this expansion followed had been opened by Macedonian and by Roman arms, and those arms had been wrought up to an irresistible efficiency in the long-drawn-out internecine warfare between the Great Powers of the Hellenic World in which Athens failed to establish her hegemony and Rome succeeded in delivering 'the knock-out blow'.

Thus, in Hellenic history, Militarism was at least partly responsible for the latter-day expansion of the Hellenic World as well as for the disintegration of the Hellenic Society with which this expansion was contemporaneous. Yet this military explanation of the correlation between expansion and disintegration does not go very deep. For mere military conquest does not in itself ensure the acceptance

[1] In IV. C (iii) (c) 3 (α), vol. iv, pp. 465–504, below.
[2] Lev. xviii. 21, xx. 2; Jer. xxxii. 35.
[3] For a symbolic illustration of this, see pp. 167–8, below.

of the victors' culture by the vanquished. And although the propagation of Hellenism through the Macedonian conquests in Syriac Asia and the Roman conquests in barbarian Europe is proof that this consequence may sometimes follow, this Hellenic example appears to be an exceptional case. It more frequently happens that the vanquished make the military victors their cultural captives—as the Romans themselves were captivated by the Greeks. And if a subject people fails to win this cultural compensation for its military and political discomfiture, it is likely to acquire a positive animus against the culture of its alien masters. For example, the cultural effect of Assyrian militarism was to make the Assyrians' Aramaean and Israelite victims impervious to the influence of the Babylonic culture of which the Assyrians were representatives—notwithstanding the fact that this Babylonic culture had the advantage over the Syriac culture in both antiquity and prestige. Moreover, when the Median barbarians, who had likewise been scarified by the Assyrian harrow, had to make their choice of a civilization among the existing civilizations that came within their horizon, they found the Babylonic culture of their Assyrian oppressors less attractive than the Syriac culture of their Aramaean and Israelite fellow sufferers.[1] Thus, in this Babylonic instance, the process of military conquest, so far from promoting the spread of the conquerors' culture, was a serious handicap to it. And this Babylonic experience has perhaps been commoner than the Hellenic.

The deeper explanation of our law that the geographical expansion of a society is facilitated by its disintegration is to be found in the nature of the social process by which such expansion is brought about. For, as we have seen, geographical expansion is an index of the encroachment of one society upon the domain of another; such social encroachment is accomplished by social assimilation; and this social assimilation is the outcome of 'social radiation'. This is not the place for any detailed consideration of this phenomenon, which is examined in other parts of this Study.[2] For our present purpose, we may confine ourselves to noting the fact that in social, as in physical, radiation a ray is a composite affair which requires to be diffracted into its elements in order to penetrate a foreign body. A composite ray of white light makes its way through a prism by disintegrating into the spectrum, in which the elementary components of white light are separated out instead of remaining fused together. The social rays in which the psychic energies of societies are radiated are similarly compounded of different elements—economic, political, and cultural—and a social ray has likewise to be

---

[1] See I. C (i) (b), vol. i, pp. 79-82, and II. D (v), vol. ii, pp. 137-8, above.
[2] See Part II. A, vol. i, p. 187, above, and V. C (i) (c) 3, vol. v, pp. 196-203, as well as Parts VIII and IX, below.

diffracted into its elementary components in order to penetrate an alien body social readily.

In successful cases of social penetration it is usually the material economic apparatus of the radiating society that works its way into the alien body social first. An Afghan or an Eskimo ventures to adopt some attractive Western 'gadget' like a rifle or a sewing-machine or a gramophone because this 'gadget' appears to be de-tachable from the main structure of the Western Civilization. In being offered an alien tool or toy, the stranger is not ostensibly being asked to adopt, along with it, the alien institutions and ideas and êthos in which this alien product has originated. If the Afghan were told that he could only obtain a rifle made in Britain on con-dition that he introduced the British Constitution into Afghanistan and became a convert to the Anglican Church and emancipated his womenfolk, then even his craving for the Western weapon would probably not suffice to overcome his consternation at the prospect of having to turn his whole life upside down. He would forgo the coveted rifle and content himself with his ancestral weapons rather than cease to walk in his ancestral ways. In other words, an expan-sive civilization does not easily penetrate an alien civilization so long as its rays remain undiffracted and therefore only play upon the alien body social in their composite form—the form in which their economic and political and cultural elements are fused together. Now this is the form in which the rays of social radiation are emitted from a civilization so long as that civilization is in process of growth. For the texture of a ray is determined by the fabric of the radiating body; and it is one of the characteristics of civiliza-tions in process of growth that all the aspects and activities of their social life are co-ordinated into a single social whole, in which the economic, political, and cultural elements are kept in a nice adjust-ment with one another by an inner harmony of the growing body social. On the other hand, when a society breaks down and goes into disintegration, it is one of the symptoms of this social malady that the previous harmony between the economic, political, and cultural elements in the body social gives way to a discord; this discord in the fabric of the radiating body is reproduced, in the form of diffraction, in the rays which the body now emits; and these diffracted rays of the disintegrating civilization have greater power to penetrate the tissues of alien social bodies than the undiffracted rays which the same civilization used to emit in the time before the breakdown, when it was still in the growth stage.

This is perhaps the underlying explanation of the law, which we have inferred from empirical observation, that social disintegration

is a more favourable condition than social growth for geographical
expansion.

On this showing, we are almost warranted in regarding geographical expansion as a social disease: an elephantiasis or fatty
growth; a running to stalk or a running to seed; the malady of the
Reptiles, who turned huge on the eve of being surpassed by the
Mammals;[1] or the malady of Goliath who grew to gigantic stature
in order to succumb to David; or the malady of the ponderous
Spanish galleons which were routed by the English mosquito-fleet.
And we may compare this disease of expansion with the mania for
big buildings, which is a well-known symptom of declines and falls.
In the realm of the social insects, this is the significance of the
titanic scale and massive structure of the sky-scrapers built by the
termites,[2] which make ants' nests look careless and shapeless by
comparison. Yet

'In termites the amount of degeneration accompanying social evolution is . . . much greater than in the ants, and this degeneration seems
to have been brought about very largely by an increasing need for protection. With greater elaboration and solidity of nest architecture the
termite colonies shut themselves off more and more from the outside
world; and all the castes, except the winged males and females, lost
their eyes and the tough consistency of their integument. They thus
came to resemble the molluscs, crustaceans and certain fishes and
reptiles which have withdrawn within a heavy protective armour and
have given up participating in the free competitive and co-operative
life of their environment. The ants, with the exception of certain subterranean species, have not been inveigled into adopting this passive
and timorous mode of life.'[3]

This illustration from the history of an insect society has its
parallels in the histories of human civilizations. In Egyptiac history,
for example, the building of the Pyramids not only celebrates the
triumph of the Egyptiac Civilization, but registers its apogee and
heralds its breakdown; and at the latter end of the story, when the
breakdown has been followed by a 'Time of Troubles' and this
'Time of Troubles' by a universal state, and when 'the New Empire'
has trodden for a second time the round which 'the Middle Empire'
had trodden before, we find the same mania breaking out once
more in the colossal temples and colossal statues of the Ramsids.[4]
In Hellenic history, again, there is no excess of bulk in the incom-

---

[1] See Wells, H. G.: *The Outline of History* (London 1920, Cassell), pp. 22-4, quoted
in IV. C (iii) (c) 2 (γ), vol. iv, pp. 425-6, below.
[2] See Part III. A, p. 107, above.
[3] Wheeler, W. M.: *Social Life among the Insects* (London, no date, Constable), p. 282.
A portion of this passage has been quoted already on p. 108, above.
[4] For this Ramsid mania, see Meyer, E.: *Geschichte des Altertums*, vol. ii, part (i),
2nd ed. (Stuttgart and Berlin 1928, Cotta), p. 429.

parable works of art which a Pheidias and an Ictinus created for
Periclean Athens; and, a century after the breakdown, Alexander
can still deprecate, as a misdirection of effort and a lapse of taste,
the flattering suggestion that Mount Athos shall be carved into a
colossal bust in Alexander's own image.[1] In the decline of Hellenic
art, the craving for colossality does not become prevalent until the
Roman age. But in that penultimate age of Hellenic history the
Colosseum and the Baths of Caracalla and the Baths of Diocletian
and the Basilica of Constantine are colossal symptoms of the same
social disease which is also manifest in the colossal dimensions of
the Roman Empire itself.

Constantine, whose pile of bricks and mortar still insolently
dominates the Forum, has had to steal from the monuments of his
predecessors the little bas-reliefs which he requires for the ornamentation of his triumphal arch, because in Constantine's day the
master of the Roman World can no longer find any living sculptor
who has either the technical skill or the creative originality to carve
new bas-reliefs for him. Is the excessive bulk of the basilica the
monument to an 'inferiority complex' in the mind of the prince
who has ordered the building and decreed its scale? Does Constantine pile concrete on concrete and rubble on rubble in order to
assert his power to command material resources and to produce
material effects, even if his sculptors cannot emulate the frieze of
Trajan's Column or the bas-reliefs of Augustus's Altar, not to speak
of the metopes of the Parthenon? And if we are right in this interpretation of Constantine's work and in this analysis of his state of
mind, how are we to interpret the colossal works on which our own
Western Society is expending its energies in our day: the 'sky-
scrapers' which we pile up on land, and the 'liners' which we launch
on the ocean? By another route, we have arrived at the same
question concerning our own Western destiny which has already
confronted us in contemplating the spectacle of the colossal expansion of our own Western Civilization over the face of the Earth.

On this interpretation, a declining society is apt to hasten the
day of its dissolution by squandering its diminishing store of vital
energy in material performances on an excessive scale, not so much
out of a wanton megalomania as in a vain effort to give the lie to its
own unacknowledged but agonizing consciousness of incompetence
and failure and doom.

(b) INCREASING COMMAND OVER THE PHYSICAL ENVIRONMENT

Perhaps we may now take it as proved that the criterion of the
growth of a civilization is not to be found in the progressive and

---

[1] Plutarch, *Life of Alexander*, ch. lxxii.

cumulative conquest of the human environment, as measured on the index of geographical expansion. We have next to see whether the conquest of the physical environment will provide us with the criterion for which we are in search; and in this field the obvious index of progress is an improvement in technique. Between an improvement in technique and a progress in the conquest of the physical environment, a definite correlation may fairly be assumed to exist. Is there evidence of an equally definite correlation between an improvement in technique and a progress in social growth?

This latter correlation is taken for granted in a classification—invented by our modern Western sociologists and readily accepted by the popular Western mind—in which a supposed series of stages in the improvement of material technique is taken as indicative of a corresponding succession of chapters in 'the progress of Civilization'. In this scheme of thought, human progress is represented as a sequence of 'ages' which are distinguished by technological labels: the Palaeolithic Age, the Neolithic Age, the Chalcolithic Age, the Copper Age, the Bronze Age, and the Iron Age, with a grand culmination—or climacteric—in the Machine Age in which our latter-day *Homo Occidentalis* has been privileged to live. In spite of the wide currency which this classification enjoys in our day, it will be wise to examine it critically; for, without prejudice to the empirical test, we can point out several grounds on which it is suspect even *a priori*.

It is suspect, in the first place, by reason of its very popularity; for the hold which this classification has obtained over the popular mind is not due to any reasoned intellectual conviction of its theoretical merits. The technological classification has been accepted widely and uncritically because it has appealed to the emotions of a society which has been fascinated by its own recent technical triumphs. In inventing this scheme of thought, our sociologists have caught the popular fancy; but in their own mental process they themselves have succumbed to the subtle and insidious influence which a historian's local and temporary environment always and everywhere exerts upon the trend of his historical studies. This is a phenomenon which we have examined in general terms already;[1] and we may therefore absolve ourselves from re-examining it here *ad hoc*, and may pass on to our next point forthwith.

A second reason for regarding the technological classification of social progress as suspect *a priori* is because it is a manifest instance of another phenomenon which we have also examined above:[2] the tendency for a student to become the slave of the particular materials

[1] See Part I. A, above, vol. i. [2] See the present Study, loc. cit.

for study which have come into his hands by chance. From the scientific standpoint, it is a mere accident of no scientific significance that the material tools which Man has made for himself should have a greater capacity to survive, after they have been thrown on the scrap-heap, than Man's psychic artifects: his institutions and feelings and ideas. Actually, while this mental apparatus is in use, it plays a vastly more important part than any material apparatus can ever play in human lives; yet because of the accident that a discarded material apparatus leaves, and a discarded psychic apparatus does not leave, a tangible detritus, and because it is the métier of the archaeologist to deal with human detritus in the hope of extracting from it a knowledge of human history, the archaeological mind tends to picture *Homo Sapiens* as *Homo Faber par excellence.*

'The spoken word does not fall to the ground, like the spent missile or the broken vessel, to be its own memorial of human achievement: it vanishes in air, so that the philologist deals not with originals, but at best with the reminiscence of an echo. To recover, therefore, what men were doing, or making, still more what they were thinking or desiring, before the dawn of History, the sole available method is that of the archaeologist, merging as it does in that of the geologist: since these alone handle and interpret original creations of men's thought and will, and contemporary elements of the physical surroundings of those men. Where the tree falls, there shall it lie, and where the lost implement or shattered potsherd or worn-out man fell, there have they lain, for all that any one cared then or knows now.'[1]

In this eloquent passage we discern the archaeologist's natural bias, against which it behoves the historian to be on his guard.

A third *a priori* ground for treating the technological classification of progress as suspect is because this is a flagrant example of the fallacy of thinking of Growth, with a big 'G', as a single movement in a straight line, and of Civilization, with a big 'C', as a unitary and unique process. This, again, is a phenomenon which we have examined before in a general way;[2] and in this place we need only observe, *ad hoc*, that even if we were to accept the technological classification as valid, we should still find it quite impossible to construct a single framework within which all the relevant facts could be brought into order.

To begin with, the framework could not be made world-wide; for, in every age of which a record survives, each stage in the technological series that has ever been passed through by any human society up to that date has always continued to be represented, side

---

[1] Myres, J. L., in *The Cambridge Ancient History*, vol. i, 2nd ed. (Cambridge 1924, University Press), pp. 1–2.
[2] In Part I. C (iii) (*b*), vol. i, above.

by side with each subsequent stage so far attained, by some living society in some locality. Scandinavia, for example, may remain in the Stone Age for thousands of years after Egypt or Shinar, or even the less distant Aegean, has taken to bronze; and then, when Scandinavia has followed the example of her neighbours by discarding stone for bronze in her own good time, she may cling to bronze for centuries after her neighbours have discarded this metal for iron.[1] Even at the present day, when the expansion of our own Western Civilization and the concomitant 'Westernization' of the other living societies has gone so far as it has towards bringing about a social unification of the whole World on a Western basis, we can still find living representatives of every stage of technique, from the recent machine-age technique, which has given our modern Western Society its unprecedented material 'drive', back to the stone-age technique which is still practised by the Esquimaux and by the Australian Blackfellows.

In fact, there is not, and never has been, any such thing as *the* Machine Age or *the* Palaeolithic Age with a capital letter. For all that we know, the older techniques, from flint-chipping to iron-smelting inclusive, may each have been invented a number of times over by different societies in different times and places. At least, this remains a possible hypothesis in the absence of any historical record of their origins. Yet even if we make the assumption that each of the earlier techniques has anticipated the history of the machine-technique in being invented at some single time and place,[2] we still cannot revert to the diagram of a unitary movement in a straight line. For if the invention of each technique has been a unique event, the new knowledge cannot have spread instantaneously, by some kind of miraculous intuition, from the minds of its inventors, at one particular place, into the minds of all the rest of Mankind in all other parts of the World. An invention does not make 'a clean cut' between two epochs of World History. It rather sets in motion a wave of mimesis; and this psychic wave behaves like other waves in other media. It travels outward in different directions from its point of origin; it takes time to travel; and it takes a different length of time in different sectors, according to the size and disposition of the local obstacles which it encounters, and the degree of the local resistance which it has to overcome. The farther a wave spreads, the more it tends to lose the original regularity of its formation; and in fact we find that the successive waves of human technique have reached different parts of the World in

[1] This technological 'time-lag' in Ancient Scandinavia has been noticed in II. D (vii), vol. ii, on p. 342, footnote 3, above.
[2] For the controversy between the advocates of the Uniformity Theory and the advocates of the Diffusion Theory, see I. C (iii) (b), Annex, vol. i, above.

different orders, and that certain societies have never been reached by certain waves at all. For example, the Egyptiac Society never transcended the Bronze Age nor the Mayan Society the Stone Age from beginning to end of their respective growths; and no known society except our own Western Society has ever converted the Iron Age into the Machine Age. Yet we shall scarcely have the audacity to measure off the growths of civilizations on this index, and to place our own civilization at the top and the Mayan at the bottom of the scale on this account.[1]

And even if we were rashly to accept the assumption that improvement in technique is the criterion of progress in growth, we should still have to define what we mean by the word 'improvement' in this context. Are we to think of improvement in the utilitarian sense, in terms of the material results accomplished, or are we to think of it in the spiritual sense, in terms of the challenge and the difficulty surmounted and the energy exerted and the creative power put forth? If we think in these latter terms—and they are the only terms tolerable to the human spirit—then we shall incline to the opinion that, in the development of technique, *c'est le premier pas qui coûte.* The transmission of the human voice by telephone or wireless is not so miraculous as the origin of articulate language (without which the technique of transmitting sounds would be of no value). The application of fire to drive steam-engines or to shoot guns is not so daring as the original mastery of fire: the discovery of how to handle it with impunity and how to keep it alight and how to rekindle it when it has gone out. The invention of fire-arms, again, has been intellectually easier than the invention of the first missile weapons: The bow-and-arrow represents a greater intellectual triumph than 'Big Bertha'. On the same showing, the solid wheel of the primitive ox-cart is more wonderful than the locomotive or the motor-car, the dug-out canoe than the liner, the flint implement than the steam-hammer. And it has been a harder task to domesticate animals and plants than to dominate

---

[1] It is in its application to the Mayan Civilization and the other civilizations of the New World that the modern Western technological index of the growths of civilizations finds its *reductio ad absurdum.*

'Not only in Peru, but also in Central America and in Mexico, the Indians lived in a high state of culture during the stone age. The copper and bronze ages are not synonyms of an essentially higher civilization in America. It only means that in certain regions the Indians had achieved a considerable measure of progress. The bronze age does not mark the adoption of a new civilization but only an amplification of the copper culture in Peru, and the transition from the stone age to the copper age means nothing more than a further step in development, and not the accession of a new people with a new culture. The earliest Maya inscriptions on immovable objects date from the first centuries A.D., and at that time the wonderful calendar of the Mayas had already been perfected. Then, as very much later, the Mayas were a stone-age people. At Paracas in Peru, Tello has discovered the remains of a civilization in which especially the art of weaving was on a marvellously high level, although no other metal than gold was known.' (Nordenskiöld, E.: *Origin of the Indian Civilizations in South America* (Göteborg 1931, Elander), p. 40.)

Inanimate Nature—to harness the horse than to harness the tide. Inanimate Nature obeys regular laws which Man has merely to work out in order to apply them mechanically for his own practical purposes. It is infinitely harder to cope with the waywardness and complexity of Life; and the peasant and the Nomad, who have discovered the art of governing the Vegetable and the Animal Kingdoms, may smile sardonically at the boastful industrialist who glories in his facile conquest of the material universe and has not paused to remind himself that 'the proper study of Mankind is Man'.[1]

'Though I have the gift of prophecy, and understand all mysteries and all knowledge; and though I have all faith, so that I could remove mountains, and have not charity, I am nothing.'[2]

The industrialist has concentrated all his effort and attention upon the relations of Man with Physical Nature to the neglect of the relations between Man and Man; and he has thus heightened the effect—for good or for evil—of every human action by putting at its disposal a terrific driving-power, without having taken thought to improve the wisdom or the virtue of the human beings whom he has been endowing so recklessly with these improved technical facilities. In the light of the event, we can see at this eleventh hour that Daedalus would have done better to follow the lead of Cain and Abel by seeking to crown their conquests of the Vegetable and Animal kingdoms with the conquest of the highest kingdom in the world of Life: the Kingdom of Man. And, in this realm of human relations, charity is of more account than clock-work.

These a priori objections to the technological diagram of human progress are almost sufficient in themselves to rule out the idea of taking an improvement in technique as the criterion of social growth. If we now apply our well-tried empirical test, we shall find that it will give this popular hypothetical correlation its coup de grâce. A survey of some of the relevant facts will show us cases of technique improving while civilizations remain static or go into decline,[3] as well as examples of the converse situation, in which technique remains static while civilizations are in movement— either forward or backward as the case may be.

For instance, a high technique has been developed by every one of the arrested civilizations. The Polynesians have excelled as navigators, the Esquimaux as fishermen, the Spartans as soldiers, the Nomads as tamers of horses, the 'Osmanlis as tamers of men.

---

[1] Pope: *Essay on Man*, Epistle ii, l. 2.
[2] 1 Corinthians xiii. 2.
[3] This point is noticed by Turgot in his *Second Discours sur les Progrès Successifs de l'Esprit Humain* (*Œuvres de Turgot*, Nouvelle Édition (Paris 1844, Guillaumin, 2 vols.), vol. ii, p. 608).

These are all instances in which civilizations have remained static while technique has improved.

An example of technique improving while a civilization declines is afforded by the contrast between the Upper Palaeolithic Age in Europe and the Lower Neolithic, which is its immediate successor in the technological series. The Upper Palaeolithic Society remained content with implements of rough workmanship, but it developed a fine aesthetic sense, and it did not neglect to discover certain simple means of giving its sense a pictorial expression. The deft and vivid charcoal sketches of animals, which survive on the walls of Palaeolithic Man's cave-dwellings, where they have been discovered by our modern archaeologists, excite our astonishment and admiration. The Lower Neolithic Society took infinite pains to equip itself with finely ground tools, and possibly turned these tools to account by using them as weapons in a struggle for existence with Palaeolithic Man in which *Homo Pictor* went down and left *Homo Faber* master of the field. In any case, the Palaeolithic Society vanished away and the Neolithic Society reigned in its stead; and this change, which inaugurates a striking improvement in terms of technique, is distinctly a set-back in terms of civilization. For the art of Upper Palaeolithic Man died out with him; and if Lower Neolithic Man had any glimmering of aesthetic sense at all, at any rate he has given no material expression to it.[1]

Another example of an improvement in technique being coincident with a set-back in civilization is to be found in the interregnum in which the Minoan Civilization went into dissolution. The Minoan Society had remained in the Bronze Age from beginning to end of its history. The latest and most barbarous swarm of Continental European barbarians who descended upon the derelict domain of the Minoan Society in the post-Minoan Völkerwanderung came armed with weapons of iron instead of bronze; and in their victorious onslaught upon the epigoni of the Minoan Civilization they doubtless profited from their acquaintance with the more potent metal. Yet this victory of the iron-sworded 'Dorians' over the bronze-sworded Minoans was a victory of Barbarism over Civilization. For an iron sword—or, for that matter, a steel tank or submarine or bombing-plane or any other killing-machine of our latter-day Machine Age—may be a talisman of victory without being a talisman of culture. When the 'Dorians' adopted weapons of iron instead of weapons of bronze, they did not cease to be barbarians. And there is no reason for crediting these barbarians even

---

[1] There is a suggestive passage on the cultural contrast between Lower Neolithic Man and Upper Palaeolithic Man in Wells, H. G.: *The Outline of History* (London 1920, Cassell), pp. 64–7.

with the technical achievement of discovering a new and better material for metallurgy. The 'Dorian' iron was probably no 'Dorian' original discovery, but simply a 'Dorian' loan which a geographical accident had put these barbarians in the way of making by mimesis from the skilled artificers of a neighbouring region.[1] In this encounter between the 'Dorians' and the Minoans, the technological criterion of progress in civilization is confuted by a *reductio ad absurdum*; for by the technological criterion we are constrained to declare that the nadir of the post-Minoan interregnum witnessed an advance in the culture of the Aegean area; that this advance was more significant than any which had been achieved in the whole history of the Minoan Civilization; and that the advance was brought about by the invading bands of iron-sworded 'Dorians' at the moment when they were using their iron weapons to deal the bronze-sworded Minoan culture its death-blow.

This example from the history of the Old World has a parallel in the history of the New World which is remarkably exact.

'The establishment of Mayan and Toltec chronology fixes, within relatively narrow limits, the beginning of the metal age in Central America and Mexico. No specimen of metal, not even a copper stain, was observed during excavations at Copan, Quirigua and other Mayan cities of the First Empire. Las Quebradas in Guatemala was actually built upon a placer mine; yet, in the sluicing operations which have almost destroyed the site, no specimen of worked gold has been found. Nor are any ornaments of metal, such as gorgets and bells, pictured on the early monuments. We therefore conclude that the metal age did not begin till after 600 A.D.; yet by 1200 A.D. metal-work was highly developed in gold, silver, copper and various alloys. Many specimens found at Chichen Itza in Northern Yucatan are of Costa Rican and Colombian origin, and the technique of metal-working is the same from

[1] According to the Hellenic tradition, the inventors of iron-working were the Chalybes: a people whose habitat in the fifth century B.C., when this tradition was current, was the Black Sea coast of Anatolia in the neighbourhood of Trebizond. If the technique of iron-working really came to the Aegean from this quarter, it might have reached the 'Dorians', via the Black Sea and the Danube, before it reached the Minoans at Cnossos or Mycenae; for the 'Dorians', on the eve of the post-Minoan Völkerwanderung, were presumably living somewhere in the Continental European hinterland of the Aegean area. The Chalybes of the Hellenic tradition, like the Tubal-Cain of the Syriac tradition who was 'an instructer of every artificer in brass and iron' (Gen. iv. 22), may be presumed to represent the Hittite culture. (The Tubal and Meshech of Gen. x. 2 stand for the Tibareni and Moschi: two swarms of barbarians from the Caucasian hinterland of the Hittite World who drifted into the former Hittite domain in Eastern Anatolia after the overthrow of the Khatti Power in the twelfth century B.C.) The historical Chalybes, as the Greeks found them when the Hellenic Society expanded into the Black Sea from the seventh century B.C. onwards, were apparently in a low state of culture. We may account for this by supposing that they were a primitive people who had simply served to transmit the art of iron-working from its Hittite homeland in East-Central Anatolia to the Balkan Peninsula via the Black Sea. Or else we may suppose that the historical Chalybes were a remnant of the Hittite Society which had been saved, by its sheltered situation, from being involved in a catastrophe which had overwhelmed the rest of the Hittite World at the beginning of the twelfth century B.C. In that case, the Chalybes must have relapsed into barbarism—in everything except their metallurgical technique—in consequence of their isolation.

Southern Colombia to Central Mexico. The art was apparently introduced from South America about A.D. 1000 and underwent a rapid
growth in the five hundred years before the Spanish conquest.'[1]

It will be seen that this illustration of our thesis from Central
America and the preceding illustration from the Aegean throw some
light upon one another. Just as in the Old World the Minoan
Society performed its achievements and lived out its life without
ever transcending the Bronze Age, so in the New World the Mayan
Society rose and fell without ever passing out of the Stone Age into
an age of metal. In Central America, the introduction of the metallurgical technique was reserved for two civilizations, both related
to the Mayan, which can neither of them compare with the antecedent civilization in respect of the general level of their cultural
attainments. And, here again, the technological advance was syn-
chronous with a cultural interregnum.

If it be a *reductio ad absurdum* of the technological criterion to
claim that the second-rate civilizations which were affiliated to the
Mayan Civilization or the barbarian invaders of the Aegean World
in the post-Minoan and pre-Hellenic interregnum were apostles of
civilization in virtue of their prowess in technique, it is amusing to
find an equally extravagant claim being submitted in all solemnity
by the last of the great Hellenic historians on behalf of the post-
Hellenic interregnum on a similar technological ground.

Procopius of Caesarea wrote a history of the wars of the Roman
Emperor Justinian (*imperabat* A.D. 527–65); and these wars were
actually the death of the ancient Hellenic Society. In obstinately
striving to realize his misguided ambition of restoring the territorial integrity of the Empire, Justinian brought financial ruin upon
the Oriental provinces, depopulation upon the Balkan provinces,
and devastation upon Italy; and even at that price he failed to
achieve his 'single-track' aim; for in extirpating the Vandals in
Africa he was clearing the way for the Moors to take their place,
and in extirpating the Ostrogoths in Italy he was creating a vacuum
which was to be filled, within three years of his own death, by the
far more barbarous Lombards. The century which followed the
wars of Justinian was actually the nadir of the post-Hellenic interregnum. This was the tragedy of the generation of Procopius, as
posterity can see it in retrospect; and indeed it was painfully apparent at the time, and was widely recognized by Procopius's own
contemporaries, that—however far or near the end of Hellenism
might be—Hellenic history had long passed its zenith. Yet in
writing the preface to his narrative of the fatal events which had

¹ *The Encyclopaedia Britannica*: Supplementary Volumes constituting the Thirteenth
Edition (London and New York 1926), vol. i, p. 195, s.v. 'Archaeology'.

just dealt Hellenism its death-blow before he took up his pen, the eminent historian goes out of his way to break a lance in a battle of his own seeking between the Moderns and the Ancients; and he awards the palm to the Moderns on the score of their technical superiority in the art of war.

'To an unprejudiced mind it will be evident that the events of these wars are at least as striking and imposing as any in history. They have been responsible for occurrences of a more extraordinary character than any of which a record survives, except (possibly) from the point of view of a reader who insists upon giving the palm to Antiquity and refuses to be impressed by anything in the contemporary world. The first example that occurs to my mind is the affectation of alluding to modern troops as "archers" and reserving such appellations as "hand-to-hand combatants" or "men-at-arms" for the warriors of Antiquity, in the confident assumption that in our day these military qualities are extinct. Such assumptions merely betray a superficiality and an utter lack of experience in those who make them. It has never crossed their minds that the archers in Homer, whose arm is cast up against them as an opprobrious epithet, had no horse-flesh between their knees, no lance in hand, and no shield or body-armour to cover them. They went into action on foot and were compelled to take cover, either by posting themselves behind the shield of a comrade or by "leaning against a tombstone"—a position which precluded them equally from extricating themselves in defeat and from pursuing a retreating enemy, and, above all, from fighting in the open. Hence their reputation for playing an underhand part in the game of war; while, apart from that, they took so little pains with their technique that, in shooting, they only drew the bow-string to the breast, with the natural result that the missile was spent and ineffective by the time when it reached its target. This was undoubtedly the level at which archery stood in earlier times. By contrast, modern archers go into action equipped with cuirasses and knee-boots and with their quiver on their right side and their sword on the other, while some troopers have a lance slung over their shoulders and a small handleless shield of just sufficient diameter to cover the face and neck. Being admirable horsemen, they are trained to bend their bow without effort to either flank when going at full gallop, and to hit a pursuing enemy in their rear as well as a retreating enemy to their front. They draw the bow-string to the face, to the level (approximately) of the right ear, which imparts such force to the missile that its impact is invariably fatal and that neither shield nor cuirass can resist its momentum. Some people, however, who choose to ignore the existence of these troops, persist in an open-mouthed adulation of Antiquity and refuse to admit the superiority of modern inventions. Misconceptions of this kind are, of course, powerless to rob the late wars of their superlative interest and importance.'[1]

Procopius's argument is an extravaganza which refutes itself; and the only comment that it seems necessary to make is that the

[1] Procopius of Caesarea: *A History of the Wars of Justinian*, Bk. I, ch. 1.

cataphract, whom Procopius presents to his readers as the *chef d'œuvre* of Greek and Roman military technique—the most efficient type of fighting-man that had ever been thrown up in the Hellenic World during the long span of time between the Homeric Age and the author's own day—was actually no more an original creation of the Greek or the Roman military genius than iron was a discovery of the 'Dorians'. This horse-archer—armed cap-à-pie and formidable by reason of his personal prowess in riding and shooting—was utterly alien from the genuine Greek and Roman military tradition, which had relegated its cavalry to a subordinate role and had put its trust in an infantry whose strength lay in the corporate cohesion and discipline of the regiment far more than in the equipment or *expertise* of the individual soldier. In the Roman Army, the cataphract was a recent innovation—an arm which had not been adopted more than a couple of centuries before Procopius's own day—and if this arm had come to be the mainstay of Roman military power within that relatively short period of time, this revolution in military technique bears witness to the historic Roman infantry's rapid and lamentable decay. In fact, in the Roman Army of Procopius's day the cataphract filled a vacuum which had been of the cataphract's own making; for the previously invincible Roman infantryman had first met his match, and finally acknowledged his superior, in the cataphract whom he encountered on the Mesopotamian plains in the armies of the Arsacidae and the Sasanidae, and on the Danubian plains in the war-bands of the Sarmatians and the Goths. The military lessons of a long trial of strength between the legionary and the cataphract, which had begun with Crassus's disaster at Carrhae in 53 B.C. and had culminated in Valens' disaster at Adrianople in A.D. 378, had ultimately led the Roman authorities to discard the historic Roman infantryman—through whose sword and trenching-tool Dea Roma had originally won her Empire—and to adopt the exotic but triumphant Oriental cataphract in the legionary's stead.

In his eulogy of the cataphract,[1] Procopius is thus really doing just the opposite of what he supposes and intends. Instead of celebrating an improvement of the Greek and Roman military tech-

---

[1] In the detailed description of the cataphract's equipment which this eulogy contains in the passage quoted above, Procopius has forgotten to mention one detail which would have been germane to his purpose and which is actually mentioned in a handbook of military technique which dates from the next generation: the *Strategikon* of the Emperor Maurice (*imperabat* A.D. 582–602). From Maurice's *Strategikon* we learn that the cataphract was equipped with 'stirrups: an invention which had cropped up since the fifth century without our being able to say from whom it had its origin'. (Oman, Sir Charles: *A History of the Art of War in the Middle Ages from the Fourth to the Fourteenth Century* (London 1898, Methuen), p. 185.) The first reference to stirrups in Chinese literature is said to date from A.D. 477 (Münsterberg, O.: *Chinesische Kunstgeschichte*, vol. i (Esslingen 1910 Neff), p. 162).

nique, he is pronouncing its funeral oration. Yet, although Procopius has chosen an unfortunate illustration of the point that he is seeking to make, his general contention that there has been a progressive improvement in Hellenic technique remains broadly true within the field of military technique to which he confines his argument. In surveying this field of Greek and Roman social history, let us rule out of account the spurious epilogue represented by the cataphract and confine our survey to the thousand years which began with the invention[1] of the Spartan phalanx in the second Messeno-Spartan War in the latter part of the seventh century B.C.[2] and which ended with the final discomfiture and discrediting of the Roman legion at the Battle of Adrianople in A.D. 378. The development of the genuinely Hellenic military technique can be traced, without any break in continuity, throughout these thousand years; and in tracing it we shall find that an arrest or a set-back in the Hellenic Civilization invariably accompanied an improvement in the Hellenic art of war.

To begin with, as we have seen already, the invention of the Spartan phalanx, which is the first signal improvement of which we have a record, was an outcome of the same events that brought the growth of the Spartan version of the Hellenic Civilization to a premature halt.[3]

The next signal improvement was the differentiation of the Hellenic infantryman into two extreme types: the Macedonian phalangite and the Athenian peltast. The Macedonian phalanx, armed with long two-handed pikes in place of short one-handed stabbing-spears, was more formidable in its impact than its Spartan precursor; but it was also more unwieldy in its manœuvres and more at the enemy's mercy if once it lost its formation; and therefore it could not safely go into action unless its flanks were guarded by peltasts: a new type of light infantry who were taken out of the

---

[1] 'Adoption', rather than 'invention', is perhaps the right word in this case, since the phalanx formation and tactics, as we have seen above (in I. C (iii) (b), Annex, vol. i, p. 428, footnote 2), appear to have originated in the Sumeric World and to have spread thence to the Hellenic World. In the *Iliad*, the phalanx-technique makes its appearance side by side with older and cruder kinds of armament and tactics. In *Iliad* xiii, ll. 126–35 (cp. l. 680), there is a detailed description of phalanx-fighting; and in *Iliad* xvi, ll. 211–17 (cp. l. 248), the Myrmidons go into battle in phalanx-order. On the other hand, in *Iliad* xiii, ll. 712–18, the Locrians are described as bowmen who are destitute of the phalangite's panoply. This panoply—the metal helmet and corselet, and the comparatively small round metal shield—appears to have been introduced into the Aegean from Assyria in the fourteenth century B.C. This material equipment, and the formation and tactics that it rendered possible, were technically as much superior to the indigenous Minoan equipment and tactics as the cataphract, in his turn, was superior to the hoplite. It is noteworthy that each of these great technical advances in the art of war was introduced during a cultural interregnum: the hoplite during the post-Minoan interregnum and the cataphract during the post-Hellenic interregnum. (See Glotz, G.: *La Civilisation Égéenne* (Paris 1923, Renaissance de Livre), pp. 100–1 and 103.)

[2] For the general social effects of this war in arresting the growth of the Spartan Society, see the present Part, Section A, pp. 53–68, above.

[3] See the preceding footnote.

ranks and trained to fight as skirmishers. In collaboration, the
Macedonian phalangite and the Athenian peltast were a far more
effective type of infantry than the old undifferentiated phalangite
on the Spartan model;[1] and this second improvement in the Hellenic military technique was the outcome of a century of internecine
warfare in the Hellenic World—the century running from the outbreak of the Atheno-Peloponnesian War in 431 B.C. to the Macedonian victory at Chaeronea in 338—which saw the Hellenic
Civilization break down and go into disintegration.

The next signal improvement in the Hellenic military technique
was made by the Romans, when they succeeded in combining the
advantages and avoiding the defects of both peltast and phalangite
in the tactics and equipment of the legionary. The legionary was
armed with a couple of throwing-spears and a stabbing-sword, and
the legion went into action in open order in two waves, with a third
wave—armed and ordered in the old-fashioned phalanx-style—in
reserve. This third improvement in the Hellenic military technique
was the outcome of a fresh bout of internecine warfare—beginning
with the outbreak of the Hannibalic War in 218 B.C. and closing
with the end of the Third Romano-Macedonian War in 168—in
which the Romans delivered a 'knock-out blow' to every other Great
Power in the Hellenic World of that age.

The fourth and last improvement was the perfection of the legion:
a process, begun by Marius and completed by Caesar, which was
the outcome of a century of Roman revolutions and civil wars.[2]
The Roman legionary was probably at his best in the army which
fought for Caesar at Pharsalus in 48 B.C.—five years after the
legions which had fought for Crassus at Carrhae in 53 B.C. had
met their match in the Parthian cataphracts. Thus the generation
of Caesar and Crassus saw the Greek and Roman military technique
both attain and pass its zenith. And the same generation saw the
Hellenic Civilization enter upon the penultimate stage in its decline
and fall. For that century of Roman revolutions and civil wars
which had begun in 133 B.C. with the tribunate of Tiberius

---

[1] The inability of the old-fashioned Spartan hoplite phalanx to cope with enemy
peltasts unaided was demonstrated in the action fought at Lechaeum in 390 B.C., when
the Athenian commander Iphicrates, with his peltasts, cut up a *mora* (division) of
Lacedaemonian infantry which was on the march unescorted by friendly cavalry. (See
Xenophon: *Hellenica*, Bk. IV, ch. v, 11–17.)

[2] In terms of our modern Western military history, the homogeneous but versatile
Roman infantry of the last century B.C. may be compared with our nineteenth-century
infantry, with its uniform equipment of rifle and bayonet. The slightly differentiated
Roman infantry of the second century B.C. may be compared with our eighteenth-
century infantry, in which the light company and the grenadier company of a battalion
were armed and trained somewhat differently from the ordinary troops of the line. The
sharply differentiated Macedonian infantry of the third century B.C. may be compared
with our seventeenth-century infantry, which was likewise sharply differentiated into
pikemen and musketeers and targeteers.

Gracchus had been the climax of the Hellenic 'Time of Troubles'; and it was Caesar's mission to bring that 'Time of Troubles' to a close by inaugurating the universal state which Augustus eventually established after the Battle of Actium.

In this history of the successive improvements in the Hellenic art of war, we have a clear case in which it is not the growth of a civilization, but its arrest and breakdown and disintegration, that goes hand in hand with the improvements in its military technique; and the histories of the Babylonic and Sinic civilizations offer us equally good illustrations of the same phenomenon. Both in the Babylonic 'Time of Troubles', when the Babylonic Society was tearing itself to pieces in the frenzy of Assyrian militarism, and likewise in the Sinic 'Time of Troubles', when the military Power of Ts'in was delivering knock-out blows to the other contending states of the Sinic World, conspicuous improvements in military technique were accomplished. In both cases, for example, the old-fashioned use of the war-horse as a draught-animal to draw a chariot was discarded in favour of its more effective use as a mount for a cavalryman.[1] Perhaps we may infer from the foregoing survey that an improvement in military technique is usually, if not invariably, the symptom of a decline in civilization.

An Englishman of the generation that has lived through the General War of 1914–18 may remind himself, in this connexion, of an incident which struck him, at the time, as painfully symbolic. As the War, in its ever-increasing intensity, made wider and wider demands upon the lives of the belligerent nations—like some great river that has burst its bounds in flood and is engulfing field after field and sweeping away village after village—a moment came in England when the offices of the Board of Education in Whitehall were commandeered for the use of a new department of the War Office which had been improvised in order to make an intensive study of trench warfare. The ejected Board of Education found asylum in the Victoria and Albert Museum, where it survived on sufferance as though it had been some curious relic of a vanished past. And thus, for several years before the Armistice of the 11th November, 1918, an education for slaughter was being promoted,

---

[1] In Sinic military history, the substitution of cavalry for chariots is known not to have been an original invention of the Sinic Society, but to have been borrowed by the Sinic World from the Nomads of Eurasia, with whom the Sinic World, in the course of its expansion, had come into contact about the fourth century B.C. The innovation is attributed to Wu-ling (*regnabat* 329–299 B.C.), the prince of the north-eastern frontier-state of Chao. (See Hirth, F.: *The Ancient History of China* (reprint: New York 1923, Columbia University Press), pp. 272–3; and Maspéro, H.: *La Chine Antique* (Paris 1927, Boccard), p. 385.) May we conjecture, on this analogy, that the introduction of the cavalry arm into the Assyrian Army at about the turn of the eighth and seventh centuries B.C. was likewise an outcome of contact with the Eurasian Nomads? This was just the time when the Cimmerian and Scythian Nomads were breaking out of the south-western corner of the Eurasian Steppe and over running Asia Minor.

in the heart of our Western World, within the walls of a public building which had been erected in order to assist in promoting an education for life. As the writer of this Study was walking down Whitehall one day in the spring of that year 1918, he found himself repeating a passage from the Gospel according to Saint Matthew:

'When ye therefore shall see the abomination of desolation, spoken of by Daniel the Prophet, stand in the holy place, (whoso readeth, let him understand), . . . then shall be great tribulation, such as was not since the beginning of the World to this time. . . . And, except those days should be shortened, there should no flesh be saved. . . .'[1]

No reader can fail to understand that when the Ministry of Education of a great Western country is given over to the study of the art of war, the improvement in our Western military technique which is purchased at such a price is synonymous with the destruction of our Western Civilization.

Nor is the art of war the only kind of technique that is apt to make its progress in inverse ratio to the general progress of the body social. War is so manifestly an anti-social activity that an antinomy between military progress and social progress is not surprising. And we shall notice in retrospect that, in all the examples of the correlation between technical improvement and social arrest or set-back which we have passed in review up to this point, the technique that has achieved improvement at Society's expense has been more or less military in each instance. Let us now take the case of a technique which stands at the furthest remove from the art of war: the technique of agriculture, which is generally regarded as *par excellence* the sovereign art of peace. If we revert to the history of the Hellenic Civilization, and trace out the course of the successive improvements in the Hellenic technique of agriculture against the general background of Hellenic history, we shall find here another instance in which an improvement in a technique has been the accompaniment of a decline in a civilization.

At the outset, perhaps, we seem to be entering here upon a different story. Whereas the first historic improvement in the Hellenic art of war was purchased at the price of an arrest in the growth of the particular Hellenic community by which this improvement had been invented, the first comparable improvement in Hellenic agriculture had a happier sequel. In the domain of agricultural technique, the first Hellenic innovators were not the Spartans but the Athenians; and when Attica, on Solon's initiative, led the way in Hellas from a régime of mixed farming for subsistence

---

[1] Matt. xxiv. 15 and 21-2.

to a régime of specialized agricultural production for export,[1] this
technical advance, so far from being followed by an arrest or decline
of civilization in the locality where the advance had been made,
was actually followed by an outburst of energy and growth in every
sphere of Attic life—an outburst which had so powerful an *élan*
that its influence was not confined to Attic soil but went coursing,
in a great current of new vitality, through the veins of the whole
Hellenic body social.

In the next chapter, however, the story of the successive improvements in the Hellenic agricultural technique takes a different,
and this time a sinister, turn. The next stage of technical advance
was an increase of scale in the operations of the new specialized
agriculture through the organization of mass-production. This
step appears to have been taken in the colonial Hellenic communities which had been planted overseas in Sicily; for the Sicilian
Greeks found an expanding market for their wine and oil among
the barbarians of the Western Mediterranean who had acquired a
taste for the fruits of the vine and the olive without having yet
learnt to plant vineyards and oliveyards for themselves. Our first
glimpse of the newfangled Attic agriculture on the new colonial
scale is in the territory of the Sicilian Greek city-state of Agrigen-
tum towards the close of the first quarter of the fifth century B.C.;
and the description which we have of it from the pen of a later
Sicilian Greek historian shows that this second advance in Hellenic
agricultural technique was vitiated socially from the start by being
bound up with the employment of slave-labour.

'After the victory [of the allied Greek city-states of Sicily over the
Carthaginians at the Battle of Himera in 480 B.C.], Gelo . . . divided the
bulk of the spoils,[2] including the prisoners of war, among the Greek
allies in proportion to the strengths of the forces which they had respectively put into the field. The Governments put the prisoners allotted to
them into fetters, and employed them on public works. The Agrigentines received the largest number, and were able to improve their countryside as well as their city. The number of captives in their hands was
so great that many private people there possessed as many as 500—the
number being due not only to the large size of the force which they had
sent on the campaign but also to the accident that, when the Carthaginian rout began, many of the fugitives retreated inland, and this mostly
into Agrigentine territory. These stragglers were all caught by the
Agrigentines, so that the city was positively packed with captives. Most
of them were nationalized, and these were put to quarrying stone for
public works [which the author goes on to enumerate and describe]. . . .

---

[1] For the causes of this Attic agrarian revolution of the sixth century B.C., see Part
II. D (ii), vol. ii, pp. 37–42, above.
[2] After disposing of some of them as rewards for distinguished valour, and reserving
others for dedication in the temples of Himera and Syracuse. A. J. T.

Besides this, they planted the whole of their territory, which had a good soil, with vineyards and with orchards of all kinds of fruit trees, which brought them in a great income from the land.'[1]

The great technical advance which was achieved in this agrarian revolution was offset by at least as great a social lapse; for the new plantation-slavery, with which the new plantation-agriculture was bound up, was a far more serious social evil than the old domestic slavery which was the only form of the institution that had existed in Hellas before. The plantation-slavery was worse, both morally and statistically. It was impersonal and inhuman, and it was on the grand scale.

This system of agricultural mass-production by slave-labour for a barbarian market spread from the Greek communities in Sicily to adjoining regions in the Western Mediterranean Basin which came within the ambit of the Hellenic Civilization: first to the Carthaginian dominions in North-West Africa and then, on a larger scale, to the great area in Southern Italy which was left derelict and devastated by the Hannibalic War.[2] Wherever this slave-plantation system of agriculture established itself, it notably increased the productivity of the land in the purely economic terms of the profits accruing to the entrepreneurs who bought or leased or squatted on the land and planted it with vines and olives and stocked it with slaves; but, by the same token, the system made the land socially sterile; for, wherever the slave-plantations spread, they displaced and pauperized the peasant and the yeoman farmer as inexorably as bad money drives out good.

The social consequence was the depopulation of the countryside and the creation of a parasitic urban proletariat in the cities;[3] and this fatal path of social development was a 'one-way street'. Not all the efforts of successive generations of Roman social reformers —not the revolutionary political measures of the hot-blooded

[1] Diodorus of Agyrium, *A Library of Universal History*, Book xi, chap. 25.

[2] It must be confessed that the malignant social effects which followed upon the second signal advance in the technique of Hellenic agriculture cannot, after all, be kept altogether distinct from the malignant effects of Greek and Roman militarism, since the invention of the new agricultural technique in Sicily was connected with the Sicilian War of 480 B.C. and its introduction into Italy with the Italian War of 218–203 B.C. When the Romans finally annihilated Carthage in 146 B.C. they gave away all the libraries of Punic literature which fell into their hands to the local African princelings who had taken sides politically with Rome against Carthage without abandoning their taste for the Punic culture. To the Roman victors, this culture meant nothing; but there was one Carthaginian book of which they made an exception for practical reasons; and this was Mago's treatise on plantation-farming. Though the work ran to twenty-eight volumes, the Roman senate ordered its translation into Latin (Pliny, *Natural History*, xviii. 22).

[3] The dispossessed peasantry of Italy tended to drift into Rome; and those who remained in the countryside sank to the status of a rural proletariat, who eked out a miserable existence by serving as casual labourers (*politores*) on the plantations at harvest time and at other busy seasons. For the depopulation of the Campagna by the time of the establishment of the Empire, see the passage from Livy which is quoted in Part II. D (i), vol. ii, on p. 17, footnote 1, above.

Gracchi, and not the private munificence of the soberly public-spirited conservatives who endowed the Italian *Alimenta* in the second century after Christ[1]—could avail to rid the Roman World of this social blight which the last advance in agricultural technique had brought upon it. In spite of such efforts at reform, the plantation slave-gang continued to usurp the yeoman farmer's place until the slave-plantation system collapsed spontaneously in consequence of the breakdown of the money economy on which this system of agricultural mass-production for a world-market was dependent for making its profits. This financial breakdown was part of the general social *débâcle* of the third century of the Christian Era; and this *débâcle* was doubtless the outcome, in part, of the agrarian malady which had been eating away the tissues of the Roman body social for the previous four centuries. Thus the social cancer of Roman plantation-slavery eventually extinguished itself by causing the death of the society upon which it had fastened.[2]

The plantation-slavery of Roman Italy has a modern Western analogy, which has often been pointed out, in the plantation-slavery which was rampant in the cotton-belt of the United States during the first half of the nineteenth century after Christ.[3] In this latter case, again, a new virulence was instilled into the ancient social disease of slavery by an improvement in economic technique. If the close of the eighteenth century had not witnessed the outbreak of the Industrial Revolution in the United Kingdom, it is probable that the nineteenth century would have seen slavery die of inanition in the Southern States of the American Union, as it had already died on the northern side of the Mason and Dixon Line. It was the Industrial Revolution that gave slavery in the Southern States a new lease of life by creating a vast new market for raw cotton in Lancashire and by inventing the machinery for carding and spinning and weaving cotton at a financial profit. In these new circumstances, which a sudden great improvement in the Western technique of manufacture had brought about, the Slave Power became a menace not only to the political integrity of the United States, but to the social welfare of the whole Western World. Happily, the Western World has responded more effectively than the Hellenic World ever succeeded in responding to this formidable challenge. We have realized that slavery becomes too terrible an evil to be tolerated when the terrific driving-power of Industrialism has once been applied to it; and, realizing this, we have paid the

[1] For the Alimenta, see Hirschfeld, O.: *Die Kaiserlichen Verwaltungsbeamten bis auf Diocletian*, 2nd ed. (Berlin 1905, Weidmann), pp. 212–24.
[2] For the spiritual reaction of the Roman plantation-slaves to the penalization to which they were subjected, see Part II. D (vi), vol. ii, pp. 213–16, above.
[3] For the spiritual reaction of the Negro plantation-slaves in the Southern United States, see Part II. D (vi), vol. ii, pp. 218–20, above.

price that has had to be paid—the price of the American Civil War —in order to stamp our modern slavery out. We have still, however, to overcome a host of other social evils which the technical improvements of the Industrial Revolution have brought in their train; and one of these still unconquered evils is the malignant growth of a parasitic urban proletariat: an evil which seems to be sapping the strength of our own society in our time as it once sapped the strength of the Roman body social in its latter days.

The lack of correlation between progress in technique and progress in civilization is apparent in all these cases in which techniques have improved while civilizations have remained stationary or have suffered set-backs. The same thing is apparent in the cases, which we have next to consider, in which techniques have remained stationary while civilizations have been moving either forward or backward.

For example, an immense step forward in human progress was made in Europe between the Lower and the Upper Palaeolithic Age.

'The Upper Palaeolithic Culture is associated with the end of the fourth glacial epoch. In place of the remains of Neanderthal Man we find the remains of several types, none of which show any affinity to Neanderthal Man. On the contrary, they all approximate more or less closely to Modern Man. At one bound we seem, when looking at the fossil remains from this epoch in Europe, to have passed into the modern period as far as human bodily form is concerned.'[1]

This transfiguration of the human type in the middle of the Palaeolithic Age is possibly the most epoch-making event that has ever yet occurred in the course of human history up to date; for at that moment Sub-Man succeeded in turning himself into Man, while Man, in all the time that has elapsed since Sub-Man's achievement made Man human, has never yet succeeded in attaining the superhuman level which is the goal of our human endeavours.[2] This comparison gives us the measure of the psychic advance which was achieved when *Homo Neanderthalensis* was transcended and when *Homo Sapiens* emerged. Yet this immense psychic revolution was not accompanied by any corresponding revolution in technique; so that, on the technological classification, the sensitive artists who drew the pictures that we still admire in the Upper Palaeolithic cave-dwellings have to be confounded with 'the Missing Link', while in reality—as measured by wisdom and stature alike, and by every trait that is distinctive of Humanity—this *Homo*

[1] Carr-Saunders, A. M.: *The Population Problem* (Oxford 1922, Clarendon Press), pp. 116–17.
[2] For the rare exceptions that prove this rule, see III. C (ii) (a), below.

Palaeolithicus Superior is divided from *Homo Palaeolithicus Inferior* by just as great a gulf as is our latter-day *Homo Mechanicus*.

This instance in which a technique has remained stationary while a civilization has advanced finds its converse in other cases in which techniques have remained stationary while civilizations have receded.

For example, the technique of iron-working, which had been originally introduced into the Aegean at the moment of the great social relapse when the Minoan Civilization went into dissolution, remained stationary—neither improving nor declining—at the time of the next great social relapse, when the Hellenic Civilization went the way of its Minoan predecessor. Our Western World inherited the technique of iron-working from the Roman World unimpaired; and it likewise inherited the technique of writing, embodied in the Latin Alphabet,[1] as well as the Greek science of mathematics.[2] Socially, there had been a cataclysm. The Hellenic Civilization had gone to pieces and a social interregnum had ensued, out of which the new Western Civilization eventually emerged. But there was no corresponding break of continuity in the realm of technique —at least, not in the histories of the three important techniques just mentioned.

Another example of a technique remaining stationary while a civilization has receded is noticed by Ibn Khaldūn[3] in his contemporary observation of his own ancestral country. He remarks that, in the fragment of the Iberian Peninsula that still remained under the Islamic dispensation in his own day, the ancient arts had survived though the ancient order of society had fallen into a lamentable decay.

Our empirical survey has made it abundantly clear that there is

[1] We might add that the Orthodox Christian World inherited the Greek Alphabet from the Hellenic Civilization, the Islamic World the Arabic Alphabet from the Syriac Civilization, the Far Eastern World the Sinic characters from the Sinic Civilization, and the Babylonic World the Sumeric cuneiform script from the Sumeric Civilization. In bringing up these further examples, however, we might be convicted of arguing in a circle; for, in all these cases, we have left it an open question whether the posterior civilization in each pair of civilizations is really an independent civilization or merely the petrified or mummified corpse of the antecedent civilization. And the continuity of script (with all the continuity of mental tradition which that implies) is of course one of the strong arguments against admitting the claims of these posterior civilizations to be allowed the status of independent civilizations in their own right. (This problem has been discussed in Part I. C (ii), vol. i, on pp. 133–46, above.)

[2] 'The Mathematics are distinguished by a peculiar privilege that, in the course of ages, they may always advance and can never recede. But the ancient geometry, if I am not misinformed, was resumed by the Italians in the same state in the fifteenth century' (Gibbon, E.: *A History of the Decline and Fall of the Roman Empire*, ch. lii). This is perhaps a reminiscence of a passage in Turgot's *Second Discours sur les Progrès Successifs de l'Esprit Humain* which was delivered at the Sorbonne on the 11th December, 1750 (*Œuvres de Turgot*, Nouvelle Édition (Paris 1844, Guillaumin), 2 vols.), vol. ii, p. 600). The topic also appears in Turgot's *Plan de Deux Discours sur l'Histoire Universelle* (op. cit., p. 666).

[3] Ibn Khaldūn: *Muqaddamāt*, translated by de Slane, Baron McG. (Paris 1863–8, Imprimerie Impériale, 3 vols.), vol. ii, pp. 360–2.

no correlation between progress in technique and progress in civilization;[1] yet, although the history of technique proves not to be, in itself, the criterion for which we are seeking, it may still provide us with a clue for finding the object of our search.

(c) 'ETHERIALIZATION'

The history of technique, which has not yet revealed to us any law of social progress, does reveal the principle by which technical progress is governed; and this principle may be described as a law of progressive simplification.

For example, in the history of our modern Western system of transportation, the technical advance which was achieved in the substitution of mechanical for muscular traction required, in its first stage, a great elaboration of material apparatus. When the horse was replaced by the locomotive, the simple carriage-road had to be turned into an elaborate 'permanent way', with cuttings and tunnels and embankments and viaducts to eliminate the gradients of the natural landscape, and with a pair of metal rails to smooth the passage of the wheels of the steam-driven train. On the other hand, in the next stage of technical advance, when the ponderous and bulky steam-engine, with its heavy consumption of water and coal, is replaced by the light and handy internal-combustion-engine, driven by a mixture of petrol vapour and air, the improvement in technique is accompanied by a notable simplification of apparatus this time. The technical advantage of mechanical traction is not only preserved but enhanced (inasmuch as the internal-combustion-engine is an improvement on the steam-engine from the mechanical standpoint); and at the same time the disadvantage of the elaborate material apparatus is partly transcended. For the motor-car liberates itself from the rails to which the locomotive is bound, and takes to the road again, with all the speed and power of a railway-train and almost all the freedom of action of a pedestrian or a horse.

The same law of progressive simplification is apparent in the history of our modern Western technique for the instantaneous long-distance conveyance of words. When electric telegraphy and telephony is first invented, the electric currents by which the Morse Code is signalled or the human voice is conveyed have to be transmitted through an artificially installed medium of metal wires. Then comes the invention of wireless telegraphy and telephony— a further technical advance which makes it possible to dispense with the artificial medium of transmission and to radiate the human voice through the natural medium of the 'aether' to the distance of

[1] The same opinion is expressed by Eduard Meyer in his *Geschichte des Altertums*, vol. i (i), 4th ed. (Stuttgart and Berlin, 1921, Cotta), pp. 164–5.

hundreds of miles in as short a time as it takes the human organs of speech to transmit the same voice a few feet through the natural medium of the air.

Or let us consider the history of writing: an older device for transmitting the sense, without the sound, of human speech across vast intervals of Space and Time. In the history of writing, there is not merely a correlation between progress in technique and simplification in form, but the two tendencies are actually identical, since the whole of the technical problem which a script has to solve, in transposing human speech into a visual medium, is the distinct representation of the widest possible range of language with the greatest economy of visual symbols.

Perhaps the most elaborate script that has ever been invented is the Sinic, in which the characters are pictograms which have been conventionalized without being simplified, and in which each pictogram represents, not a sound nor even a word, but an idea. Since there is an infinite diversity of nuance among the ideas that arise in the human mind, the number of characters in the Sinic script runs into five figures, and a single one of these characters may contain more strokes than there are letters in our Alphabet. This Sinic script is certainly the most incompetent in technique, as well as the most elaborate in form, of any system of writing that is now in use.

This still current Sinic script is technically inferior to two extinct scripts—the Egyptiac hieroglyphic and the Sumeric cuneiform—which have each independently taken the step of using conventional pictures to represent sounds as well as ideas, or, in technical terms, to serve as phonograms as well as ideograms. The technical advantage of this step lies precisely in the economy of visual symbols which it renders possible; for while there is no limit to the number of distinct ideas in the human mind which may demand distinct representation in a system of ideograms, there is only a limited range of sounds in any given human language. Accordingly, a script that is based on phonograms instead of ideograms can provide for all its requirements out of a relatively small stock of visual symbols. If the Egyptiac and Sumeric scribes had only had the courage of their invention, and had discarded the use of ideograms altogether when once they had hit upon the use of phonograms to take their place, their scripts might perhaps now be holding the field which our own Alphabet actually occupies at the present day. As it was, they deprived themselves of the advantage of their invention by persisting in the use of phonograms and ideograms side by side (a perverse practice which made the invention of phonograms a source of confusion instead of a step towards greater clarity). All the same, both scripts are technically superior to the Sinic in almost all respects. Their pictograms are both fewer in number and simpler in form. The Egyptiac scribes, in particular, carried simplification of form very far in the cursive versions of their script, while, in their analysis of the sounds of human speech, they went the length of making phonograms for syllables containing only one consonant: an advance which brought them to the verge of inventing a consonantal alphabet.

In the historic Alphabet, which was invented by some Syriac scribe after the Egyptiac scribes had just failed to hit upon it, the simplification of writing, which is the same thing as its technical improvement, has been carried almost as far as it can go. The essence of the Alphabet is the analysis of the sounds of human speech into their primary elements, and the representation of each of these elements by a separate visual symbol which combines distinctiveness with simplicity of form. The Phoenician inventors of the Alphabet analysed out, and gave representation to, the consonants. The Greeks borrowed this Phoenician invention and then improved upon it by analysing and representing the vowels as well. And the Latin Alphabet, which is the script of our own Western Society, is simply a variant of the Greek Alphabet without any change, for better or worse, in technical principle. In a vowelled alphabet of the Greek and Latin type, it is possible to give visual representation—with sufficient accuracy and distinctiveness for practical purposes, if not for the scientific requirements of the phonetician—to almost any sound that is used in almost any language that has ever been spoken.

In the history of writing, with its culmination in the Alphabet, the law of correlation between improvement in technique and simplification in apparatus is admirably illustrated. And its operation can be discerned again in the history of language: a technique of articulate and significant sounds which is both logically and chronologically prior to the invention of writing and indeed is perhaps coeval with Humanity itself.

In the history of language, as in the history of writing, simplification is the path of technical progress. The tendency of language, when it is in course of improvement, is to abandon the elaborate apparatus of inflexion, in which the parts of speech that express relations are welded on to the parts that express meanings, and to resort, instead, to the use of prepositions and auxiliary verbs and particles, in which the same relations are expressed in the form of separate words which can be attached to, or detached from, any of the other separate words that express meaning, without the necessity of altering the internal form of either word in either class.

It will be seen that this tendency in the technique of language has the same effect as the tendency in the technique of writing to progress from ideographic pictograms to conventional symbols representing the elementary sounds. The effect in both cases is to render possible an economy of forms: visual forms in the case of writing and sound forms in the case of speech. It will also be seen that the relation-word sits as loosely to the meaning-word as the tool to the human hand, which can pick up or put down any tool at will or exchange one tool for another, while the nexus between the inflexion and the root on to which it is welded is like the nexus between a sword-fish's sword and the sword-fish, in contrast to the casual relation of a man's sword to the man.[1] In an inflective language, the root can no more let go of its inflexion than the swordfish can let go of his sword; and therefore, if the meaning has to be put into a different relation to other meanings than the particular relation which any one given inflexion happens to express, a separate form has to be coined for the combination of the old root with the new inflexion, with which it has now to enter into another indissoluble partnership, just as, when Nature wishes to use the snout as a prehensile implement instead of using it as a piercing instrument, she cannot just unship the sword-fish's sword and fit a trunk to the creature's snout instead, but can only provide herself with a trunk by creating quite another creature—an elephant—to wear this other implement as an integral part of his elephantine bodily organism.

The tendency of language to simplify itself by abandoning inflexions in favour of auxiliary words may be illustrated by a comparative view of the histories of certain representatives of the Indo-European family of languages. As the two extreme poles in this series we may take Classical Sanskrit and Modern English. Sanskrit happens, by an historical accident, to have been stabilized in a standard literary form before it had deviated very far from the now extinct *Indo-europäische Ursprache*: the primitive mother tongue from which all the members of the Indo-European family are descended. Accordingly we find in Sanskrit what, to an English-speaking student, seems an amazing wealth of inflexions side by side with a surprising poverty in particles, while, at the other end of the scale, Modern English has retained only a few miserable vestiges of the wealth of inflexions bequeathed by the *Ursprache*, but has recouped itself by developing a wealth of prepositions and particles and, above all, auxiliary verbs. In this linguistic gamut in which English and Sanskrit represent the extremes, Attic Greek

[1] For this contrast between animal fixity and human adaptability, see in general Part III. A, pp. 79–88, above.

lies somewhere near the middle. An English student of Attic Greek is struck by its conformity with Sanskrit in having retained an abundance of inflexions; but closer inspection shows that the Greek and the Sanskrit wealth in inflexions is differently distributed between the different parts of speech. Greek is poorer than Sanskrit in the inflexions of the noun, but on the other hand it is richer in the inflexions of the verb; and this difference is significant, because the verb, unlike the noun, has relation as well as meaning in its essence. But a Hindu Sanskrit scholar who turned his attention to Greek would probably not be struck by the Greek inflexions at all—neither by the verbal inflexions nor by the nominal. The feature in the Attic Greek language that would impress the Sanskrit scholar would be its wealth in particles; and on the strength of this feature he might be inclined to think of Attic Greek and Modern English as representing an identic tendency, in common contrast to Sanskrit. If the three languages are to be judged by their relative powers of expression, we shall probably come to the conclusion that our hypothetical Indian has come nearer to hitting the mark in classing Greek with English than our hypothetical Englishman in classing it with Sanskrit. For the English composite verb has at least as wide a range and as subtle a nuance as the Greek inflective verb for expressing relations, while the Sanskrit verb is equally inferior to them both.

Again, the Arabic verb impresses the English student at first sight by its wealth of 'aspects' expressed through internal inflexions; but he soon discovers that the English verb, with the aid of its auxiliaries, can express all the nuances of these 'aspects' as well as all the distinctions of Time, whereas the Arabic verb with its single pair of tenses—a perfect and an imperfect—is virtually incapable of expressing the elementary Time-distinction between past, present, and future.

The Ottoman Turkish language, again, manages to express as wide a range and as subtle a nuance of relations by means of an inflective verb as Attic Greek itself; but its inferiority to Greek is revealed by its poverty in particles. Such particles as it possesses are mostly loans from Persian and Arabic. But the greatest weakness of Turkish is its lack of relative pronouns; and it is in vain that it calls all its gerunds and gerundives into action to do duty for them. The result is a complication of syntax which makes the most ponderous Ciceronian or Miltonian period seem simple by comparison. The Turkish language would be better off if it could drop half its verbal inflexions and acquire a handful of relatives in exchange.

The line of progress in the technical improvement of language

which the foregoing survey reveals seems to suggest that a technically perfect language would dispense with inflexions altogether in
favour of auxiliary words, and perhaps eventually dispense with
these auxiliaries as well, and express itself entirely in uninflected
words of meaning whose relations with one another would be
indicated simply by their relative order. Modern English has
travelled this path a very long way; and the Classical Chinese language—which seems to have been as progressive as the Classical
Chinese script is backward—has possibly travelled the whole path
to its logical end.

Our law of correlation between improvement in technique and
simplification in apparatus, which we have now illustrated by
examples taken from the diverse fields of transportation and telegraphy and telephony and writing and language, can be illustrated
equally well from the histories of astronomy or philosophy or
fashions in dress.

If we turn the pages of some illustrated history of fashion in our
own Western World, we shall be struck by the steadiness of the
trend which is apparent, in the course of the last four centuries,
from elaborateness towards simplicity and from diversity towards
uniformity. In the costume of a Queen Elizabeth or a King
Louis XIV there is a profusion and extravagance of ornament, and
an exaggeration and distortion of the natural lines of the human
figure, which smells strongly of the savage.[1] Elizabeth, with her
enormous ruff and her tight-laced waist, has essentially the same
conception of finery as the primitive African or Melanesian who
files his teeth to a point and distends his lips and ear-lobes by in-
serting wooden plugs into the living flesh. And Louis, when he
caricatures the beauties of the natural human head of hair in the
fantastically dense tresses and crimped curls of his enormous bag-
wig, is really aiming at the same effect as the Abyssinian chieftain
who envelops his head in a lion's mane. The excruciating effect
which is made upon our modern sensibilities by Louis' and Elizabeth's taste is enhanced when we notice the contrast between the
costliness of the dress of the fashionable world in the sixteenth and
seventeenth centuries and the scantiness and raggedness of the
clothing of the common people, who have to go unshod and un-
protected against cold and rain. As we turn over the pages, we are
conscious of a growing sense of relief as we approach the fashion-
plate of our own 'post-war' generation.[2] For in our generation the

[1] For an interpretation of the latter-day savage's penchant towards puerility and
monstrosity as a kind of pathological 'compensation' for the absence of progress in his
social life, see Bergson, Henri: *Les Deux Sources de la Morale et la Religion* (Paris 1932,
Alcan), pp. 142-4.
[2] Peter the Great, whose tastes (both for good and for evil) were some two centuries
ahead of his age (even if we reckon his age on the Western and not on the, by then,

old invidious class-distinctions are no longer flaunted so flagrantly in the field of dress: a field in which they have no rhyme or reason, whatever there may be to be said for them or against them in other spheres. In dress, there has been a remarkable and salutary approximation towards uniformity between class and class within living memory; and the main factor in this approximation has not been the cheap imitation of the finery of the rich which has been brought within the means of the poor by the mass-production of the Machine Age. A more striking and significant tendency has been the voluntary simplification in the dress of the minority which disposes of the means to set the fashion. There has been a tendency towards the use of plainer materials, and—even more markedly—towards a simpler cut, which aims at following and setting off the natural lines of the human body instead of contradicting or caricaturing them.[1]

It is interesting to rediscover the same trend in the history of Hellenic fashion as in the history of our own. Thucydides, writing on the morrow of the Great War of 431–404 B.C., describes the finery which had been worn by well-to-do male Athenians not so very long before the historian's own day, in contrast to the simple modern style of dress which had been introduced by the Spartans and had spread from Lacedaemon to the rest of Hellas. In the same passage Thucydides also mentions a modern tendency—which unfortunately has no counterpart as yet in our modern Western World —for the well-to-do minority to accept equality with the masses, not only in the matter of dress, but in their whole material standard of living.[2] This tendency towards simplification which is manifest,

relatively belated Byzantine Time-scale), already experienced this sense of relief in England when he visited that country at the close of the seventeenth century. When King William III asked his eccentric Russian guest: 'What has pleased you most in London?' Peter replied: 'That the richest people go about in clothes that are plain but clean' (Brückner, A.: *Peter der Grosse* (Berlin 1879, Grote), p. 224. Cp. p. 515).

[1] In the modern Western male costume, this tendency set in with the invention of the coat and waistcoat towards the close of the seventeenth century, and was confirmed in the opening decades of the nineteenth century when bright colours and showy materials were abandoned and breeches were superseded by trousers. In the Western female costume, the corresponding revolution has been later but more rapid. While much the same kind of taste is expressed, *mutatis mutandis*, in the feminine as in the masculine dress of our 'post-war' age (in which the two costumes both incline equally towards simplicity, as in the Elizabethan age they both inclined towards a certain style of extravagance), there is a violent contrast between the male and female costume of the mid-nineteenth century, when the Empress Eugénie revives the worst extravagances of Queen Elizabeth, while the Emperor Napoleon III already anticipates the sober and almost sombre garb of a President Mustafā Kemāl or a President Calvin Coolidge.

[2] 'The Athenians were among the first to lay aside their arms and change to a more comfortable and refined way of living. The older men of the well-to-do class have only recently abandoned the luxuries of wearing linen shirts and fastening their hair in a bunch with gold grasshopper clasps. Among the kindred population of Ionia, these fashions long retained their hold over the older generation. The simple dress which we wear to-day was first introduced by the Lacedaemonians, who reduced the whole outward standard of living to approximately the same level for rich and poor. They were also the first to take exercise naked, and to strip in public and oil themselves for this purpose. Originally, even at the Olympic Games, the athletes used to cover their nakedness with a

for all who have eyes to see, in the histories of fashions in dress, appears to reveal itself to instructed eyes in the progress of Physical Science, and it has also been acclaimed as the royal road of philosophic intuition by one of our greatest living Western philosophers.

In the history of Physical Science, the Ptolemaic system of astronomy, which was the first attempt to give a coherent explanation of all the observed movements of all the known heavenly bodies, had to postulate an elaborate geometrical apparatus of epicycles. The Copernican system, by which the Ptolemaic has latterly been replaced, presents us, in far simpler geometrical terms, with an equally coherent explanation of the vastly wider range of movement of the innumerable host of heaven that has now been revealed by the invention of the telescope. And to-day Einstein's system— for those who comprehend it—appears to be introducing a still further simplification into the hypothetical structure of the physical universe by bringing the dimensions of Time and Space, and the laws of Gravity and Radiation and Magnetism, into a single synthesis.

In the domain of Philosophy, a corresponding tendency towards simplification has been taken as an index of progress in intuition by Monsieur Henri Bergson.

'Something which, when viewed from without, is susceptible of being decomposed into an infinite number of inter-coordinated parts might perhaps appear, if viewed from inside, as one single act. For instance, a movement of the hand, which feels to us indivisible, will be perceived externally as a curve which can be defined by an equation: that is, as a juxtaposition of points which are infinite in number and which at the same time all satisfy a single law. In the place where our analysis, remaining outside its object, discovers positive elements in greater and ever greater numbers and in more and ever more astonishing coordination with one another (in virtue of the very fact that their numbers increase), an intuition which succeeded in planting itself in the interior would be aware no longer of means combined but rather of obstacles surmounted. An invisible hand passing brusquely through a heap of iron filings would be simply brushing aside resistance; but the sheer simplicity of this act would appear, when viewed from the side of resistance, in the guise of a juxtaposition of the filings in a positively determined order.'[1]

The simile of the movement of the hand in its outward and its inward aspects is applied by the same philosopher, in another

loin-cloth while competing, and it is not many years since this practice has been given up. Among the non-Hellenic peoples of the present day, especially in Asia, when there are boxing and wrestling competitions, they still wear loin-cloths for the occasion; and it would be possible to point out many other similarities between ancient Hellenic and modern non-Hellenic life.' (Thucydides: 'Prolegomena' (Bk. I, chs. 1–5).)

[1] Bergson, Henri: *Les Deux Sources de la Morale et de la Religion* (Paris 1932, Alcan), pp. 118–19.

passage of the same work, to the relation between Man and the material universe.

'When one speaks of the smallness of Man and the vastness of the Universe, one is thinking of the complexity of the Universe at least as much as of its dimensions. A personality makes an effect of simplicity, whereas the material world is of a complexity that baffles the imagination: the most minute particle of matter that is visible to the human eye is already a world in itself. How persuade oneself that Personality can be the sole *raison d'être* of Matter? But we will not allow ourselves to be intimidated. When we find ourselves in the presence of parts which can be enumerated *ad infinitum*, it is possible that the whole may be simple, and that we are just looking at it from the wrong end. Carry your hand from one position to another: for you, who perceive the movement from within, it is something that is indivisible. But I perceive it from outside and fix my attention on the line that has been traversed; and so I say to myself that the first half of the space has first had to be traversed, and then half the second half, and then half of what remains, and so on and on: I might continue for milliards of centuries, and still I should never have exhausted the enumeration of the acts into which my eyes decompose the movement that feels indivisible to you. Similarly the gesture which evokes the Human Species—or, in general terms, evokes objects of love for the Creator—might very well demand conditions which demand other conditions which lead on step by step into an infinite regress. The mere thought of this multiplicity turns the thinker giddy; yet it is nothing but the reverse side of an indivisible something. It is true that the infinitely numerous acts into which we decompose a movement of the hand are purely virtual, and that they are absolutely determined in their virtuality by the actuality of the movement itself, whereas the constituent parts of the Universe, and the parts of these parts, are realities—and realities which, when they are living creatures, enjoy a spontaneity which can reach the point of free activity. So we will not claim that the relation of the complex to the simple is precisely the same in the two cases. The purpose of the parallel that we have drawn has merely been to show that sheer complexity—even when it is a boundless complexity—is not a sign of importance; and that an existence which is simple in itself may demand conditions that stretch away in an endless chain.'[1]

Thus a modern Western philosopher applies the historic *solvitur ambulando* to the ancient sophism of the Eleatics in order to equate complexity with Matter and simplicity with Life, and this not merely with Life at its lowest levels, but with the Life of Man and the Life of a Creative Godhead.

The foregoing illustrations seem to indicate that our law of the correlation between simplification in apparatus and improvement in technique has no limits to its field of operation. We have discovered

[1] Bergson, op. cit., pp. 278–9.

this same tendency towards simplification at work in the most diverse spheres. But perhaps 'simplification' is not quite an accurate, or at least not altogether an adequate, term for describing the tendency which we have just been investigating. 'Simplification' is a negative word. It connotes omission and elimination; whereas, in the concrete examples of the phenomenon from which we have inferred the validity of our law, the ultimate effect which the law produces by its operation is not a diminution, but an enhancement, of practical efficiency or of aesthetic satisfaction or of intellectual understanding or of godlike love. In fact, the result is not a loss but a gain; and this gain is the outcome of a process of simplification because this process liberates forces that have been imprisoned in a more material medium and thereby sets them free to work in a more etherial medium with a greater potency. We are witnessing here the release of

'A fiery soul which, working out its way,
Fretted the pigmy-body to decay
And o'er-informed the tenement of clay.'[1]

In other words, the process which we are examining involves not merely a simplification of apparatus but a consequent transfer of energy, or shift of emphasis, from some lower sphere of being or sphere of action to a higher sphere. Perhaps we shall be describing the process in a more illuminating way if we call it, not 'simplification', but 'etherialization'.

This phenomenon of 'etherialization' may be observed in many different spheres.

In the sphere of human control over Physical Nature it may take the form of a transfer of the field of operation from a grosser to a subtler mesh in the texture of the material universe: from coal-fuel to oil-fuel (as in the illustration which we have drawn from the history of our modern Western methods of transportation); or from water-power to steam-power and from steam-power to electric-power; or from the transmission of electric waves through metallic wires to their transmission through the 'aether'. This trend in the development of our modern Western application of Physical Science is indicated, with a finely imaginative touch, in the following passage from the pen of an anthropologist of the present generation:

'We are leaving the ground, we are getting out of touch, our tracks grow fainter. Flint lasts for ever, copper for civilizations, iron for generations, steel for a lifetime. Who will be able to map the route of the London-Peking air express when the age of movement is over or to-day

[1] Dryden: *Absalom and Achitophel.*

to say what is the path through the "aether" of the messages which are radiated and received? But the frontiers of the petty vanished kingdom of the Iceni still sweep defensively across the southern frontier of East Anglia, from drained marsh to obliterated forest.'[1]

The consummation towards which this historic tendency may conceivably be advancing (on the assumption that it persists) has been anticipated in imagination by a nineteenth-century English novelist in a phantasia in which he pictures the then prevalent methods of controlling Physical Nature—the methods of the early Industrial Revolution—as having been rendered obsolete by the discovery, and superseded by the application, of an incomparably subtle and powerful physical force.

'I went with my host and his daughter Zee over the great public museum, which occupies a wing in the College of Sages, and in which are hoarded, as curious specimens of the ignorant and blundering experiments of ancient times, many contrivances on which we pride ourselves as recent achievements. In one department, carelessly thrown aside as obsolete lumber, are tubes for destroying life by metallic balls and an inflammable powder, on the principle of our cannons and catapults, and even still more murderous than our latest improvements. My host spoke of these with a smile of contempt, such as an artillery officer might bestow on the bows and arrows of the Chinese. In another department there were models of vehicles and vessels worked by steam, and of a balloon which might have been constructed by Montgolfier. "Such," said Zee, with an air of meditative wisdom—"such were the feeble triflings with Nature of our savage forefathers, ere they had even a glimmering of perception of the properties of Vril." '[2]

This imaginary 'Vril'-force, with which Bulwer Lytton endows 'the Coming Race', performs the magic which our more sanguine physicists look forward to exercising in our own day if they succeed in discovering a method for 'breaking up the atom'. In both the nineteenth-century and the twentieth-century conceptions, the ultimate form of human control over Physical Nature—the form which is to give Man boundless material power—is conceived as being incomparably etherial in its mode of operation.

The phenomenon of 'etherialization' which thus asserts itself in the domain of Applied Science may also be observed in the domains of Theology and Mathematics and Art and Philosophy.

The etherialization of Theology is compared with the corresponding development in the history of Mathematics by Monsieur Bergson:

'The gradual ascent of Religion towards Gods whose personality is more and more plainly marked and who enter into more and more

[1] Heard, Gerald: *The Ascent of Humanity* (London 1929, Cape), pp. 277–8.
[2] Bulwer Lytton: *The Coming Race*, ch. xvi.

clearly defined relations with one another or tend to become absorbed into one single divinity . . . has gone forward until a moment has come at which the religious spirit has turned away from the Outward towards the Inward, from the Static to the Dynamic, by a process of conversion analogous to that accomplished by the Pure Intellect when it passed from the consideration of finite magnitudes to that of the Differential Calculus.'[1]

An etherialization of our modern Western Art which took place in the course of the eighteenth century, when the sceptre passed from the art of Architecture to the art of Music and when the *élan* of the Western artistic impulse was thus, as it were, translated from the grosser medium of stone into the subtler medium of sound, has been traced out by Oswald Spengler in one of the most interesting passages of his *magnum opus*.

'About the year 1740, when Euler was beginning to establish the definitive formulation of Functional Analysis, there arose the Sonata, which is the maturest and the highest form of the instrumental style. . . . Therewith begins the reign of Music over all the other arts. In the field of the plastic arts Music banishes statuary and tolerates nothing but the completely musical and finikinly un-Hellenic and counter-Renaissance *Kleinkunst* of porcelain, which was invented at a time when chamber music was winning its way to a position of decisive importance. Whereas the plastic art of the Gothic age is architectonic ornament—rows of human figures—through and through, the plastic art of the Rococo period is a significant example of an art which is only plastic superficially, while in reality it is under the domination of Music—which is its opposite in the circle of the arts—and is speaking in the language of musical form. This reveals the degree to which it is possible for the technique that governs the foreground of artistic life to be in contradiction with the spirit of the world of forms which this technique creates (*pace* the usual aesthetic theory which assumes that spirit and technique stand to each other in the relation of a cause and an effect). Compare the crouching Venus of Coyzevox (A.D. 1686) in the Louvre with her Hellenic forerunner in the Vatican, and you will see the difference between plastic art treated as music and plastic art working in its own right. In Coyzevox's work, the sense of movement, the flow of the lines, and the fluidity that has been imparted to the very essence of the stone—which, like porcelain, has somehow lost its solidity and mass—can be described most aptly in musical terms: staccato, accelerando, andante, allegro. Hence the feeling that somehow the close-grained marble is here out of place. Hence, too, the altogether un-Hellenic reliance on effects of light and shade: a device which corresponds to what has been the leading principle of oil-painting since Titian. The quality which the Eighteenth Century called colour—whether in an engraving or in a drawing or in a group of statuary—really means music. This quality governs the painting of Watteau and Fragonard and the art of the Gobelins and

[1] Bergson, op. cit., p. 189.

Pastelle. Do we not talk, from that day to this, of "colour-tones" and "tone-colours"? And is this not a recognition of an equivalence finally attained between two arts that are superficially so different? And are not all such designations meaningless in reference to all Hellenic Art? Music even succeeded in recasting, in its own spirit, the Baroque architecture of Bernini. It re-cast it into Rococo; and the transcendental Rococo ornamentation is "played" over by lights which are virtually musical tones, and which perform the function of resolving roofs, walls, arches and everything that is constructive and concrete into polyphony and harmony: an architectural music whose trills, cadences and passaggios carry to the point of identity the assimilation of the architectural semantic of these halls and galleries to the music which was conceived for them. Dresden and Vienna are the homes of this late and shortlived wonderland of chamber music and billowy furniture and mirror-rooms and pastoral poetry and porcelain-groups. This is the last expression of the Western soul: an expression of autumnal ripeness with a touch of autumn sunshine. The Vienna of the Vienna Congress saw it die and disappear.'[1]

While Spengler's brilliant historical analysis lays bare the process of 'etherialization' in the domain of Art, an illustration of the corresponding process in the domain of Philosophy may be found in a famous passage in which Plato represents Socrates as recounting the history of his own personal intellectual development.

'"In my own early days", said Socrates, "I had an extraordinary passion for this branch of study which they call Physical Science. It seemed to me a sublime science to know the causes of all phenomena and to understand the reasons for the genesis and disintegration and existence of each of them. And often I used to rack my brains with such preliminary speculations as whether there is any truth in the theory that living organisms arise out of a kind of fermentation of Heat and Cold; or whether the material instrument of our thought is blood or air or fire; or whether, perhaps, this is a wrong approach to the problem, and we must rather think of the brain as providing the senses of hearing and sight and smell, and think of memory and supposition as arising from the senses, and then think of knowledge as arising at the end of the chain, from memory and supposition when these are brought into a steady focus. And then again I used to speculate on the ways in which all these phenomena pass out of existence, and about the natural history of the stellar universe and of our own planet, until, at the end of it all, I came to the conclusion that I had less gift for conducting this kind of research than any creature in the World. I will give you a conclusive piece of evidence about my state of mind. I was blinded by this kind of research to such an extreme degree that I actually unlearnt the things which it had seemed to me—and to others as well—that I had known

[1] Spengler, Oswald: *Der Untergang des Abendlandes*, vol. i (Munich 1920, Beck), pp. 318–20. Compare the passage quoted in III. C (iii), below, on pp. 388–9. The same theme is developed by Heard, G., in *The Ascent of Humanity* (London 1928, Cape), pp. 226–8.

quite clearly before. . . . But one day", he went on, "I happened to hear Anaxagoras giving a recitation from a book in which he said that it is Mind which is the directive force in the Universe and the cause of all phenomena; and here I found at last an explanation that delighted me. It seemed to me somehow right that the cause of all phenomena should be Mind; and I thought that, if this were the truth, a directive force like Mind in the Universe must be directing the whole thing and arranging each detail of it to the best possible purpose." '[1]

In the experience here described, which was evidently a turning-point in Socrates' mental history, the Athenian philosopher transferred his interest and attention from the physical to the psychic sphere, from the Macrocosm to the Microcosm, and discovered in the hypothesis of a spiritual cause that clue to an explanation of the mystery of existence which had eluded him so long as he had been working on the hypothesis that the cause was material. Thus Socrates found intellectual salvation; and, in finding that, he found moral salvation as well; for this change in the field of his research involved a simultaneous change in the goal. In the act of transferring his quest from the physical to the psychic sphere, Socrates transcended Metaphysics and made his entry into the realm of Ethics. As appears in the last sentence in the passage just quoted, the scope of his inquiry now broadened out to include the Good as well as the True; and when the problems of Physical Science had thus ceased to trouble him, he became receptive to the promptings of his δαιμόνιον.

This δαιμόνιον that spoke to Socrates after he had grown in wisdom[2] and had put away childish things[3] was no other than the still small voice in which Elijah heard at last the Godhead whom he had not seen in the fire and not encountered in the earthquake and not felt in the great and strong wind which had rent the mountains and broken in pieces the rocks.[4] And this experience, which came alike to the Syriac prophet and to the Hellenic philosopher, was also attained by the Sinic sage Lao-tse,[5] when he made the same spiritual transit to the Microcosm from the Macrocosm. This Socratic path led Lao-tse to his intuition of Wu Wei: the ultimate principle whose nature cannot be indicated in the language of the discursive reason except by way of verbal paradox. Wu Wei is that utter emptiness which is the acme of plenitude, and that utter immobility which is the acme of motion, and that utter relaxation which is the acme of intensity, and that utter tranquillity which is the ecstasy of creation.

---

[1] Plato: *Phaedo*, 96–7.   [2] 1 Sam. ii. 26, and Luke ii. 52.
[3] 1 Cor. xiii. 11.   [4] 1 Kings xix. 11–12.
[5] Or (perhaps it is more accurate to say) by the anonymous originators of the school of Sinic philosophy that passes under the name of Lao-tse.

These paradoxical lights on the nature of Wu Wei may perhaps be further illuminated by a parable. For Wu Wei was assuredly the unconscious philosophy of the hero in the story of the Chinese pilot and the English crew: a story which, *se non è vero, è ben trovato*.

Some time about the middle of the nineteenth century, there was an English sailing-ship which used to make the voyage to China, year by year, with the same English crew and used to finish the voyage, each time, by going up the Yangtse, three days' sail up stream, with the same Chinese pilot. Now these were the years when, in England, the Industrial Revolution was making rapid headway; and one year the owners scrapped the old sailing-ship and sent their men out on the China voyage this time in a new-fangled steamer instead. The English crew were as pleased as the English owners with their new mechanical toy; and all the way out they speculated about the impression which the steamer would make upon their old friend the Chinese pilot. To navigate a steamer was quite a sensation even for these seamen from Liverpool, where the wheels had been whirring and the steam had been whizzing all around them since their childhood. How, then, would a steam-propelled vessel strike John Chinaman, when he was suddenly confronted with this miracle of mechanical ingenuity which had no parallel or precedent in his own Chinese social background? Would he react like the Queen of Sheba when she had seen all Solomon's wisdom and there was no more spirit in her? Would wonder or terror be his dominant emotion when he was asked to take the wheel of a ship which, with no visible means of propulsion, was able to travel at a greater velocity than any junk or sampan that had ever been rowed by oars or wafted by sails of bamboo matting? As the Englishmen entertained themselves with these speculations at their Chinese friend's expense on the long voyage out (for the China voyage was still long enough, even when it was made under steam), their curiosity was titivated; and as they approached the point off the China coast where the pilot always came on board they had quite a tense feeling of expectancy. When they saw their old friend mounting the ladder from the pilot-boat, they could hardly restrain themselves from calling his attention to the marvellous difference between the new and the old; but they just managed to hold their tongues, for they had decided beforehand that it would be more amusing to let John Chinaman's comments burst out of his mouth spontaneously.

The pilot stepped on to the steamer's deck, made his customary salutation to the Captain, walked to the wheel, and prepared to steer the vessel when she got under way again. 'Now he will have his surprise', thought the Englishmen, 'when he finds the ship moving forward with not a sail bent on the yards. Now he will realize that there is something about this ship that he has never come across in any ship before.' But it was the Englishmen's fate to have the surprise on this occasion; for, when the engines started, they were astonished to see that not a muscle moved on the Chinese pilot's face, and that he kept his place at the wheel without uttering a word. 'Well, John Chinaman is a cautious fellow', they said as they talked the pilot's conduct over. 'His mind works slowly. He will ruminate all day and tell us his thoughts this evening.' But the day passed, and the evening, and the night, and the pilot still said nothing, but kept his place at the wheel and quietly did his business as he had always done it before. The second day and night passed likewise, and the pilot had still said nothing when the third and last day arrived—the day on which he was to take his leave after having piloted the steamer up river to her destination. At this point the Englishmen were unable to contain themselves any longer. They forgot their resolution to leave it to the pilot to break the silence first; and they asked him outright what impression their magic ship had made on him. 'Oh! This ship?' said the Chinese (and his face remained as expressionless when he spoke as it had been since he had come on board). 'This ship? Why, once upon a time we used to make ships like this in China too; but we gave them up again some time ago. It must be about two thousand years since we used them last!' And, with his customary salutation the pilot stepped down the ladder into the little boat that was waiting to take him off, and rowed away without so much as one glance back at the master-piece of Western industry which he had treated so cavalierly. In the game of making an impression, which the English seamen had started in a patronizing vein, the Chinese pilot had won a crushing victory.

The point of this legendary Chinese pilot's retort to the English seamen's curiosity is, of course, not the same as the point of the passage from the pen of an authentic English novelist of the same period which has been quoted above. When the imperturbable Chinese conveyed his contempt for a steamship, or for any other piece of clockwork, by affecting to believe that his own people had invented and discarded that sort of thing a long time ago, he did not mean to say that in China they had replaced steam-power by electric-power and electric-power by 'Vril-power' or by some other imaginary device of incomparable potency for harnessing the material forces of Physical Nature in the service of human purposes. In dismissing his English contemporaries' new mechanical toy as a childish thing—one of 'the feeble triflings with Nature' which his own forefathers had perpetrated and afterwards outgrown—he was making a criticism of the Western Industrial Revolution that cuts much deeper than the 'meditative wisdom' of Bulwer Lytton's equally fictitious heroine. He meant to say that his own people had anticipated 'the South Sea Barbarians'—and this perhaps by many centuries—in trying their hand at the exploitation of Physical Nature, but that they had been convinced by their experience that this material world was not the place where human beings should lay up their treasure, and had acted upon this conviction by transferring their interest and energy, not from a less efficient to a more efficient industrial technique, but right away from Industrialism to some wholly different sphere.

This mythical transfer of the treasure of the Sinic Civilization in ancient times has a historic parallel, in the present-day Hindu World, in the preaching of the Mahatma Gandhi to his co-religionists and fellow countrymen. In wrestling with the problem of the penetration of India by the Western system of Industrialism and by the Western spirit with which this system goes hand in hand, the Mahatma has come to the conclusion that India must repudiate not only the present-day apparatus of Western technique, but the whole system and spirit for which this apparatus stands, if she is to find her own salvation. This is the doctrine for which he has found a concrete symbol, understanded of the people, in the *khaddar*, or hand-woven cloth of hand-spun home-grown cotton-thread, which he urges all Indian men and women to make for their own wear. The return, which he commends, from the elaborateness of the Western technique of spinning and weaving by power-driven machinery to the simplicity of handwork, is not commended in the belief that there is any intrinsically superior virtue in the simpler, as against the more elaborate, method of providing for one of the primary material necessities of human life. The Mahatma's advocacy of hand-spinning is really an advocacy, in symbolic terms, of a transfer—or reversion—of Indian interest and Indian energy from a material to a spiritual plane of action.

The doctrine and the policy for which the genius of Mr. Gandhi has found this particular form of expression are not, of course, peculiar to this Mahatma of this 'post-war' generation. The spirit of Gandhism is such a strong and persistent and prominent element in the êthos of Hinduism that even a Western observer of Hindu life who is so incorrigibly Western-minded as Mr. Rudyard Kipling has seized and expressed this trait in the beautiful story of Purun Dass:[1] the competent, sophisticated, and ostensibly Westernized prime minister of an Indian autonomous state under the British Raj who suddenly renounces his whole worldly position at the height of his worldly success, and deliberately adopts the life of a

[1] 'The Miracle of Purun Baghat', in *The Second Jungle Book*.

hermit. The career of this Hindu hero of a Western work of fiction, which was conceived and written before Mr. Gandhi was heard of, actually foreshadows the historic career of the Gujerati Banya, educated in London and established in business in South Africa, who renounced a successful legal practice in order to follow Religion. The path of Purun Bhagat and of Mahatma Gandhi is a path that is familiar in the history of Hinduism and its antecedents. It is the path which the Emperor Açoka trod in his youth when he renounced the use of war as an instrument of his Imperial policy, and again in middle life when he virtually renounced the Imperial throne itself in order to lead the life of a Buddhist monk. And the same path had been trodden by the Emperor's master the prince Gautama, when he renounced throne and wife and child in order to become the Buddha.

Thus the way of life which is being preached in our generation by the Hindu Mahatma Gandhi has a host of precedents and inspirations in the Hindu tradition. Yet, since the Mahatma himself has freely acknowledged his spiritual indebtedness to Christianity as well as to Hinduism, we may perhaps conjecture that his preaching reflects in part the influence of a passage in the New Testament in which the principle of 'etherialization' has received its supreme expression.

'Take no thought for your life, what ye shall eat or what ye shall drink; nor yet for your body, what ye shall put on. Is not the life more than meat, and the body than raiment?

'Behold the fowls of the air: for they sow not, neither do they reap nor gather into barns; yet your heavenly father feedeth them. Are ye not much more than they? . . .

'And why take ye thought for raiment? Consider the lilies of the field, how they grow; they toil not, neither do they spin:

'And yet I say unto you that even Solomon in all his glory was not arrayed like one of these. . . .

'Therefore take no thought, saying, What shall we eat? or, What shall we drink? or, Wherewithal shall we be clothed? (For after all these things do the Gentiles seek). . . .

'But seek ye first the Kingdom of God, and His righteousness.'[1]

This passage from the Gospel according to Saint Matthew may conclude our chain of quotations to illustrate the wide range and extreme diversity of the spheres in which the phenomenon of 'etherialization' manifests itself. In each sphere, the same fundamental tendency can be discerned under some different aspect. In morphological terms, 'etherialization' appears as a progressive change in organization from complexity towards simplicity; in

[1] Matt. vi. 25–6, 28–9, and 31–3.

biological terms, it appears as a *saltus Naturae*[1] from Inanimate
Matter to Life; in philosophical terms, as a re-orientation of the
mind's eye from the Macrocosm towards the Microcosm; in religious terms, as a conversion of the soul from the World, the Flesh,
and the Devil to the Kingdom of Heaven. If we chose to extend
our survey further, no doubt we should find different manifestations
of 'etherialization' in other spheres again; but the illustrations
which we have gathered in already are sufficient for our purpose;
for they point the way unmistakably towards the object of our
present inquiry.

(d) THE TRANSFERENCE OF THE FIELD OF ACTION

Etherialization has come to our notice as a concomitant of growth;
and our illustrations of the phenomenon make it clear that the
criterion of growth, for which we are in search, and which we have
failed to discover in the progressive and cumulative conquest of the
external environment, either human or physical, lies rather in a
progressive change of emphasis and transfer of energy and shifting
of the scene of action out of this field into another field in which—
as we have noted already in passing[2]—the action of Challenge-and-
Response may find an alternative arena. In this other field, challenges do not impinge from outside but arise from within, and
victorious responses to challenges do not take the form of surmounting an external obstacle or overcoming an external adversary
but manifest themselves, instead, in an inward self-articulation or
self-determination. When we watch an individual human being
or a human society making successive responses to a succession of
challenges, and when we ask ourselves the question whether this
particular series of responses to challenges is to be interpreted as
a manifestation of growth, we shall arrive at the answer to our
question through observing whether, as the series proceeds, the
action does or does not tend to shift from the first to the second of
the two fields aforesaid. The presence or absence of this tendency
gives us our criterion for the presence or absence of growth; and
we may add that it is always a tendency that is in question; for,
if we look narrowly, we shall find it impossible to cite a case of
Challenge-and-Response in which the entire action takes place on
either the one or the other of our two fields exclusively. Even in
those responses which look like sheer conquests of an external
environment at first sight, an element of inward self-determination
can always be detected as well and, conversely, there is always some

---

[1] *Pace* the dictum that *Natura non facit saltum*: a view which cannot be reconciled
with our present insight into the inwardness of natural phenomena.
[2] See III. B, p. 126, and III. C (i) (a), p. 128, above.

residue of action in the external area, even when the shifting of the scene of action to the internal arena has been carried as far as it will go. The action is never fought solely on one single field in any of those successive bouts of Challenge-and-Response in which the victorious responses accumulate into growths. At the same time, if growth is being achieved, this implies that, in each successive bout, the action on the external field is counting for less, and the action on the internal field for more, in deciding the issue between victory and defeat.

This truth comes out very clearly in those presentations of history in which the attempt is made to describe processes of growth exclusively in terms of the external field from start to finish. Let us take as examples two outstanding presentations in these terms which are each the work of a man of genius : Monsieur Edmond Demolins' *Comment la Route Crée le Type Social*,[1] and *The Outline of History* which has been written by Mr. H. G. Wells.[2]

The environmentalist thesis is set out by Monsieur Demolins in his preface[3] with uncompromising terseness :

'Il existe à la surface du globe terrestre une infinie variété de populations; quelle est la cause qui a créé cette variété? . . . La cause première et décisive de la diversité des races, *c'est la route que les peuples ont suivie.* C'est la route qui crée la race et qui crée le type social.'

When this provocative manifesto fulfils its purpose by stimulating us to read the substance of the book in which the author's thesis is worked out, we find that he manages quite well so long as he is drawing his illustrations from the life of societies which have remained on the primitive level. In such cases, the state of society can be explained with approximate accuracy and completeness in terms of responses to challenges from the external environment exclusively; but this, of course, is not an explanation of growth, since these primitive societies are now static. Monsieur Demolins is equally successful in explaining the state of the arrested civilizations. He has done a brilliant piece of work in his chapter on the Eurasian Nomads. But conditions are static here again; and this chapter, which comes first in the book, is also an acme, with all the rest of the book for its anti-climax. When the author applies his formula to patriarchal village communities, the reader begins to be uneasy. The explanation seems too plausible, the course too much plain sailing. In the chapters on Carthage and Venice, one feels sure that he has left something out, without being able quite to say

[1] Demolins, E.: *Comment la Route Crée le Type Social*. (Paris, no date, Firmin-Didot, 2 vols.)
[2] Wells, H. G.: *The Outline of History* (London 1920, Cassell).
[3] Demolins, op. cit., vol. i, p. vii.

what this omission may be. When he seeks to explain the Pytha-
gorean philosophy in terms of a portage-trade across the Toe of
Italy, one feels tempted to smile, but checks oneself in deference to
Monsieur Demolins' impressive ability and disarming enthusiasm.
But the chapter entitled 'La Route des Plateaux—Les Types Al-
banais et Hellène' pulls one up short. Albanian Barbarism and
Hellenic Civilization to be unhesitatingly bracketed together, just
because their respective exponents happen to have arrived once
upon a time at their respective geographical destinations by way of
the same *terrain*! And the great human adventure and human experience which we know as Hellenism to be reduced to a kind of
epiphenomenal by-product of the Balkan plateaux! In this un-
lucky chapter, the argument of *Comment la Route Crée le Type
Social* confutes itself by a palpable *reductio ad absurdum*. When a
civilization goes so far in its growth as the Hellenic Civilization went
before it suffered breakdown, an attempt to describe its growth
exclusively in terms of responses to challenges from the external
environment becomes positively ridiculous.

Mr. Wells, again, seems to lose his sureness of touch when he
handles something mature instead of handling something primitive.
He is in his element when he is exercising his imaginative powers in
order to reconstruct some dramatic episode in some remote æon of
Geological Time. His story of how 'these little theriomorphs, these
ancestral mammals', survived when the overgrown reptiles went
under is almost worthy to rank with the Biblical saga of David and
Goliath, and in its own vein it is inimitable. As we read the passage,[1]
we look forward eagerly to coming chapters, in which this brilliant
mind is to play upon the famous events of human history; but
we are destined to experience a certain disappointment. When
the little theriomorphs turn into Palaeolithic Hunters or Eurasian
Nomads, Mr. Wells, like Monsieur Demolins, still comes up to our
expectations; and he does passably well when some individual
theriomorph, here and there, develops the personality of a Ts'in
She Hwangti, or even the personality of a Nabonidus. But he comes
to grief in the recent annals of our own Western history when he
has to size up that singularly etherialized theriomorph William Ewart
Gladstone. In appreciating—or failing to appreciate—Mr. Gladstone, Mr. Wells has allowed his judgement to be perverted by
conscious prejudice and—still graver intellectual crime—by involuntary obtuseness. No doubt, in Mr. Wells's own mind, his
passing references to Mr. Gladstone, whether felicitous or not, are
only a niggling detail in the great sweep of his historical panorama;
and yet, in a sense, they are a touchstone for trying the quality of the

[1] Wells, op. cit., pp. 22–4. The passage is quoted textually in IV. C (iii) (c) 2 (γ),
vol. iv. pp. 426–7, below.

whole monumental work. For, in handling Mr. Gladstone, Mr. Wells is handling a great man of his own culture and his own country and his own century; and, to an author with Mr. Wells's imaginative gift, such a subject offers an opportunity of apprehending human character, not by a mere description and classification and docketing of the outer man, but by an intuitive sympathy of one soul with another. Mr. Wells has failed to rise to the occasion here because he has failed to transfer his spiritual treasure, as his narrative proceeds, from the Macrocosm to the Microcosm; and this failure reveals the limitations of the magnificent intellectual achievement which *The Outline of History* represents.[1]

Mr. Wells's failure may be measured by Shakespeare's success in solving the same problem. If we arrange the outstanding characters of the great Shakespearian gallery in an ascending order of etherialization, and if we bear in mind the fact that the playwright's technique is to reveal characters by displaying personalities in action, we shall observe that, as Shakespeare moves upward from the lower to the higher levels in our character-scale, he constantly shifts the field of action in which he makes the hero of each drama play his part, and shifts it always in the same direction—giving the Microcosm an ever larger share of the stage and pushing the Macrocosm ever farther into the background. We can verify this fact if we follow our series of Shakespearian heroes from Henry V through Macbeth to Hamlet. The relatively primitive character of Henry V is revealed almost entirely in his responses to challenges from the human environment around him: in his relations with his boon-companions and his relations with his father and in his communication of his own high courage to his comrades-in-arms on the morning of Agincourt, and in his impetuous wooing of Queen Kate. When we pass to Macbeth, we find the scene of action shifting; for Macbeth's relations with Malcolm or Macduff, and even his relations with Lady Macbeth, are equalled in importance, in the action of the play, by the hero's own relations with himself. Finally, when we come to Shakespeare's revelation of Hamlet, we see him allowing the Macrocosm almost to fade away, until the hero's relations with his father's murderers, and with his spent flame Ophelia, and with his outgrown mentor Horatio, become absorbed into the internal conflict which is working itself out in the hero's own soul. In Hamlet, the field of action has been transferred from the Macrocosm to the Microcosm almost completely; and in this masterpiece of Shakespeare's art, as in Aeschylus's Prometheus or in Browning's *Dramatic*

---

[1] This criticism of *The Outline of History* is made with all respect, in the belief that frankness in criticism is the best evidence of sincerity in appreciation. For a positive appreciation of Mr. Wells's achievement as an historian, see Part I. A, vol. i, pp. 4–5, above.

Monologues, a single actor virtually monopolizes the outward stage, in order to leave the greater scope for action to the surging spiritual forces which this one personality holds within him.

This transference of the field of action, which we discern in Shakespeare's presentation of his heroes when we arrange these fictitious personalities in an ascending order of spiritual growth, can also be discerned in the histories of civilizations. Here too, when a series of responses to challenges accumulates into a growth, we shall find, as this growth proceeds, that the field of action is shifting, all the time, from the external environment of the growing society into the interior of the society's own body social.

For example, we have noticed above, in another connexion, that, when our Western forefathers in France and England succeeded in repelling the onslaught which the Scandinavians made upon Western Christendom in the earliest age of our Western history, one of the means by which they achieved this signal victory over their human environment was by forging the potent military and social instru-ment of the Feudal System.[1] The creation of the Feudal System was of the essence of the Western response to the Scandinavian challenge; and we may now go on to observe that Feudalism was also the element in this response that caused its momentary equili-brium to overbalance and thus opened the way for the Promethean *élan* of our Western life to pass the dead point that is reached whenever a challenge is successfully met, and to make the transit from one dynamic bout of Challenge-and-Response to another. The social and economic and political differentiation between different classes of society, which Feudalism entailed, set up certain stresses and strains in the structure of the Western Society; and these strains produced the next challenge with which the growing society was confronted. Western Christendom had hardly rested from its labours in beating back the Vikings before it found its next task in the problem of replacing the Feudal System of relations between classes by a new system of relations between sovereign states and their individual citizens.[2] In this example of two successive challenges in the history of our Western Civilization, the shift of the scene of action from the exterior to the interior field is plainly apparent.

We can observe the same tendency in other passages of history which we have likewise examined already in different contexts.

In Hellenic history, for example,[3] we have seen that the earlier challenges in the series of challenges and responses of which Hel-

[1] See Part II. D (v), vol. ii, pp. 199–200, above, with the quotations there given from Paul Vinogradoff's *English Society in the Eleventh Century* (Oxford 1908, Clarendon Press). See further op. cit., pp. 88–9.
[2] For the role of this challenge in Western history, see further III. C (ii)(b), p. 343, below.
[3] See Part III. B, pp. 120–2, and the present chapter, section (a), pp. 139–40, above.

lenic history consists all emanated from the external environment. The earliest challenge of all was the human challenge of the highlanders to the lowlanders in Hellas itself. The victorious lowlanders were then exposed to the physical challenge of the Malthusian problem; and they met it by an expansion overseas which exposed them to a new human challenge from the rival Phoenician and Etruscan colonists of the Western Mediterranean and from the indigenous barbarians. This challenge was actually presented when the expansion of the Greeks was checked for some two centuries (*circa* 525–325 B.C.) by the counter-pressure of their non-Greek neighbours[1]—a counter-pressure which became so strong that Hellas was thrown on to the defensive and was compelled, in the critical year 480 B.C., to fight for her existence on two fronts simultaneously: against the Carthaginians in Sicily and against Xerxes in Continental European Greece itself. Thereafter, this formidable challenge from the human environment was triumphantly surmounted in the course of the four centuries beginning with Alexander's passage of the Hellespont. Alexander overthrew the Achaemenian Empire, and thereby opened the way for Hellenism to dominate the main body of the Syriac World, and the Egyptiac and Babylonic and Indic worlds into the bargain. The Romans overthrew the Carthaginian Empire and gained the upper hand over the European barbarians— thus opening the way for a fresh expansion of Hellenism towards the west on a scale commensurate with the eastward expansion that had been inaugurated by Alexander. Thanks to these triumphs of Macedonian and Roman arms, the Hellenic Society now enjoyed a respite of some five or six centuries—from the latter part of the fourth century B.C. to the early decades of the third century of the Christian Era—during which no serious challenge from the external environment was presented to it. During those centuries, the Hellenic Society was dominant over all other societies—civilizations and barbarisms alike—that came within its range, and dominant over Physical Nature likewise. It was not until the third century of the Christian Era that the external environment obtruded itself upon the Hellenic World once again by presenting simultaneously the economic challenge of diminishing returns from the social institution of the city-state[2] and a military challenge from the Sasanian Power on the Euphrates and from barbarian war-bands on other frontiers of the Roman Empire. During the five or six preceding centuries, the Hellenic World was practically exempt from challenges emanating from the external environment, either physical

---

[1] See the quotations from Herodotus and Thucydides on p. 139, above.
[2] See Rostovtzeff, M.: *The Social and Economic History of the Roman Empire* (Oxford 1926, Clarendon Press), *passim*.

or human, for the first time in Hellenic history. But this did not mean that, during those centuries, the Hellenic Society was exempt from challenges altogether. On the contrary, as we have noted already, these centuries were a period of decline: that is to say, a period in which Hellenism was being confronted by challenges to which it was failing to respond with success. We have seen what these challenges were; and, if we now look into them again, we shall observe that they were all of them new versions of old challenges which had been met victoriously in the external field but had been translated, in that very act, from the environment of the Hellenic Society into the society's own internal life.

For example, the external challenge of Achaemenian and Carthaginian military pressure had stimulated the Hellenic Society in self-defence to forge two potent social and military instruments—the Athenian Navy and the Syracusan Tyrannis—and these two instruments had performed their immediate function by giving Hellas the strength to fling back her external assailants. But the same instruments also produced certain stresses and strains in the internal structure of the Hellenic body social—a competition for hegemony between Athens and Sparta, a degeneration of the Athenians' hegemony over their maritime allies into a tyranny, and a reaction against Syracuse on the part of both her Sicilian barbarian subjects and her Sicilian Greek allies—and these new internal stresses and strains presented the Hellenic Society with a fresh challenge which it failed to meet: a failure which resulted in social breakdown. Thus a challenge which had originally presented itself, in 480 B.C., as an impact of external political forces reappeared in 431 B.C. as a conflict of political forces which were all internal to the Hellenic body social.

In the next chapter of Hellenic history, corresponding effects followed from the expansion of Hellenism, east and west, in the tracks of the Macedonian and the Roman armies. The military victories of Hellenic arms, which exempted Hellenism from any further external challenges for some five or six hundred years, could only achieve this result by transferring the field of Challenge-and-Response from outside to inside the ambit of the Hellenic World. The long military struggles of Hellenism with its external enemies—the Achaemenidae and the Carthaginians and the Barbarians—were brought to a victorious close by Alexander and the Scipios, only to be translated forthwith into the civil wars of rival Macedonian diadochi and rival Roman dictators. The economic competition between the Hellenic and Syriac societies for the mastery of the Western Mediterranean reappeared within the bosom of the Hellenic Society, after the Syriac competitor had succumbed, in the still more devastating domestic warfare between the gangs of

Oriental plantation-slaves and their Siceliot or Roman masters—a warfare which was carried on in the former arena of the Carthagino-Syracusan and Carthagino-Roman Wars.[1] The cultural conflict between Hellenism and the Oriental civilizations—Syriac and Egyptiac and Babylonic and Indic—likewise reappeared within the bosom of the Hellenic Society, after the Hellenic culture had successfully asserted its supremacy over the others, as an internal crisis in Hellenic, or Hellenized, souls: the crisis that declared itself in the emergence of Isis-worship and Astrology and the Mahayana and Mithraism and Christianity and a host of other syncretistic religions.

> They cease not fighting, East and West,
> On the marches of my breast.[2]

In our own Western history, so far as it has gone up to date, we can detect a corresponding trend. In earlier ages, the most conspicuous of the challenges with which Western Christendom had to contend were presented by the human environment. In its infancy, Western Christendom had to hold its own against the Arab empire-builders of a new Syriac universal state in the Iberian Peninsula and against the abortive Far Western Christian and Scandinavian civilizations along its Atlantic seaboard and against the Continental European barbarians. In the age of the Crusades, when the Western Christians expanded temporarily over the Mediterranean and permanently over the Baltic, they were expanding at the expense of other societies: the Muslims and the Orthodox Christians and the surviving Continental European barbarians. Thereafter, their expansion was temporarily checked by the successful resistance of their victims, and they were subjected in their turn to counter-pressure from formidable alien powers: on one front from the Muscovites and on others from the 'Osmanlis. And after that, again, the West broke out into its latter-day expansion: a movement which is comparable, scale for scale, with the feats performed in Hellenic history by the Macedonians and the Romans, and which has brought the West into collision with the whole of the non-Western World.

Our modern Western expansion has been literally world-wide; and for the time being, at any rate, it has relieved us completely from our old pre-occupation with challenges from alien human societies. The last challenge of the kind in our modern history was presented some two-and-a-half centuries ago, when the 'Osmanlis

[1] For this Hellenic plantation-slavery, see Part II. D (vi), vol. ii, pp. 213–16, and the present chapter, section (b), pp. 169–71, above.
[2] Housman, A. E.: *A Shropshire Lad*, xxviii. The lines are equally applicable to the religious war in France which was waged in the sixteenth century between Catholicism and Protestantism and which reappeared in the seventeenth century—within the bosom of a victorious Catholic Church which had driven the Huguenots off the field—as the controversy between the Jesuits and the Jansenists.

made their second attempt to capture Vienna; and, since the
failure of that last great Ottoman offensive in A.D. 1683, *Homo
Occidentalis* has forgotten how it feels to face a serious menace from
an external human force. Since that day he has constantly inspired
this feeling in others, without ever again experiencing it himself,
until, in these latter days, he has attained a position of world-wide
dominance which is absolute on the economic plane and pre-
ponderant on the political plane, while even on the cultural plane
it is at any rate unrivalled.

The only semblance of an effective external challenge which has
been presented to *Homo Occidentalis* since the 'Osmanlis raised
their siege of Vienna in 1683 has been the challenge of Bolshevism,
which has confronted the Western World since Lenin and his companions made themselves masters of the *ci-devant* Russian Empire
in the second Russian revolution of 1917. Yet Bolshevism, for all
its breathings of fire and slaughter, has not yet seriously threatened
the ascendancy of our Western Civilization, as we know it, outside
the frontiers of the U.S.S.R.; and even if one day the Communist
dispensation were to fulfil the Russian Communists' hopes by
spreading from Russia over the whole face of the planet, a world-
wide triumph of Communism over Capitalism would not mean the
overthrow of the present world-wide supremacy of the Western
Civilization by an alien culture, since Communism, unlike Islam, is
itself derived from a Western source. In its origin, the Communist
doctrine is a nineteenth-century Western criticism of the nineteenth-century Western social order; and the adoption of this
exotic Western doctrine as the revolutionary creed of twentieth-
century Russia, so far from signifying that the ascendancy of Western
culture is in jeopardy, really shows how potent this ascendancy has
come to be.[1]

There is a profound ambiguity in the nature of Bolshevism which
is manifested in Lenin's career. Did Lenin come to fulfil or to
destroy the work of Peter the Great? And does the substitution of
Lenin's for Peter's name in the translation of Petersburg into Lenin-
grad signify that Lenin has made or marred the fortune of the city
which Peter founded? In re-transferring the capital of Russia from
an eccentric position on the western threshold of the country to a

[1] The truth that the Russians could not succeed in establishing an ascendancy over
the Western World except in so far as they had previously succeeded in Westernizing
their own way of life, was already apparent to Gibbon, as may be seen from a passage
in the 'General Observations on the Fall of the Roman Empire in the West' at the end of
chapter xxxviii of *The History of the Decline and Fall of the Roman Empire*:
'Europe is secure from any future irruption of barbarians; since, before they can
conquer, they must cease to be barbarous. Their gradual advances in the science of war
would always be accompanied, as we may learn from the example of Russia, with a
proportionable improvement in the arts of peace and civil policy; and they themselves
must deserve a place among the polished nations whom they subdue.'

central position in the interior,[1] Lenin seems to be proclaiming himself the successor of the Arch-Priest Avvakum[2] and the Old Believers and the Slavophils. Here, we feel, is a prophet of Holy Russia who has been great enough to gather up into his own career and personality the whole reaction of the Russian soul against the Western Civilization—a reaction which had been gathering momentum during the two centuries that had passed since the ordeal of Westernization was first forced upon Russia by Peter. And yet, when Lenin casts about for a creed to express this spiritual revolt, he does not find an anti-Western creed of Russian origin. There is a significant touch of irony in the fact that he is constrained to arm Russia for her fight against the West with a borrowed Western weapon, and to take his indictment of the Western Civilization at second-hand from a Western critic: the German Jew Karl Marx.

It is true that the Marxian creed comes nearer to a total repudiation of the Western order of society than any other creed of Western origin which a twentieth-century Russian prophet could have adopted. And this explains the paradox that a Utopia which was conceived in a Western environment, as a protest against the industrialization of Western life, should have been erected for the first time into an officially established social régime in a non-Western country in which the process of Westernization had hardly gone skin-deep, and in which the solvent of Industrialism had not yet begun to disintegrate the primitive agrarian economy which was the traditional economic basis of the Russian Society. It was the negative and not the positive element in the Marxian creed—its denials and not its affirmations—that made it congenial to a Russian revolutionary mind; and this explains why in Russia, in 1917, the exotic Western apparatus of capitalism was successfully overthrown by the equally exotic Western doctrine of Communism. This explanation is borne out by the metamorphosis which the Marxian philosophy appears to be undergoing in the Russian atmosphere. For in Russia, since 1917, we seem to see Marxism turning, before our eyes, into an emotional and intellectual substitute for Orthodox Christianity, with Marx for its Moses and Lenin for its Messiah and their collected works for the Scriptures of this new atheistic Russian Church Militant. In this apparent metamorphosis of Marxism, it looks, at first glance, as though, in Russia, the spirit of the intrusive Western Civilization had been overcome at last, and the indigenous spirit of the Orthodox Christian Civilization had reasserted itself. But the phenomena take on a different aspect when we turn our

[1] For this oscillation of the capital of modern Russia between Moscow and Petersburg, see Part II. D (v), vol. ii, pp. 157–8, above, and Part IX, below.
[2] See *The Life of the Archpriest Avvakum, by himself,* translated by J. E. Harrison and Hope Mirrlees (London 1924, Woolf).

attention from faith to works, and examine what Lenin and his successors have actually been doing to the Russian people.

When we ask ourselves what is the significance of the Five Years' Plan, we are constrained to answer that, whether the Plan be destined, in the long run, to succeed or to fail, there can be no mistake about its intention. This is an attempt to mechanize agriculture as well as industry and transportation, to change a nation of peasants into a nation of mechanics, to transform the old Russia into a new America. In other words, it is a latter-day attempt at Westernization which is so ambitious and so radical and so ruthless that it puts Peter the Great's work into the shade. If Peter could have had foreknowledge of this Bolshevik Five Years' Plan, he would have gasped. 'I only chastised these miserable Russians with whips', he would have exclaimed, 'but my audacious successors are chastising them with scorpions! I only scratched the surface of Russian life, but these giants, with their mighty engines, are ploughing up the Russian soil and pulling up the tree of indigenous Russian culture by the roots!' Thus, willy-nilly, the prophet Lenin and his successors are playing Balaam's and not Jonah's part. They are working—and this with demoniac energy—to ensure the triumph in Russia of the very civilization which they are denouncing in the World at large. No doubt they dream of creating a new society which will be American in equipment but Russian in soul. Yet this is a strange dream to be dreamed by statesmen for whom a materialistic and deterministic interpretation of History is an article of faith! On Marxian principles, we must expect that, if a Russian peasant is taught to do the work and live the life of an American mechanic, the peasant will also learn to think as the mechanic thinks and to feel as he feels and to desire what he desires. And in this tug-of-war which we are witnessing in Russia between the ideals of Lenin and the methods of Ford we may look forward to seeing the modern ascendancy of the Western over the Russian Civilization paradoxically confirmed.

The ambiguity in Lenin's career, which we have just analysed, is likewise apparent in the career of the Russian prophet's Hindu contemporary and compeer Gandhi, whose involuntary furtherance of the same ubiquitous process of Westernization is still more ironical. The Hindu prophet sets out to sever the threads of cotton which have entangled India in the activities of the Western World. 'Spin and weave our Indian cotton', he preaches, 'with your Indian hands. Do not any longer clothe yourselves in the products of Western power-looms; and do not, I conjure you, seek to drive those alien products out of the Indian market by setting up on Indian soil new Indian power-looms on the Western pattern!' This message, which is Gandhi's real message,[1] is not accepted by Gandhi's countrymen. They revere the spirit of the saint, but they only follow his guidance in so far as he resigns himself to leading them along the path of Westernization. And thus we see Gandhi to-day promoting a political movement with a Western programme —the transformation of India into a sovereign independent parliamentary state—and with a Western procedure (the whole Western political apparatus of conferences, resolutions, votes, platforms, newspapers, and publicity). In this political campaign, the prophet's most effective—though not his most obtrusive—supporters are those very Indian industrialists who have done the most to defeat the prophet's real mission—the men who have acclimatized the technique of Western industrialism in India itself. Their factory chimneys, which the prophet, in his heart of hearts, must regard with dismay, rise almost within view of his retreat at Sabarmati.[2] Stranger still, Western thoughts colour and inform the prophet's own mind. He seeks inspiration in Western works of philosophy and devotion at least as much as in the Hindu Scriptures[3].

In this spiritual travail of a Gandhi and a Lenin in our generation, we can watch the impact of the Western Civilization upon Hinduism and upon Russian Orthodox Christendom in the act of transformation from an external encounter between the Western Society and its neighbours into an inner experience of a Westernized World. Strive as they will to win a decisive victory for an anti-Western reaction, the Hindu and the Russian zealot of these latter days can only succeed in giving an impetus to the very process of Westernization against which they are up in arms. The life and energy with which they inspire their anti-Western 'holy wars' is actually drawn—and this is the secret of its vigour—from a Western source; and thus, in the crucible of these ardent souls, an anti-Western movement is transmuted into a new manifestation of the spiritual force against which it is directed. A Gandhi and a Lenin find it impossible to take spiritual action without being moved by the spirit of the Western Civilization; and, conversely, the Western-born heirs of this Western Civilization find it impossible to be indifferent to the thoughts and feelings and acts of a Gandhi and a Lenin. We are aware that, in the titanic careers of these two Janus-faced figures, our own Western destinies are involved, as they were never involved in the careers of a Sivaji or an Ivan the Terrible or a

[1] For Gandhi's role as a preacher of simplification and etherialization, see pp. 190–1, above.

[2] For the discord between Ancient and Modern in the architecture of the City of Ahmadabad, see Toynbee, A. J.: *A Journey to China* (London 1931, Constable), ch. xxi, pp. 140–4.

[3] For the Christian element in the Mahatma Gandhi's inspiration, see p. 191, above.

Saladin or a Suleymān or any other champion of an alien civilization who has taken up the challenge of our Western power without
being touched, in his own soul, by the influence of the Western
spirit. It is as though this Western spirit were a kind of psychic
electricity which had now electrified the whole of Mankind with
such effect that there could no longer be any exertion of human
psychic force which was not either a positive or a negative charge
of this all-pervasive Western current.

This change which is signalized in the careers of Gandhi and
Lenin is not confined to the relations of the West with the two once
alien societies that have now given those two great personalities to
a Westernized World. The transformation of an external conflict
between two separate societies into an internal conflict in the bosom
of one of the two, when this one has succeeded in absorbing the
other into its own body social, is a phenomenon which might be
illustrated alternatively from the history of the relations between the
modern West and any of the other societies with which the West
has come into contact in the course of its world-wide expansion in
these latter days. In fact, the virtual elimination of external challenges emanating from the human environment, which has been
one of the remarkable features of our Western history during the
last two hundred and fifty years, has been followed by the presentation of equivalent challenges in the internal life of a Western Society
which has expanded into an oecumenical system. On the economic
plane, one of these transmuted challenges is the new problem arising
from the differences in standards of living which continue to divide
different fractions of Mankind after they have been brought into
economic relations with one another by the world-wide nexus of
our modern Western commerce and industry and finance. On the
political plane, the challenge of 'holy wars' waged by alien civilizations against Western Christendom has been transmuted, since the
triumph of the West over these external adversaries, into a Western
problem of 'imperialism' and 'colonial administration'. On the
cultural plane, the conflict between Western culture and alien cultures has been transmuted into a conflict, within the bosom of a
Western-made 'Great Society', between different classes and different races.

Corresponding transmutations of external into internal challenges
have followed the triumph of the Western Civilization over its
material environment—a victory which it has won with its left hand
while its right hand has been occupied in mastering its human
neighbours. In this material sphere, the process of transference
comes out very clearly in the recent economic history of Great
Britain: the country in which the modern Western Industrialism

first emerged a century-and-a-half ago in order to spread thereafter far and wide over the World, as molten lava flows abroad over
the landscape from the crater through which it has welled up out
of the depths of the Earth.

In England, the first round of the stubborn contest between Man
and Physical Nature out of which the new force of Industrialism
arose was fought under the same conditions as the first bout in the
mythical wrestling-match at Peniel between Jacob and the angel,[1]
when Jacob's superhuman adversary immobilized the human combatant by putting out of joint the hollow of his thigh. On the eve
of the triumph of Man over Physical Nature which inaugurated the
Industrial Revolution, the pioneers of Industrialism in England
found themselves caught and held by the geographical location of
the raw materials and the potential sources of mechanical power
which they were striving to make subject to their own human wills.
The potters were constrained to establish their potteries where they
happened to find the beds of potter's clay, and the iron smelters
their furnaces at some half-way house between the deposits of the
ore from which their metal was to be extracted and the seams of
the coal by which the operation was to be performed. Even the
textile manufacturers were constrained to aline their mills along the
foot of the Pennines, in order to tap the streams descending from
the fells for water-power to drive their machinery.[2] At this stage,
Physical Nature was able to dictate to Man the place where he
should try conclusions with her; and the industrial map of England
was governed by the geological and physiographical map *a priori*.

In the next stage, Man triumphed over Nature as Jacob overcame the angel at the breaking of the day, when he refused to let
him go unless he would give him his blessing. In this second round
of the contest, the fathers of Industrialism solved the problem of
transportation and thereby liberated their industrial operations
from their previous bondage to the vagaries of Geology and
Physiography.

'Where does that there clay come from?' asked Edwin. For not
merely was he honestly struck by a sudden new curiosity, but it was
meet for him to behave like a man now, and to ask manly questions.

'Runcorn,' said 'the Sunday' scornfully. 'Can't you see it painted all
over the boat?'

'Why do they bring clay all the way from Runcorn?'

'They don't bring it from Runcorn. They bring it from Cornwall.
It comes round by sea—see?' He laughed.

'Who told you?' Edwin roughly demanded.

[1] Genesis xxxii. 24-32.
[2] For the original location of the industrial districts in England, see Part II. D (ii),
vol. ii, pp. 60-4, above.

'Anybody knows that!' said 'the Sunday' grandly, but always maintaining his gay smile.

'Seems devilish funny to me,' Edwin murmured, after reflection, 'that they should bring clay all that round-about way just to make crocks of it here. Why should they choose just *this* place to make crocks in? I always understood . . .'

'Oh! Come on!' 'the Sunday' cut him short. 'It's blessed well one o'clock and after!' . . .

'The Sunday' was satisfied with his bit of accidental knowledge. Edwin was not. Edwin wanted to know why, if the clay for making earthenware was not got in the Five Towns, the Five Towns had become the great seat of the manufacture. Why were not pots made in the South, where the clay came from?[1]

We know, of course, the answer to this question which an English novelist, born and bred in the Staffordshire potteries in the latter part of the nineteenth century, has placed in the mouth of one of his characters whom he presents to his readers as his own fellow-townsman and contemporary. Long before the end of the nineteenth century, the invention of the steamship and the railroad had made it possible for the potter to fetch his clay, and the iron-master his ore, and the textile-manufacturer his raw wool and cotton, not only from the other end of England but from the very ends of the Earth, and to carry the stuff so cheaply that the cost of transportation did not wipe out or even perceptibly diminish the manufacturer's profits. And why—as Edwin Clayhanger went on to ask—did Muhammad prefer to perform the *tour de force* of making the mountain come to him instead of taking the line of lesser resistance and migrating, himself, to the mountain? 'Why were not pots made in the South, where the clay came from?' Why had the Five Towns in Staffordshire not only become, but remained, the great seat of manufacture? The answer was that, in the course of a century, as industrial technique had gone from strength to strength, the relative importance of the two fundamental factors in industry had gradually shifted. In the eighteenth century, the dominant factor in pot-making had been the clay, which dictated to the potter the place where he should set up shop. A century later, the dominion had passed from Physical Nature to Man, until the site of the Potteries had come to be determined no longer by the location of the raw material, but rather by the local presence or absence of the human skill that fashioned the clay into pots. In the geographical nexus between the clay and the potter, the original relations were thus actually inverted. In the eighteenth century, the potter had gone to Staffordshire to find his clay; in the nineteenth

---

[1] Arnold Bennett: *Clayhanger*, Bk. I, chs. (i) and (ii).

century, when the Staffordshire clay-beds had become utterly inadequate to supply the needs of an industry which had increased
the scale of its operations in the meantime by a hundred or a thousand fold, the clay was coming to Staffordshire from Cornwall to
find its potter. And thus the Five Towns remained the great seat
of the manufacture for a different reason from that which had
caused them to become the seat of the manufacture originally. In
the beginning, the lode-stone had been the clay; in the next chapter of the story, the magnetic power had come to be transferred
from the inanimate clay to the human skill which the clay had
originally attracted to itself.

If we now turn our attention from the industry of clay to the industries of metal and of fibre, a further chapter in the history of
Industrialism unfolds itself. For when once human skill has established its ascendancy over raw materials and over mechanical
driving force as the dominant factor in industrial production, it is
only a matter of time for the volatile human spirit to break loose
from its obsolete material moorings and to blow where it lists.

In the metal industry in England, this tendency has been perceptible since the close of the General War of 1914–18, as the
corollary of a technical change: the transfer of plant and capital
from the production of the old-fashioned staple heavy-work to that
of newfangled implements—such as motor-cars—in which the
sheer bulk of mineral consumed in the productive process counts
for very much less in proportion to the amount of the human skill
which is brought into play. In 1931, it was remarked by a sharp-
sighted French observer of English social life that

'One can already perceive a spontaneous movement of population
from the north of England towards the south, from the mining areas
towards London and the Thames Valley. This tentative migration may
be considered as the first visible after-effect of the attack on the coal
monopoly. In the nineteenth century the centre of gravity of the British
economic structure was irresistibly attracted towards the coal basins of
the north; the twentieth century may produce a new equilibrium, less
strictly dependent on the Black Country.'[1]

In the cotton industry—which operates with a raw material that
is vastly lighter than that employed in even the most finikin lines of
our 'post-war' metallurgy—the liberation of human skill from the
bondage of gross matter has become virtually complete. In this
industry, the skill once mobilized by water-power in Lancashire
and New England has been able to attract to itself, from the ends of
the Earth, a raw material which cannot be produced at all by the
local soil and climate of New England or Lancashire themselves;

[1] Siegfried, A.: *England's Crisis* (London 1931, Cape), pp. 125–6.

and, in the next chapter of this story, the diffusion of the skill which used to be concentrated in the classic seats of the industry has been equally wide in its range. At the present time, the raw cotton is produced in almost every part of the tropical and sub-tropical belt in which the soil and water required for cotton cultivation can be found; and at the same time the World's cotton-crop is spun into cotton-thread and woven into cotton cloth in mills that are no longer confined to the purlieus of Manchester or Lowell, but have sprung up like mushrooms—east and west and north and south— round Kobe and Shanghai and Ahmadabad and on the Polish plains and on the piedmont of North Carolina.

In this thoroughgoing diffusion of the cotton industry, we have a classic instance of a challenge from the Physical Environment being met and mastered triumphantly by *Homo Faber*. And the result which has been attained in textiles to-day (and this in every stage of the economic process, from the production of the raw material to the marketing of the finished product) seems likely to be attained in other industries to-morrow. In fact, we may look forward to a time when Industry of all kinds will have shaken itself free from the ties of locality and will have solved the technical problem of per- forming its operations at any point on the surface of the Earth at which it may elect to instal itself. But the plight of the cotton in- dustry in the very hour of its technical victory plainly shows that the old contest between Man and Physical Nature has not really been transcended, but has rather been transmuted into a new con- flict between Man and Man.

The pioneers of the cotton industry wrestled with, and eventually triumphed over, the technical difficulties of cultivating the cotton plant, and of transporting the cotton crop from field to mill, and of carding and spinning and weaving the cotton fibre by mechanical power; but these very triumphs in the technical sphere have created new problems in the realm of human relations. The extension of the area of cotton-cultivation has produced a competition between the cotton-growers of America and Asia and Africa to supply the mills; the diffusion of the technique of cotton-manufacture has produced another competition between the manufacturers of Great Britain and New England and North Carolina and Japan and China and India and Poland to supply the world-market; and, over and above these local rivalries, a conflict of interests has arisen between Capital and Labour, and between Producers and Consumers. These human problems have been bequeathed to the latter-day heirs of the cotton industry by their predecessors, from whose victories over Physical Nature they have also inherited the solutions of those technical problems which used to obsess the industry in its infancy.

In this history of our modern Western cotton industry we can detect, once again, as we follow out a sequence of challenges and responses, the tendency for the scene of action to shift from the external environment to the internal life of the society or the individual that is the subject of the experience.

The self-same tendency appears in the history of the technique of communications, which has latterly played so important a role in our modern Western industrial development.

The invention of sailing-ships overcomes the barrier of the estranging sea; the invention of twin-screw steamships liberates the navigator from his bondage to the winds, even as an auxiliary or emergency source of driving-power. Again, the invention of the wheel enables Man to transport overland a load of greater bulk and weight than the maximum that he is capable of carrying on his own shoulders, while the invention of railways enables him to increase the load almost *ad infinitum* and to whirl it across the breadth of a continent almost as easily as a ship could waft it across the breadth of an ocean. Tunnels pierce the barriers interposed by mountains; six-wheeled motor-cars and caterpillar-tractors skim over quaking bogs and yielding sands; and finally aeroplanes make transportation wholly independent of sea and land and mountain and swamp and desert and all the other physical obstacles by which the movement of goods and persons was impeded so long as it was tied down to the aquatic and terrestrial surface of the globe. More wonderful still, we have now discovered means of communication between human intelligences which render the transportation of human bodies superfluous. For the arts of writing and telegraphy and telephony and television, and the organization of the newspaper press and the broadcasting radio, have lengthened the range of the human eye and ear and voice from a few miles or a few yards to the great circle of the Earth's circumference. The age-long human ambition to 'annihilate distance' has been realized at last in our day; but here again, in the act of overcoming a challenge presented by the external environment, we have evoked a new challenge in the internal field of our own social life. We have 'annihilated distance' by equipping our physical movements and our physical senses with a vastly enhanced material 'drive'; and this technical triumph—which has been achieved substantially within the last hundred and fifty years—has given 'the traffic problem' a wholly new meaning.

Let us call up in our minds the now fast-fading picture of the pre-mechanical road. This antique road is thronged with all kinds of primitive wheeled vehicles: wheel-barrows, and rickshaws, and ox-carts, and dog-carts, with the stage-coach as the *chef-d'œuvre* of muscular traction, and with a foot-propelled bicycle here and there as a portent of things to come. Since this road is already rather crowded, there are a certain number of collisions; but nobody minds, because nobody is hurt and the traffic is scarcely interrupted. For the fact is that these collisions are not serious. They cannot be serious, because the traffic is so slow, and the muscle-power—human, bovine, equine—by which the vehicles are propelled is so feeble, that these vehicles can collide and rebound without mishap. 'The traffic problem' on this road is not the problem of avoiding collisions, but the problem of hauling the loads and covering the distances. Accordingly, there is no sort of traffic-regulation: no policeman on point duty, and no system of signal-lights.

And now let us turn our eyes to the familiar road of to-day on which a mechanized traffic hums and roars. On this road, the problems of speed and of haulage have been solved, as is testified by this motor-lorry with its train of trucks that comes lumbering along with the momentum of a charging elephant, and by this sports-car that goes whizzing past with the swiftness of a bee or a bullet. But, by the same token, the problem of collisions has become 'the traffic problem' *par excellence*. For while the chauffeur commands a traction-power which puts the teamster out of the running so long as the chauffeur is competent and sober, a fool or a knave at the driving-wheel of a motor-vehicle is far more dangerous both to the public and to himself than a fool or a knave on the driver's seat of a hay-wagon. Hence, on this latter-day road, the crucial challenge is no longer technological but psychological. Instead of being concerned to transport larger and heavier loads at higher speeds, we are rather concerned nowadays to avoid collisions by regulating the traffic: by introducing a lighting-system, by teaching the drivers what the signals mean, and by having the road patrolled by police in order to see that these signals are obeyed. The old challenge of physical distance has been transmuted into a new challenge of human relations between drivers who have learned how to 'annihilate distance' and have thereby put themselves in constant danger of annihilating one another.

This change in the nature of the traffic problem on our roads has, of course, a symbolic as well as a literal significance. It typifies the general change that has occurred over the whole range of our modern Western social life since the emergence of the two dominant social forces of the age: the economic force of Industrialism and the political force of Democracy.[1] Owing to the extraordinary progress which our latter-day inventors have made in harnessing the energies of Physical Nature and in organizing the concerted action of millions

[1] For the rise of these two forces to their present position of supremacy, see Part I. A, *init*.

of human beings, everything that is now done, for good or evil, in our society is inevitably done with a stupendous 'drive'; and this has made the material consequences of individual acts far greater and the moral responsibility of the agents far heavier than these used to be under our previous social régime.[1] It may be that in every age of every society some moral issue is always the challenge that is fateful for the society's future; but, however that may be, there is no doubt, in the case in point, that it is a moral challenge and no longer a technical challenge that confronts our own society in our own day.

'In the present-day thinker's attitude towards what is called mechanical progress, we are conscious of a changed spirit. Admiration is tempered by criticism; complacency has given way to doubt; doubt is passing into alarm. There is a sense of perplexity and frustration, as in one who has gone a long way and finds he has taken the wrong turning. To go back is impossible: how shall he proceed? Where will he find himself if he follows this path or that? An old exponent of applied mechanics may be forgiven if he expresses something of the disillusion with which, now standing aside, he watches the sweeping pageant of discovery and invention in which he used to take unbounded delight. It is impossible not to ask: Whither does this tremendous procession tend? What, after all, is its goal? What its probable influence upon the future of the Human Race?

'The pageant itself is a modern affair. A century ago it had barely taken form, and had acquired none of the momentum which rather awes us to-day. The Industrial Revolution, as everybody knows, was of British origin; for a time our island remained the Factory of the World. But soon, as was inevitable, the change of habit spread; and now every country, even China, is become more or less mechanized. The cornucopia of the engineer has been shaken over all the Earth, scattering everywhere an endowment of previously unpossessed and unimagined capacities and powers.

'Beyond question many of these gifts are benefits to Man, making Life fuller, wider, healthier, richer in comforts and interests, and in such happiness as material things can promote. But we are acutely aware that the engineer's gifts have been and may be grievously abused. In some there is potential tragedy as well as present burden. Man was ethically unprepared for so great a bounty. In the slow evolution of morals he is still unfit for the tremendous responsibility it entails. The command of Nature has been put into his hands before he knows how to command himself.'

These moving words propound a question which has been struggling to find expression in all our hearts; and they are words spoken with authority, for they were uttered by the President of

[1] On this point see Toynbee, A. J.: *Survey of International Affairs: 1928* (London 1929, Milford), pp. 7-8.

the British Association for the Advancement of Science in his opening address at the hundred-and-first annual meeting of that historic body.[1] Is the new social driving-power of Industrialism and Democracy to be employed in the great constructive task of organizing a Westernized World into an oecumenical society in which the new forces may find free play to work on a world-wide scale for the benefit of all Mankind? Or are we going to turn our new power to our own destruction by putting its unprecedentedly powerful 'drive' into a number of ancient anti-social institutions—into War and Tribalism and Slavery and Property—at the risk of turning these once not wholly lethal vehicles of evil into veritable Juggernaut cars? This is the latter-day traffic-problem of our Western Civilization in its inward spiritual essence.[2]

The foregoing analysis of the latest chapter in our Western history incidentally throws light on a phenomenon in Egyptiac history which we have already noted for a fact without having hit upon the explanation: the ambiguous significance of the Pyramids as monuments of the breakdown as well as the triumph of the Egyptiac Civilization.[3] This ironic ambiguity is due, as we can perceive now by analogy, to a shift which occurred, in the Pyramid-Builders' age, in both the theatre and the nature of the challenge in which the Egyptiac Society's destiny was at stake.

When we inquired into the genesis of the Egyptiac Civilization,[4] we found that it had been brought to birth by the audacity and

[1] The full text of Sir Alfred Ewing's address on this occasion, which was delivered in York on the 31st August, 1932, will be found in *The Times* of the 1st September, 1932.

[2] The same simile of the traffic on the road has been drawn, with the same application, by Professor Gilbert Murray in a speech delivered in 1932 at the Annual General Meeting of the English National Federation of Women's Institutes:

'This is a time of rapid change. The ends of the Earth are being brought closer together. News travels all round the World in a few moments. People travel ever so much more and ever so much faster than they did in our grandmothers' time. The consequence is that all the civilized nations are crowded close together and constantly treading on each other's toes and, as always happens in a crowd, everyone has to be careful and considerate or else there will be trouble.

'Think of any of our big towns—Manchester, Liverpool, Glasgow, or London itself: think of the great stretches of country round them which used to be open fields or moors and which are now streets full of traffic. They used to be open fields and moors. Our fathers and grandfathers could gallop over those moors on horseback, could tear about wherever they liked, without any danger of running into other people or knocking them down. They need hardly ever think of anyone but themselves. The horse only went about twelve miles an hour and there was plenty of room in every direction. But now those moors have become crowded streets. People are driving about them in motors which go at thirty or forty miles an hour and there is no spare room at all. They have to be very careful indeed and always thinking about other people. They have to have red signs and green signs and policemen at point duty to direct them. They have to be very obedient. And even so they kill some four thousand people a year!

'That is exactly the change that has taken place in the World. The World has become crowded: people are moving about faster and faster and the engines that carry them are terribly powerful. There are all sorts of disastrous accidents waiting for us, unless we move with great care and particularly care for others. And when I say care for others I mean people other than ourselves, classes other than our own class and nations other than our own nation.'

[3] See the present chapter, section (a), p. 153, above, as well as I. C (ii), vol. i, pp. 141–3.

[4] See II. C (ii) (b) 2, vol. i, pp. 302–15, above.

determination of pioneers who had met the challenge of desiccation
on the Afrasian Steppe by plunging into the forbidding and apparently impenetrable jungle-swamp of the Lower Nile Valley and
turning the formless wilderness into a pattern of ditches and embankments and fruitful fields. This heroic victory of human wills
over the wantonness of Physical Nature demanded not only a sus-
tained individual courage, but also a continuous co-operative effort;
such co-operation demanded discipline; and the discipline through
which the fathers of the Egyptiac Civilization won the day in their
battle with the jungle-swamp was purchased at the price of sub-
ordinating the wills of the rank and file to the wills of a few outstanding leaders. Thus the physical ordeal out of which the Egyptiac
Civilization emerged, like the human ordeal which Western Christendom underwent in the Scandinavian onslaught, left a mark on the
internal articulation of the growing society in addition to the change
which it produced in the society's relations with its external environment.[1] By the time when this Egyptiac ordeal came to an end, the
water and soil and vegetation of the Lower Nile Valley were subject to the wills of human beings; and at the same time the great
majority of these human victors, in the very act of subduing
Physical Nature, had themselves fallen into subjection to a small
minority of their own human kind who happened to be endowed
with exceptional power of command or with exceptional intellectual
ability.

This differentiation in authority and knowledge and wealth and
prestige between the ruling minority and the subject majority in
the Egyptiac Society of 'the Old Kingdom' went to far greater
lengths than the corresponding differentiation between the social
positions of different classes in medieval Western Christendom
under the feudal régime. The command which the King of the
Two Lands, and his hierarchy of administrators and technicians
and priests, had acquired over the wills and imaginations and
actions and lives of the Egyptian peasantry was indeed as absolute
as the control which he had established, through this command of
'man-power', over the soil and water of the Land of Egypt itself.
In other words, the challenge originally presented to Man in the
encounter between Man and Nature in the Lower Nile Valley had
been transmuted into a challenge which found its arena—and
demanded its response—in the internal articulation of the new-
born Egyptiac Society.

The destinies of the Egyptiac Civilization now turned upon the

---

[1] For the internal effect of the Western Christian response to the Scandinavian
challenge upon the structure of the Western Christian Society, see II. D (v), vol. ii, pp.
199-200, and the present chapter, p. 196, above.

question of how the royal lord and master of Egypt and the Egyptians would use his enormous power. Would he respond to this new challenge, which was a moral challenge, in the spirit of Prometheus or in the spirit of Zeus?[1] Would he employ the material power and the 'man-power' at his command in order to improve the lot of the peasantry who had made him master of the material wealth of Egypt when they had placed at his disposal their own human wills? Would he lead them onward and upward to the level of the well-being that had been attained already by the King himself and by his handful of peers? Or would the dizzy height of his pinnacle upset the King of Egypt's moral and intellectual balance? As he surveyed his Land of Egypt and saw that it was very good, would he yield to the illusion that he, and he only, was its creator? Would he forget that, without the disciplined co-operation of a docile peasantry, the King alone could have created nothing? And would he treat the wealth and power which was the co-operative product of an entire society as though it were his private property, to be devoted to his own gratification and glorification in this life and to his immortalization in the life to come? Would he act like Zeus, whose plan of empire, when first he mounted on his father's throne, was to call the Gods—his superhuman companions in arms in his victorious struggle with the Titans—and to give each one of these elect his place and honours, but to have no care of unhappy Man?[2]

Under the first and the second of the dynasties that ruled the Egyptiac World after the union of the two crowns, this fateful question remained open; but under Snefru, the last king of the Third Dynasty, and his successors of the Fourth Dynasty, it received its answer; and in this answer it was the voice of Zeus and not the voice of Prometheus that made itself heard; for those kings were the Pyramid-Builders;[3] and the pyramids have immortalized these autocrats, not as ever-living gods, but as never-to-be-forgotten grinders of the faces of the poor. In the long run, the Egyptian peasantry has had its revenge upon King Cheops and King Chephren; for it handed down their evil reputation through the centuries, until these Egyptiac folk-tales found their way at last into Hellenic literature in the immortal work of Herodotus. In our own age, when the society that produced the Pyramids has long been extinct, their indestructible piles commemorate still the endurance of the peasants who built them and the tyranny of the sovereigns who caused them to be set up.

[1] For the myth of Prometheus and an essay in the interpretation of it, see Part III. B, above.
[2] Aeschylus: *Prometheus Vinctus*, ll. 230–4, quoted above in Part III. B, on pp. 114–15.
[3] The builders of the three classic Pyramids at Gīzah were King Khufu (Cheops), King Khafre (Chephren), and King Menkaure (Mycerinus).

The spirit that inspired—or, rather, exacted—the building of the Pyramids possessed the Egyptiac Society ever after, and this with fatal consequences. For the power and knowledge which the creation of Egypt out of the wilderness had placed in a minority's hands could only have fructified if its benefits had been shared by this minority with the majority in the next chapter of Egyptiac history. When this new challenge evoked the response of Zeus, and not the response of Prometheus, from the epigoni of the pioneers, the penalty was paid in the first instance by the mass of the people, and in consequence by the society as a whole, and therefore ultimately also by the ruling minority itself. The building of the Pyramids seems to have broken the spirit of the Egyptian peasantry; and the cruel experience of that generation left its impress upon the êthos of their descendants, as though the weight of the piles which the fathers had been compelled to raise were weighing, *in saecula saeculorum*, upon the children's souls.[1] This peasantry degenerated into a sullen agrarian proletariat; and the ruling element in the Egyptiac Society degenerated, on its side, into a 'dominant minority' which ruled by repression because it had lost the art of ruling by leadership.[2] In losing the art of leadership, the Egyptiac 'Heirs of the Kingdom'[3] lost, into the bargain, their initiative and their originality in all their activities. The êthos of the Egyptiac Society during its long-drawn-out decline displays a rigidity and a conventionality and a barrenness of all inspiration[4] which present the sharpest contrast to the creative energy displayed in this self-same society's epic birth and growth.[5]

In Egyptiac history, Death laid his icy hand on the life of a growing civilization at the moment when the challenge that was the stimulus of its growth was transferred from the external to the internal field, because, in this new situation, the shepherds of the people betrayed their trust. In the somewhat similar situation of our world in our day, when the challenge of Industrialism is being transferred from the sphere of technique to the sphere of morals, the outcome is still unknown, since our reaction to the new situation is still undecided. On the other hand, in that earlier chapter

---

[1] For the religious consequences of the tyrannical egotism of the Pyramid-Builders, see I. C (ii), vol. i, pp. 142–3, above.

[2] For the schism of societies into 'proletariats' and 'dominant minorities', which is one of the symptoms of social breakdown and disintegration, see Part I, vol. i, pp. 41–2 and 53–62, above, and Part V, below. For the sharpness of this schism in the life of the Egyptiac Society, see Meyer, E.: *Geschichte des Altertums*, 3rd ed., vol. i, part (ii) (Stuttgart and Berlin 1913, Cotta), p. 68.   [3] James ii. 5.

[4] For the role of Ikhnaton, as one of those exceptions which prove a rule, see I. C (ii), vol. i, pp. 145–6, above.

[5] The vices of the Egyptiac êthos during the long ages of decline are so conspicuous that they are often mistakenly attributed to the Egyptiac êthos *tel quel*—a mistake which ignores the almost antithetical virtues which are equally conspicuous during the relatively short age of this society's genesis and growth.

in our history when the challenge of the Scandinavian onslaught
upon Western Christendom was met by the creation of a new
Western military technique, with a consequent modification of the
Western social system, there was a transfer of the challenge which
manifestly stimulated the challenged civilization to achieve a further
degree of growth. In this instance, as we have seen,[1] the challenge
was transferred from the battle-field between Western Christendom and the Vikings to the field of conflict between the different
classes into which the Western body social had been impelled to
articulate itself in the process of resisting the Scandinavian pressure;
and in this new situation our Western Civilization responded as
successfully to the challenge of an internal problem as it had
previously responded to an external attack, with the result that it
continued to grow in wisdom and stature and went forward from
strength to strength.

On this showing, we may perhaps persist in the view that a given
series of successful responses to successive challenges is to be interpreted as a manifestation of growth if, as the series proceeds, the
action tends to shift from the field of the external environment—
whether physical or human—to the *for intérieur* of the growing
personality or the growing civilization. In so far as this grows and
continues to grow, it has to reckon less and less with challenges
delivered by alien adversaries and demanding responses on an outer
battle-field, and more and more with challenges that are presented
by itself to itself in an inner arena. Growth means that the growing
personality or civilization tends to become its own environment and
its own challenger and its own field of action. In other words, the
criterion of growth is progress towards self-determination; and
progress towards self-determination is a prosaic formula for describing the miracle by which Life enters into its Kingdom.

This miracle is described by the Hellenic mythology in the
parable of Pygmalion's statue, and portrayed by our Western art
in Watts's picture of Chaos. In the Hellenic myth, a piece of marble
turns to human flesh and blood in response to the prayer of a
sculptor who has fallen in love with the creature of his own creative
hands. In Watts's *Chaos*, huge figures of titans are pictured in the
act of shaking themselves free from the frame of their Mother
Earth. They are still clay of her clay—glowing-red forms of one
earthy substance and one fiery heat with the glowing-red landscape.
Some of them are drowsily stirring in a flux of volcanic flames; others,
wholly liberated and fully come alive, are leaning, stupefied, upon
the Earth-Mother's breast. But we know that in a moment—the
moment after this which the artist has caught in his vision—these

---

[1] See II. D (v), vol. ii, pp. 199–200, and the present chapter, p. 196, above.

giants will surely rise to their feet and then stride forward over land and sea. We know it because already, on the peaks of the mountains, the grim chthonic glow is turning miraculously into the ethereal flush of dawn; and because, down here in the shadow, unhurried but unhindered, there floats or dances through Space and Time a living chain of Goddesses, hand linked in hand: the endless procession of the Hours.

II. AN ANALYSIS OF GROWTH

(a) THE RELATION BETWEEN GROWING CIVILIZATIONS AND INDIVIDUALS

The argument of the preceding chapter has led us to the conclusion that the criterion of growth is to be found in progress towards self-determination. If this conclusion is right, it may offer us a clue for analysing the process of the growths of civilizations, which is the next problem that lies before us.

If self-determination is the criterion of growth, and if self-determination means self-articulation, we shall be analysing the process by which growing civilizations actually grow if we investigate the way in which they progressively articulate themselves. In a general way, it is evident that a society in process of civilization articulates itself through the individual human beings who 'belong' to the society, or to whom the society 'belongs'. We can express the relation between Society and Individual indifferently by either of these two mutually inverse formulae; and this ambiguity seems to show that either formula is inadequate and that, before setting out on our new inquiry, we shall have to consider what is the relation in which societies and individuals stand to one another.

This is, of course, one of the stock questions of sociology, and there are two stock answers to it. One answer is that the individual human being is a reality which is capable of existing, and of being apprehended, by itself, while the society is nothing but a sum or aggregate of atomic and autonomous individuals who bring societies into existence by coming together and dissolve them by parting company again. The other stock answer is just the opposite. According to this second view, the reality is the society and not the individual: the society is a perfect and intelligible whole, while the individual is simply a part of this whole, who can neither exist nor be conceived as existing in any other capacity or in any other setting. If we examine each of these two antithetical views in turn, we shall find that neither of them will bear examination; and we may also find incidentally what the true answer to our question is.

The classic picture of an imaginary atomic individual is the celebrated Homeric description of the Cyclops Polyphemus and his kind, which is quoted by Plato in his *Laws*:[1]

> Mootless are they and lawless. On the peaks
> Of mountains high they dwell, in hollow caves,
> Where each his own law deals to wife and child
> In sovereign disregard of all his peers.[2]

It is perhaps significant that, in this fantasy of Hellenic mythology, the atomic way of life is ascribed to no race of ordinary human beings, but to fabulous monsters who are represented as living at the ends of the Earth. The truth is that no human beings have ever actually lived in this mythical Cyclops-fashion; for Man, as we have seen already, is essentially a social animal, in the sense that social life is a condition which the evolution of Man out of Sub-Man pre-supposes, and without which that evolution could not conceivably have taken place.[3]

'The purely individualist Self or mere individual is a figment of abstraction. For the Self only comes to realization and consciousness of itself, not alone and in individual isolation and separateness, but in Society, among other selves with whom it interacts in social intercourse. I would never come to know myself and be conscious of my separate individual identity were it not that I become aware of others like me: consciousness of other selves is necessary for consciousness of self or self-consciousness. The individual has therefore a social origin in experience. Nay, more, it is through the use of the purely social instrument of language[4] that I rise above the mere immediacy of experience and immersion in the current of my experience. Language gives names to the items of my experience, and thus through language they are first isolated and abstracted from the continuous body of my experience. Through the naming power of language, again, several items of experience can be grouped together under one name, which becomes distinctive of their general resemblances, in disregard of their minor differences. In other words, the power of forming general concepts becomes possible only through the social instrument of language. Thus the entire developed apparatus of thought with which I measure the Universe and garner an untold wealth of personal experience is not my individual equipment and possession, but a socially developed instrument which I share with the rest of my fellows. The individual Self or Personality rests not on its individual foundations but on the whole Universe.'[5]

---

[1] *Odyssey*, ix, ll. 112–15, quoted in Plato, *Laws*, Bk. II, 640 B.

[2] Τοῖσιν δ᾽ οὔτ᾽ ἀγοραὶ βουληφόροι οὔτε θέμιστες,
    ἀλλ᾽ οἵγ᾽ ὑψηλῶν ὀρέων ναίουσι κάρηνα
    ἐν σπέσσι γλαφυροῖσι, θεμιστεύει δὲ ἕκαστος
    παίδων ἠδ᾽ ἀλόχων, οὐδ᾽ ἀλλήλων ἀλέγουσι.

[3] See I. C (iii) (c), vol. i, pp. 173–4, above, and the passages there quoted from Aristotle and from Eduard Meyer.

[4] For the social origin of language, see the passage quoted from Eduard Meyer in vol. i, p. 174, above.—A. J. T.

[5] Smuts, J. C.: *Holism and Evolution*, 2nd ed. (London 1927, Macmillan), pp. 253–4. See also Webb, C. C. J.: 'Our Knowledge of One Another,' in *The Proceedings of the British Academy*, vol. xvi (London 1930, Milford), especially pp. 8–9.

So much for the imaginary Cyclopean human being who is pictured as being free to live and die unto himself or alternatively to enter into a 'social contract' with others of his kind, according as he chooses. The human social animal's relation to his society is evidently not that of an arithmetical integer to an arithmetical sum; and we have next to ask ourselves whether the truth is to be found in the antithetical view. Is the individual's relation to his society the relation of a part to a whole?

'There are communities, such as those of bees and ants, where, though no continuity of substance exists between the members, yet all work for the whole and not for themselves and each is doomed to death if separated from the society of the rest.

'There are colonies, such as those of corals or of Hydroid polyps, where a number of animals, each of which by itself would unhesitatingly be called an individual, are found to be organically connected, so that the living substance of one is continuous with that of all the rest. Sometimes these apparent individuals differ among themselves and their energies are directed not to their own particular needs but to the good of the colony as a whole. Which is the individual now?

'Histology then takes up the tale and shows that the majority of animals, including Man, our primal type of individuality, are built up of a number of units, the so-called cells. Some of these have considerable independence; and it soon is forced upon us that they stand in much the same general relation to the whole man as do the individuals of a colony of coral polyps, or better of Siphonophora, to the whole colony. This conclusion becomes strengthened when we find that there exist a great number of free-living animals, the Protozoa, including all the simplest forms known, which correspond in all essentials, save their separate and independent existence, with the units building up the body of Man: both, in fact, are cells; but while the one seems to have an obvious individuality, what are we to say of the other? . . .

'In a sense . . . the whole organic world constitutes a single great individual, vague and badly co-ordinated, it is true, but none the less a continuing whole with interdependent parts: if some accident were to remove all the green plants, or all the bacteria, the rest of Life would be unable to exist.'[1]

Do these observations of Organic Nature hold good for Mankind? Is the individual human being so far from possessing a Cyclopean independence that he is actually no more than a cell in the body social of the society to which he belongs, or, on a wider view, a cellule in the vaster body of 'a single great individual' which is constituted by 'the whole organic world'? The well-known original frontispiece to Hobbes's *Leviathan* pictures the human body social as an organism built up out of a host of Anaxagorean *homoeo-*

[1] Huxley, J. S.: *The Individual in the Animal Kingdom* (Cambridge 1912, University Press), pp. 36–8 and 125.

meriae[1] which are individual human beings—as though the 'social contract' could have the magical effect of degrading a Cyclops into a cell. The same picture of the individual human being as an only partially emancipated part of a social whole which has acquired for itself some elements of individuality is presented, rather more tentatively, by the twentieth-century English biologist whom we have just been quoting:

'One interesting property gained by brains and sense-organs:—organisms possessing them can easily enter into more than one individuality. . . . A man can very well be at one time a member of a family, a race, a club, a nation, a literary society, a church and an empire. "Yes, but surely *these* are not individuals"—I seem to hear my readers' universal murmur. . . . Here we can but express a pious opinion:—that they *are* individuals, that here once more the tendency towards the formation of *closed systems* has manifested itself, though again in very varying degrees, so that some of the systems show but a glimmer of individuality, others begin to let it shine more strongly through. That their individuality is no mere phantasm I think we must own when we find men like Dicey and Maitland admitting that the cold eye of the Law, for centuries resolutely turned away, is at last being forced to see and to recognize the real existence, as single beings that are neither aggregates nor trusts, of corporate personalities.'[2]

A state of human life in which the corporate personality of a society has completely overshadowed and dominated and subordinated to itself the individual personalities of the human beings belonging to it is pictured, in an eschatological phantasy, by a twentieth-century English biochemist.[3]

'After the immense efforts of the first colonisers [of the Planet Venus], we have settled down as members of a super-organism with no limits to its possible progress. The evolution of the individual has been brought under complete social control, and besides enormously enhanced intellectual powers we possess two new senses. The one enables us to apprehend radiation of wave-lengths between 100 and 1,200 metres, and thus places every individual at all moments of life, both asleep and awake, under the influence of the voice of the community. It is difficult to see how else we could have achieved as complete a solidarity as has been possible. We can never close our consciousness to those wave-lengths on which we are told of our nature as components of a super-organism or deity, possibly the only one in Space-Time, and of its past, present and future. It appears that on Earth the psychological equivalent of what is transmitted on these wave-lengths included the higher forms

---

[1] See Lucretius, *De Rerum Natura*, Bk. I, ll. 830 seqq.
[2] Huxley, op. cit., p. 143.
[3] See the sketch entitled 'The Last Judgement' in Haldane, J. B. S.: *Possible Worlds* (London 1928, Chatto and Windus), especially pp. 302–5 and 308–9. The author works out very ingeniously the implications of 'a life completely dedicated to membership of a super-organism' (op. cit., p. 303).

of art, music and literature, the individual moral consciousness, and, in the early days of Mankind, religion and patriotism. The other wavelengths inform us of matters which are not the concern of all at all times, and we can shut them out if we so desire. Their function is not essentially different from that of instrumental radio-communication on Earth. The new magnetic sense is of less importance. . . .'[1]

This conception of a human society as a super-organism is presented in a fantasia by the twentieth-century English biochemist because he does not regard it as anything more than a speculative curiosity. But a nineteenth-century English social philosopher once argued that human societies were super-organisms in sober earnest;[2] and a twentieth-century German social philosopher has ventured to reaffirm dogmatically that the historic societies that we call civilizations are actual examples of super-organisms—and this, apparently, in the literal sense, with all its implications.

'Civilizations (*Kulturen*)[3] are organisms. The History of Civilization (*Kulturgeschichte*) is the biography of these organisms. The history (*Geschichte*) of the Chinese [i.e. the Sinic] or the Antique [i.e. the Hellenic] Civilization, which presents itself to us, before our mind's eye, as "History" in the conventional sense (*in historischer Erscheinung*), is the exact counterpart of the history (*Geschichte*) of the individual human being, or of an animal or of a tree or of a flower. If we wish to gain insight into its structure, the proper method has been worked out long ago in the science of the comparative morphology of plants and animals. . . .

'A civilization is born at the moment when, out of the primitive psychic conditions of a perpetually infantile [raw] Humanity, a mighty soul awakes and extricates itself: a form out of the formless, a bounded and transitory existence out of the boundless and persistent. This soul comes to flower on the soil of a country with precise boundaries, to which it remains attached like a plant. Conversely, a civilization dies if once this soul has realized the complete sum of its possibilities in the shape of peoples, languages, creeds, arts, states, and sciences, and thereupon goes back into the primitive psyche from which it originally emerged.'[4]

In this remarkable passage, the conception of a society as a super-

[1] Haldane, J. B. S.: *Possible Worlds* (London 1928, Chatto and Windus), pp. 304–5.
[2] This was, of course, Herbert Spencer in his *Principles of Sociology*, vol. i (London 1876, Williams and Norgate). The thesis that societies are organisms is worked out systematically, in detail, in part (ii). See, for example, pp. 514–15, in which 'the classes engaged in manual occupations' are equated with 'the components of the alimentary surfaces'; the trading class with the vascular system; and the 'controlling' class with the brain.
[3] In Spengler's terminology, a *Kultur* means what, in this Study of History, is called a civilization, so long as the civilization is in process of growth. *Zivilisation*, which for Spengler is the antithesis of *Kultur*, means the condition into which a civilization (in our sense) falls when it breaks down and goes into disintegration.—A. J. T.
[4] Spengler, Oswald: *Der Untergang des Abendlandes*, vol. i, 15th–22nd ed. (Munich 1920, Beck), pp. 150 and 153.

organism is formulated in such uncompromising terms that it virtually refutes itself; but we may cite a formal condemnation of it from the work of an English publicist which happened to appear in the same year as Spengler's book.

'Again and again, social theorists, instead of finding and steadily employing a method and a terminology proper to their subject, have attempted to express the facts and values of Society in terms of some other theory or science. On the analogy of the physical sciences they have striven to analyse and explain Society as *mechanism*, on the analogy of biology they have insisted on regarding it as an *organism*, on the analogy of mental science or philosophy they have persisted in treating it as a *person*, sometimes on the religious analogy they have come near to confusing it with a God.

'These various analogies have very different degrees of value and disvalue. The mechanical analogy and the organic analogy have been alike definitely harmful and have led theory seriously astray; for they both invoke a material analogy in what is essentially a mental or spiritual study.[1] The analogies drawn from psychology and mental philosophy are far less harmful and may be even extremely suggestive if they are not pushed too far; for though neither Society nor the various associations which it includes are "persons", they approach far more nearly to being persons than to being either mechanical or organic.'[2]

The biological and psychological analogies are perhaps least harmful and least misleading when they are applied to primitive societies in their present static condition or to those exceptional and unsuccessful civilizations that have fallen into a state of arrest.[3] But they are manifestly unsuited to express the relation in which the growing civilizations stand to the individual human beings who 'belong' to them—or to whom such societies 'belong'. The inclination to introduce these particular analogies in this context seems to be a peculiar infirmity of our own Western social philosophers; and we may trace this infirmity to the special penchant— noted in an earlier passage of this Study[4]—which we in our Western Society seem to have for personifying groups or classes or associations of human beings, or human social institutions, by the device of labelling them with mythological proper names: 'Britain', 'France', 'Czechoslovakia'; 'His Majesty's Government' and 'The London County Council'; 'the Church', 'the Bar', 'the Press', 'the Turf', 'the Trade'. The distorting effect of these fictitious personifications upon historical thought and historical narrative has been discussed

---

[1] 'We may, if we will, speak of the "organs of the body social" or of the "machinery of society", but we must beware of regarding such phrases as more than metaphors or of basing any conclusions at all upon them.' (Ibid., p. 21.)
[2] Cole, G. D. H.: *Social Theory* (London 1920, Methuen), pp. 13–14.
[3] For the arrested civilizations, see the present Part III. A, above.
[4] See I. C (iii) (*e*), Annex, vol. i, pp. 442–5, above.

in this Study already[1] and need not be re-emphasized here. It is sufficiently evident that the representation of a society as a personality or as an organism does not offer us an adequate or accurate expression of the society's relation to its individual human 'members'. A human society is not a whole of which the individual human beings are parts, any more than it is an aggregate of individual human atoms that are free to associate or dissociate at will.

What, then, is the true relation between human societies and individuals? The truth seems to be that a human society is, in itself, a relation: a particular kind of relation between human beings who are not only individuals but are also social animals in the sense that they could not exist at all—or at any rate not humanly—without being in this social relation with one another. The species of human relation of which our human societies are one sample is known to us already. At an earlier point in this Study,[2] we have noticed that 'the social relations of human beings extend beyond the furthest possible range of personal contacts, and' that 'these impersonal relations are maintained through social mechanisms called institutions. Without institutions, societies could not exist. Indeed, societies themselves are simply institutions of the highest order—institutions, that is, which comprehend without being comprehended by others. The study of societies and the study of institutional relations are one and the same thing.'

The nature of these social or institutional relations between individual human beings is thus the ultimate object of our present inquiry into the relations between individuals and societies. But, before we can go further, we shall have to remind ourselves of the nature of these human individuals, or social animals, whose relations with one another we are trying to study; and we shall have to consider incidentally the nature of 'relations' in general.

The very concept of 'relations' between 'things' or 'beings' involves the logical contradiction that something which is *ex hypothesi* separate and self-contained and individual and exclusive has also to be conceived as somehow overlapping with other entities of the same order. How is this contradiction to be transcended? Only, perhaps, by substituting 'actions' for 'things' and 'agents' for 'beings' and 'interaction' for 'overlapping' as our formulae for describing 'the nature'—or, rather, 'the working'—of the Universe. Let us follow, along this path, the South African philosopher-statesman whose guidance we have sought on many occasions.

'Action does not come to a stop in its structures; it remains Action, it remains in action. In other words, there is more in bodies, things and events than is contained in their structures or material forms. All

---

[1] In loc. cit.   [2] In I. C (iii) (e), Annex, vol. i, pp. 454-5, above.

things overflow their own structural limits, the inner Action transcends the outer structure, and there is thus a trend in things beyond themselves. This inner trend in things springs from their very essence as localised, imprisoned Action. From this follow[s] . . . the concept of things as more than their apparent structures, and their "fields" as complementary to their full operation and understanding. A thing does not come to a stop at its boundaries or bounding surfaces. It is overflowing Action, it passes beyond its bounds, and its surrounding "field" is therefore essential not only to its correct appreciation as a thing, but also to a correct understanding of things in general, and especially of the ways in which they affect each other.'[1]

This suggestive concept of 'fields' is applied by the philosopher to Action of diverse kinds on different planes.

'Round every luminous point in experience there is a penumbra, a gradual shading off into haziness and obscurity. A "concept" is not merely its clear luminous centre but embraces a surrounding sphere of meaning or influence of smaller or larger dimensions, in which the luminosity tails off and grows fainter until it disappears. Similarly a "thing" is not merely that which presents itself as such in clearest definite outline, but this central area is surrounded by a zone of vague sense-data and influences which shades off into the region of the indefinite. The hard and abrupt contours of our ordinary conceptual system do not apply to reality and they make reality inexplicable, not only in the case of causation, but in all cases of relations between things, qualities and ideas. Conceive of a cause as a centre with a zone of activity or influence surrounding it and shading gradually off into indefiniteness. Next conceive of an effect as similarly surrounded. It is easy in that way to understand their interaction, and to see that cause and effect are not at arm's length but interlocked, and embrace and influence each other through the interpenetration of their two fields. In fact, the conception of fields of force which has become customary in Electro-magnetism is only a special case of a phenomenon which is quite universal in the realms of thought and reality alike. Every "thing" has its field, like itself, only more attenuated; every concept has likewise its field. It is in these fields and these fields only that things really happen. It is the intermingling of fields which is creative or causal in Nature as well as in Life. The hard secluded thing is barren because abstract, and but for its field it could never come into real contact or into active or creative relations with any other thing or concept. Things, ideas, animals, plants, persons: all these, like physical forces, have their fields, and but for their fields they would be unintelligible, their activities would be impossible, and their relations barren and sterile.'[2]

If we realize the existence of fields and recognize their importance, our thought runs on to explore their ranges; and our philosopher-statesman cites a contemporary philosopher-mathematician

[1] Smuts, J. C.: *Holism and Evolution*, 2nd ed. (London 1927, Macmillan), p. 336.
[2] Smuts, op. cit., pp. 17–18.

for the view that the field of any given 'thing' or 'event' extends to the totality of the Universe. Professor Whitehead, General Smuts observes,

'arrives at the result that a thing or event is not confined to its own simple Space-Time location, and is thus not itself alone, but that it reflects the aspects of all other things and events from its particular standpoint, and thus in a sense involves their locations also. In the larger context of Nature the thing or event is therefore a synthesis of itself with the aspects or perspectives of everything else as mirrored from its standpoint. Whitehead's searching analysis leads to results which closely resemble those of Leibniz's Monadology.'[1]

On the plane of physical phenomena, this doctrine means that each single atom or proton or electron, and each single ray of radiation, embraces the entire Physical Universe, inasmuch as its field of action has no narrower range than that. And a modern French philosopher, Monsieur Henri Bergson, argues, on the same principle, that the entire material universe is virtually included in the material body of each single human being.

'People never tire of repeating that Man is an insignificant speck on the Earth, and the Earth in the Universe. Yet, even in respect of his body, Man is far from occupying merely the tiny place which is usually assigned to him, and with which Pascal himself was content when he reduced "the thinking reed" to no more than a reed materially. For if

[1] Smuts, op. cit., p. 22, referring to Whitehead, A. N.: *Science and the Modern World* (Cambridge 1927, University Press). See also Smuts's note, in *Holism and Evolution*, pp. 121-4, on 'Whitehead's doctrine of Organic Mechanism'. This doctrine, which is Whitehead's central theme in *Science and the Modern World*, is enunciated there, in precise terms, on pp. 99 and 134, while on p. 193, ibidem, Whitehead touches upon the relation of his own philosophy to that of Leibniz. In Leibniz's philosophy, the ultimate substances or entities or realities—for which Leibniz has coined the term 'monads'—are individual centres of perception, each of which mirrors the Universe:
'Chaque monade est un miroir vivant de l'univers suivant son point de vue.' (*Leibnitii Opera Philosophica*, edited by Erdmann, J. E. (Berlin 1840, Eichler), p. 725.) 'Et comme une même ville regardée de différens côtés paroît tout autre et est comme multipliée perspectivement, il arrive de même que par la multitude infinie des substances simples, il y a comme autant de différens univers, qui ne sont pourtant que les perspectives d'un seul selon les différens points de vue de chaque monade' (op. cit., p. 709).
From this faculty of reflecting or perceiving the Universe, which Leibniz ascribes to his monads, he argues that each monad enjoys self-determination:
'Les monades qui sont les véritables et uniques substances, ne sauroient être empêchées naturellement dans leurs déterminations intérieures, puisqu'elles enveloppent la représentation de tout externe' (op. cit., p. 722). 'Elles ont en elles une certaine perfection; il y a une suffisance qui les rend sources de leurs actions internes et pour ainsi dire des automates incorporels' (op. cit., p. 706).
But this very self-determination implies that one monad cannot be acted upon by—and therefore, conversely, cannot itself act upon—any other monad:
'Il n'y a pas moyen . . . d'expliquer comment une monade puisse être altérée ou changée dans son intérieur par quelque autre créature, puisqu'on n'y sauroit rien transposer ni concevoir en elle aucun mouvement interne qui puisse être excité, dirigé, augmenté ou diminué là-dedans. . . . Les monades n'ont point de fenêtres, par lesquelles quelque chose y puisse entrer ou sortir' (op. cit., p. 705. Cf. pp. 680 and 709 and 728).
Thus, while the Leibnizian monads have the whole Universe for their field of perception, they apparently have no fields of action at all.
For further light, see Russell, Bertrand: *A Critical Exposition of the Philosophy of Leibniz* (Cambridge 1900, University Press).

our body is the matter to which our consciousness attaches itself, then it is coextensive with our consciousness, it comprehends all that we perceive, it stretches to the stars. But this immense body changes every instant—and sometimes radically—through the slightest displacement of one particular part of itself which occupies its centre and which keeps within a tiny space. This interior and central body, which is relatively invariable, is always present. And it is not only present; it is active: it is through it, and through it alone, that we are able to move other parts of the great body. Since it is action that counts, and since it is taken for granted that we are in the place where we act, it is customary to confine the consciousness within the tiny body and to ignore the immense body . . . [yet], if the surface of our very small organized body (which is organized precisely with a view to immediate action) is the locus of our actual movements, our very large inorganic body is the locus of our eventual and our theoretically possible movements. No doubt, everything happens *as though* our external perceptions were constructed by our brain and projected by it into space; but this is merely because the perceptive centres of the brain perform the necessary explorations and preparations for these eventual actions and sketch the design of them within. The truth is quite different; and we *are* really *in* everything that we perceive, though we happen to be represented there by parts of ourselves which vary without ceasing and which are occupied by actions that are only virtual.'[1]

In this passage, the modern Western philosopher contents himself with equating the individual human body, by virtue of its 'field', with as much of the material universe as happens at any given moment to come within the individual human being's range of action and perception and thought. An old school of Western thinkers went the length of equating the individual human soul with the entire Universe, on all its planes and in all its aspects, when they made their dichotomy between Microcosm and Macrocosm: a dichotomy which applies alike to the Soul and to the Universe itself. In the Microcosm, the Universe is mirrored or concentrated in the Soul; in the Macrocosm, the Soul ranges over a 'field' that is coextensive with the Universe; and the sum of things—the ultimate Whole which remains undivided and indivisible in reality, notwithstanding the logical dichotomy that has been practised upon it by human thought—is Soul and Universe in one.

In this now old-fashioned anticipation (or implementation) of a modern idea, we have found one answer to the question before us. It seems that individual human beings are related with one another through having individual fields of action that are each coextensive with the Universe and therefore all coextensive *inter se*. But, like so many of the intuitions of the medieval scholastic genius, this answer

1 Bergson, H.: *Les Deux Sources de la Morale et de la Religion* (Paris 1932, Alcan), pp. 276–7.

to a practical question is no answer for practical purposes. For to say that people are related with each other through fields that have no limits short of the Universe is virtually to say that they enter into their mutual relations at Infinity; and this leaves as obscure as ever the nature of their empirically observed relations in those mundane human societies, with their unique locations in Space-Time, that are the actual objects of this Study. Empirical observation has informed us, in objective terms, that these societies are institutions which, for our practical purposes, are of the highest order, in the sense that they comprehend other institutions without being comprehended by others in their turn.[1] In subjective terms we have found, by the same empirical test, that, for the same practical purposes, these same societies are also 'intelligible fields of study'.[2] In practice, therefore, our question will not have received a satisfactory answer until we have grasped the nature of the empirically observed relations between human individuals in these social fields which are neither universal in their range nor infinitely remote.[3] Does the philosophically true but practically unsatisfying answer which we have obtained from the oracle of Scholasticism furnish any clue for discovering an answer in our own practical terms? Perhaps we can make the transit from the theoretical to the practical answer to our question by way of a mathematical simile.

Let us represent our human individuals, whose social relations we are trying to grasp, by any number of points on a plane; and from each one of these points, as an apex, let us produce a cone to represent each individual's field of action. Some of these cones may expand rapidly, at an obtuse angle; others may expand gradually, at angles that are more acute; and the central spine or axis of each cone may take off at any angle from the common plane on which all the apices lie. Our only postulate is that the cones shall all be produced into the third dimension on one and the same side of our original plane (which offers, of course, two alternative sides on which our three-dimensional figures may be constructed). Let us now decree that every one of these cones shall be produced,

<hr>

[1] See Part I. C (iii) (e), Annex, vol. i, p. 455, above.
[2] See Part I. A and also I. C (iii) (e), Annex, vol. i, p. 443, above.
[3] The problem that confronts us here has been formulated as follows, in 'holistic' terms, by General Smuts:
'What limits are there to the field of an inorganic body or an organism or a personality? Leibniz represented each monad as containing or mirroring the whole Universe in its own way and from its own particular angle; lower monads, of course, more imperfectly than higher monads; but each in its own degree is a sort of Microcosm or miniature Universe. In other words, each tiniest least monad is in a sense cosmic and universal. This description would not apply to a "field". As we have seen, a "field" is of the same character as the inner area of the whole, only more attenuated in its force and influence, and the farther it recedes from that area the greater the attenuation; so that the field, though theoretically indefinite in extent, is in effect quite limited in practical operation.' (Smuts, op. cit., pp. 347-8.)

on the (conventionally determined) productive side of our plane, from its apex on and on into Infinity. This decree ensures mathematically that, notwithstanding the diversity of the respective angles at which our cones take off from our plane, the ultimate cross-section of every cone will coincide in area with the ultimate cross-section of every other cone; for, on a plane that lies at an infinite distance from our original plane of departure, all our cones alike will project themselves in cross-sections with infinite and therefore coextensive areas. At the same time, we shall find that the sections of a certain number—though only a certain number—of our cones do coincide in area at each and every distance, short of infinity, from the productive face of our original plane, at which we choose to describe another plane parallel to it. For, as our cones which we are producing from our original plane traverse any one of these other planes, at some finite distance from the first, on their way towards Infinity, they will each leave their mark on the second plane in the shape of a conic section; and while these conic sections will naturally differ from one another in location and size and form according to the point on the original plane from which each particular cone has taken off, and according to the angles that govern its production, it will be found, as a matter of fact, that the conic sections imprinted on the second plane by a certain number of different cones that have taken off from the first plane at different points and at different angles will actually coincide with one another—coinciding, in this case, at a finite and not at an infinite distance from their respective apices, and in a finite and not in an infinite area.

Before we proceed to the interpretation of this simile, it may be well to make the mathematical construction clearer by translating it into concrete terms. For our original plane let us take the surface of the Earth; let our points on this surface be represented by search-light projectors; and let these projectors be without those prisms of crystal or glass by means of which the beams of light that are projected from ordinary search-lights are diverted, at the outset, from their natural paths and are made to travel parallel to one another in the form of a shaft instead of following their natural bent and diverging cone-wise. These natural cones of radiating light will thus take off from the surface of the Earth at different points and at different axial angles and at different degrees of obtuseness or acuteness according to the particular structures and locations and bearings of the particular projectors from which they respectively emanate; and—just as in the case of our abstract mathematical cones—their cross-sections will all be coextensive with one another at Infinity. In the concrete illustration, however, we are confronted at once with the gulf between theory and practice; for it is evident that, in practice, this theoretical coincidence of all the cross-sections of all our light-cones will never be realized. It will not be realized because the light-cone—which is the 'field' of radiation of the projector—becomes more and 'more attenuated in its force and influence the farther it recedes from' the lamp that is the source from which the radiation is emitted, 'so that the field, though theoretically indefinite in extent, is in effect quite limited in practical operation'.[1] Moreover, in the particular concrete case that we are imagining, the field of our search-light's cone-shaped radiation is limited in a double way: not only by the attenuation of the light as it travels, but also by the interposition of opaque bodies that prevent its further progress—even before it has petered out—towards the Infinity which it would never actually reach in any event. These obstructive bodies are the layers of cloud that float in the atmosphere on planes that are roughly parallel to the Earth's solid and liquid surface; and the under-surface of one of these cloud-layers will receive the imprint of a conic section from each one of the light-cones, emanating from our projectors, whose further progress this particular cloud-layer happens to bar. With this cloud-surface to play upon, the expert human manipulators of the projectors will be able so to adjust their angles of projection that the conic sections of the light-cones that are projected on to the cloud-surface from different points and at different angles will overlap with one another so closely as virtually to coincide. Indeed, this power of making the sections of the beams of search-lights coincide, for practical purposes, at distances but little removed from the solid or liquid surface of the Earth is the power that gives the invention of the search-light its practical value for Man. As *Homo Belligerans*, he focuses his convergent beams upon a single point on an aerial plane that is determined by the momentary presence of a hostile piece of aircraft; as *Homo Coponans*, he focuses upon a point on a plane that is embodied materially in the under-surface of a cloud in order to advertise his wares by 'sky-writing'.

The concrete version of our simile has probably made an interpretation superfluous; but, for the reader's possible convenience, we will give the key nevertheless. The points on the surface of a mathematical plane, or the search-light projectors on the surface of the Earth, represent individual human beings; the mathematical cones, or light-cones, represent these individuals' respective fields of action; the second plane, or the under-surface of the cloud-layer, upon which the cones impinge at some finite range in the course of their production towards Infinity, represents the social animal's

[1] See the passage quoted from Smuts, op. cit., on p. 227, footnote 3, above.

sociality; and the coincidence of a certain number of the conic sections imprinted on this surface represents the coincidence of the fields of action of a certain number of individual human beings—a coincidence which constitutes a society.

If this simile has any substance in it, it may now yield us a definition of what a human society is. A society, we may say, is a relation between individuals; and this relation of theirs consists in the coincidence of their individual fields of action; and this coincidence combines the individual fields into a common ground; and this common ground is what we call a society. Inasmuch as an individual's field of action is a part or aspect of the individual himself, each single individual is in a sense coextensive and indeed identical with the whole of the society in which he is a shareholder or in which he has a vested interest—to apply a metaphor from the business practice of the modern Western World. On the other hand, inasmuch as the Microcosm is distinct and distinguishable from the Macrocosm—and it is only in the field of the Macrocosm, and not in the fastness of the Microcosm, that the different individuals interact—it cannot be said that every individual is identical with every other, in spite of their being each identical with the society through which they are related. In this 'political arithmetic' or 'social geometry', the Euclidean axiom that 'things which are equal to the same thing are equal to one another' apparently does not hold.

The foregoing investigation into the nature, or the working, of human societies has incidentally brought out a point which is of great importance for the next stage of our inquiry. Our analysis of phenomena into agents and their fields of action implies not only that 'the stuff or material of the Universe' is 'activity instead of matter',[1] but also that this activity originates in one, and one only, of its two poles and can only flow in the one direction. The mathematical cones in our simile were produced from their apices; the light-cones were radiated from the search-light projectors; the Macrocosm is apprehended and acted upon by the Microcosm; and the action which is the theme of human history is the action of individual human beings on that common ground of their respective fields of action which we call a society.

A field of action—and, *a fortiori*, an intersection of a number of fields of action—cannot be a source of action. The source of action is other than the field of action *ex hypothesi*. And—to apply this truism to the case in point—the source of social action cannot be the society, but can only be each or some or one of the individuals whose fields of action constitute a society on the ground where they coincide. A 'field' or a 'relation' is condemned, by its very nature,

---

[1] Smuts, op. cit., p. 335.

to the impotence which is ascribed to the abstract human intellect in the Aristotelian aphorism.[1] It 'moves nothing'. A 'field' merely provides a locus for the action of an agent who operates in the field but who is not the field itself; a 'relation' merely provides a common ground for the interaction of two or more agents with one another. Just as mathematical Space takes no action itself, but merely lends itself to the action of particular electrons or atoms or vibrations, each of which occupies the whole of Space for its field, so a human society is inherently incapable of playing an active, creative role in human affairs. The society is not, and cannot be, anything more than a medium of communication through which the individual human beings interact with one another. It is human individuals and not human societies that 'make' human history.[2]

This truth is stated forcibly and insistently by Bergson in the work which we have been quoting repeatedly in this part of our Study.

'We do not believe in the "unconscious" [factor] in History: the "great subterranean currents of thought", of which there has been so much talk, only flow in consequence of the fact that masses of men have been carried away by one or more of their own number. . . . It is useless to maintain that [social progress] takes place of itself, bit by bit, in virtue of the spiritual condition of the society at a certain period of its history. It is really a leap forward which is only taken when the society has made up its mind to try an experiment; this means that the society must have allowed itself to be convinced, or at any rate allowed itself to be shaken; and the shake is always given by *somebody*. It is useless to allege that this leap forward does not imply any creative effort at the back of it, and to argue that there is not here any invention comparable to the artist's. This is to ignore the fact that the majority of the great successful reforms have appeared at first unrealizable and have been so in fact. They could only be realized in a society whose spiritual condition was already that which these reforms were to induce through their realization; and there was a vicious circle here from which no issue would have been found if the circle had not been broken by one or more privileged souls which had dilated the social soul in themselves and which then drew the society after them [through the breach which they had made]. Now, this is just what we mean by the miracle of artistic creation.'[3]

1 Διάνοια δ' αὐτὴ οὐθὲν κινεῖ, ἀλλ' ἡ ἕνεκά του καὶ πρακτική· αὕτη γὰρ καὶ τῆς ποιητικῆς ἄρχει. (Aristotle, *Ethica Nicomachea*, Z 2 (pp. 1139 A–B).)
2 'Aller Fortschritt geht von einzelnen Persönlichkeiten aus'—Meyer, E.: *Geschichte des Altertums*, vol. i (i), 4th ed. (Stuttgart and Berlin 1921, Cotta), pp. 145–6. Compare Schweitzer, A.: *The Decay and Restoration of Civilisation* (London 1923, Black), p. 73; Bagehot, W.: *Physics and Politics*, 10th ed. (London 1894, Kegan Paul), pp. 30–8 and 87–97.
3 Bergson, op. cit., pp. 333 and 73–4. Compare p. 102. In another passage (in op. cit., p. 124) Bergson suggests that 'it is only in Humanity that the effort of invention, which

The individuals who perform this miracle of creation, and who thereby bring about the growth of the societies in which they arise, are more than mere men. They can work what to men seem miracles because they themselves are superhuman in a literal and no mere metaphorical sense.

'In giving to Man the moral conformation which he required in order to be a social animal, Nature has probably done all that she was able to do for the Human Species. But, just as men of genius have been found to push back the bounds of the human intelligence (which means that, at long intervals, individuals have been granted far more than it was originally possible to give, all at once, to the species), so there have arisen privileged souls who have felt themselves related (*apparentés*) to all souls, and who, instead of remaining within the limits of their group and keeping to the [restricted] solidarity that has been established by Nature, have addressed themselves to Humanity in general in an *élan* of love. The apparition of each of these souls has been like the creation of a new species composed of one unique individual—the thrust of Life arriving, at long intervals, in the person of a particular human being, at a result which could not have been attained all at once for the aggregate of Mankind. Thus each of these souls has marked the attainment of a certain point by the evolution of Life; and each of them has manifested in an original form a love which seems to be the very essence of the creative effort.'[1]

For Bergson, it is the mystics who are the superhuman creators *par excellence*, and he finds the essence of the creative act in the supreme moment of the mystical experience.

'Shaken to her depths by the current that is to carry her away, the Soul ceases to turn upon herself and escapes for one instant from the law which requires the species and the individual to condition one another in a vicious circle. The Soul stops still, as though she heard a voice calling her. Then she lets herself go—straight forward.'[2]

What is the new specific character of these rare and superhuman

manifests itself in the whole domain of Life through the creation of new species, has discovered the means of carrying on through individuals who are endowed with intelligence and who are therewith made the repositories of the faculties of initiative, independence and liberty.'

[1] Bergson, op. cit., pp. 96–7. Compare pp. 228 and 289. It is interesting to find the same conception appearing a few years earlier in the work of a contemporary English writer whose mental background would appear to be very different from our French philosopher's.

'Jesus . . . was a new kind of man, literally, scientifically; a new species of the *Genus Homo*. . . . A new species of the *Genus Homo*, for the ordinary biologist, would mean a man with an extra eye, or a rudimentary fin where his tail should be. . . . But . . . the coherence which we discern in the life of Jesus . . . is organic on a higher level than the pure biological. . . . The differentiating characteristic of this new man, as we regard him, lies first in his apprehension in immediate experience of an all-pervading Unity, and second, and more importantly, in the perfection of his obedience to it. . . . Jesus is not the unique example of the new man. One very clear and relatively modern example is the English poet, John Keats. . . . I find very evident traces of the same kind of development in Spinoza, in Goethe, in Shakespeare, in Blake, and in some of the great Christian mystics.' (Murry, John Middleton: *God* (London 1929, Cape), pp. 111–18.)

[2] Bergson, op. cit., pp. 245–6. Compare p. 84.

souls that break the vicious circle of primitive human social life and resume the work of creation? The new factor may be described as 'Personality'.

'Personality is still a growing factor in the Universe, and is merely in its infancy. Its history is marked by the thousands of years, whereas that of Organic Nature is marked by millions. Personality is as yet but an inchoate activity of the whole, but nevertheless its character is already distinct and well marked; and its future evolution is the largest ray of hope in human, if not terrestrial, destiny. . . . The level of its power and activity is gradually rising; more and more it is gathering the unorganized centrifugal tendencies of the individual into an effective central control, and often it wins even in the most discouraging circumstances those moral victories which form the great landmarks of personal and human progress.'[1]

It is through the inward development of Personality that individual human beings are able to perform those creative acts, in their outward fields of action, that cause the growths of human societies; and so we find that this enhancement of the individual's mastery over the Macrocosm is the consequence of a corresponding achievement in the Microcosm—of a progress in self-articulation or self-determination within. The outward and the inward advance in organization and increase in power are so intimately connected that either can be described in terms of the other.

'The nature of Personality is distinguished by its departure from the processes of Organic Nature and an approximation to the forms of action which are characteristic of Society. Just as in a well-organized society or state there is a central legislative and executive authority which is for certain purposes supreme over all individuals composing that society or state, and controls their activities in certain definite directions deemed necessary for the welfare of the state, so the human personality is distinguished by an even more rigorous inner control and direction of the personal actions to certain defined or definable ends. . . . The ideal personality is he in whom this inner control is sufficiently powerful, whether exercised by conscious will or some unconscious activity, to harmonize all the discordant elements and tendencies of the personal character into one harmonious whole, and to restrain all wayward, random activities which are in conflict with that harmony.'[2]

In the South African philosopher's analysis of Personality and

[1] Smuts, op. cit., pp. 306 and 308.
[2] Smuts, op. cit., pp. 305–6. On p. 107 the author draws the following contrast between the soul which has achieved Personality and the soul which has not succeeded in achieving it:
'Consider for a moment what distinguishes the formed and developed personality from the unformed and incomplete personality; the strong character from the weak; the master of his fate from him who is blown about by every wave of impulse or opinion. In the latter case—the case of the weak, or flabby, or irresolute person—you have usually the same elements of character as in that of the strong man. But the difference is that while in the case of the strong man or personality all these elements are unified into one central whole which shapes and directs their separate activities, in the case of the weak

in the French philosopher's account of the mystical experience[1] we are given a glimpse of the process by which, in the souls of certain individual human beings, a new spiritual species—a veritable Superman—emerges. The mystically illumined Personality evidently stands to ordinary Human Nature as civilizations stand to primitive human societies. In both cases, the new species is evolved from the old through a passage from a temporary state of quiescence into a bout of dynamic activity. In both cases, likewise, the new chapter of history implies, and in fact demands, a sequel; for 'all things overflow their own structural limits . . . and there is thus a trend in things beyond themselves'.[2] Civilizations that have succeeded in coming to birth not only tend to grow, but also tend to impinge upon other societies in the pluralistic social universe which has been the field of human history up to date.[3] Similarly, personalities that have succeeded in attaining self-determination through self-mastery find, in the act, that they cannot live and cannot die unto themselves;[4] that, having been lifted up, they cannot rest until they have drawn all men unto them;[5] because it is for this that they are come into the World.[6]

'The soul of the great mystic does not come to a halt at the [mystical] ecstasy as though that were the goal of a journey. The ecstasy may indeed be called a state of repose, but it is the repose of a locomotive standing in a station under steam pressure, with its movement continuing as a stationary throbbing while it waits for the moment to make a new leap forward. . . . Henceforward, the soul has a superabundance of life; it has an immense *élan*; it has an irresistible thrust which hurls it into vast enterprises. . . . The great mystic has felt the truth flow into him from its source like a force in action. He could no more stop himself from spreading it than the Sun could stop himself from pouring out his light. . . . His desire is with God's help to complete the creation of the Human Species and to make of Humanity what it would have been from the beginning if it had been capable of constituting itself definitively without the help of Man himself. Or, to use words which . . . say

man these elements of thought, emotion, will, and passion have never been harmonized or fused into one whole; the sovereign legislative and executive authority in the personality has never been properly constituted or exerted, or is so weak as to be regularly disobeyed and defied; the unorganized and uncoordinated factions in the character fight for their own hand and keep up a constant state of inner warfare in the personality, with the result that the stronger passions or impulses carry the day and ruin the character, which depends on a harmonious subordination of all the various elements of character under one supreme ethical authority. The inner discord may even proceed the length of apparent dissociation of the personality and lead to the singular phenomenon of multiple personality in the same individual.'

The spiritual struggle in which the emergent personality brings psychic order out of psychic anarchy in the Microcosm, and social growth out of social stagnation in the Macrocosm, is delineated with the poetic imagination and the emotional intensity of genius in the seventh chapter of the Epistle to the Romans.

[1] Bergson, op. cit., pp. 243–9.   [2] Smuts, op. cit., p. 336, quoted on pp. 223–4, above.
[3] The phenomena arising from the contacts between civilizations are discussed in Parts IX and X, below. For the contacts between civilizations and barbarians, see Part VIII, below.   [4] Romans xiv. 7.   [5] John xii. 32.   [6] John xvi. 28.

the same thing in different language, the mystic's direction is the very direction of the *élan* of Life. It is that *élan* itself, communicated in its entirety to privileged human beings whose desire it is thereafter to set the imprint of it upon the whole of Mankind and—by a contradiction of which they are aware—to convert a species, which is essentially a created thing, into creative effort; to make a movement out of something which, by definition, is a halt.'[1]

This contradiction is the crux of the dynamic social relation which arises between human beings upon the emergence of mystically inspired personalities and which resolves itself—if it achieves a resolution of its forces—in the growths of civilizations.[2] The necessity which impels a creative personality to transfigure his fellow men into fellow creatures by re-creating them in his own image is both internal and external. The internal necessity lies in the identity of Life and Action. No being can be what he is unless he is putting his essence into action in his field. But a human being's field of action lies in a society which is common ground between his field and the fields of a host of other people; and it is here that the necessity translates itself into external pressure when the individual agent happens to be a genius who represents 'a new species composed of one unique individual'.[3] The creative mutation in the Microcosm requires an adaptative modification in the Macrocosm before it can become either complete or secure; but, *ex hypothesi*, the Macrocosm of the transfigured personality is also the Macrocosm of his untransfigured fellow men; and accordingly his effort to transform the Macrocosm in consonance with the change in himself will be resisted by their inertia, which will tend to keep the Macrocosm in harmony with their unaltered selves by keeping it just as it is.

---

[1] Bergson, op. cit., pp. 246–51.

[2] The crux does not present itself in situations where the social relations between human beings are not dynamic but static: e.g. in civilizations that have suffered arrest, or in stagnant or quiescent primitive societies that have not entered upon the path of civilization at all. In primitive societies in their latter-day 'Yin-state' of integration— which happens to be the only condition in which we have direct knowledge of them— social activity is crystallized or solidified in a 'cake of custom' (see the quotation from Bagehot in II. B, vol. i, p. 192, above); and the social relations established between each individual and every other on the common ground of their respective fields are repetitive and uniform and invariable or, in other words, stable. The crux only presents itself when 'the cake of custom' breaks. Presumably it did present itself in the 'Yang-activity' of differentiation to which the latter-day 'Yin-state' of Primitive Humanity is the sequel. In that phase of evolution, Humanity was achieved through a mutation of Sub-Man into Man (see I. C (iii) (e), vol. i, pp. 179–80, and II. B, vol. i, pp. 192–5, above); and since it appears that our pre-human ancestors who accomplished this mutation were already social or at any rate gregarious animals (see I. C (iii) (c), vol. i, pp. 173–4, above), it is conceivable that this pre-human mutation worked, like the post-human mutation that is struggling to achieve itself in the growths of civilizations, through a social conflict between individuals: in this case between incipient human beings and their recalcitrant sub-human kin and kind. But we have no record of this momentous chapter of history; and Bergson (op. cit., p. 124) may be right in his view that it is only in our own post-human phase of evolution that the instrument and agent of creation has come to be the individual.   [3] Bergson, op. cit., pp. 96–7, quoted on p. 232, above.

This social situation presents a dilemma. If the creative genius fails to bring about in his milieu the mutation which he has achieved in himself, his creativeness will be fatal to him. He will have put himself out of gear with his field of action; and in losing the power of action he will lose the will to live—even if his former fellows do not harry him to death, as abnormal members of the swarm or hive or herd or pack are harried to death by the rank and file in the static social life of gregarious animals or insects. This is the penalty of the genius whose failure to transform his social milieu convicts him of having been 'before his time'. On the other hand, if our genius does succeed in overcoming the passive inertia or active hostility of his former fellows and does triumphantly transform the social milieu which has hitherto been common ground between him and them into a new order in harmony with his transfigured self, he thereby makes life impossible for men and women of common clay unless they can succeed in adapting their own selves, in turn, to the new social milieu that has now been imposed upon them by the triumphant genius's masterfully creative will.

This is the meaning of a saying attributed to Jesus in the Gospels:

'Think not that I am come to send peace on Earth: I came not to send peace but a sword.

'For I am come to set a man at variance against his father, and the daughter against her mother, and the daughter-in-law against her mother-in-law.

'And a man's foes shall be they of his own household.'[1]

The emergence of a superman or a great mystic or a genius or a superior personality inevitably precipitates a social conflict. The conflict will be more or less acute, according to the degree in which the creative individual happens to rise above the average level of his former kin and kind. But some conflict is inevitable, since the social equilibrium which the genius has upset by the mere fact of his personal emergence has eventually to be restored either by his social triumph or by his social defeat.

'A work of genius, which begins by being disconcerting, may by its mere presence create, bit by bit, a conception of art and an artistic atmosphere which will permit of its being understood. It will then receive the hall-mark of genius retrospectively. Failing that, it would have remained what it was at the beginning: that is, simply disconcerting. In a financial speculation, it is success that decides that the idea has been a good one. There is something of the same sort in the case of artistic creation, with this difference that here the success, if it eventually comes to the work which has shocked people at first, is the

[1] Matthew x. 34–6. Compare Luke xii. 51–3.

effect of a transformation in public taste which has been produced by the work itself. On this showing, the work has been a force as well as a material object. It has communicated the impress of an *élan* which the artist has imparted to it, or, rather, which is the artist's own *élan*, invisibly present in it. . . . It is only the thrust of genius that has ever forced the inertia of Humanity to yield.'[1]

How is it possible for social equilibrium to be restored when once the discordant, disturbing thrust of genius has made itself felt?

The simplest solution would be that uniform thrusts—uniform in vigour and uniform in direction—should be made by each and every individual member of Society simultaneously. In that event, no strain or tension or disturbance of equilibrium would be felt on the common ground of the individuals' respective fields of action, because all the individuals, in seeking to adapt their respective fields to the uniform mutations that had occurred simultaneously in their inner selves, would be feeling their way towards uniform adaptations. This easy solution, however, is only a fanciful conceit; for, *ex hypothesi*, a creative mutation of Human Nature is the act of an individual soul which is acting independently; and a simultaneous uniform mutation in every one of a number of individual human beings would be a sheer miracle.

There are not, of course, any authentic instances of this convenient miracle in human history. The most that we find is that the same—or more or less the same—creative thought or plan occurs, at approximately the same time and place, to two or three individuals instead of occurring exclusively to one.

In the history of our modern Western mechanical inventions, for example, the steam-engine and the locomotive and the aeroplane and the tank were invented at almost the same moment by several people. Indeed, the highly involved and long-drawn-out dispute between the several claimants of the reward which was offered for the invention of the tank by His Britannic Majesty's Government in the United Kingdom illustrates the difficulty of tracing an invention indisputably to a single author even when the invention in question is only a few years old, and when the society in which it has been made is in the habit of keeping exact and voluminous records of its transactions. And whatever the upshot of this British controversy may be—whether the invention of tanks in Great Britain was really singular or plural—it seems to be admitted that 'the ideas which had been thought out by the British originators in 1914 were reinvented separately and independently by the French

---

[1] Bergson, op. cit., pp. 74 and 181.

in 1915'.[1] Similarly, in the history of modern Western mountaineering and exploration, there was actually a race between different parties to scale the Matterhorn[2] and to reach the North and South Poles;[3] and in the history of modern Western Physical Science it was for a time an open question whether the concept of Evolution would receive its classical expression—'the struggle for existence' and 'the survival of the fittest'—from the mind of Charles Darwin or from the mind of Alfred Russel Wallace, while the abstruse calculations which led to the discovery of the planet Neptune—on the slender clue of certain unexplained irregularities in the motion of the planet Uranus—were actually worked out independently and simultaneously by Adams and Leverrier. This phenomenon of simultaneous pluralistic creation is particularly conspicuous in the histories of religions. The feat of providing the Arabian external proletariat of the Roman Empire with a vernacular version of the monotheism which had come to prevail in the Roman World was being attempted by Muhammad's contemporary Maslamah in the Najd at the very time when it was being accomplished, in the Hijāz, by Muhammad himself;[4] and this simultaneous appearance of Muhammad and Maslamah in Arabia has parallels in the contemporaneity of Jesus and John the Baptist in Jewry, and in the encounter between Paul and Apollôs in the Hellenic mission-field of Primitive Christianity,[5] and in the simultaneous appearance, in different parts of Western Christendom, of the Protestant Reformers: a Wyclif and a Huss in one generation and a Calvin and a Zwingli and a Luther in another.

The phenomenon of which these are a few familiar examples is described in the popular phrase that this or that new thing 'is in the air'; and there is nothing surprising about it. When we consider that a number of human beings who are in social relations with one another share more or less the same social background and social heritage and are exposed to more or less the same social challenges, it would rather be surprising if more or less the same response were never hit upon by several people at once. And the really surprising point in the actual operation of social dynamics is that a new thing 'in the air' should not be breathed in as a matter of course by

---

[1] *Encyclopaedia Britannica*, 13th ed., supplementary volume iii, p. 726. See further Swinton, Major-General Sir E. D.: *Eyewitness* (London 1932, Hodder and Stoughton).

[2] In the year 1865, the summit of the Matterhorn was reached for the first time by a party ascending from the Swiss side and by a party ascending from the Italian side within three days of one another—the two parties working quite independently.

[3] The South Pole was reached independently by Amundsen on the 14th December, 1911, and by Scott on the 18th January, 1912. Peary's claim to have been the first human being to reach the North Pole—a feat which he achieved on the 6th–7th April, 1909—was disputed (though not convincingly) by Cook.

[4] For Muhammad's career, see further III. C (ii) (*b*), pp. 276–8, with Annex II, below.

[5] Acts xviii. 24–8, and xix. 1–7; 1 Corinthians i. 10–16, and iii, *passim*.

everybody. This, however, is not what happens in fact; for while
it is true that a new creative thought or plan does often occur to
more than one member of a society simultaneously, it is also true
that it never occurs simultaneously to more than a minority.

The importance of such creative minorities in human history has
struck the imagination of Mr. H. G. Wells:

'I am building my expectation of a new phase in human affairs upon
the belief that there is a profoundly serious minority in the mass of our
generally indifferent species. I cannot understand the existence of any
of the great religions, I cannot explain any fine and grave constructive
process in history, unless there is such a serious minority amidst our
confusions. They are the Salt of the Earth, these people capable of
devotion and of living lives for remote and mighty ends.'[1]

In this passage, the fact on which emphasis is laid is not that
these creative personalities are more than one in number, but that
they are fewer—and far fewer—than the total membership of the
societies in which they succeed in producing such dynamic social
effects. And indeed this is the aspect of the situation which will
make the strongest impression on us if we survey those contemporary instances of the phenomenon in the political sphere which the
English writer of this passage had in mind: the Japanese Samurai,
the Russian Communists, the Italian Fascisti.

The truth seems to be that the intrinsic uniqueness and individuality of any act of creation is never counteracted to more than
a trifling extent by the tendency towards uniformity which arises
from the fact that every individual member of Society is a potential
creator and that all these individuals are living in the same social
atmosphere; so that the creator, when he arises, always finds himself overwhelmingly outnumbered by the inert uncreative mass of
his kin and kind, even when he has the good fortune to enjoy the
companionship of a few kindred spirits. In all acts of social creation
the creators are either creative individuals or, at most, creative
minorities; and, at each successive advance which these pioneers of
growing civilizations achieve, the great majority of the members
of the society are left behind.

If we take, for example, the growth of the Hellenic Civilization
between its infancy, as portrayed in the Homeric Epic, and its acme,
which was attained in Athens during the half-century immediately
preceding the catastrophe of 431 B.C., we notice at once that almost
all the women have been left behind and almost all the slaves. The
Homeric Odysseus has blossomed into the Attic Themistocles; but
as for the Homeric Penelope and the Homeric Eumaeus, where, in
fifth-century Athens, are they? We shall not rediscover Penelope

---

[1] Wells, H. G.: *Democracy under Revision* (London 1927, Hogarth Press), p. 42.

in the virtuous but colourless housewife of Xenophon's *Oecono-micus*,[1] nor Eumaeus in the Aristophanic slave who culminates in the sharp and shady Carion of the *Plutus*.[2] The creative minority in Periclean Athens is exclusively free-born and exclusively male; and, even so, it is only a small fraction of the free male population of Attica that has any part or lot in it.

We shall find the same situation if we take a glance at any or all of the five civilizations—the Western and the Orthodox Christian and the Islamic and the Hindu and the Far Eastern—that happen to be alive in our own day. The differentiation is perhaps most conspicuous in Hinduism, where the whole gamut of known human standards, from the lowest to the highest, is represented in the gradations that extend from the Ghonds and Bhils and Criminal Castes and 'Untouchables' and 'Depressed Classes' at one end of the scale to a Tagore or a Bhose or a Gandhi at the other. On Western tongues, it is a common reproach to Hinduism to point out that it may stand for anything, from the loftiest moral and intellectual level to the most degraded; and the abandonment of the Hindu masses to their degradation is the central point in Miss Katherine Mayo's indictment of the Hindu *élite*.[3] It is interesting to observe that the Hindu apologia has followed both of two mutually contradictory lines. Some of the Hindu apologists prefer to glory in their infirmities[4] and claim for Hinduism, as its peculiar merit, that it translates into action, in everyday life, the Latin tag *Homo sum, humanum nihil a me alienum puto*.[5] At the same time, other Hindu apologists pass over into a counter-offensive on the

---

[1] Milesian Aspasia is, of course, the exception which proves the Attic rule that is exemplified by the housewife in the *Oeconomicus* (an early fourth-century portrait which is equally true to life in the fifth century).

[2] In Carion, the lineaments of the typical slave of the Attic 'New Comedy' are already manifest.

[3] Mayo, K.: *Mother India* (London 1927, Cape). Between the moment when the writer of this Study wrote these lines and the day when he first re-read them, a conference between the leaders of the Caste Hindus and the leaders of the 'Untouchables' had issued in the Poona Agreement of the 24th September, 1932. On the morrow of this agreement, in which the Caste Hindus undertook to give the 'Untouchables' a fair share in the political power which was on the point of devolving upon the Hindu community as a whole through the transfer of political authority in India from British to Indian hands, it looked as if this enfranchisement of the 'Untouchables' on the political plane might lead on to the removal, or at any rate the alleviation, of their social disabilities, to which they had been subject from time immemorial. If that sequel did follow, it would stamp the Poona Agreement of the 24th September, 1932, as the most signal event that had occurred in the history of Hinduism for many centuries. It is noteworthy that the achievement of the Poona Agreement was directly due to the personality of the Mahatma Gandhi, who had announced his intention of fasting to death unless the Caste Hindus and the 'Untouchables' were able to agree upon some alternative to the British Government's scheme for the political enfranchisement of the 'Untouchables'—a scheme which, in Mr. Gandhi's opinion, would have had the effect of stereotyping the ancient unhappy cleavage within the bosom of the Hindu community. The Poona Agreement—which may perhaps take rank, in retrospect, as the greatest triumph in Mr. Gandhi's career—may prove to be one recent example of a saint's power of transforming his social milieu into conformity with the creative evolution in himself.

[4] 2 Corinthians xi. 30, and xii. 9.   [5] Terence: *Hauton Timorumenus*, i, 1, l. 25.

lines of the Parable of the Mote and Beam. Instead of directly defending themselves, they seek to confound their Western critics by pointing out, in their turn, that the differentiation of cultural levels between one class and another, which shocks a Western observer when he contemplates the structure of the Hindu Society, stares us Westerners in the face in the present aspect of our own Western World.

Our Western scientific knowledge of which we boast, and even our Western technique for turning this knowledge to practical account—a technique on which we depend for the maintenance of our wealth and strength—is perilously esoteric. The great new social forces of Democracy and Industrialism, which our Western Civilization has thrown up in the course of its growth, have been evoked from the depths by a tiny creative minority. Even this minority is wondering to-day whether it will be able to control and guide much longer these forces that it has let loose—as witness Sir Alfred Ewing's presidential address to the British Association in 1932.[1] And the main reason why this would-be Western Salt of the Earth is in fear, to-day, of losing its savour is because the great mass of the Western body social has remained unsalted.

To-day this great mass of humanity still remains on substantially the same intellectual and moral level on which it lay—a century ago, or a century and a half—before the titanic new social forces began to emerge. The measure of this intellectual and moral retardation or stagnation or degradation of the mass is given with remorseless accuracy by the character of 'the Yellow Press'. In the latter-day perversion of our Western Press, we see the 'drive' of Western Industrialism and Democracy being employed to keep the mass of Western Humanity culturally depressed at, or perhaps even below, its pre-industrial and pre-democratic spiritual level; and the same new 'drive' has been put, with similar evil consequences, into the old institutions of War and Tribalism and Slavery and Property.[2] The creative minority in the modern Western World is in danger of seeing its advance brought to a standstill and the ground that it has conquered filched away by an act of betrayal that has prostituted the new-won powers and the new-made apparatus of this handful of pioneers to the anti-social function of debauching the rest of Society. This betrayal is a dastardly crime; and yet, in exposing it, we have not really probed to the bottom of the mischief. For the life of the many could never have been debauched so effectively by adroitly misapplying the inventions of the few if the many had not remained morally and intellectually stationary all

[1] See the passages quoted from this address in III. C (i) (d), p. 211, above.
[2] See III. C (i) (d), p. 212, above, and IV. C (iii) (b) 2–7, vol. iv, pp. 137–98, below.

the time while the few were making their tremendous moral and intellectual advance. This stagnation of the masses is the fundamental cause of the crisis with which our Western Civilization is confronted in our day. And the intensity of this crisis seems to bear out the Hindu controversialist's contention that the blemish which the Western observer perceives in the social structure of Hinduism is not peculiar to the Hindu Society, but is likewise discernible in the contemporary Western World.[1] This common predicament of two living societies may be regarded as a regular phenomenon in the life of all civilizations that are, or at any time have been, in process of growth.

The very fact that the growths of civilizations are the work of creative individuals or creative minorities carries the implication that the uncreative majority will be left behind unless the pioneers can contrive some means of carrying this sluggish rear-guard along with them in their eager advance. And this consideration requires us to qualify the definition of the difference between civilizations and primitive societies on which we have hitherto worked. At an earlier point in this Study,[2] we found that the primitive societies, as we know them, are in a static condition, whereas the civilizations —or, at any rate, the growing civilizations—are in dynamic movement. We should now rather say that growing civilizations differ from static primitive societies in virtue of the dynamic movement, in their bodies social, of creative individual personalities; and we should add that these creative personalities, at their greatest numerical strength, never amount to more than a small minority in the society which their action pervades and animates. In every growing civilization, even at the times when it is growing the most

---

[1] In estimating our Western Society's prospects of surmounting this crisis, we may perhaps venture to encourage ourselves by recalling certain instances in our own past history in which a gulf that had opened between an advancing minority and a lagging majority was after all successfully closed by bringing the majority into line. A noteworthy instance presents itself in the history of Parliamentarism in England. The successful establishment of responsible parliamentary government as a result of 'the Glorious Revolution' of A.D. 1688 was followed by a *de facto* limitation of the exercise of political power through this new constitutional channel to an oligarchy which represented a much smaller fraction of the total population of the country than the class which had effectively enjoyed the franchise in previous chapters of parliamentary history, when the control of Parliament over the Government had been imperfect or negligible. Moreover, this oligarchy succeeded in maintaining its virtual monopoly for nearly a century and a half—from A.D. 1688 to A.D. 1832—with the result that the mass of the population was practically disfranchised and the new system of government threatened to lose its vitality. Yet, even thus late in the day, it proved not impossible to bring the rear-guard into line with the van-guard; and in the course of the century beginning in A.D. 1832 succcessive extensions of the franchise have enabled almost the whole adult population to participate in the political life which the Whig oligarchs won for themselves in A.D. 1688. Similarly, the social gulf which opened, in an earlier chapter of English history, between the thegns, who had played the leading part in beating off the Vikings, and the militarily subordinate rank and file of the freemen, was successfully closed again without the permanent establishment of a rigid caste-system. (See II. D (v), vol. ii, p. 200, and III. C (i) (d), vol. iii, pp. 196 and 215–16, above.) These historical precedents may serve to put us in better heart to-day.   [2] In Part II. B, vol. i, pp. 192–5.

lustily, the great majority of the participant individuals are in the
same stagnant quiescent condition as the members of a primitive
society which is in a state of rest. More than that, the great
majority of the participants in any civilization in any phase are
men of like passions—of identical human nature—with Primitive
Mankind.

'The truth is that, if Civilization has profoundly modified Man, it
has done so by making the social milieu into a kind of reservoir
for accumulating habits and skills which are poured into the individual by Society in each successive generation. Scratch the surface
and efface what we receive from an education which never ceases, and
we shall rediscover something very like primitive humanity in the
depths of our nature. . . . Human Nature is the same to-day as it always
has been.'[1]

It will be seen that, although the difference between static primitive societies and growing civilizations is traceable to a difference
in nature between two types of individual which are respectively
characteristic of the two species of society, the individual participants in societies of the higher species do not conform exclusively,
or indeed predominantly, to the type of individual which is characteristic of this species of society. The characteristic type of
individual whose action turns a primitive society into a civilization
and causes a growing civilization to grow is the 'superior personality'
or 'genius' or 'great mystic' or 'superman'; but in any growing
society at any given moment the individuals of this type are always
in a minority. They are no more than a leaven in a lump of ordinary
humanity; and this ordinary humanity is no different in nature from
the human type which is typical of primitive societies.

Thus the line of spiritual demarcation between superior personalities and ordinary human beings does not coincide with the
line of social demarcation between civilizations and primitive
societies. There is an overwhelming majority of ordinary people
in the membership of even the most advanced and progressive
civilization; and the humanity of all these people is virtually primitive humanity.

'Those beliefs and customs of Savage Man are "primitive" which are
the product of that "primitive" type of mind, or of non-primitive mind

    [1] Bergson, op. cit., pp. 133 and 169. See further pp. 106–7 and 150–70 for the author's
whole argument against the thesis that primitive Human Nature in primitive societies
differs in kind from ordinary Human Nature in the societies that are in process of civilization. The great French philosopher's opinion on this question is shared by a great
English anthropologist: 'The truth seems to be that to this day the peasant remains a
pagan and savage at heart; his civilization is merely a thin veneer which the hard knocks
of Life soon abrade, exposing the solid core of paganism and savagery below.' (Frazer,
Sir J. G.: *The Golden Bough*, 3rd ed., Part VII: 'Balder the Beautiful' (London 1913,
Macmillan), Preface, pp. viii–ix. Cp. Meyer, E.: *Geschichte des Altertums*, vol. i (i), 4th
ed. (Stuttgart and Berlin 1921, Cotta), p. 145.)

which from some cause or other keeps the co-ordinative reasoning controlling power in abeyance. That man is "primitive", whether he is a Veddah of Ceylon or a European peasant, whose ideas and practices are of that character.'[1]

Conversely, we have no warrant for assuming that the Arcadian village or the Ethiopian kraal or even the most backward and stagnant primitive society is destitute of superior personalities *in posse*[2]—individuals who have lived and died obscure because they have failed to break 'the cake of custom' and have therefore failed to win for their potential genius the field which it needs in order to realize and manifest itself in action.

> Along the cool sequester'd Vale of Life
> They kept the noiseless tenour of their way.

We are still left at grips with the problem of how those dynamic personalities who do succeed in breaking 'the cake of custom' in their own *for intérieur* are actually able to consolidate their individual victory, and save it from being converted into a social defeat, by going on to break 'the cake of custom' in their social milieu and so drawing all men unto them. In order to solve this problem,

'a double effort is demanded: an effort on the part of some people to make a new invention, and an effort on the part of all the rest to adopt it and adapt themselves to it. A society can be called a civilization as soon as these acts of initiative and this attitude of docility are both found in it together. As a matter of fact, the second condition is more difficult to secure than the first. The indispensable factor which has not been at the command of the uncivilized societies is, in all probability, not the superior personality (there seems no reason why Nature should not have had a certain number of these felicitous vagaries at all times and places). The missing factor is more likely to have been the opportunity for individuals of this stamp to display their superiority and the disposition in other individuals to follow their lead.'[3]

This problem of securing that the uncreative majority shall in

---

[1] Murphy, J.: *Primitive Man: His Essential Quest* (London 1927, Milford), p. 10.

[2] 'Le génie est répandu sur le genre humain à peu près comme l'or dans une mine. Plus vous prenez de minerai, plus vous recueillez de métal. Plus il y aura d'hommes et plus vous aurez de grands hommes ou d'hommes propres à devenir grands. Les hasards de l'éducation et ceux des événements les développent ou les laissent enfouis dans l'obscurité. . . . On est forcé d'avouer que si Corneille, élevé dans un village, eût mené la charrue toute sa vie, que si Racine fût né au Canada chez les Hurons . . . ils n'eussent jamais déployé leur génie.'—'Plan de Deux Discours sur l'Histoire Universelle' in *Œuvres de Turgot*, nouvelle édition (Paris 1844, Guillaumin, 2 vols.), vol. ii, pp. 645–6.

[3] Bergson, op. cit., p. 181. Compare the following passage of Plato (in *Laws*, 951 B–C): 'Among the mass of Mankind there is always a certain number—though a very small number—of godlike individuals whose inspiration is of priceless social value. These rare individuals are no more apt to emerge in socially progressive societies than in others; so the members of the socially progressive societies ought to be constantly on their tracks, scouring sea and land in order to discover sterling representatives of the species [and to derive from them inspiration for] revising the existing body of social institutions.'

fact follow the creative minority's lead appears to have two solutions, the one practical and the other ideal.

'How is one to get purchase upon the will [of another person]? There are two ways open to the educator. The one way is by drill (*dressage*) . . . the other is by mysticism. . . . The first method inculcates a morality consisting of impersonal habits; the second induces the imitation of another personality, and even a spiritual union, a more or less complete identification, with it.'[1]

The classic description of this second, mystical method is given in Plato's indignant refusal of Dionysius's request for a short and simple exposition of the Platonic philosophy in writing.

'I have one thing to say about all writers, past or future, who claim to understand my philosophy either as a result of oral communications received from me or from others or by the unaided light of their own genius. All such claimants stand convicted of charlatanism on my showing. At any rate there is no written work of my own on my philosophy, and there never will be. For this philosophy cannot possibly be put into words as other sciences can. The sole way of acquiring it is by strenuous intellectual communion and intimate personal intercourse, which kindle it in the soul instantaneously like a light caught from a leaping flame; and, once alight, it feeds its own flame thenceforward. Of course I know very well that the best presentation of it, oral or written, would be my own. I also know that I should be the first to be pained by a written presentation which failed to do it justice. And if I believed that an adequate popular presentation, either written or verbal, were possible, what finer life-work could I have set myself than to write something of real benefit for Mankind; something which would bring the nature of the Universe into the light of day for all eyes to see? Unhappily, I do not consider that the study of my philosophy is good for people, with the exception of a few who are capable of discovering it for themselves with the aid of a minimum of demonstration. As for the rest, I fancy that some would be filled perversely with a misguided contempt and others with a soaring, windy expectation—in the belief that they had learnt something tremendous.'[2]

The direct kindling of creative energy from soul to soul, which Plato here enjoins, is no doubt the ideal way. Yet to enjoin this way exclusively is a counsel of perfection. The problem of bringing the uncreative rank and file of a growing society into line with the creative pioneers, in order to save the pioneers' own advance from being brought to a halt, cannot be solved in practice, on the social scale, without also bringing into play the faculty of sheer mimesis— one of the less exalted faculties of Human Nature which has more in it of drill than of inspiration.

To bring mimesis into play is indispensable for the purpose in

---

[1] Bergson, op. cit., pp. 98-9. [2] Plato's Letters, No. 7, 341 B-E.

hand because mimesis, at any rate, is one of the regular faculties of
ordinary Primitive Man.

'The original drill, the drill that has been intended by Nature, consists in the adoption of the habits of the group; it is automatic; and it
is performed spontaneously in situations where the individual feels himself half merged in the collective life.'[1]

Thus, when the Promethean *élan* summons mimesis to its aid
in order to express itself in the growths of civilizations through the
action of creative individuals or creative minorities, it is not called
upon to perform the *tour de force* of evoking, in the other individuals
who constitute the uncreative majority, some new faculty which has
hitherto been alien from their nature. Creative Evolution has set
herself here the easier task of utilizing an existing faculty for the
performance of a new function by merely giving the faculty a new
orientation; and this historic reorientation of an intrinsically unaltered faculty of mimesis has engaged our attention already in our
first inquiry into the specific difference between primitive societies
and civilizations. We have noticed already that mimesis is a generic
feature of social life and that its operation can be observed in
societies of both species. But we have also noticed in the same context that while, in primitive societies, mimesis is directed towards
the older generation of the living members and towards the dead
ancestors, in whom 'the cake of custom' is incarnated, the mimetic
faculty is reoriented, in societies in process of civilization, towards
creative personalities who have broken new ground.[2] The 'elements'
of the old faculty 'persist; but they have been magnetized and have
been turned by this magnetization in a new direction'.[3]

Can this revised version of a primitive social drill—this perfunctory and almost automatic right or left incline—really serve as
an effective substitute for the 'strenuous intellectual communion
and intimate personal intercourse' which Plato declares to be the
sole way in which the spark of creative energy can be genuinely
transmitted?[4] It can only be replied that the inertia of Mankind

[1] Bergson, op. cit., p. 99. This metaphor of 'drill' is also employed by Bagehot, W.,
in *Physics and Politics*, 10th ed. (London 1894, Kegan Paul), p. 27.

[2] See Part II. B, vol. i, pp. 191–2, above.

[3] Bergson, op. cit., p. 230. 'This is the principal mode in which the greatest minds of
an age produce their effect. They set the tone which others take, and the fashion which
others use. There is an odd idea that those who take what is called a "scientific view"
of history need rate lightly the influence of individual character. It would be as reasonable to say that those who take a scientific view of Nature need think little of the influence
of the Sun. On the scientific view a great man is a great new cause.' (Bagehot, W.:
Physics and Politics, 10th ed. (London 1894, Kegan Paul), pp. 96–7.)

[4] This question is raised by de Gobineau: 'L'imitation n'indique pas nécessairement
une rupture sérieuse avec les tendances héréditaires, et l'on n'est vraiment entré dans
le sein d'une civilisation que lorsqu'on se trouve en état d'y progresser soi-même, par
soi-même et sans guide.' (*Essai sur l'Inégalité des Races Humaines* (Paris 1853–5, Firmin-
Didot, 4 vols.), vol. i, p. 122.)

in the mass has never in fact been overcome by the exclusive use of the Platonic method; and that, in order to draw the inert majority along in the active minority's train, the ideal method of direct individual inspiration has always had to be reinforced by the practical method of wholesale social drill—a habitual exercise of Primitive Mankind which can be made to serve the cause of social progress when new leaders take command and issue new marching orders.

The creative personality who makes play with the primitive habit of mimesis in order to move a mass of ordinary people on whom he has no hope of getting purchase in any other way is in much the same quandary as a chauffeur who turns and turns his crank on the chance that the engine may start up in the end if only he persists. The chauffeur resorts to this primitive donkey-work because experience has taught him that these apparently 'vain repetitions'[1] are actually capable of striking the essential spark which he has failed to conjure up with his 'self-starter'. A similar capacity is latent in the apparently perfunctory and automatic spiritual motions of mimesis.

'Formulae that are almost void of meaning have a way of evoking here and there, like veritable magic phrases, the spirit that can fulfil them. A mediocre teacher, giving mechanical instruction in a science that has been created by men of genius, may awake in some one of his pupils the vocation which he has never felt in himself, and may convert him all unconsciously into an emulator of those great men whose personalities are invisibly present in the message which our teacher transmits.'[2]

It is this mysterious possibility of kindling fire by rubbing dry sticks that invites, and justifies, the play which is made with mimesis in those relations between creative minorities and inert majorities that bring about the growths of civilizations. Mimesis, as we have seen,[3] may lead to the acquisition of social 'assets'—aptitudes or emotions or ideas—which the acquisitors had not originated for themselves and which they might never have possessed if they had not encountered and imitated other people in whose possession these assets were already to be found. This, of course, is as much as to say that mimesis is a 'short cut'; and, at a later point in this Study,[4] we shall find that this 'short cut', though it may be an inevitable path

[1] Matt. vi. 7.
[2] Bergson, op. cit., pp. 229–30. Compare p. 47, *ad init.* An historic social illustration of Bergson's point is offered, in the sphere of Art, by the extraordinary yet well-established fact that the sublime and vital and creative art of Mahayanian Buddhism was actually kindled into flame by the spark of divine fire which was invisibly present in the mediocre works of Hellenic art—produced mechanically on standardized patterns for commercial profit—which were current in the Oxus-Jaxartes Basin and North-Eastern Iran and the Panjab round about the beginning of the Christian Era.
[3] In Part II. B, vol. i, p. 191, above.   [4] In IV. C (iii) (a), vol. iv, pp. 123–31, below.

towards a necessary goal, is also a dubious expedient which no less inevitably exposes a growing civilization to the peril of break-down. It would be premature, however, to discuss that peril in this place. For, now that we have come to the end of our inquiry into the relation between growing civilizations and individuals, we have next to inquire into the interaction between individuals in growing civilizations.

(b) THE INTERACTION BETWEEN INDIVIDUALS IN GROWING CIVILIZATIONS

The Movement of Withdrawal-and-Return

In the last chapter we have studied the course which is followed by creative personalities when they are taking the mystic path which is their highest spiritual level. We have watched the mystic's soul passing first out of action into ecstasy and then out of ecstasy into action again.[1] In this language, we have been describing the creative movement in terms of the personality's inward psychic experience. In terms of his external relations with other individual human beings in the social life which is the common ground of his and their respective individual fields of action, we shall be describing the same movement if we call it a disengagement and temporary withdrawal of the creative personality from his social milieu, and his subsequent return to the same milieu transfigured: in a new capacity and with new powers. The disengagement and withdrawal make it possible for the personality to realize individual potentialities which might have remained in abeyance if the individual in whom they were immanent had not been released for a moment from his social toils and trammels. The withdrawal is an opportunity, and perhaps a necessary condition, for the anchorite's transfiguration; but, by the same token, this transfiguration can have no purpose, and perhaps even no meaning,[2] except as a prelude to the return of the transfigured personality into the social milieu out of which he has originally come: a native environment from which the human social animal cannot permanently estrange himself without repudiating his humanity and becoming 'either a beast or a god'.[3] The return is the essence of the whole movement, as well as its final cause.

---

[1] See the passage quoted from Bergson on pp. 234-5, above.

[2] The transfiguration of a creative personality is a change in his aspect which, *ex hypothesi*, is perceived in him by fellow human beings; and it can only be perceived by men and women who have associated with him after, as well as before, he has enjoyed the personal spiritual experience of which his transfigured countenance is the outward and visible sign. (See Exodus xxxiv. 29-35, for a description of such transfiguration in mythological imagery.)

[3] Aristotle, *Politics*, i. 1, 9-12 (p. 1253 A), quoted in I. C (iii) (c), vol. i, on p. 173, above.

This is apparent in the Syriac myth of Moses' solitary ascent of Mount Sinai. Moses ascends the mountain in order to commune with Yahweh at Yahweh's call; and the call is to Moses alone, while the rest of the Children of Israel are charged to keep their distance and not to touch the mount, under pain of being blasted by a force which only Moses can confront unscathed. Yet Yahweh's whole purpose in calling Moses up is to send him down again as the bearer of a new law which Moses is to communicate to the rest of the people because they are incapable of coming up to receive the communication themselves.

'And Moses went up unto God; and the Lord called unto him out of the mountain, saying: "Thus shalt thou say to the house of Jacob and tell the Children of Israel. . . ."

'And he gave unto Moses, when he had made an end of communing with him upon Mount Sinai, two tables of testimony . . . written with the finger of God.'[1]

The emphasis upon the return is equally strong in the account of the prophetic experience and the prophetic mission which is given by the Arabic philosopher Ibn Khaldūn.

'The human soul has an innate disposition to divest itself of its human nature in order to clothe itself in the nature of the angels and to become an angel in reality for a single instant of time—a moment which comes and goes as swiftly as the flicker of an eye-lid. Thereupon, the soul resumes its human nature, after having received, in the world of angels, a message which it has to carry to its own human kind. This is the meaning of the terms Revelation and Discourse of Angels.'[2]

In this philosophic interpretation of the Islamic doctrine of prophecy we seem to catch an echo of a famous passage of Hellenic philosophy: the Platonic simile of the Cave.[3]

' "And now," he said . . ., "Picture to yourself people in a kind of cave-like underground dwelling. The place has its entrance open to the light, and this entrance stretches along the whole length of the cave. Picture these people living in this place from their infancy with their limbs fettered and likewise their necks, so that they cannot change their position and can only see in front of them, because the fetters make it impossible for them to turn their heads. And then imagine fire-light coming to them, from behind their backs, from a fire which is burning at a higher level and at a long distance off, with a raised road running between this fire and the prisoners. And now picture a parapet built along the side of the road, like the screens in front of the performers in a Punch and Judy show—the screens over the top of which they display their puppets."

[1] Exodus xix. 3, and xxxi. 18. See chapter xix, *passim*.
[2] Ibn Khaldūn: *Muqaddamāt*, French translation by Baron M. de Slane (Paris 1863–8, Imprimerie Impériale, 3 vols.), vol. ii, p. 437.
[3] Plato, *Republic*, 514 A–521 C.

' "I see the picture," he said.

' "Well, now imagine people carrying past this parapet all kinds of material objects which show up over the top of it—particularly models of living creatures: figures of human beings and figures of animals made of stone and of wood and of all kinds of materials. And imagine that some of the people will be talking—as they naturally will—and others keeping silence as they carry the objects by."

' "A strange simile," he said, "and strange prisoners!"[1]

' "The prisoners are ourselves," said I.'

The prisoners, of course, take it for granted that the moving shadows cast by the fire-light upon the back wall of the cave are the ultimate realities, since these are the only realities that they have ever been able to see. They cannot guess that these are mere shadows of solid objects that are in motion, outside the cave, behind the prisoners' backs; or that these objects themselves are only inanimate models of living beings—models whose motions are imparted to them by genuine living agents whose very shadows are intercepted by the parapet and therefore never appear on the cave-wall screen. When the voices of the passengers on the road actually penetrate the cave and echo from the wall on which the moving shadows of their burdens are cast, the prisoners imagine—inevitably—that the voices are being emitted by the shadows of the objects that are being carried by the speakers, and never suspect the existence of the speakers themselves. This fantasy is presented by Plato as an apt simile for the ordinary state of ordinary people in the ordinary world.

Plato then imagines a prisoner being suddenly released from his fetters and compelled to stand up and turn his head and walk and face the light and finally come out into the open. The first result of this sudden compulsory reorientation of vision is that the liberated prisoner is dazzled and confused. He finds himself in an agonizing and incomprehensible blaze of light, and wishes himself back in the comfortable and familiar underground environment in which he has been brought up. But this is only the first effect of his translation from the fire-lit cave into the sun-lit upper world. The faculty of vision is already in him, and it only needs this drastic reorientation of direction and change of medium in order to accustom his eyes gradually to take in the real world, until at last he is able to look the Sun himself in the face. And when the

---

[1] The simile is more strange to a reader of Plato's generation in Plato's world than to one of our generation in ours; for Plato is really picturing, by a brilliant effort of imagination, the situation of an audience in a cinematograph theatre with its eyes glued to the screen on which a lantern at their backs projects the lights and shadows of a moving film. Plato even anticipates the distinction between silent films and 'talkies'. If Plato had happened to live in this Western World in this twentieth century, he would assuredly have taken the simile which he requires at this point in *The Republic* from real life, instead of resorting to an elaborate and inevitably somewhat bizarre fantasy.

liberated prisoner has thus adapted himself to living in sunlight and freedom completely, his previous condition is exactly inverted. If he is now suddenly compelled to turn his back on the light of day and go down into the cave again, he is just as much dazzled and confused by the twilight now as he was by the sunlight before. He experiences all the agonies and uncertainties of translation once again; and again he regrets, and now if possible still more poignantly, the environment which he is being compelled to leave. Moreover, this time his regrets are fully justified; for this time he is being compelled to leave a better world for a worse (as he knows now, for certain, through having had some experience of either); and, in returning to his old companions in the cave who have never yet seen the sunlight, he will be exposed to the risk of a hostile reception.

'There will assuredly be laughter at his expense, and it will be said of him that the only result of his escapade up there is that he has come back with his eye-sight ruined. Moral: it is a fool's game even to make the attempt to go up aloft; "and as for the busybody who goes in for all this liberating and translating to higher spheres, if ever we have a chance to catch him and kill him, we will certainly take it".'

When Plato has painted the ordeal of the return in these unattractive colours, it is almost startling to find him imposing this ordeal remorselessly upon his elect philosophers. If it is essential to the Platonic system that the elect should acquire philosophy, it is equally essential that they should not remain philosophers only. The purpose and the meaning of their philosophic enlightenment is that they should ultimately become philosopher-kings.

' "Our business," I said, "is to compel the most highly gifted individuals in our society to address themselves to the study which we have called the greatest study of all. We have to make them see the Good by ascending the ascent which we have pictured in our simile. But when they have duly ascended and seen their fill, then it becomes our business not to give them the licence which is actually given them nowadays."

' "What licence?"

' "The licence," I said, "of remaining up there and refusing to come down again to the prisoners who have remained in bondage—refusing to share, for better or for worse, in the trials and triumphs of that underworld. . . . We must say to them . . .: *You have each of you to come down again in your turn to the common dwelling-place of your kin and kind; and you have to accustom yourselves again to using your eyes in the dark. When you have recovered the habit, you will find yourselves infinitely sharper-sighted then the denizens of the underworld. You will know exactly what each of the shadows is, and what it is a shadow of, thanks to the vision which you have had of Reality in the several realms of Beauty and Justice and Goodness. And so our society—which is also*

III   I

your society—will be taught to live its life in the clear light of consciousness instead of having to live it in the nightmare in which most societies have been kept hitherto by people who have been fighting over shadows— struggling for power, as though power were a prize worth winning—while the actual truth is, and must be, that social life is happiest and most harmonious where those who have to rule are the last people who would choose to be rulers, and is least happy and least harmonious where the rulers are of the opposite disposition." '

The path which Plato here lays down for his philosopher-kings is unmistakably identical with the path that has been trodden by the Christian mystics.[1] The pain and bewilderment which the Platonic prisoner suffers for a time after he has been forced to come up out of the cave into the sunlight correspond to the raptures and hallucinations which are the prelude to the Christian mystic's transfiguration through his ecstatic union with God.[2] The still sharper pain and still deeper bewilderment which the liberated prisoner suffers when he is forced to re-descend into the chthonic 'prison-house' and feels its 'shades' beginning 'to close around' him[3] correspond, in turn, to 'the dark night' through which the soul of the Christian mystic has to pass when it is returning from ecstasy into action. Yet, while the path is identical, the spirit in which it is traversed by the Hellenic and the Christian soul is not the same.

In the Simile of the Cave, it is taken for granted that the personal interest, as well as the personal desire, of the liberated and enlightened philosopher must be in opposition to the interest of the mass of his fellow men who still 'sit in darkness and in the shadow of death, . . . fast bound in misery and iron'.[4] For these unliberated prisoners of the underworld, the crying need—though they themselves may be blind to it—is that the philosopher should return, 'trailing clouds of glory', 'from God who is' his 'home',[5] like 'a day-spring from on high' to give them light: 'to give knowledge of salvation', and 'to guide' their 'feet into the way of peace'.[6] On the other hand, the philosopher, on Plato's showing, cannot minister to these needs of Mankind without sacrificing his own happiness and his own perfection. For, when once he has attained enlightenment, the best thing for the philosopher himself, in Plato's own view, is to remain in the light and live happily there ever after.

[1] For a penetrating analysis and description, in small compass, of the Christian mystic experience, see Bergson, H.: *Les Deux Sources de la Morale et de la Religion* (Paris 1932, Alcan), pp. 243–9. Portions of this passage have been quoted already in the present Study on pp. 234–5, above.
[2] For these raptures and hallucinations, see Bergson, op. cit., p. 244.
[3] William Wordsworth: *Ode on Intimations of Immortality from Recollections of Early Childhood*.
[4] Psalm cvii. 10.   [5] Wordsworth, op. cit.   [6] Luke i. 77–9.

It was indeed a fundamental tenet of Hellenic Philosophy that the best state of life is the state of 'contemplation' ($\theta\epsilon\omega\rho\iota\alpha$): a philosophic term with a religious association[1] which pitches its meaning somewhere between 'intellectual speculation' and 'mystical ecstasy'. The life of contemplation is placed by Pythagoras above the life of action, as well as above the life of pleasure;[2] and this doctrine runs through the whole Hellenic philosophical tradition from Pythagoras to the Neoplatonists. It is accepted, explicitly or implicitly, by Plato himself in many places besides the passage here quoted; and in this passage, as we have seen, Plato assumes that nothing but compulsion will bring the philosopher down again to the underworld and back again to Mankind to perform the social task which his fellow men require of him. The compulsion which the Platonic philosophers obey when they become philosopher-kings may not be really external; but even if they are driven into action by a Spartan sense of duty rather than by a Median lash, they are being driven all the same; and, however admirably they may behave, they are handicapped by a fatal lack of zest which checks the impetus of their *élan*. This negative, weary, melancholy temper is manifest in the *Meditations* of Marcus Aurelius, the historic philosopher-king who dutifully carried on his shoulders the burden of governing the whole *Orbis Romanus*.

'Human life! Its duration is momentary, its substance in perpetual flux, its senses dim, its physical organism perishable, its consciousness a vortex, its destiny dark, its repute uncertain—in fact, the material element is a rolling stream, the spiritual element dreams and vapour, life a war and a sojourning in a far country, fame oblivion. What can see us through? One thing and one only—Philosophy; and that means keeping the spirit within us unspoiled and undishonoured . . . and taking what comes contentedly as all part of the process to which we owe our own being.'[3]

The state of mind of the historic philosopher-king which is revealed in this passage reflects upon the pious hope which is expressed by Plato at the close of his allegory. Plato affects to believe that his enlightened philosophers, when they receive their orders to return, will duly obey and duly consent to take a hand in the work of the World (on the understanding that they are to take it turn and turn about, so that they can spend the greater part of their time apart, in exclusive communion with one another, in a

[1] A $\theta\epsilon\omega\rho\iota\sigma$ means, in the technical terminology of Hellenic public life, an ambassador from a city-state to the holy place of some Pan-Hellenic divinity: e.g. to the oracle of Apollo at Delphi.
[2] Burnet, J.: *Greek Philosophy: Thales to Plato* (London 1914, Macmillan), p. 42.
[3] Marcus Aurelius Antoninus: *To Himself*, Bk. II, *ad fin.*

pure moral atmosphere and a clear intellectual daylight).[1] But while this Platonic Wisdom might be justified of her children[2] in the rare personality of a Marcus, who carried his heavy burden of social responsibility in the spirit of a conscientious sentry who would not desert his post,[3] this was not the characteristic spirit of Hellenic philosophers and not their common practice; and the example of Marcus in the second century of the Roman Empire was not followed by Plotinus in the next century, when the breakdown of the Hellenic universal state was making the duty of returning to the World less attractive to Hellenic philosophers than ever. In Plotinus, both Hellenic Philosophy and Hellenic Mysticism reached their term; and Plotinus's repudiation of the Platonic injunction to return is taken by Bergson as a sign that the Hellenic form of Mysticism was incomplete.

'In our eyes, the culmination of Mysticism is an entry into contact, and in consequence a partial coincidence, with the creative effort that is manifested by Life. This effort comes from God, if it is not identical with God himself. The great mystic would be an individual who transcended the limits assigned to the Human Species by its materiality, and who thus continued and prolonged God's action. . . . To Plotinus . . . it was given to see the Promised Land, but not to set foot upon its soil. He went as far as Ecstasy: a state in which the Soul feels itself, or thinks that it feels itself, in the presence of God, with God's light illuminating it. But Plotinus did not transcend this last stage and so arrive at the point where contemplation plunges into action and the human will becomes merged in the divine will. Plotinus believed himself to be at the summit: to go further would have been, for him, to go downwards. And this is what he has expressed in language which is admirable in itself but which is not the language of Mysticism in its plenitude. "Action," he says, "is a weakened form of contemplation."[4] Herein Plotinus remains faithful to the intellectualism of the Hellenic genius. In fact, he sums it up in a striking formula. . . . In a word, Mysticism, in the absolute sense in which we have decided to take the term, was never attained by Hellenic thought. No doubt Mysticism was seeking here for realization; and, as an unrealized possibility, it knocked several times on the door. The door actually opened to it wider and wider, but never wide enough to allow it to enter complete.'[5]

This ultimate refusal of the Hellenic philosophers to return from the world of contemplation into the world of action out of which they had originally come may explain why it was that the breakdown which the Hellenic Civilization had suffered in the generation

---

[1] Plato, *Republic*, 520 D.   [2] Matt. xi. 19; Luke vii. 35.
[3] For this simile of the sentry see Plato, *Phaedo*, 62 B, where it is placed in Socrates' mouth.
[4] Ἐπεὶ καὶ ἄνθρωποι, ὅταν ἀσθενήσωσιν εἰς τὸ θεωρεῖν, σκιὰν θεωρίας καὶ λόγου τὴν πρᾶξιν ποιοῦνται. (Ennead III, viii, 4).
[5] Bergson, op. cit., pp. 235–6.

preceding Plato's generation was never retrieved. For here we see the same 'great refusal' that the creators of the Egyptiac Civilization made in the age of the Pyramid-Builders,[1] and that Zeus would have made at the dawn of Hellenic history if he had not been saved from it, in spite of himself, by Prometheus.[2] The reason why 'the great refusal' was made by the Hellenic philosophers is also clear. Their moral limitation was the consequence of an error in belief. Believing that the ecstasy and not the return was the be-all and end-all of the spiritual Odyssey on which they had embarked, they saw nothing but a sacrifice on the altar of duty in the painful passage from ecstasy to return which was really the purpose and meaning and culmination of the movement in which they were engaged. The supreme importance of this passage, which the Hellenic philosophers just failed to divine, is brought out in Bergson's penetrating account of the experience of the Christian mystics.

'If [in the mystic ecstasy] the Soul is absorbed into God in its thought and in its feeling, there is still some part of it that remains outside, and that is the will. Its action, if it acted, would still proceed simply from itself. Its life, therefore, is not yet divine. Of this it is aware; the knowledge causes it a vague disquietude; and this agitation in repose is characteristic of what we call complete Mysticism. It indicates that the *élan* has been acquired for the sake of going further; that, while the ecstasy certainly engages the perceptive and emotional faculties, there is also the will; and that the will, likewise, has to be restored to God. When this feeling has grown to the point of occupying the whole field of consciousness, the ecstasy has fallen away, the Soul finds itself alone again, and sometimes it is desolated by the experience. Accustomed as it has been for a time to dazzling light, it can no longer distinguish anything in the shade. It does not take account of the profound travail that is being accomplished in obscurity within. It feels that it has lost much; it does not yet know that it has suffered that loss in order to gain all. This is the "dark night" of which the great mystics speak, and it is perhaps the most significant, and in any case the most instructive, feature that the Christian Mysticism has to show. The definitive phase—the phase that is characteristic of the Great Mysticism—is at hand. . . . The soul has already felt God's presence; it has already believed itself to have perceived Him in symbolic visions; it has already even attained to union with Him in the ecstasy; but none of this has been lasting because it has all been nothing but contemplation: action has [always hitherto] recalled the Soul to itself and has thus detached it from God. [But] now it is God who is acting in the Soul and through it: the union is entire, and consequently definitive. . . . Now the visions are things of the past; for how could the Godhead manifest itself from outside to a Soul which is now and henceforward filled with the Godhead? There

---

[1] See III. C (i) (*d*), pp. 212–15, above.   [2] See III. B, above.

is nothing more now in the appearance of such a human being to indicate that there is any essential distinction between him and the other human beings among whom he moves. He alone is aware of a change which raises him to the rank of the *adjutores Dei* who are passive in their relation to God but active in their relation to Mankind.'[1]

This movement of Withdrawal-and-Return, which culminates in 'the dark night of the Soul' in the Christian mystical experience, is not a peculiarity of human life which is only to be observed in the relations of human beings with their fellows. It is something that is characteristic of Life in general; and it becomes manifest to Man in the life of the plants as soon as Man has made this plant-life his own concern by taking to agriculture. In the World of Vegetation the withdrawal and the return are enacted in the annual procession of the seasons. The corn withdraws in the autumn when the stubble wilts and the seed is sown in the bosom of the Earth; the buried seed undergoes its mystic unseen trans-figuration in the winter; and the corn returns in the spring when the green blade rises out of the ground in order to ripen for a fresh harvest in the summer. This movement of Withdrawal-and-Return in the Vegetable Kingdom, which has entered into the economic life of Mankind in consequence of the invention of agri-culture, pulsates through our human economic activity in all its post-agricultural transformations. Withdrawal-and-Return is the rhythm of the Nomad's annual trek on a recurrent orbit with his flocks and herds; and we bear testimony to the operation of the same *motif* in the rhythm of our own modern Western Industrial-ism when we talk of 'sinking' capital or of making 'a reproductive investment'.

The manifest parallelism between the life of plants and the life of men has led the human imagination to express its thoughts and feelings and hopes and fears about each of these two realms of life in terms of the other.

The Withdrawal-and-Return of the corn has been translated into anthropomorphic terms in ritual and mythology, as witness the rape and restoration of a Korê or Persephonê,[2] and the death and resurrection of a Dionysus or Adonis or Osiris or whatever may be the local name for the universal corn-spirit or ἐνιαυτὸς δαίμων whose ritual and myth are as ubiquitous as the art of agri-culture itself. It is a frequent feature of the agrarian myth that the

---

[1] Bergson, op. cit., pp. 246–8.

[2] If the mythical adventure of Persephonê represents the movement of Withdrawal-and-Return when it is carried to completion (as we have seen it carried in the experience of the Christian mystics), we may perhaps take the myth of Eurydicê as an allegory of the movement when it comes to a halt just short of the triumphant return (as we have seen it come to a halt in the experience of the Hellenic philosophers).

transfiguration which is accomplished during the period of with-drawal should likewise be translated into human terms by intro-ducing a difference of personality and a diversity of sex. The springing corn is thus pictured as a male child who is born from the womb of the Earth Mother.

Conversely, the human imagination has found an allegory of human life in the phenomena of Withdrawal-and-Return which are apparent in the life of plants and trees and flowers; and in terms of this allegory it has wrestled with the problem of Death: a problem which begins to torment human minds from the moment when, in growing civilizations, the higher personalities, whose value and significance lie in their unique originality and therefore appear to be annihilated by their death, begin to disengage them-selves from the mass of Mankind.

There is a passage in the Homeric Epic in which the poet's apprehension of the common lot of leaves and men casts a shadow over the husbandman's glad confidence in the return of spring—the shadow of the thought of the transitoriness of the lives of men:

> Mark ye the leaves, for men are like thereto.
> When leaves by winds into the dust are whirled
> Soon the green forest buddeth millions new,
> And lo, the beauty of Spring is on the World.
> So come, so pass, all that are born of Man.[1]

In the dirge for the Sicilian Greek poet Bion—an anonymous Greek poem of the third century B.C.—the annual reappearance of the plants and flowers is represented, in the antique vein of the agrarian ritual, as a happy resurrection, and not in the Homeric vein as a ruthless replacement of old life by new; but this is only to point a pathetic contrast between the resurrection of the flower and the last sleep of a man from which there is no waking.

> Alas, when mallow in the garden dies,
>   Or parsley green, or crinkled anise dear,
>   They rise again, they bloom another year;
> But we, great men, so powerful and so wise,
> Once dead, beneath the hollow earth must keep
> A long, dumb, changeless, unawakening sleep.[2]

In this passage from a poem of the Hellenic decline, the return of a human being to the society of his fellows, when once he has been withdrawn from the material world of men by the stroke of Death, is ruled out of the bounds of possibility. But there was a subterranean stream of Hellenic feeling and thought in which

---

[1] *Iliad*, vi, ll. 146–9, translated by Gilbert Murray.
[2] *Anonymi Epitaphios Bionis*, ll. 99–104, translated by Gilbert Murray.

the annual resurrection of the vegetation—represented anthropo-
morphically as the ἐνιαυτὸς δαίμων—was taken as an earnest of
immortality for individual human beings; and this underground
spiritual current, which was the spirit of the Eleusinian and the
Orphic mysteries, welled up to the surface of thought and belief
in the allegorical imagery of Primitive Christianity.

'Except a corn of wheat fall into the ground and die, it abideth alone;
but if it die, it bringeth forth much fruit.'[1]

The allegory suggested in this passage from the Gospel according
to Saint John is introduced and followed out in an older document
of the collection that constitutes the New Testament:

'Some man will say: "How are the dead raised up? And with what
body do they come?"

'Thou fool, that which thou sowest is not quickened except it die;

'And that which thou sowest, thou sowest not that body that shall
be, but bare grain, it may chance of wheat or of some other grain;

'But God giveth it a body as it hath pleased him, and to every seed
his own body . . .

'So also is the resurrection of the dead. It is sown in corruption, it
is raised in incorruption;

'It is sown in dishonour, it is raised in glory; it is sown in weakness,
it is raised in power;

'It is sown a natural body, it is raised a spiritual body . . .

'And so it is written: "The first man Adam was made a living soul;
the last Adam was made a quickening spirit." . . .

'The first man is of the earth, earthy; the second man is the Lord
from Heaven.'[2]

In this passage from the First Epistle of Paul to the Corinthians,
four ideas are presented in a succession which is also a crescendo.
The first idea is that we are witnessing a resurrection when we
behold the return of the corn in the spring after its withdrawal in
the autumn. The passage thus begins by reaffirming the ancient
faith in the resurrection of plants and flowers which had been
enacted in the agrarian ritual and expressed in the agrarian myth,
but which had been shaken in the soul of the Homeric poet by his
dismay at the appalling human experience of Death. The second
idea is that the resurrection of the corn is an earnest of the resurrection of dead human beings: a reaffirmation of a doctrine which
the Hellenic Mysteries had taught and which a third-century Greek
poet had sorrowfully abandoned. The third idea is that the resurrection of human beings is possible and conceivable in virtue of
some kind of transfiguration which their natures undergo through
the act of God during the time of waiting that has to intervene

<hr>

[1] John xii. 24.   [2] 1 Corinthians xv. 35–8 and 42–5 and 47.

between their death and their return to life. The earnest of this hypothetical transfiguration of dead human beings—a hypothesis which has to be taken on faith—is the manifest transfiguration of seeds into flowers and fruits: a miracle which repeats itself year by year for every human eye to see. This parallel also foreshadows the quality of the transfiguration which human beings are to undergo. This change in human nature is to be a change in the direction of greater endurance, greater beauty, greater power, and greater spirituality; and this last term in the poetic imagery in which Paul describes the change reveals it as identical with the tendency which we have taken as our criterion of growth and which we have called 'etherialization'.[1] The fourth idea in the passage is the last and the most sublime. In the concept of the First and Second Man, the problem of Death is forgotten and the concern for the resurrection of the individual human being is momentarily transcended. In this climax of Paul's thought, the transfiguration of the seed into the fruit, which is apparent in the life of plants and flowers, is taken as an earnest and an allegory of a transfiguration of human nature which is of even greater moment than the destiny of any individual human soul. In the advent of 'the second man who is the Lord from Heaven', Paul hails 'the creation of a new species composed of one unique individual': the *adjutor Dei* whose mission it is to raise the rest of Mankind to a superhuman level by inspiring his fellow-men with his own inspiration from God.[2]

Thus the same *motif* of withdrawal and transfiguration leading up to a return in glory and power can be discerned in the spiritual experience of Mysticism and in the physical life of the Vegetable Kingdom and in the speculations of the human mind on human death and human immortality and in the creation of a higher out of a lower species. This is evidently a *motif* of cosmic range; and it is therefore not surprising to find that it has furnished one of the 'primordial images' of Mythology, which is an intuitive form of apprehending and expressing universal truths.[3]

One mythical variant of the *motif* is the story of the foundling. A babe born to a royal heritage is cast away in infancy—sometimes (as in the stories of Oedipus and Perseus) by his own father or grandfather who is warned by a dream or an oracle that his child is destined to supplant him; sometimes (as in the story of Romulus)

---

[1] See III. C (i) (c), above.

[2] See the passages from Bergson which are quoted on pp. 232 and 234–5 and 255–6, above.

[3] For the nature of Mythology, see I. C (iii) (e), Annex, vol. i, p. 442, above. It was a discovery of Plato's that the mythopoeic activity of the human spirit was 'primary' not only in the sense of being 'primitive', but also in the sense of being 'profound', so that even the philosopher, in his highly sophisticated quest, might succeed in penetrating beyond the furthest limits to which reason and logic could carry him by bringing his mythopoeic faculty into play.

by a usurper, who has killed the babe's father or driven him out and fears lest the babe should grow up to avenge him; and sometimes (as in the stories of Jason and Orestes and Zeus and Horus and Moses and Cyrus) by friendly hands that are concerned to save the babe's life from the villain's murderous design.[1] The next chapter in the story is that the infant castaway is miraculously saved alive. Romulus is suckled by a she-wolf and Cyrus by a bitch[2] and Zeus by the goat—or nymph—Amalthea.[3] Jason is reared by the Centaur Cheiron. Oedipus and Cyrus and Romulus are retrieved by shepherds.[4] Moses floating in his ark of bulrushes among the flags is adopted by Pharaoh's daughter.[5] Perseus and his mother, cast out to sea from Argos in a crazy chest, come safe to shore on Seriphos. In the third and last chapter the child of destiny—now grown to manhood and wrought to a heroic temper by the hardship through which he has passed—returns in power and glory to enter into his kingdom. Oedipus unwittingly slays and then succeeds his father Laius; Perseus unintentionally slays and then succeeds his grandfather Acrisius; Cyrus deliberately deposes and succeeds his grandfather Astyages; Jason compasses the death of his father's brother and supplanter Pelias; Orestes slays his father's cousin and slayer and supplanter Aegisthus; Romulus takes his revenge upon his father's brother and supplanter Amulius by founding a new city which eclipses Alba Longa; Horus overthrows his father's brother and slayer and supplanter Set and recalls Osiris to life and to power; Moses discomfits Pharaoh by delivering the Children of Israel from out of his hand; Zeus overthrows his own father Cronos. This is the story of the foundling; and in the Hellenic imagination this story loomed so large that it came to be a literary commonplace: a regular ingredient in the

---

[1] In the stories of Jason and Orestes and Horus the villain is a usurper who is the hero's uncle or cousin (a Pelias and an Aegisthus and a Set; compare Hamlet's usurping uncle who not only deposes but also murders his royal brother who is the father of the hero—as Set slays and dismembers Osiris). In the story of Moses the villain is a legitimate but tyrannical sovereign (Pharaoh; compare Herod in the story of Jesus). In the story of Cyrus the villain is a grandfather (Astyages; compare Acrisius in the story of Perseus). In the story of Zeus, the villain is the hero's father.

[2] In the Herodotean version of the Cyrus-myth, Κυνώ or Σπακώ is the name of the child's foster-mother (Herodotus, i. 110). In the Hellenic Mythology, the child who is suckled by a bitch is Neleus.

[3] It is pointed out by M. P. Nilsson (in *Minoan-Mycenaean Religion and its Survival in Greek Religion* (London 1927, Milford), p. 501) that, in the Greek Mythology, the divine child who is reared by some one who is not his mother appears in Hyacinthus, Plutus, Erichthonius, and the Phrygian Dionysus, as well as in the Cretan Zeus. For this Cretan Zeus, see I. C (i) (b), vol. i, p. 98, above.

[4] The Roman twins Romulus and Remus who are retrieved by a shepherd have their Hellenic prototypes in the twins Neleus and Pelias. Neleus (though not, apparently, Pelias) is suckled by a bitch, in consonance with the suckling of Romulus and Remus by a she-wolf.

[5] Compare the story of Attis, who is hidden as a child among the reeds of the River Gallos and is afterwards taken up by the Goddess Cybele. (See Evans, Sir Arthur: *The Earlier Religion of Greece in the Light of Cretan Discoveries* (London 1931, Macmillan), p. 35.)

plots of the Attic 'New Comedy' and of the Hellenistic Novel. In our own Western folk-lore we find the same story in the fairy-tale of Hop-o'-my-Thumb.

In another mythical variant of the Withdrawal-and-Return *motif*, the hero is not cast out to perish of exposure as an infant, but is sent out as a youth to meet his death on some perilous quest. Perseus is sent by King Polydectes to bring the Gorgon's head; Jason is sent by King Pelias to bring the Golden Fleece; Bellerophon is sent by King Proetus to meet his death in Lycia from the Chimaera or the Solymi or the Amazons; Hêraklês is sent by King Eurystheus to perform his Twelve Labours. In this variant of the story, the final chapter is the same. The hero defeats the villain's design by triumphantly performing his perilous task and returning from his ordeal in power and glory.[1]

In the story of Jesus, the Withdrawal-and-Return *motif* perpetually recurs. Jesus is the babe born to a royal heritage—a scion of David or a son of God Himself[2]—who is cast away in infancy. He comes down from Heaven to be born on Earth; he is born in David's own city of Bethlehem yet finds no room in the inn and has to be laid in a manger, like Moses in his ark or Perseus in his chest. In the stable, he is watched over by friendly animals, as Romulus is watched over by the wolf and Cyrus by the hound, and as Bellerophon is befriended by Pegasus; and he also receives the ministrations of shepherds, and is reared by a foster-father of humble birth, like Romulus and Cyrus and Oedipus. Thereafter he is saved from King Herod's murderous design by being taken away privily to Egypt, as Moses is saved from Pharaoh's murderous design by being hidden in the bulrushes, and as Jason is placed beyond King Pelias' reach by being hidden in the fastness of Mount Pelion, and Cyrus beyond King Astyages' reach by being banished to the highland marches of Media.[3] And then, at the end of the story, Jesus returns, as the other heroes return, to enter into His Kingdom. He enters into the Kingdom of Judah when, riding into Jerusalem, He is hailed by the multitudes as the Son of David. He enters into the Kingdom of Heaven in the Ascension.

In all this, the story of Jesus conforms to the common pattern of the story of the foundling babe; but in the Gospels the under-

[1] With this variant of the *motif* we must perhaps class Moses' flight in early manhood from Egypt to Midian, where he receives Yahweh's commission and then returns to Egypt with Yahweh's power working for and through him. Perhaps we should also regard as another variant of the Withdrawal-and-Return *motif* the curious masquerade of the youthful Achilles on Scyros and of the toil-worn Hêraklês in the house of Omphalê. In masquerading as a woman, the mighty man of valour seems, at first sight, to have repudiated his own nature; but the masquerade is temporary, and the hero resumes his proper role in order to perform thereafter the mightiest deeds in his career.

[2] Compare the lineage of Perseus, who is both a grandson of Acrisius and a son of Zeus.   [3] Herodotus, loc. cit.

lying *motif* of Withdrawal-and-Return presents itself in other shapes as well. It is present in each one of the successive spiritual experiences in which the divinity of Jesus is progressively revealed. When Jesus becomes conscious of His mission upon His baptism by John, He withdraws into the wilderness for forty days and returns from His Temptation there in the power of the spirit;[1] 'and they were astonished at his doctrine, for his word was with power',[2] 'for he taught them as one having authority, and not as the Scribes'.[3] Thereafter, when Jesus realizes that His mission is to lead to His death, He withdraws again into the 'high mountain apart'[4] which is the scene of His Transfiguration and returns from this experience resigned and resolved to die. Thereafter, again, when He duly suffers the death of mortal man in the Crucifixion, He descends into the tomb in order to rise immortal in the Resurrection. And, last of all, in the Ascension, He withdraws from Earth to Heaven in order to 'come again with glory to judge both the quick and the dead: whose kingdom shall have no end'.[5]

These crucial recurrences of the Withdrawal-and-Return *motif* in the story of Jesus likewise have their parallels. The withdrawal into the wilderness reproduces Moses' flight into Midian;[6] the Transfiguration on the 'high mountain apart' reproduces Moses' transfiguration on Mount Sinai;[7] the death and resurrection of a divine being is anticipated in the Hellenic Mysteries and is derived by the Mysteries themselves from the world-wide agrarian ritual and myth; the tremendous figure who is to appear, and dominate the scene, at the catastrophe which is to bring to an end the present mundane order, is anticipated in the Zoroastrian Mythology in the figure of the Saviour (*Saosyant*) and in the Jewish Mythology in the figures of the Messiah and 'the Son of Man'.[8] There is, however, one feature in the Christian Mythology which seems to have no precedent; and that is the interpretation of the future coming of the Saviour or Messiah or 'Son of Man' as the future return to Earth of an historical figure who has already lived on Earth the life of a human being. In this flash of intuition, the timeless past of the Foundling Myth and the timeless present of the Agrarian Ritual are translated into the historical striving of Mankind to reach the goal of human endeavours, or, on a wider than human

---

[1] Luke iv. 14. [2] Luke iv. 32. [3] Matt. vii. 29.
[4] Matt. xvii. 1. [5] The Nicene Creed.
[6] There is, however, a significant difference in the nature of the spiritual experience in the wilderness by which the hero's soul is fortified. Moses in the wilderness encounters a benevolent numen, and receives an assurance of the kind of supernatural aid that Odysseus obtains from Athena. On the other hand, Jesus in the wilderness is fortified through being tempted by the Devil, like Job or Faust.
[7] The parallel here is an intentional feature in the story; for the three apostles who witness the Transfiguration see Moses as well as Elijah communing with Christ.
[8] See Gall, A. von: Βασιλεία τοῦ Θεοῦ (Heidelberg 1926, Winter).

range, into the unceasing travail of creation.[1] In the concept of the Second Coming, the *motif* of Withdrawal-and-Return attains its deepest spiritual meaning.[2]

After this attempt to grasp what Withdrawal-and-Return really means, we are perhaps in a better position to take an empirical survey of its working in human history through the interaction of creative personalities and creative minorities with their fellow human beings. There are famous historical examples of the movement in many different walks of life. We shall encounter it in the lives of mystics and saints and statesmen and soldiers and historians and philosophers and poets, as well as in the histories of nations and states and churches.[3] In each instance, we shall see the creative personality or creative minority taking the path of Withdrawal-and-Return in order to rise to some occasion of social crisis: in order, that is to say, to cope with some challenge that is confronting the society to which the individual or the minority belongs.

Saint Paul

Among the mystics and the saints—to begin our survey with these—we see Paul of Tarsus being born into Jewry in a generation when the impact of Hellenism upon the Syriac Society was presenting a challenge which no living Jew could evade. How was the Syriac genius to react? In the spirit of the Jewish Zealots, who sought to meet the Hellenic challenge by putting on the whole armour of the Jewish Law and violently repudiating Hellenism and all its works—both material and spiritual? This was in fact the original reaction of Paul:[4] a born propagandist who had received the conventional education of a Pharisee in the Jewish 'Diasporà.[5] And the first chapter in Paul's career was devoted to persecuting the Jewish followers of Jesus, who were guilty, in Jewish Zealot eyes, of making a breach in the Jewish community's ranks. In the last chapter of his career, Paul employed his gifts of propaganda in responding to the challenge of Hellenism in a totally different way. He sought to solve the problem of Helleno-Syriac relations by peace instead of war. He preached a new dispensation 'Where there is neither Greek nor Jew, circumcision nor uncircumcision, Barbarian, Scythian, bond nor free'[6]—and he preached this in the name

[1] Romans viii. 22.
[2] For this concept of the Second Coming, see further the first Annex to this chapter on pp. 462–5, below.
[3] 'All the great nations have been prepared in privacy and in secret. They have been composed far away from all distraction.' Bagehot, W.: *Physics and Politics*, 10th ed. (London 1894, Kegan Paul), p. 214.
[4] Paul's own account of his career will be found in his Epistle to the Galatians, ch. i, vv. 13–24.
[5] For the Jewish Diasporà, see II. D (vi), vol. ii, above.
[6] Colossians iii. 11.

of Jesus, whose Gospel of non-violence and universal brotherhood and divine love he carried to its logical conclusion in his mission to the Gentiles. Paul's *volte-face* not only scandalized the Zealots whose camp he had abandoned; it even caused some searchings of heart among the leaders of the Jewish Christian Church. Yet this last chapter was the creative chapter in Paul's career; the first chapter was a false start; and between the two chapters a great gulf was fixed. After his vision on the road to Damascus, in which he was suddenly enlightened, Paul withdrew into the wilderness, as Jesus himself had withdrawn after his sudden enlightenment at the moment of his baptism by John.

'When it pleased God,' Paul writes, 'to reveal his Son to me, that I might preach him among the heathen, immediately I conferred not with flesh and blood, neither went I up to Jerusalem to them which were apostles before me, but I went into Arabia and returned again unto Damascus. Then after three years I went up to Jerusalem to see Peter.'[1]

In the Arabian wilderness, Paul thought out—or felt out—a new philosophic and emotional interpretation of Christianity; and from this creative withdrawal he returned, with all the native powers of his genius heightened and focused upon his life-work, in order to preach this Pauline Christianity to the *Orbis Romanus*.

A Pair of Saviours

The challenge presented by the final bankruptcy of the Hellenic culture to the stricken and stunned population of the derelict Roman provinces in the West was taken up by two saints—one a born educator and the other a born administrator—who lived through the blackest years of the sixth century of our era in Italy. Benedict of Nursia (*vivebat circa* A.D. 480–543)[2] was born just after the first barbarian 'successor-state' of the Roman Empire was set up by Odovacer in Italy, and he died in the throes of the long-drawn-out and devastating war between the Ostrogothic 'successor-state' and the Imperial Government of Constantinople—a war which was the worst that Italy had undergone since the War of Hannibal, and which completed the destruction of the ancient order of society in the peninsula. Gregory the Great (*vivebat circa* A.D. 540–604) was born in the middle of the Great Romano-Gothic War, a few years before Benedict's death, and he lived to see the brief Imperial Restoration in Italy, which followed the overthrow of the barbarian Goths, undone by the irruption and permanent lodgement of the far more

---

[1] Galatians i. 15–18.
[2] Dom John Chapman interprets the evidence as showing that Benedict lived on into the sixth decade of the sixth century (*Saint Benedict and the Sixth Century* (London 1929, Sheed and Ward), ch. viii).

barbarous Lombards. Both saints were launched by their parents
on the conventional career of their society and class and generation;
both showed their creative genius in rebelling against the outworn
convention and breaking away; and both brought their genius to
fruition by withdrawing for a time from the World and disen-
tangling themselves from the trammels of Society in order to return
in due course with a new moral power and a new practical policy
for dealing with a new state of affairs to which the old conventional
order had no application. In these two returning anchorites, the
lost sheep of Western Christendom found shepherds to convert their
soul and to comfort them with pastoral rod and staff as they walked
through the valley of the shadow of death.[1]

Saint Benedict. Benedict,[2] sent as a child from his Umbrian
birthplace to Rome in order to receive the traditional upper-class
education in the humanities, revolted at the life in the capital and
withdrew into the wilderness at this early age. In a cave—the *Sacro
Speco*—in the Valley of Subiaco he lived for three years of his
youth the life of a complete anchorite in utter solitude; but the
turning-point in his career—an event of still greater importance
than his original break-away—was his return to social life upon
reaching manhood when he consented to become the head of a
monastic community: first in the valley of Subiaco and eventually
on Monte Cassino. In this last creative chapter of his career, the
saint improvised in the wilderness a new education to take the place
of the obsolete system which, years before, in Rome, the child had
rejected. And Benedict's Senatorial contemporaries, who had never
departed in their own careers from the traditional rut, now sent
their sons out into the wilderness to be brought up there in a new
discipline by a Christian Cheiron. Moreover, the Benedictine community on Monte Cassino became the mother of monasteries which
increased and multiplied until they had spread the Benedictine
Rule into the uttermost parts of the West; and this Rule was one
of the main foundations of the new social structure which was
eventually raised in Western Christendom on the ruins of the
ancient Hellenic order.

'This Rule, extending to only seventy-three short chapters . . . and
not probably designed by its author for use much beyond the bounds
of the communities under his own immediate supervision, proved to be
the thing which the world of religious and thoughtful men was then
longing for: a complete code of monastic duty. Thus, by a strange
parallelism, almost in the very year when the . . . Emperor Justinian
was codifying the results of seven centuries of Roman secular legislation

---

[1] Psalm xxiii.
[2] For Benedict's career see Hodgkin, T.: *Italy and her Invaders*, vol. iv, 2nd ed.
(Oxford 1896, Clarendon Press), ch. xvi.

—[a Herculean task which was virtually labour lost]—Saint Benedict on his lonely mountain-top was unc nsciously composing *his* code for the regulation of the daily life of the great civilizers of Europe for seven centuries to come.'[1]

One of the most important features in Benedict's rule was the prescription of manual labour; for this meant, first and foremost, agricultural labour in the fields.[2] The Benedictine movement was, in fact, on the economic plane, an agricultural revival: the first successful revival of agriculture in Italy, after innumerable abortive attempts, since the destruction of the ancient Italian peasant-economy in the Hannibalic War seven-and-a-half centuries earlier. The Benedictine Rule achieved what had never been achieved by Gracchan agrarian laws or by Imperial alimenta because it did not work, as state action works, from above downwards upon individuals who would not and could not have taken the initiative for themselves if the authorities had not taken it on their behalf, but worked, on the contrary, from below upwards, by evoking the individual's initiative through enlisting his religious enthusiasm.[3] By virtue of this spiritual *élan*, the Benedictine Order not only turned the tide of economic life in Italy at the moment when it was at its lowest ebb. It also performed in medieval Transalpine Europe that strenuous pioneer work of clearing forests, draining marshes, creating fields and pastures, and starting manufactures which were performed in modern North America by the French and English backwoodsmen.

[1] Hodgkin, op. cit., p. 440. At the point in this passage where the writer of this Study has inserted his own parenthesis, Dr. Hodgkin describes Justinian as working 'for the benefit of the judges and the statesmen of the new Europe'. It is true that, after the interregnum and the Dark Age, the Justinianean *Corpus Juris* was, so to speak, rediscovered—in Orthodox Christendom in the tenth century and in Western Christendom in the eleventh—and this discovery undoubtedly produced a profound effect thereafter upon legal thought and practice in both these societies. This, however, was in the nature of a legal 'renaissance'; and, in making a comparison between Justinian's and Benedict's legislative work, it is perhaps more pertinent to bear in mind that, whereas Benedict's Rule was a new kind of legislation which broke new ground and, in breaking it, fulfilled an urgent need, Justinian was codifying a law which was not merely old, but was on the verge of becoming an anachronism owing to the disappearance of the social conditions which the Roman Law had been designed to meet. For fully three centuries after the Justinianean codification was completed, this code was altogether inapplicable to the new social conditions that supervened upon the final bankruptcy of the Hellenic culture. And, in view of this, Justinian's work may fairly be called 'labour lost'.—A. J. T.

[2] *Benedicti Regula Monachorum*, ch. xlviii, 'De Opera Manuum Cotidiana': 'Otiositas inimica est animae, et ideo certis temporibus occupari debent fratres in labore manuum, certis iterum horis in lectione divina. . . . Si autem necessitas loci aut paupertas exegerit ut ad fruges recolligendas per se occupentur, non contristentur, quia tunc vere monachi sunt si labore manuum suarum vivunt sicut patres nostri et apostoli. Omnia tamen mensurate fiant propter pusillanimes.'

[3] Unlike either the recipients of the Gracchan land-allotments or the farmers who received the loans in which the capital applied to the Alimenta Italiae was invested, the Benedictine workers on the land were not free men but slaves. Their master, however, was no human slave-owner but God; and the ex-slaves of human masters found themselves on a footing of perfect equality with ex-freemen when they entered the Benedictine Order. 'Non convertenti ex servitio praeponatur ingenuus, nisi alia rationabilis causa existat, . . . quia, sive servus sive liber, omnes in Christo unum sumus et sub uno Domino aequalem servitutis militiam baiulamus' (*Regula*, ch. ii).

The Benedictine pioneers, however, were no mere hewers of wood and drawers of water for the civilization which they served; for their manual labour included the work of the pen as well as the work of the spade. Wherever they founded a new cell, they introduced a mental as well as a material culture; and one of the incidental results of their industry was the preservation of the Classical Latin literature—the vehicle of that traditional Roman education which Benedict himself had rejected at the outset of his career.

Saint Gregory the Great. In the career of Gregory the Great,[1] the break-away was not achieved at so early an age. Born and bred in Rome itself, Gregory appears to have acquiesced not only in the conventional education, but also in the conventional bureaucratic career until he found himself occupying the post of *Praefectus Urbi*[2]—civil governor of the Imperial City—in or about the year 573; and it seems to have been his experience in this office that led him, at this stage, to make an abrupt change in his course.

The fact was that, in A.D. 573, the *Praefectus Urbi* was faced with an impossible task; for in 573 the City of Rome was in much the same predicament as the City of Vienna in 1920. A great city which had become what it was—in its government and its livelihood and its population—in virtue of having been the capital of a great empire for a number of centuries, now suddenly found itself cut off from its former provinces, deposed from its traditional rank, deprived of its historic functions, and thrown back, all unprepared, upon its own resources. In most of these respects, the reversal of fortune which Rome suffered in the sixth century of the Christian Era was even more extreme than the similar experience of Vienna in the twentieth century. At her zenith, Rome had been the political capital of the entire Basin of the Mediterranean and the social and economic capital, likewise, of the western half of it—including a Transalpine annex that extended to the Rhine and the Tyne.[3] By A.D. 573, the political capital of the Roman World had been transferred from Rome to Constantinople, while in the West the Roman dominions had been cut short until the frontiers had fallen back to the outskirts of Rome itself. The brief Imperial Restoration in Italy that had followed the devastating Romano-Gothic War had been brought to an end by the avalanche of the Lombard invasion which had overwhelmed Northern Italy in A.D. 568 and had spread

---

[1] For Gregory's career see Hodgkin, op. cit., vol. v (Oxford 1895, Clarendon Press), ch. vii; Dudden, F. H.: *Gregory the Great: His Place in History and Thought* (London 1905, Longmans, Green and Co., 2 vols.). Little is added to these two studies by Batiffol, P.: *Saint Gregory the Great* (London 1929, Burns, Oates, and Washbourne).

[2] The better attested reading in the manuscripts is 'praeturam'; but since the urban praetorship was extinct in Gregory's time, whereas the urban praefecture was a still surviving office, the less well attested reading 'praefecturam' is to be preferred. (See Dudden, op. cit., vol. i, p. 101.)

[3] For this annex, see I. B (iv), vol. i, pp. 39 and 40, above.

to the Centre and the South in 570–2, when roving Lombard war-bands had established themselves in Spoleto and Benevento. In the year of Gregory's prefecture, the *Ager Romanus* in the environs of Rome itself was restricted approximately to the area which it had occupied, some nine centuries back, before the Romans had em-barked on their struggle with the Samnites for the hegemony over Italy.[1] The territory which had supported the tiny rural market-town of that age had now to support a vast parasitic ex-capital city; and the Imperial bureaucracy, of which the *Praefectura Urbis* was a part, was impotent to cope with a problem that had never been envisaged by the Imperial statesmen who had installed the bureau-cratic machine.

This impotence of the old order to deal with the new state of affairs must have been borne in upon the mind of a Roman magnate who held the *Praefectura Urbis* in or about A.D. 573; and that pain-ful experience would fully account for Gregory's break-away, which occurred two years later, about A.D. 575. Gregory now withdrew entirely from the secular world. He applied his estates in Sicily[2] to the foundation and endowment of six Benedictine monasteries and distributed the rest of his property to the poor—except for his ancestral palace in Rome, which he turned into another monastery in order to enter it himself, not as the abbot but as an ordinary monk. Gregory's withdrawal—like Benedict's and Paul's—was of three years' duration; and at the end of that period he was in the act of withdrawing still farther—to Ultima Thule—on the enter-prise of converting the heathen English; but at that moment—and this was the true turning point in Gregory's career—he was recalled to Rome by the Pope, in deference to an urgent popular demand, and was constrained to bring his administrative gifts into play once more in the service of the afflicted City. He served Rome hence-forth in capacities in which he could use those gifts effectively.

Gregory's life-work, which began with his return and never ceased until his death in harness, was performed in the role of an ecclesiastical administrator and diplomatist and statesman. He per-formed it first as Seventh Deacon of the Roman See (the officer responsible for the social welfare work of the Church in the City); then, from about 579 to 585, as Apocrisiarius (the Papal representa-tive at the Imperial Court of Constantinople); and finally as Pope, from 590 to his death in 604. Gregory was elected to the Papacy by *force majeure* in a year of war and pestilence and famine,[3] and he

---

[1] For details see Hodgkin, op. cit., p. 350.

[2] We may conjecture that these Sicilian estates were the only part of Gregory's property in agricultural land, outside the walls of Rome, that had not been lost in conse-quence of the Lombard invasion.

[3] After his return from his diplomatic mission in Constantinople he had withdrawn again to his monastery in Rome—this time as its abbot.

bore heroically the burden which he had shrunk from accepting.[1]
On the Papal throne, he accomplished three great achievements.
In the first place, he reorganized the administration of the Patrimonia Petri—the estates of the Roman Church in Italy and overseas—with such efficiency that the condition of the serfs was
improved while at the same time revenues were raised for relieving,
on the grand scale, the distress of the destitute population of the
derelict Imperial City.[2] Gregory's second achievement—a labour
of ten years—was to negotiate a *modus vivendi* in Italy between the
Imperial authorities and the Lombards on a basis of *uti possidetis*.[3]
His third achievement was to lay the foundations of a new empire
for Rome in the place of her old empire which now lay in ruins.
This new Roman Empire, established by religious propaganda and
not by military force, was eventually to conquer new worlds whose
soil the legions had never trodden and whose very existence had
never been suspected by the Scipios and Caesars. And the first step
towards this re-establishment of the Roman Empire in a new and
more etherial form was the recovery of a Roman foothold in Britain
through the mission of Augustine: the Abbot of Gregory's own
monastery in Rome, whom Gregory the Pope dispatched in A.D.
596 to carry out an enterprise which Gregory the anchorite had
aspired to undertake in person nearly twenty years earlier. Thus,
at Rome's darkest hour, when the Lombards were at her gates, her
sacerdotal shepherd and captain audaciously out-manœuvred
the Continental Barbarians by sending his lieutenant overseas
to acquire new allies for Rome, and to win her a new sphere
of influence, in the enemy's rear. The spirit of the Roman
Pontiff in A.D. 596 is worthy of comparison with that which
had been shown, eight centuries back, by the Roman Senate
in 211 B.C. when, with Hannibal at the Gates, they had shipped
troops out of Rome down the Tiber to reinforce their armies
in Spain.[4]

[1] For Gregory's distress at leaving the life of contemplation, once for all, for the life
of action see his letter to Theoctista, the sister of the Emperor Maurice, in which he
analyses his feelings about his appointment (*Letters*, Bk. I, letter 5). See further
Hodgkin's observations in op. cit., pp. 304–6.
[2] For Gregory's administration of the Patrimonia of the Roman Church, see Dudden,
op. cit., vol. i, pp. 296–320. For his organization of relief work in the City, see vol. i,
pp. 247–51.
[3] See Hodgkin, op. cit., pp. 418–21.
[4] 'Cum ipse [Hannibal] ad moenia urbis Romae armatus sederet, milites sub vexillis
in supplementum Hispaniae profectos audiit' (Livy xxvi. 11). Another parallel in Roman
history to Gregory's dispatch of Augustine to Britain—a parallel, in this case, from the
history of Gregory's own age—is the Emperor Heraclius's audacious and successful
strategy of sailing with the flower of his troops from Constantinople in the spring of
A.D. 622, when a Persian army lay encamped at Calchedon, just across the Golden Horn,
in order to take the enemy in the rear by disembarking his expeditionary force at
Alexandretta. The preceding winter had been spent by Heraclius in retirement (see
Bury, J. B.: *A History of the Later Roman Empire* (London 1889, Macmillan, 2 vols.),
vol. ii, pp. 224–5).

Saint Ignatius Loyola

Another saint whose life-work had its overture in a withdrawal and a return is Ignatius Loyola. Loyola was born into Catholic Christendom in an age when the medieval standing of the Roman Church as the master-institution of the Western World had been challenged, and when its very existence as well as its supremacy had been placed in jeopardy, by the renaissance of Paganism in Italy and the eruption of Protestantism in Transalpine Europe. In this religious and social crisis Loyola, born a Spanish nobleman, was brought up in the Spanish nobility's conventional atmosphere and served in the Spanish Army till his twenty-seventh year,[1] when he was badly wounded in a siege of Pamplona by the French. The wound necessitated an operation from which the patient almost died; but he was just able to recover; and during his convalescence he underwent a religious conversion. In the year following these events, which had all taken place in A.D. 1521, Loyola dedicated himself to fight thenceforward as a soldier for God; but he did not rush straight into action in this new form of warfare. He spent the next twelve years in retreat: on pilgrimage, in asceticism, in study, and in meditation. It was only after this long withdrawal that he returned to the World at last in order to establish the Society of Jesus. The Society did not begin to take shape till the year 1534; it did not receive recognition from the Pope until 1540; and Loyola himself was not elected to be its first General until 1541. In Loyola's career, the *motif* of Withdrawal-and-Return is conspicuously manifest.

The Buddha

The *motif* is almost equally conspicuous in the career of a genius who was born into a wholly different time and place and whose temperament was at the opposite extreme of the human gamut: Siddhārtha Gautama the Buddha. Gautama was born into the Indic World in its 'Time of Troubles'.[2] In the devastating internecine warfare between contending states, he lived to see his native city-state Kapilavastu sacked, and his Sakyan kinsmen massacred. The small aristocratic republics of the early Indic World, of which the Sakya community was one, appear, in fact, to have been succumbing in Gautama's generation to rising monarchies which were autocratically governed and were built on a larger scale. Thus

---

[1] We have Loyola's own authority for the statement that he was twenty-six years old at the time of his conversion; and since the conversion evidently took place immediately after he received his wound at the siege of Pamplona—i.e. in A.D. 1521—it follows that he was born in A.D. 1495. (See Sedgwick, H. D.: *Ignatius Loyola* (London 1923, Macmillan), pp. 392-3.)

[2] For the symptoms, see I. C (i) (*b*), vol. i, pp. 86-7, above.

Siddhārtha Gautama was born a Sakya aristocrat at a moment when the older Indic social order, in which this aristocracy had its recognized place, was being challenged by new social forces. Gautama's personal retort to this challenge was to renounce a world which was becoming inhospitable to aristocrats of his ancestral kind. According to the tradition, it was at the age of twenty-nine that he abandoned his wife and son and wealth and rank and inheritance—he was the son of a 'king'[1]—and 'went out from the household life into the homeless state',[2] in order to seek enlightenment through asceticism. This quest continued without result for seven years during which Gautama constantly increased the severity of his physical self-mortification until he had carried it to the furthest extremity consistent with remaining alive. It was not until he had taken the first step towards returning to the World by breaking his fast that the light broke in upon him. And then, after he had attained the light for himself, he spent the rest of his life in imparting it to his fellow human beings.[3] In order to impart it effectively, he allowed a company of disciples to gather round him and thus became the centre and head of a fraternity.

The return of the ascetic Gautama to Society as the enlightened Tathāgata is remarkable when we consider what the mental content of the Buddha's enlightenment was. In his philosophy, the highest aim and happiest state of the human soul was something still more remote from action than the contemplative $\theta\epsilon\omega\rho\iota\alpha$ which was the Hellenic ideal of Pythagoras and Plato and Plotinus. It was nothing short of spiritual self-annihilation. And while Plato paid lip-service to the duty of return, the Buddha proclaimed the philosopher's right to escape into the freedom of Nirvana if only he could win his own way thither. Nevertheless, the Buddha did return to the World more sincerely, and therefore more effectively, than Plato. The foundation of the Sangha was a greater social achievement than the foundation of the Academy; and in the record of the Buddha's relations with princes there is none of the pedantry which appears in Plato's relations with Dionysius. The subsequent histories of Buddhism and Platonism point and accentuate this contrast. We have seen already[4] that Plato's injunction to return was repudiated, both in doctrine and in practice, by the first of the Neo-Platonists. On the other hand, the actual return of the Buddha—which was in logical contradiction with his doctrine, besides being

---

[1] The 'kingship' of Gautama's father seems to have been no more than a primacy *inter pares*. The constitution of the Sakya Commonwealth was oligarchical rather than monarchic. (See Eliot, Sir Charles: *Hinduism and Buddhism* (London 1921, Arnold, 3 vols.), vol. i, p. 131.)

[2] Eliot, op. cit., vol. i, p. 135.

[3] Eliot, op. cit., vol. i, pp. 138–40.

[4] On p. 254, above.

against his personal inclination[1]—became the central feature of the
Neo-Buddhism which took shape in the Mahayana or Great Vehicle.
One of the new and distinguishing features of the Mahayana is 'a
code of altruistic ethics which teaches that everyone must do good
in the interest of the whole World and make over to others any
merit he may acquire by his virtues. The aim of the religious life
is to become a Bodhisattva, not to become an Arhat.'[2] The Arhat
is an adept who has attained the Buddhist goal of self-annihilation
for himself; and according to the Mahayana 'the Arhat, engrossed
in his own salvation, is excused only by his humility and is open to
the charge of selfish desire, since the passion for Nirvana is an
ambition like any other'.[3] The Bodhisattva is a potential Arhat or
aspirant Buddha who voluntarily postpones his own entry into
Nirvana when he has reached the threshold and stands before the
open door, and thus sacrifices his own happiness by prolonging his
own existence as a sentient being among sentient beings, in order
to help his fellow-creatures to reach the point which he himself has
reached already on their common path.[4] It would seem that the
impulse to consummate a movement of withdrawal by a counter-
movement of return must be deeply grounded in the nature of the
human soul, and perhaps in the nature of the Universe itself, if it has
asserted itself so insistently in Buddhist practice, in despite of
Buddhist teaching and Buddhist belief.

David

When we pass from the lives of mystics and saints to those of
statesmen and soldiers, the Withdrawal-and-Return *motif* reveals
itself in this field again.

In the Syriac saga, for example, David begins his career as a
mighty man of valour in Saul's war-band. In other words, the

---

[1] See Eliot, op. cit., vol. i, p. 140. This inclination to remain aloof, which the enlightened Buddha overcame in his own soul, was a vestige of the ordinary attitude of the
unregenerate Indic anchorites of Gautama's generation; and, according to the legend,
the conventional opinion of these anchorites had been scandalized by Gautama's very
first step towards his return, when he broke his fast. 'There were five monks living near
him, hoping that when he found the Truth he would tell it to them. But when they saw
that he had begun to take food, their faith failed and they went away' (Eliot, op. cit.,
vol. i, p. 139). The Buddhist legend goes on to relate that the Buddha succeeded—
though not without difficulty—in converting these five monks to a recognition of his
Buddhahood, in spite of the scandal of his return to 'a life of ease' (Eliot, op. cit., vol. i,
pp. 140–1). In the story of Jesus, this incident has its parallel in the scandal caused
among the Pharisees by the formal breach of the Sabbath when the disciples of Jesus
satisfied their hunger, with their master's approval, by plucking and eating ears of corn
on the Sabbath day (Matt. xii. 1–8). For the Pharisees, the return of Jesus to ordinary
social intercourse after his forty days of ascetic withdrawal in the wilderness was an
insuperable stumbling-block.

'The Son of Man came eating and drinking, and they say: "Behold a man gluttonous
and a wine bibber, a friend of publicans and sinners".' (Matt. xi. 19.)

[2] Eliot, op. cit., vol. ii, p. 6.

[3] Eliot, op. cit., vol. ii, p. 8.   [4] See Eliot, op. cit., vol. ii, pp. 7–11.

future hero first appears on the scene as just an outstanding representative of what is, in itself, a common type in the society into which he has been born. It is not until Saul's jealousy has driven David into the wilderness, to lead the precarious life of an outlaw in the no-man's-land between Israel and Philistia, that David begins to acquire the statesmanship which eventually marks him out to be Saul's successor. And it is this statesmanship, thus acquired, that enables David, after his return from the wilderness, to solve for Israel the urgent problem of the age which Saul has failed to solve effectually: the problem of endowing the people of the hill-country with a political organization that will enable them to hold their own against the people of the coast.

Solon

Solon, again, was born into a rustic Attica in an age when Attica, in common with the whole Hellenic World, was confronted with the problem of continuing to provide for a population which was not ceasing to increase, yet which could not any longer be provided for by the old method of geographical expansion.[1] Solon's personal reaction to this social challenge was to withdraw from the agrarian life amid which he had been brought up and to take to the life of a merchant: a life which was something exotic in Attica at the turn of the seventh and sixth centuries B.C. While the majority of Solon's countrymen were still engrossed in the desperate business of obtaining diminishing returns from sowing and reaping increasing quantities of the traditional crops, Solon took to buying and selling and exporting and importing and travelling overseas and acquainting himself with the newfangled technique of a money economy. But he only withdrew for a season from the common round of Attic rural life in order to return to the land with a practicable scheme of economic salvation. By applying the new mercantile technique to the old industry of agriculture, Solon discovered the secret of substituting intensive development for extensive expansion; and he returned to teach his countrymen how to enhance the economic productivity of their land and labour by giving up 'subsistence farming' in favour of 'cash-crop farming' in specialized crops produced for export. Thus Solon's withdrawal from Attic agriculture to overseas trade was a prelude to his return to Attic agriculture in a new capacity. The first change in Solon's career—the change from farmer to merchant—led up to the second, and vital, change from merchant to statesman. And it was in his return to the land as a statesman that Solon accomplished his life-work.

[1] See vol. i, pp. 24–5, and vol. ii, pp. 39–42, as well as the present volume, pp. 122 and 139–40 and 168–9, above.

Philopoemen

In the history of Philopoemen of Megalopolis, we find a Hellenic analogue of the Syriac saga of David. Born in the heart of the Peloponnese in an age when the city-states of Greece were being dwarfed by the new Powers of vastly greater calibre that had sprung up all around them on the periphery of an expanding Hellenic World, Philopoemen started his career as a spirited young soldier in the Macedono-Lacedaemonian War of 224–221 B.C.; and he covered himself with distinction at Sellasia. When the overthrow of Cleomenes in that decisive battle had restored peace to Continental Greece for the time being, Philopoemen withdrew for ten years (*circa* 220–210 B.C.) to Crete in order to train himself in the arts of generalship and statesmanship in that miniature island-world apart within the great and growing oecumenical society of Philopoemen's day. From this Cretan apprenticeship, into which he had entered as a mere soldier, Philopoemen returned to the Peloponnese at the end of ten years as an experienced man of affairs; and it was only after that, upon his first election to the annual generalship of the Achaean Confederacy in 208 B.C., that he began his life-work—the work of piloting the frail and puny Achaean ship of state through perilous seas over which new storm-clouds were gathering from beyond the western horizon.[1]

Caesar

The same *motif* reveals itself in a far more famous political career. When Caesar withdrew from Rome to Gaul in 58 B.C., he was still to outward appearance nothing more than a virtuoso in the regular role of the Roman politician of the day: a player of the conventional game for the sake of the conventional prizes. During the nine years that passed before he re-emerged from Gaul in 49 B.C. and crossed the Rubicon, he grew in political and moral stature till even his bitterest opponents were compelled to recognize him, in their heart of hearts, as the one possible Saviour of Society—if Society would consent to allow itself to be saved.

Leo Syrus

The *motif* reappears in the career of Leo Syrus[2] (*imperabat* A.D.

---

[1] For the metaphor of 'the clouds from the west', which was first employed, apropos of Rome and Carthage, by Agelaus of Naupactus in the peace-pourparlers of 217 B.C. between the Aetolian Confederacy and the Macedonian Alliance, see Polybius, Bk. V, chs. 103–5.

[2] The grounds for regarding Leo as a 'Syrian' (i.e. as a native of the administrative area which was known in the political geography of the Later Roman Empire as Oriens or Ἀνατολή) are given by Bury in his edition of Gibbon (Gibbon, E.: *The History of the Decline and Fall of the Roman Empire*, edited by Bury, J. B.: *Editio Minor* (London 1900–2, Methuen, 7 vols.), vol. v, p. 185, footnote 17). Leo's family appear to have been natives of the city of Germanicea, in Commagene, among the south-eastern foot-

717–40): the great statesman who saved the infant civilization of Orthodox Christendom from meeting its death before it was out of the cradle.

In the history of Leo, there are some features that recall the Syriac saga of David, and others that recall the Hellenic myths of Jason and Bellerophon.[1] Like David, Leo first appears upon the scene as a mighty man of valour in a prince's war-band. He comes to the notice of the Emperor Justinian Rhinotmetus, as David comes to the notice of King Saul, by presenting himself in the prince's camp as a shepherd-boy bringing rustic gifts from the produce of his father's flocks; and in the prince's service he displays a prowess which only serves to draw down upon him his royal master's deadly jealousy. The historical Emperor Justinian II was in fact, throughout his history, a by-word for that demoniac vein of passion and implacability that is attributed in the Syriac saga to Saul. But, in the saga of Leo, the hero's master, when he seeks to compass the hero's death, does not adopt the direct methods of a Saul but resorts to the guile of a Pelias or a Proetus. Leo is sent by Justinian, as Jason is sent by Pelias, on a perilous quest to the Caucasus; and Justinian takes treacherous measures to ensure that his victim shall meet his death which are quite in the manner of Proetus's treacherous dealing with Bellerophon. Leo, however, like his mythical and historical prototypes, achieves the impossible and not only escapes alive but triumphantly fulfils his mission, so that when he returns—leading home from the Caucasus a marooned Roman army in a Xenophontic catabasis that duly ends at Trebizond—he is greeted as the heaven-sent saviour of the Roman People and eventually takes the place of his long since discomfited and discredited and evicted master on the Imperial throne.

Whatever may be the respective ingredients of fact and fable in the story of Leo up to this point, it is certain that Leo returned to Romania from the Caucasus in A.D. 713 as a seasoned statesman who was ripe to enter upon his life-work; and it was in the last chapter of his career, which opened now, that he performed his three historic achievements. In A.D. 716–18, he defeated the second and supreme effort of the Arabs to overwhelm Orthodox Christendom by force of arms and to make themselves masters of Con-

---

hills of the Taurus Range. The family left their Asiatic home as refugees, and found a new home in Thrace, when Commagene was conquered from the Romans by the Arabs some time during the first reign of Justinian II (A.D. 685–95).

[1] Leo's personal history (which has been touched upon in this Study, by anticipation, in I. C (i) (b), vol. i, on p. 64, footnote 3, above) is recounted in the *Chronographia* of Theophanes retrospectively, *sub Anno Mundi* 6209, which was the year of Leo's accession to the Imperial throne of Constantinople. The story reads like a genuine record of fact which has become suffused with traditional or legendary *motifs*—a well-known tendency in the stories of historical personalities that have made a deep impression upon the popular imagination.

stantinople. Thereafter, he provided for the future security of the infant civilization whose life he had saved from out of the jaws of destruction by evoking, in Orthodox Christendom, a ghost of the Roman Empire[1]—and this with a thoroughgoing efficiency and an enduring effect that stand out in impressive contrast to the superficial and ephemeral re-establishment of the same great institution in the West by Charlemagne half a century later. Leo not only consolidated his East Roman Empire territorially, with Anatolia—now salvaged from the Arabs—as its centre of gravity and Constantinople as its European bridge-head. He gave his new state such solid administrative and military and financial and legal and economic foundations that it remained 'a going concern' for little short of five centuries after his reign, whereas 'the Holy Roman Empire' of the West faded away into the nullity of 'a ghost of a ghost' almost immediately after the death of the founder and was never successfully resuscitated—not even by the energy of an Otto I or by the genius of a Frederick II. Leo's third historic achievement was the impress which he set upon the history of the Orthodox Church: a permanent impress in the supremacy over the Church which he vindicated for his re-animated State, and a temporary yet nevertheless profoundly important impress in his initiation of the Iconoclastic Movement. In both the successful and the abortive part of his ecclesiastical policy, Leo, in the eighth century of the Christian Era, brought about developments in Orthodox Christendom which did not take place in Western Christendom until the time of the Protestant Reformation, some seven centuries later. It will be seen that in Leo's career the movement of Withdrawal-and-Return, represented by the Caucasian episode, was the prelude to a titanic output of creative activity after the hero's restoration to the society of which he became the saviour.

Muhammad

A still more effective statesman in whose career the Withdrawal-and-Return *motif* is strongly marked is the Prophet Muhammad, who was born into the Arabian external proletariat of the Roman Empire in an age when the relations between the Empire and Arabia were coming to a crisis. At the turn of the sixth and seventh

[1] This ghost of the Roman Empire was evoked by Leo to serve as a 'carapace' for Orthodox Christendom against the assaults of the Syriac universal state, which had been reintegrated in the shape of the Arab Caliphate. Thus the East Roman Empire, during the eighth, ninth, and tenth centuries of the Christian Era, performed for Orthodox Christendom the service which was performed for Western Christendom during the sixteenth, seventeenth, and eighteenth centuries by the Danubian Hapsburg Monarchy, when it was serving as a 'carapace' against the assaults of the Ottoman Empire (which, it may be recalled in passing, was the universal state of the Orthodox Christian Society). For the simile of the 'carapace' see I. C (iii) (*b*), vol. i, p. 156, footnote 1, and II. D (v), vol. ii, p. 177, footnote 1.

centuries of the Christian Era, the saturation-point had been reached in the impregnation of Arabia with cultural influences from the Empire through the cumulative effect of a long-continuing process of social radiation.[1] Some reaction from Arabia upon the Empire, in the form of a counter-discharge of energy, was bound to ensue; and the destinies of both parties to the Arabo-Roman interaction were deeply involved in the open question of what direction this imminent Arabian recoil would take and what plane of social activity it would choose for its principal field of action. It was the career of Muhammad (*vivebat circa* A.D. 570–632) that gave these questions their historic answers; and a movement of Withdrawal-and-Return was the prelude to each of the two crucial new departures upon which Muhammad's life-history hinges.

There were two features in the social life of the Roman Empire in Muhammad's day that would make a particularly deep impression upon the mind of an Arabian observer because, in Arabia, they were both conspicuous by their absence. The first of these features was monotheism in religion.[2] The second was law and order in government. Muhammad's life-work consisted in translating each of these elements in the social fabric of 'Rūm' into an Arabian vernacular version and incorporating both his Arabianized monotheism and his Arabianized imperium into a single master-institution—the all-embracing institution of Islam—to which he succeeded in imparting such titanic driving-force that the new dispensation, which had been designed by its author to meet the needs of the barbarians of Arabia, burst the bounds of the Peninsula and captivated the entire Syriac World from the shores of the Atlantic to the coasts of the Eurasian Steppe.

This life-work, upon which Muhammad seems to have embarked in about his fortieth year (*circa* A.D. 609), was achieved in two stages. In the first of these stages, Muhammad was concerned exclusively with his religious mission; in the second stage, the religious mission was overlaid, and almost overwhelmed, by the political enterprise. Muhammad's original entry upon a purely religious mission was a sequel to his return to the parochial life of Arabia after a partial withdrawal (*circa* A.D. 594 seqq.)[3] into the exotic life of a caravan-

[1] For this phenomenon of social radiation, see Part II. A, vol. i, p. 187, and III. C (i) (a), pp. 151–3, above, and V. C (i) (c) 3, vol. v, pp. 196–203, as well as Parts VIII and IX, below. [2] See III. C (ii) (a), p. 238, above.

[3] The dates of Muhammad's caravan-expeditions are instructive. They fall within the short interval of peace (A.D. 591–603) between the two long-drawn-out and devastating Romano-Persian Wars of A.D. 572–91 and A.D. 603–28. We do not know the exact year in which Muhammad's expeditions between Mecca and Syria ceased, but we may conjecture that they were brought to an end by the general paralysis of economic life in the Asiatic provinces of the Roman Empire that must have resulted from the Persian invasions. The expeditions had evidently ceased before Muhammad's entry upon his prophetic mission, and, if that is to be dated about A.D. 609, we may bring this date into relation with the Persian invasion of Syria in A.D. 606 and with the occupation of Calche-

trader between the Arabian oases and the Syrian desert-ports of the
Roman Empire along the fringes of the North Arabian Steppe.
The second or politico-religious stage in Muhammad's career was
inaugurated by the Prophet's withdrawal (*Hijrah*) from his native
oasis of Mecca to the rival oasis of Yathrib (thenceforward known
par excellence as Medina: 'The City' [of the Prophet]). In the
Hijrah—which has been recognized by Muslims as such a crucial
event in the Prophet's career that it has been taken as the inaugural
date for the Islamic Era—Muhammad left Mecca as a hunted
fugitive. After a seven years' absence (A.D. 622–9), he returned to
Mecca, not as an amnestied exile, but as lord and master, not only
of Mecca itself, but of half Arabia. It will be seen that the first
stage in Muhammad's career is comparable with the career of
Solon[1] and the second stage with the career of Caesar.[2]

Peter the Great.

The drastic and effective statesmanship of Muhammad, which
changed the face of the Arabian Barbarism, has its analogue in the
work of Peter the Great and Lenin, who, in two successive chapters

---

don by a Persian expeditionary force in A.D. 608. May we conjecture that Muhammad's
commercial activities were abruptly and unexpectedly cut short by these catastrophic
events and that it was an enforced resumption of a sedentary life of economic inactivity in Mecca that diverted the ex-merchant's spiritual energies from the economic
into the religious channel? This would explain—in so far as there can be any external
explanation of a psychic event—why Muhammad's creative religious experience came
to him at just this point in his life.

[1] In Part III. A, pp. 7–8, above, the Steppe has been compared to the Sea, and
the life of the camel-caravanner, who conveys merchandise across the Steppe on board
'the ship of the desert', to the life of the merchant-seaman. Thus, from the technical
or professional standpoint, there is an affinity between the early commercial phases of
Muhammad's and Solon's careers. There is also this further point of resemblance that,
in Muhammad's Arabia, this commercial life—which brought the individual or the
minority that took to it into social intercourse with the Great World—was just as exotic
as it was in Solon's Hellas. In Arabia *circa* A.D. 600, as in Hellas *circa* 600 B.C., commerce
was the pursuit of a small minority, whose adoption of this profession was tantamount
to a withdrawal from the common run of life in the surrounding society. In one respect,
however, the situations of the two statesmen were different; for, while Solon the
Athenian belonged to a relatively backward local community in which the merchant was
a much rarer type than he was in contemporary Corinth or Miletus, Muhammad the
Meccan belonged to a local community in which commerce was the prevailing economic
activity—in contrast to the more primitive conditions of the rest of the Hijāz in Muhammad's day. Perhaps this difference explains why the first stage of Muhammad's career,
which corresponds to Solon's career, was a failure, in contrast to Solon's success. In
rustic Attica, Solon's profession had a rarity-value which must have enhanced Solon's
personal prestige in the eyes of his countrymen and have thereby facilitated the accomplishment of Solon's mission. On the other hand, Muhammad the merchant had no
peculiar honour in his own commercially-minded city. It is significant that Muhammad, when he had been despised and rejected at Mecca, found a welcome at Yathrib:
a rustic oasis (see Margoliouth, D.S.: *Mohammed*, 3rd ed. (London 1905, Putnam),
pp. 185 and 191, and the present Study, II. D (ii), vol. ii, p. 57, footnote 3, above)
where an immigrant with Muhammad's Meccan commercial experience was a valued and
an honoured guest. In fact, Muhammad proved himself valuable to the Yathribis not
only by introducing them to political law and order, but also by teaching them to take
advantage of their geographical situation in order to supplant Mecca as the half-way-
house on the caravan-route between Syria and the Yaman.

[2] For the significance of Muhammad's political success, see further the second Annex
to this chapter, on pp. 466–72, below.

of a single social revolution, have succeeded in changing the face of Russian Orthodox Christendom.

By a freakish stroke of Fortune, there was born into the purple of the Russian Orthodox Christian universal state at Moscow, on the 30th May, 1672, a genius endowed with a completely Western êthos—and this not even the êthos of his own Western contemporaries, but the êthos of their descendants in the sixth or seventh generation, whose time was not to come till some two centuries had gone by! Peter the Great[1] was an incomprehensible and therefore disagreeable *lusus Naturae* in the eyes of an English Bishop Burnet or a Dutch King William III, as well as in the eyes of a Russian Arch-Priest Avvakum. When Burnet met Peter in A.D. 1698, he pronounced him sordid-minded, and saw nothing more in him than a young barbarian potentate who happened to be a good ship's carpenter. When William met him, he complained that he had no aesthetic sense, and no knowledge of the Dutch language apart from a jargon of nautical technicalities. These worthy representatives of the modern culture of the West did not, and could not, guess that, in their encounter with this repulsive mechanically-minded barbarian they were being given a glimpse into their own society's future and were being shown a prototype of the typical *Homo Occidentalis* who was to adorn an age two centuries beyond their own! For us, their descendants, who have the fortune to live in these latter days, the figure of Peter has ceased to be enigmatic. We have no hesitation in placing Peter the Great in the same portrait-gallery as Edison and Ford and Rhodes and Northcliffe and Mark Twain's Yankee at the Court of King Arthur and Mr. Shaw's Straker in *Man and Superman*.

The leading traits of *Homo Occidentalis Mechanicus Neobarbarus* appear in Peter's character unmistakably, both for good and for evil. He displays an American vitality, an American impatience of pomp, an American delight in manual skill, and also an American ruthlessness.

When Peter wanted anything done, he always took the initiative by setting the example of doing the hard work himself. He worked with his own hands as a ship-wright; and, in his new Western-model Russian Army and Navy, he worked his way up the ladder of promotion from the bottom, as though he were a self-made man instead of being, as he actually was, the creator as well as the master of these two new Russian public services.[2] Moreover, he

---

[1] The account of Peter which is given here is taken for the most part from Brückner, A.: *Peter der Grosse* (Berlin 1879, Grote).

[2] In the triumphal procession through the streets of Moscow in A.D. 1696 with which Peter celebrated the capture of Azov—his first signal success—Peter himself marched among his comrades in the uniform of a naval captain. Compare his admiration for

chose a genuine self-made man in the person of Menshikov to be
his Russian right-hand man (his other principal coadjutors were
imported Westerners). He threw off the Byzantine ceremonial of
the Muscovite Court[1] and preferred to live at ease: not only among
the relatively cultivated Western merchants and professional men
in the German suburb of Moscow,[2] but also among his Western
craftsmen at Preobrazhensk. (At Zaandam in Holland, which he
visited on his Western tour, he stayed in the house of an artisan
whose acquaintance he had made in Russia.) His method of visiting the West was to send his Swiss adviser Lefort on a diplomatic
mission to the Western Courts and then to travel incognito in his
own ambassador's suite as one of a party of naval apprentices. As
for his mechanical bent, he had already learnt the use of all manner
of tools and mechanical apparatus by his twelfth year, before ever
he had stirred abroad. In 1697 the Kurfürstin Sophie Charlotte
of Brandenburg found him master of no less than fourteen trades;
he took the opportunity of his visit to the West to add dentistry
and etching to his accomplishments and to make some study of
anatomy; and he astonished the Saxon Court by his technical
knowledge of artillery. The most 'American' of all Peter's traits
was the combination of this manual ability with the lynx eye of
the prospector and the entrepreneur. When he temporarily occupied the Caspian Provinces of Persia in 1722-3 his first step was
to organize a systematic inquiry into their natural resources; and
he himself divined the commercial future of coal in an age when
coal was as yet of no account at Newcastle. More remarkable still,
a passing visit to Baku in the course of a military campaign revealed
to Peter's uncannily perspicuous vision the future of mineral oil![3]

It will be seen that Peter was a *lusus Naturae* in two degrees.
He was a Westerner born into Russian Orthodox Christendom;
and he was a Westerner born into the World two centuries before
the West itself succeeded in producing human beings of Peter's
type. When we have added that Nature endowed Peter with genius
and that Fortune placed in his hands the autocratic government
of a great state, we shall find that we have left ourselves only one
historical figure with whom Peter can be treated as comparable,
and that is Ikhnaton.

Ikhnaton, inheriting despotic power in a society in which he
was a spiritual stranger, attempted to remake Society in his own
image and ended in utter failure. Peter, attempting the same *tour*

English simplicity in dress, which comes out in the anecdote cited in III. C (i) (c) on
p. 179, footnote 2, above.
[1] Throughout his reign, Peter restricted himself to a modest personal income.
[2] This suburb was known in Russian as 'the Svoboda' or 'free town'. The proportion
of self-made men among its bourgeoisie was high. For its êthos, see vol. ii, p. 232, above.
[3] See II. D (vii), vol. ii, pp. 278-9, above.

de force in the same circumstances, achieved a resounding success. What accounts for this extreme difference between the fortunes of these two historic human 'sports'? Partly, no doubt, the difference in temperament (for in temperament, as opposed to circumstances, Peter and Ikhnaton were poles apart). There is, however, another factor which was manifestly of the utmost importance in Peter's career and which was lacking in Ikhnaton's career; and this factor is the movement of Withdrawal-and-Return. Ikhnaton did indeed withdraw from the Egyptiac Society into the enchanted palace which he conjured up for himself at Tell-el-Amarna. But, once within the precincts of this asylum, he could never bring himself to face the return to reality. Peter likewise withdrew from the alien Orthodoxy of Russia into the Western World towards which he was drawn by spiritual affinity; but his whole absence in the West, on the momentous tour of A.D. 1697–8, only lasted eighteen months; and the absentee autocrat cut his travels short, upon the news of the outbreak of the Streltzy, in order to return to Russia post-haste and crush the mutineers. Moreover, the Peter who returned to Russia in the autumn of 1698 was a different man from the Peter who had left Russia less than two years before.

The change in Peter which actually took place is symbolically described in a Russian fairy-tale. On the Western tour, as the tale is told, the real Peter disappeared;[1] and the man who came back to Russia in 1698 was neither Peter nor indeed a real man at all, for he was none other than Antichrist in Peter's shape! There is more in this fairy-tale than the naïve peasants who tell it comprehend; for Peter really did return with a life-work to carry out which is aptly described as the work of Antichrist from the standpoint of Russian Orthodox Christendom. When he left Russia for the West, Peter was still just a boy who had found his hobby in carpentry and had applied this hobby, when Fortune gave him the power, to building himself a navy and building it on Western lines because those lines happened to be technically the best. If this gifted boy had simply stayed at home, immersing himself in his hobby and making himself an *enfant terrible* to the conservative Byzantine Court which was his native social milieu, he might well have met the same untimely and violent end as Scyles the Scythian;[2] and his vagaries would certainly have had no greater effect

[1] He is said to have disappeared in Sweden—a country which he did not actually visit—but the Sweden of the fairy-story is a mythical German Kingdom which is ruled by a virgin—a wraith, perhaps, of the famous Queen Christina (*regnabat* A.D. 1633–54).

[2] Scyles (*florebat circa* 450 B.C.) was the prince of a Scythian Nomad horde which ranged the steppes in the hinterland of the north coast of the Black Sea. Through the Greek colonies planted on this coast, Scyles made the acquaintance of the Hellenic Civilization, and he fell in love with it. For a time he led a double life—living part of the year, unbeknown to his fellow-Nomads, in the Greek city of Borysthenes in Greek clothes and in the Greek manner, with a Greek wife. (Compare Peter's visits to 'the

than those of Ikhnaton upon the subsequent course of history. The very different course which Peter's life-history actually took was the outcome of his brief Western tour of A.D. 1697–8—as far as it can be ascribed to any external event. At any rate, Peter returned to Russia from this tour with his mental horizon immensely widened and with his mind made up to carry out a design which might seem to be beyond the compass of any one man's powers but which, nevertheless, was the one possible way of safeguarding 'the changeling's' own personal fortunes. Peter returned with the resolve to make life possible for Russia in the contemporary World—and, incidentally, to make life possible for Peter himself in Russia—by bringing this derelict remnant of Byzantinism into the comity of Western nations as one of the Great Powers of the Western political system.

This broadening of Peter's aim can be discerned in those records of his Western tour that have come down to us. The interests that took him abroad in 1697 were not social and political but technical. Out of his eighteen months in Western Europe, he spent nine on improving his knowledge of the technique of ship-building. He worked for five months and a half on a frigate that was under construction in the Dutch Admiralty dockyard at Amsterdam; and he went on from Holland to England because the Dutch naval designers were not sufficiently scientific in their methods to satisfy him! The impression which he made, in England, upon King William and Bishop Burnet has been described already. Yet a broadening of outlook is indicated by the fact that, in England, Peter sometimes turned aside from his technical pursuits in order to attend Anglican church services and Quaker meetings; and such indications are confirmed by his action after his return, when he launched his campaign of Westernization along the whole front of the battle-ground between his own subversive personality and the traditional social life of Russian Orthodox Christendom. On every sector of this front, he took the offensive and won a victory. He overcame the Streltzy,[1] he overcame the Boyars,[2] he overcame the

Svoboda', and his ten-years-long liaison with Anna Mons.) When the Nomads discovered their prince's secret Hellenism, they did him to death. The story is told by Herodotus in Bk. IV, chs. 78–80.

[1] The Streltzy were destroyed by Peter in A.D. 1698–9. In non-Western communities that have entered upon the path of Westernization, the destruction of a turbulent and inefficient 'Old Guard', in order to make room for a new-model army on the Western pattern, has been a common first step in the campaigns of political Westernizers. Compare the destruction of the Mamlūks in Egypt by Mehmed 'Alī in A.D. 1811 and the destruction of the Janissaries in Turkey by Sultan Mahmūd II in A.D. 1826. The exception which proves the rule is the voluntary renunciation of traditional privileges in Japan by the Daimyos and their Samurai in A.D. 1868–9. For these phenomena, see further Part IX, below.

[2] The noble cadets attached to Lefort's suite (of whom Peter himself was one!) were given exacting instructions to master certain particular Western techniques. If they did not bring home satisfactory evidence that they had done what had been laid upon them,

Byzantine social tradition,[1] he overcame the Orthodox Church,[2] and he overcame the Swedes.[3] This astonishing list of victories is a summary of Peter's life-work; and this life-work was a sequel to his withdrawal-and-return in A.D. 1697–8.

Lenin

Withdrawal-and-Return is likewise the key to the career of

they were to forfeit their estates! Peter even went so far as to prohibit any nobleman from marrying until he had passed an examination in geometry, arithmetic, and navigation! Moreover, all hereditary boyars were conscripted by Peter for a lifelong term of compulsory public service—and this without even the compensation of being given a monopoly of the field. For at the same time the public service was thrown open to all classes; and self-made men were automatically ennobled upon the attainment of quite modest ranks in the new political hierarchy. More than that, the Russians of all classes in Peter's service were subordinated to the imported Westerners, of whom more than a thousand were engaged on long-term contracts during the Western tour of A.D. 1697–8. It will be seen that Peter passed his boyars under the harrow, without mercy.

[1] Peter's declaration of war upon the Byzantine social tradition was delivered in his celebrated gesture of shaving, with his own hand, the beards of the grandees who came to congratulate him on his return from the West in A.D. 1698. A ukase of the 4th January, 1700, made the wearing of Western dress compulsory by a certain date 'for the glory and beauty of the State and the improvement of the Army'. This was confirmed in a second ukase of the 20th March, and detailed instructions were issued in 1701. Compare Mehmed 'Ali's imposition of Western uniforms upon his troops, and Mustafā Kemāl's imposition of Western dress upon the entire male civil population. (The compulsory change of dress which was carried through by Peter in Russia was confined to the upper class, and the obligation to shave might be bought off by the payment of a beard-tax.) Peter, however, was not content with imposing Western dress. He arranged for the compilation of elaborate manuals of Western fine manners; and in the houses of the nobility in the new capital, Petersburg, 'receptions' à la française were organized by the Police.

[2] Peter re-converted the Orthodox Church in Russia into the docile instrument of state which had been the church's function in the minds of Peter's Byzantine precursors Constantine the Great and Justinian the Caesaro-papist and Leo the Iconoclast; but Peter's model in this matter was probably the contemporary practice in the Protestant countries of the Western World rather than the original practice in Orthodox Christendom itself. In A.D. 1690 (just on the morrow of his effective accession to power) Peter failed to secure the election of his own well-educated and progressive candidate, the Metropolitan Marcellus of Pskov, to the Patriarchate of Moscow. But when the Patriarchate fell vacant next time, which happened in 1700, Peter deliberately left it vacant for 20 years, until 1721, when he substituted for the Patriarchate, as the supreme authority over the Russian Orthodox Church, a Holy Synod which was simply a secular department of the Petrine State. The measure of Peter's victory over the Orthodox Church is given by the fact that he attended Protestant and Catholic church services, not only abroad, but in 'the Svoboda' under the very walls of Moscow. In a prospectus, issued in 1702, inviting foreign experts to come to Russia—a document which was printed in German and was circulated in the West—Peter gave an express and explicit guarantee of religious toleration. (Text of the relevant passage in Brückner, op. cit., p. 204.)

[3] Having realized Russia's need to acquire a seaboard, Peter began, in A.D. 1695–6, with the relatively easy conquest of Azov from the Turks. It is significant that, after his return from the Western tour of A.D. 1697–8, he addressed himself to the far more formidable task of conquering the Baltic Provinces from the Swedes, and persevered in this arduous enterprise for twenty years (A.D. 1700–21) until he finally achieved his aim. He had come to the conclusion that a seaboard on the Baltic was worth acquiring at any price because it would open the door for direct intercourse between Russia and the West. (For the significance of the new capital which Peter founded on the Neva, see II. D (v), vol. ii, pp. 157–8, above.) On the other hand, the conquest of Azov was not worth following up, because the further passage from this port to the open sea was blocked by the Ottoman Government's control of the Straits of Kertch and of the Bosphorus and of the Dardanelles. And even if the Russian ships had been able to run the gauntlet of these three successive 'Symplegades', they would have merely found themselves at large in the Eastern Mediterranean—a sea which, in Peter's day, before the opening of the short-cut from the Atlantic to the Indian Ocean, was a sluggish backwater, remote from the principal ocean-highways of the World.

III   K

Lenin:[1] the second Russian 'Antichrist' whose intention it was to undo, and whose achievement it has been to consummate, the work of Westernization which was originally initiated by Peter.[2] Born in 1870, Lenin entered, in 1893, upon the conventional revolutionary career of the Russian intellectual of his generation: an abortive agitation which ended in 1897 in banishment to Siberia. It was after his withdrawal from Russia to Switzerland in 1900, after his Siberian sentence had been served out, that Lenin came to know his own mind and began to impose his will upon the minds of his fellow revolutionaries. He came to the front in 1903, when a conference of Russian Marxian Socialists in exile, which was held that year in Brussels and London, resulted, by reason of Lenin's masterful intransigence, in the historic split of the Russian Marxian Socialist Party into the two sects of Minoritarians (*Mensheviki*) and Majoritarians (*Bolsheviki*). From that time onwards Lenin, as leader of the 'majoritarian' Bolshevik faction in the Russian Marxian Socialist camp, continued to gain in authority and prestige through the long course of an absence from Russia which extended, from first to last, from 1900 to 1917. And though this potent exile's first return missed fire in the failure of the abortive Russian Revolution of 1905–7,[3] his second return, when he appeared again in Russia from the West on the 4th April, 1917, will assuredly rank as one of the decisive events in the history of our Western Civilization and perhaps in the history of Mankind, as well as in the history of Russia. After twenty-four years of revolutionary work, of which some eighteen years had been spent at work in exile in Siberia and Europe, Lenin now returned, with seven more years of life before him, to carry out his tremendous life-work. Before he died in 1924 he had made himself master of the territory and population and resources of the *ci-devant* Russian Empire; and he had turned this mastery to account in order to put in hand—with a ruthlessness equal to Peter's—the great experiment of translating the Marxian Utopia into real life on the grand scale.

Garibaldi

Before we pass on from the 'practical men' to the 'intellectuals', we may observe the Withdrawal-and-Return *motif* appearing again in the careers of two famous Western heroes of the modern age: Giuseppe Garibaldi (*vivebat* 1807–82) and Paul von Hindenburg (*vivebat* 1847–1934).

[1] See Mirsky, D. S.: *Lenin* (London 1932, Holme Press).
[2] For the function of Bolshevism as an instrument of Westernization, see III. C (i) (*d*), pp. 200–2, above.
[3] On this occasion, Lenin returned to Russia in November 1905 and withdrew again in December 1907.

The first chapter in Garibaldi's career is not unlike the first chapter in Lenin's. Born in 1807, Garibaldi entered, in 1833, upon the conventional revolutionary career of the post-Napoleonic Western Liberal: an abortive conspiracy against the régime of the Restoration, which ended in the conspirator's ignominious flight from the territory of the Sardinian Government instead of ending in the Government's overthrow. The next stage in Garibaldi's life-history recalls a stage which has come to our notice in the life-history of Philopoemen. As the young Philopoemen withdrew for ten years from his native Peloponnese in order to practise the arts of war and statesmanship overseas in the training-school of Crete, so the young Garibaldi now withdrew for twelve years (1836–48) from his native Italy in order to learn the same perennial arts in the New World of Latin America. It was in a Latin-American war between the Republic of Rio Grande do Sul and the Empire of Brazil that Garibaldi won his spurs as a guerilla leader; and it was in another Latin-American war—this time between Monte Video and Buenos Ayres—that he recruited the nucleus of his Italian 'Red-Shirts'.

'[The] Italian Legion of Monte Video was the origin of the Garibaldians proper. It was the first considerable body of his countrymen whom he ever commanded on land; most of the men were political exiles; it was they who first wore the famous "red shirt"; and those of them who came back with him to Europe in 1848 imported the Garibaldian dress, tradition, and methods in war and politics. The idea with which they enlisted was to fight for the liberties of Monte Video in return for the shelter it had given them, refusing all rich rewards; but the idea behind was to prepare for another struggle, which, as Garibaldi said, he had never forgotten even "in the depths of the American forests".'[1]

Thus, when the news of the European Revolution of 1848 reached the opposite shores of the Atlantic, Garibaldi in Monte Video was ready for the call to enter upon his life-work. As they sailed homewards across the ocean in order to turn their prowess to account in fighting for the liberation of Italy, the returning hero and his companions 'knew that they were going "towards the attainment of the passion and desire of their lives" '.[2] And the People of Italy, on their part, were already aware of what Garibaldi's life-work was to be,[3] before ever he re-entered the country which he had left, twelve years before, as an obscure and defeated fugitive. Garibaldi's fame had outstripped Garibaldi himself and

[1] Trevelyan, G. M.: *Garibaldi's Defence of the Roman Republic, 1848–9* (second impression: London 1928, Longmans, Green and Co.), p. 35.
[2] Trevelyan, op. cit., p. 40.
[3] Read the anecdote recounted by Trevelyan in op. cit., on pp. 39–40.

come home to Italy before him. 'Already the names of Garibaldi and his Italian Legion were household words'[1] as far afield as Rome. In the chapter of his life-history which began when he once more set foot on Italian soil in 1848, Garibaldi stepped straight into that place in the hearts of his countrymen and in the history of his age which he was to occupy from that time onward.[2]

Hindenburg

As for Hindenburg, in the summer of 1914 he was already some four years older, at the age of 67, than Garibaldi had been at the time when the task which had been Garibaldi's life-work was carried to completion by the entry of the Italian troops into Rome in the autumn of 1870. And yet, at the outbreak of the General War, the life-work of Hindenburg had not really begun. Born in 1847, and born the son of a Prussian officer, he had almost automatically embraced his father's profession and had passed in his turn through the conventional career of a Prussian officer from start to finish. Nor had his career been particularly eventful; for, while he had come to manhood just in time to serve in the campaigns of 1866 and 1870–1, the whole of the rest of his time of service had elapsed in a period of unbroken peace, until he had been placed on the retired list in his sixty-fourth year as a worthy but undistinguished General Officer. Yet this retirement, which seemed to write 'finis' upon his record, was destined to last for no longer than three years. On the 22nd August, 1914, less than a month after the outbreak of the General War, von Hindenburg re-emerged from his retirement at Hanover, and entered upon his life-work, when he rescued East Prussia from her Russian invaders. For this was the first step in a new career which culminated in the command of the whole German Army on all fronts; and the veteran Generalissimo justified the trust which had been placed in him by his countrymen in the stress of national danger when he stood by his troops at the moment of débâcle instead of running to earth on neutral soil at the heels of his sovereign and his chief-of-staff. Thereafter, when the fighting had ceased and the armies had been demobilized, von Hindenburg retired to Hanover for the second time in July 1919, and remained in retirement this time for twice as many years as before, until his countrymen summoned him out of retirement once again by electing him President of the German Reich in April 1925. Thereupon, at the age of seventy-seven, the veteran entered

---

[1] Trevelyan, op. cit., loc. cit.
[2] Compare the life-history of Hereward the Wake, who left England before the Norman Conquest as a young sprig seeking his fortune on the Continent, and returned to England after the Norman Conquest to step at once into the position of being the one Englishman who knew how to defy the Conqueror.

upon a third career in which he was required to bear the highest responsibility in an unfamiliar field of action. In this remarkable life, the *motif* of Withdrawal-and-Return has asserted itself at the eleventh hour in order to transform the retired Prussian officer of 1911 into the Pater Patriae of 1925 by miraculously adding a cubit to an old man's stature.

A Pleiad of Historians

If we pass on now, in our survey, from the lives of soldiers and statesmen to the lives of historians and poets and philosophers, our attention will first be attracted by a Pleiad of historians—Thucydides and Xenophon and Polybius; Josephus and Ibn Khaldūn; Machiavelli and Clarendon and Ollivier—who have started life as soldiers or statesmen and have made the transit from one field of action to another in their own life-histories by returning as historians to a world from which they have previously been expelled as prisoners-of-war or deportees or exiles.

Born into their social milieux in generations whose fortune it has been to encounter tremendous challenges and to live through momentous experiences, these eventual observers and recorders of the histories of their own times have all begun their careers by taking a hand in 'practical affairs': participating, that is to say, in the direct interactions between individual human wills in which current history works itself out. This original orientation of their energies towards 'practical' action may have been determined by different causes—by inward inclination or by external accident—but in every case the effect upon their activities has been the same. So long as they have been swept along in the stream of 'practical' action into which they have stumbled or plunged, they have found no occasion for exercising their latent historical abilities. In each of these lives, the occasion has been offered by some accidental breach in the future historian's career as a 'practical man'; and, here again, the effect of this compulsory abandonment of their original role in Society has been the same, whether the reversal of fortune has been greeted by the victim of it as a welcome relief from an onerous public duty or has been endured as a painful banishment from a field of action for which the exile's heart has never ceased to ache. As it happens, these opposite personal reactions to the break are illustrated in the respective attitudes of those two members of our historical Pleiad who have attained the highest distinction in the 'practical' sphere—the only two, in fact, who would undoubtedly have made their mark in history as statesmen if Fortune had allowed them to hold their ground in the political field from beginning to end and had never compelled them to withdraw in order to make their mark otherwise by turning their historical talents to account. Yet in Clarendon's and in Machiavelli's life alike, the break in the career has actually been the making of it; and this apparent paradox applies *a fortiori* to the life of Thucydides, who lives on in living minds to-day as a greater historian than either of these, although there is no indication that he would ever have emerged from obscurity if his service as a soldier in the Twenty-Seven Years' War had continued to the bitter end. Without exception, every member of our Pleiad has made a greater mark and achieved a greater distinction in the last chapter of his career, which has opened with his return as an historian, than he would ever have achieved if the first chapter had not been cut short by his withdrawal as a defeated general or a fallen minister of state.

In these eight broken lives we have a conspicuous example of that process of 'etherialization' which we have taken as our criterion of growth. In the 'practical' first chapter of their careers, these future historians have all set themselves to produce an effect upon their fellow men by the obvious and crude and finite 'direct method' of bringing their wills to bear upon the wills of their neighbours. The compulsory withdrawal, which has inhibited the exercise of their activities on this 'practical' plane, has compelled them to find a new vent by transferring their action to another plane and transmuting their energies into a new medium. In prison or internment or exile, the energies that can now no longer discharge themselves in the impact of will upon will have been transmuted from will-power into a heightened intensity of perception and thought and imagination and feeling; and, in virtue of this transfiguration, the same energies have been able, in the fullness of time, to return to action by evoking an answering note of heightened perception and thought and imagination and feeling in the souls of other human beings. On this higher plane, and through this more etherial medium, action duly begets action in the end, as it does when will strikes will; for the heightening of perception and thought and imagination and feeling cannot take place without producing some tension in the will of the personality that enjoys the experience. In this subtler form of interaction, however, the second will responds to the first by a spontaneous movement that arises from within, and not under a duress that has been imposed upon it *more mechanico* or *manu militari*.

This new form of action on a new plane has been made possible by the employment of a new method of expression and approach. The *ci-devant* soldiers and statesmen who once produced an effect on their fellow men by the direct exertion of will-power, have been taught by Necessity to invent the alternative method of creating works of art; and, just because it is more etherial, this alternative method is also more effective. It is more effective in the double sense of being wider in its range and of going deeper in its penetration. For the influence of soul on soul that is transmitted through the medium of will-power is as narrow and as superficial as it is sensational. In every kind of action, the agent's scope is limited by the nature of his field; and the scope of the 'practical' man of action is bounded by the confines of the personal and institutional relations through which he is operating. It is only when human action is transmuted—by the purging out of all its human passion and its human animus[1]—from the gross medium of will into the etherial media of perception and thought and feeling and imagination, that it is able to transcend all limits of Time and Space and to win its way into a field that extends to Infinity.

Let us search, in our own time and place, for vestiges of the living presence of Thucydides and Xenophon the Athenian soldiers, or Polybius the Megalopolitan statesman, or Josephus the defender of Jotapata, or Ibn Khaldūn the vizir and the qādi, or Machiavelli the Secretary to the Signoria of Florence, or Clarendon the mentor and minister of Charles the First and Charles the Second, or Ollivier the minister of Napoleon III. Search as we may, we shall not find one vestige of life to-day in any of these souls in their original 'practical' capacities. In these capacities, their only monument is Shirley's remorseless stanza:

> Some men with swords may reap the field
> And plant fresh laurels where they kill;
> But their strong nerves at last must yield:
> They tame but one another still.
> Early or late
> They stoop to Fate
> And must give up their murmuring breath
> When they, pale captives, creep to death.

It is the break in their careers that has saved these abortive soldiers and statesmen from a Caesar's or Napoleon's fate by compelling them to withdraw from the field of 'practical affairs' in order to return to action on the plane on which they have achieved their immortality.

> Ergo vivida vis animi pervicit, et extra
> Processit longe flammantia moenia mundi
> Atque omne immensum peragravit mente animoque.[2]

---

[1] For purgation (κάθαρσις) as the function of the Hellenic art of tragic drama, see Aristotle's famous definition of Tragedy in the *Poetics*, vi. 2 (1449 B).

[2] Lucretius: *De Rerum Natura*, Bk. I, ll. 72–4, quoted already in II. C (ii) (b) 1, vol. i, on p. 299, above.

If we search now for Thucydides and Xenophon and Polybius and
Josephus and Ibn Khaldūn and Machiavelli and Clarendon the
historians, we shall find each one of them just as much alive and
just as effectively in action in his etherial communion with posterity
as ever he was in his 'short and narrow-verged' life in the flesh. As
creative artists, these *ci-devant* soldiers and statesmen are proof
against Shirley's taunt:

> The garlands wither on your brow;
> Then boast no more your mighty deeds.

They can answer in the language of Wren's epitaph *Si monumentum
requiris circumspice*[1] or in the language of Horace's ode *Non omnis
moriar*.[2] For, in withdrawing on one plane to return on another,
they have found life in losing it;[3] and their action sweeps on, immortal and infinite.

> O love, they die in yon rich sky,
> They faint on hill or field or river:
> Our echoes roll from soul to soul
> And grow for ever and for ever.

This is the spiritual significance of the *motif* of Withdrawal-and-
Return as it manifests itself in the lives of our Pleiad of historians.
At a later point in this Study, when we come to consider the inspirations of historians,[4] we shall have to examine this particular
type of Withdrawal-and-Return once again for the sake of the light
which it may be found to throw upon the nature of the historian's
art. For the purpose of our present inquiry, we have merely to
review the circumstances in which each of these eight withdrawals
and returns took place.

On a comparative view, these eight lives fall into three groups.
In five of them—the lives of Thucydides and Xenophon and
Josephus and Ollivier and Machiavelli—the *motif* appears in its
simple form. The break which cuts short the chapter of 'practical'
action concludes it once and for all, and the chapter of literary
activity fills the rest of the life to the end. In two other lives—the
lives of Polybius and Clarendon—the pattern is more complicated.
Instead of there being only one break, there are two or three; and
the periods of 'practical' and literary activity are interwoven in a
series of alternate chapters. Finally, there is the life of Ibn Khaldūn, in which a single short period of literary activity is followed,
as well as preceded, by a long period of immersion in 'practical'
affairs—the posterior period of 'practical' activity lasting, in this
case, right down to the philosophic qādi's death.

---

[1] Inscribed in St. Paul's Cathedral on a tablet over the architect's tombstone.
[2] Horace: *Carmina*, iii. 30.   [3] Matt. x. 39.
[4] This is the subject of Part XIII, below.

Thucydides

Thucydides (*vivebat circa* 454–399 B.C.) was a citizen of Athens who lived through the Twenty-Seven Years' War of 431–404 B.C., and who was overtaken by the outbreak of the war in his early manhood. He thus belonged to a generation which was just old enough to have known the pre-war Hellenic World as an adult member of the pre-war society; and at the same time he lived long enough to see the denouement of the great catastrophe that brought the growth of the Hellenic Civilization to an end and set in motion the long and tragic movement of decline and fall. The definite breakdown of the Hellenic Civilization was, in fact, the challenge which the generation of Thucydides had to encounter and the experience through which they had to live; and Thucydides was fully alive to the significance of the catastrophe. 'This war', he says in the preface to the first part of his work,[1] 'was . . . the greatest upheaval ever experienced by Hellas and by a part of the non-Hellenic World (it would hardly be an exaggeration to say: by the Human Race)'; and he informs his readers in the same passage that, 'in the belief that this war would eclipse all its predecessors in importance, he began to write as soon as war broke out'. In the Athens, however, of Thucydides' day an able-bodied adult male citizen was constrained in peace-time, and *a fortiori* in war-time, to devote the best part of his time and energy to public service if the State made the demand; and we may suppose that, as soon as war broke out, this 'practical' demand upon Thucydides became exacting. At any rate, in the eighth year of the war, we find Thucydides serving as one of the ten Athenian Generals: a board of public officers, elected annually for a twelve months' term, who exercised the chief executive authority in the civil government in addition to their command over military operations.

It was in this position of 'practical' responsibility, which Thucydides held in 424–423 B.C., that he suffered the break in his career which was the turning-point in his life-history. In the winter of 424–423 B.C., when Thucydides was in command of an Athenian naval squadron stationed at Thasos, he failed to prevent a Lacedaemonian expeditionary force commanded by Brasidas from capturing Amphipolis. The lost fortress was a key-position, since it commanded the passage across the River Strymon on the land-route leading from Continental Greece towards the Dardanelles:

---

[1] Thucydides' *History of the Twenty-Seven Years' War* is in two parts, each introduced by a preface. The preface to Part I = Bk. I, chs. 1–23; the preface to Part II = Bk. V, chs. 25–6. Part II is unfinished. (The work was apparently interrupted by the author's death.) The narrative breaks off abruptly in the middle of the record of the twenty-first year of the war (411 B.C.) out of the total of twenty-seven years (431–404 B.C.) which the author intended to cover.

the only route along which it was possible for the Peloponnesians to strike, with their superior land-power, at a vital point in the Athenian Empire, so long as Athens retained her command of the sea. The Athenian People sought relief for their feelings of chagrin and alarm at the news of this reverse by cashiering Thucydides and sentencing him to exile. And it was thanks to this personal mishap to Thucydides the soldier that Thucydides the historian at last obtained the opportunity to accomplish his life-work.

'I lived', he writes in the preface to the second part of his work, 'through the whole of [the Twenty-Seven Years' War], and I was not only of an age of discretion, but I took special pains to acquire accurate information. It was my fate to be exiled from my country for twenty years after my command at Amphipolis; and in this situation I was enabled to see something of both sides—the Peloponnesian as well as the Athenian—and to make a special study of the War at my leisure.'

Thanks to this fortunate misfortune, Thucydides was able to complete rather more than two-thirds of his projected work,[1] though he seems to have died a premature death before he was out of his fifties. What is more, he has triumphantly achieved his ambition, declared in the preface to the first part of the work, to produce 'an everlasting possession'—a permanent contribution to knowledge—'rather than an ephemeral *tour de force*'. In his own austere intellectual way, this cashiered Athenian officer has anticipated the injunction

'Lay not up for yourselves treasures upon Earth. where moth and rust doth corrupt, and where thieves break through and steal;
'But lay up for yourselves treasures in Heaven, where neither moth nor rust doth corrupt, and where thieves do not break through nor steal;
'For where your treasure is, there will your heart be also.'[2]

The passing agony of one unhappy generation of Hellenes who dealt their own Hellas a mortal blow and knew that her blood was on them and on their children[3] has been transmuted by Thucydides, in a great work of art, into an ageless and deathless human experience.

Xenophon

Xenophon was the continuator of Thucydides' work; and he carried on the tale of ruin, from the point at which Thucydides' narrative broke off, for another fifty years,[4] until he, too, dropped his pen

---

[1] The title of Part II, as given by the author himself in the preface to this part, is: 'The History of the Second Phase of the War down to the Overthrow of the Athenian Empire by the Lacedaemonians and their Allies and the Occupation of the Long Walls and the Peiraeus.'
[2] Matt. vi. 19–21.   [3] Matt. xxvii. 25.
[4] Xenophon's *Hellenica* covers the years 411–362 B.C.

from a hand which was arrested, not by the accident of death, but by the inward inhibition of despair.[1] Born an Athenian citizen in a generation which did not come to manhood until the Twenty-Seven Years' War was in full swing, and which therefore was inclined to take the state of war for granted, Xenophon can scarcely have seen his first military service until some time after Thucydides had seen his last;[2] and his experience of the Atheno-Peloponnesian War did not sate Xenophon's appetite for the military career. After the restoration of peace in Hellas he went off to seek his fortune in the service of Cyrus the Lesser: a young pretender to the Achaemenian throne; and this gratuitous military adventure —on which Xenophon embarked against the advice of his mentor Socrates[3]—resulted, as Socrates had feared, in Xenophon's being penalized at Athens by a sentence of banishment;[4] but this political mishap simply impelled the incorrigible soldier of fortune to find a new opening for military adventure by irrevocably throwing in his lot with the Spartans. He attached himself to the staff of King Agesilaus, and was actually present, in the Spartan king's suite, at an important engagement in which his own Athenian countrymen were on the opposing side.[5]

It was after this, when Xenophon was perhaps some ten years older than his predecessor Thucydides had been when he retired, after his banishment, to his Thracian asylum at Scaptê Hylê, that at last the change took place in Xenophon's life which transformed Xenophon the soldier into Xenophon the author. The Lacedaemonian Government now showed its appreciation of Xenophon's services by endowing him with an estate at Scillus, a quiet, rural neighbourhood in the Peloponnese;[6] and at Scillus Xenophon lived in peace and wrote at leisure for some twenty years, until eventually

[1] After recounting the Battle of Mantinea which was fought in 362 B.C., and in which Xenophon's own son met his death as well as the great Theban statesman Epaminondas (the one man of his generation who might conceivably have saved Hellas, if his life had been spared), Xenophon winds up his history with the following sentence: 'There was more unsettlement and disorder in Hellas after the battle than before it—but I do not propose to carry my narrative further, and will leave the sequel to any other historian who cares to record it' (Xenophon: *Hellenica*, Bk. VII, *ad fin.*). The bitterness of this sentence comes with peculiar pungency from the pen of a writer with Xenophon's placid temperament.

[2] Xenophon is said to have been in action, in the summer of 4?4, at the Battle of Delium, and to have had his life saved on this occasion by Socrates. This story, however, is probably apocryphal; and Xenophon was perhaps some ten years younger than the story assumes.

[3] See Xenophon's own account of this incident in his *Cyri Anabasis*, III. i. 4–8.

[4] The decree of banishment appears to have been issued against Xenophon in 399 B.C., the same year in which Socrates was put to death. His final offence, in the eyes of his own Athenian countrymen, seems to have been his action in inducing the remnant of his ten thousand fellow-Greek mercenaries, after their catabasis from Babylonia to the Aegean, to take service with the Spartan commander Thibron in his operations against the Achaemenian Power in western Asia Minor.

[5] The Battle of Coronea, fought in 394 B.C.

[6] See Xenophon's own charming description of his estate at Scillus in *Anabasis*, V. iii. 7–13.

he was expelled by the Eleans after the downfall of his Lacedaemonian patrons.[1] It was those twenty years in Scillus that ensured
the achievement of Xenophon's life-work.

Josephus

Josephus was a Jew who lived through the Romano-Jewish War
of A.D. 66–70, and who was overtaken by the outbreak of the war in
his late twenties.[2] Born into a distinguished family of the hereditary Jewish priesthood, and brought up at Jerusalem in the traditional Jewish culture,[3] Josephus was old enough to have known
the pre-war Jewish life in Palestine as an adult member of the
pre-war society; and at the same time he lived to witness the great
catastrophe which ended in the destruction of the Palestinian
Jewish community root and branch, and which thereby reduced
Jewry to a mere diasporà.[4] The Great Romano-Jewish War of
A.D. 66–70 was the last and the decisive bout in a long-drawn-out
combat which had opened with the armed insurrection of the Maccabees against the Seleucid Power in 168 B.C. This Jewish attempt
to resist the impact of Hellenism by force of arms had been a forlorn hope from the outset; and the tragedy of the inevitable outcome was only heightened by the accidental prolongation of the
unequal struggle over a period of little less than two and a half
centuries.[5] The annihilation of the Palestinian Jewish community
through the knock-out blow which was delivered, in the end, by
the military power of Rome, was the experience which had to be
endured by Jewry in the generation of Josephus; and Josephus
writes of this great Jewish catastrophe in terms that recall Thucydides' description of the great Hellenic catastrophe of 431 B.C.
'The Judaeo-Roman War', he says in the opening sentence of the
preface to his history of it, 'is the greatest war of our own times,
and it would hardly be an exaggeration to add that it is the greatest
of any wars on record between either city-states or nations.'[6]

In the early part of the war, Josephus, like Thucydides, parti-
cipated as a combatant; and, like Thucydides again, he was com-

[1] The Eleans were former allies of the Lacedaemonians who had shown themselves
recalcitrant and had therefore been chastised by the Lacedaemonian Government in
398–397 B.C. as soon as the downfall of Athens had set Spartan hands free to attend to
minor matters. Scillus was a former possession of the Eleans which had been taken from
them by the Lacedaemonians on this occasion. The Eleans promptly resumed possession
after the Lacedaemonian *débâcle* at Leuctra in 371 B.C.

[2] See Josephus's *Autobiography*, chs. 3 and 4 and 15.

[3] See Josephus, op. cit., chs. 1 and 2. He records that, between the ages of sixteen and
nineteen, he spent three years in self-mortification in the Wilderness, as the disciple of an
ascetic anchorite, as a prelude to becoming a Pharisee.

[4] See II. D (vi), vol. ii, p. 236, and II D (vii), vol. ii, pp. 285–6, above.

[5] The militant anti-Hellenic reaction of Jewry in Palestine was respited by a series
of accidents: the overthrow of the Seleucidae by Rome; the rise of the Arsacid Power
east of Euphrates; and the adroit temporizing policy of the Herods.

[6] Josephus: *The Romano-Jewish War*: Preface = Bk. I, chs. 1–16.

pelled to change his role by the fortune of war, which broke his
military career and thrust him into the position of an observer who
was penalized in one sense and privileged in another. Josephus was
penalized in the sense that the circumstances in which his change
of fortune came about were such as to produce a moral breach
between the prisoner-of-war and his own people, in whose eyes he
was a traitor to the Jewish cause.[1] He was privileged inasmuch as
he won the confidence and esteem and patronage of Vespasian—
the Roman commander in Palestine who rose, while the war in
Palestine was still in progress, to be the lord and master of the
Roman World. When the war was over and the last embers of
the great conflagration had been stamped out, Josephus left Palestine for Rome in the same ship as Vespasian's son and lieutenant
and successor Titus; and in Rome he settled down in comfort[2] to
his life-work of writing *The History of the Romano-Jewish War* and
The Ancient History of the Jews and the other historical and con-
troversial works through which he lives to this day. Josephus's
own account of the stroke of Fortune which turned Josephus the
soldier into Josephus the historian is given in the following terms:

'By descent I am a Hebrew from Jerusalem, by profession a priest.
I saw service against the Romans in the initial phase of the War, and
was a compulsory spectator of its latter stages.[3] . . . My own record of
the War as a whole and of the incidental details is correct, since I was
a first-hand witness of all the events. I was in command of our Gali-
laeans so long as resistance was possible, while after my capture I was
a prisoner with the Romans. Vespasian and Titus compelled me to
remain in constant attendance upon them under guard, at first in chains,
though afterwards I was released and was sent from Alexandria, on the
staff of Titus, to the siege of Jerusalem. During this period nothing
was transacted that escaped my observation. The events in the Roman
camp I sedulously recorded at first hand, while I was the only person
present who could understand the reports of the deserters from the

[1] Josephus became a prisoner-of-war in the campaign of A.D. 67 upon the capture of
the Galilaean fortress of Jotapata, of which he had been the commandant. During the
siege of Jotapata and in the earlier operations in which he had taken part, Josephus
had shown himself an energetic and able soldier; but his record down to this point did
not subsequently count to him for righteousness in Jewish eyes. The Jewish people
could not forgive Josephus for having been the only survivor of the garrison of Jotapata
to give himself up alive, instead of falling in action or committing suicide; nor could
they forgive him for having made favour thereafter with Vespasian and for having
attempted, in the final campaign, to persuade the fanatical defenders of Jerusalem to
capitulate before it was too late. No doubt Josephus had been in the black books of the
Zealots from the outset as an original opponent of the war, who had only taken up arms
against his better judgement after he and his party had lost control of the political
situation. (For Josephus's part in the war down to the siege of Jotapata, see his *Autobiography*, chs. 4–74. For the siege of Jotapata and the circumstances in which Josephus
not only escaped with his life but promptly established himself in the good graces of
Vespasian, see *The Romano-Jewish War*, Bk. III, chs. 127–408.)
[2] See Josephus's own rather self-complacent account of his life after becoming the
protégé of Vespasian in his *Autobiography*, chs. 75–6.
[3] *The Romano-Jewish War*, Bk. I, ch. 3.

Jewish side. When all my material was in the proper state of preparation, I took advantage of a period of leisure at Rome to employ the
services of collaborators to help me with the Greek language, and I thus
wrote out my narrative.'[1]

It will be seen that, in their external aspect, the career of Josephus and the career of Thucydides ran an almost identical course,
but that there is a profound difference in the spiritual response
which the same challenge evoked from the two personalities. The response of Thucydides is a noble example of the tragic *catharsis*;
and, in 'the everlasting possession' into which the Athenian exile
has transmuted his transitory experience, the dross of egotism and
animus has all been refined away. As we read Thucydides' history,
we are conscious that the author's personal misfortune is genuinely
of no account in the author's own eyes by comparison with the
public catastrophe which has overtaken Athens and Hellas; and
even the deep emotion which the consciousness of this catastrophe
awakens in Thucydides' soul is so rigorously held in control that
we are only made aware of its intensity now and again by the
quivering tension which reveals itself, here and there, through the
texture of the historian's calm and measured words. In the soul
of Josephus, on the other hand, the *catharsis* has been imperfect;
and the note which his writing strikes has a tart and polemical
tone. While one element in his soul is seeking to transmute the
agonizing experience of a war of annihilation into an everlasting
memorial of the people and the culture that have been blotted out
of the book of life,[2] there is all the time another Josephus who is
seeking a personal relief for a private spiritual malaise. This other
Josephus is attempting to heal his personal breach with Jewry by
making himself the classic interpreter of Jewry to Hellenism; and
he is trying to assuage the stings of his conscience—which will
not leave him in peace, in his pampered life of exile in Rome, while·
Jerusalem lies in ruins—by conducting a perpetual polemic against
Hellenism with his pen, as an amends for his having once bought
personal immunity and advancement from the lords of the Hellenic
World by giving up his sword. In other words, Josephus, in his
latter-day literary work, is in some sense pursuing his previous
'practical' activities in a new medium. And this fault is still more
conspicuously apparent in the literary work of the French member
of our Pleiad: Émile Ollivier.

Ollivier

Ollivier is not without excuse for his frailty, for his personal
identification with the disaster that overtook his country in his day

¹ *A Reply to Apion*, Bk. I, chs. 47–50.   ² Exod. xxxii. 32; Rev. iii. 5.

was much more intimate, and much more serious, than Thucydides' identification with the fall of Athens or Josephus's with the fall of Jewry. Ollivier was a Frenchman who lived through the Franco-Prussian War of 1870–1. For France, this war, which brought to an end a French political and military hegemony of two centuries' standing on the European Continent, was not only a supreme national catastrophe; it was also a supreme national humiliation, since the war was lost by no honourable defeat but by a lamentable *débâcle*. And for Ollivier this tragic experience of France was a personal tragedy of equal magnitude; for, at the moment when the disaster occurred, Ollivier occupied in France the principal position of political responsibility next to the Emperor Napoleon III himself. While the Emperor was saved from the fury of the French people by falling into the enemy's hands, his minister had to fly the country. Ollivier took refuge in Italy, and when he ventured to return to France in 1873 his life was in ruins. Born in 1825, engaged in politics from 1848 to 1870, and virtually Prime Minister in the Imperial Government during the fatal days between the end of 1869 and the 9th August, 1870, Ollivier now found himself, at the age of forty-eight, a scapegoat in the wilderness, with all the transgressions of the Second Empire heaped upon his devoted head.[1]

Ollivier's retort to the outrageous Fortune which had felled his country and himself by the same terrific blow was to write, on the grand scale, a history of the whole unhappy chapter in French history in which he had played his own unhappy part. The prologue to the drama, as he presents it in *L'Empire Libéral*,[2] begins with the morrow of the peace-settlement of 1815; the curtain descends upon the *débâcle* of 1870 after Ollivier's fall from office on the 9th August of that year and his subsequent abortive private mission to Italy. The first volume was published in 1895, a quarter of a century after the catastrophe, when the author himself was already seventy years old;[3] and thereafter volume followed volume

---

[1] Ollivier applies the simile of the scapegoat to himself in *L'Empire Libéral*, vol. i, p. 30.

[2] *L'Empire Libéral: Études, Récits, Souvenirs*, par Émile Ollivier (Paris 1895–1912, Garnier Frères, 16 volumes).

[3] The final and effective decision to write seems to have been taken by Ollivier as a consequence of Bismarck's outright avowal that he had deliberately precipitated the war by tampering with the text of the famous 'Ems Telegram'. This outright avowal was not made until 1892, after Bismarck's dismissal from the Chancellorship of the German Reich by the Emperor William II. Ollivier appears to have been stirred by this revelation in two ways. He was elated to see the responsibility for the outbreak of the war transferred from the shoulders of France to the shoulders of Germany by so conclusive an authority as Bismarck himself; and he was outraged to find that Bismarck's confession was not being taken by public opinion as an exoneration of Ollivier for his own part in those transactions. *L'Empire Libéral* seems to have been committed to writing under this twofold stimulus. The context in which Ollivier gives his account of Bismarck's avowal is illuminating. (See *L'Empire Libéral*, vol. i, pp. 24–31.)

year by year until the sixteenth and last volume was published in
1912, when the author was eighty-seven and when the greater war
of 1914–18, which was to reverse the result of the war of 1870–1,
was only two years ahead in the future.[1] In thus transferring to
historiography the energies that had been expelled from the field
of politics twenty-five years earlier, Ollivier was not achieving a
spiritual *catharsis* and was not pursuing the path of 'etherialization'. To parody a notorious maxim of his Prussian enemies,[2] he
was rather taking up the historian's pen in order to pursue the
politician's aims by the best alternative means that still remained
at his disposal. The driving force that impels him to write and
write from his seventy-first to his eighty-eighth year is a burning
desire to vindicate France and to vindicate Ollivier.

The first of these two motives is proclaimed at the beginning
of the book:

'À la veille de disparaître de ce monde, je veux donner une dernière
preuve de dévouement à la patrie bien aimée à laquelle j'ai consacré
toutes mes pensées. Je veux la laver devant la posterité de la tache
d'avoir déchaîné parmi les hommes la misère, la défiance, la haine, la
barbarie. Je veux démontrer qu'en 1870 elle n'a pas été plus agressive
qu'elle ne l'avait été en 1792 et en 1806; qu'alors comme autrefois elle
a défendu son indépendance, non attenté à celle d'autrui. Laissant aux
contempteurs de son droit les gémissements dont depuis tant d'années
ils affaiblissent son courage, je lui tends la coupe où l'on boit le cordial
qui rend la foi, la force, l'espérance. Si elle l'accepte, tant mieux pour
elle!'[3]

The patriotic motive, here confessed, is plain to read; but the
personal motive, which Ollivier is at pains to deny, is equally unmistakable. It is revealed in the author's chagrin that Bismarck's
avowal of his responsibility for precipitating the war has not served
to vindicate his own—Ollivier's—reputation.[4] It is revealed in the
ostentation with which he abstains from vindicating himself (for
'on s'excuse même en renonçant aux excuses'). Above all, it is
revealed in his grand finale, which is not the *débâcle* at Sedan and
is not the fall of Metz and is not the fall of Paris and is not the
signature of the Peace of Frankfurt, but is—at the end of sixteen
volumes—the fall of the Ministère Ollivier!

[1] The writer of this Study, who was an undergraduate at Oxford at the time when the
last volumes of *L'Empire Libéral* were appearing, can well remember the interest which
their publication aroused.
[2] 'War is only a continuation of State policy by other means' (Clausewitz, General
Karl von: *On War.* Translated by Colonel J. J. Graham from the third German edition
(London 1893, Trübner), p. vii).
[3] Ollivier, E. O.: *L'Empire Libéral*, vol. i, pp. 32–3.
[4] Ollivier, op. cit., vol. i, p. 30.

Machiavelli

If Émile Ollivier is the dimmest member of our Pleiad, Niccolò Machiavelli is as bright a star as Thucydides himself.

Machiavelli (*vivebat* A.D. 1469–1527) was a citizen of Florence who was twenty-five years old when King Charles VIII of France crossed the Alps and overran Italy with a French army in A.D. 1494. He thus belonged to a generation which was just old enough to have known Italy as she had been during her age of immunity from 'barbarian invasions'; and he lived long enough to see the peninsula become the international arena for trials of strength between sundry Transalpine or Transmarine Powers, which found the prize and the symbol of their alternating victories in snatching from one another's grasp an oppressive hegemony over the once independent Italian city-states. This impact upon Italy of non-Italian Powers was the challenge which the generation of Machiavelli had to encounter and the experience through which they had to live; and the challenge was the more difficult for the Italians of this generation to meet inasmuch as the experience had not been tasted, either by these Italians or by their forefathers, for the best part of two and a half centuries.

The immunity which was broken (for nearly four centuries to come) by the French invasion of A.D. 1494 had been enjoyed down to that date, with little or no interruption, since the death of the Holy Roman Emperor Frederick II in A.D. 1250. Between those two dates, the Italian city-states had not only lived their own parochial lives in political freedom and security from external attack behind the 'natural frontiers' of the Alps and the sea, but on the economic plane their merchants and manufacturers had dominated the business-life of three worlds: the Arabic World and the main body of Orthodox Christendom, as well as the whole of Western Christendom. The coasts of the Levant and the Black Sea had been bespangled with Italian trading-ports and naval stations and colonies. The Republic of Venice had made herself mistress of Crete; Florentine dukes had ruled in Athens; the Greek Emperor in Constantinople had been browbeaten by his Genoese neighbours across the Golden Horn at Galata; and the Genoese flag had flown as far afield as Caffa in the Crimea and Tana at the mouth of the Don, in the far corner of the Sea of Azov. Moreover, Italian explorers had pushed their way beyond the farthest limits of Italian empire and commerce. Some twenty-five years after Frederick II's death three Venetian explorers, the Polos, had made their way to China across the whole breadth of the Eurasian Steppe; and, just two years before Charles VIII's passage of the

Alps, a Genoese explorer, Columbus, had made his way across the whole breadth of the Atlantic to the West Indies.

But the greatest achievements of the Italian genius during those two and a half centuries of immunity had not been extensive but intensive, not material but spiritual. In architecture, in sculpture, in painting, in literature, and in almost every other province in the realm of aesthetic and intellectual culture, the Italians, during those centuries, had been performing works of creation that bear comparison with the creative achievements of the Greeks during an equal period of time in the sixth and fifth and fourth centuries B.C.[1] In fine, the Italians had used their long-sought, hard-won immunity from alien military and political domination in order to create, within their sheltered peninsula, a miniature Italian World apart within the wider world of Western Christendom—an Italian World in which the level of the Western Civilization had been raised precociously to such a high degree that the difference of degree became tantamount to a difference in kind. By the close of the fifteenth century the Italians were, and felt themselves to be, so far superior in civilization to all other Westerners (with the possible exception of the Flemings) that—half in conceit and half in earnest—they revived the term 'barbarians' to describe the Western peoples on the farther side of the Alps and beyond the Tyrrhene Sea. And then, in this very generation, the latter-day 'barbarians' began to act in character by showing themselves militarily and politically wiser than the Italian children of light.[2]

As the new Italian culture radiated out of the peninsula in all directions, it had quickened the cultural growth of the peoples round about, and quickened it first in the grosser elements of culture—such elements as political organization and military technique—in which the effect of radiation is always most prompt to make itself felt.[3] In consequence, the 'barbarian' peoples of Western Christendom, while remaining little less barbarous than before in everything else, had begun to overtake their Italian teachers in the mastery of the military and political arts; and when once they had mastered them they were able to apply them on a vastly larger scale than the scale of the Italian city-states. Their ability to surpass the Italians in this material way was not, of course, a symptom of any greater inborn genius. On the contrary, the 'barbarians' were manifestly inferior in political and military

---

[1] The Italians, of course, sought inspiration from this ancient Greek genius by evoking the ghost of the extinct Hellenic culture, first in its latter-day second-hand Latin version and eventually in its original Greek form. (For this Italian Renaissance of Hellenic Culture, see further IV. C (iii) (c) 2 (α), vol. iv. p. 275, footnotes 1 and 2, as well as Part X, below.) [2] Luke xvi. 8.
[3] For this phenomenon of social radiation, see Part II. A, vol. i, p. 187, and Part III. C (i) (a), pp. 151–3, above, and Parts VIII and IX, below.

as well as in artistic and literary genius to the Italians of Machiavelli's age. The explanation of the 'barbarians'' relative success in achieving a scale of social organization which the Italians had found to be beyond their own powers lies in the fact that the 'barbarians' were applying the political lessons which the Italians had taught them in far easier circumstances than those with which statesmanship had to contend in contemporary Italy.

In Machiavelli's generation, Italian statesmanship was being handicapped, and 'barbarian' statesmanship was being facilitated, by the operation of one of the regular laws of 'the Balance of Power'.[1]

The Balance of Power is a system of political dynamics that comes into play whenever a society articulates itself into a number of mutually independent local states; and the Italian Society that had differentiated itself externally from the rest of Western Christendom during the second chapter in the history of our Western Civilization (*circa* A.D. 1075–1475) had at the same time articulated itself internally in this very way. The political movement to extricate Italy from the Holy Roman Empire had been initiated and carried through by a host of 'communes' or city-states which were striving, each for itself, to assert a right to local self-determination; so that the creation of an Italian World apart and the articulation of this world into a multiplicity of local states were coeval events in Italian history. Thus the Balance of Power had been introduced from the outset into the political structure of this new Italian version of the Western Civilization; and indeed the Italian city-states were already contending fiercely with one another in order to maintain or modify or restore this balance among themselves long before they had completed their common task of shaking themselves free from the old Imperial trammels. At this stage of Italian history, however, the loss of energy and the destruction of wealth and life and happiness which were caused by this internal political strife were not yet so serious as to check the new Italian Society's growth in civilization. This growth made headway in all those fields of activity that have been cited above; and, as Italy grew in spiritual stature, she radiated her culture, as has been described, into the regions round about her. The effect of this continuing radiation of culture from an Italian source of social energy was to bring an ever widening circle of surrounding countries and peoples within the ambit of the Italian Civilization in this or that sphere of social activity and in this or that degree. It has been mentioned already that (as always happens) the first

---

[1] The various laws of interaction between mutually independent states that follow from 'the Balance of Power' are examined in greater detail in Part XI, below.

sphere of activity in which the 'barbarians' made substantial progress in learning from their Italian teachers was the sphere of
military and political technique. And at this point one of the laws
of the Balance of Power comes into play.

The Balance of Power operates in a general way to keep the
average calibre of states low in terms of every criterion for the
measurement of political power: in extent of territory and in head
of population and in aggregate of wealth. It operates in this way
through a system of pressures; a state which threatens to increase
its calibre above the prevailing average becomes subject, almost
automatically, to pressure from all the other states that are members of the same political constellation; and it is one of the laws
of the Balance of Power that, in any given constellation of states
in which the political units are in this dynamic relation with one
another, the pressure is greatest at the heart of the constellation
and relaxes progressively towards the periphery.

At the centre, every move that any one state makes with a view
to its own aggrandizement is jealously watched and adroitly
countered by all its neighbours, and the sovereignty over a few
square feet of territory and a few hundred 'souls' becomes a subject
for the bitterest and stubbornest contention. For this reason, it
commonly happens that, at the centre of the constellation, no
appreciable political result is produced by the application of even
the highest genius or by the mobilization of the utmost energy.
The severity of the mechanical pressure under which the statesman
has to operate here effectively counteracts the statesman's ablest
efforts; while, on the other hand, on the periphery, a second-rate
statesman is capable—thanks to the relatively slight degree of pressure under which he has to work—of producing results that arouse
the astonishment and envy of the first-rate statesman at the centre.
In the easy circumstances of the periphery quite a mediocre political talent is often able to work wonders. In this field, the second-
rate statesman can carry out his naïve moves without their being
frustrated or even being suspected by his local rivals; and he can
annex a province or a kingdom or even a whole continent without
arousing as much opposition as his brilliant contemporary in the
central region has to face when he seeks to annex a single fortress
or a single village. The domain of the United States can be expanded unobtrusively right across North America from Atlantic
to Pacific, the domain of Russia right across Asia from Baltic to
Pacific, in an age when the best statesmanship of France or Germany cannot avail to obtain unchallenged possession of an Alsace
or a Posen.

This extreme unevenness in the distribution of political pressure prescribes a law of the Balance of Power which can be formulated as follows: If a given society is articulated politically into a multiplicity of mutually independent local states, with the result that the Balance of Power has been introduced into the dynamics of this society's political structure; and if this society proceeds to grow in civilization, with the result that it radiates its culture out abroad and thereby enlarges its own geographical ambit:[1] then the states that occupy the heart and homeland of this civilization will sooner or later be dwarfed and overshadowed and dominated by the rise, around the periphery of the expanding constellation, of a whole new order of Great Powers with an overwhelmingly greater average calibre.

There are many historical examples of this phenomenon; and, to look no farther than our own present predicament,[2] we can see that the multiplicity and the discord of the national states of Europe is being challenged collectively in our generation by the rise, in Asia and overseas, of a new order of Great Powers of a vastly greater average magnitude. The United States, which has been the first of these giants to grow to full stature, is to-day a match, not merely for this or that European state or group of states, but for all Europe put together (if Europe ever can be put together by the genius of any European statesman). And to-morrow we Europeans must look forward to seeing our little European World encircled by a dozen giants of the American calibre when Canada and Argentina and Australia have peopled their empty spaces, and when Russia and India and China and Brazil have acquired the knack of efficiency, and when the Union of South Africa has expanded its domain from the Tropic of Capricorn to the Equator.

[1] In the case of an expanding civilization, the unevenness in the distribution of the political pressure as between the centre and the periphery is accentuated by a psychological factor which the process of geographical expansion brings into play. Two common forms which expansion takes are the cultural assimilation of outer barbarians and the physical occupation of outlying regions by colonists from the homelands of the expanding society. The effect of both these forms of expansion is to create 'new countries'; and in 'new countries' of both kinds there is a high degree of psychological plasticity which works powerfully in favour of political consolidation. The political value of this psychological factor is illustrated by the relative ease with which the statesmanship of the Roman Republic was able to incorporate the semi-barbarous mountaineers of the Sabina and Picenum into the Roman body politic, by contrast with the strength of the resistance that was offered by a Veii or a Capua. Another illustration is the relative ease with which British statesmanship has succeeded in creating new self-governing nations out of the bi-national White populations of Canada and South Africa, by contrast with that fissiparous tendency in European multi-national states which disrupted the pre-war Austria and which is threatening to disrupt the post-war Belgium. (For the plasticity of colonial populations and the way in which this factor has worked in favour of the construction of the British Commonwealth of Nations, see further Toynbee, A. J.: *The Conduct of British Empire Foreign Relations since the Peace Settlement* (London 1928, Milford), pp. 37–8.)

[2] Other examples are to be found in the history of the Sinic World *post Confucium*, during 'the period of contending states', and in the history of the Hellenic World *post Alexandrum*. This latter example is dealt with on pp. 310–12, below, apropos of the career of Polybius.

When that day comes, the pygmy countries of Europe, instead of being confronted by a single giant, will be encircled by half a dozen; and these encompassing giants, who already overtop us as they grow in stature, all owe their gigantic strength to the currents of vitality that have been flowing into their frames, through one medium or another, from Europe itself. These gigantic countries of the extra-European World have either been colonized by European immigrants or they have been overrun by European conquerors or they have been opened up by European traders or else they have been spiritually irradiated by European techniques or institutions or ideas without any physical inoculation with European flesh and blood; but, whatever the process may have been, they have all been brought to life by being brought within the ambit of that Western Civilization of which Europe has been the fountain-head. And thus it would appear that—to invert a famous phrase[1]—we Europeans have called a new world into being not to *redress* but to *upset* the balance of the old.[2]

In the light of the political laws which we have analysed above, we can see objectively that this 'dwarfing' of Europe is the natural and indeed the inevitable result of the expansion of our Western Civilization when it has expanded out of a continent that is partitioned politically into a multiplicity of states and when its inter-state relations are governed by the principle of the Balance of Power. At the same time, the result is, subjectively, a strange sensation for us Europeans who, in our generation, are living through this experience. It is strange to find Europe being dwarfed and put out of countenance by the outer world which she has succeeded in bringing within her ambit through the radiation of her higher culture. It is strange to realize that she may emerge from her last four centuries of triumphal progress as the servant, and not as the mistress, of the other continents round about her. An uncomfortable blend of bewilderment and misgiving and pique and irony is the characteristic state of mind of a European in our generation when he gazes out at the 'Brave New World' which he sees arising all around him. And this was likewise the state of mind of an Italian in Machiavelli's generation, when he looked abroad and saw the 'barbarians' looming up from outer darkness into the penumbra of the light that was shining out from Italy into the rest of Western Christendom.

---

[1] The phrase was uttered by the British statesman Canning in a debate in the House of Commons at Westminster on the 26th December, 1826, in allusion to the part which British statesmanship had played in the liberation of a score of new nations that had come to life in South and Central America within the chrysalis of the Spanish Empire.

[2] 'The dwarfing of Europe' in our generation is examined further in Part XII, below, apropos of the prospects of our Western Civilization.

It was just this Italian light that had given the 'barbarians' their new and formidable vitality. A France politically Italianized by Louis XI and a Spain politically Italianized by Ferdinand and Isabella and an England politically Italianized by Henry VII were the new 'barbarian' Powers which, in Machiavelli's day, were dwarfing an Italian Florence or Venice or Milan and were putting the whole of Italy out of countenance.[1] It is curious to reflect that these raw 'barbarian' Powers which were overshadowing the city-states of Italy at the turn of the fifteenth and sixteenth centuries are the self-same nation-states of Transalpine Europe which, in their turn, are being overshadowed now, four centuries after, by the rising continent-states of an extra-European World. By A.D. 1527, the year of Machiavelli's death, his Florence and Venice and Milan had come to stand to France and Spain and England as our England and France and Spain were standing in A.D. 1927 to Canada and Russia and the United States.

This situation is a challenge to statesmanship. If the pygmy states at the centre take no preventive action, it is obvious that the giant states on the periphery are bound to overwhelm them by sheer weight of metal; and this means that, on the political plane, the creators and sustainers of the common civilization will lose their power of initiative and perhaps their independence, and that the sceptre will pass to the outer 'barbarians' who are not yet fit to wield it. This will not only be a political calamity for the pygmy central states; it will also be a cultural calamity for Society as a whole. From every point of view, it is in the public interest that this calamity should be averted; and the duty of averting it devolves upon the statesmen of the central states whose political existence is threatened. It is for them to act, but how are they to perform their task? The solution manifestly lies in somehow transmuting political pluralism and political strife into political concord and political solidarity; but how is this miracle to be achieved? For, as we have observed, it is precisely here, in the centre of the international constellation, that the forces working for political disunity

[1] There were also two other Great Powers which began to press heavily upon Italy in Machiavelli's lifetime, but which had not been brought to life by the radiation of Italian influence. One of these other two Powers was the Ottoman Empire, which engulfed the Italian enclaves in the Levant as soon as it had finished its conquest of the Orthodox Christians. (The 'Osmanlis made themselves masters of Genoese Galata in A.D. 1453 and of Florentine Athens in 1456; and in 1470 they conquered Venetian Negrepont in the course of a great Veneto-Ottoman War which lasted from 1463 to 1479, and which did not end until the Ottoman cavalry had appeared in Friuli (in 1477–8). In 1475 they annexed Genoese Caffa and Tana, and in 1480 an Ottoman expeditionary force momentarily occupied Otranto.) The other Great Power which arose on Italy's eastern flank was the Danubian Hapsburg Monarchy, which took shape in A.D. 1526—a few months before Machiavelli's death—as a carapace to protect the eastern borders of Western Christendom against Ottoman onslaughts. (For this function of the Danubian Hapsburg Monarchy see II. D (v), vol. ii, pp. 177–90, above.)

and discord exert their strongest pressure. It will be seen that the task which confronted Italian statesmanship in Machiavelli's generation, and which likewise confronts European statesmanship in ours, is a task of peculiar difficulty; if the problem can be solved at all, it can only be solved by some stroke of genius; and, in the Italy of Machiavelli's generation, Niccolò Machiavelli himself had many of the qualities for serving as the man of the hour.

Machiavelli was endowed by Nature with consummate political ability; he had an insatiable zest for exercising his talents; and Fortune conspired with merit to give him his opportunity. Fortune made him a citizen of Florence, one of the leading city-states of the peninsula; and merit won him, at the age of twenty-nine, the post of secretary to the Government of the Republic. Appointed to this important office at Florence in A.D. 1498, four years after the passage of the 'barbarian' Charles VIII, Machiavelli acquired a first-hand knowledge of the new 'barbarian' Powers in the course of his official duties; for the Florentine Government sent their Secretary abroad on frequent diplomatic missions, and these not only to other Italian Governments but also to the Courts of the formidable potentates beyond the Alps. In the course of the fourteen years during which he held his Secretaryship, Machiavelli was sent on one mission to the Emperor and on no less than four missions to the Court of France; and his writings show how ably he turned these occasions to account.[1] With his genius for political observation, he studied and apprehended and recorded exactly those features in the political structure of the new Transalpine nation-states which were of practical interest and importance for contemporary Italian statesmanship. After fourteen years of this experience, Machiavelli had become perhaps better qualified than any other living Italian for taking in hand the urgent task of helping Italy to work out her political salvation, when a turn in the wheel of Florentine domestic politics suddenly expelled him from his whole field of 'practical' activity. On the 7th November, 1512, Machiavelli was deprived of his Secretaryship of State; in the February and March of the following year he suffered imprisonment and torture; and, although he was lucky enough to emerge again alive, the price which he had to pay for his release from prison was a perpetual rustication on his farm in the Florentine countryside at San Casciano, where he found himself wholly cut off from all those affairs of state in which he had hitherto lived

---

[1] See the instructions, dispatches, and reports, relating to these five diplomatic missions, which are printed in Machiavelli's collected works, as well as his four special studies on France and Germany (*Ritratti delle Cose della Francia, Ritratti delle Cose dell'Alamagna, Rapporto delle Cose della Magna, Discorso sopra le Cose di Alamagna e sopra l'Imperatore*).

and moved and had his being. The break in his career was complete; yet, in putting him to the proof of this tremendous personal challenge, Fortune did not find Machiavelli wanting in the power to make an effective response.

The fallen and imprisoned statesman had already decided on his response before he had obtained his release, as is apparent from the following passage in a letter of the 9th April, 1513, which he wrote to a friend and former colleague from his place of confinement:

'Fortune has decided that, as I do not know how to talk about the *Arte della Seta* or the *Arte della Lana*,[1] or about profits and losses, my cue must be to talk about the State. I have to talk about that or else resign myself to keeping quiet.'[2]

Already, the *ci-devant* Secretary of State was preparing to return as a political philosopher to a world which had cast him out as a practical politician; and the circumstances in which this change of role was actually achieved are described by the philosopher himself in another letter addressed to the same correspondent and written before the close of the same calendar year:

'Here I am on the farm; and, since those last experiences of mine, the number of days that I have spent in Florence does not amount to twenty, all told. I have spent my time since then in fowling—thrushes —with my own hand, rising before daylight. I have been setting bird-lime and going along with a bundle of cages on my back, for all the world like Geta when he came from the harbour with Amphitryon's books. I have been catching at least two thrushes a day, and sometimes as many as seven. In this way I occupied myself for the whole of September. After that, this sport came to an end (to my regret, in spite of its being odd and not worth caring about); and I will now tell you what my life has been since then.

'I rise with the Sun, and go my ways to my wood, which I am having cut. I stay there two hours inspecting the previous day's work and passing the time with the wood-cutters, who always have some trouble on hand, with their neighbours if not among themselves. About that wood I have a thousand tales to tell of the things that have happened to me. . . .

'After leaving the wood, I go off to a spring, and from there to a fowling-place of mine, with a book stowed away: a Dante or a Petrarch or one of these minor poets: say, Tibullus or Ovid or the like. I read those tales of lovers' passions and call to mind my own and indulge myself a little in such reminiscences. Then I transfer my quarters to the roadside inn, talk with the passers-by, ask them the news of their villages, hear all kinds of things and note the various tastes and diverse fantasies of Mankind. Then comes the hour for dinner, when I eat, with my household, of such viands as this poor farm of mine and this tiny property can afford me. So soon as I have eaten, I return to the inn; and, here, most days, I find the inn-keeper, a butcher, a miller, and two kiln-tenders. With this company I amuse myself to day's end playing cards—source of a thousand disputes and a thousand bouts of mutual abuse. Most times the stakes are a farthing; and, for all that, our shouts can be heard from San Casciano. Thus, amid these trifles in which I am enveloped, I drag my brain out of the mildew in which it moulders and purge out the malignity of my fortune—content to let Fate trample on me in this way, if only to see whether she won't become ashamed of herself.

'When the evening comes, I return to the house and go into my study; and at the door I take off my country clothes, all caked with mud and slime, and put on court dress; and, when I am thus decently re-clad, I enter into the ancient mansions of the men of ancient days. And there I am received by my hosts with all lovingkindness, and I feast myself on that food which alone is my true nourishment, and which I was born for. And here I am not abashed to speak with these Ancients and to question them on the reasons for their actions. And they, in their humanity, deign to answer me. And so, for four hours long, I feel no gêne, I forget every worry, I have no fear of poverty, I am not appalled by the thought of death: I sink my identity in that of my Ancient mentors. And since Dante says that there can be no science without some retention of that which Thought has once comprehended, I have made notes of the mental capital that I have acquired from their conversation, and have composed an essay *De Principatibus*, in which I try to penetrate as deep as I can into the theory of the subject—discussing what Sovereignty is, what varieties of it there are, how these are acquired, and how they are maintained, and through what causes they are lost. And if ever any conceit of mine has pleased you, you should not be displeased by this, while a sovereign—and especially one newly installed —should find it acceptable. Accordingly, I am dedicating it to His Magnificence Giuliano [de' Medici]. Filippo Casavecchia has seen it and will be able to regale you with the substance of the thing and with the arguments I have had with him—though all the time I am enriching it and re-polishing it.'[1]

This was the origin of *The Prince*; and the concluding chapter of the famous treatise, which is an 'Exhortation to liberate Italy from the Barbarians', reveals the intention that Machiavelli had in mind when he took up his pen to write. He was addressing himself once more to the one vital problem of contemporary Italian statesmanship in the hope that perhaps, even now, he might help to

[1] Machiavelli, Niccolò: Letter of the 10th December, 1513, to Francesco Vettori (*Lettere Familiari*, No. xxvi).

bring that problem to solution by transmuting into creative thought the energies which had been deprived of their practical outlet. If *The Prince* had happened to inspire some living Italian princeling —if a Medici or Este or Sforza or Gonzaga had employed the author's methods to attain the author's ends—it is not inconceivable that Machiavelli might have lived to see the political union of Italy accomplished; and, had this Italian political problem been solved in that age, the consequences would assuredly have been far-reaching. In the *Cinquecento*, a politically united Italy would have easily driven the Transalpine 'barbarians' beyond her borders, and she might even have established over her discomfited invaders as decisive an ascendency in the cruder commerce of politics and war as the politically disunited Italy of the *Quattrocento* had established already over the rest of Western Christendom on the etherial planes of Literature and Art.

In fact, of course, the political hope that animates *The Prince* was utterly disappointed. The problem of Italy's political disunity was not solved by Italian statesmanship in Machiavelli's lifetime; and therefore it was Italy's fate to serve for centuries as the battlefield of 'barbarian' armies and the prize of 'barbarian' victories— a prize that fast depreciated in value as it was bandied to and fro between alternate 'barbarian' victors. Spanish and Austrian and French hegemonies came and went and monotonously came again. It was only in the nineteenth century, when more than four hundred years had passed since Machiavelli's birth, that the political union of Italy was belatedly accomplished; and, *au fin du compte*, the Italian people had to pay a heavy price for the long incompetence of Italian statesmanship. While an Italy united in the sixteenth century might have made herself mistress of Europe and have contended with the 'Osmanlis on equal terms for the dominion of the Levant, the Italy who completed her union on the 20th September, 1870, was content to take her place in the rank and file of European states as the last and least of the latter-day Great Powers.

Thus *The Prince* failed to achieve its author's immediate aim, as this aim is presented in the final chapter; but this is not to say that *The Prince* was a failure; for 'the pursuit of practical politics by literary means' was not the essence of the business which Machiavelli was going about when, evening after evening in his remote farm-house, he entered into the mansions of the men of ancient days and ate of the ambrosia which he had been born to eat. In these rare hours of mental retreat, the fallen politician was freer from the burden of practical politics than at any other times in his life; yet, in virtue of this complete withdrawal from the plane of activity on which he had made his first effect upon the World, Machiavelli was able to return to the World on a more ethereal plane on which his effectiveness has been vastly greater. Even if he had retained his Secretaryship to the end of his days, and even if the political union of Italy had been accomplished in his lifetime through his instrumentality, Machiavelli the practical politician would never have influenced the course of history as it has actually been influenced by Machiavelli the political philosopher. For, in finding his 'true nourishment' in his communion with the Ancients, Machiavelli was really finding his opportunity to perform his life-work. In those magic hours of *catharsis* when he rose above his vexation of spirit, Machiavelli succeeded in transmuting his 'practical' energies into a series of mighty intellectual works—*The Prince* and the *Discourses on Livy* and *The Art of War* and *The History of Florence*—and these fruits of a Florentine politician's broken career have been the seeds of our modern Western political philosophy. The thought which these famous books put out into the World is still living and working in our thought to-day.

Polybius

Polybius of Megalopolis (*vivebat circa* 206–128 B.C.) was born a citizen of a Hellenic city-state in the heart of Continental Greece in an age when Greece was in the same general predicament as Europe in our time or Italy in the age of Machiavelli.[1] In the Hellenic World of the second century B.C., as in our Great Society of the twentieth century of the Christian Era and in the Western Christendom of the *Cinquecento*, the little states in the centre of the World, at the fountain-head of Civilization, were ringed round by a circle of gigantic Powers which the quickening outflow of the living waters had called into life on the periphery. Eastward, the Greek core of the Hellenic World was overshadowed by the Greek 'successor-states' of the Achaemenian Empire: the political progeny of the military conquests of Alexander. Westward it was overshadowed by the even greater Powers of Carthage and Rome: two non-Greek city-states which had been stimulated into empire-building in the process of resisting the impact of Hellenic arms and succumbing to the influence of Hellenic culture. The general situation was one with which we are familiar; but in the Hellenic World of Polybius's day this situation worked itself up to a climax —and out to a catastrophe—which our Western World has hitherto escaped.

[1] The following sketch was written before the writer of this Study had read the sympathetic and penetrating appreciation of Polybius and his work by Mr. T. R. Glover in *The Cambridge Ancient History*, vol. viii (Cambridge 1930, University Press), ch. i.

In the Western World of to-day, the encirclement of Europe by the giant Powers of the penumbra is recent and still incomplete. And the Western World of yesterday, which did see Machiavelli's Italy both encircled and overrun by the Transalpine 'barbarians', was at least spared the spectacle of seeing the giants collide on Italian soil in a war of annihilation. Though Northern Italy had to suffer the damage and humiliation of serving as 'the battle-field of Europe' from A.D. 1494 to A.D. 1866, this evil was mitigated by the fact that, in all the European warfare of this age, 'the European forces' were 'exercised by temperate and undecisive contests'. And the great European historian who wrote these words in 1781 was able to declare his confident belief that 'the Balance of Power will continue to fluctuate, and the prosperity of our own or the neighbouring kingdoms may be alternately exalted or depressed; but these partial events cannot essentially injure our general state of happiness, the system of arts and laws and manners, which so advantageously distinguish, above the rest of Mankind, the Europeans and their colonists'.[1] The confidence here proclaimed was based on the experience of three centuries of European history, and it was to be justified by the subsequent course of events for another century to come.

In all the warfare between French and Spanish armies, and French and Austrian armies, that met in battle on Italian soil in the course of nearly four centuries of European contests from the days of Charles VIII to the days of Napoleon III, no combatant, from first to last, ever dealt his adversary a mortal blow; and the Balance of Power between the great Transalpine states continued to fluctuate without being overthrown until the day when Italian statesmanship at length succeeded in abating the nuisance of this high-handed usage of Italy as an arena for Transalpine military exercises by fulfilling Machiavelli's dream and consolidating Italy herself into a single united nation-state of the Transalpine calibre—a state strong enough to guard its own frontiers and to warn off, for the future, the habitual Transalpine trespassers. This has been the relatively fortunate history of the relations between Europe and Italy during the epoch of Western history that began in Machiavelli's lifetime and came to a close in 'the eighteen-seventies'. Let

[1] Gibbon, Edward: *The History of the Decline and Fall of the Roman Empire*, ch. xxxviii, *ad finem*: 'General Observations on the Fall of the Roman Empire in the West.' The passage here quoted appears to have been written some time during the first quarter of the year 1781, at a moment when the author's own country happened to be engaged in fighting a losing battle. At that moment, the American Revolutionary War was approaching its crisis. His Britannic Majesty was at war with France and Spain and Holland, as well as with the Thirteen American Colonies; the Northern Powers of Europe were maintaining an unfriendly 'armed neutrality'; and the decisive campaign of the war, which was to end at Yorktown so disastrously for British arms, was about to open! And yet Gibbon's confidence was justified in the event by the peace settlement of A.D. 1783.

us hope that the history of the comparable relations between a latter-day Great Society and Europe may be no more unhappy than this during the centuries to come. For the history of the relations between the Hellenic Great Society and Greece in the lifetime of Polybius shows that a general situation of this kind is fraught with potential dangers which may work out to a disastrous outcome.

In the Hellenic World of Polybius's age, the new Great Powers of the periphery duly found their battlefields on Greek soil, but they did not 'exercise' their forces there 'in temperate and undecisive contests'. In their Greek arena, they fought one another to the death; and Greece was devastated and the Hellenic Civilization destroyed before these gladiatorial combats between Rome and Carthage and Rome and Macedon were brought to an end by a series of 'knock-out blows', which wiped the defeated Powers off the face of the Earth and left Rome, the victor, as the sole surviving Power in the whole circuit of the Mediterranean.

In this deadly warfare on Greek battle-fields between 'barbarian' Powers, a helpless and defenceless Greece suffered only less severely than the vanquished titans. The wars between Rome and Carthage were fought out mainly on Greek soil in Sicily and Magna Graecia; and the Hannibalic War entailed the sack of the two chief Greek cities of the West: Syracuse in 212 B.C. and Tarentum in 209. A larger number of smaller Greek cities suffered the same fate in the wars between Rome and Macedon, which were fought out on the soil of Continental Greece. In the first Romano-Macedonian War, the victims were Aegina and Anticyra (sacked in 211–210) and Oreus (sacked in 208); in the Third Macedonian War they were Haliartus and Coronea (sacked in 171)[1] and seventy cities in Epirus (sacked in 168). And the overthrow of Macedon at Pydna by Roman arms did not spell the end of Greek disasters. A desperate revolt of Macedon against her Roman conquerors in 150–148 B.C. excited the Achaean Confederacy in the Peloponnese to make a declaration of war on Rome next year: a suicidal gesture which resulted in the annihilation of Corinth in 146 B.C., a few months after the annihilation of Carthage. The annihilation of Corinth and the dissolution of the Achaean Confederacy in 146 B.C. dealt the final blow to Greek prosperity and Greek independence.

This was the overwhelming experience through which Polybius lived and of which he eventually became the historian.

'The events which he has chosen as his subject are sufficiently extraordinary in themselves to arouse and stimulate the interest of every reader, young or old. What mind, however commonplace or indifferent,

[1] See II. D (v), vol. ii, p. 213, above.

could feel no curiosity to learn the process by which almost the whole
World fell under the undisputed ascendancy of Rome within a period
of less than fifty-three years,[1] or to acquaint itself with the political
organization to which this triumph—a phenomenon unprecedented in
the annals of Mankind—was due? What mind, however infatuated with
other spectacles and other studies, could find a field of knowledge more
profitable than this?'

That is how Polybius apostrophizes his readers in the preface
to his *Oecumenical History*;[2] but although this panoramic history
of his own times was Polybius's life-work, it was not as a historian
that he started his career; for all the circumstances of his birth
and upbringing drew him in his youth towards the life of a practical
politician.

Polybius's native city, Megalopolis, was an Arcadian community
which was one of the leading states-members of the Achaean Confederacy. Its accession to the Confederacy, some thirty years before the date of Polybius's birth, had been an historic event, which
had given the Achaean Confederacy a prospect of achieving the
political unification of all the Peloponnese, and perhaps of all Continental Greece. The accession of Megalopolis, which had opened
this prospect up, had been the work of a high-minded and clear-
sighted Megalopolitan statesman, Lydiadas, who had found himself despot of his native city and had voluntarily abdicated from
this post of personal power in order to serve the public interest
both of Megalopolis and of Greece. In making this generous
gesture, Lydiadas of Megalopolis was taking up the policy of his
contemporary Aratus of Sicyon—the Greek statesman who had
started the movement for turning the ancient parochial Achaean
Confederacy into the nucleus of a wider Greek political union by
persuading his own city Sicyon to enter the Confederacy, as its
first non-Achaean state-member, after he had liberated Sicyon
from Macedonian occupation.

It will be seen that Aratus and Lydiadas dreamed the same
dream for Greece that Machiavelli dreamed for Italy.[3] They

---

[1] 220–168 B.C.

[2] Polybius: *Historiae*, Bk. I, chs. 1–4.

[3] In the history of the Sinic World, in which the process of geographical expansion
produced its usual result of encircling the little states at the centre with an outer ring of
younger states of larger calibre (see p. 303, footnote 2, above), the central states sought
to protect themselves in the same way as in ancient Greece and in modern Italy: that is
to say, by forming a confederacy; and this confederacy 'remained one of the fundamental elements in Sinic politics' for two-and-a-half centuries (Maspéro, H.: *La Chine
Antique* (Paris 1927, Boccard), p. 299). Ultimately, however, the Sinic Central Confederacy failed, and this for the same reason as the Achaean League. Though its history
bore out the rule that 'union is strength', it never succeeded in making itself quite strong
enough to shake itself free from the toils of the surrounding Powers; and thus the Confederacy sank in the end into the position from which its constituent members had hoped
to extricate themselves once for all when they joined forces. It became a pawn on the
Great Powers' chess-board.

realized that the age-long disunion and strife of the Greek city-
states could not continue with impunity in an age when Greece
was encompassed about by gigantic Powers of a vastly superior
calibre. 'They should be profoundly thankful if they succeeded,
by maintaining absolute unanimity and by linking hands like
people crossing rivers, in flinging back the onslaughts of the barbarians[1] for the common salvation of their countries and themselves.'[2] This policy was originally propagated in the Peloponnese
by Aratus and Lydiadas; and while it was Aratus of Sicyon who
had initiated the idea, it was in Megalopolis, the city of Lydiadas,
that the word became flesh in an hereditary school of statesmen.
The work of Lydiadas was carried on in the next generation by
two other distinguished Megalopolitans, Philopoemen and Lycortas; and Lycortas was the father of Polybius.

Thus Polybius was brought up in a social milieu in which there
was a long tradition of public service; and he went into politics as a
matter of course. Indeed, his first political appointment was given
him by special favour before he had attained the legal minimum
age. In 181 B.C. he was appointed member of a diplomatic mission
which was to represent the Achaean Confederacy at the Court of
Alexandria. Polybius's fellow envoys were his own father Lycortas
and Aratus, the son of Aratus the Great; and it was in virtue of his
family connexions that the statutory age-qualification was waived
on this occasion in the young man's favour.[3] After this favourable
start in politics, Polybius doubtless looked forward to living the life
of 'a practical politician' for the rest of his days; but political events
which were beyond the Achaean Government's control were to give
quite a different turn to Polybius's career. The young Megalopolitan
had happened to come of age during a momentary lull in the great
political tornado that was sweeping across his world. Continental
Greece had enjoyed a respite from serving as the battle-field of the
Powers since 189 B.C., when the Aetolian Confederacy had laid
down its arms after a vain attempt to wage war against Rome in
alliance with the Seleucid Monarchy. But the respite was brief;
for the Third Romano-Macedonian War broke out in 171 B.C.;

---

[1] The word 'barbarians' is used here as a half-jesting half-serious nickname for the
non-Greek Great Powers on the periphery of the Hellenic World and in the penumbra
of the Hellenic Civilization. Compare the similar usage, cited above, in fifteenth-
century and sixteenth-century Italy.

[2] This statement of the problem to be solved by Greek statesmanship might well have
been made by either Aratus of Sicyon or Lydiadas of Megalopolis, though it was actually
made by Agelaus of Naupactus: a statesman of the rival Aetolian Confederacy which was
attempting in the same age to achieve the same aim of unifying Greece politically, though
round a different nucleus. Agelaus's speech on this theme, which was delivered at a
peace conference which was held at Naupactus in 217 B.C., is reported by Polybius in
Bk. V, chs. 103–5.

[3] See Polybius's own notice of this transaction in Bk. XXIV, ch. 6. The mission never
actually sailed for Egypt, after all!

and one of the sequels to the overthrow of Macedon by Rome in 168 was the precautionary deportation to Italy, *en masse*, of leading politicians from the states of Greece. The deportees included a thousand Achaeans; Polybius was one of the number; and this sudden break in his political career was the turning-point in his life.

From that point onwards, Polybius's life was an alternation between periods of compulsory withdrawal from practical politics and other periods of painful return to public affairs. His internment in Italy lasted for more than sixteen years (166–150 B.C.); and during this first compulsory withdrawal he accepted the challenge of Fortune by taking advantage of the break in his political career at home in order to enlarge, in his Italian exile, both the range of his political horizon and the circle of his personal acquaintance.[1] At Rome he learnt to know the Roman Commonwealth from within;[2] at Rome, likewise, he became the friend and mentor of the most promising young Roman of the next generation: Publius Cornelius Scipio Aemilianus;[3] and these two experiences governed the course of Polybius's life thereafter.

Released from internment in 150 B.C., Polybius was drawn back into public affairs by the catastrophic international events of the next five years. In 147 Scipio was elected consul in order to take command in Africa and break the desperate resistance which the Carthaginians were offering to the now overwhelmingly superior force of Rome in the Third Romano-Carthaginian War;[4] and Poly-

[1] The challenge presented to Polybius and his fellow deportees was severe; for the uncertainty in which they were kept by the deliberate policy of the Roman Senate must have imposed a heavy nervous strain upon their spirits. The nominal reason for which they had been brought to Rome was in order to give them an opportunity of vindicating themselves in person from the charge of having adopted a hostile attitude towards the Roman cause during the Third Romano-Macedonian War. Upon their arrival in Rome, the Senate professed astonishment that it should be asked to pass judgement on citizens of foreign states on whom judgement had already been passed at home. Thereupon, the Achaean Government sent an embassy to Rome to point out that the Achaean deportees had not, as a matter of fact, had any sentence passed upon them in Achaea, and to ask the Senate either to try the deportees itself or to send them home for trial forthwith. Thereupon the Senate—being determined to prevent the deportees from returning to political life in their own countries, and at the same time desiring to avoid the juridical irregularity of passing judgement itself on individuals who in theory were not under Roman jurisdiction—replied, in writing, to the Achaean embassy that: 'In the opinion of the Senate, it is not in the interests either of the Roman Government or of your Governments that these individuals should return home.' Polybius, who narrates this diplomatic transaction himself (in Bk. XXX, ch. 32), has recorded that 'when this reply came out, it not only threw the deportees themselves into a state of utter despair and mental paralysis, but it excited public grief throughout Greece, where the reply was taken as depriving the unfortunates of all hope of salvation. When the terms of the reply became generally known, the feelings of the Greek public were devastated, and people were overcome by a wave of hopelessness.'

[2] Compare the knowledge of France and Germany which Machiavelli acquired on his more transient Transalpine missions.

[3] The origin and history of this friendship between Polybius and Scipio Aemilianus is recorded by Polybius himself in Bk. XXXI, chs. 22–30. It was through Scipio's intercession that Polybius was permitted by the Roman authorities, as a special favour, to continue to reside in the capital when his fellow deportees were distributed for internment among the country towns of Italy.

[4] Scipio, on this occasion, like Polybius some **thirty-four years earlier**, had the honour

bius accompanied his Roman friend to the African front. Polybius was thus an eyewitness of the last act of the long tragedy that ended now in the literal annihilation of a commonwealth which had been one of the greatest of the Great Powers in the World at the time of Polybius's birth.[1] And then, from Scipio's camp by the smouldering ruins of Carthage, Polybius was called post-haste to Greece by the news of the outbreak of war between Rome and the Achaean Confederacy; and he arrived in his own country to find Corinth already overtaken by the same awful fate which Carthage had just suffered under his eyes.

Thereupon, Polybius was required, after a twenty years' absence, to resume his political career at home in circumstances which were at once more honourable and more painful for him than any which he could have foreseen or imagined. The Board of Ten Commissioners which the Roman Government, according to its usual practice, had sent out after the termination of hostilities to wind up the affairs of the conquered enemy country now courteously invited Polybius to serve as their expert adviser; and after they had performed their own major task—which was to dissolve the Achaean Confederacy and to confiscate the property of communities and individuals convicted of war-guilt—they left it to Polybius to regulate the affairs of the ex-member-states on the new footing on which they were thenceforth to live.[2] In this transaction, Polybius deserved as well of his country as in anything that he had ever been able to do for her; and his countrymen were not ungrateful for his services; but it was a transaction which was final by its very nature; and after Polybius had followed the Commissioners to Rome to make his report, he found himself again—and now irrevocably—cut off from practical politics. His second retirement, which now followed, was to last until the end of his long life (he lived to be eighty-two), with one interval when his faithful friendship for Scipio conspired with his insatiable desire for knowledge to draw him out of his retreat and lure him into the heart of Spain

of receiving his appointment in advance of the legal minimum age. Scipio had, in fact, been the only Roman officer to distinguish himself in the first two campaigns of the Third Romano-Carthaginian War—a war which had been forced upon Carthage by the Roman Government with the deliberate intention of destroying Carthage root and branch.

[1] In a passage which has only been preserved at second-hand (in Appian's *Punica*, 132), Polybius himself has recorded how, at the final scene of destruction, Scipio broke down; and how he afterwards quoted two foreboding lines of Homer (*Iliad* vi, ll. 448–9); and how, when Polybius asked him point-blank what he meant by his quotation, Scipio confessed that he was thinking that Rome would suffer one day what Carthage was suffering then.

[2] Though the Achaean Confederacy was dissolved, the individual states-members (with the exception of Corinth, which forfeited its juridical existence, besides being physically destroyed) retained their juridical sovereignty and *de facto* autonomy as isolated *civitates liberae* under the supervision of the Roman Governor of Macedonia (which, unlike Achaia, was now annexed by Rome and converted into a Roman province).

in order to witness the last phase of the war between Rome and Numantia.[1]

In this strange alternation between periods of enforced leisure and other periods of strenuous participation in public affairs, Polybius continued, through his personal merit, to gain experience and achieve distinction while all the World around him, including Rome herself,[2] was going to wrack and ruin; and as he 'watched the workings of Fortune' and learnt to 'know her genius for envious dealing with Mankind',[3] he answered her challenge by transmuting his unemployed ability and frustrated zeal for practical politics into the literary activity of 'depicting the operation of the laws of Fortune upon the grand scale' in an oecumenical history of his own times.[4] In this work, Polybius the historian has performed an act of creation which could never have been emulated by Polybius the politician; and though the *Oecumenical History* may not be a pearl of as great a price as the work of Polybius's predecessor Thucydides, it is nevertheless, in its own way, 'an everlasting possession' likewise; for Polybius, like Thucydides, had the genius to divine the character of his time and to catch its reflexion in a work of art;[5] and, like Thucydides again, he also had the strength of mind to bring his genius into play by seizing the unique opportunity that was offered to the historian by the politician's adversity. Expelled from the political life of their respective countries at an age when they were at the height of their personal powers, both men returned after an absence of twenty years to find their countries politically prostrate. But this physical return in the flesh to a home in ruins was not the true return of Polybius and Thucydides; 'for here' they had 'no

[1] Scipio had been appointed to the Spanish command in 134 B.C., as he had been appointed to the African command in 147 B.C., in order to break the resistance of an enemy who was outmatched by Rome in every element of military strength except the vital elements of generalship and *moral*.

[2] In Bk. XXXI, ch. 25, Polybius describes the general demoralization of the rising generation of the Roman governing class after the destruction in 168 B.C. of Macedon—the last surviving Great Power that had been capable of disputing Rome's ascendancy; and he lived to see the outbreak, in 133 B.C., of the Hundred Years' Revolution which was the nemesis of the devastation of Southern Italy in the Hannibalic War and which was to end in autocracy.

[3] Polybius, Bk. XXXIX, ch. 8.

[4] The work consists of forty volumes (only the first six survive intact), of which thirty contain the main body of the work, two the prologue, and eight the epilogue. The main body (Bks. III–XXXII) records the history of the conquest of the whole Hellenic World by Rome between 220 B.C. and 168 B.C. The epilogue (Bks. XXXIII–XL) carries the story down to the annihilation of Carthage and Corinth in 146 B.C. The prologue (Bks. I–II) carries the story back to the outbreak of the First Romano-Carthaginian War in 264 B.C.

[5] 'The coincidence by which all the transactions of the World have been oriented in a single direction and guided towards a single goal is the extraordinary characteristic of the present age, to which the special feature of the present work is a corollary. The unity of events imposes upon the historian a similar unity of composition in depicting for his readers the operation of the laws of Fortune upon the grand scale; and this has been my own principal inducement and stimulus in the work which I have undertaken' (Polybius: *Oecumenical History*, Preface = Bk. I, chs. 1–4).

continuing city'.[1] Megalopolis and Athens were in truth the cities from which they withdrew; but the city to which they have both returned, to abide in it for ever, is not the City of Cecrops but the City of Zeus.[2]

Clarendon

The English statesman and historian Edward Hyde, Earl of Clarendon (*vivebat* A.D. 1609–1674), saw his life rudely shattered and still more strangely remade by a social convulsion which was scarcely less violent in its way than the terrible experience that fell to the lot of Polybius. In Clarendon's generation, the modern Western World was shaken to its spiritual depths; and out of those depths there emerged a titanic new force—the political force which, under the name of Democracy, is still in the ascendant in our world in our generation, three centuries later.[3] This tremendous political movement which is still in motion to-day—expanding in a wave which has latterly submerged the greater part of the Habitable Earth—welled up three centuries ago in a huge eruption of molten lava from the mouth of a single crater. England was the place in Western Christendom where this crater opened in order to discharge to the ends of the Earth a stream of energy that rose, with terrific impetus, from the vast subterranean reservoirs of Western social experience; and Clarendon's generation was the time in which the volcano erupted. Born in 1609, Edward Hyde had reached the age of thirty-three in the year in which the English Civil War between Crown and Parliament broke out, and the outbreak of that war broke up Hyde's life into periods of alternate storm and calm on the pattern which we have detected in the life of Polybius.[4] The Englishman's lifework, like the Greek's, was the outcome of his inward response to these external vicissitudes; and this truth became manifest to Clarendon himself when, in the haven of his final exile, he reviewed his life-history and saw it in retrospect as a whole. The noble passage in which Clarendon describes his own experience of Withdrawal-and-Return must be given in his own words, which cannot be paraphrased, though they must perforce be abbreviated.

'He was wont to say that, of the infinite blessings which God had vouchsafed to confer upon him almost from his cradle, amongst which he delighted in the reckoning up many signal instances, he esteemed himself so happy in none as in his three acquiescences, which he called

---

[1] Heb. xiii. 14.   [2] Marcus Aurelius: *Meditations*, iv. 23.
[3] See the present Study, Part I, *ad init.*, vol. i, above, and the present chapter, pp. 359–63, below.
[4] If the parallel between the lives of Clarendon and Polybius is to be worked out in detail, we shall have to confess that Polybius was more fortunate in his friendship with Scipio than Clarendon in his service to Charles II.

his three vacations and retreats he had in his life enjoyed from business of trouble and vexation; and in every of which God had given him grace and opportunity to make full reflections upon his actions, and his observations upon what he had done himself, and what he had seen others do and suffer; to repair the breaches in his own mind and to fortify himself with new resolutions against future encounters, in an entire resignation of all his thoughts and purposes into the disposal of God Almighty, and in a firm confidence of his protection and deliverance in all the difficulties he should be obliged to contend with; towards the obtaining whereof, he renewed those vows and promises of integrity and hearty endeavour to perform his duty, which are the only means to procure the continuance of that protection and deliverance.

'The first of these recesses or acquiescences was his remaining and residing in Jersey, when the Prince of Wales, his now Majesty, first went into France upon the command of the Queen his Mother . . .; and his stay there, during that time that his Highness first remained at Paris and St. Germain's, until his expedition afterwards to the fleet and in the Downs.[1] His second was when he was sent by his Majesty as his ambassador, together with the Lord Cottington, into Spain; in which two full years were spent before he waited upon the King again.[2] And the third was his last recess, by the disgrace he underwent and by the act of banishment.[3] In which three acquiescences he had learnt more, knew himself and other men much better, and served God and his country with more devotion, and he hoped more effectually, than in all the other more active part of his life.

'He used to say that he spent too much of his younger years in company and conversation, and too little with books. . . . He accused himself of entering too soon out of a life of ease and pleasure and too much idleness into a life of too much business, that required more labour and experience and knowledge than he was supplied for; for he put on his gown as soon as he was called to the Bar;[4] and, by the countenance of persons in place and authority, as soon engaged himself in the business of the profession as he put on his gown, and to that degree in practice that gave him little time for study, that he had too much neglected before; besides that he still indulged to his beloved conversation. Few years passed before the troubles in Scotland appeared, and the Little Parliament was convened; which being dissolved and presently a new one called, he was a member in both, and wholly gave himself up to the public affairs agitated there. . . . And in the beginning of the rebellion he was sworn of the Privy Council and made Chancellor of the Exchequer: and from this time the pains he took, and the great fatigue he underwent, were notorious to all men; insomuch as, the refreshment of dinner

[1] Clarendon's residence in Jersey lasted from the 17th April, 1646, to the 26th June, 1648.—A. J. T.
[2] Clarendon was actually in Madrid from the 26th November, 1649, until the December of 1650.—A. J. T.
[3] Clarendon was required to deliver up the Great Seal on the 30th August, 1667; he had to leave England as a fugitive on the 29th November; and he reached France on the 2nd December of the same year. He died abroad on the 9th December, 1674.—A. J. T.
[4] Clarendon was called to the Bar in 1633 at the age of 24.—A. J. T.

excepted, for he never supped, he had very little of the day, and not much of the night, vacant from the most important business. . . .

[His] 'first retreat gave him opportunity and leisure to call himself to a strict account for whatsoever he had done, upon revolving of all his particular actions and the behaviour of other men; and to compose those affections and allay those passions which, in the warmth of perpetual actions and chafed by continual contradictions, had need of rest and cool and deliberate cogitations. He had now time to mend his understanding, and to correct the defects and infirmities of his nature, by the observation of and reflection upon the grounds and successes of those counsels he had been privy to, upon the several tempers and distempers of men employed both in the martial and civil affairs of the greatest importance, and upon the experience he had and the observation he had made in the three or four last years, where the part he had acted himself differed so much from all the former transactions and commerce of his life. . . .

'These unavoidable reflections first made him discern how weak and foolish all his former imaginations had been, and how blind a surveyor he had been of the inclinations and affections of the heart of Man; and it made him likewise conclude from thence how uncomfortable and vain the dependence must be upon any thing in this World, where whatsoever is good and desirable suddenly perisheth, and nothing is lasting but the folly and wickedness of the inhabitants thereof. In this first vacation, he had leisure to read many learned and pious books; and here he began to compose his Meditations upon the Psalms, by applying those devotions to the present afflictions and calamities of his King and country. He began now by the especial encouragement of the King,[1] who was then a prisoner in the Army, to write The History of the late Rebellion and Civil Wars, and finished the first four books thereof; and made an entry upon some exercises of devotion which he lived to enlarge afterwards.

'When he had enjoyed, in that pleasant island of Jersey, full two years, in as great serenity of mind as the separation from country, wife and children can be imagined to admit, he received . . . an express order from the King . . . that he should forthwith attend the person of the Prince of Wales . . . and then without any delay he used all possible diligence to find the Prince. . . .

[In] 'his second retreat and recess' [when he was sent as ambassador into Spain], though he underwent in this employment many mortifications of several kinds, yet he still acknowledged that he learned much during the time of his being in Spain, from whence he returned a little before the Battle of Worcester; and after the King's[2] miraculous escape into France he quickly waited upon his Majesty, and was never separated from his person till sixteen or seventeen years after by his banishment.

'This he called his third and most blessed recess, in which God vouchsafed to exercise many of his mercies towards him. And though

[1] i.e. Charles the First, not Charles the Second!—A. J. T.
[2] i.e. Charles the Second.—A. J. T.

AN ANALYSIS OF GROWTH

he entered into it with many very disconsolate circumstances; yet in a short time, upon the recovery of a better state of health, and being remitted into a posture of ease and quietness, and secure from the power of his enemies, he recovered likewise a marvellous tranquillity and serenity of mind, by making a strict review and recollection into all the actions, all the faults and follies, committed by himself and others in his last continued fatigue of seventeen or eighteen years. . . .

'In all this retirement he was very seldom vacant, and then only when he was under some sharp visitation of the gout, from reading excellent books or writing some animadversions and exercitations of his own, as appears by the papers and notes which he left. He learned the Italian and French languages, in which he read many of the choicest books. Now he finished the work which his heart was most set upon, The History of the late Civil Wars and Transactions to the Time of the King's Return in the Year 1660; of which he gave the King advertisement. He finished his Reflections and Devotions upon the Psalms of David, which he dedicated to his children; which was ended at Montpelier before the death of the Duchess. He wrote and finished his Answer to Mr. Hobbes's Leviathan, to which he prefixed an epistle dedicatory to the King, if his Majesty would permit it. He wrote a good volume of Essays, Divine, Moral and Political, to which he was always adding. He prepared a Discourse Historical of the Pretence and Practice of the successive Popes from the Beginning of that Jurisdiction they assume; in which he thought he had fully vindicated the power and authority of kings from that odious usurpation. He entered upon the forming a Method for the better disposing the History of England, that it may be more profitably and exactly communicated than it hath yet been. He left so many papers of several kinds, and cut out so many pieces of work, that a man may conclude that he never intended to be idle.'[1]

Ibn Khaldūn

The last member of our Pleiad of historians is 'Abd-ar-Rahmān ibn Muhammad ibn Khaldūn al-Hadramī of Tunis (*vivebat* A.D. 1332–1406)—an Arabic genius who achieved in a single 'acquiescence' of less than four years' length, out of a fifty-four years' span of adult working life, a life-work in the shape of a piece of literature which can bear comparison with the work of a Thucydides or the work of a Machiavelli for both breadth and profundity of vision as well as for sheer intellectual power. Ibn Khaldūn's star shines the more brightly by contrast with the foil of darkness against which it flashes out; for while Thucydides and Machiavelli and Clarendon are all brilliant representatives of brilliant times and places, Ibn Khaldūn is the sole point of light in his quarter of the firmament. He is indeed the one outstanding personality in the

[1] *The Life of Edward Earl of Clarendon, written by himself, ad fin.* (Oxford 1817, Clarendon Press), vol. ii, pp. 549–67.

history of a civilization whose social life on the whole was 'solitary, poor, nasty, brutish, and short'.[1] In his chosen field of intellectual activity he appears to have been inspired by no predecessors[2] and to have found no kindred souls among his contemporaries and to have kindled no answering spark of inspiration in any successors; and yet, in the Prolegomena (*Muqaddamāt*) to his *Universal History* he has conceived and formulated a philosophy of history which is undoubtedly the greatest work of its kind that has ever yet been created by any mind in any time or place. It was his single brief 'acquiescence' from a life of practical activity that gave Ibn Khaldūn his opportunity to cast his creative thought into literary shape.

Ibn Khaldūn was born into the Arabic World in an age when the infant Arabic Civilization was struggling (as it proved, in vain) to bring order out of the chaos which was its legacy from a recent social interregnum. This interregnum (*circa* A.D. 975–1275) had been the sequel to the break-up of the Umayyad and 'Abbasid Caliphates, which had been the final embodiments of the Syriac universal state; and at the western extremity of the derelict Syriac World—in North-West Africa and in the Iberian Peninsula—the last vestiges of the old order had been swept away by a conflux of barbarians from three continents: European Asturians and Franks from the Pyrenees; African Nomads from the Sahara[3] and highlanders from the Atlas[4] who made themselves a name as the 'Berbers' *par excellence*;[5] and Asiatic Arab Badu from the North Arabian Steppe who were perhaps the most barbarous and destructive of them all.

The destruction which these barbarians had worked was brought home to Ibn Khaldūn by his family history as well as by his personal experience. The Khaldūns were a prominent house of the aristocracy of Seville[6] who had emigrated from Andalusia to Africa, about a century before 'Abd-ar-Rahmān ibn Khaldūn's birth, in anticipation of the conquest of Seville by the Castilians;[7] and in the

---

[1] The famous description of the life of Primitive Man in the State of Nature which is given by Thomas Hobbes in *Leviathan*, part i, ch. 13. For the history of the Arabic Civilization into which Ibn Khaldūn happened to be born, see I. C (i) (*b*), vol. i, pp. 70–2, with Annex I, above.

[2] The education which he received from his masters—of whom he gives an account in his *Autobiography*—seems to have been exceedingly thorough but entirely scholastic. (See the relevant passage, in French translation, in Ibn Khaldūn: *Muqaddamāt*, translated by de Slane, McG. (Paris 1863–8, Imprimerie Impériale, 3 vols.), vol. i, Introduction, pp. xix–xxvi.)

[3] The Murābits. [4] The Muwahhids.

[5] See II. D (v), vol. ii, p. 204, above.

[6] By origin, the family were Yamanīs from the Hadramawt who had migrated to Andalusia, after the Umayyad conquest, in one of the military colonies which were then drafted out to the Iberian Peninsula from the five garrisons of Arab troops in Syria (de Slane, op. cit., vol. i, pp. ix–x).

[7] Ibn Khaldūn, in his *Autobiography* (translation in de Slane, op. cit., vol. i, p. xv), mentions that his ancestors migrated from Seville to Ceuta some twenty years before the fall of Cordova (A.D. 1236), Carmona (A.D. 1243), Seville (A.D. 1244), and Jaen (A.D. 1246).

family's new home in Ifrīqīyah 'Abd-ar-Raḥmān, comparing the local conditions in his own generation, as he saw them, with the descriptions of Ifrīqīyah in earlier ages which he read in historical works, was evidently impressed by the greatness of the contrast between present and past and was convinced that the immense change for the worse which had taken place within the last three centuries was the handiwork of the Arab Badawī tribes—the Banu Hilāl and the Banu Sulaym—who had been unleashed in A.D. 1051 upon a rebellious Maghrib by the Fāṭimid rulers of Syria and Egypt.

'Ifrīqīyah and the Maghrib',[1] he writes, 'are suffering still from their devastation by the Arabs. The Banu Hilāl and the Sulaym broke their way in during the fifth century of the Hijrah [the 11th century of the Christian Era]; and they have continued to wreak their fury on these countries for three centuries and a half. Hence devastation and solitude still reign there. Before this invasion, the whole region extending from the [Western] Sudan to the Mediterranean was thickly populated: the traces of an ancient civilization, the débris of monuments and buildings, the ruins of towns and villages, are there to testify to the fact.'[2]

Ibn Khaldūn was conscious of the difference between this purely destructive Arab invasion during the post-Syriac interregnum and the movement which, some three or four centuries earlier, had brought his own ancestors westward from the Hadramawt to Andalusia. For these Arab emissaries of the Umayyads had come to the Maghrib not to destroy but to fulfil. They had come to step into the shoes of the previous Roman garrisons and Roman officials and to retrieve for the ancient Syriac Society, in its latter days, the former colonial domain of which it had been deprived during eight or nine centuries of alien rule.[3]

'After the preaching of Islam,' Ibn Khaldūn observes, 'the Arab armies penetrated into the Maghrib and captured all the cities of the country; but they did not establish themselves there as tent-dwellers or as Nomads, since their need to make sure of their dominion in the

[1] In the language of Arabic political geography, the Maghrib (i.e., 'the West') means in a general way the whole of the Arabic World west of Egypt, though the term is apt to be confined to the Arabic domain in North-West Africa to the exclusion of the Arabic domain in the Iberian Peninsula (Andalūs). Maghrib al-Aqṣā (i.e., 'the Far West') means Morocco. Ifrīqīyah (an Arabization of the Latin name 'Africa') means a region of rather wider extent than the modern Tunisia in which urban and agricultural life had the ascendancy over Nomadism. The successive capitals of Ifrīqīyah have been Carthage, Qayrawān, Mahdīyah, and Tunis.
[2] Ibn Khaldūn: *Muqaddamāt*, translation by de Slane, vol. i, p. 312. Cp. pp. 66–7.
[3] The Syriac culture had been planted on the coasts of North-West Africa and Spain by Phoenician colonists from about the ninth century B.C. onwards. The interval of alien rule between the end of the Carthaginian régime and the beginning of the Umayyad régime had lasted in Spain from the close of the third century B.C. to the beginning of the eighth century of the Christian Era, and in Africa from the middle of the second century B.C. to the middle of the seventh century of the Christian Era.

Maghrib compelled them to keep to the towns. So in the Maghrib at this stage the Arabs did not occupy the open country. It was not until the fifth century of the Hijrah that they came to take up their abode there and to spread tribe-wise in order to camp all over this immense region.'[1]

The first of the two passages here quoted from the *Universal History* of Ibn Khaldūn occurs in a chapter[2] which is perhaps the most crushing indictment of Nomad rule over sedentary populations that has ever been delivered from the mouth of a first-hand witness.[3] But the thought which had been set in motion in Ibn Khaldūn's mind by his apprehension of the ruin which the Nomads had brought upon the Maghrib did not come to a standstill here. It moved on, with a gathering momentum, to contemplate the contrast between the Nomadic and the sedentary way of life and to analyse the nature of each; to ponder over the group-feeling or sense of social solidarity or *esprit de corps* ('*asabīyah*) which is the Nomad's psychological response to the challenge of life in the desert; to trace out a connexion of cause and effect between *esprit de corps* and empire-building and between empire-building and religious propaganda; and thence to broaden out until at last it embraced, in a panoramic vision, the rises and falls of empires and the geneses and growths and breakdowns and disintegrations of civilizations.[4]

This mighty tree of thought, with its towering stem and symmetrically branching boughs and delicate tracery of twigs was the eventual outcome of the seedling that germinated in the young 'Abd-ar-Rahmān's mind under the early impression of the contrast between present and past in his native Ifriqīyah. But Ibn Khaldūn did not begin his career by sitting down to put these burgeoning thoughts into order. It seemed a more pressing task to be putting some rudiments of order into the struggling, chaotic social life of

---

[1] Ibn Khaldūn: *A History of the Berbers* = *A Universal History*, vols. vi and vii, French translation by de Slane (Algiers 1852–6, 4 vols.), vol. i, p. 28. The passage here quoted is taken for the text of his tenth chapter by Gautier, E. F.: *Les Siècles Obscurs du Maghreb* (Paris 1927, Payot). See further Marçais, G.: *Les Arabes en Berberie du XIᵉ au XIVᵉ Siècle* (Paris 1913, Leroux).

[2] Ibn Khaldūn: *Muqaddamāt*, Bk. I, section ii, *ad fin.* The chapter-headings speak for themselves: 'Every country that is conquered by Arabs rapidly goes to ruin'; 'In general, Arabs are incapable of founding an empire unless they have received a tincture of religion of a certain strength from some prophet or saint'; 'Of all peoples, Arabs are the least capable of governing an empire.'

[3] The indictment is the more remarkable when we consider that the particular Nomads at whose expense Ibn Khaldūn makes his *argumentum ad hominem* shared the name of Arab with the author himself; but perhaps it is actually this ostensible kinship which inspires Ibn Khaldūn with his animus against the Banu Hilāl; for the House of Khaldūn had not only been bourgeois for centuries; there was no Nomadic chapter at all in their past; for the peasantry of the Hadramawt is just as sedentary as the bourgeoisie of Mecca or Medina or San'ā. The very accent and argot of the Banu Hilāl set Ibn Khaldūn's teeth on edge. (For this, see the passages quoted by Gautier in op. cit., p. 387.)

[4] See, further, Annex III, below.

contemporary Ifriqīyah; and this was the task to which the young man found himself called both by family tradition and by personal need of a livelihood. The Macrocosm called him; the Microcosm could wait. And so, at the age of twenty, ʿAbd-ar-Rahmān ibn Khaldūn followed in his forbears' footsteps by plunging into local politics as a courtier and a minister of state.

The Arabic adventurer's own account, in his *Autobiography*, of his life during the next twenty-two years reminds a modern Western student of history, who re-reads the story in A.D. 1935, of nothing so much as the life of some latter-day Western-style Chinese politician during the equal span of time which has elapsed since the outbreak of the Chinese Revolution. It was, indeed, a life of 'meeting at night and parting at morning'; for, within this span of twenty-two years, Ibn Khaldūn saw service with no less than seven different princelings; and from almost every one of these successive royal masters his parting was abrupt and violent. In his native principality of Tunis, where he made his début, he remained no longer than a few weeks; and thereafter we find him making a series of brief appearances now in Fez and now in Granada (whence his momentary employer sends him, in A.D. 1363, on an embassy to the court of Peter the Cruel in Seville)[1] and now again in this or that city of Ifriqīyah. In all these peregrinations, his only tranquil 'getaway' was the last; and this, too, was effected *more sinico*.

In the spring of A.D. 1375 Ibn Khaldūn had just settled down at Tilimsān (Tlemçen), under the patronage of the local prince, to give public instruction as a change from practical politics, when it pleased the prince to send his accomplished guest on a political mission to a Nomad Arab tribe in the interior.

'As I had renounced public affairs,' Ibn Khaldūn proceeds, 'in order to live in retreat, the prospect of this mission filled me with repugnance; but I affected to accept it with pleasure. [On my road], I fell in with the ʿAwlād ʿArīf [who appear to have been a branch of the Duwāwidah tribe which Ibn Khaldūn had been instructed to visit]; and they welcomed me with gifts and honours. I took up my abode with them; and they sent to Tilimsān to fetch my family and my children. They promised at the same time to represent to the Sultan that it was positively impossible for me to fulfil the mission with which he had charged me; and in fact they induced him to accept my excuses. Thereupon I established myself with my family at Qalʿat ibn Salāmah, a castle situated in the country of the Banu Tujīn which was held from the Sultan by

[1] This was how ʿAbd-ar-Rahmān ibn Khaldūn visited, for the first and last time, the home of his ancestors. 'When I arrived at Seville', he writes, 'I remarked a number of monuments of my ancestors' greatness'. Peter received ʿAbd-ar-Rahmān with honour, and actually offered to reinstate him in his ancestral property if he would consent to enter his service—an offer which ʿAbd-ar-Rahmān politely declined. (See the relevant passage from the *Autobiography* in de Slane's translation of the *Muqaddamāt*, vol. i, p. xliv.)

the Duwāwidah in feudal tenure. I remained there for four years, entirely free from worries and from the turmoil of public affairs; and it was there that I began the composition of my work [on universal history]. It was in this retreat that I completed the *Muqaddamāt*:[1] a work which was entirely original in its plan and which I made out of the cream of an enormous mass of research. When I settled at Qal'at ibn Salāmah, I installed myself in a large and solid suite of rooms that had been built there by Abu Bakr ibn 'Arīf. During the prolonged stay which I made in this castle, I completely forgot the kingdoms of the Maghrib and of Tilimsān and thought of nothing but the present work.'[2]

This light-hearted 'acquiescence', secured by chicane, was obtained in strangely different circumstances, and was accepted in a profoundly different spirit, from the three 'acquiescences' in the life of Clarendon. Yet the volatile Maghribī's single sojourn in Qal'at ibn Salāmah evoked a greater work of genius than anything that came of the sober Englishman's successive sojourns in Jersey and Madrid and Montpelier—and this notwithstanding the fact that Ibn Khaldūn's quadrennium in the wilderness was the solitary incident of the kind in the whole of his long career. For, when once he quitted the friendly walls of Qal'at ibn Salāmah, Ibn Khaldūn was sucked back into the turmoil of affairs; and he never extricated himself again.

From the author's own account, it is not clear whether scholarship or boredom was the magnet that drew him back into the World. It is only certain that he was not responding, like Clarendon, to the call of public duty.

'When I had finished the *Muqaddamāt* and passed on to the history of the Arabs and Berbers and Zenāta, I had a keen desire to consult a number of books and collections that are only to be found in great cities; and I had to correct and to make a fair copy of a work that had been dictated almost entirely from memory. . . . Impelled by the desire to visit the Sultan Abu'l-'Abbās and to set eyes again on Tunis, the home of my fathers, . . . I set to work to obtain from this prince his permission to re-enter the dominions of the Hafsid Government. Shortly after, I received letters of amnesty, with an invitation to join the prince forthwith; so I hastened on the preparations for my departure and took my leave of the 'Awlād 'Arīf.'[3]

From that autumn of A.D. 1378 till his death in the spring of 1406, nearly twenty-eight years after, Ibn Khaldūn never found

---

[1] It is amusing to reflect that the great work on the philosophy of history which had been originally inspired in Ibn Khaldūn's mind by the portent of Arab barbarism in the Maghrib was actually composed under the aegis of the very barbarians who were the author's *bêtes noires*. We may conjecture that Ibn Khaldūn found means of excusing himself from reading aloud to his ingenuous hosts the biting satire on their ancestral way of life which he had been composing under their hospitable roof!

[2] Ibn Khaldūn: *Autobiography*, in op. cit., vol. i, pp. lxvii–lxviii.

[3] Op. cit., vol. i, p. lxviii.

another haven where his mind could be 'entirely free from worries'. His experiment of returning to public life in his home country was not a success; and four years later he sailed from Tunis for Alexandria—never again to return to his native Maghrib. But this was one of the cases in which *caelum non animum mutant qui trans mare currunt*;[1] and, even in the stabler society of Egypt, Ibn Khaldūn contrived to enliven his old age with as many chances and changes as had given zest to his youth in the chaotic West. The high personal distinction which he had now attained only gave him so much the greater scope for making enemies; and in the twenty years ending with his death in A.D. 1406 he was no less than six times appointed to one of the four highest judicial posts of Cairo[2] and five times deposed—to die at last triumphantly in office, within ten days of his fifth reinstatement. In each successive tenure, he put his colleagues and rivals out of countenance by exposing with equal ruthlessness their venality in administering the law and their ignorance in interpreting it—a double humiliation for which they were unable to forgive him. Nor were these legal feuds the only sensational incidents in the Egyptian chapter of the Maghribī philosopher's life. On the eve of his first deposition, his whole family, with all his worldly goods, were lost at sea on their way from Ifriqīyah to join him in his new Egyptian home; and, in the interval between his second and his third tenure of his judicial office at Cairo, he had an encounter at Damascus with Timur the Lame[3] which was a vastly more hazardous adventure than his youthful encounter, thirty-seven years before, with Peter the Cruel.

These were the turbulent circumstances in which 'Abd-ar-Rahmān ibn Khaldūn completed the life-work upon which he had embarked when he started to dictate his incomparable *Muqaddamāt*

---

1 Horace: *Epistles*, I. xi. 27.

2 The post of Qādi'l-Qudāt of the Mālikī School of Islamic jurisprudence.

3 Ibn Khaldūn's encounter with Timur was involuntary; for he seems to have been included more or less by *force majeure* in the suite of the Mamlūk Sultan Nāsir Nāsir-ad-Dīn Faraj when the Sultan marched out, towards the close of A.D. 1400, to dispute Timur's passage through Syria. The philosopher was deposited in Damascus while the Sultan went to meet his redoubtable adversary on the battle-field; but a brief engagement with the Transoxanian invaders was sufficient to damp the martial ardour of the Mamlūks; and their retreat was so precipitate that Ibn Khaldūn found himself, without warning, marooned in Damascus, with Timur's victorious army beleaguering the city. In this predicament, the resourceful philosopher headed a deputation from the citizens of Damascus to the conqueror's camp. (Since the enterprise was vetoed by the Mamlūk military governor of Damascus, Ibn Khaldūn and his fellow ambassadors made their exit from the city by having themselves let down over the city-wall with cords: a traditional Damascene expedient which had once saved the life of Saint Paul!) When the deputation found themselves in Timur's presence, Ibn Khaldūn contrived to engage Timur in conversation and then won the Emperor's heart by reciting to him the section of his *Universal History* in which he had recorded Timur's career up to date, with the request that Timur would deign to correct any errors of fact in the narrative! Timur treated Damascus with little less than his customary harshness, but he let Ibn Khaldūn depart to Cairo in peace. (For this encounter between Ibn Khaldūn and Timur, see the passages quoted from the original authorities by de Slane in op. cit., vol. i, pp. lxxxvi–xcii.)

during his creative 'acquiescence' at Qal'at ibn Salāmah. The task of committing to writing the *Universal History* which was in his mind was not at an end until the Prolegomena had been followed by six further volumes; and we may conjecture that these last six-sevenths of the work might never have seen the light if the successful composition of the prelude, during those four exceptional years of tranquillity, had not inspired the philosopher with an impetus to write which persisted through the subsequent years of recurrent turmoil. We must add that the relative value of the different parts of the work as 'everlasting possessions' is not to be measured by any quantitative standard; and that if Posterity were confronted with the cruel choice between losing the first volume alone of Ibn Khaldūn's *Universal History* or saving the *Muqaddamāt* at the price of losing all the other six, we should unhesitatingly sacrifice the six volumes which the author contrived to compose after his re-emergence from Qal'at ibn Salāmah in order to preserve the single volume which came to birth in that tranquil retreat. In fact, Ibn Khaldūn's life-work is the work which he accomplished in the four years devoted to creation out of half a century spent in a whirl of public activity. And the great philosopher's true return from his brief withdrawal was not the second chapter of practical life in which he emulated the vagaries of the first. In one aspect, the Ibn Khaldūn who bade farewell to Qal'at ibn Salāmah in the autumn of A.D. 1378 reassumed, at Tunis and in Cairo, the role of the restless politician who had whimsically taken his congé from the Court of Tilimsān in the spring of A.D. 1375. In another aspect, the ephemeral man of affairs re-emerged from his retreat transfigured, once for all, into the immortal philosopher whose thought still lives in the mind of every reader of the *Muqaddamāt*.

Confucius

The same *motif* of Withdrawal-and-Return appears in the life of the Sinic social philosopher Confucius (*vivebat circa* 551–479 B.C.) —a life which was outwardly not unlike the life of Ibn Khaldūn.

Born into the Sinic World within a century of the breakdown of the Sinic Civilization,[1] at a time when the destructive internecine warfare between a plurality of sovereign states was rapidly gathering momentum, the young Confucius aspired to enter politics in order to arrest the disintegration of the Sinic Society by systematizing and enforcing the observance of its traditional ceremonies and customs and institutions. Unlike Ibn Khaldūn, who evidently took

---

[1] If this breakdown is to be dated by any external event, a convenient date is the outbreak of war, in 634 B.C., between the peripheral states of Tsin and Ch'u for the hegemony over the cluster of smaller states at the centre of the Sinic World. (See Maspéro, H.: *La Chine Antique* (Paris 1927, Boccard), p. 323.)

his politics lightly as a profitable and diverting outlet for his practical energies, Confucius placed his whole treasure in the life of practical action, and found little consolation in imparting to a band of admiring disciples the precepts which he yearned to put into practice as a minister of state. Hence Confucius's life was a life of personal disappointment;[1] for the local princes of the contending states had little use for the services of a pedant in their cynical and perilous struggle for existence. Accordingly, Confucius had difficulty in obtaining an official appointment at all; and when at last he did attain a minor administrative post in his native state of Lu (one of the smaller states of the centre), he did not succeed in retaining it. His resignation was followed by his withdrawal from his native country; and he spent the next fourteen years in a peripatetic way of life—presenting himself in the capital of one state after another in the hope that some foreign prince might offer employment to a prophet who had found too little honour at home. This hope was never fulfilled; and Confucius's wanderings abroad were only brought to an end by an invitation to return to Lu which was extended to him as an act of grace without any accompanying offer of reinstatement in office. By then Confucius was sixty-eight years old; and when death overtook him five years later he was still in a private station. But this disappointing return to his little native state of Lu at the close of his life in the flesh was not the final way in which Confucius returned to the public life which he had quitted *à contre-cœur* fourteen years earlier. For the energies which the unsuccessful administrator was no longer able to apply to practical affairs found their outlet thereafter through literary and educational channels.

Confucius in exile collected and edited the literary monuments of the traditional lore which Confucius in office had sought to put into practice; the disciples who gathered round the philosopher's person and accompanied him in his wanderings from place to place followed suit by collecting and editing their master's oral precepts; and some three and a half centuries after Confucius's death, when the long crescendo of internecine warfare between the contending states had ended in the 'knock-out blow' of 221 B.C., and when bitter experience had taught the Sinic World to appreciate the stabilizing power of the pedantic Confucian êthos, the *Corpus Confucianum* was actually adopted by the Government of a Sinic universal state as its official canon of statesmanship.[2] The final

---

[1] For a critical sifting of the attested facts in Confucius's life-history, see Maspéro, op. cit., pp. 454–9. For the traditional biography, see Hirth, F.: *The Ancient History of China to the End of the Chou Dynasty* (New York (reprint of) 1923, Columbia University Press), pp. 241–8.

[2] See Hu Shih: 'The Establishment of Confucianism as a State Religion during the Han Dynasty' (in the *Journal of the North China Branch of the Royal Asiatic Society*,

step was taken in 125 B.C.,[1] when a competitive public examination in the Confucian Classics was instituted as the avenue of entry into the Imperial Civil Service; and the official reign of Confucius, which dates from that year, may be said to have lasted until the abolition of the examination system in A.D. 1905.

During these two thousand years, the posthumous ascendancy of Confucius survived the interregnum (*circa* A.D. 175–475) which followed the break-up of the Empire of the Han; it survived the influx of the barbarians, and the far more revolutionary influx of the Mahayana, into the new Far Eastern World; and it survived the latter-day barbarian invasions of Khitan and Kin and Mongol and Manchu. The one power that has ever seriously disputed the hold of Confucius over Chinese minds since the sage's ethereal reign began is the Civilization of the West, which is making its forcible impact upon the traditional life of China in the present generation. For the moment, maybe, the Western impact has driven Confucius from his millennial throne; yet, even if he has been officially deposed, the unconquerable sage is still contriving to govern where he no longer reigns by ruling incognito. For the essence of the Confucian social system, as it was instituted two thousand years ago, is government by students under the auspices of a sage whose personality and precepts are regarded with all the more veneration since the man of flesh and blood has departed this life and has received his apotheosis; and the lineaments of this system can still be detected in the life of a revolutionary China beneath all the scum and froth that have gathered on its agitated surface. In this twenty-eighth year after the abolition of the Confucian examinations, China is still being governed by students in a dead philosopher's name. The veneration long paid to Confucius has been transferred provisionally to Sun Yat-sen; and the borrowed prestige of the founder of the Kuomintang has secured the long-suffering acquiescence of the Chinese People in the conduct of public affairs by Dr. Sun's political legatees, who (to China's undoing) have received their education abroad in the social and physical sciences of the West, instead of being educated in the Confucian Classics like their predecessors for sixty generations. The moral and political bankruptcy of these Western-educated student-politicians of the Kuomintang may conceivably bring King Confucius back into his own again; and thus, even now, we cannot foresee the end of the mighty kingdom which this Sinic sage unwittingly acquired when he lost his official post in the petty principality of Lu.

vol. lx, 1929, pp. 26–7). See also Shryock, J. K.: *The Origin and Development of the State Cult of Confucius* (London 1932, Century Company).

[1] This is Hu Shih's date in op. cit., p. 27. The date is given as 124 B.C. by Franke, O.: *Geschichte des Chinesischen Reiches*, vol. i (Berlin and Leipzig 1930, de Gruyter), p. 301.

Kant

The *motif* reappears in the life of a modern Western philosopher who was more academic than Confucius himself. Immanuel Kant of Königsberg (*vivebat* A.D. 1724–1804) withdrew from the World deliberately. Though he had to wait fifteen years to obtain a professorial chair in his native city, he steadfastly refused all calls to other universities. In all his life, he never travelled more than forty miles from his birthplace or took a voyage upon the waters of the Baltic on whose shores he lived; and the daily round of his activities was so monotonously regular that the townspeople learnt to set their watches by his punctual passage past their windows on his daily 'constitutional ' walk. Yet within his own lifetime the retiring philosopher lived to draw a host of students to the outlying Prussian city from which he refused to move; and the insignificant-looking man who never transported his body more than forty miles has radiated his thought from Königsberg to the ends of the Earth.

Dante

When we turn our attention from the philosophers to the poets, we find the same *motif* in the life-history of Dante (*vivebat* A.D. 1265–1321). For this greatest of all Florentines did not accomplish his life-work till he had been driven to withdraw from his native city. In Florence, Dante fell in love with Beatrice, only to see her die before him after marrying another man. In Florence he went into politics, only to be sentenced to exile.[1] And from this banishment the Florentine *exul immeritus*[2] never returned in the flesh. Yet, in losing his birthright in Florence, Dante was to win the citizenship of the World; for, in exile, the genius which had been crossed in politics after being crossed in love found its life-work to achieve in creating the *Divina Commedia*.[3] To judge by an allusion in the first ode of Paragraph Nineteen of *La Vita Nuova*,[4] the first

[1] Dante was a philosophic Ghibelline, who broke away from the prevailing Guelf tradition of Florence because he divined—two centuries before Machiavelli—that the supreme political need of the Italian Society was for some supreme authority to bring peace and order into the relations between the contending city-states. While Machiavelli looks for an Italian dictator to be his saviour of Italian Society, Dante, in his less sophisticated generation, feels no repugnance against calling in a 'barbarian' to perform the same service for Italy in the traditional role of a Holy Roman Emperor.

[2] 'Dantes Aligherius Florentinus et Exul Immeritus' is the superscription over four out of ten extant letters written by Dante in exile.

[3] Dante was condemned to exile *in absentia* (under pain of death if he returned) on the 10th March, 1302. He is believed to have composed the *Divina Commedia* in exile during the last seven years of his life (A.D. 1314–21). The date in which the action of the poem is placed in the poem itself is A.D. 1300, when the poet was still living in Florence; but this date, which represents the middle-point of Dante's life on the conventional life-span of three-score years and ten, is evidently fictitious.

[4] Dante: *La Vita Nuova*, § 19, Canzone Prima, ll. 45–7:
Là, ov' è alcun che perder lei s'attende,
E che dirà nell' Inferno a' malnati:
'Io vidi la speranza de' beati.'

conception of the *Commedia* must already have arisen in Dante's mind before the death of Beatrice in A.D. 1290. Yet it was not until a quarter of a century later, when Beatrice had been twenty-four years in her grave and Dante himself twelve years in exile, that the extinction of the Florentine statesman's last political hopes, by the death of the Emperor Henry VII in A.D. 1314, at last set the poet free to escape from the trammels of Time and Space into the writing of his ageless and deathless masterpiece.

Hamlet

We may conclude our survey of the working of Withdrawal-and-Return in the lives of individuals by reverting from the realm of fact to the realm of myth from which we started, and contemplating the hero of a Scandinavian myth who has been transfigured by the genius of Shakespeare into the archetype of 'the intellectual'. In Shakespeare's tragedy of *Hamlet*, the dreamy student of Wittenberg is suddenly confronted, by the revelation of his mother's guilt, with the prospect of having to do the deed of Orestes. In face of this dreadful challenge, which finds him unfitted by temperament and unprepared by experience for making the response that his conscience demands, Hamlet does not resort to a physical withdrawal from the tragic scene in the fashion of his Hellenic counterpart. Orestes is conveyed away secretly, as a child, from the clutches of his mother and her lover and is brought up in distant Phocis in order to return to Argos in his manhood as his father's avenger. Since his earliest memory, Orestes has grown up with the knowledge that this is the deed which it has been laid upon him to do. Hamlet learns his fate by a sudden intimation at an age when he has already passed the threshold of maturity; and the manner in which he withdraws in order to return is characteristically different. Understanding, from the first, that his spiritual agony cannot be escaped by physical flight, he deliberately assents to his mother's request that he stay in Denmark instead of returning to Wittenberg; and thereupon he withdraws—on a far longer spiritual voyage—into the innermost depths of the Microcosm, in order to return to the Macrocosm, in the fullness of time, transformed, for the Orestian deed, into a demonic 'man of action'.

Puberty

Having now completed our survey of Withdrawal-and-Return in the lives of individuals, we may trace the same *motif* in the histories of minorities.

The *motif* presents itself conspicuously in the case of one minority of a natural order which always exists of necessity in every society: the minority consisting of those male members of any given society who, at any given moment, are in course of passing out of boyhood into manhood through the metamorphosis of puberty. The withdrawal of the boys from the common life of Society on the eve of puberty in order that they may return as men when they are ripe for marriage is a social movement which is not only common in the life of primitive societies, but is also traceable in the lives of societies that are in process of civilization—sometimes as a theme of Mythology and sometimes as a custom that lingers on in practice in some by-way of practical life. The temporary segregation of the boys of a primitive society during their years of puberty is a commonplace of Anthropology.[1] The reflexion of this custom in Mythology is illustrated by the Hellenic myth of the Centaur Cheiron's school of heroes in the wilderness of Mount Pelion. Its survival, as 'a going concern', into the history of a civilization is illustrated by the Spartan institution of the so-called 'Lycurgean Agôgê' and by the English institution of the so-called 'Public Schools'.[2]

Penalized Minorities

Other illustrations of the same *motif* are to be found in the experiences of some among those 'penalized minorities' whose histories we have already surveyed in another connexion.[3]

In the history of Jewry, for example, in face of the challenge presented by the impact of Hellenism, the Pharisees withdrew[4] in the second century B.C. not only from the cultural movement of Hellenization which had been unsuccessfully promoted by the High Priest Joshua-Jason but also from the triumphant military and political reaction against the Hellenic Seleucid Power which was captained by the Maccabees. And then, in the first century of the Christian Era, the greatest Pharisee that ever lived returned from this two-centuries-long segregation, with a mighty spiritual impetus, to sweep away all cultural barriers between Jew and Greek[5] by preaching the transfigured Judaism of Jesus as a means of salvation for the whole of Humanity.[6]

[1] For a survey of the prevalence of this institution in the lives of extant primitive societies, see Schurz, H.: *Altersklassen und Männerbunder* (Berlin 1902, Reimer).

[2] For an examination of the Lycurgean Agôgê and its analogies in the English 'Public Schools', see Part III. A, above. It is to be noted that while the English boy who is segregated from his family on the eve of puberty by being sent to a 'public school' does return to ordinary life upon reaching manhood, the Spartiate never returns, after his entry into the Agôgê at the age of seven, until he is superannuated from military service at the age of sixty.   [3] In II. D (vi), vol. ii, above.

[4] The name 'Pharisees' literally means 'those who separate themselves'.

[5] Col. iii. 11.

[6] For the *motif* of Withdrawal-and-Return in the personal life-history of Paul, see the present chapter, pp. 263–4, above. It is to be noted that the particular Pharisee who accomplished this Christian return from the Pharisaic withdrawal was an exceptional individual. The rank-and-file of the Pharisaic minority of Jewry marched into the same blind alley as the rank-and-file of the Spartiate soldiers and the Hellenic philosophers. They duly withdrew, but they never made their withdrawal fructify by returning in new capacities to create new worlds.

In a similar movement, the Nestorians withdrew, under pressure from the following wave of Islam, right out of the domain of their native Syriac Society into the remote interior of the Eurasian Steppe; and thence in due course they returned as conquerors on the crest of the wave of the Mongol invasion.[1] The Constantino-politan Greeks, driven out of public life by the Ottoman conquest, withdrew into the realm of private business in order to emerge again into public life, some two centuries later, as the Phanariots—the efficient secretaries of state whose business training made their political services indispensable to the Ottoman Government in its hour of adversity.[2] The English Nonconformists,[3] who had made their stormy entrance on to the stage of English history in the Civil War and the Commonwealth, thereafter withdrew and returned in somewhat similar circumstances to those that evoked the correspond-ing movement among the Ottoman Greek Orthodox Christians. Dropping out of public life from the **morrow** of the Restoration until the eve of the passage of the Reform Bill,[4] they likewise re-acted by withdrawing into the realm of private business in order to return omnipotent, a century and a half later, as the authors of the Industrial Revolution.[5]

[1] See II. D (vi), vol. ii, pp. 236–8, above.
[2] Ibid., pp. 222–8, above.
[3] Ibid., pp. 220–1 and 250, above.
[4] The exclusion of the Nonconformists from public life may be dated from the passage of the Corporation Act in A.D. 1661 and the Test Act in A.D. 1673. Their re-admission may be dated from the repeal of these two Acts in A.D. 1828.
[5] In the examples of Withdrawal-and-Return here cited from the histories of certain 'penalized minorities', the two beats of the movement make a sequence in Time—the withdrawal coming first and the return following after a perceptible Time-interval. But there is also a sense in which the very response of a penalized minority to the challenge of penalization is in itself an example of Withdrawal-and-Return, even when the two beats of the movement are virtually simultaneous. Some of the most conspicuous representa-tives of the 'penalized minorities'—e.g. the Jewish Diasporà—have never returned at all in the literal sense; but in the ethereal sense they undoubtedly have returned to the World in a new capacity and with enhanced power in the act of concentrating their social energies on other fields, and excelling in these fields, in response to the challenge of being handicapped in, or altogether excluded from, the most highly regarded fields of social activity. (See II. D (vi), vol. ii, p. 209, above.)
   This 'timeless' exhibition of the Withdrawal-and-Return *motif* is characteristic of what may be called the 'institutional penalized minorities': e.g. the Buddhist and Christian monastic orders or the Roman Catholic celibate clergy. It is indeed a common practice in primitive societies to penalize, by the imposition of tabus, those minorities or indi-viduals who serve as institutions incarnate. The notion underlying this practice seems to be that, the more drastically such incarnate institutions are compelled to withdraw from the ordinary activities of social life, the more vigorously they will return to Society on the plane of magical or religious activity which has been assigned to them as their special field. In fact, their fellows deal with them as the man with the pollarding-axe deals with the willow (See I. C (iii) (b), vol. i, p. 168, above) or the pruner with the vine or the mower with the meadow. A classic example of such compulsory withdrawal being imposed upon an incarnate institution by tabu is the treatment of the Toda 'palol', or sacral dairyman, by the pastoral Toda Society of the Nilgiri Hills in Southern India. (See Rivers, W. H. R.: *The Todas* (London 1906, Macmillan), pp. 98–105.) The 'palol', who is solely charged with the management of the sacral dairy, is not allowed to visit his home or any ordinary village. He has to do all his business with ordinary people through an intermediary. He may not cross a bridge. He must be celibate (except in the celebra-tion of his eighteenth year of office!). He may not attend a funeral under pain of having to resign his office. He may not be approached at all by ordinary Todas on two days

Barbarian Rear-guards

The *motif* reappears in the histories of other minorities which we have already had occasion to examine in the course of this Study.

We have seen, for example, how the Celtic and Teutonic rear-guards of the European Barbarism parted company with the van-guard and held themselves in reserve when the van-guard threw itself upon the derelict provinces of the Roman Empire in the Völkerwanderung of *circa* A.D. 375–675; and we have noted the historic difference in the outcome of these two alternative barbarian strategies. The barbarian van-guard, recklessly rushing in, was easily and rapidly overcome by the internal proletariat of the defunct Hellenic Society, which was able, through the institution of the Catholic Church, to deliver an irresistible counter-attack on its own ground.[1] On the other hand, the Celtic and Teutonic rear-guards, which held aloof and concentrated their efforts in the first instance upon begetting embryonic civilizations of their own, were able to contend with Catholic Christendom on equal terms when they emerged from their withdrawal at last in their own good time. In the embryonic Far Western Christian Civilization of the Irish and the embryonic Scandinavian Civilization of the Vikings, the Catholic Church found adversaries of a very different metal from the temper of the Goths and the Franks, which had been as flexible as the iron of a Galatian sword-blade. And there were moments in the seventh century of the Christian Era, and again in the ninth, when it was really an open question which of two contending Powers would win for itself the privilege of giving birth to the future civilization of the West.[2] In the narrowness of the margin by which the abortive Far Western Civilization and the abortive Scandinavian Civilization were defeated in their struggle with the Catholic Church we have the measure of their superiority over the Gothic Barbarism from which they had parted company; and this

---

in the week. Neither he nor his dairy must be touched by any ordinary person. He may not cut his hair or nails. Compare the tabus imposed upon the Grand Lama in Tibet. And compare likewise the role of 'the prisoner in the Vatican' which, in modern Western Christendom, has been played by the Pope for more than half a century, from A.D. 1870 to A.D. 1929. As 'the prisoner in the Vatican', the Pope has been able to move the feelings and imaginations of Roman Catholics all over the World more powerfully than he had ever moved them when he was the temporal sovereign of an Italian principality extending from the Mediterranean to the Adriatic and from the Po to the Garigliano. At the time of writing, it remains to be seen what will be the ultimate psychological consequences of the Lateran Agreements of 1929 between the Holy See and the Kingdom of Italy, under which 'the prisoner in the Vatican' has emerged from his masterly captivity to resume the role of a territorial sovereign over the miniature territory of the Vatican City. (For the Lateran Agreements, see further Toynbee, A. J., and Boulter, V. M.: *Survey of International Affairs for 1929*, Part V (i).)

[1] See II. D (vii), vol. ii, pp. 320–1, above.

[2] For the successive combats in which the Roman Church had to engage with the embryonic Far Western Christian Civilization and the embryonic Scandinavian Civilization for the privilege of becoming the embryo of our modern Western Civilization, see II. D (vii), vol. ii, pp. 322–60, above.

superiority can be traced to the special impetus which the two barbarian rear-guards acquired, before coming into action, from their
previous movement of Withdrawal-and-Return.

Athens in the Second Chapter of the Growth of the Hellenic Society

A still more conspicuous example of Withdrawal-and-Return,
which has come to our attention repeatedly,[1] is the behaviour of the
Athenians in the crisis into which the Hellenic Society was thrown
by the presentation of the Malthusian challenge in the eighth
century B.C.

We have noticed that the first reaction of Athens to this problem
of over-population was ostensibly negative. She did not react to the
pressure of over-population, as her neighbours Eretria and Chalcis
and Corinth and Megara reacted to it, by seizing and colonizing
new agricultural land overseas; and she did not react, as the Spartans reacted, by conquering the territories of adjoining Greek city-
states and turning the Greek inhabitants into serfs.[2] In this age,
so long as her neighbours were content to leave Athens alone,
Athens was content to play an apparently passive role on a Hellenic
stage on which the action was all the time becoming more intense
all around her. The first glimpse of her demonic latent energy that
she gave to the rest of Hellas was in her violent and victorious
reaction against King Cleomenes' attempt, towards the close of the
sixth century B.C., to bring her under the Lacedaemonian hegemony, as his predecessors had brought the Isthmian states.[3] And

---

[1] See vol. i, pp. 24–5; vol. ii, pp. 37–42; and vol. iii, pp. 122, 139–40, 197, above.
[2] The definitive boundaries of Attica as they had been established by Solon's time, at
the turn of the seventh and sixth centuries B.C., certainly embraced an area which was
exceptionally large for a *Continental* Greek city-state (the territorial scale of the Greek
colonies in Magna Graecia and Sicily was distinctly larger than that of the mother-states
in Continental Greece). In fact, Attica was by far the largest city-state territory in
Continental Greece with the one exception of the territory of Sparta. Yet there is no
indication, either in tradition or from presumptive evidence, that Attica was a product of
conquest. It is probable, though unattested, that Eleusis was originally an independent
city-state; but, if so, the unrecorded act of union between Eleusis and Athens must have
been an agreed measure, on a footing of equality, like the union of A.D. 1707 between
Scotland and England. The sole apparent exception to the pacific process by which
Attica grew was the acquisition of the Island of Salamis from Megara by force of arms; but
this did not become a precedent. When Athens next extended her territorial sphere on
the Continent by the attachment of Plataea, she attached her, not as a conquered and
recalcitrant enemy, but as an enthusiastic and devoted ally.
[3] The Lacedaemonian Government attempted to establish its ascendancy in Athens,
as it had established it in Corinth and Sicyon and Epidaurus and Megara, by overthrowing a local despotic régime and setting up in its place a more or less reactionary
oligarchy which could only make itself secure against a restoration of the radical despotism by continuing to lean upon Lacedaemonian support. When King Cleomenes applied
this policy to Athens, he was successful in the first step. In 511 B.C., a Lacedaemonian
expeditionary force duly expelled the despots of Athens and set up an oligarchy in their
stead. But at Athens this was not the end of the story. The local restoration of the
oligarchy was followed here by a struggle for power between the moderates and the
extremists; in 508 B.C. the leader of the moderates, Cleisthenes, gained the upper hand
by 'taking the Dêmos into his party' (Herodotus, Bk. V, ch. 66); the extremists appealed to
Sparta; and Cleomenes led a new Lacedaemonian military expedition to Attica with surprising consequences. When he put the Athenian extremists back into power and drove

thus, by her passive non-participation in the general movements of the age, and by her active resistance to any attempt to coerce her into conformity, Athens more or less deliberately segregated herself from the main body of the Hellenic World for upwards of two centuries. Yet these two centuries of Athenian withdrawal were not centuries of Athenian inactivity. On the contrary, we have seen how Athens took advantage of this long seclusion, which left her free from foreign entanglements, to concentrate her energies upon solving the general Hellenic problem of over-population by an original solution of her own—an Athenian solution which proved its superiority by continuing to work when the Spartan solution and the Chalcidian solution were bringing in diminishing returns. It was only in her own good time, when she had remodelled her traditional institutions to suit her newfangled way of life, that Athens at last returned to the arena from which she had so long absented herself. But when she returned in these circumstances, she returned with an impetus that was unprecedented in Hellenic history.

Athens proclaimed her return by the sensational gesture of throwing down the gauntlet to the Achaemenian Power. It was Athens who responded—when Sparta hung back—to the appeal of the Asiatic Greek insurgents in 499 B.C.; and from that day onwards Athens stood out as the protagonist in the Fifty Years' War (*gerebatur* 499–449 B.C.) between Hellas and the Syriac universal state. For upwards of two centuries from the beginning of the fifth century B.C., the role of Athens in Hellenic history was the absolute antithesis of the role which she had been playing for an equal period of time before.[1] From the outbreak of the Ionian Revolt in

the moderates into exile, he was answered by a general rising of the population of Attica; he found himself blockaded, with his little expeditionary force, in the citadel of Athens; and he was compelled to capitulate on condition of evacuating Attica unconditionally. Thereupon, Cleisthenes returned and immediately introduced his famous democratic constitution. In 507 B.C., Cleomenes sought to avenge this humiliation by unleashing against Athens her three strongest neighbours: Thebes, Chalcis, and Aegina. But, in face of this fresh attack, the Athenians displayed their latent energy once again. On land, they decisively defeated the combined Theban and Chalcidian forces in a single campaign (after which they dealt with Chalcis as Sparta had dealt with Messene). At sea, they successfully carried on a desultory naval warfare against the Aeginetan sea-power for some twenty years, until the imminence of Xerxes' great offensive against European Greece put a temporary stop to local inter-state hostilities.

[1] In the earlier period of Athenian history, the prevalent Athenian policy was only departed from by the despot Peisistratus, who anticipated, in the third quarter of the sixth century B.C., the Athenian imperialism of the fifth century by attempting to secure strategic and political and economic control over the two key-points in the Aegean area: the Black Sea Straits and the mouth of the River Strymon together with the mineral deposits of Mount Pangaeus. Peisistratus found his opportunity at Athens because his predecessor Solon had insisted upon implementing the Solonian economic policy by non-revolutionary methods which worked too slowly for the stress of the times. On the whole, Peisistratus came to fulfil the Solonian programme and not to destroy it; but he used his despotic power in order to 'speed up' the agrarian reconstruction of Attica by revolutionary methods. After his final triumph, he appears to have taken a leaf out of the Spartans' book and to have carried out in Attica an internal redistribution of landed property at the expense of the defeated and exiled aristocrats.

499 B.C. down to the end of the Chremonidean War in 262, Athens was always in the thick of the mêlée of Hellenic international politics; and it was not until she found herself hopelessly out-classed by the new titans of the periphery that she reluctantly renounced the status and the burdens of a Hellenic Great Power. Nor was her would-be withdrawal from the arena of international politics after her final overthrow by Macedon in 262 B.C. the end of her active participation in the general life of the Hellenic World. For, long before she fell behind in the military and political race, she had made herself 'the education of Hellas' in every other field. She had given the Hellenic culture a permanent Attic impress which it still retains in the sight of Posterity.

Ionia in the First Chapter of the Growth of the Hellenic Society

In the history of Athens, we have discerned our *motif* of With-drawal-and-Return in the creative activity of a minority which taught the Hellenic Society how to continue its growth by teaching it how to solve one of its crucial problems. Athens made herself 'the education of Hellas' in the literal sense by discovering how to solve the general Hellenic problem of over-population by a special Athenian method of intensive economic development. We have seen, however, at an earlier point,[1] that this Malthusian challenge which received an Athenian response was not the first crucial challenge with which the Hellenic Society had been confronted in the course of its history. The Malthusian challenge was actually evoked by the previous success of the Hellenic Society in replying to the prior challenge of Chaos. And it is natural to inquire whether, in this first chapter of Hellenic history, we can detect the same *motif* of Withdrawal-and-Return that is apparent in the second. We have seen that this primary challenge of Chaos was victoriously met in Hellenic history by the invention of the city-state: an institution which enabled the relatively orderly and progressive population of the rare and narrow plains to establish their ascendancy over the wild highlanders. Was the Hellenic city-state, like the later Hellenic economic system of specialized production for export, the invention of some creative minority which temporarily withdrew from the rest of the Hellenic Society, like Athens in a later age, in order to return in its own good time with a solution of a common problem which it had worked out for itself in its period of retreat?

We are here in the realm of conjecture; for we have no contemporary records of this first chapter of Hellenic history; but in

[1] In Part III. B, on pp. 120–1, above.

an earlier passage of this Study[1] we have found some reason for believing that the Hellenic city-state was originally invented, at the end of the post-Minoan Völkerwanderung, by those refugees from the 'Dorian' avalanche who parted company from their neighbours in Continental Greece by taking to their ships and finding new homes overseas on the coast of Anatolia. The transmarine migration which brought into existence the historic city-states of Aeolis and Ionia and Doris may fairly be regarded as a 'withdrawal' in our present usage of the term; and there are indications, as we have seen, that the historic city-states of Continental Greece were later foundations which were established on the overseas pattern artificially by mimesis. If we have interpreted these indications aright, then the eventual 'return' of the transmarine settlers into full communion with the rest of the Hellenic Society may be traced in the spread of the new institution of the city-state over the greater part of the Hellenic World. And, whether or not the Hellenic city-state can properly be regarded as a specifically Ionian invention, it is beyond dispute that there was an Ionian 'return' in the cultural if not in the political sphere. The monument of this return is the historic conquest of Continental Greece by the Ionian Epic,[2] which became 'an everlasting possession' of all Hellas. In fact, the Hellenic culture had received a definitely Ionian impress before Athens withdrew and returned to give it the Attic impress which it subsequently bore. Nor, even then, did the second impress wholly efface the first; for, although the Attic êthos and the Ionian êthos were notably different,[3] the Athenians did not begin to perform original acts of creation on their own account until they had saturated themselves with the Ionian spirit. The Athenian poet Aeschylus himself, in whom the Attic Promethean *élan* is incarnate, is content to describe his plays as 'slices from Homer's banquets';[4] and it was the Athenian 'reception' of the Ionian Epic that secured for the Iliad and the Odyssey an unchallenged supremacy in the realm of Greek literature as 'the Hellenic Bible'—a supremacy from which the Ionian 'Homer' was never to be ousted by any of his Attic successors.

The Achaean Confederacy in the First Chapter of the Disintegration of the Hellenic Society

Thus it would appear that, in each of two successive chapters in the history of the growth of the Hellenic Civilization, a challenge

---

[1] In II. D (iii), vol. ii, pp. 97–8, above.
[2] Ibid., pp. 94–6, above.
[3] See the illuminating analysis of the difference, as it comes out in a comparison of the Aeschylean with the Homeric treatment of an originally identical theme, in Murray, Gilbert: *The Rise of the Greek Epic*, 2nd ed. (Oxford 1911, Clarendon Press), pp. 289–95.
[4] Athenaeus 347 E, quoted in this Study already in vol. i, p. 449, footnote 1, above.

was met by the withdrawal and return of a creative minority
which withdrew temporarily from the rest of Society in order to
discover an original solution for the common problem and then
returned in the fullness of time in order to communicate to the rest
of Society the solution which it had duly discovered during its
temporary retreat. In the growth-phase of the Hellenic Society,
there are no more chapters than these two, since the growth of
the Hellenic Civilization was brought to an end by a failure to
meet the next challenge—the challenge of international anarchy—
which the Athenian response to the Malthusian challenge evoked in
its turn.[1] The consequence was the breakdown of 431 B.C. and the
long disintegration which followed; but this disintegration was
not a constant process. It consisted in an alternation of lapses and
rallies and relapses;[2] and in the first rally the *motif* of Withdrawal-
and-Return appears again.

One of the features of this first Hellenic rally was an attempt to
solve a problem which had been presented to the central states of
the Hellenic World by the renewal of the process of geographical
expansion—the problem of saving the central states from being not
only dwarfed but overwhelmed by the rise of new Great Powers of
titanic calibre on the expanding periphery. Athens; as we have
seen, had confessed herself worsted by this problem when she
sought to retire from active participation in international politics
after her last disastrous experience in the Chremonidean War of
266–262 B.C. In her foregoing attempt to pose among the titans as
the Great Power which in their presence she had ceased to be,
Athens had not succeeded in adding a cubit to her stature. She
had merely exposed herself to being treated—and sacrificed—as a
pawn in the war-game between giant Antigonus and giant Ptolemy.
When she shook herself free at last from Macedonian military
occupation in 228 B.C., her impulse, upon which she acted, was to
repeat the gesture of withdrawal which had turned out so fortu-
nately for her when she had made it for the first time some five
centuries earlier. By this time, however, there were other statesmen in Greece who perceived that, in the new Hellenic World
which had been called into existence by Alexander the Great, the
little city-states at the centre were so utterly at the mercy of the
titans round about that they were not even free to withdraw from

---

[1] The Athenian response to the Malthusian challenge of over-population was to obtain an enhancement of local productivity by specializing in production for exchange;
but this economic solution of an economic problem confronted the Hellenic Society with
the new political problem of establishing some international system of political peace
and order as a framework for an international system of economic interdependence. This
was the problem which the Hellenic World failed to solve. (See Part III. B, p. 122,
footnote 3, above, and IV. C (iii) (b) 10, vol. iv. pp. 206–14, below.)

[2] For the movement of Lapse-and-Rally-and-Relapse in the disintegrations of civilizations, see V. C (ii) (b), vol. vi. pp. 278–321, below.

the field at their pleasure. They were no longer actors on a stage; they were pawns on a board; and the all-powerful players of the diplomatic and military game would replace them on the board, and sacrifice them once again, whenever this might happen to suit their convenience. If the city-states of Greece were to recover their freedom even to withdraw, they could only hope to succeed by joining forces in order to establish in the heart of Greece a confederacy of city-states which would be sufficiently strong to compel a Macedon or an Egypt to respect its neutrality. This was the policy of the statesmen who attempted to turn the ancient parochial Achaean Confederacy into a wider union.[1] We need not enlarge upon this policy here, for we have noticed it already in our inquiry into the social milieu of Polybius.[2] We need only mention that in this instance the movement of withdrawal was followed by no movement of return because the policy of Aratus failed and the first rally of the Hellenic Civilization broke down into a relapse.[3] Yet in the policy which Aratus pursued with persistence and success for a quarter of a century, from 251 B.C. to 225, the first beat of the familiar rhythm is unmistakably recognizable.

Italy in the Second Chapter of the Growth of the Western Society

We have seen that Aratus in Greece was at grips with a problem of the Balance of Power which likewise exercised Machiavelli in Italy;[4] and we have also seen that both statesmen's efforts ended in failure. But in one important respect the two situations were different. While Aratus, in the third quarter of the third century B.C., was attempting to extricate the city-states of Greece from an entanglement with the Great Powers of the periphery from which they had been suffering for the best part of a century without ever having succeeded in shaking themselves free, Machiavelli, at the

---

[1] For the failure of both Athens and Sparta, the ci-devant leaders of Greece, to take the lead in this later chapter of Hellenic history in a movement which was manifestly the sole chance of salvation that Greece still had open to her, see, further, IV. C (iii) (c) 2 (α), vol. iv, pp. 265–6, below. In the critical year 228 B.C., Athens refused to join the Achaean Confederacy and Sparta went to war with it!

[2] See the present chapter, pp. 310–14, above.

[3] The policy of Aratus came to grief in 228 B.C., when the Achaean federal movement came into collision with the Spartan revolutionary movement. There was not room for both movements in the Peloponnese; and when Aratus found himself being worsted by Cleomenes, he undid his own life-work by purchasing the military assistance of Macedon in 225–224 B.C. at the price of allowing the Achaean Confederacy to become a Macedonian pawn. The joint Achaean and Macedonian war against Sparta (224–222 or 223–221 B.C.) was immediately followed by a joint Achaean and Macedonian war against the Aetolian Confederacy—the rival of the Achaean Confederacy which had been attempting to carry out the Aratean policy round a different nucleus for a whole generation before Aratus himself had appeared in the field. The last hope of extricating Greece from the internecine warfare between the titanic Powers of the periphery disappeared in 212 B.C. when the Aetolians involved Greece in the Hannibalic War by entering into an alliance against Macedon with the Romans.

[4] For a general exposition of this problem, see the present chapter, pp. 301–6, above.

turn of the fifteenth and sixteenth centuries of the Christian Era, was attempting to preserve for the city-states of Italy an immunity from molestation on the part of Transalpine Europe which they had actually enjoyed, without any serious break, for more than two centuries before the apparition of Charles VIII in A.D. 1494. In other words, the withdrawal of Italy from the international politics of Transalpine Western Christendom, unlike the attempted withdrawal of third-century Greece from the international politics of the Macedonian 'successor-states', was not a pathetically abortive gesture but a successfully accomplished fact. In this respect it is comparable, not to the Achaean movement in the third century B.C., but rather to the withdrawal of Athens in the eighth, seventh, and sixth centuries B.C. which we have been studying in this chapter already.

On a comparative view, we can see that the Athenian withdrawal of the eighth, seventh, and sixth centuries B.C. and the Italian withdrawal of the thirteenth, fourteenth, and fifteenth centuries of the Christian Era display a strong resemblance to one another. In both cases, the withdrawal—on the political plane—was complete and persistent. In both cases, the self-segregating minority devoted the energies that were liberated by its release from foreign political entanglements to the task of finding an original solution of its own for a problem that confronted the whole of Society. And in both cases the creative minority returned to the Society which it had temporarily abandoned in the fullness of time, when its work of creation was accomplished, in order to set its impress upon the whole body social. We have already noticed how the Hellenic Society took an Attic impress after the return of Athens at the beginning of the fifth century B.C. We may now remind ourselves that our own Western Society took just as strong an Italian impress when Italy returned—not voluntarily, but under protest—at the beginning of the *Cinquecento*.

Moreover, the actual problems which Athens and Italy solved, in retreat, on their respective societies' behalf were much the same. Like Attica in Hellas, Lombardy and Tuscany in Western Christendom served, after withdrawal, as a segregated social laboratory in which the experiment of transforming a locally self-sufficient agricultural society into an internationally interdependent commercial and industrial society was successfully carried out. And in the Italian, as in the Athenian, case there was a radical remodelling of traditional institutions in order to bring them into conformity with the newfangled way of life. A commercialized and industrialized Athens changed over, on the political plane, from an aristocratic constitution based on birth to a bourgeois constitution based on property.[1] A commercialized and industrialized Milan or Bologna or Florence or Siena changed over from the prevalent Feudalism of medieval Western Christendom to a new system of direct relations between individual citizens and locally sovereign governments whose sovereignty resided in the citizens themselves. These concrete economic and political inventions, as well as the impalpable and imponderable cultural creations of the Italian genius, were communicated by Italy to Transalpine Europe from the close of the *Quattrocento* onwards.

At this stage, however, the respective courses of Western and Hellenic history diverge in consequence of one essential point of dissimilarity between the position of the Italian city-states in Western Christendom and the position of Athens in Hellas. Athens was a city-state which had withdrawn from a society of city-states in order to return to a society that had not ceased to consist of city-state units. And accordingly, when Athens became 'the education of Hellas', the process of education was facilitated by the fact that the creative minority and the imitative majority had one important feature in common. They were both alike organized on the city-state pattern; and thus, while the non-Athenian majority of Hellas had to change over from agriculture and aristocracy to industry and democracy in order to catch up with the progress that the creative Athenian minority had made, the majority was not required to make any change in the nature or the scale of the local communities into which it was articulated. It was merely a question of changing a number of agricultural aristocratic city-states into the same number of industrial democratic city-states. There was no question of altering the city-state basis which was the common social heritage of Athens and her Hellenic neighbours.

In the relations between the creative Italian minority and the non-Italian majority of Western Christendom, the problem of assimilation was more difficult because in this case there was no corresponding common ground between the two parts of Society. For the city-state pattern, on which the Italian minority was organized, was not the original basis of articulation in Western Christendom. The original basis—the basis on which Western Christendom, in the first chapter of its history, had met the challenge of Chaos and had triumphed over the rival Scandinavian

---

[1] This change, which was made in principle, and indeed in substance, by Solon himself at the beginning of the sixth century B.C., was the really radical change in the constitution of Athens. Compared with this, the transition from oligarchy to democracy which followed in the course of the next century-and-a-half was secondary. When once the change of basis from the birth-qualification to the property-qualification had been made, Athens was a potential democracy already. It was merely a question of lowering to zero the amount of the property-qualification for the exercise of political power without any further change in its essential nature.

Civilization—was not the city-state but Feudalism.[1] The city-state, in fact, was not one of the original institutions of the Western Society. In Western history, the city-state only emerged in the second chapter; and then it emerged as a newfangled institution of the minority which withdrew and returned in this age. The withdrawal of the Italian minority from political entanglements with Transalpine Christendom was accompanied by a change-over, on the part of the self-segregating Italian communities, from a feudal to a city-state basis. This change in the basis of social articulation was one of the most conspicuous ways in which the Italians differentiated themselves from the majority of Western Christendom in their temporary retreat.[2] There was no simultaneous change in the same sense in the social structure of the Western Society at large; and when the creative Italian minority returned in due course to become 'the education of Western Christendom', the greater part of the Western World was still organized on the original feudal basis, and not on the new city-state basis on which the Italians had built their new model for a progressive Western Society.

This situation presented a problem to Western Christendom for which, *a priori*, there were two conceivable alternative solutions. In order to place itself in a position to adopt the new social inventions which Italy had to offer, Transalpine Europe might either break with its feudal past and rearticulate itself throughout on the Italian city-state basis; or else it might modify the Italian inventions in such a way as to make them workable on the feudal basis and on the kingdom-state scale of the old-fashioned Transalpine World. Theoretically, the problem might be solved along either of these lines. The only thing that was not practically possible was for the Italian inventions, as they stood, to be applied in the Transalpine kingdoms, as they stood, without some far-reaching measure of adaptation on the one side or on the other. In the event, the city-state articulation of the Italian minority was rejected and the Italian inventions were only adopted in Transalpine Europe in so far as they could be applied on the kingdom-state scale. But the alternative solution of rearticulating Transalpine Europe into an Italianized society of city-states was not left untried; and although the experiment eventually proved abortive, it was carried a considerable distance and came within sight of success before it irrevocably failed.

Northern Italy, in fact, was not the only place in Western

---

[1] See II. D (v), vol. ii, pp. 199–200, and III. C (i) (*d*), p. 196, above.
[2] For the emergence of the institution of the city-state in the Italian part of medieval Western Christendom as a 'throw-back' to the 'apparented' Hellenic Society on the part of the 'affiliated' Western Society, see Part X, below.

Christendom in which, during the second chapter of Western history, a creative minority extricated itself from the general political life of the Western Society by building city walls and learning to live a new life of its own behind them. While Italy was the region in which this movement declared itself the most conspicuously, and where it achieved its greatest works of creation, the movement was not exclusively Italian in origin. It was a general movement of the Western Society, which came to the surface wherever it was favoured by the presence of certain social conditions. These conditions were presented in some measure in other parts of Western Christendom besides Italy; and wherever they were to be found, the movement asserted itself.

The main conditions were two: the one economic and the other political. The economic condition was that the emergent city-states should command a sufficient field of commercial and industrial activity—a sufficiency of markets and of sources of supply—to enable them to live by commerce and industry instead of continuing to depend upon agriculture. The political condition was that there should be a sufficiently exact equilibrium—or sufficiently prolonged stalemate—in the local Balance of Power between the large-scale Powers of Western Christendom—the Papacy and the Empire and the peripheral kingdoms—to enable new Powers on the small scale of city-states to take possession of the no-man's-land between the evenly-matched and therefore temporarily immobilized titans.[1] These conditions were fulfilled in the case of Northern Italy; for Northern Italy was the pier-head[2] from which medieval Western Christendom was bound to conduct its overseas trade with the Syriac World and with Orthodox Christendom—two neighbouring worlds which in that age were both larger and richer than Western Christendom itself;[3] and Northern Italy was also the no-man's-land in the long and stubborn contest for the headship over Western Christendom which was waged between the Papacy and the Holy Roman Empire. These were the conditions under which Northern Italy disengaged herself (*circa* A.D.

---

[1] It is one of the laws of the Balance of Power that, when and where it falls into an exactly stable equilibrium, this situation gives an opportunity for the emergence of new Powers, of lesser calibre, in the interstices between the existing Powers who are temporarily immobilized by the exactness of their balance with one another. This law is examined further in Part XI, below.

[2] For this function of Northern Italy in the primitive geographical structure of Western Christendom, see I. B (iv), vol. i, p. 38, above.

[3] Italy was the physical bridge between Western Christendom and these two alien worlds; for when Western and Orthodox Christendom emerged simultaneously from the interregnum that followed the break-up of the Roman Empire, the Italian Peninsula was partitioned between them; and, thereafter, the possession of the Orthodox Christian part of Italy—that is, the 'heel' and the 'toe' and the Island of Sicily—was disputed between Orthodox Christendom and the re-emergent colonial Syriac Society of North-West Africa.

1158–1250) from the mass of Western Christendom as a constellation of virtually sovereign city-states. But the same conditions offered themselves in certain other places with similar results.

In Germany, for example, the rise of city-states was promoted economically by the debouchure, on German soil, of the overland trade-routes from Italy to Transalpine Europe through the Alpine passes and also by the northward and eastward expansion of Western Christendom—an expansion which gave Germany a seaboard on the Baltic and brought Scandinavia and Poland and Hungary within the radius of the German pioneers of Western trade.[1] At the same time, on the political plane, the rise of city-states in Germany was promoted indirectly by the struggle between the Empire and the Papacy in Italy—a struggle which sapped the strength of the Imperial Power in its German homeland and thus gave an opportunity for the Emperor's German feudatories to erect themselves into virtually independent princes. The resulting Balance of Power between the princes and the Emperor enabled rising city-states to shake themselves free in Germany as their elder sisters in Italy had been enabled to win their freedom through the Balance of Power between the Empire and the Papacy. In Flanders, again, the rise of city-states was promoted economically by the junction on Flemish soil of the overland trade-route from the Mediterranean (over Northern Italy and Southern and Western Germany) with the maritime trade-routes along the Atlantic and North Sea coasts and across the Straits between the Continent and the British Isles. Thereafter, the Flemish city-states were enabled to complete the achievement of their *de facto* political independence from the authority of the Count of Flanders, who was a feudatory of the Crown of France, by taking sides with the Crown of England in the Hundred Years' War (*incepit* A.D. 1337).

Thus, by the middle of the fourteenth century of the Christian Era, the feudal darkness of the Western World was thickly sown with constellations of city-states; and these constellations were disposed in a commanding formation. At each of two points on opposite fringes of the Western firmament, in Italy and in Flanders, there was a star-cluster of such density that, within its own circumference, it wholly occupied the field of vision with a continuum of stellar light which left no rifts of darkness visible. Between the Italian and the Flemish cluster, across Swabia and the Rhineland, there stretched a star-riband of looser mesh and lesser luminosity, in the likeness of the Milky Way; and from the north-eastern flank of this terrestrial galaxy, in the neighbourhood of Cologne, the star-stream of the Hansa Towns shone out across Westphalia from the

[1] For this expansion, see II. D (v), vol. ii, pp. 167–70, above.

banks of the Rhine to the shores of the Baltic. It will be seen that
the new cosmos of city-states, which was taking shape in Western
Christendom within the framework of the old cosmos of feudal
tenures, had increased and multiplied with remarkable vitality
during the three centuries or so that had elapsed since the beginning of its creation. The light was shining in the darkness from
which it had been divided by the creative act; but the darkness
comprehended it not. Would the light prevail over the darkness or
the darkness reabsorb the light?[1] The moment had come when the
Western Society must choose which world, of these two alternative
and incompatible worlds, it was henceforth to be: the old feudal
world or a new world of city-states.[2]

Before the end of the fourteenth century this issue had been

[1] In the ephemeral overseas world (*terre d'outre mer*) which medieval Western
Christendom won for itself in 'the Crusades' at the expense of the moribund Syriac
Society and the prematurely decadent Orthodox Christendom, the feudal cosmos which
the Crusaders created in this new colonial domain in the twelfth and thirteenth centuries
of the Christian Era actually was swallowed up, in the fourteenth and fifteenth centuries,
by the new city-state cosmos which had latterly come into being in Italy.

At the time of the original conquests, which were mainly achieved in the First Crusade
and in the Fourth, the lion's share of the conquered territories was parcelled out into
feudal principalities, while the Italian maritime city-states, whose sea-power had contributed so much to the success of these joint Italian and Transalpine enterprises, had to
content themselves with the acquisition of a number of comparatively small (though
commercially and navally important) enclaves. By the end of the story, on the eve of
the total extinction of Latin dominion in the Levant at the hands of the 'Osmanlis,
the relative extent of the Italian and the Transalpine holdings of Latin territory in the
Levant had been completely reversed. In so far as the *ci-devant* Frankish feudal principalities had not been reconquered by the Orthodox Christians and the Muslims, the
remnants had been mostly preserved in virtue of their transfer from incompetent Transalpine to competent Italian hands. The change of régime which this transfer involved was
striking; for, in the Frankish principalities overseas, the principles of feudalism had been
carried to greater logical extremes, under artificial cultivation, than they had ever
attained in their spontaneous growth on their native European soil, whereas the Italian
colonial régimes which eventually took their place were anticipations of the modern
Western methods of colonial exploitation.

The outstanding example of this process is the history of the Latin Kingdom of
Cyprus, which was founded in A.D. 1191-2. As a result of a local conflict which broke
out in A.D. 1372 between the Genoese and Venetian colonies in Cyprus, the reigning
French dynasty of the House of Lusignan fell foul of the Genoese and was compelled to
cede to the Genoese Republic the sovereignty over the port of Famagusta, with a
monopoly of the foreign trade of the island. Famagusta was reconquered from the
Genoese by the Cypriot Crown in A.D. 1464, but the enfeebled feudal power could only
maintain itself by inviting a Venetian protectorate in A.D. 1466; and this protectorate duly
led on, in the usual manner of protectorates, to annexation. In the last chapter of its
history, from A.D. 1489 until the Ottoman Conquest in 1571, Latin Cyprus was a
Venetian colony.

Another example is the Levantine career of the Acciajuoli—a family of Brescian steel-
manufacturers who had settled in Florence and taken to banking. In A.D. 1334, Niccolò
Acciajuoli, who was the confidential banker of the Angevin Court of Naples, took advantage of his financial and political transactions on behalf of his royal clients in order to
acquire estates for himself in the Frankish feudal principality of Achaia. In 1358,
Niccolò obtained from the ruling Angevin prince of Achaia the hereditary governorship
of Corinth. Niccolò's sons mortgaged Corinth to their second cousin Nerio Acciajuoli;
and in 1385-8 Nerio conquered the Frankish Duchy of Athens (which included Boeotia
as well as Attica) from the Catalans, who had conquered it themselves from the French
in 1311. The Florentine dominion in Central Greece which was thus established in
1388 lasted until the Turkish annexation of Athens in 1456 and of Thebes in 1460.

[2] For a comparison between the situations in fourteenth-century Western Christendom and in fifth-century Hellas, see further III. C (ii) (*b*), Annex IV, below.

decided, and decided against the new dispensation. A twentieth-century historian, looking back over the intervening span of Western history to the year 1400, can see plainly in retrospect that, by that date, the brilliant new world of city-states was already doomed to be abortive. But perhaps this decision would have been less readily apparent to a contemporary observer than it is to us to-day; for, although its historical consequences have been momentous, its actual execution was not sensational. The medieval Western cosmos of city-states was not blotted out in any single overwhelming cosmic catastrophe. Its fate was decided by the outcome of a number of local conflicts, no one of which was of oecumenical importance in itself. Their importance was the consequence of their aggregate effect; and this was largely hid from the eyes of the generation that took part in them.

In Italy, the light was dimmed by the destructive War of Chioggia (*gerebatur* A.D. 1378–81) between the two principal Italian maritime commonwealths, Genoa and Venice: an equivalent of the Atheno-Lacedaemonian War of 431–404 B.C. which left both protagonists permanently enfeebled. The year A.D. 1378 may also be taken as the beginning of an era of chronic and ubiquitous warfare between the Italian city-states on more scientific and professional and therefore more exhausting and ruinous lines than the earlier Italian fashion of conducting hostilities. The hundred and sixteen years between the outbreak of the War of Chioggia and the apparition of Charles VIII (A.D. 1378–1494) were the heyday of the Italian Condottieri. Thus, in the last quarter of the fourteenth century, the Italian city-states were setting themselves seriously to break one another's strength; and in the same decades the South and West German city-states allowed their strength to be broken by the local feudal princes.[1]

The policy of these German city-states was ambitious. The example of the Swiss Confederation, which had found in its union the strength to contend against the Hapsburg Power since the turn of the thirteenth and fourteenth centuries, inspired the formation of a Swabian League of Cities in 1376 and a Rhenish League of Cities in 1381. These two leagues entered into an alliance with one another shortly afterwards; and in 1385 this alliance was extended to include some of the leading members of the Swiss Confederation. At the end of the year 1385, the efficacy of this new federal movement among the Central European city-states was put to the test by the outbreak of war between the Swiss Confederation and Leopold Hapsburg; and the Swabian and Rhenish allies of

---

[1] For this crisis in the fate of the city-states of Southern and Western Germany, see Clarke, M. V.: *The Mediaeval City State* (London 1926, Methuen), pp. 175–8.

the Swiss proclaimed as their war aim: 'Between the Forests of the Vosges, Thuringia, Bohemia, and the Lower Alps shall be a great union of free cities.'[1] If this large aim had been achieved, the fourteenth century of the Christian Era might have seen the ancient feudal body social of Western Christendom riven asunder by a solid wedge of confederated city-states extending right across the middle of Continental Europe from the Mediterranean and the Adriatic to the Channel and the North Sea and the Baltic.[2] In that event, the forces of Feudalism, divided by the enemy in their midst and unable to render one another mutual aid, might eventually have been driven off the field, to leave a new society of city-states in possession. But this prospect was barely opened up before it was decisively blotted out. At the critical moment, the Rhenish and Swabian cities hung back; the Swiss defeated Leopold Hapsburg at Sempach (in A.D. 1386) and 'set the seal on their independence' unaided; and two years later, when the Rhenish and the Swabian League found themselves at war, in their turn, with their own local feudal enemies, no Swiss help came to save them from defeat. Both these German Leagues were defeated decisively by the local German princes in A.D. 1388; and thereafter, in 1389, they were formally dissolved—'as contrary to God, the King, the Empire and the Law'—by the Holy Roman Emperor Wenceslas.

At about the same time, misfortunes of equal gravity befell the older and larger and stronger North German League of the Hansa, and also the Flemish cluster of city-states.

Flanders—which, as a stronghold of the new city-state régime in Western Christendom, was only second in importance to Italy itself—became subject in A.D. 1384 to a new line of Counts of the House of Burgundy; and in these Burgundian princes the Flemish burghers found their masters. It had been one thing to assert their civic liberties against the feudal lordship of a Count of Flanders who had no external resources beyond the fitful support of his usually embarrassed suzerain the King of France. It was quite another thing for them to contend with a Power which commanded the resources of territories outside Flanders itself[3] and which was learning to make the most of these resources by applying the new-fangled Italian military and fiscal and administrative methods to

[1] This watchword was an adaptation of the Swiss watchword: 'Between the four forest cantons shall be a great Switzerland' (Clarke, op. cit., p. 177).

[2] It will be noticed that the fourteenth-century zone of city-states (Northern Italy–Rhineland–Netherlands) approximately coincided in area (apart from the replacement of a Burgundian by a Swabian corridor) with the central slice of the Carolingian Empire which was assigned to Charlemagne's eldest grandson Lothaire in A.D. 843. (For the historical importance of Lothaire's portion, see I. B (iv), vol. i, pp. 37–9, above.)

[3] In the same year, 1384, in which the House of Burgundy acquired the County of Flanders, it enlarged its home territory—the French Duchy of Burgundy—by acquiring both the French County of Nevers and the Imperial County of Burgundy.

an old-fashioned Transalpine feudal principality.[1] From the establishment of Burgundian rule in Flanders in A.D. 1384 down to the incorporation of Flanders into Revolutionary France in A.D. 1795, the Flemish city-states remained subject to the House of Burgundy and its successive heirs, the Spanish and the Austrian Hapsburgs.

As for the Hansa League, it was overtaken before the end of the fourteenth century by the nemesis of the political pressure which, in furtherance of its commercial interests, it had brought to bear upon the converted barbarians on the northern and eastern periphery of an expanding Western Christendom. The *ci-devant* barbarians, finding themselves outmatched in efficiency by the Hansa and its partners the Teutonic Order, brought their quantitative superiority into play to compensate for their qualitative inferiority, and thereby succeeded in redressing the unequal balance.[2] The political union of Lithuania with Poland in A.D. 1386 was as great a blow to the Hansa Towns as it was to the Teutonic Knights; and the subsequent union of the three Scandinavian Kingdoms in A.D. 1397 completed the Hansa's discomfiture.[3] For the next five centuries, the history of the Hansa Towns is the history of their successive absorption into other bodies politic of different structure and larger build. And the long process was completed in A.D. 1866 when the last three survivors—Hamburg, Lübeck, and Bremen—decided to merge themselves in the North German Confederation.[4] Indeed, that merger may be regarded as the extinction of the last three stars of the innumerable host of city-states which had covered the face of Western Christendom five centuries earlier.

England in the Third Chapter of the Growth of the Western Society

Thus it was decided that Western Christendom should not be rearticulated into a society of city-states in order to facilitate the transmission of the new Italian version of the Western culture from Italy to Transalpine Europe. And since there was no room in Western Christendom for a kingdom-state cosmos and a city-state cosmos to exist side by side in perpetuity, this decision spelled the doom of the city-state régime even in its Italian and Flemish

[1] The House of Burgundy was a pioneer among the Transalpine dynasties which set themselves, in the fifteenth century, to transform their feudal principalities into autocracies by devices borrowed from Italy.   [2] See II. D (v), vol. ii, pp. 172–5, above.

[3] The arrest of the expansion of the German city-states into the Baltic which was brought about by the political unification of the Scandinavians and of the Polono-Lithuanians in the fourteenth century of the Christian Era may be compared with the similar arrest of the expansion of the Greek city-states into the Western Mediterranean which was brought to a standstill in the sixth century B.C. by the political unification of the Etruscans and of the Transmarine Phoenicians.

[4] The final completion of the process ought possibly to be dated in this year 1933, when Hamburg, Lübeck, and Bremen, together with all the other *Länder* of the German *Reich*, have lost the last vestige of their political individuality in the course of the German National-Socialist Revolution.

strongholds. Accordingly, if the new Italian culture was to be transmitted to the Western World at large or even to be preserved in its place of origin, it was thenceforth necessary that it should be adapted to the prevailing kingdom-state scale. It was only in so far as this adaptation could be accomplished that the Italian culture had a prospect of becoming 'the education of the Western World' under the actual conditions which had been set for its propagation before the end of the fourteenth century. In these circumstances, the Western Society was confronted with a new problem which may be formulated as follows. In the preceding chapter of Western history, a change-over from an agricultural aristocratic way of life to an industrial democratic way of life had been achieved by the Italians and the Flemings in two localities in Western Christendom at the price of reducing the unit-size of the local communities from the traditional and generally prevalent kingdom-state scale to a new city-state scale which had failed to acquire a general currency. In the next chapter of Western history, the problem was to discover how the new Italian and Flemish way of life could be lived, on the kingdom-state scale, by the Western World as a whole. This challenge was taken up in Switzerland and Holland and England, and it eventually received an English response.[1]

In another connexion, we have noticed already[2] that all these three countries have been sheltered to an unusual degree by the inaccessibility of the local physical environment from challenges presented by the surrounding human environment. In other words, the inhabitants of all these three countries are well placed for withdrawing, if they choose, from the trammels of a regional society of which they find themselves members; and in the third chapter of the history of our Western Society the Swiss and the Dutch and the English have all in fact made efforts to shake themselves free from the entanglements of Western international politics in order to concentrate their energies upon the task of finding original solutions for the general Western problem of the age.

The Swiss, who had successfully surmounted the crisis of the city-state cosmos in the latter part of the fourteenth century, when

---

[1] A student of social geography will observe that in this new chapter of Western history the general pattern of the social map of Western Christendom is still the same as in the last chapter. The creative minorities that temporarily withdraw in order to find a response to the challenge of the day arise in the same two neighbourhoods on either flank of the Western World. England and Holland represent the same geographical 'node' as Flanders; Switzerland represents the same 'node' as Northern Italy. It will be noticed, however, that there is a general shift towards the North-West—from Italy to Switzerland across the Alps and from Flanders to England across the Straits—and also that the relative importance of the two 'nodes' is reversed. In the Italian-Flemish chapter, the South-Eastern Node is more important than the North-Western; in the English-Dutch-Swiss chapter, the North-Western Node is the principal focus of action. In the modern period, Holland and England count for more than Switzerland, whereas in the medieval period Italy counts for more than Flanders.

[2] In II. D (vii), vol. ii, on pp. 262–4 and 268, above.

the German and Flemish city-states had succumbed, succeeded in maintaining their political freedom, in the Swiss–Burgundian War of A.D. 1474–7, against the nearest of the new Italianized Transalpine Powers. *Vis-à-vis* the Holy Roman Empire, the Swiss Confederation secured *de facto* independence in A.D. 1499 and *de jure* independence in the Westphalian Peace Settlement of 1648.

The Dutch succeeded in winning their political freedom from the Spanish Hapsburg Power in the Dutch–Spanish War of A.D. 1572–1609; and, like the Swiss, they obtained the recognition of their *de jure* independence from the Holy Roman Empire in 1648, as part of the Westphalian Settlement.

The English, after having squandered their energies in the Hundred Years' War (A.D. 1337–1453) in order to win a Continental European empire, had found themselves at the end of the struggle in possession of less Continental territory than they had held at the moment when they embarked on this Continental adventure. In 1337 they had held Aquitaine; in 1453 they were left with nothing but Calais; and Calais went the way of all the other English possessions on the Continent in 1558. This experience cured the English of Continental ambitions; and then, in the next generation, they encountered the Continent in a still more disagreeable guise: not, this time, as a hazardous field for English military adventures in which England might burn her fingers, but as a formidable breeding-ground for aggressive Great Powers of supra-insular calibre which might use the Continent as a base of operations for bringing the island into political subjection. From the moment of Queen Mary's marriage to King Philip of Spain in A.D. 1554 the English were confronted by this new Continental danger; and the danger was only banned, after a generation of warfare against heavy odds, by the destruction of the Spanish Armada in 1588. The triumph of that year confirmed the outlook which had been first induced in English minds by the humiliations of 1429–53 and 1558. From that time onwards until the General War of A.D. 1914–18, the avoidance, as far as possible, of Continental European political entanglements was accepted, without further question, as one of the fundamental and perpetual aims of English foreign policy.[1]

Thus the same policy of withdrawal was adopted, in their different circumstances, by the English, the Dutch, and the Swiss; but these three local minorities in the modern Western body social were not equally well placed for carrying this policy out, though they were all better placed for this purpose than any of their neigh-

---

[1] This statement requires some qualification in regard to British foreign policy during the period A.D. 1689–1815.

bours. In an age before the field of warfare had been extended to the air, the Swiss mountains were less effectually protective than the Dutch and English waters; and in an age before the invention of the steamship but after the invention of artillery, there was all the difference in the world between the breadth of a Dutch dyke, which was already too narrow to insulate Holland from the Continent, and the breadth of the English Channel, which was still broad enough to make the British Isles an *alter orbis*. The Dutch were found out by their Continental situation when they emerged incurably exhausted from their forty years' struggle (A.D. 1672–1713) against Louis XIV;[1] and thereafter, at the turn of the eighteenth and nineteenth centuries, both Holland and Switzerland were temporarily engulfed in the Napoleonic Empire.[2] On the other hand, England remained an *alter orbis* for three whole centuries until, in our own generation, she has been re-welded on to the military and political system of the Continent—and this time more closely than ever before in her history—by the ever-accelerating progress of those recent mechanical inventions which are largely the fruits of English ingenuity.[3] In this post-war age, the English Channel is no broader—in the subjective human terms of measurement which have to be applied in this context—than a Dutch dyke in the age of Alva and William the Silent; and the Atlantic itself is no broader than the Channel at the time when Napoleon's army of invasion was encamped at Boulogne. It now seems not improbable that the fate of Holland in the eighteenth century may be the fate of England in the twentieth; but this possible coming change in England's position belongs to a new chapter in Western history which is only just beginning. The chapter that concerns us here is the last; and in that chapter the prolongation of England's period of privileged insulation for some two centuries beyond the term of Holland's enjoyment of the same privilege has been an historical fact of capital importance. Her prolonged immunity has enabled England to surpass and supplant Holland, in this chapter, in the role of the creative minority that withdraws from communion with Society in order to return in the fullness of time with an original solution for a general social problem.

---

[1] The experience of Holland in the General War of A.D. 1672–1713 was not unlike the experience of Athens in the Atheno-Peloponnesian War of 431–404 B.C. 'The Old Oligarch' (Pseudo-Xenophon: *Respublica Atheniensium*, ch. ii. 14–16) observes that the one defect of Athenian sea-power is that Attica itself is not an island. The observation is equally applicable to Holland, *mutatis mutandis*.

[2] Switzerland was as much in Napoleon's power *de facto* as Holland, though only the fringe of Switzerland was formally incorporated into France.

[3] For this, see further Toynbee, A. J.: *The Conduct of British Empire Foreign Relations since the Peace Settlement* (London 1928, Milford), pp. 7–8, and the passages there quoted from an address on 'The Dominions and Foreign Policy' which was broadcast on the 14th November, 1924, by Lord Grey of Fallodon.

In the competition for this role between the three minorities in question the English also had the advantage over the Dutch and the Swiss in another way. The Kingdom of England—and *a fortiori* the subsequent United Kingdom of Great Britain—was a state of large calibre on the traditional Transalpine scale. Indeed, in the eighteenth century, after the Union between England and Scotland in A.D. 1707, Great Britain, while by no means the largest state in the Western World in point of sheer territorial magnitude, was by far the largest single area that had been consolidated into a really effective political and economic unity. And her political and economic unification on this large scale made Great Britain an admirable laboratory for solving the crucial Western problem of the day: the problem of finding ways and means of adapting to the original kingdom-state scale of the Western Society the latter-day city-state achievements. In this matter, both Holland and Switzerland were at a disadvantage because both these states were really survivals of the abortive city-state cosmos—a régime which had been preserved in these two localities behind the shelter of dykes and mountains when it had perished in other parts of Western Christendom. The Swiss Confederation and the United Netherlands were virtually two local combines of city-states;[1] and, from the institutional standpoint, they were anachronisms in the modern Western World—in the same category as the two surviving Italian city-states of Venice and Genoa. They were incapable, *a priori*, of solving the problem of the age, because they themselves were constructed on the city-state basis and therefore on the city-state pattern. For these several reasons, it was not in Switzerland or in Holland but in England that the problem was eventually solved.

The problem, as we have seen, was to emulate the social achievements of the city-state régime in kingdom-states with a feudal heritage; and these achievements had been three in number: the substitution of a democratic for an aristocratic form of government; the substitution of a commercial and industrial for a purely agricultural economy; and the introduction of a new standard of business-like efficiency into the conduct of both economics and politics. All these achievements had now to be emulated on the supra-city-state scale of the feudal kingdom; and the accomplishment which was actually translated on to the larger scale most rapidly and easily was efficiency on the political plane.

The first attempt to translate the accomplished political efficiency of the city-state on to a supra-city-state scale was made within the

---

[1] Juridically, the Swiss Confederation was a union of cantons and the United Netherlands a union of provinces; but in both commonwealths the principal constituent states were city-states *de facto*.

city-state cosmos itself. It declared itself in a widespread movement to weld local clusters of city-states together into larger
commonwealths which should be as solid and as enduring as their
individual city-state constituents. This movement was particularly
active in Italy. At the opening of the fourteenth century of the
Christian Era, the North and Central Italian regions of Lombardy,
Romagna, Tuscany, Umbria, and the Marches were partitioned
between seventy or eighty city-states; or, in other words, there was
a larger number of fully-self-governing states in one-half of Italy
in A.D. 1300 than can be counted in 1935 in the whole World. On
the other hand, by the time of Machiavelli's death, in A.D. 1527,
the number of sovereign states in the same Italian area had been
reduced from seventy or eighty to ten, including the Papal Principality. Switzerland and Holland are monuments of the spread of
the same movement of consolidation, at a later date, to those portions of the city-state cosmos that lay beyond the Alps. But the
Swiss and the Dutch were more successful than the Italians in one
respect. Swiss and Dutch statesmanship succeeded in welding a
number of city-states together into larger commonwealths without
abandoning the democratic kind of government that was the soul
of political life under the city-state régime; and though their city-
state federal structure debarred the Swiss and the Dutch from
going on to make those new experiments in democratic government
that were eventually made by the English, the Swiss and the Dutch
did avoid the loss of their hereditary form of political liberty. In
Italy, on the other hand, the benefits of territorial consolidation
were purchased at the price of a forfeiture of political liberty in
a twofold sense.

In the first place, when the seventy or eighty Italian city-states
were welded together into ten agglomerations of seven or eight
city-state units each on the average, the unification was not brought
about here through the voluntary federation of the component
states on an equal footing, but through the conquest and subjugation, in each case, of half a dozen weaker city-states by some powerful and domineering neighbour. The Grand Duchy of Tuscany
was the outcome of the conquest of Fiesole and Volterra and
Arezzo and Pistoia and Pisa and Siena[1] by Florence. The Venetian
dominions on the Continent were built up by the imposition of

[1] The territory of Siena was only annexed by Florence or, rather, partitioned between
Florence and Spain, in A.D. 1557, thirty years after Machiavelli's death. It was after this,
again, that the Florentine Commonwealth was officially transformed into the Grand
Duchy of Tuscany. (The title was conferred on the ruling Medici Duke of Florence by
the Pope in A.D. 1567 and was recognized by the Holy Roman Emperor in A.D. 1576.)
The foregoing siege and capture of Siena, in 1555, by a combined Florentine-Spanish
expeditionary force was as brutal an act of conquest as any of the preceding steps in the
formation of the Florentine empire.

Venetian rule upon Treviso and Padua and Vicenza and Verona and Brescia and Bergamo. The Papal State was rounded off—or, in theory, reconstituted—by the political degradation of the former city-states of Bologna and Ferrara to the status and style of 'the Legations'. There was, of course, a considerable variety in the imperial policy of these different empire-building Italian Powers. The city-states that fell under the Venetian hegemony were comparatively well treated, whereas Pisa was deliberately and malignantly ruined by her Florentine conquerors in the fifteenth century. As for the vigorous and turbulent Bolognesi, they could never reconcile themselves to being governed as a satrapy of the Holy See by Papal Legates. The local conditions and reactions varied; but the forfeiture of political liberty was the general rule, and downright oppression at the hands of the conquering Power was not infrequent. This was one sense in which the territorial consolidation of Italy entailed the loss of political freedom; and in the second place the empire-building city-states—with the notable exception of Venice[1]—all paid for their dominion over their neighbours by the loss of their own domestic liberties before the process of empire-building was completed. The formation of these miniature Italian empires was contemporary with the rise of the Italian despots who were the miniature predecessors of a Transalpine Louis XI or Henry VII; and these two Italian political developments were not only contemporary but were inter-connected. A city-state which had set its heart upon conquering its neighbours could not accomplish this formidable ambition with the amateur instruments of a civic militia and a republican constitution. Imperialism required a professional army of mercenaries; and a mercenary force required in its turn a despotic government with the twofold function of keeping the mercenaries in order and organizing the city's resources to maintain them. Venice was the only Italian city-state that succeeded in building up an Italian empire without finding itself driven to place the lives and fortunes of its own citizens in the hands of an autocrat.

This price which was paid in Italy for the reduction of the number of Italian states from seventy or eighty to ten was actually paid in vain from the Italian standpoint; for the new Italian principalities, large as they were by comparison with the former Italian city-states, were still not large enough to serve the purpose of enabling them to hold their own against the Transalpine Powers. They might, perhaps, have held their own if the Transalpine Powers

---

[1] Genoa, of course, besides Venice, retained her republican institutions, as well as her independence, until she was engulfed in the Napoleonic Empire; but Genoa can hardly be reckoned among the empire-building Italian city-states, for none of the communities on the Riviera which she brought under her rule were of anything like her own calibre.

had remained enveloped in their ancient feudal darkness without receiving any irradiation of Italian light; and there was possibly a period in the fourteenth century when the Duchy of Milan or the Commonwealth of Venice was capable of holding its own against the House of Anjou or the House of Luxemburg. This theoretical equilibrium, however, was of short duration, if it ever really existed; for Italian political efficiency in the shape of Italian despotism proved to be the easiest of all Italian accomplishments to acclimatize in Transalpine Europe and to accommodate to the Transalpine scale; and before the end of the fifteenth century every one of the latter-day Italian principalities had been decisively out-classed in political strength by the new Italianized autocracies of Louis XI in France and Ferdinand and Isabella in Spain and Henry VII in England.[1]

This propagation of Italian autocracy beyond the Alps was

[1] In Hellenic history, the analogue of the relation between political despotism and territorial consolidation in the history of modern Italy is to be found, not in the Hellenic World at large and not in Continental Greece or in the Aegean, but in the colonial domain of Hellas in Sicily and Magna Graecia.

In Continental Greece, despotism and consolidation did not go together. On the contrary, the city-states round about the Isthmus of Corinth were associated in an inter-state union for the first time in their histories at the moment when they were liberated from the despots who had ruled them during the seventh and the sixth centuries B.C. The overthrow of the Isthmian despots and the formation of the Peloponnesian League were both the work of the Spartan Government; and these two Spartan acts were not only simultaneous but were actually two complementary parts of a single policy.

In Sicily and Magna Graecia, on the other hand, Hellenic history developed on lines which are parallel to the modern Italian developments which we have just been examin-ing. In this western region of the Hellenic World, the movement towards consolidation in the fifth and fourth centuries B.C. was more radical and more persistent than any corresponding movement in Continental Greece until the Aetolian and Achaean move-ments of the third century. And whereas these Achaean and Aetolian movements, when they came, resembled the modern Swiss and Dutch movements in seeking to reconcile solidarity with liberty and equality, the earlier movement in Sicily and Magna Graecia resembled the modern Italian movement in both its leading characteristics. In Hellenic Sicily and Magna Graecia, as in modern Italy, the process of consolidation did not take place voluntarily on a footing of equality, but was accomplished through the subjugation of the weaker city-states by the stronger (a subjugation which went much further than the 'hegemonies' that were being imposed in the same age upon the weaker city-states of Continental Greece and the Aegean by Athens and Sparta and Thebes). A Catana and a Leontini were dealt with by a Syracuse as ruthlessly as Florence dealt with Arezzo or with Pisa, while the dominion which was established by Tarentum over Metapontum and Heraclea and Messapia was as positive as the Venetian dominion over Treviso and Padua and Friuli. Again, the persistent republicanism of empire-building Tarentum was as much of an exception in Magna Graecia and Sicily as the persistent republicanism of Venice in Italy. The typical story was the story of Syracuse, in whose history empire-building went hand in hand with despotism at home, as it went in Milan or Florence. The Milanese Visconti and the Florentine Medici of our modern Western history have their Hellenic analogues in the successive dynasties of Syracusan despots: the Deino-menidae (circa 485–466 B.C.), the Dionysii (405–344 B.C.), Agathocles (316–289 B.C.), and Hiero with his grandson Hieronymus (266–214 B.C.).

Finally we may observe that the consolidation of the Greek city-states of Sicily and Magna Graecia under the empires of Syracuse and Tarentum in the fifth and fourth and third centuries B.C. was as ineffectual as the consolidation of the Italian city-states under the empires of Milan and Venice and Florence in the fourteenth and fifteenth and six-teenth centuries of the Christian Era for the purpose of enabling these little principalities to hold their own against the surrounding 'barbarians'. The Greeks of Sicily and Magna Graecia suffered the same fate at the hands of the Carthaginians and the Oscans and the Romans that the Italians suffered at the hands of the Hapsburgs and the Bourbons.

It will be seen that the parallel works out with remarkable exactitude.

Italy's undoing; but it brought the Transalpine countries no equivalent gain because this Italian political efficiency was only one of the Italian accomplishments which Transalpine Europe had to assimilate. Transalpine Europe would not be laying hands upon the greatest political gift that Italy had to give her until she found for herself some equivalent of the Italian political democracy which Italy herself had already lost; and without the achievement of some kind of political democracy it was difficult for the Transalpine countries to emulate the Italian economic accomplishment of advancing from agriculture to commerce and industry.

The difficulty lay in the very nature of Society; for every social system is a coherent whole; and it is therefore inherently difficult to acquire any one part of an alien social system without acquiring the rest. In the natural evolution of the medieval Italian city-state, the growth of democracy and the growth of industry and commerce had been complementary to one another. They had been synonymous with the political and the economic rise of the bourgeoisie; and no class can rise beyond a certain point in any one sphere of social life without rising simultaneously and proportionately in the others.[1] In Italy, the old bourgeoisie began to decline in economic prosperity as soon as its political liberty had been taken from it by the new autocracy. On this showing, it was hardly likely that, when this Italian autocratic form of government was transplanted to the Transalpine kingdoms, a vigorous new Transalpine bourgeoisie would grow up under its shadow in communities that had remained till then predominantly agrarian and feudal. And, in the event, there was no such miraculous departure in the Transalpine countries from the regular order of Nature.

In Spain, the autocracy of Ferdinand and Isabella grew in stature until it became the grander autocracy of Philip II; and in France, in similar fashion, the autocracy of Louis XI rankled into that of Louis XIV; but two centuries passed without any creative political advance from autocracy towards democracy in either of these two Transalpine countries.[2] In both Spain and France, the introduction

---

[1] This is the limitation of our law (which we have traced out in II. D (vi), above) that specialization is the response to the challenge of penalization. It is quite true that a penalized minority which responds to its challenge does find compensation for being excluded from certain spheres of social activity by winning for itself a supremacy or monopoly in other spheres. But it is also true that the responsive penalized minority cannot succeed beyond a certain point, even in the restricted sphere which it has made peculiarly its own, unless it ultimately returns to communion with the general life of the society from which it has been ostracized. A pertinent case in point is the history of the English Nonconformists (see the present chapter, p. 334, above). The English Nonconformists responded to the challenge of their partial exclusion from public life for a century and a half (circa A.D. 1673–1828) by starting the Industrial Revolution; but they could hardly have carried the Industrial Revolution through if they had not returned to public life (without forfeiting their supremacy in private business) in the nineteenth century. It was after this that Industrialism in England attained its apogee.

[2] The transformation of the indigenous Transalpine feudal monarchy into an Italianized

of the new Italian institution of despotic government caused the traditional feudal institutions to atrophy, without evoking any new institutions to take their place. The result was political stagnation; and in this dead-alive political atmosphere it is not surprising to observe that the wealth of the New World did not save Spanish commerce and industry from decadence and that the governmental patronage of French commerce and industry under the administration of Colbert did not enable France to compete successfully on the economic plane with Holland and England.[1] It was in England that the problem of translating democracy from the city-state scale to the kingdom-state scale was successfully solved; and it was therefore in England thereafter that Western commerce and industry first entered upon a new phase of activity on a scale that dwarfs the medieval commerce and industry of Italy or Flanders or the Hansa Towns in the measure of the difference in calibre between a United Kingdom of Great Britain and an isolated city-state like thirteenth-century Florence or Venice.

For some reason, the introduction of the new despotism, which had a deadening political effect in Spain and France, had the opposite effect in England. In England it was taken as a challenge which demanded a response; and the English response was to breathe new life and import new functions into the traditional constitution of the Transalpine body politic which was an English as well as a French and a Spanish heritage from the common past of Western Christendom.

One of the traditional Transalpine institutions[2] was the periodical holding of a parliament or conference between the Crown and the Estates of the Realm for the double purpose of ventilating grievances and obtaining a vote of supply for the Crown from the Estates as a *quid pro quo* for an honourable undertaking on the Crown's part that well-founded grievances should be redressed. In the gradual evolution of this institution of Parliament, the Transalpine king-

autocracy had in general much the same effect as the transformation of the indigenous Macedonian 'Homeric' monarchy into an Atticized autocracy. (For the modernization and revival of the institution of monarchy in Hellenic history, see III. C (ii) (b), Annex IV, below.) Both expedients failed because both were 'short cuts'. (For the peril of 'short cuts', see IV. C (iii) (a), vol. iv, pp. 123–31, below.)

[1] There were, of course, movements in both Spain and France to anticipate or emulate the commercial and industrial achievements of the Dutch and the English. But it is significant that in both countries these movements were made by penalized minorities who were ultimately driven out to find an asylum among their step-mother countries' economic rivals. It was Holland and England, and not Spain and France, that ultimately benefited by the business ability of the Spanish Jews and the French Huguenots.

[2] The institution of Parliament was not, of course, exclusively Transalpine in origin; for assemblies of states were not unknown in medieval Italy; and the congressional method of dealing with public business may have been part of the common social heritage of Western Christendom from the Church (see p. 360, footnote 2). In Northern and Central Italy, however, the growth of the institution was cut short by the rise of city-states, so that it became, in effect, a Transalpine institution as it developed.

doms had discovered how to overcome their regional problem of material scale—the problem of unmanageable numbers and impracticable distances—by inventing, or rediscovering, the legal fiction of 'representation'. The duty or right of every person concerned in the business of Parliament to take a personal part in the proceedings—a duty or right which is self-evident in a polity on the scale of a city-state—was attenuated in these unwieldy Transalpine feudal kingdoms[1] into a right to be represented by proxy, and a duty, on the proxy's part, to shoulder the burden of travelling, even from the extremity of the Kingdom, to the place where the Parliament was being held.[2]

This feudal institution of a periodical representative and consultative assembly was well fitted for its original purpose of serving as a liaison between the Crown and its subjects in a feudal monarchy. In particular, it enabled the Crown to raise larger revenues by consent, in exchange for concessions on matters of policy, than it could raise by mere insistence upon exacting its customary feudal dues. On the other hand, the medieval Transalpine Parliament was originally not at all well fitted for the task—to which it was success-

---

[1] It is only since the invention of railways and telegraphy and other mechanical means of communication that modern England and France have become smaller—in terms of human geography—than Attica or Laconia were in the Hellenic World.

[2] Where and when the institution of Parliament came to be of sufficient political importance for membership to become a contested privilege instead of a detested duty, the practice arose of choosing between rival candidates by the method of election (in the modern sense of selection by majority vote, as opposed to the original sense of the Latin word *eligere* = simply 'to pick out', without connoting that the act of selection is performed by the majority of an electorate rather than by the individual will of a personal sovereign or his representative). Among students of parliamentary history, it appears to be a still unsettled question whether the application of the electoral system, in its modern sense, in the parliamentary field was an original invention or whether it was suggested to the minds of its inventors by analogy from the ecclesiastical field, in which the idea of election was familiar to the medieval Western Society as a traditional device for appointing, not the members of consultative bodies, but individual executive officers. The election of executive officers was a part of the constitutional machinery of the Hellenic city-state, which had been borrowed by the Christian Church as a method of appointing abbots, bishops, patriarchs, and other ecclesiastical dignitaries. When the Christian Church was taken into partnership by the Roman Empire in the fourth century of the Christian Era, autocracy tended to encroach upon self-government in the ecclesiastical field, as it had already superseded it in the secular field. But this process was arrested by the break-up of the Empire; and since in Western Christendom, unlike Orthodox Christendom, the Imperial Power was not effectively revived, the system of electing executive officers survived in the Western Church as 'a going concern' to a sufficient extent to make the notion of election familiar to the minds of medieval Western constitution-builders. The new Western constitutional invention (which may or may not have been inspired by ecclesiastical precedents) was to apply the device of election to secular feudal consultative bodies as a means of making them 'representative'. The idea of 'representation', as well as the device of election, had made its appearance in Hellenic constitutional history; but in Hellenic history the two things had never been combined. The device of election had been reserved for the appointment of executive officers, while the 'representativeness' of consultative bodies had been secured, logically enough, by employing the device of the lot. At Athens, for example, the Council of Five Hundred, which was instituted by Cleisthenes in 508–507 B.C., was appointed annually by lot on a fixed allocation of seats. (Fifty seats were allocated to each of the ten Cleisthenic 'tribes' (Aristotle: *The Constitution of Athens*, xliii. 2), and within each 'tribe' these fifty seats were distributed among the 'demes' (parishes) in proportion to their populations.)

fully adapted in England in the seventeenth century—of undertaking the Crown's work instead of merely consulting with and bargaining with the Crown as to the manner in which the royal prerogatives should be exercised.

Between deliberation and diplomacy on the one hand and executive action on the other there is a great gulf fixed. The two lines of political activity demand, and evoke, quite different outlooks and habits and capacities; and although the institution of Parliament had become well established in Transalpine Europe in general, and in the Kingdom of England in particular, in the course of the fourteenth and fifteenth centuries, there was still no indication at the turn of the fifteenth and sixteenth centuries that this Transalpine institution was capable of becoming the germ of a new form of self-government for bodies politic on the kingdom-state scale. In that generation, these things were hidden from the wise and prudent.[1] There is no inkling of the future course of Transalpine constitutional development in Machiavelli's otherwise penetrating studies of France and Germany;[2] and if the lynx-eyed Florentine publicist had happened, in the course of his official career, to have been sent on a diplomatic mission to England, we may doubt whether he would have divined the future even on the spot. Indeed, an Italian observer visiting England a hundred years after Machiavelli's day, in the early decades of the seventeenth century of the Christian Era, would probably have pronounced that the old-fashioned local institution of Parliament was destined to succumb to the newfangled Italian institution of autocracy in England as surely as in the other Transalpine countries. He would hardly have guessed that, before the century ran out, the English would have brought the triumphal Transalpine progress of autocracy to a halt by achieving the constitutional *tour de force* of turning the medieval Transalpine institution of Parliament into a still more effective engine of executive political action than the personal government of a Matteo Visconti or a Henry Tudor or a Louis Valois.

[1] Matthew xi. 25.
[2] In the dispatches relating to his embassies to the French Court, and in the *Ritratti delle Cose della Francia*, there appears to be no allusion at all to the French Estates. (The five Parlements are mentioned in the *Ritratti*; but these, of course, were courts of law and not parliamentary bodies in the English sense.) In the dispatches relating to his embassy to the Emperor, and again in the *Ritratti delle Cose dell'Alamagna* and the *Rapporto di Cose della Magna*, there are a few references to certain sessions of the Imperial Diet and to one session of the local Diet of the Tyrol; and here Machiavelli does show a clear realization of the power of the purse which was exercised by these parliamentary bodies in the Holy Roman Empire. Perhaps the most interesting reference to a Transalpine parliamentary body in Machiavelli's works is the notice of the Swiss Federal Diet in the second dispatch (dated Botzen, the 17th January, 1507) relating to his mission to the Emperor. Machiavelli here reports that 'il corpo principale de' Svizzeri sono dodeci comunanze collegate insieme, le quali chiamano cantoni. . . . Costoro sono in modo collegati insieme, che quello che nelle loro Diete è deliberato, è sempre osservato da tutti, nè alcun cantone vi si opporrebbe'.

Why was it that England took up, and met successfully, a challenge with which no other contemporary Transalpine kingdom proved able to cope? Why did the Transalpine feudal monarchy grow into a constitutional monarchy in England when it gave way to an absolute monarchy in France?

'It was because the English monarchy became national before it ceased to be feudal, at a time when the French monarchy still remained feudal only. When then the feudal element disappeared, as it ultimately did in both kingdoms, in England its place was taken by a government in which the Estates had already begun to share; in France there was no power in existence to replace the feudal monarchy but the uncontrolled power of an absolute king. The difference is owing to the regular participation of the Estates in England before the feudal monarchy disappeared—a participation which existed in that period of French history, with one exception, only on the rare occasions of popular unrest. On the decline of Feudalism in France, there was no authority, and no body of men, politically prepared permanently to take over or even to share with the king in the centralized government that was replacing feudal decentralization. That place could be taken only by an authority that was at once centralized and national, and the only one then in existence to do it was a strong, national, but practically absolute monarch. To put it otherwise, in England there was participation and there was representation while feudal conditions still remained, and therefore when these conditions disappeared the strong centralized national power which emerged was one which retained the participation of the Estates. In France, since this participation had not begun during the period when feudal conditions flourished, so it could not continue when they began to decline, and the feudal monarchy was replaced by one practically, even if not theoretically, absolute. . . . The decisive factor in determining [the] results for England was the *early* centralization of administration—a centralization which came far sooner there than elsewhere. It was this that made England the only Western country with a common law little influenced by Rome, and this too ultimately made her a constitutional instead of an absolute monarchy.'[1]

These were the predisposing conditions that stimulated the English body politic to take up and meet successfully a challenge which the other Transalpine bodies politic scarcely attempted to face. Yet, even when full allowance for these favourable conditions has been made, the English achievement of pouring the new wine of Renaissance Italian administrative efficiency into the old bottles of medieval Transalpine parliamentarism, without allowing these old bottles to burst, is a constitutional triumph that can only be regarded as an astonishing *tour de force*. And this English constitutional *tour de force* of carrying Parliament across the gulf that

---

[1] Professor C. H. McIlwaine in *The Cambridge Medieval History*, vol. vii (Cambridge 1932, University Press), pp. 709–10.

divides the conduct from the criticism of government was the political act of creation which was performed for the Western Society by the English creative minority during its period of withdrawal. This political invention provided a propitious social setting for the subsequent English economic invention of Industrialism.[1] 'Democracy' in the sense of a system of government in which the executive is responsible to a parliament which is representative of the people, and 'Industrialism' in the sense of a system of machine-production by 'hands' concentrated in factories to tend the machinery, are the two master-institutions that still dominate the life of the Western World in our age;[2] they have come to prevail because they offer the best solutions which the Western Society has been able to find for the problem of transposing the achievements of the Italian city-state culture from the city-state scale to the kingdom-state scale; and both these solutions have been worked out for the Western Society in England in an age when England has been temporarily aloof from the general life of the Western World.

What is to be Russia's Role in our Western History?

In the contemporary history of the Great Society into which our Western Christendom has grown, can we again discern symptoms of that tendency to overbalance which is a symptom that the process of growth is still continuing? Now that the problems set to us by Italian solutions of earlier problems have received their English solutions, are these English solutions giving rise to new problems in their turn? We are already alive, in our generation, to two new challenges to which we have been exposed by the triumph of Democracy and Industrialism in the current meaning of these terms. In particular, the economic system of Industrialism, which means local specialization in skilled and costly production for a world-market, demands the establishment of some kind of political world-order as a framework for the operation of Industrialism on its indispensable world-wide scale. And, in general, both Industrialism and Democracy demand from Human Nature a greater individual self-control and mutual tolerance and public-spirited co-operation than the human 'social animal' has been apt to practise, because these new institutions have put an unprecedentedly powerful material 'drive' into all human social actions. We shall have to consider these two challenges more closely when we come to estimate the future prospects of our Western Civilization.[3] In this

---

[1] It is noteworthy that the English, in making their political invention of parliamentary government in the seventeenth century, took advantage of a previous industrial invention, namely the art of printing. The printing-press was a powerful aid to the efficient and expeditious conduct of parliamentary business.

[2] See I. A, *init.*, in vol. i, above.   [3] In Part XII, below.

place, we will merely suggest, in this connexion, that these challenges which confront us here and now are not altogether different in kind from those which have confronted our own society and other societies in other times.[1] Our purpose at the moment in reminding ourselves of our current challenges is not to investigate them for their own sakes but simply to observe whether they have yet evoked any fresh examples of the movement of Withdrawal-and-Return.

This observation is difficult to make, for the practical reason that these challenges themselves are very recent, so that any responses to them that may be on foot must *ex hypothesi* still be in a very rudimentary stage. We can, therefore, look for nothing more definite than inklings which may turn out to be false scents. Subject to this *caveat*, we may perhaps venture to speculate whether we have not here found an explanation of the present posture of Russian Orthodox Christendom, which has baffled us by its apparent self-contradiction when we have attempted, at an earlier point in this Study, to analyse it in a different context.[2]

In the Russian Communist Movement, we have detected, under a Westernizing masquerade, a 'Zealot' attempt to break away from the policy of Westernization which had been imposed upon Russia, two centuries before Lenin's day, by Peter the Great; and at the same time we have seen this masquerade passing over, willy nilly, into earnest. We have concluded that a Western revolutionary

---

[1] For example, the challenge of being called upon to create a political world-order the framework for an economic world-order is bound to confront any society that has accomplished the economic change from a locally self-subsistent and 'extensive' economy to an 'intensive' and oecumenically interdependent economy. The Hellenic Society was confronted by this challenge after it had adopted the new economy of Solonian Athens (see Part III. B, p. 122, footnote 3, and the present chapter, p. 340, footnote 1, above, and IV. C (iii) (b) 10, vol. iv, pp. 206–14, below); and the same challenge confronted the medieval Western city-state cosmos, which practised an economy of the intensive interdependent type from the outset. (We may note in passing that this challenge, which now confronts our modern Western society, was never successfully met either in the medieval Western city-state cosmos or in the Hellenic World and that their failure to meet this challenge caused both these societies to break down.) Again, the challenge of the increase in material 'drive' which Industrialism and Democracy entail was not unknown to either of these two other societies, though it perhaps confronts our own society in our day in an unprecedentedly high degree. The increase in material 'drive' which Hellas acquired in the course of the half-century between the repulse of Xerxes' invasion and the outbreak of the Atheno-Peloponnesian War is reflected in the Thucydidean usage of the word παρασχυνή. (For the significance of the subsequent change in the meaning of this Greek word, see Part VII, below.) As for the medieval Western city-states, they too were defeated by the challenge of the increase in 'drive', as well as by the challenge of the demand for a world-order. Indeed, it is the internal failure of the medieval Western city-state cosmos to respond successfully to these two challenges that accounts for its subsequent external failure to refashion the rest of Western Christendom in its own image. This latter failure, as we have seen, had the consequence that the problem of changing over from the city-state scale to the kingdom-state scale became, for the time, the major problem of the Western Society as a whole; and the two problems of 'world-order' and 'material drive' were in abeyance so long as the problem of 'change of scale' was in the forefront. This latter problem was substantially solved in the latter part of the nineteenth century; and now, in the twentieth century, the problems of 'world-order' and 'material drive', which found no solution in the medieval city-state cosmos, have presented themselves again—and this time more insistently than ever—on the newly-achieved scale of the Great Society. [2] See III. C (i) (d), pp. 200–2, above.

movement which has been taken up by an unwillingly Westernized Russia as an anti-Western gesture has turned out, unintentionally and unexpectedly, to be a more potent agency of Westernization in Russia than any application of the conventional Western social creed; and we have tried to express this outcome of the latest phase of the social intercourse between Russia and the West in the formula that a relation which was once an external contact between two separate societies has been transformed into an internal experience of the Great Society into which Russia has been incorporated. Can we now go on to discern more clearly and define more closely what form this experience is taking? Can we explain the apparent contradiction of Communist Russia's simultaneous centrifugal and centripetal movement *vis-à-vis* the Western Society in the formula that Russia, while resigning herself to her incorporation into the Great Society, is at the same time attempting to make a temporary withdrawal from the general life of the society in which she has been enrolled by *force majeure*; and that she is making this attempt to withdraw in order to play the part of a creative minority which will strive to work out some solution for the Great Society's current problems? If this is really the explanation of Russia's present course, it is not difficult to understand why it is that Russian minds are drawn in this direction; for a withdrawal in these circumstances and with this aim promises to give some satisfaction to two strong Russian desires. It satisfies the impulse, which the Russians have inherited from their own non-Western past, to escape from the Western toils; and it also holds out the prospect that if, after all, it proves impossible for Russia to break away permanently from her Western entanglements, she may at least make her return to the bosom of the Western Society in a creative role which will enable her to re-cast the general shape of Western life on a more or less Russian pattern.

The Working of Withdrawal-and-Return in the Histories of Civilizations

Having now completed our survey of the withdrawals and returns of creative minorities, we may find ourselves able to establish what the general features of these movements are when a creative minority and not a creative individual is the protagonist.[1]

---

[1] There are, of course, creative individuals at the back of all creative minorities, on the hypothesis that some individual human being is the ultimate author of every creative human act. (For this hypothesis, see III. C (ii) (*a*), above.) In the case of several of the creative minorities that we have passed under review, the originating individuals can be identified. Behind sixth-century and fifth-century Athens we can discern the personality of Solon, and behind the third-century Achaean Confederacy the personality of Aratus. But who was the architect of the Aetolian Confederacy in the preceding generation? Or the nameless Ionian or Aeolian refugee who invented the Hellenic city-state in the Dark

The first step in any group-movement of Withdrawal-and-Return is the extrication of the potentially creative minority from the general life of the society to which it belongs. This step may be accomplished in any one of several different alternative ways. The minority may be relieved of its entanglements against its own will, by *force majeure*, as the English were relieved of theirs on the Continent of Europe between A.D. 1429 and A.D. 1558. Or it may deliberately seek to shake off entanglements and fight with might and main to win its liberty, as the Dutch fought against the Spanish Hapsburg Power from A.D. 1572 to 1609 or the Lombards against the Hohenstaufen Power from A.D. 1158 to 1250 or the Athenians against the Spartan Power in 508–507 B.C. Or, having originally been extricated against its own will, it may come to realize that this dénouement has been a blessing in disguise, and may thereafter fight as vigorously to save itself from being involved in entanglements as it once fought to debar itself from being relieved of them. This has been the history of the English, who have resisted the successive attempts of a Philip II of Spain and a Louis XIV of France and a Napoleon to incorporate England into a Continental European empire as doggedly as they resisted the victorious efforts of a Joan of Arc to relieve England of the English empire which she had established on the Continent in the earlier chapters of the Hundred Years' War. Or, again, the withdrawal may take the negative form of a persistent abstention, on the part of the minority, from commitments which are being entered into by the majority of its neighbours—as when Athens, in the eighth and seventh and sixth centuries B.C., abstained from taking any part in the contemporary movement of territorial expansion either along the Spartan line of conquering the territory of neighbouring Greek city-states or along the Chalcidian and Eretrian and Megarian and Corinthian line of conquering the territory of barbarians overseas. The alternative forms of withdrawal are diverse, but in each case the result is the same. In each case the minority that undergoes the experience finds its energies set free from the pre-occupation of dealing with its neighbours in order to concentrate these energies upon creative work.

The second stage in the movement is the stage of relative isolation in which this creative work is performed; and this stage is apt to fall into two distinct phases which may be called the originative phase and the constructive phase respectively. The first, or origina-

Age? And can we put our finger on the individual Italians or the individual Englishmen who have been ultimately responsible for the contributions that have been made by a creative Italian minority and by a creative English minority to the growth of our Western Civilization? In these cases we may infer the unseen presence of a creative individual from the visible existence and activity of a creative group; but since we cannot identify the creative individual in fact, we are constrained to deal with such cases either in terms of a group or not at all.

tive, phase is a youthful age of poetry and romance and emotional upheaval and intellectual ferment; the second, or constructive, phase is a comparatively sedate and 'grown-up' age of prose and matter-of-fact and common sense and systematization; and the psychological transition between the two phases is sometimes abrupt.

In Italian history this transition is apparent in the contrast in êthos between Dante (*vivebat* A.D. 1265–1321) and Boccaccio (*vivebat* A.D. 1313–75); in English history in the comparable contrast between Milton (*vivebat* A.D. 1608–74) and Dryden (*vivebat* A.D. 1631–1700); in Attic history in the contrast between the radical spirit of Athens before, and her conservative spirit after, the great Athenian disaster of 404 B.C. In the Athens of that generation, the transition from poetry to prose is registered in the change that comes over the style of the Athenian playwright Aristophanes. His latest extant play, the *Plutus* (produced in 388 B.C.), is already more akin to 'the New Comedy', which reaches its zenith a century later, than it is to Aristoph nes' own earlier work, which belongs unmistakably to the same world of thought and feeling as the art of Aeschylus.[1]

Approximately, we may say that in Attic history the originative phase lasts from the generation of Solon to the Atheno-Peloponnesian War and the constructive phase from that decisive catastrophe down to the generation of Alexander, by whose time the Attic 'education of Hellas' has been put into an Isocratean shape in which it is ready for export to the ends of the Earth. In Italian history, the originative phase is represented in the field of politics by the democratic movement and in the field of art by the Tuscan School of painting, while the constructive phase is represented by the Venetian School and by the mastery of the despots, with their autocratic methods of administrative efficiency. In English history, the originative phase may be regarded as beginning with the accession of Queen Elizabeth and as being divided by the Restoration from the constructive phase, which lasts from 'the sixteen-sixties' to 'the eighteen-sixties' and has to its credit such solid achievements as the foundation of the Royal Society and 'the Glorious Revolution of 1688' and the peopling of the North American Continent with an English-speaking population and *The History of the Decline and Fall of the Roman Empire* and the invention of the steam-engine and the passage of the Reform Bill of 1832 and the establishment of the Indian Empire and *The Origin of Species* (which was

[1] For an appreciation of the change in the outlook and êthos of Aristophanes in the course of his life, as mirrored in his literary work, see Murray, Gilbert: *Aristophanes: A Study* (Oxford 1933, Clarendon Press).

published in 1859) and the invention of the British Commonwealth of self-governing nations (an invention which dates from the creation of the Dominion of Canada in 1867).

The third stage in the movement of Withdrawal-and-Return is the return of the creative minority into communion with the general life of the society from which it has temporarily withdrawn in order to perform its work of creation. And the way for this return is prepared, as we have seen, by the transition, during the preceding stage of isolation, to a constructive from an originative phase of creative activity; for in this constructive phase the creator is really anticipating his return by giving his work a shape in which it will be possible for him to transmit it eventually to the non-creative majority when he enters into full social intercourse with them again.

The return, when it comes, is sometimes deliberate, as when Athens threw herself in 499 B.C. into the oecumenical conflict between Hellas and the Syriac universal state. In other cases it is involuntary, as when the Achaean Confederacy was forced in 228 B.C., by its collision with Sparta, to allow itself once more to be used as a pawn in the game between the Great Powers of the periphery, or when Holland was drawn back into Continental European entanglements by the General War of A.D. 1672–1713, or England by the General War of A.D. 1914–18. Yet in whatever fashion and whatever mood the return is made—whether the returning minority makes a virtue of necessity or whether it kicks against the pricks—this experience of return is apt to be as painful and as humiliating, in its own way, as the foregoing experience of withdrawal. The returning minority has to suffer the disillusionment of the child in Wordsworth's ode who comes from Heaven to Earth 'trailing clouds of glory' to find 'the shades of the prison house' closing around him; and it has to expect from the uncreative majority the hostile reception that awaits the Platonic philosopher when he re-descends into the cave.[1]

The encounter between the minority and the majority when they meet again does in fact take the form of a challenge which is reciprocal. The returning minority challenges the uncreative majority to accept its own original solution of their common problem or else to take the consequences of continuing to confront the problem helplessly without finding any solution for it at all. Reciprocally, the majority challenges the minority to convert it to the new way of life which the minority has worked out for itself in isolation, or else to stand convicted, by 'the acid test' of experiment, of having

[1] For the relevant passages from Wordsworth and Plato, see the present chapter, pp. 249–52, above.

failed, after all, to discover a solution for the common problem that will actually work in the workaday world. If the minority does fail, upon its return, to convert the majority, then the whole of its movement of Withdrawal-and-Return is exposed in retrospect, in the last act, as ineffective and abortive. On the other hand, if the minority, going out into the highways and hedges like the servant in the parable at the bidding of his lord, does compel the multitudes to come in,[1] then the readjustment in the life of the majority which is required for the performance of this act of mimesis is sometimes so drastic that it can only take the form of revolution.[2] In any event, the reciprocal challenge is apt to produce all manner of friction and conflict and storm and stress; and in the most signal triumphs of creative minorities and creative individuals there is often a note of tragic irony.

Sometimes the creator only wins his converts posthumously, after he has testified to the worth of his revelation by sacrificing his life for its sake.

'Ye build the sepulchres of the prophets, and your fathers killed them.

'Truly ye bear witness that ye allow the deeds of your fathers; for they indeed killed them, and ye build their sepulchres.'[3]

In other cases, the creator only wins his converts indirectly, through the intervention of an intermediary. When Moses has led the Children of Israel out of the land of Egypt and out of the house of bondage,[4] and has shepherded them through the Wilderness, it falls not to Moses but to Joshua to lead them on into the Promised Land. When David has won the Kingdom of Israel and Judah for the House of Jesse, and has conquered Jerusalem from the Jebusites, and has prepared abundantly for the building of the Temple, it falls not to David but to Solomon to build it.[5] The poetry of 'Homer' reaches the listener's ear through the voice and hand of the rhapsodist, and the music of the composer of a symphony through the fingers or the lips of the executants. The Gospel of Jesus of Nazareth makes its grand conquest of the Hellenic World through its interpretation by Paul of Tarsus. And the successive contributions which an Italian and an English creative minority have made to the growth of the Western Civilization have not passed into general currency until they have been filtered through a French medium. It was in a French version that the new culture of the Italian Renaissance made its triumphal progress beyond the Alps until, in the eighteenth century, it reigned supreme throughout

---

[1] Luke xiv. 23.
[2] For revolutions as incidents in the mimesis of a creative minority by an uncreative majority, see further Part IV, below.
[3] Luke xi. 47–8. Cp. Matthew xxiii. 29–31.
[4] Exodus xiii. 3, and xx. 2.   [5] 1 Chronicles xxii.

the Western World; and it is in a French version, again, that the English invention of responsible representative parliamentary government has been spreading, in the nineteenth and twentieth centuries, over the Old World and the New.

It is indeed ironical that the prophet should be venerated by the children of his slayers and that the creator should depend on the propagandist for giving currency to creative work which the propagandist himself could never have originated. Yet the irony is only a cross light which falls upon the creative personality's experience when it is regarded subjectively from the individual's point of view; and as soon as we contemplate this experience in another aspect as one incident in that interaction between individual actors out of which the act of creation springs, we perceive that the sacrifice or effacement of the creator himself does conduce, in the nature of things, to the furtherance of the creator's work.

The canonization of the prophet by the children of his slayers, which is so ironical an outcome of the prophet's return from the prophet's personal standpoint, seems almost a matter of course when we view it in the light of the normal psychology of the uncreative majority of Mankind. For familiarity breeds acquiescence as well as contempt; and the sheer passage of time may work potently to win acceptance for the martyr's gospel by fructifying the outpoured blood which is 'the seed of the Church'.

Again, the effacement of the creator by the interpreter is a tribute, on the imitator's part, to the greatness of the creator's work. 'The letter killeth, but the spirit giveth life';[1] yet, just because this is true, it is also true that the miracle of creation which the spirit performs is ineffable and inimitable, whereas the deadening letter of the scribes stands out stiff and steady to be copied, however clumsily, by the novice's hand.

A very prosaic illustration of the convenience of the letter as a medium of transmission is offered by the history of the spread of the institution of responsible representative parliamentary government in the modern Western World. We have seen that this institution is an English invention which has spread for the most part in a non-English form. If we take a survey of the constitutions of the sixty or seventy fully-self-governing states which exist in our 'post-war' World, we shall find that the great majority of them have acquired at least a tincture of parliamentarism, but that the particular form of parliamentarism which is practised in the United Kingdom—the country in which the institution was originally invented—is hardly current elsewhere except in half a dozen communities which have been brought into existence by British colonization and

[1] 2 Corinthians iii. 6.

which have continued to retain their political association with Great Britain as members of the British Commonwealth of Nations. Outside this British Commonwealth, hardly any of the present parliamentary constitutions of parliamentarily governed states are directly inspired by the British Constitution, which is the mother of the whole parliamentary system; the majority are copies of either the United States or the French or the Belgian or some other non-British constitution in which the principles of British parliamentarism have been embodied.

Why have the great majority of the countries of the World preferred to take their parliamentarism at second-hand, instead of drawing it from the fountain-head? When we put the question, the answer is obvious. The American and French and Belgian constitutions have been the popular models because these are written constitutions set down in black and white on paper, so that any constituent assembly in any part of the World can imitate them—if only likewise on paper—by the simple procedure of purchasing a copy from a stationer and adopting the text as it stands with the mere substitution of 'the Portuguese Republic' for 'the French Republic' or 'the United States of Brazil' for 'the United States of North America'. This cannot be done with the British Constitution, because this is an unwritten constitution which can only be mastered by making a long and close study on the spot of how it actually works. But why is the British Constitution left elusively unwritten, while the French and Belgian and American constitutions are set down plainly in black and white? When we ask ourselves this second question, we see that the British Constitution is unwritten just because it is the living, growing, original, while the American and Belgian and French constitutions are written, and rigid, because they are themselves copies of this British model; and the rest of the World has found it easier to make copies of copies than to make fresh attempts at copying the original itself. This illustration goes far to explain the interpreter's role because it shows that the very creativeness of the creator may in itself be an impediment to the direct imitation of his work.[1]

So much for the third stage in our movement of Withdrawal-and-Return; but if the return of the creative individual or minority is duly consummated by the conversion of the uncreative majority, then this third stage has a sequel in which storm gives place to calm, conflict to peace, and a sense of malaise to a sense of well-being.

'In the development of single communities and groups of communities there occurs now and again a moment of equilibrium, when

---

[1] The same illustration of the same point is touched upon further in IV. C (iii) (c) 2 (β), vol. iv, pp. 414–18, below.

institutions are stable and adapted to the needs of those who live under them; when the minds of men are filled with ideas which they find completely satisfying; when the statesman, the artist, and the poet feel that they are best fulfilling their several missions if they express in deed and work and language the aspirations common to the whole society. Then for a while Man appears to be the master of his fate; and then the prevailing temper is one of reasoned optimism, of noble exaltation, of content allied with hope. The spectator feels that he is face to face with the maturity of a social system and creed. These moments are rare indeed; but it is for the sake of understanding them that we read history. All the rest of human fortunes is in the nature of an introduction or an epilogue. Now by a period of history we mean the tract of years in which this balance of harmonious activities, this reconciliation of the real with the ideal, is in course of preparing, is actually subsisting, and is vanishing away.'[1]

The particular moment of equilibrium that was in the historian's mind when he wrote this eloquent and imaginative passage was the moment in the second period of our Western history at which the two institutions of the Papal Church and Feudalism were found satisfying by men and women in Western Christendom. We may perhaps equate this moment with those five years in the thirteenth century of the Christian Era when Saint Dominic and Saint Francis of Assisi and the Emperor Frederick II and Saint Louis King of France were all in the World together. And in the third period of our Western history we may possibly discern an equivalent moment in the eighteenth century between the end of the Wars of Religion and the beginning of the Wars of Democracy and Industrialism, when the Western World as a whole was finding satisfaction in the culture that had been broadcast through a French medium by the Italian Renaissance. If these two illustrations are apt, they both confirm the author's judgement that the moments of which he writes in this passage are not only rare but are also transitory. The Emperor Frederick II himself, who is one of the most brilliant representatives of the medieval Western Civilization at its zenith, is a witness whose life-history proclaims that the equilibrium of his age was ephemeral; and the Papal *Respublica Christiana*, which was the master-institution of the age, and which Frederick assailed in vain, was to be disrupted by the new culture of the Italian city-states which in Frederick II's day were fighting as the allies of the Holy See against the House of Hohenstaufen.

In truth, this moment of reconciliation between the real and the ideal, which is the sequel to a successful movement of Withdrawal-and-Return in the history of a society in process of civilization, is bound to be ephemeral *a priori*. The sense of well-being and the

1 Davis, H. W. C.: *Mediaeval Europe* (London, no date, Williams & Norgate), p. 6.

sense of mastery which pervade Society at a moment such as this give an inkling of the happiness which Mankind would enjoy if it were ever to attain the goal of human endeavours. But that goal will only be attained when the whole of Society has come to consist of individuals of the new species which is represented by the Saints alone in human history up to date. In a society of Saints, well-being might endure because the crux of social relations might be over-come. But the Saints who have appeared in the World so far have only been able to transfigure Human Nature in their own per-sonalities and in those of the rare kindred souls who have risen to Sainthood through communion with the Saints by catching the divine fire. The Saints have not been able to evoke the creative change from Primitive Humanity to Sainthood in Mankind at large; and they have made their effect upon the uncreative majority, not by the direct kindling of creative energy from soul to soul, but by a resort to the primitive social drill which we have called mimesis.[1] This social expedient of mimesis is a 'short cut'; and the resort to it is proof in itself that the goal of human endeavours has not yet been attained. The climber has not yet reached the ledge above him where he may hope to find rest. He is still in jeopardy on the face of the cliff; and here there is no rest for him; for unless he continues to climb on upward until he reaches the next ledge, he is doomed to fall to his death, either through a sudden false step[2] or through an arrest at high tension which entails the same fall in the end when the arrested climber's energies have been exhausted by the effort of keeping his position[3].

'For every form which has improved, dozens have degenerated. Probably all the birds are derived from one ancestral species which took to the air, but very many have independently lost the power of flight. The ostriches and their allies, the dodo, the kiwi, the flightless parrots and rails of New Zealand, have all lost their flying power and gained nothing in exchange. Only the penguins have transformed their wings into fairly effective firs. Very numerous groups whose ancestors were motile have taken to sessile habits or internal parasitism. Degeneration is a far commoner phenomenon than progress. It is less striking because a progressive type, such as the first bird, has left many different species as progeny, while degeneration often leads to extinction, and rarely to a widespread production of new forms. Just the same is true with plants. Many primitive forms have not progressed. A few have done so, but relapses of various kinds are equally common. Certainly the study of evolution does not point to any general tendency of a species to progress. The animal and plant community as a whole does show such a tendency, but this is because every now and then an evolutionary

---

[1] See III. C (ii) (a), above, ad fin.
[2] For the breakdowns of civilizations, see Part IV, below.
[3] For the arrested civilizations, see Part III. A, above.

advance is rewarded by a very large increase in numbers, rather than because such advances are common. But if we consider any given evolutionary level, we generally find one or two lines leading up to it and dozens leading down.'[1]

Haud igitur leti praeclusa est ianua;[2] for what is true of the evolution of the Plants and the Birds is also true of the growths of civilizations.

If a growing society is tempted to cling to some momentary equilibrium for fear of losing the happiness which the moment has brought, it will lose its life and its happiness into the bargain because the moment cannot really be prolonged. And the moment is inexorably transient because the gesture of mimesis that has conjured it up is only an improvisation which the remorseless test of Time exposes as something superficial and insincere. In the gesture of mimesis, the uncreative majority is making an outward movement of conformity and not an inward adaptation. Spiritually, the gulf between the majority and the minority remains unbridged. And if, in this situation, the creative minority and the imitative majority remain immobile face to face, it is not the imitative majority that will be 'levelled up' but the creative minority that will be 'levelled down'. The salt will have lost its savour; and Faust, in bowing down and worshipping the moment with his 'Verweile doch! Du bist so schön!'[3] will have delivered himself over into the power of Mephistopheles.

We can now perceive that the reciprocal challenge which is the relation between minority and majority in the movement of Withdrawal-and-Return resembles the movement of a walker's legs when he is taking a step. The withdrawal of the minority is like the walker's action in lifting one leg while he keeps the other leg on the ground to give him his purchase for carrying the lifted leg forward. The period of isolation corresponds to the time when the advancing leg is in the air; and the return corresponds to the moment when this leg returns to the ground. In the act of mimesis, the rear leg is trailing forward in its turn to catch up with the front leg, whose turn it now is to stay planted on the earth; and the sense of well-being is experienced in the moment when both legs are side by side and the muscular effort demanded of the walker is at its minimum. Yet if the walker seeks to prolong that easy moment by stopping his advance and coming to attention, he will not only fail to reach his goal and so stultify all the steps which he has taken already; he will also soon find that the stationary posture is more

---

[1] Haldane, J. B. S.: *The Causes of Evolution* (London 1932, Longmans, Green & Co.), pp. 152–3.
[2] Lucretius: *De Rerum Natura*, V, 373.
[3] Faust, l. 1700, quoted in II. C (ii) (b) 1, vol. i, on p. 281, above.

irksome and more fatiguing than a steady continuation of his advance towards his objective. For a single step—and *a fortiori* a half-step—is not a complete or satisfactory movement in itself. A step is an incident in a journey; and each single step presupposes and demands another, until the walker has traversed the whole distance between his starting-point and his goal.

The growth of a civilization is a succession of steps; and the gait of social progress is really not a walk but a run, for there are moments when both feet[1] are off the ground simultaneously. There are moments, that is to say, when a new creative minority has separated itself out from the rest of the body social and has begun to execute a new movement of Withdrawal-and-Return in response to a new challenge, before the body social which is thus being rearticulated and reinvigorated has yet completed the process of adopting by mimesis the response to a previous challenge which has been worked out by an older creative minority in an earlier movement of Withdrawal-and-Return. In our own Western history, for example, there was a time during the thirteenth and fourteenth centuries when the new problem of transforming a locally self-sufficient agricultural society into an internationally interdependent commercial and industrial society was being worked out in the city-states of Northern Italy and Flanders while in Western Christendom at large the agricultural economic conditions and the corresponding feudal and ecclesiastical institutions, from which the rising city-states were already breaking away, were still in process of gaining ground and winning acceptance. And in the next chapter there was another time during the seventeenth and eighteenth centuries when the new problem of translating the Italian inventions of Democracy and Industrialism from the city-state scale on to the kingdom-state scale was already being worked out in England while the Western World at large was still engaged in assimilating those other elements in the Italian city-state culture which were capable of being translated as they stood on to the larger scale without being remodelled.[2]

---

[1] To say 'both feet' may seem to imply that the creative minority and the uncreative majority are two permanent articulations of the growing body social; but of course our simile, like all similes, only works out imperfectly. For a society, being not an organism itself, but merely a relation between organisms, is able to articulate and rearticulate itself much more freely than either a human body or a human soul; and accordingly, in order to make sure of 'putting its best foot forward' every time, a growing society is apt to articulate out of its members a new leg to take each new step, or, in other words, a new creative minority to find an original response for each new challenge. It is exceedingly rare for any community or other group of individuals which has played the part of creative minority in one chapter of a growing society's growth to play the same part in the next chapter. (This last point is dealt with further in IV. C (iii) (c), *passim*, in vol. iv, below.)

[2] This overlap between successive bouts of Challenge-and-Reponse and Withdrawal-and-Return confronts the historian with the minor technical problem of choosing between alternative systems of naming his periods. Assuming that the successive periods in the

It will be seen that this periodic movement of growth, in which the solution of one problem gives rise to a new problem even before it has secured a general acceptance for itself, is a plain instance of that alternating rhythm of Yin and Yang which we have studied already in another connexion.[1] We have first put our finger on the pulse of this rhythm in observing the contrast between the static condition of extant human societies of the primitive species and the dynamic movement of those societies of another species that are in process of civilization. In the particular sequence of Challenge-and-Response and Withdrawal-and-Return in which the two known species of human societies have their place, we are only in a position to observe a single pulsation: the impulse that has launched a small number of human societies out of the Yin-state attained by Primitive Humanity into the Yang-activity in quest of a goal which the Saints themselves only dimly and fitfully apprehend. In going on to study the process by which civilizations grow, we have now rediscovered in this process the alternating rhythm of Yin and Yang; but this time the rhythm is tuned to a shorter 'wave-length', and we are able to observe it in a number of examples which extend over two or three successive pulsations each.

Perhaps this is as far as we can hope to carry our analysis of the interaction between individuals in growing civilizations. In the next chapter, which is the last section of this Part, we have

growth of any given civilization will be labelled most distinctively and most characteristically if they are named after the successive creative minorities that have risen to meet successive challenges by discovering original responses through withdrawals and returns, we have still to decide whether we are to name any given period after the old minority which has not yet completed the act of return or after the new minority which has entered already upon the process of withdrawal. To take, for example, the second chapter of our own Western history—the 'medieval' chapter which runs, in conventional dates, from about A.D. 1075 to A.D. 1475—are we to call this chapter 'the Romanistic-Feudalistic period of Western history' after the *Respublica Christiana* and the Feudal System which were the master-institutions of the age? It was these institutions that presided over the moment of equilibrium and harmony which Mr. H. W. C. Davis has described in the passage quoted above. Yet it would seem equally appropriate to call this same chapter 'the Italian period of Western history' after the Italian city-states which were engaged, at that very moment, in working out a new way of life in order to solve new problems which the medieval harmony had left unsolved. Or again, to take the last chapter of Western history before the chapter in which we are living now—the chapter, that is to say, which runs, in conventional dates, from about A.D. 1475 to A.D. 1875—are we to call this chapter 'the Italistic period of Western history' after the Italian minority whose culture was being progressively adopted during these centuries by the non-Italian majority of the Western Society; or are we to call it 'the English period of Western history' after the English minority which was engaged during the same centuries in working out in relative isolation those new versions of Democracy and Industrialism on the kingdom-state scale which in this latest age are apparently conquering the World? And how will future historians conceive of the present chapter of our Western history which began about half a century ago? Will they think of it as 'the Britannistic period', in deference to the British origin of the two master-institutions and prevailing forces of the age; or will they rather associate it with the name of the new creative minority, whatever it may be, that will find—or attempt to find—a solution for the new problems to which Industrialism and Democracy are already giving rise? It will be seen that there are two alternative systems, which we may call the Promethean and the Epimethean, for giving our historical periods their names.

[1] In Part II. B, vol. i, on pp. 195–204, above.

to take a glance at the differentiation in character between one growing civilization and another which the process of growth brings with it.

III. DIFFERENTIATION THROUGH GROWTH

We have now completed our investigation of the process by which civilizations grow, and, in the several instances which we have examined, the process appears to be one and the same. Growth is achieved when an individual or a minority or a whole society replies to a challenge by a response which not only answers the particular challenge that has evoked it but also exposes the respondent to a fresh challenge which demands a fresh response on his part. And the process of growth continues, in any given case, so long as this recurrent movement of disturbance and restoration and overbalance and renewed disturbance of equilibrium is maintained. This is the process of growth as we have observed it in a comparative study of a number of cases; but, although the process may be uniform, the experiences of the various parties that undergo the process are not the same.

The variety of experience in confronting a single sequence of common challenges is manifest when we compare the experiences of the several different communities into which any single society is articulated at any given moment. For under the test of a common challenge a certain number of the communities that are exposed to it are apt to succumb, whereas others strike out a successful response through a creative movement of Withdrawal-and-Return, while others, again, neither succeed in responding along original lines nor fail to respond altogether, but manage to survive the crisis by waiting until some creative individual or creative minority has shown the way through, and then following tamely in the footsteps of the pioneers.[1] Each successive challenge that any growing civilization undergoes is apt to differentiate the experiences of its constituent individuals and communities in this way; and it is evident that the differentiation is cumulative. The longer the series of recurrent Challenge-and-Response-and-Challenge, the greater the progressive differentiation in the experiences of the parties concerned. And if the process of growth thus gives rise to differentiation within the body social of a single growing society, where the successive challenges to which the parties are subjected are common to all these parties, then, *a fortiori*, the same process must differentiate one growing society from another, since the series of Challenge-and-Response-and-Challenge through which the growths of different societies are achieved are not identical but separate and

[1] See I. B (ii), vol. i, pp. 22-6, above.

diverse. Thus the growths of civilizations entail a progressive differentiation between the experiences of one growing society and another; and we have now to consider what the implications of this differentiation of experiences may be. Does a variety of experience produce, in its turn, a variety of outlook and aptitude and êthos?

In the matter of outlook, one signal example of a variety that is traceable to a variety of experience has engaged our attention already. Our first step in entering upon this Study of History was to take account of the relativity of historical thought;[1] and, in studying this characteristic of historical thought empirically in the work of our own contemporary Western historians, we came to the conclusion that the outlook of Western historians in our time has been governed by the modern Western versions of 'Industrialism' and 'Democracy'—the two master-institutions which the Western World has thrown up in the most recent chapter of its history in the process of working out its responses to the dominant challenges of the age.[2] In this connexion, we observed that the historians of this particular society in this particular age have been apt to view the histories of all societies in all ages from the Industrial and Democratic angles of vision; and we came to the conclusion that this local and temporary standpoint has given our historians a false perspective, not only for studying the histories of all other societies beside our own,[3] but even for studying the history of our own society in its earlier chapters, before the modern Western versions of 'Industrialism' and 'Democracy' were worked out. Here, then, in the domain of historical thought, we have one clear case in which the variety in the experience of different civilizations is reflected in a variety of outlook. Are there other cases of the kind?

A conspicuous case presents itself in the domain of Art. For while the concept of the relativity of historical thought is an unfamiliar idea which has to be explained and justified, the concept of unique artistic styles that can be apprehended by direct aesthetic intuition is an accepted commonplace. There is nothing new or startling or paradoxical in the proposition that every civilization

---

[1] In Part I. A, vol. i, above.

[2] For this aspect of modern Western 'Industrialism' and 'Democracy', see III. C (ii) (b), pp. 358–63, above.

[3] On this point see also Spengler, Oswald: *Der Untergang des Abendlandes*, vol. i (Munich 1920, Beck), pp. 183–4. In this passage, as so often, Spengler does injury to his own thesis by pressing it too far. 'It is altogether impossible', he writes, 'to penetrate completely, with the forces of one's own soul, into the historical *Weltaspekt* of alien civilizations (*Kulturen*)—the picture of the process of growth as it has taken shape in souls that have quite a different "lay-out" from ours'. This sentence sounds the characteristic note of over-emphasis and hyper-dogmatism which is the serious blemish in Spengler's remarkable work.

creates an individual artistic style of its own; and, if we are attempting to ascertain the limits of any given civilization in any dimension, either spatial or temporal, we find, as a matter of fact, that the aesthetic test is the surest as well as the subtlest.

For example, a survey of the successive artistic styles that have prevailed in Egypt brings out the fact that the art of the 'predynastic age' is not yet characteristically Egyptiac, whereas the Coptic art has discarded the characteristically Egyptiac traits; and on this showing we are able to establish the Time-span of Egyptiac history, from the birth to the dissolution of the Egyptiac Society, more accurately than we can establish it by any other method of measurement. By the same aesthetic test, we can establish the respective dates at which the Hellenic Civilization emerged from beneath the crust of the Minoan Society and at which it disintegrated in its turn in order to make way for the Orthodox Christian Civilization to rise to the surface. Here, too, Art speaks in clearer accents than either Politics or Economics. The aesthetic test, again, enables us to establish, with some assurance, the distinction between an 'apparented' Sinic Society, with an art that was indigenous, and an 'affiliated' Far Eastern Society with an art that owed its individual style to an Indo-Hellenistic inspiration. By the same test, we can distinguish the chapters of Indic history that precede from those that follow the Hellenic intrusion upon the Indic World. In the spatial dimension, likewise, the style of the Minoan artifacts which our modern Western archaeologists have brought to light enables us to ascertain the geographical extension of the Minoan culture at different epochs with approximate accuracy, though the history of this Minoan Civilization is known to us exclusively through the archaeological record without any reinforcement in the shape of written documents or oral tradition—so true it is that 'if these should hold their peace, the stones would immediately cry out'.[1]

The individuality of artistic style is indeed so profound that it sets its imprint upon the simplest and crudest works of craftsmanship. The chiselling of a stone or the moulding of a brick or the texture and varnish of a potsherd is capable of bearing testimony to the existence of the culture that fashioned it with as clear a voice as the masterpiece of a great poet or the life of a great saint or the career of a great statesman.

'The phenomenon of Style springs from the nature of the Macrocosm. It expresses the fundamental symbolism (*Ursymbol*) of a civilization (*Kultur*). . . . [And] in the historical panorama of any given civilization there is only room for one single style, which is the style of that

---

[1] Luke xix. 40.

civilization itself. . . . A masterpiece of the purest Renaissance, like the
courtyard of the Palazzo Farnese, is actually nearer—immeasurably
nearer—to the vestibule of St. Patroclus at Soest or to the interior of
Magdeburg Cathedral or to the propylaea of eighteenth-century South
German mansions than it is to the temple at Paestum or to the Erech-
theum. There is the same relation between Doric and Ionic; and that
is why Ionic columns can enter into a combination with Doric architectural forms which is just as complete as the combination of late
Gothic and early Baroque in St. Lawrence at Nuremberg or the combination of late Romanesque and late Baroque in the beautiful upper
portion of the West Choir at Mainz. And this is also why our eye is
still only just beginning to distinguish, in the Egyptiac Style, the
respective contributions of "the Old Kingdom" and "the Middle Kingdom": contributions which correspond respectively to the Doric-Gothic
youth of a style and to its Ionic-Baroque age, and which, in Egyptiac
history, interpenetrate one another with complete harmony in the
semantic of all works of art of any greatness from the time of the
Twelfth Dynasty onwards.'[1]

In the light of the evidence which we have marshalled for ourselves, we may be disposed to agree with Spengler when he maintains in this passage that every society in process of civilization
creates a unique and unmistakable artistic style of its own. But if
we accept the view that every civilization has its individual outlook
and aptitude and êthos in the domain of Art, this conclusion raises
a further question; for civilizations—as we shall find when we
come to study their contacts with one another in Space and in
Time[2]—are wholes whose parts all cohere with one another and
all affect one another reciprocally. If, therefore, it is accepted that
every civilization has a style of its own in the domain of Art, we
have to inquire whether the qualitative uniqueness which is the
essence of style can appear in one single domain of social life without pervading all the parts and organs and institutions and functions and activities of the whole body social.

Spengler answers this question with an emphatic negative; for
he maintains that the relativity which we have recognized in the
domains of Art and of Historical Thought is also recognizable in
the domains of Mathematics and of Physical Science; and he even
imports his dogma of relativity into the Kantian Categories of
Thought in general, and into the realm of Ethics into the bargain.

'There is not and cannot be any such thing as Number-in-Itself.
There is a plurality of worlds of numbers because there is a plurality

---

[1] Spengler, O.: *Der Untergang des Abendlandes*, vol. i (Munich 1920, Beck), pp. 275
and 284-5. In the passages here omitted, the author gives interesting characterizations
of the Egyptiac Style and the Hellenic Style. For Spengler's conception of the *Ursymbol*,
which he equates with the Platonic *Idea*, see further op. cit., p. 243.
[2] For the contacts of civilizations in these different dimensions, see Parts IX and X,
below.

of civilizations. We find an Indic, Arabic, Hellenic, and Western type of numbers; and each type is something individual and unique from the foundations upwards; each is the expression of a different sensation of the Universe; each is the symbol of a validity which, even in the scientific sense, is strictly limited; each is the principle of an arrangement of the statically existent (*des Gewordnen*) which reflects the innermost essence of a unique soul and of no other soul but this: the soul, that is to say, which is the centre of just this civilization and no other. It follows that mathematics are not singular but plural. . . . Number as conceived in and through the spirit . . . bears witness not to a universal but in each case to a quite specific Humanity. Accordingly, when a new system of mathematics arises, its style depends entirely upon the particular civilization in which it has its roots and upon the particular kind of human beings in whose minds it is thought out. . . .[1]

'There is no Physical Science without unconscious pre-suppositions which it is beyond the scientific researcher's power to control. Moreover, these pre-suppositions can be traced back to the earliest days of the civilization—the days in which it first awakened to consciousness. The existence of a physical science implies the previous existence of a religion. In this matter there is no distinction between the Catholic and the Materialistic view of Physical Nature: they are both statements of the same creed in different words. Even the atheistic presentation of Science has religion in it: modern mechanics are a reproduction of Christian dogmas, point for point. No science is *mere* system, law, number or arrangement; every science is also an historical phenomenon, and as such it is a living organism which realizes itself in the thoughts of human beings and is governed by the destiny of a particular civilization. In the science of modern Physics there is an historical as well as a logical necessity. It is not only a matter of intellect; it is also a matter of race. . . . The notion of a universally valid Science which is true for all civilizations is an illusion. . . .[2]

'In the [concept of the *a priori*], Kant assumes not only that the form of all mental activity is unalterable, but also that it is identical for all human beings. In consequence, he has entirely overlooked a circumstance of inestimable importance (the main reason for this lapse being his failure to test his thought by reference to any mental resources or any intellectual standpoint except those of his own time). The point in question is the variation in the degree of this "universal validity". While there are certain factors in Thought which are no doubt valid over a wide range and which are at least ostensibly independent of the civilization or the century to which the thinker belongs, there is also, underlying all Thought, another necessity, in respect of the forms of Thought, which is of quite a different kind: the necessity to which a human being is subject in his capacity as a member of one particular civilization and no other. . . .[3] The categories of Thought, Life, and Consciousness of the Universe are as various as the physiognomies of

---

[1] Spengler, op. cit., vol. i, pp. 85–6. See further the whole of this chapter: 'Vom Sinn der Zahlen' (pp. 75–131).
[2] Spengler, op. cit., vol. i, pp. 531–2.   [3] Spengler, op. cit., vol. i, pp. 87–8.

individual human beings. There are intellectual as well as physical "races" and "peoples": communities constituted by the possession of some particular mental form or idea; and they have as little knowledge of their own intellectual idiosyncrasies as they have of other people's perceptions of "redness" or "yellowness". The common system of symbols which is especially characteristic of Human Speech fosters the illusion that there is an identity of inner life and an identical picture of the Universe. [In reality], the great thinkers of the individual civilizations are comparable in this respect to victims of colour-blindness who do not realize their own condition and who therefore each make merry over their neighbours' mistakes. . . .[1]

'There are exactly as many systems of morality as there are civilizations. In this matter no one has a free choice. In the activity of every painter and musician there is assuredly some factor, of which the artist himself is never conscious, which nevertheless governs from the outset the semantic of his works and distinguishes them from the artistic performances of all other civilizations; and it can be stated with equal assurance that every manifestation of life by any human being who belongs to any civilization is stamped from the outset—*a priori*, in the strictest Kantian sense—with an idiosyncrasy which goes far deeper than any conscious judgement or endeavour and which is recognizable, by its style, as belonging to a particular civilization. The individual may behave morally or immorally, "well" or "badly", in terms of the primordial moral sense of his own civilization; but the form of his behaviour is not a matter of personal choice. Every civilization has its own ethical standard; and the validity of this standard begins and ends with that civilization itself. There is no such thing as a universal human ethic.'[2]

In the foregoing series of passages, in which Spengler carries his dogma of relativity from the domain of Art into almost every other domain of social life, there is a magnificent logic; and an English empiricist might find this German transcendentalist a formidable antagonist if he were rash enough to challenge him to a tournament with his own German weapons. If we admit that there are qualitative differences between the styles of different civilizations in the domain of Art, and also admit that every civilization is an indivisible whole consisting of parts which are interdependent with one another, then it is certainly difficult to refute Oswald Spengler's logic by counter-syllogisms. But an empiricist will be inclined to reply by approaching the same problem from a different angle. He will begin by submitting that the attribute of absolute and all-pervasive qualitative individuality, which Spengler ascribes to each and every society of the species Civilizations, carries with it the implication that a civilization is something qualitatively constant and therefore static; and this would mean, in Spengler's own

[1] Spengler, op. cit., vol. i, p. 251.   [2] Spengler, op. cit., vol. i, p. 471.

metaphysical terms, that civilizations belong to the realm of *das Gewordnes*, and not to the realm of *das Werden*: a consequence which is in contradiction with Spengler's own doctrine[1] and with the empiricist's own observation.

The empiricist will go on to point out that a civilization, as he observes it 'in real life', is not a static thing but a dynamic process or movement or *élan*: an endeavour to create something Super-human out of primitive Human Nature. He may be prepared to contemplate the possibility of a specific difference of character between the raw material and the eventual work of art which the demiurge is striving to fashion out of it; for experience reveals what is tantamount to a specific difference between primitive or ordinary Human Nature and the nature of the Saints who are Superman's heralds and forerunners;[2] and from this experience we may infer, *a fortiori*, that 'the first man Adam was made a living soul, the last Adam was made a quickening spirit', and that 'the first man is of the earth earthy, the second man is the Lord from Heaven'.[3] But how can we accept the conclusions of logic when it ascribes this specific individuality—this absolute qualitative dif-ference, not only from all primitive societies but also from one another—not to saints or to supermen but to civilizations, when these civilizations are nothing but alternative and parallel and philosophically contemporary efforts to move on from *das Ge-wordnes*—from the accomplished fact of Human Nature—to an-other nature, superhuman or divine, which is the unattained goal of human endeavours: the goal towards which 'the whole creation groaneth and travaileth'?[4] If a civilization is a movement from one kind of being to another, and is not a thing in itself, then surely it cannot be absolutely constant and self-consistent; and if it is a representative of a species, then surely, again, it cannot be abso-lutely unique. Logic or no logic, we cannot follow Spengler as far as this.

On the other hand, we shall probably feel that he is opening up an interesting line of inquiry on firmer ground when he interprets the variety of social style as arising not from a difference of essence but rather from a difference of emphasis.

'We talk of the *habitus* of a plant—by which we mean the specific outward appearance that belongs to this plant alone, and the character and the style in which it presents itself in the realm of static existence and spatial extension (*in den Bereich des Gewordnen und Ausgedehnten*),

[1] See Spengler, op. cit., vol. i, p. 243, *ad init.*
[2] For this conception of the Saints as precocious representatives of a new species in process of creation, see the passages quoted from Bergson and from Middleton Murry in III. C (ii) (*a*), on p. 232, above.
[3] 1 Corinthians xv. 45 and 47. [4] Romans viii. 22.

whereby every plant is distinguished, in every one of its parts and at every single stage of its life, from the representatives of all other species. This notion is so important for the study of physiognomy that I propose to apply it to the great organisms of History and to speak of the *habitus* of the Indic, the Egyptiac or the Hellenic Civilization or History or Mentality. A vague sense of the conception is already to be found underlying the notion of Style, and we are merely clarifying this notion and giving it greater depth if we talk of the religious, mental, political, social, and economic style of a civilization, or, in general terms, of the style of a soul. This *habitus* of conscious being, which covers sentiments and thoughts and bearing and behaviour in the life of an individual human creature, has a wider scope in the life of entire civilizations. In this sphere it embraces the total expression of Life in its higher manifestations: for example, the choice of particular branches of Fine Art (the choice of sculpture in the round and fresco-painting by the Hellenes, and the choice of counter-point and oil-painting in the West) and the decisive rejection of other branches (the rejection of sculpture by the Arabs). The style of a civilization reveals itself again in a penchant towards esotericism (Indic) in contrast to a penchant towards publicity (Hellenic); or a penchant towards the spoken word (Hellenic) in contrast to a penchant towards the written word (in the Sinic World and the West).'[1]

This interpretation of the variety of social style as the outcome of a differentiation in penchant or bent or trend or emphasis will carry conviction to the empirical student of history, because he will find it borne out by actual examples 'in real life'.

The Hellenic Civilization, for instance, displays a manifest tendency towards a predominantly aesthetic *habitus* (to borrow Spengler's terminology). This Hellenic tendency to view life as a whole in distinctively aesthetic terms is illustrated by the well-known fact that the Ancient Greek adjective καλός, which properly denotes what is aesthetically beautiful, is employed indiscriminately to stand in addition for what is morally good. In other words, in the Hellenic Society the emphasis upon the aesthetic outlook has become so strong that the moral outlook has been confounded with it on the showing of the Ancient Greek vocabulary.

The Indic Civilization, again, as well as the 'affiliated' Hindu Civilization, displays an equally manifest tendency towards a *habitus* which is predominantly religious.

'One general observation about India may be made at the outset. Here more than in any other country the national mind finds its favourite occupation and full expression in religion. This quality is geographical rather than racial, for it is possessed by Dravidians as much as by Aryans. From the raja to the peasant most Hindus have

---

[1] Spengler, op. cit., vol. i, p. 156.

an interest in theology and often a passion for it. Few works of art or literature are purely secular: the intellectual and aesthetic efforts of India, long, continuous and distinguished as they are, are monotonous inasmuch as they are almost all the expression of some religious phase.'[1]

When we come to our own Western Civilization, we find no difficulty in detecting our own bent or bias. It is, of course, a penchant towards machinery: a concentration of interest and effort and ability upon applying the discoveries of Natural Science to material purposes through the ingenious construction of material and social clockwork (material engines such as steamships and motor-cars and sewing-machines and wrist-watches and fire-arms and bombs; and social engines such as parliamentary constitutions and military mobilization systems). We are acutely—and, to-day, no longer complacently[2]—aware that this is our Western bent; but we are possibly apt to under-estimate the length of the time during which our Western energies have been flowing in this direction.

We sometimes talk as though our Western 'Machine Age' were no older than the modern Western Industrial Revolution which began little more than a century and a half ago; and it is true, as we have seen in another connexion,[3] that less than two centuries and a half ago the polite society of Holland and England (which were the two most commercially-minded Western countries of the day) was disgusted at the base mechanic êthos of Russian Peter. Peter the Great, however, was manifestly a *lusus Naturae*; and the disgusting impression which he made upon the sensibilities of a Bishop Burnet and a King William III as a barbarian whose barbarism was accentuated and not redeemed by his amazing but unedifying mechanical talent is precisely the impression which *Homo Occidentalis* himself has usually made upon the children of other civilizations since very early days. This is how *Homo Occidentalis* was regarded in China and Japan in the earlier decades of the nineteenth century of the Christian Era; and he was regarded in just the same way in the Orthodox Christian World eight centuries earlier when he burst upon the East Roman Empire in the First Crusade. Anna Comnena's description of the cross-bow— 'a barbarian weapon which is entirely unknown to the Hellenes' —might serve, *mutatis mutandis*, for a description of a modern Western rifle from the pen of a nineteenth-century Confucian *literatus*. The Byzantine authoress brings out the ingenuity of construction and length of range and power of penetration and deadliness of effect of this Western lethal weapon, and sums it up

[1] Eliot, Sir Charles: *Hinduism and Buddhism* (London 1921, Arnold, 3 vols.), vol. i, pp. xiii–xiv.
[2] For our recent awakening from complacency, see III. C (i) (*d*), pp. 210–12, above.
[3] See p. 279, above.

as 'a really devilish contrivance'.[1] There are a number of other symptoms that indicate how early this mechanical trend declared itself in Western history. Clock-work, for example, in the literal sense, appears to have been invented in the West in the same century as the cross-bow;[2] and in the thirteenth century of the Christian Era Roger Bacon, within the bosom of the Western Society, was as notable a forerunner of the latter-day *Homo Occidentalis Mechanicus* as the alien Peter Alexeyevich four centuries later.

It is even possible that the first stirrings of our Western mechanical activity may be discerned at a much earlier date, when the 'apparented' Hellenic Society was still in being and the 'affiliated' Western Society was only in gestation, awaiting the hour of its birth. It is at any rate one of the curiosities of history that the sole instance of the application of mechanical invention to practical economic life which appears to be recorded in Hellenic annals had its locus in Gaul: a region which was not incorporated into the Hellenic World until its latter days, and which always remained on its fringe, but which has been the homeland and heart of the Western World in every age of the Western Civilization. This Gallic apparatus—the existence of which is attested in the first century of the Christian Era, and again in the fourth[3]—seems 'rudimentary' and 'clumsy' to the modern Western scholar[4] when he studies the original accounts of it at second-hand with the masterpieces of modern Western mechanical ingenuity in his mind as a standard of comparison. Yet if we consider this labour-saving appliance in its Hellenic environment and appraise it on a Hellenic standard from a Hellenic standpoint, we shall be inclined to regard it as being almost as great a portent in the Roman Empire as the genius of Peter Alexeyevich was in Holy Russia. We feel ourselves here in the presence of something profoundly alien from the Hellenic genius.[5] Is it fanciful to see in this 'rudimentary' and 'clumsy' Gallic reaping-machine a precocious pre-natal manifestation of the Western mechanical bent?

At any rate, however far it may or may not be possible to trace our Western mechanical trend back towards the origins of our Western history, there is no doubt that a mechanical penchant is as characteristic of the Western Civilization as an aesthetic penchant

---

[1] Τὸ μὲν οὖν τῆς τζάγγρας πρᾶγμα τοιοῦτόν ἐστιν ὡς ὄντως δαιμόνιον. (Anna Comnena: *Alexias*, Bk. X, ch. 8.) [2] Spengler, op. cit., vol. i, pp. 18–19.

[3] See Pliny, *Historia Naturalis*, xviii. 296, and Palladius, *Opus Agriculturae*, vii. 2, cited by Heitland, W. E.: *Agricola* (Cambridge 1921, University Press), p. 398.

[4] Heitland, op. cit., loc. cit.

[5] For a conspectus of the mechanical equipment of the Hellenic World in the latest age of Hellenic history, see Usher, A. P., *A History of Mechanical Inventions* (New York, 1929, McGraw-Hill Book Company), chaps. 4 and 5. The water-wheel seems to have been more widely diffused than the Gallic reaping-machine, but there is no evidence that it, too, was of Gallic origin.

is of the Hellenic Civilization or a religious penchant of the Indic and the Hindu. And in our comparative study of the progressive differentiation between growing civilizations we are possibly warranted in going on one step farther than this. With all circumspection, we may possibly venture to suggest in certain instances that this or that interest or aptitude or activity which manifestly plays an important part in the history of some one particular civilization is in some sense the counterpart of some other interest or aptitude or activity which appears to play a corresponding role in the history of another particular civilization.

It may be suggested, for example, that our modern Western sensitiveness to ugliness in moral action when it takes the form of cruelty, coupled with our obtuseness to ugliness in visual form when it takes the shape of a modern Western industrial area, is not only inverse to, but is also in some sense equivalent to, or compensatory for, the obtuseness to cruelty which was coupled, both in medieval Italy and in ancient Greece, with an acute sensitiveness to ugliness in the field of vision.

'It is often said that the modern man has entirely lost the Greek love of beauty. This is, I think, untrue, and unjust to our present civilization, unlovely as it undoubtedly is in many ways. It is curious that modern critics of the Greeks have not called attention to the *aesthetic* obtuseness which showed itself in the defective reaction of the ancients against cruelty. It was not that they excluded beautiful actions from the sphere of aesthetics; they never thought of separating the beautiful from the good in this way. But they were not disgusted at the torture of slaves, the exposure of new-born children, or the massacre of the population of a revolted city. The same callousness appears in the Italian cities at the Renaissance; Ezzelino was a contemporary of the great architects and painters. I cannot avoid the conclusion that it is connected in some obscure way with the artistic creativeness of these two closely similar epochs. The extreme sensibility to physical suffering which characterizes modern civilization arose together with Industrialism, and is most marked in the most highly industrialized countries. It has synchronized with the complete eclipse of spontaneous and unconscious artistic production, which we deplore in our time. . . . The explanation of this extreme susceptibleness must be left to psychologists; but I am convinced that we have here a case of transferred aesthetic susceptibility. We can walk unmoved down the streets of Plaistow, but we cannot bear to see a horse beaten. The Athenians set up no Albert Memorials, but they tortured slave-girls in their law-courts and sent their prisoners to work in the horrible galleries of the Laureion silver-mines.'[1]

On the same line of thought, it may be suggested that the

[1] Inge, W. R., in *The Legacy of Greece* (Oxford 1921, Clarendon Press), pp. 39-40.

luxuriance of Religion in India corresponds in some sense to the
luxuriance of Politics in Europe.

'Hinduism has often and justly been compared to a jungle. As in the
jungle every particle of soil seems to put forth its spirit in vegetable life
and plants grow on plants, creepers and parasites on their more stalwart
brethren, so in India art, commerce, warfare, and crime, every human
interest and aspiration seek for a manifestation in religion, and since
men and women of all classes and occupations, all stages of education
and civilization, have contributed to Hinduism, much of it seems low,
foolish and even immoral. The jungle is not a park or garden. Whatever can grow in it, does grow. The Brahmans are not gardeners but
forest officers. To attempt a history or description of Indian creeds
seems an enterprise as vast, hopeless and pathless as a general account
of European politics. As for many centuries the life of Europe has
expressed itself in politics, so for even longer ages the life of India,
which has more inhabitants than Western Europe,[1] has found expression
in religion, speculation, and philosophy, and has left of all this thought
a voluminous record, mighty in bulk if wanting in dates and events.
And why should it chronicle them? The truly religious mind does not
care for the history of religion, just as among us the scientific mind
does not dwell on the history of science.'[2]

Or, again, we may follow Spengler when he suggests that the
art of sculpture in the round, with the human figure as its theme,
corresponds, as the master-art of the Hellenic Civilization, to the
art of music in the West, where it is music and not sculpture that
has played the leading role.

Spengler distinguishes an 'Apollinean' and a 'Faustian' group
of arts which he regards as being characteristic of the Hellenic and
the Western Civilization respectively.

'In the Apollinean group, which includes vase-painting, fresco-
painting, bas-relief sculpture, an architecture based on ranks of columns,
the Attic Drama and the dance, the central point is the sculpture of the
naked statue. The Faustian group, on the other hand, gravitates round
the ideal of pure spatial Infinity; and its central point is to be found
in counter-point music. From this central point outwards, fine-spun
threads extend into all fields of mental life and weave themselves into
the infinitesimal system of mathematics, the dynamic system of physics,
the Catholicism of the Society of Jesus and the Protestantism of the
Enlightenment, the modern machine-technique, the credit system and
the dynastic-social organization of the State—a stupendous sum of
spiritual self-expression. . . .

'The nearer the [two] civilizations have approached towards their
complete self-realization, the more decided has been their leaning towards an art of inexorable symbolic clarity. . . . From [the generation

[1] The population of India (about 315 millions) is larger than that of Europe without
Russia.
[2] Eliot, Sir Charles: op. cit., vol. ii, p. 166.

of Bach and Handel] onwards, music—and this a pure instrumental and not a vocal music—becomes the Faustian art *par excellence*. The corresponding artistic crisis occurs in Hellenic history about the year 470 B.C., when the last of the great fresco-painters, Polygnotus, yields the primacy, once and for all, to his pupil Polycleitus—yields it, that is to say, to the art of statuary.

'With this music and this sculpture the goal is attained. A pure symbolism of a mathematical stringency has now become possible. That is the meaning of the *Canon* (Polycleitus's work on the proportions of the human body); and Polycleitus's *Canon* has its analogue in the canon of counter-point which was established by Polycleitus's Western "contemporary" Bach. In clarity and intensity of pure form, these arts attain the acme and the final term of achievement. We may test this by comparing the tone-body (*den Tonkörper*) of the Faustian instrumental music, and within this again the stroke-body (*den Streichkörper*), and in Bach's music the body of the wind-instruments (which operates as a unity) as well, with the body of Attic statues. We may likewise compare the two things that are called "figures" by Haydn and by Praxiteles respectively: that is to say, the figure of a musical theme and the figure of an athlete. The use of the word "figure" itself is borrowed from mathematics and it reveals the fact that this goal, which has now been attained at last, has been found in a union of the artistic with the mathematical spirit. In music and in sculpture, the analysis of Infinity and the Euclidean geometry have each apprehended its own respective task, its specific problem of numbers, with complete clarity. The greatest masters of these mathematical systems are contemporaries of the great masters of these thoroughly mathematical arts. It will be recollected that, at an earlier point in this work, mathematics has been described as an art and the great mathematician as an artist and a visionary. The explanation now lies before us. The mathematics of Beauty and the beauty of Mathematics can no longer be distinguished from each other. The Infinite Space of musical tones and the Pure Body of marble or bronze are a direct interpretation of that which has spatial extension and static existence (*des Ausgedehnten und Gewordnen*). They belong respectively to Number conceived as Relation and to Number conceived as Mass. Both in fresco-painting and in oil-painting, the relevant laws of proportion and perspective yield no more than a bare intimation of mathematical system. On the other hand, the two latest and strictest arts [i.e. statuary and music] *are* mathematics. Counter-point and the statue-canon alike are absolute worlds of numbers. In these worlds, laws and formulas are enthroned. At this height of attainment, the Faustian and the Apollinean art are both manifested in their completeness.'[1]

This is perhaps as far as we can follow out the differentiation which accompanies the growth of civilizations without losing our way in a maze of fantasy. We have explored far enough to have

[1] Spengler, op. cit., vol. i, pp. 380–3. See further the whole of the chapter entitled 'Musik und Plastik' (pp. 297–402).

established the fact that a differentiation of some kind does take place; and thus we have returned, at the close of this third part of our Study, to the point from which we started at the beginning of the first part, when we dwelt upon the fact that in any age of any society all social activities, including the study of history itself, are governed by the dominant tendencies of the time and the place. Yet if we were merely to dwell on this point once again, we should be ending this part of our Study on a false note; for, as we have observed in our critique of the concept of Race,[1] the variety that is manifested in Human Nature and in human life and institutions is a superficial phenomenon which masks, without impairing, an underlying unity.

We have compared our civilizations to rock-climbers;[2] and on the showing of this simile the several climbers, though they are certainly separate individuals, are also all representatives of a single species and are all engaged upon an identical enterprise. They are all attempting to scale the face of the same cliff from the same starting-place on a ledge below towards the same goal on a ledge above. The underlying unity is apparent here; and it appears again if we vary our simile and think of the growths of civilizations in terms of the Parable of the Sower. The seeds which the sower sows are separate seeds; and every grain has its own different destiny. Some fall by the wayside and some fall upon stony places and some fall among thorns (the breakdowns and disintegrations of the unsuccessful civilizations will engage our attention in the parts of this Study that follow next). It is only a residue that falls into good ground and brings forth fruit. Yet the seeds are all of one kind, and they are all sown by one sower in the hope of obtaining one harvest. And even the seeds that are devoured by the fowls or scorched by the sun or choked by the thorns are serving the sower's purpose, as well as the seeds which bring forth fruit an hundredfold. The differentiating Yang-movement of growth is leading towards a goal which is a Yin-state of integration. For 'ilayhi marji'ukum jamī'an':[3] 'to Him return ye every one'.

[1] In II. C (ii) (a) 1, vol. i, above.
[2] In Part II. B, vol. i, on pp. 192–5, above.
[3] Qur'ān, x. 4. Literally: 'To Him in your return, universally.'

THE 'CONDUCTIVITY' OF NOMADISM AS ILLUSTRATED IN THE DIFFUSION OF LANGUAGES

THE high social 'conductivity' of both the Steppe and the Sea is particularly well brought out by some of the phenomena of the geographical distribution of languages.

It is a well-recognized fact that a seafaring people is apt to spread its own language round all the coasts of any sea or ocean in which it has made itself at home. Ancient Greek navigators once put the Greek language into currency round the whole circumference of the Mediterranean, and their Modern Greek successors still keep Greek alive round the narrower compass of the Aegean. The prowess of Malayan seamanship has propagated the Malay family of languages as far as Madagascar on the one hand and the Philippines on the other. And, in the Pacific, the Polynesian language is still spoken with extraordinary uniformity throughout an archipelago that extends from Fiji to Easter Island and from New Zealand to Hawaii, though many generations have now elapsed since the vast spaces of 'estranging sea' which separate these Pacific islands from one another were regularly traversed by Polynesian canoes. Again, it is because 'Britannia rules the waves'—or did rule them for a century or so—with a world-wide thalassocracy that English has latterly become a world-language with a currency from China to Peru. This 'conductive' effect of maritime navigation in propagating languages over wide areas with rapidity and ease is notorious; but it is perhaps not so commonly recognized that the same 'conductivity' is also one of the properties of the Nomadism of the Steppes.

This property of Nomadism can be verified by examining the geographical distribution of four living languages, or families of languages, which are all very widely disseminated in the world of our day: namely Berber, Arabic, Turkish, and Indo-European.

The Berber languages are spoken to-day by the Nomads of the Sahara (i.e. the African section of the Afrasian Steppe) and also by the sedentary peoples along the northern and southern 'coasts' of the Sahara, in the Maghrib and in the northern fringe of the Nigerian and Senegalese Sudan. It is natural to infer that the northernmost and the southernmost branches of this family of languages were propagated into their present domains by Saharan Nomads, speaking Berber as their mother-tongue, who trespassed, in times past, out of the Desert into the Sown.

Again, Arabic is spoken to-day not only in the Arabian section of the Afrasian Steppe but on its northern coasts, in Syria and 'Irāq, and on its southern coasts, in the Hadramawt and the Yaman, and on its western coasts, in the Basin of the Nile, from the Delta up to the Sudanese Jazīrah. More than that, the Arabic language has spread still farther westward—trespassing here upon the Berber family's domain—until it has reached the North-African coast of the Atlantic and the northern shore of Lake Chad; and in this instance we happen to have an historical record of how the propagation of Arabic across the whole breadth of Northern Africa was accomplished. We know that this was the work of Arabic-speaking Nomads—the Banu Hilāl and the Banu Sulaym—who, by the deliberate policy of the Fātimid Caliphate, were first transplanted from the North Arabian Steppe to Upper Egypt and were then let loose upon North-West Africa about the middle of the eleventh century of the Christian Era.[1]

If we look next at the present distribution of the Turkish languages, we can infer with assurance from the linguistic map that their original centre of distribution must have been the Eurasian Steppe. Turkish dialects are spoken to-day throughout a solid block of Central Asian territory extending from the east coast of the Caspian to the Lob Nor and from the Northern escarpment of the Iranian Plateau to the western face of the Altai, with a fringe of outlying enclaves in the regions round about: in Azerbaijan and Anatolia; in the Crimea and the Dobruja; in Western Siberia and Bashkiristan; and, far away to the north-east, in the Basin of the Lena, where the Yakut dialect of Turkish survives to show that Turkish-speaking peoples must once have occupied not only, as now, the western but also the eastern half of the Eurasian Steppe which now constitutes Zungaria and Mongolia and Manchuria. The inference is that the Turkish family of languages was propagated over its present domain by Turkish-speaking Eurasian Nomads; and this inference from the linguistic map is of course proved correct by our historical records.

This explanation of the present distribution of the Turkish family of languages gives the key to the present distribution of the Indo-European family, which (as its name implies) is now so strangely sundered into two isolated geographical groups: one domiciled in Europe and the other in India and Iran. The present Indo-European linguistic map becomes intelligible if we assume that the languages of this family were originally propagated by Nomads who were tenants of the Eurasian Steppe before the pro-

[1] See Gautier, E. F.: *Les Siècles Obscurs du Maghreb* (Paris 1927, Payot), pp. 385–90; Marçais, G.: *Les Arabes en Berberie du xie au xive siècle* (Paris 1913, Leroux).

pagators of the Turkish languages made themselves at home there. Europe and Iran both have 'seaboards' on the Eurasian Steppe, and this great waterless ocean is the natural medium of communication between them. This explanation of the present Indo-European linguistic map is confirmed by the researches of our modern Western archaeologists, who have recently discovered the records of now extinct Indo-European languages which were once current on another 'seaboard' of the Eurasian Steppe, in the Tarim Basin.

We can fortify the foregoing evidence for the 'conductivity' of Nomadism by an instance in Tropical Africa and another instance in North America.

It is one of the well-known curiosities of Tropical African sociology that, among the African Negro peoples, there is a violent contrast between the extreme linguistic uniformity which is characteristic of one part of their habitat and the equally extreme linguistic diversity which is characteristic of another part. From Uganda and Kikuyu to Basutoland and Kaffraria, over a span of more than thirty degrees of latitude, the African Negroes all speak dialects of the one great Bantu family of languages.[1] On the other hand, in the Sudan (in the widest sense of the term, in which it covers a belt of territory stretching right across Africa from the western foot of the Abyssinian Plateau to the Guinea Coast), a different language, with no discernible affinity to the neighbouring languages, is spoken in every district and, in some districts, in almost every village.[2] In the Sudan, the rare *lingue franche*, e.g. Haussa and Fulani, are apt to be of at least partly alien origin.[3] This contrast which the linguistic diversity of the Sudan presents both to the uniform Bantu area on the south and to the uniform Berber and Arabic area on the north is a phenomenon which demands explanation; and the most obvious explanation is to be found in the fact that the Bantu-speaking and Fulani-speaking peoples, like the Imoshagh and like the Badawī Arabs, are by origin stock-breeding Nomads, whereas the Sudanese Negroes are sedentary agriculturists.

A parallel case in North America is the contrast between the

[1] 'To the south of a zigzag boundary which stretches from Fernando Pô on the west to Mombasa on the east, lies the sphere of the Bantu speech.... There is but one indigenous language-family over the whole of Central and South Africa, the only exceptions to this universality of type being a few patches of Sudanian tongues on the Northern Congo, Nilotic dialects in East Africa, a click language south of the Victoria Nyanza, and the nearly extinct Hottentot and Bushman languages of South-West Africa' (Johnston, Sir H. H.: *The Opening Up of Africa* (London, no date, Williams & Norgate), pp. 131–2).
[2] 'West Africa and the south-western part of the Egyptian Sudan are perhaps the most bewildering in their innumerable language types. A few hundred or few thousand people will speak a language in one group of villages totally distinct in vocabulary and in grammar from the equally isolated language of the next group of villages, and so on' (Johnston, op. cit., p. 131).
[3] See Johnston, op. cit., p. 130 and pp. 117–18.

narrowness of the geographical domain of the Mayan language and the vast extent of the Nahuan-Shoshonean group of languages (the group to which the Aztec language belongs). The Nahuan-Shoshonean family ranges from Idaho to Costa Rica;[1] and we know that these languages were propagated, not indeed by stock-breeding Nomads, but by equally mobile tribes who made their livelihood on the North American prairies by hunting.

Thus the 'conductivity' of Nomadism and of Seafaring accounts for a number of the most conspicuous examples of the wide geographical diffusion of languages.[2] Indeed, the examples are so conspicuous that, although the number of instances is not really large, we have mistakenly come to regard wide distribution as the normal state of affairs which can be taken for granted, and narrow distribution as something exceptional which requires explanation.[3]

[1] Spinden, H. J.: *The Ancient Civilizations of Mexico and Central America* (New York 1922, American Museum of Natural History), p. 32.
[2] Nomadism and Seafaring are not, of course, the exclusive agencies of wide diffusion. Another manifest cause of wide diffusion is military conquest—the cause which accounts for the present diffusion in Europe of the Romance languages. The diffusion of the Russian language from the Basin of the Dniepr to the shores of the Pacific has been achieved, as we have seen (in II. D (v), vol. ii, pp. 154–7, above), by Cossack pioneers who had mastered the arts of the Nomad as well as those of the waterman.
[3] 'The current notion about languages is much too much dominated by the impression that is produced by the diffusion of a few families of languages over areas of immense extent: a phenomenon which has really been, in all cases, a gradual outcome of the course of history. This is true of the Indo-Germanic and the Semitic languages, as well as of the Turkish, Melanesian, and Bantu languages; and it also holds good for the diffusion of the Hamitic languages over North Africa. This creates a deceptive appearance of there being something anomalous when a number of languages which are fundamentally different from one another are crowded together within the limits of one small area—a phenomenon which is to be found in overwhelming abundance among the native Indians of all parts of America, and which, in the Old World, has survived in the Caucasus. . . . This is a state of affairs which is almost universal in primitive regions that have been left nearly or completely untouched by the main current of history' (Meyer, E.: *Geschichte des Altertums*, vol. ii, part (i), 2nd ed. (Stuttgart and Berlin 1928, Cotta), pp. 7–8).

THE CAUSES OF THE OCCASIONAL ERUPTIONS OF THE
NOMADS OUT OF THEIR OWN DOMAIN ON THE STEPPES
INTO THE ADJOINING DOMAINS OF THE SEDENTARY
SOCIETIES ROUND ABOUT THEM

IN our inquiry into the life of the Nomadic Civilization, we have
seen that Nomadism involves two kinds of movement which are
quite distinct, and are in fact in sharp contrast to one another,
though they are frequently confused in the popular notion of what
Nomadism is.

The normal movement of a Nomadic community or horde is a
regular movement of a cyclic kind in which the horde never tres-
passes beyond the limits of a definite range but keeps moving perpetually within these limits—coming round again and again to each
particular station on this range periodically. Since the economic
incentive which keeps the Nomad on the move is the necessity of
extracting out of his range the utmost pasturage obtainable for his
flocks and herds by taking advantage of the local seasonal variations
in the vegetation of the Steppe, it follows that the period of the
Nomad's cyclic movement is the year-period; that the geographical
direction of the movement is alternately south to north in spring and
north to south in autumn; and that the geographical extent of
the Nomad's range runs from hundreds into thousands of miles in
its north-and-south extension—the area required by any given
horde being determined by the ratio between its head of cattle and
the pastoral resources of its range, both in their totality and in their
local distribution between the different seasonal stations.[1] This
regular cyclic annual movement of a Nomadic horde differs in degree
only, and not in kind, from the regular cyclic daily movement of the
factory workers and the clerical workers in a modern Western industrial community between the factories and offices where they
work and the residential districts where they sleep.

This yearly periodic movement within a limited range is what
'Nomadism' (the Greek word for 'cattle-driving') literally and
properly means. But the Nomads are also subject to another movement which differs from their normal movement in every way.
This other movement occurs at intervals, not of twelve months, but
of decades or centuries; it is at first sight difficult to discern any
regular periodicity in it; its direction is as often as not from east to
west or from west to east, in contrast to the normal northward

[1] See Part III. A, pp. 7, 14 and 16, above.

movement in spring and southward movement in autumn; and the
distances traversed by the Nomads in this occasional movement are
out of all comparison with the range of the normal seasonal movement. In the occasional movements of this second kind, a Nomad
horde is apt not only to trespass out of its own recognized range on
to the ranges of its Nomadic neighbours, but actually to burst out
of the Steppes altogether and to flood over the fields and cities of
the sedentary societies on the further side of the border between
the Desert and the Sown.

These occasional migrations or eruptions of the Nomads, right
out of the Steppes, have of course affected the lives and fortunes and
histories of the sedentary societies round about much more profoundly and sensationally than these have been affected by the
Nomads' regular annual movements within their own domain; and,
since the history of the Nomads has been written almost entirely by
observers belonging to one or other of the sedentary societies with
which the Nomads have happened to collide, these violent eruptions have come to be regarded as the characteristic manifestations
of Nomadism, though really they are exceptional interludes in a
round of annual movements which are regular in time, limited in
geographical range, and intrinsically peaceful in character.

The impact of these Nomad eruptions upon the lives of the
sedentary victims is so catastrophic that the sedentary observers
have been inclined to postulate a demonic force of will and strength
of purpose in the Nomads to account for such vast effects upon the
sedentary societies' fortunes. In opposition to this popular view,
we have suggested, in passing,[1] that these eruptions are not, as a
matter of fact, the spontaneous expressions of the Nomads' human
initiative, but are all produced mechanically by the action upon the
Nomads of either one or other of two alternative external forces:
either a pull exerted by one of the sedentary societies in the neighbourhood of the Steppes, or else a push exerted by the climate of
the Steppes themselves.

Evidently this proposition requires proof; and the first step towards putting it to the test is to tabulate as many of the historic
eruptions as we can ascertain from the surviving records.

In setting out to compile this table, there are several obvious
considerations which we must keep in mind.

In the first place, the eruptions which we shall be entering on our
list are not all precisely comparable with one another from the
sociological standpoint. At one end of the social scale there are
migrant hordes, like the [pseudo-] Avars who burst out of the heart
of the Eurasian Steppe into the Hungarian Alföld in the second

---

[1] See Part III. A, p. 15, above.

half of the sixth century of the Christian Era, who have been so
utterly uprooted before the moment when they break into the historical record that the whereabouts of their previous ranges is
quite unknown. Then there are others, like the Magyars, who
burst into the same Alföld at the close of the ninth century of the
Christian Era, whose previous ranges may be conjectured[1] but
cannot be ascertained with certainty. There are others again, like
the Banu Hilāl and the Banu Sulaym, who migrated out of Arabia
into Africa in the eleventh century of the Christian Era, or like the
various hordes of Calmucks who migrated out of the western parts
of the Mongolian Plateau in all directions—to the Obi, to the Volga
and to the Kuku Nor—during the first half of the seventeenth
century, whose previous ranges are on record but who lost touch
with their former homes when once their migration was under way.
The migrations of the Calmucks and the Banu Hilāl, like those of
the Magyars and the Avars, were mass-movements in which the
migrants brought their flocks and their herds and their women and
their children with them. On the other hand, the eruption of the
Calmucks' kinsmen the Mongols or Tatars in the thirteenth century
of the Christian Era was only secondarily a displacement of population and was primarily a military operation carried out by a horde
which extended its domain principally by means of imposing its
political dominion upon other peoples.[2] The Mongols had a fixed
capital in Mongolia at Qaraqorum (besides the subsidiary capitals
which they established in, or on the fringes of, the conquered
countries); and they depended upon the secretarial and administrative abilities of the Nestorian and Manichaean and Buddhist
Uighurs in the Central Asian oases, as well as upon the strength of
their own right arms.[3] Among the Primitive Muslim Arabs who
burst upon the Roman and Sasanian Empires out of the Arabian
Peninsula in the seventh century of the Christian Era, there was
likewise an association between Nomads and oasis-dwellers, but in
this case the merchants of the city of Mecca and the husbandmen
of the oasis of Medina were the dominant partners, and the Badu
went into action under their command. Finally, in the Palmyrene
eruption of the third century of the Christian Era, which was
an abortive anticipation of the Muslim Arab eruption of the
seventh century,[4] the patricians of the Palmyrene city-state, whose

---

[1] See Macartney, C. A.: *The Magyars in the Ninth Century* (Cambridge 1930,
University Press).
[2] This contrast between the Mongol eruption and the subsequent Calmuck eruption
is pointed out by Courant, M.: *L'Asie Centrale aux xviime et xviiime siècles: Empire
Kalmouk ou Empire Mantchou?* (Lyon 1912, Rey), p. 35.
[3] For the relations between the Mongols and the Uighurs, see II. D (vi), vol. ii,
pp. 237-8, above.
[4] On this point, see I. C (i) (*b*), vol. i, p. 74, footnote 4, above.

magnificent public buildings represent the antithesis of the Nomadic life, so completely eclipsed their Nomad satellites that it is perhaps doubtful whether this particular eruption ought to find a place in our table at all.

Another pertinent consideration is that the dates which we assign to these eruptions are bound to be more or less arbitrary on several accounts.

For one thing, the border between the Desert and the Sown is not a fixed line which can be crossed at a single step at a precise moment which can be timed with a stop-watch. It is not a boundary line but a transitional zone; and both the location of this zone and its breadth are perpetually changing in accordance with changes in the local social or the local climatic conditions. Then, again, the sensational eruptions will often be found to have been preceded and prepared for by long continuing and hardly perceptible seepages. For example, the Arabs who flooded over the interior of the Roman and Sasanian Empires in the seventh century of the Christian Era had been heralded during the preceding two hundred years by the Arabs whose seepage into the Arabian borderlands of the Roman and Sasanian Empires had given rise already, before Muhammad's birth, to the Ghassanid Arab and the Lahmid Arab Principality on ground that had been under direct Roman and direct Sasanian administration at an earlier date. Again, the Saljūqs, who flooded over the ʿAbbasid Caliphate and burst into the East Roman Empire in the eleventh century of the Christian Era, had been heralded by the Turkish slaves and freedmen who, since the ninth century, had been making themselves the masters in Baghdad and in Samarra and in the provinces. At the same time, there have been a certain number of Nomad outbreaks which have taken their victims as completely unawares as the most malign of the eruptions of Vesuvius, and the catalogue of these bolts from the blue includes not only the impacts of the Avars, Magyars, and Mongols upon Europe, but also the outbreak of the Muslim Arabs from Arabia—in spite of the seepage which had been giving warning of its imminence during the preceding two centuries. These sudden explosive discharges of Nomad invaders out of the Desert into the Sown seem to be peculiar to those Nomads who have succeeded in acquiring a certain amount of sedentary technique and organization from the oasis-dwellers in their midst, and whose outbreaks are in the nature of military operations rather than migrations *en masse*. At least, this conclusion seems to emerge from a comparison of the thirteenth-century eruption of the Mongols with the seventeenth-century eruption of the less sophisticated Calmucks, or a comparison of the seventh-century eruption of the Primitive Muslim

Arabs either with the pre-Muslim seepage or with the subsequent eruption of the Banu Hilāl. The tide of Nomad invasion also seems to acquire its greatest impetus when it is flooding up one of those gulfs of the steppe-ocean that penetrate into the interior of the sedentary world around, just as the physical tides of the sea attain their greatest velocity and mount to their greatest heights within the confines of the estuaries of tidal rivers. In the physiography of the Steppe, the most notable estuary of the kind is, of course, the bay which opens between the northern coast of the Caspian and the southern limit of the 'forest-fleece' of the Urals; for this bay runs due westward from that point, along the north shore of the Black Sea and the north bank of the Danube, through more than thirty degrees of longitude, till it comes to an end at last at the Iron Gates.

In the reckoning of dates, we have also to take account of the fact, referred to already, that our extant records of Nomad eruptions are almost all derived from the sedentary peoples into whose domains the Nomads have burst, so that we have usually to be content with ascertaining the date at which this or that horde crossed this or that sedentary society's threshold, without our being able to discover precisely where and when the movement which has burst across this threshold in full swing originally took its start and gathered its momentum in the depth of the Steppe—in the absence of any sedentary observer on the spot who might have noticed and recorded this first phase. For practical purposes, we have to date these eruptions by the moments at which they burst across one or other of the different sectors into which we may conveniently divide the vastly long border between the Steppes and the surrounding sedentary territories. And, in many cases that are extremely pertinent and important, our records only begin at stages in the Nomads' penetration of the sedentary world which are two or three degrees removed from the original line at which the invaders began to trespass upon alien ground and left their native haunts behind them. In other words, we have not only to dissect the border between the Desert and the Sown into a number of distinct sectors, but on some of the most frequently and most energetically violated frontiers we have to distinguish between a series of thresholds or limina, in échelon one behind the other, which the Nomad trespassers are apt to cross successively before the cumulative effect of the resistance which they encounter ultimately counteracts their momentum and brings their invasion to a halt.

Tentatively, we may divide the frontiers of the Eurasian Steppe into six sectors and the frontiers of the Afrasian Steppe into nine.

The first sector of the Eurasian frontiers extends between the mountainous base of the Korean Peninsula on the east and the

Khingan Range on the west; and the eruption of Nomads on this sector out of the Steppe into China may be dated by their successive passages of three thresholds or limina: first, the Pale covering the Liaotung Peninsula; second, Shanhaikwan (the Chinese Thermopylae); and, third, the watershed between the Hwangho Basin and the Yangtse Basin.

The second sector extends from the western slopes of the Khingan Range to the Pamir Plateau via the Tien Shan; and here the first threshold is marked by the line of the Great Wall of China, while the second threshold falls into three sub-sectors, according to whether the invaders who have passed the Wall then fall upon the eastern plain of North China, or upon Tibet, or upon the Tarim Basin.[1] On the sub-sector where the second threshold is marked by the western edge of the North-China Plain, there is a third threshold (identical with Threshold (iii) of Sector I) at the watershed between the Hwangho and the Yangtse, and a fourth at the watershed between the basins of the Yangtse and the West River on the one side and the river-systems of Indo-China on the other. This fourth threshold was actually crossed by the Mongols about seventy years after their passage of the Great Wall.

The third sector extends from the Pamirs to the east coast of the Caspian Sea; and here the first threshold is the border between the Dasht-i-Qipchāq and the oases of the Oxus-Jaxartes Basin, while the second threshold is the northern escarpment of the Iranian Plateau. Eurasian Nomad invaders of South-Western Asia who succeed in mounting the Iranian Plateau and then crossing it may either turn south-eastward and descend upon the plains of the Panjab, or turn south-westward and descend upon the plains of 'Irāq, or turn north-westward and reach the Plateau of Anatolia. Thus, on this sector, the third threshold is divided into three sub-sectors which are geographically remote from one another; and a still greater distance divides the several sub-sectors of the fourth threshold of this Pamir-Caspian sector *a fortiori*. The third threshold in the Panjab leads to a fourth threshold at the line of the Ganges and to another fourth threshold at the north-western foot of the Plateau of Maharashtra; and the third threshold in 'Irāq leads to a fourth threshold on the verge of Syria and Egypt. Both Egypt and Maharashtra may seem, at first sight, inordinately remote, not only from one another, but from their common first threshold along the line between the Caspian and the Pamirs. Yet Nomad invaders who have once crossed this original line have

---

[1] The Tarim Basin, of course, is left uncovered by the western terminus of the Wall; but, at various times in history, the frontier of China over against the Nomads has extended beyond this point, north-westward, to Hami and Urumchi.

penetrated simultaneously, on more than one occasion, to Egypt in the one direction and to Maharashtra in the other. The Aryas in the first half of the second millennium B.C. (who broke upon Egypt as the Hyksos) and the Turks in the first half of the second millennium of the Christian Era (who reached Egypt as the Mamlūks and India as the Slave Kings) are two cases in point.[1]

The fourth sector, which extends from the north coast of the Caspian to the southern end of the forest-clad Urals, is comparatively short; but the shortness of the front is compensated for by the depth of the steppe-gulf, beyond this front, which assists any horde that crosses the first threshold on this sector to push on readily and rapidly to a second, third, and fourth threshold. On this sector, the first threshold is marked by the line of the River Emba and the second by the line of the River Volga. A horde which succeeds in crossing the Volga has the choice between three lines of advance. Either it may push straight on across the Don and occupy the steppe between the west bank of the Don and the eastern face of the Carpathians; or, without crossing the Don, it may turn southward and occupy the Ciscaucasian Steppe—to be pushed, perhaps, eventually, right round the eastern end of the Caucasus Range into the steppes of Azerbaijan;[2] or, in the third place, it may ascend the course of the Volga and lodge itself in the northern bay of the Steppe where the Volga is joined by the Kama. Thus the second threshold on this front splays out into three sub-sectors: the Don-to-Carpathians sub-sector, the Caucasian sub-sector, and the Volga-Kama sub-sector. The Don-to-Carpathians sub-sector of the second threshold leads on, in its turn, to three choices of a third threshold. A horde which is in occupation of the Don-to-Carpathians Steppe may either turn south and enter the Crimea, or it may turn south-west and occupy Wallachia, or it may make its way across the Carpathians and ensconce itself in the basin which contains the Hungarian Alföld. Finally, a horde which has occupied Wallachia may cross the Danube and occupy the Basin of the River Maritza or even the Basin of Thessaly.

The fifth sector of the frontiers of the Eurasian Steppe extends from the Urals to the Altai and has a single threshold which approximately coincides with the line of the Trans-Siberian Railway between Sverdlovsk (Yekaterinburg) and Novo-Nikolayevsk.

The sixth and last sector extends from the Altai to the Khingan, and approximately coincides with the present frontier between the Soviet Republic of Outer Mongolia and the U.S.S.R.

[1] For the identity of the tracks of the Aryas and the Turks on the Pamirs-Caspian front and beyond it, see I. C (i) (b), vol. i, pp. 104-7, above.

[2] This seems to have happened to the Albanian Sarmatians and to a section of the Sevordik Magyars.

Before passing on from the Eurasian to the Afrasian Steppe, we may observe that the Eurasian Steppe is engirdled by a ring of detached and more or less outlying enclaves of steppe-country, which have sometimes played an important part in the history of Nomad eruptions out of the main body of the Eurasian Steppe because, in these enclaves, the Nomads have found new homes after their own hearts, in which they have been able to go on leading the Nomadic life under favourable conditions in the very midst of an alien sedentary world. The most famous of these enclaves is the Alföld or Puszta of Hungary. Others are the Dobruja or Scythia Minor between the right bank of the Danube, in the penultimate reach in which it flows south-and-north, and the coast of the Black Sea; the Basin of the Maritza and the Basin of Thessaly; the Axylon or treeless high steppe at the centre of the Anatolian Plateau; the Steppe of Azerbaijan, in the lower basin of the Rivers Aras and Kur; the Dasht-i-Lūt or salt desert at the centre of the Iranian Plateau; the Basin of Seistan; the Thar or Indian Desert (which is sociologically an enclave of the Eurasian Steppe, though it belongs to the Afrasian Steppe physiographically); the Kuku Nor Basin in North-Eastern Tibet; and finally the so-called 'Eastern Gobi', on the eastern side of the Khingan Range, which has been the mustering place for the Nomads who have invaded China on the sector between the Khingan Range and Korea.

Turning now to the frontiers of the Afrasian Steppe, and numbering our sectors continuously—since, in the study of Nomad eruptions, the two great steppes have to be treated as one whole—we may take, as the seventh sector in our series, the Lower Euphrates front of the Arabian portion of the Afrasian Steppe. On this Lower Euphrates front, the first threshold is the line of the Euphrates itself; the second is the south-western escarpment of the Iranian Plateau; and the third is the northern escarpment of the Iranian Plateau. (All these three thresholds were passed, in succession, by the Primitive Muslim Arabs.)

The eighth sector is the Upper Euphrates front, which has one threshold—marked by the line of the river between Hit and Jarābis —leading over into an outlying enclave of the North Arabian Steppe in the Jazīrah.

The ninth sector is the Syrian front of the Arabian portion of the Afrasian Steppe, with its first threshold along the border between the North Arabian Steppe and Syria, from Jarābis on the Euphrates to 'Aqabah on the Red Sea. The second threshold on this Syrian front splays out into two sub-sectors, one leading out of Syria into Anatolia and the other out of Syria into Egypt. The Egyptian subsector of the second threshold leads on, in its turn, to two further thresholds: one leading across the Nile into the Maghrib and the other up the Nile into the Nilotic or Eastern Sudan. Finally, the third threshold towards the Maghrib leads on into the Iberian Peninsula across a fourth threshold which is marked by the Straits of Gibraltar. (The Primitive Muslim Arabs passed all these four thresholds likewise.)

Turning, now, to the African portion of the Afrasian Steppe, we may take as our tenth sector the Nile front of the Libyan Desert, over against Egypt and Nubia. This sector has a first threshold, marked by the west bank of the River Nile itself, and a second, marked by the border between Egypt and Syria. (This second threshold was passed by the Katāma Berber followers of the Fāti-mids when, after occupying Egypt in A.D. 969, they invaded Syria in or about A.D. 970.)

The eleventh sector is the border between the Libyan Desert and the cultivable plateau of the Cyrenaica.

The twelfth sector is the border between the Sahara and the Maghrib. The first threshold here is the southern escarpment of the mountains and plateaux that stretch continuously from Cape Nun on the Atlantic to Cape Bon on the Mediterranean. The second threshold is marked by the Straits of Gibraltar, across which the Saharan invaders of the Maghrib have sometimes passed over into the Iberian Peninsula.

The thirteenth sector is the opposite border of the Sahara over against the Sudan.[1]

The fourteenth sector is the frontier of the South Arabian Desert over against the highlands of the Yaman. The first threshold here is the borderline between the relatively low and arid interior and the high-lying parts of the Yaman that are watered by the monsoons. There is a second threshold at the Straits of Bāb-al-Mandab, across which the Nomad invaders of the Yaman have made their way, on one occasion at least, on to the Plateau of Abyssinia.

The fifteeenth sector is the frontier between the detached enclave of the Afrasian Steppe in Somaliland and Tropical Africa.

If we take an historical survey of the eruptions of Nomads out of the Steppes on all these fifteen sectors of the immensely long frontier along which the Desert marches with the Sown, and if we watch for the passage of the Nomad invaders at the fourth or third or second of the successive thresholds, as the case may be, as well as at the first, we shall make reasonably certain of including in our table all the important eruptions of which a record survives. The

---

[1] The Sudan is here used in the proper sense of the term which includes the whole northern fringe of Tropical Africa that is inhabited by a sedentary Negro population, from the coast of the Atlantic to the western escarpment of the Abyssinian Plateau.

Hyksos eruption, for example, will come within our ken as it
crosses its fourth threshold and bursts upon Syria and Egypt, some
two thousand miles beyond the line at which these Hyksos originally
broke out of the Eurasian Steppe when they crossed the Jaxartes.
Again, the eruption of the Cimmerians and the Scythians will come
within our ken, some fifteen hundred miles from the same starting-
line, as it crosses its third threshold and bursts simultaneously
upon Assyria and upon Cappadocia. Conversely, there are sectors
on which our earliest records, at any threshold, are of relatively
recent date. On the Thirteenth or Sudanese Sector, for instance,
we have no record of any Nomad eruption earlier than the eleventh
century of the Christian Era. And there is one sector, the Fifteenth
or Somali Sector, where we are entirely destitute of dated records,
though the vast extension of Nomadic and Semi-Nomadic Bantu-
speaking Negroid peoples over the central and southern parts of
Africa is a monument of the vigour of at least one Nomad eruption
in this quarter at some unknown date in the past.

In compiling our table, we shall naturally carry it down to the
present day; but, in choosing the *terminus post quem* we are to start,
we shall scarcely find it worth while to make any systematic survey
of any period anterior to the beginning of the second millennium
B.C., considering the extreme scantiness of the record in these
earlier chapters of the story. In another connexion, we have found
reason for believing that the genesis of Nomadism was coeval with
the geneses of the Egyptiac and Sumeric civilizations;[1] and there is
no reason to imagine that the occasional eruptions of the Nomads
into the domains of their sedentary neighbours—a phenomenon
which presents itself as far back in history as our continuous record
extends—would not present itself equally in the earlier chapters if
our record of these were fuller than it actually is. As a matter of
fact, we are not without some evidence for Nomad eruptions in the
third millennium B.C. and even in the fourth. The Asiatic invaders
of Egypt who were met and repulsed by the Government of 'the
Old Kingdom' in the age of the Sixth Dynasty, about the middle
of the third millennium B.C., were perhaps the front line of the
Amorite horde which is found already established in Syria and in
process of drifting into Shinar in the latter part of that millennium;
and these Amorites were not the earliest wave of Semitic-speaking
Nomads to break out of the Arabian Steppe into the regions round
about. The forefathers of the Semitic-speaking Akkadians, who are
found established in Northern Shinar, as next-door neighbours to
the Sumerians, when the curtain rises upon the history of the Tigris-
and-Euphrates Basin, must have been the descendants of a Nomad

---

[1] See II. C (ii) (*b*) 2, vol. i, pp. 304–5, above.

horde which broke out of the Arabian Steppe into the Jazīrah, on
the Upper Euphrates front, at some date in the fourth millennium
B.C.—and this, perhaps, nearer to the beginning of that millennium
than to the end of it.[1] Again, we must suppose that the first, or
'Centum-speaking', wave of Indo-European-speaking Nomads
must have broken out of the Eurasian Steppe upon both Europe on
the one side and the Tarim Basin on the other[2] at some date in the
third millennium B.C., since the second, or 'Satem-speaking', wave,
which subsequently followed in the first wave's wake, undoubtedly
broke upon the sector of the Eurasian front between the Pamirs and
the Caspian, and washed across this front as far afield as Egypt in
one direction and the Panjab in the other, in the early centuries of
the second millennium B.C. These fragments of evidence indicate
that it may ultimately be possible to fill in our table, upwards, at
least as far as the beginning of the fourth millennium if our knowledge of this age continues to be enlarged by the progress of
archaeological discovery. Meanwhile, we may be content to take
the beginning of the second millennium as our present starting-
point for practical purposes.

In using the table that here follows, the reader is advised to keep
the key-plan, on p. 420, of the fifteen 'fronts' or 'sectors', and their
successive 'thresholds' or 'limina', folded out, so that he may have
it under his eye all the time together with each of the pages on which
the passages of particular hordes across particular 'thresholds' are
set out under their dates—since, on these pages, the various
'thresholds' and 'fronts' are indicated by reference numbers only
and not by name.

In order to give the reader a visual impression of the constant
oscillation between the boundaries of the Nomadic and the sedentary worlds, the writer has supplemented the entries in roman type,
which record the eruptions of the Nomads out of the Desert into
the Sown, with a complementary series of entries in italics, which
record the encroachments of the sedentary peoples upon the Steppe.

---

[1] The respective locations of the Akkadians and Sumerians in the third millennium,
after the Land of Shinar had come to be partly in Akkadian hands, show that the Upper
Euphrates front and not the Lower Euphrates front must have been the sector on which
the Nomad ancestors of the Akkadians broke out of Arabia in the fourth millennium
B.C. This was also the track of the Shammar and 'Anazah in the seventeenth century of
the Christian Era. On the other hand, the Lower Euphrates front was the sector on
which the Chaldaeans broke through at the turn of the second and the last millennium
B.C. and the Primitive Muslim Arabs in the seventh century of the Christian Era.

[2] The spread of this 'Centum-speaking' wave in an easterly as well as in a westerly
direction is proved by the recent discovery, in the Tarim Basin, of written records in a
Centum-language that has been labelled 'Tokharian'.

Vent	Threshold I		Threshold II		Threshold III		Threshold IV	
	Horde	Date	Horde	Date	Horde	Date	Horde	Date
				2025–1725 B.C.				
1								
2								
3	Aryas + Iranians		Aryas + Iranians		1. Aryas 2. Hyksos + Mitanni	prae 1750	3. Hyksos	prae 1680
4	?Thracians + Slavs		1. ?Thracians + Slavs					
5								
6								
7								
8								
9								
10								
11								
12								
13								
14								
15								

	Threshold I		Threshold II		Threshold III		Threshold IV	
Vent	Horde	Date	Horde	Date	Horde	Date	Horde	Date
				1725–1425 B.C.			3. *New Empire* v. Hyksos	post 1580
1								
2								
3								
4								
5								
6								
7								
8								
9								
10								
11								
12								
13								
14								
15								

1425–1125 B.C.

Vent	Threshold I		Threshold II		Threshold III		Threshold IV	
	Horde	Date	Horde	Date	Horde	Date	Horde	Date
1								
2								
3								
4					2. *Assyria v. Mitanni*	c. 1375		
5					{ 2. ? Thracians			
6					{ 3. ? Thracians		? 'Centaurs'	
7	Chaldaeans	post 1200						
8	Aramaeans	post 1200						
9	Hebrews+ Aramaeans	post 1400						
10	Libyans	post 1300						
11								
12								
13								
14								
15								

Vent	Threshold I		Threshold II		Threshold III		Threshold IV	
	Horde	Date	Horde	Date	Horde	Date	Horde	Date
				1125–825 B.C.				
1								
2								
3								
4								
5								
6	Chaldaeans	continue						
7	*Tiglath-Pileser I* v.	prae 1100						
8	Aramaeans							
9								
10	Libyans	continue						
11								
12								
13								
14								
15								

825–525 B.C.

Vent	Threshold I Horde	Threshold I Date	Threshold II Horde	Threshold II Date	Threshold III Horde	Threshold III Date	Threshold IV Horde	Threshold IV Date
1								
2								
3	{ Cimmerians (? = Pactyes) } +Scythians		Cimmerians +Scythians / Medes v. Scythians	post 610	1. ? Pactyes / 2. Scythians / 3. Cimmerians / Lydians v. Cimmerians	post 700 / prae 700 / post 650	3. Scythians	c. 630
4	Cimmerians +Scythians +Sarmatians		1. Cimmerians +Scythians / Greek colonies / 1. Sarmatians / 2. Budini	post 650	1. Tauri (Thracians) / 2. Getae / 3. Agathyrsi		Odrysae	
5	Scythians							
6								
7	? Arabs	? prae 700						
8	Arabs	prae 700						
9	Nabataeans	post 586						
10								
11	Greeks colonize Cyrene	c. 630						
12	Phoenicians colonize the Maghrib	post 825	? Iberians from Africa					
13								
14								
15								

525–225 B.C.

Vent	Threshold I Horde	Date	Threshold II Horde	Date	Threshold III Horde	Date	Threshold IV Horde	Date
1	Yen v. predecessors of Sienpi	post 400						
2	T'sin v. predecessors of Hiongnu	post 400						
3	Achaemenidae v. Massagetae	prae 525						
4			1. 'Agricultural' Scythians 1. Bastarnae 3. Geloni } v. Nomad Scyths	prae 450 c. 280 prae 450	3. Celts v. Agathyrsi	? prae 300	Celts v. Odrysae	c. 280
5								
6								
7								
8								
9								
10								
11								
12	Carthaginians v. Numidians	prae 400						
13								
14								
15								

III

O

Vent	Threshold I		Threshold II		Threshold III		Threshold IV	
	Horde	Date	Horde	Date	Horde	Date	Horde	Date
				225 B.C.–A.D. 75				
1								
2	Hiongnu / *Han* v. Hiongnu in Kansu	c. 225 B.C. / post 135 B.C.						
3	Sakas (= Massa-getae = Jats) + Yuechi (= Tochari = Doghras)	c. 135 B.C.	Sakas (into Seistan) / *Arsacids* v. Sakas	130 B.C. / post 123 B.C.	1. Sakas / 1. Kushans (Yuechi)	c. 75 B.C. / post 50 A.D.	1. Sakas / 2. Sakas	c. 50 B.C. / c. 100 A.D.
4			1. Sarmatians / 2. ?Sarmatians (Albani) into Azerbaijan	c. 225 B.C. / prae 66 B.C.	1. Scythians / 3. Sarmatians (Iazyges)	c. 200 B.C. / prae 30 B.C.		
5								
6								
7								
8	Arabs	127 B.C.						
9	Arabs	post 100 B.C.						
10								
11	Numidians	post 200 B.C.						
12								
13								
14								
15								

A.D. 75–375

Vent	Threshold I		Threshold II		Threshold III		Threshold IV	
	Horde	*Date*	*Horde*	*Date*	*Horde*	*Date*	*Horde*	*Date*
1	Sien Pi ('Pe Yen')	c. 300						
	⎧ *Posterior Han* expand north-west	post 73						
2	⎨ Hiongnu ('Pe Han')+To Pa ('Wei')	c. 300						
	⎩ *Wei* expand north-west	c. 370						
3								
4			⎧ 1. *Goths* v. Sarmatians	c. 200	2. *Goths*	prae 249		
			⎩ 1. *Goths* on Black Sea	post 250				
5								
6								
7								
8	⎧ *Christianity* converts Osrhoene	prae 200						
	⎩ Palmyrenes	264						
9	*Romans* annex Nabataea	106	⎧ 1. Palmyrenes	prae 270				
	Palmyrenes	post 260	⎩ 2. Palmyrenes	prae 270				
10	Blemmyes	c. 270						
11	Nubians	post 284						
12	⎧ *Romans* advance v. Berbers	1st & 2nd cents.						
	⎩ Berbers	238						
13								
14								
15								

A.D. 375–675

Vent	Threshold I		Threshold II		Threshold III		Threshold IV	
	Horde	Date	Horde	Date	Horde	Date	Horde	Date
1	Khitan							
	{Juan-Juan v. Juan-Juan	post 550						
	{Kao-chang v. Juan-Juan	c. 400						
2	Turks	507						
	T'ang v. Northern Turks	post 546						
	Ephthalites	post 628						
3	Turks	c. 375	Sasanidae v. Ephthalites	c. 425	1. Ephthalites + Gurjaras	455		
	T'ang v. Western Turks	post 563						
		post 656						
4	Huns	c. 372	1. Huns	c. 375	1. *Goths* v. Sarmatians	c. 375	*Slavs*	post 500
	Avars + {(Sevordik) +Khazars / ((Magyars)) +?Pechenegs}	?c. 550	1. *Slavs* v. Huns	post 550	2. Huns	post 500	Cotrigurs (= Huns)	558
			1. Avars	post 550	2. *Slavs*	c. 400	{Bulgars	680
			2. Sevordik Magyars + Khazars	post 550	3. Huns	c. 454		
			3. White Bulgars = Huns	post 550	3. *Gepidae*	c. 454		
			3. Bashkird Magyars	post 550	3. Avars	c. 567		
5	? Turks	?c. 375						
6	? Qipchaq	?c. 550						
	? Yakuts	?c. 550						
7	Arab infiltration	post 375	Arabs	642	Arabs	705	Arabs	710
	Arab invasion	633						
8	Arab infiltration	post 375	{1. Arabs	651	1. Arabs	647		
	Arab invasion	639	{2. Arabs	639				
9	Arab infiltration	post 375						
	Arab invasion	629						
10	*Monophysitism* converts Nubians	post 550						
11	Berbers	post 400						
12	Berbers	post 363						
13								
14	{*Abyssinians* v. Hijaz	c. 570	*Abyssinians* v. Yaman	c. 525				
15	{Arabs	post 632						

A.D. 675–975

Vent	Threshold I — Horde	Date	Threshold II — Horde	Date	Threshold III — Horde	Date	Threshold IV — Horde	Date
1	{ Khitan	696						
	{ Khitan occupy 16 frontier districts	post 927						
	{ W. Turks + N. Turks revolt v. T'ang	681+699						
2	Ilek Khan v. W. Turks + Uighurs v. N. Turks	750+744						
	Manichaeism converts Uighurs	762						
	Sāmānids conquer Talas	893						
3	{ Islam converts Saljūqs + Ilek Khans	956+960						
4	{ Judaism converts Khazars	c. 750	1. Sevordik Magyars on Black Sea	c. 830	3. Charlemagne v. Avars	791		
	{ Ghuzz	c. 889	1. Russians	c. 860	3. Slovaks	post 800		
	{ Russians v. Khazars	966	1. Pechenegs	c. 889	3. Magyars	c. 895		
			3. Islam converts White Bulgars	post 900	2. Pechenegs	c. 895		
5								
6								
7	Carmathians	914						755
8	Banu Hamdan	prae 900					{ Franks conquer Septimania	
9	{ Carmathians	923					{ Franks conquer Catalonia	788
	{ Banu Hamdan	944						
10	Katāma Berbers	969	Katāma Berbers	c. 970				
11								
12	Katāma Berbers	c. 800						
13	Ghāna dominate Tuareg	prae 975						
14								
15								

A.D. 975–1275

Vent	Threshold I		Threshold II			Threshold III		Threshold IV	
	Horde	Date	Kin	Horde	Date	Horde	Date	Horde	Date
1	Kin	post 1114	Kin		post 1125				
2	Mongols	post 1207	Mongols		post 1213	Mongols	post 1258	Mongols	post 1277
3	{ Ilek Khans; Mongols	992; 1219		Saljūqs; Ghuzz; Mongols	1026; 1157; 1221	1. Ghaznawis; 2. Saljūqs; 3. Saljūqs; 2. Mongols	986; 1041; 1037; 1258	1. Ghōris; 2. Saljūqs (Syria); 3. Atabeks (Egypt); 3. Mongols (Syria)	1191; 1071; 1162; 1260
4	{ Qïpchāq = Cumans; Mongols	c. 1050; 1238		1. Ghuzz+Cumans; 1. Mongols; 3. Mongols	c. 1055; 1238; 1237	2. Ghuzz; 3. Pechenegs+Cumans; 3. Cumans+Mongols	prae 1065; 1067; 1241	Pechenegs; Gagauz	1026; 1065
5	Mongols	post 1221							
6	? Buriats	[?post 1200							
7	[Carmathians; Banu Mazyad; Banu 'Uqayl	prae 975]; 1012; 980							
8									
9	[Carmathians; Mirdasids	prae 975]; 1011		2. Banu Hilāl	prae 1046	1. Banu Hilāl; 2. Juhaynah	1052; post 1319		
10	[Katāma Berbers]	969]							
11									
12	Murābits; *Normans* v. Murābits; Muwaḥḥids	post 1068; post 1134; post 1140		Murābits; *Franks* v. Murābits; Muwaḥḥids; *Franks* v. Muwaḥḥids	1086; prae 1144; 1144; 1212				
13	Sanhāja (on Niger); Murābits (on Niger); 'Sayfī' Arabs (on Chad)	c. 1000; post 1054; prae 1100							
14									
15									

A.D. 1275–1575

Vent	Threshold I Horde	Date	Threshold II Horde	Date	Threshold III Horde	Date	Threshold IV Horde	Date
1								
2	*Chinese v. Mongols* Mongol backwash	post 1368 c. 1525	1. *Chinese v. Mongols* 2. *Lamaism* converts Mongols	c. 1355 post 1566	*Chinese v. Mongols*	c. 1351		
3	*Islam* converts Chag-hatays *Timur* v. Nomads Uzbegs	c. 1321 1362 1500	*Islam* converts Il-Khans Uzbegs	1295 1507				
4	*Islam* converts Golden Horde Muscovy conquers Saray	post 1313 1502	1. *Moldavians* 1. *Lithuanians* } v. Nogay Horde 1. *Cossacks on* Dniepr 3. Muscovy conquers Qazan	post 1350 post 1350 post 1350 1552	1. *Genoese* at Caffa 2. *Wallachians* v. Nogay Horde	c. 1275 post 1300		
5	*Islam* converts Sibir *Cossacks* v. Sibir	post 1570 1586						
6								
7								
8								
9					2. *Fung* v. Arabs	c. 1500		
10								
11								
12								
13	*Empire of Malle* Tuareg take Timbuktu *Songhay* v. Tuareg *Moroccans* cross Sahara	post 1313 1434 1469 1590						
14								
15	*Muhammad Gran*	c. 1525						

A.D. 1575–1875

Vent	Threshold I		Threshold II		Threshold III		Threshold IV	
	Horde	Date	Horde	Date	Horde	Date	Horde	Date
1	Manchus v. Inner Mongols	1618	Manchus	1629	Manchus	1645		
	Manchus v. Outer Mongols	1634	2. Calmucks invade Tibet	1642				
	Manchus v. Zungaria	1691	3. Zungar Calmucks	1678				
	Zungar Calmucks	1755	1. Don Cossacks on Black Sea	post 1637				
3	Russians v. Türkmens	1608	1. Russians v. Nogay Tatars	post 1768				
		post 1870	2. Russians conquer Ciscaucasia	post 1552				
4	Torgut Calmucks	1616	2. Torgut Calmucks	1616	1. Russian annexation	1783		
	Russians v. Torguts	1771	2. Russians v. Torguts	1771				
			2. Russians conquer Azerbaijan	post 1800				
5	Zungar Calmucks	c. 1621						
	Russians v. Qāzāqs	post 1730						
6	Manchus v. Qāzāqs	post 1754						
7	Shammar + 'Anazah	post 1650						
	Wahhābis	1801						
8	Northern Shammar	prae 1800						
9	Wahhābis	1805	2. Mehmed 'Ali v. Wahhābis	1810				
10								
11	Sanūsiyah	post 1850			2. Islam converts Wadai	1612		
12					2. Wadai v. Tujjār Arabs	1612		
13	Tuareg (Niger)	post 1770						
	Fulbe (Niger)	post 1802						
	Awlād Sulaymān (Chad)	? post 1750						
	Sanūsiyah (Wadai)	post 1850						
14								
15	Galla (v. Abyssinia)	post 1575						

A.D. 1875–2175

Vent	Threshold I			Threshold II		Threshold III		Threshold IV	
	Horde	*Date*		*Horde*	*Date*	*Horde*	*Date*	*Horde*	*Date*
1	*Chinese* colonization	post 1911							
2	*Chinese* colonization	post 1911							
3									
4									
5									
6									
7	Wahhābīs	1922							
8	Refugee Shammar	1921							
9	Wahhābīs	1924							
10	{ Baqqara Arabs (Mahdists)	1883							
	{ *British* conquer E. Sudan	1898							
11	*Italians* v. Sanûsîyah	1930							
12	*French* conquer Sahara	post 1900							
13	*French* conquer Wadai	1901							
14	Wahhābīs	post 1926							
15									

The Vents from the Steppes	I	II	III	IV
A. Eurasian Steppe			*Successive Thresholds*	
1. Between Korea and Khingan	Liaotung Pale	Shanhaikwan	Hwangho-Yangtse Watershed	
2. Between Khingan and Tien Shan	Great Wall	1. Eastern Plain 2. Tibet 3. Tarim Basin	Hwangho-Yangtse Watershed	Tongking+Burma
3. Between Pamirs and Caspian	Jaxartes	Iran	1. Panjab+Thar 2. 'Iráq 3. Anatolia	1. Ganges Basin 2. Maharashtra 3. Syria+Egypt
4. Between Caspian and Urals	Emba	1. Volga and Don 2. Lower Volga 3. Kama	1. Crimea 2. Lower Danube 3. Hungary	Thrace+Thessaly
5. Between Urals and Altai	West-Siberian Steppe			
6. Between Altai and Khingan	Baikal Basin			
B. Afrasian Steppe				
7. Lower Euphrates Front	'Iráq			
8. Upper Euphrates Front	Jazirah	Iran	Oxus-Jaxartes Basin	
9. Syrian Front	Syria	1. Anatolia 2. Egypt 3. Syria	1. Magrib 2. Eastern Sudan	Andalusia
10. Nile Front (from the Libyan side)	Egypt+Nubia			
11. Cyrenaica Front	Cyrenaica	Andalusia		
12. Maghrib Front	Maghrib			
13. Sudan Front	Western Sudan			
14. Yaman Front	Yaman	Abyssinia		
15. East Africa Front	Somaliland			

This table is an attempt to display the eruptions of the Nomads and the encroachments of the sedentary peoples on a synoptic view; and, though the presentation is imperfect, it enables us to make certain general observations which may throw some light upon the causes to which these movements are to be ascribed.

One easy observation is that the Nomadic way of life is not the monopoly, nor even the special perquisite, of particular 'races' or particular linguistic groups. On the Afrasian Steppe, there have been both Semitic-speaking and Hamitic-speaking Nomads ranging side by side throughout the ages that are covered by our records; and in spite of the encroachments of the Arab Badu upon the Berber Nomads' domain from the eleventh century of the Christian Era onwards, both these linguistic families are still represented among the Afrasian Nomads at the present day. The Eurasian Steppe has witnessed more drastic vicissitudes in racial and linguistic fortunes.

At the present day, for example, the Indo-European-speaking peoples are no longer represented among the Eurasian Nomads at all—unless we count the Ossetian survivors of the Iranian-speaking Sarmatians who have been driven right out of the Ciscaucasian Steppe on to the northern slopes of the Caucasus Range and have been transformed, in effect, from Nomads into mountaineers. Yet, as far as we can see, the Indo-European-speaking Nomads had the Eurasian Steppe to themselves from the third millennium B.C. to the third century B.C. The earliest Eurasian Nomad neighbours of the Sinic and Sumeric worlds alike appear to have been Indo-European-speakers; it is not until the third century B.C. that the Turkish-speaking Hiongnu Nomads become prominent; and, even then, their predominance is limited at first to the hinterland of the second sector of the Eurasian frontiers, between the Khingan Range and the Tien Shan. Thereafter, in successive eruptions, these Turkish-speaking Nomads gain more and more ground in Eurasia at the Indo-European-speaking Nomads' expense, until at last, at the turn of the fourth and fifth centuries of the Christian Era, the Huns, who are the Turkish-speaking Nomads' westward advance guard, drive the Sarmatian rear-guard of their Indo-European-speaking predecessors right out of their last asylum in the great western bay of steppe-country between the Emba and the Carpathians—to lose their identity as they tumble pell-mell upon the western provinces of the Roman Empire in the company of the Goths and the Vandals.[1] From the fifth century of the Christian

---

[1] The absorption of a few scattered drops of this Sarmatian flood into the soil of Gaul is commemorated in the place-name Sermaises or Sermaizes, which survives down to this day here and there in France.

Era to the twelfth, the Turkish-speaking peoples had the Eurasian Steppe almost as much to themselves as their Indo-European-speaking predecessors had had it before the rise of the Hiongnu in the third century B.C. But in the thirteenth century of the Christian Era the tremendous eruption of the Mongol-speaking Tatars—in the very region which had witnessed the emergence of the Turkish-speaking Hiongnu some fourteen or fifteen centuries earlier—marked the first stage in the eviction of the Turkish-speaking peoples from the Steppes in their turn, as the Turkish-speaking peoples had formerly evicted their Indo-European-speaking predecessors. The process which was begun by the Mongol-speaking Tatars in the thirteenth century was carried farther by the Mongol-speaking Calmucks in the seventeenth century. For while the Tatars had been content, for the most part, to conquer their Turkish-speaking neighbours without displacing them, the Calmucks, who migrated en masse,[1] were in process of absorbing the western as well as the eastern half of the Eurasian Steppe into a Mongol-speaking domain extending from the Eastern Gobi to the Don and from the Kuku Nor to the Obi, when the process was cut short in the third quarter of the eighteenth century by the simultaneous intervention of two sedentary Powers: the Muscovite and the Manchu Empires. But for the crushing blows which were dealt, at that stage, to the expanding Calmuck Power on the Steppe by these two great external forces, the Calmuck expansion would doubtless have continued; and then the Turkish-speaking Qāzāqs, who still range to-day over the Dasht-i-Qipchāq from the Altai to the Caspian, would have suffered, in the eighteenth century, the fate which was inflicted upon the Iranian-speaking Sarmatians in the fourth century by the Qāzāqs' Hunnish predecessors and kinsmen.

Thus, within the centuries covered by our record, the supremacy on the Eurasian Steppe has passed successively from Indo-European-speaking to Turkish-speaking and from Turkish-speaking to Mongol-speaking hordes; and these are not the only linguistic families whose representatives have successfully taken up the Eurasian Nomad way of life. On several occasions in history, the Tungus-speaking reindeer-Nomads from the sub-arctic Tundras or Tungus-speaking hunters from the Siberian and Manchurian forests have acquired the art of horse-and-cattle Nomadism on the Eastern Gobi, between the Khingan Range and Korea, and have made their mark in history by erupting—under the successive names of Sien Pi and Khitan and Kin—across the Liao Pale and

[1] For this contrast between the Mongol movement in the thirteenth century and the Calmuck movement in the seventeenth century, see p. 397, above.

through the Shanhaikwan into China.[1] Even the Ugrian-speaking peoples, who are hunters and forest-dwellers *par excellence*, have been represented in the history of the Eurasian Nomadism by the famous horde of the Magyars, as is testified by the close affinity between the present national language of Hungary and the dialects of the West-Siberian Voguls and Ostyaks.

More important, for our present purpose, than the linguistic and racial variety of the Nomads are the synchronisms, which our table brings to light, between their eruptions out of the Desert into the Sown on different fronts.

The most striking of these synchronisms are those which cover both the Eurasian and the Afrasian Steppe at once. For example, *circa* 700 B.C., when the Cimmerians and the Scythians had arrived at the third successive 'threshold' in the course of their eruption through the passage between the Pamirs and the Caspian, the Arabs, erupting out of the Arabian portion of the Afrasian Steppe, were likewise pressing upon the Upper Euphrates from the opposite direction. Again, at the turn of the fourth and fifth centuries of the Christian Era, when the Juan Juan were breaking upon China between the Khingan and the Tien Shan and the Huns were erupting simultaneously between the Pamirs and the Caspian and between the Caspian and the Urals, the Arabs were once again pressing upon the Euphrates and upon Syria and the Berbers were invading the Roman dominions in Cyrenaica and North-West Africa. Similarly, in the middle of the eleventh century of the Christian Era, when the Saljūqs were erupting between the Pamirs and the Caspian, and the Cumans between the Caspian and the Urals, the Banu Hilāl were breaking out of Arabia across Syria and Egypt into the Maghrib, and the Murābits were breaking out of the Western Sahara into the Sudan in one direction and into Morocco and Andalusia in the other. Finally, round about the middle of the seventeenth century of the Christian Era, when the Calmucks were flooding over their Mongol kinsmen's ranges towards the east and over the alien Qāzāqs' ranges towards the west, the Shammar and the 'Anazah were breaking out of Arabia and were crossing the Upper Euphrates into the Jazīrah.

There are other synchronisms which also catch the eye, though the movements here concerned are confined to the one or the other of the two great areas.

For example, on the Afrasian Steppe, the fourteenth, thirteenth, and twelfth centuries B.C. saw the Libyans pressing upon the west

---

[1] The most famous Tungus-speaking invaders of China hitherto have been, of course, the Manchus; but the Imperial Manchus passed straight out of a primitive hunting economy into the influence of the Far Eastern Civilization—leaving the Nomadic way of life to be adopted by their poor relations, the Solons, from their neighbours the Mongols.

bank of the Nile out of the Libyan Desert and the Aramaeans
breaking out of the North Arabian Steppe into Syria. Again, at the
beginning of the nineteenth century of the Christian Era, when the
Wahhābīs were attempting to break out of the North Arabian
Steppe into Syria and 'Irāq, the Fulbe were breaking over the
Western Sudan out of the Western Sahara.

On the Eurasian Steppe, at the turn of the third and second
centuries B.C., when, at one extremity, the Hiongnu were pressing
upon China between the Khingan and the Tien Shan, at the other
extremity the Sarmatians (Roxalani and Iazyges) were crossing the
Don and occupying the western bay of the Steppe up to the eástern
foot of the Carpathians. Again, about the middle of the sixth
century of the Christian Era, when the [pseudo-] Avars—with the
Khazars at their heels—were sweeping out of the heart of the
Steppe across the Emba and the Volga and the Don and the Carpathians into the Hungarian Alföld, the Khitan were pressing upon
China between the Khingan Range and Korea. Finally, in the first
half of the thirteenth century, the Tatars or Mongols erupted out
of the Eurasian Steppe on almost every front simultaneously: between Khingan and Tien Shan, between Pamirs and Caspian,
between Caspian and Urals, between Urals and Altai. Conversely,
round about the middle of the fourteenth century, there were
simultaneous encroachments upon the epigoni of Chingis Khan on
the part of almost all the sedentary peoples round about. In the
Far East, the founder of the Ming Dynasty overthrew the Yuen
Dynasty and expelled its Mongol henchmen out of China into the
Steppes, on the northern side of the Great Wall, out of which they
had issued a century and a half before.[1] In the Oxus-Jaxartes
Basin, Timur Lenk simultaneously established the ascendancy of
the oasis-dwellers over the hordes of Chaghatāy and Jūjī.[2] And, in
the great western bay of the Steppe, the Nomads' cattle-ranges
were simultaneously reclaimed for the plough by the Rumanian
highlanders who descended out of Transylvania into the plains at
the foot of the Carpathians which they converted into Wallachia
and Moldavia; and by the Lithuanians who broke out of the North
European forest between the Bug and the Dniepr and pushed their
way right down to the Black Sea coast;[3] and by the Cossacks who
ensconced themselves on an island in the River Dniepr itself.[4]
There was a corresponding synchronism in the middle of the
eighth century of the Christian Era when the Nomadism of the
Khazar Power on the Volga and the Nomadism of the Uighur

[1] See II. D (v), vol. ii, pp. 121–2, above.
[2] See II. D (v), vol. ii, pp. 144–50, above.
[3] See II. D (v), vol. ii, p. 172, above.
[4] See II. D (v), vol. ii, pp. 154–7, above.

Power in Zungaria were conquered simultaneously—not by alien ploughs but by alien faiths.[1]

Having observed these synchronisms both in the eruptions of the Nomads out of the Desert into the Sown and in the encroachments of their sedentary neighbours from the Sown upon the Desert, we are now in a position to observe that the eruptions and the encroachments are apt to alternate with one another.

This observation is easiest to make in the outlying enclaves of the Steppe and in its tapering gulfs.

For example, in the Hungarian Alföld, when the curtain rises upon its history at the moment of Darius's expedition against the Scythians towards the close of the sixth century B.C., we find in occupation a Nomad horde: the Agathyrsi.[2] About the fourth century B.C., the Agathyrsi are superseded on the Alföld by Celts who have pushed their way down the valley of the Danube out of the Central European forests. Before the end of the last century B.C., however, the Βοίων ἐρημία[3] is once more occupied by Nomads —this time by the Sarmatian Iazyges, who have made their way, since Darius's day, from the east bank of the Don to the western side of the Carpathians. Thereafter, the Romans succeed in cooping the Iazyges up into the quadrilateral between the Danube and the Theiss, until, about A.D. 400, the Alföld is recovered for Nomadism by the horde of Huns that produces Attila. After the evaporation of Attila's power, the Alföld is occupied for a century by a fresh band of sedentary North European barbarians: the Gepidae. In A.D. 567 the Gepidae are destroyed and replaced by the Nomad [pseudo-]Avars. In A.D. 791 the Avars, in their turn, are crushed by Charlemagne, and the Alföld is again occupied by sedentary North European barbarians: the Slovaks. In A.D. 895 it

[1] The Khazars were converted at this time to Judaism and the Uighurs to Manichaeism.

[2] It is assumed here that the Agathyrsi were Nomads, and that they were a fraction of the same horde as the Odrysae who were the contemporary masters of the Maritsa Basin. (The names are very close to one another if we may suppose that the δ in 'Odrysae' is the Macedonian δ for θ and that the Ag- in 'Agathyrsi' is a distinguishing prefix.) On the strength of Herodotus iv. 48, where the River Maros is said to rise among the Agathyrsi, it is sometimes suggested that the Agathyrsi were a sedentary people inhabiting Transylvania; but this does not necessarily follow, since Transylvania has often been under the rule of Nomads whose own home has been on the Alföld. For example, at any time during the last 1,000 years, it would have been a natural thing to say that the Maros rises 'in the country of the Magyars'. In their European settlements, the Agathyrsi in the Alföld and the Odrysae in the Maritsa Basin were separated from one another by the Getae, who ranged over the plains of the Lower Danube Basin between the Carpathians and the Haemus (i.e. the European Balkan). Further eastward, in the mouth of the great western bay of the Eurasian Steppe, between the Volga and the Emba, there was a contemporary horde called the Thyssagetae, whose name may possibly record a coalescence of one branch of the Getae with one branch of the Athyrsi or Odrysae into a single people.

[3] Strabo, p. 292. The country was desolate in Strabo's time because the Boii had been exterminated by Boerebistas, the Dacian prince of Transylvania (Strabo, pp. 213, 304, 313). In creating this vacuum on the Alföld, the Dacians were unintentionally preparing the ground for the Iazyges, as, some six centuries later, the Lombards exterminated the Gepidae for the benefit of the Avars.

is won back for Nomadism, once more, by the irruption of the
Magyars. At the beginning of the eleventh century, the Magyars
are converted to Western Christianity and are incorporated into
the body social of the Western Society; but in A.D. 1241 this work
of conversion and civilization is almost undone when the Alföld is
half swamped by the pagan Nomad Cumans who burst in from
the east, on the track of the Magyars, with the Mongols at their
heels. It is only after the sudden ebb of the Mongol tide in the
same year that the Cuman refugees on the Alföld are gradually
converted and assimilated, like the Magyars before them. Therewith, the sedentary civilization of the West prevails in the Alföld
over the Eurasian Nomadism. Yet, in this year 1935, it would be
rash to assert too confidently that the Hungarian Alföld will never
be the home of a Nomad horde again.

We can observe a still longer series of alternations in the adjacent
bay of the Eurasian Steppe between the eastern foot of the Carpathians and the west bank of the Don.

In this field, when the curtain rises in the sixth century B.C.,
we find the Nomad Scythians in possession; but their domain is
already being nibbled away simultaneously by interlopers from two
sides: from the sea side by the Greek commercial establishments
that have been planted along the north coast of the Black Sea, and
from the interior by 'the agricultural Scythians' whose presence
and activity on the Black Earth Belt has been tolerated by their
Nomad masters, 'the Royal Scythians', in order that they may pay
in exports of grain for imports of Hellenic luxuries. Soon after
the turn of the fourth and third centuries B.C., the Nomad Scythians
are supplanted altogether in their westernmost ranges by a band
of North European barbarians the (German?) Bastarnae, as the
Scythians' neighbours and fellow Nomads, the Agathyrsi in the
Alföld, had been supplanted in the fourth century by the Celts.
Before the end of the third century, however, the north-to-south
movement of the Bastarnae down the valley of the Dniestr is
countered by a fresh east-to-west movement of Nomads: this time,
the Sarmatians from the east bank of the Don. In the third century
of the Christian Era, the westernmost of these Sarmatians, the
Roxalani, are effaced in their turn by another band of North
European barbarians, the Goths, who migrate, down the valley
of the Dniepr, from the seaboard of the Baltic to the seaboard of
the Black Sea. About A.D. 375, the Goths are blown right off the
Steppes into the heart of Europe by the explosive irruption of
the Huns from the far side of the Volga; but the Huns recede,
and in the sixth century of the Christian Era the western end of
the Don-to-Carpathians Steppe is occupied by fresh North Euro-

pean barbarians, the Slavs, who drift southward on the track of
the Bastarnae and the Goths. This drift is so strong that it silts
up into Wallachia, passes the Danube, and fills the depopulated
interior of the Balkan Peninsula with a Slavonic population right
down to the Morea.[1] But in the middle of the sixth century this
Slav drift is cut short by the irruption of the Nomad [pseudo-]
Avars; and at the close of the seventh century the Nomad Bulgars,
whom the Avars have cut through and left still in being in their
wake, cross over from the north to the south bank of the Danube
and impose their rule upon the Slav vanguard in the Balkan Peninsula. In the middle of the ninth century a fresh band of North
European barbarians, the Scandinavian Varangians or Russians,
make their way down the Dniepr, in the track of the Goths, from
the Baltic to the Black Sea. Between A.D. 889 and A.D. 895, the
Russians' track is crossed by the Magyar Nomads, who are driven
westward, by the Pechenegs at their back, first across the Dniepr
and then across the Carpathians into the Alföld. In the tenth
century, the Russians return again. About A.D. 966, they exterminate the Khazars at the mouths of the Don and the Volga; and
Svyatoslav's ensuing invasion of the Bulgarian and East Roman
dominions, on the south side of the Danube, in A.D. 967–72, has
its counterpart in the contemporary maritime raids against the
Caspian provinces of the 'Abbasid Caliphate.[2] But in the middle
of the eleventh century the Russians are cut off, once more, from
the Caspian and the Black Sea and the Balkans by the irruption,
from the far side of the Volga, of the Nomad Ghuzz followed up
by the Nomad Cumans or Qipchāq; and in the middle of the
thirteenth century this Nomad counterstroke is repeated, with
vastly greater force, by the irruption of the Mongols, who establish
their suzerainty over Russia itself. But the Mongol flood-tide ebbs
almost as swiftly as it has flowed. Before the thirteenth century
is over, the Venetian and Genoese mariners are establishing their

---

[1] If Morea is not the Greek word for mulberry-leaf but is really a Slavonic word
meaning 'sea-country' (like the names of the present German province of Po-*mer*ania on
the Baltic and the present Russian province of Po-*mor*skaya on the Sea of Japan), then the
word Morea is a living record of the Slavonic occupation of the peninsula which is more
famous under its previous name of the Peloponnese. Some of the Moreot Slav communities retained their identity down to the French conquest of the Morea in the thirteenth century; and the present place-names testify to their former ubiquity. At the
present day, the language introduced into the Balkan Peninsula by these Slav immigrants via Moldavia and Wallachia in the sixth century survives as the Slavonic language
which is now called Bulgarian (though the original Bulgars were Turkish-speaking
Nomads from the Steppe by whom the Balkan Slavs were conquered at the close of the
seventh century). The other living Slavonic language in South-Eastern Europe, which
is known as Serbo-Croat, was introduced by a different swarm of Slavs—the Serbs (or
Sorabians) and the Croats (or Chrobatians)—whose right wings replaced the previous
German occupants of Galicia and Silesia and Lusatia, while the left wings of the same
two Slav peoples made their way through the Moravian Gap and pushed across the
Alföld, or worked their way round the western rim of the Alföld, till they reached the
Adriatic.   [2] See II. D (vii), Annex VI, vol. ii, p. 438, above.

trading-posts along the same coast on which the Ancient Greek mariners had established themselves some eighteen or nineteen centuries back, in the age when the same steppe was occupied by the Scythians. And, in the middle of the fourteenth century, the pasture-lands of the Nomads in this quarter are nibbled away, along their inland border, by the encroachments of the Wallachians and Moldavians and Lithuanians and Cossacks. In the sixteenth century the Muscovites deal the Nomads a still heavier blow by conquering from the epigoni of the Mongols those points of vantage on the Volga which had been conquered by the Varangian Russians, six hundred years before, from the epigoni of the Khazars. In the seventeenth century, the Don Cossacks emulate the Varangians of the ninth century and the Goths of the third century by launching their piratical craft upon the waters of the Black Sea. But at this moment history makes a motion to repeat itself yet again; for in the seventeenth century the newly established Muscovite frontier along the Lower Volga is broken by the irruption of a fresh horde of Nomads from the east, the Torgut Calmucks. It is only in A.D. 1771, when the Calmuck tide ebbs back across the Volga and right back across the Kazak Steppes,[1] that the ascendancy of the sedentary life over Nomadism in the western gulf of the Eurasian Steppe is asserted decisively; and even to-day it would be rash to declare that the last chapter in this chequered story had now unfolded itself.[2]

Thus, in the Hungarian enclave and in the Ukrainian gulf of the great Eurasian Steppe, we have two recorded series of alternate advances and retreats in a secular conflict between the Eurasian Nomads on the one hand and the sedentary peoples of Central and Northern Europe on the other. In the Ukrainian series, the alternations are: Scythians, *Bastarnae*, Sarmatians, *Goths*, Huns, *Slavs*, Bulgars, *Russians*, Pechenegs, *Russians*, Cumans+Mongols, *Wallachians+Moldavians+Lithuanians+Cossacks+Muscovites*, Calmucks, *Muscovites*. In the Hungarian series, the alternations are: Agathyrsi, *Celts*, Iazyges, *Romans*, Huns, *Gepidae*, Avars, *Franks +Slovaks*, Magyars, *Conversion of the Magyars*, Cumans+Mongols, *Recession of the Mongols and Conversion of the Cumans*.

If we take a comparative view of the histories of the Scythians and the Khazars and the Golden Horde of the Mongols on the western bay of the Eurasian Steppe, we can draw something like a typical pic-

---

[1] See Thomas de Quincey's *Revolt of the Tartars: or, Flight of the Calmuck Khan and his People from the Russian Territories to the Frontiers of China* (reprinted in the *Collected Writings of Thomas de Quincey*, edited by David Masson, vol. vii (London 1897, Black), pp. 368–421).

[2] Even after the Calmuck recession of A.D. 1771, the Calmuck flood of the seventeenth century has left its mark in the isolated pool of Calmuck Nomads that still lies between the lower courses of the Volga and the Don.

ture of the history of a Nomad horde which happens to be carried away in one of the eruptive movements that we are now studying.

In the first chapter of the story, the horde erupts out of the heart of the Steppe into the debatable borderland, in the bay, from which these incoming Nomads evict a previously-settled sedentary population. In this chapter, the Nomadism of the Desert gains ground at the expense of the sedentary culture of the Sown; but in the second chapter a reaction declares itself; for, as the Steppe simmers down from effervescence into quiescence, the new Nomad occupants, who have arrived as unmitigated Nomads from the far interior of Eurasia, become more and more affected and diluted by sedentary influences. The Royal Scythians allow the Greek maritime traders, and the Golden Horde allows the Italian maritime traders, to establish themselves on the north coast of the Black Sea; and, simultaneously, the agricultural peoples of Central and Northern Europe, who have been driven temporarily right off the field by the first impact of the Nomad new-comers in the first chapter of the story, begin to recover their ground either as tolerated and exploited subjects of the Nomad lords of the Steppe (the relation of 'the Agricultural Scythians' to 'the Royal Scythians' in the fifth century B.C. and of the Slav peoples in the Dniepr Basin to the Khazars in the ninth century of the Christian Era) or else as their conquerors (the relation of the Wallachians and Moldavians and Lithuanians and Dniepr Cossacks to the western outposts of the Golden Horde). In either situation, the economic outcome is the same. The grain of the Black Earth Belt and the furs of the northern forests come to be exchanged for the sea-borne luxuries of the Levant, and in this trade the Nomad masters of the Steppe sink into the position of parasites who take their toll, as far as their force avails, without contributing any positive economic service. In the third and last chapter, the parasitism of the Nomads eliminates itself. The Nomads succumb to the charms of the civilizations of the South. The Scythian prince Scyles 'goes Hellene';[1] the Khaqan of the Khazars is converted to Judaism, and the Khan of the Golden Horde to Islam. This penchant towards the sedentary life and culture, which declares itself first among the

---

[1] For the Philhellenism of Scyles, see Herodotus, Bk. IV, chs. 78–80; and compare the attraction which was exerted upon the Calmucks, in the same region, by the Russian variety of the Orthodox Christian Civilization in the eighteenth century of the Christian Era, as described by Courant in op. cit., on pp. 132–3. Compare, in particular, the foundation, in A.D. 1737, of the town of Stavropol for the Calmuck converts from Lamaistic Mahayanian Buddhism to Orthodox Christianity. The privilege of residence within the urban precincts of Stavropol was confined to the notables, while the rank-and-file continued to live in the surrounding open country. This is a precise parallel to the relation between Scyles and his tribesmen when Scyles was leading his double life as a Scythian chieftain and a citizen of the Hellenic city-state of Borysthenes—except that Scyles had to apostatize *sub rosa* because, in the fifth century B.C., Nomadism was politically dominant in the western bay of the Steppe and Urbanism was only there on sufferance.

notables, is violently, though unsuccessfully, resisted by the rank
and file; and, in the event, the antipathy of the irreconcilables is
justified; for the converted Nomad fails to hold the ground which
his unconverted forbears had won for him in their original eruption. In the grand finale of the third and last chapter of the story,
the epigoni of the Nomad intruders, having been demoralized by
the cultural influences of the sedentary South, are overwhelmed
by a fresh descent of the sedentary Northern barbarians. The
Scythians are partially disinherited by the Bastarnae, the Khazars
are annihilated by the Varangians; the Golden Horde are annihilated by the Muscovites. And, therewith, the debatable territory
passes back out of Nomad hands into sedentary hands, until a fresh
irruption of another Nomad horde out of the heart of the Steppe
starts a repetition of this social cycle.

If we now view these alternations in connexion with the synchronisms which we have noticed above, we shall perceive that
our table of Nomad eruptions is beginning to reveal a regular pattern of movements which are periodical in Time and uniform in
Space over the whole extent of the Steppes from the Atlantic coast
of the Sahara to the Great Wall of China. In order to make this
pattern clearer to the reader's eye, the eruptions recorded in the
table have been grouped in periods of three hundred years each;
and the reader will see at a glance that the alternating movement
which we have brought to his attention above in two local fields
reappears in the picture of the entire field when the eruptions are
grouped in these three-hundred-year periods. The overwhelming
majority of the recorded eruptions fall within the periods 2025–
1725 B.C., 1425–1125 B.C., 825–525 B.C., 225 B.C.–A.D. 75, A.D. 375–
675, A.D. 975–1275, and A.D. 1575–1875. Conversely, the overwhelming majority of the entries in the alternate periods—1725–
1425 B.C., 1125–825 B.C., 525–225 B.C., A.D. 75–375, A.D. 675–975,
and A.D. 1275–1575—are records of movements in the contrary
direction: that is to say, records of encroachments on the Nomads'
domain on the part of the surrounding sedentary peoples and
cultures and religions.

If we concentrate our attention in the first place upon the alternate three-hundred-year periods of effervescence, and look into the
dates more closely, we shall see that, within each of these spans
of three centuries, it is the first century of the three that is the
most vigorously eruptive. The century A.D. 1575–1675 contains
the eruptions of the Zungar and the Torgut Calmucks and the
Shammar and the 'Anazah Arabs; the century A.D. 975–1075 contains the eruptions of the Saljūq and the Cuman Turks and the
Banu Hilāl Arabs and the Murābit Berbers; the century A.D. 375–

475 contains the eruptions of the Juan Juan and the Huns; the
century 225–125 B.C. contains the eruptions of the Hiongnu and
the Yuechi and the Sarmatians; the century 825–725 B.C. contains,
in all probability, the eruption of the Cimmerians and the Scythians
(though our earliest news of the eruption dates from not much
earlier than 700 B.C., with the arrival of the stream of invaders at
the third of the successive 'thresholds' beyond the line of their
original exit from the Eurasian Steppe on the sector between the
Pamirs and the Caspian);[1] the century 1425–1325 B.C. contains
the eruption of the Aramaeans and probably also the eruption of
the Libyans; the century 2025–1925 B.C. contains, in all probability, the eruption of the Aryas who break upon Egypt subsequently, *circa* 1680 B.C., as the Hyksos. This list does not include
all the principal eruptions that are on record. For example, the
eruption of the Primitive Muslim Arabs occurred in the last and
not in the first century of the effervescent period A.D. 375–675; the
eruption of the Mongols in the last and not in the first century of
the effervescent period A.D. 975–1275; the eruption of the Turks
and [pseudo-]Avars in the second and not in the first century of
the effervescent period A.D. 375–675. And these are some of the
most celebrated Nomad eruptions in history. At the same time,
from the statistical standpoint, the concentration of Nomad eruptions into the particular centuries which we have enumerated is
clearly marked; and the reader will have perceived that these centuries of maximum effervescence occur at regular intervals of six
hundred years. On this showing, it looks as though the phenomenon of occasional Nomad eruptions out of the Desert into the Sown
has a rhythm of its own which is as regular, on its own scale, as
the Nomad's annual trek in search of seasonal pasture. While the
movement in search of pasture has a year period, the eruptive
movement appears to have a six-hundred-year period.

[1] Herodotus (Bk. IV, ch. 12) says that the Cimmerians who invaded Anatolia and the
Scythians who invaded Iran both came via the Ciscaucasian Steppe—the Cimmerians
down the east coast of the Black Sea, the Scythians round the south-eastern end of the
Caucasus Range. If these tracks were proven, they would be unique; for *all* other known
Eurasian Nomad invaders of South-Western Asia have erupted out of the Steppe through
the gap between the Caspian and the Pamirs; and though some Nomads (Albanians,
Alans, Huns, Sevordik) have occasionally forced the passage of the Caspian Derbend,
their raids have been ephemeral and their settlements no further afield than Azerbaijan. As a matter of fact, Herodotus's statement is not valid evidence that the Cimmerians and Scythians who burst upon Assyria *circa* 700 B.C. did not take the usual route
south of the Caspian and across the Iranian Plateau; for the context shows that the
statement rests not upon testimony but upon inference. Herodotus finds that in his
own day there are real live Scythians on the western bay of the Steppe, north of the Black
Sea, and that the former presence of Cimmerians in the same region is attested by the
local place-names. He infers that the Cimmerians and Scythians who had harried South-
Western Asia two or three hundred years earlier must have come from this region. This
inference, however, is discredited by the historical analogies, which make it far more
likely that the Cimmerians and Scythians on the Black Sea Steppe and the Cimmerian
and Scythian invaders of South-Western Asia were two parallel streams which had
separated already before their respective passages of the Emba and the Jaxartes.

If the reality of this six-hundred-year cycle of eruption is a fair inference from the facts and dates that are assembled synoptically in our table, it is immediately evident that this cycle cannot be explained as an effect of the pull which is exerted upon the Nomads by their sedentary neighbours; for this would mean that, every six hundred years, a vacuum, inviting a Nomad irruption, simultaneously arises in the social structure of every sedentary society that marches with every sector of the frontiers of the Afrasian and Eurasian steppes, from the Sudan to Western Siberia and from Hungary to Manchuria; and it is manifest that the histories of the sedentary societies display no trace whatever of any such symmetrical periodicity. On the other hand, if we think of explaining our six-hundred-year cycle of Nomad eruption as the effect of a climatic push and not of a human pull, we shall find that our hypothesis is reconcilable with the climatic theories of at least one modern school of climatologists.

This school, whose most eminent representative is Dr. Ellsworth Huntington, believes that there is a periodic shift in the location of the successive climatic zones that encircle the globe latitudinally, so that, in the Northern Hemisphere (with which we are exclusively concerned for present purposes), the arid sub-tropical zone, which lies between the humid tropical zone and the temperate zone, is oscillating all the time, with a regular periodicity, between two extreme geographical positions, in one of which it is nearer to the Equator, while in the other it is nearer to the North Pole. This theory of a periodic shift in the geographical location of the climatic zones has engaged our attention in this Study already, apropos of the geneses of the Mayan and Yucatec civilizations and the floruit of the Syriac Civilization in the oases of the North Arabian Steppe.[1] Let us now consider the bearings of the theory upon our present problem of periodic Nomad eruptions out of the Desert into the Sown.

From our present standpoint, we shall observe that, if and when the arid zone shifts northwards, there will then be an accentuation of its aridity (and, therewith, a diminution in its capacity for supporting life, even on the Nomadic economy) in the parts adjoining the temperate zone. The former southern fringe of the temperate zone will turn into the northern fringe of the Steppe, while the former northern fringe of the Steppe, in which the aridity has previously been at its minimum, will become the region of maximum desiccation. (Simultaneously, of course, the former southern fringe of the Steppe will turn into the northern fringe of the Tropics, while the region in which the aridity has been previously at its

---

[1] See II. D (vii), Annex I, vol. ii, above.

maximum will now be moistened by the northernmost precipitation of the monsoons.) Conversely, if and when the arid zone shifts southwards, there will be a mitigation of its aridity (and, therewith, an increase in its capacity for supporting life, even by means of agriculture in substitution for Nomadism) in the parts adjoining the temperate zone. The recent northern fringe of the Steppe will once more become the southern fringe of the temperate zone, while the northern fringe of the Steppe will fall back southwards into the area which has recently been the region of maximum aridity. (And simultaneously, on the southern border of the arid zone, the Steppe will compensate itself for its losses to the temperate zone in the north by recovering ground at the expense of the tropical forest.)

Now, if the frontiers between the several climatic zones were ideally straight lines, all running precisely parallel to the Equator and to one another, and if the geneses and growths of sedentary societies were just as rife in the tropical zone as they are in the temperate zone, then the social effect of a periodic oscillation in the positions of the climatic zones would be that, during the northward swing of the climatic pendulum, the Nomads would erupt out of the Steppes northwards into the domains of the temperate-zone sedentary societies, while during the southward swing of the pendulum they would erupt into the domains of the tropical-zone sedentary societies, southwards. In other words, the alternating rhythm of the climate would duly translate itself into an alternating rhythm of Nomad eruptions, but this latter rhythm would not be the actual rhythm which we have detected by empirical observation. The direction of the eruptions would alternate, but the phenomenon of eruption itself would be unintermittent, whereas the alternating rhythm of eruption which we have actually observed is not an alternation in direction between northward and southward outbreaks but an alternation in intensity between bouts of relative effervescence and bouts of relative quiescence.

At first sight, it may look as though these empirically observed social facts could not be explained by the theory of oscillating climatic zones after all. But the social facts and the climatic theory fall into harmony with each other as soon as we take account of the disposition of the climatic zones *de facto*. *De facto*, the ideal *a priori* disposition of the climatic zones in precisely parallel bands, all running due east and west, is thrown out entirely, on the real map, by a number of potent disturbing factors, such as the distribution of the land and water surfaces of the globe and the articulation of the land-surface into highlands and lowlands. In the outcome, the arid zone is deflected, on the African and Asiatic

land-surfaces of the Northern Hemisphere, from a west-and-east
to a south-westerly-to-north-easterly direction; and, in consequence of this deflexion, the arid zone, instead of running evenly
between the temperate zone and the tropical zone from side to side
of these two continents, breaks contact altogether with the tropical
zone and burrows its way into the heart of the temperate zone
before it reaches its eastern extremity in Asia.

In the terminology which we are employing in this Study, this
means that the Steppes march with the temperate zone on no less
than twelve, and with the tropical zone on only three, out of the
fifteen sectors into which we have divided the total length of the
frontiers between the Desert and the Sown on the African and
Asiatic land-surfaces of the Northern Hemisphere. The Eurasian
Steppe actually marches with the temperate zone on every front,
and the Afrasian Steppe marches with it on six fronts out of nine.
The three fronts on which the Afrasian Steppe marches with the
tropical zone are the Sudan Front and the Yaman Front and
the East Africa Front, and it is only on rare occasions that, on the
two African fronts in this group of three, the Afrasian Nomadism
has been in contact with a sedentary civilization. Except on the
Yaman front, the Afrasian as well as the Eurasian Nomadism has
been in contact with sedentary civilizations almost exclusively on
the fronts that march with the temperate zone.

The upshot of all these facts taken together is that, if the climatic
zones did really shift to and fro periodically on the 'lay-out' of the
de facto climatic map, then the eruptions of the Nomads out of
their own domain into the domains of the adjoining sedentary
civilizations would occur almost exclusively in times when the shift
of climates was taking place from south to north, and only to a
negligible extent during the contrary shifts from north to south.
In other words, the north-to-south phase of the cycle would translate itself, in the life of the Nomad occupants of the Steppes,
vis-à-vis the sedentary civilizations, into a phase of relative social
quiescence, and the south-to-north phase of the climatic cycle into
a phase of relative social effervescence. Now these are precisely
the alternating phases which we have detected in the life of the
Nomads by empirical observation; and this means that these results
of our empirical social observation do admit of an explanation in
terms of the climatological theory of a periodic oscillation of
climatic zones which Dr. Ellsworth Huntington has built up out
of his study of lake-strands and river-beds and tree-rings.

The way in which the Eurasian and Afrasian Nomad is affected
by the accentuation of the aridity of his physical environment
during a northward shift in the periodic oscillation of the

climatic zones is depicted by Dr. Ellsworth Huntington himself
as follows:

'Under the influence of climatic pulsations, the change from prosperity to adversity is usually much more abrupt than from adversity to
prosperity. . . . In the deserts, the Nomads increase in number, and
their flocks attain great proportions. The crest of a climatic wave is
reached. The settled nations, dwelling in the best agricultural lands,
feel no distress. The change is too slight to trouble them. They proceed
with their plans for expansion and growth. The Nomad, on the contrary, feels the difference at once. At first it does not disturb him
greatly unless the population has attained an uncommon degree of
density. Soon, however, he comes into conflict with his fellow Nomads,
for all move to the best pasturage and most permanent waters. Conditions become similar to those under which the herdsmen of Isaac
strove with those of Abimelech in Gerar after a time of famine. The
weaker party is driven out, and begins to wander in search of new
pastures and springs. Conflict follows conflict. At length the tribes
which have often been driven forth grow desperate. Impelled by despair, they pour forth in wild hordes upon the nations round about.'[1]

The same tension, resulting in the same resolution of forces,
is expressed in mathematical terms in a communication which
the writer has been so fortunate as to receive from an eminent
physicist:

[If we isolate the climatic factor from other factors,] 'the different
effects of a change of climate on an agricultural and on a pastoral community may be realized at a glance.

'Suppose, for instance, that we are considering an agricultural community of n families spread over an area of s square kilometres. Each
family will have an average holding of s/n square kilometres which in
a steady state will be sufficient to support it. Presumably they will take
all steps by irrigation and intensive cultivation to get as much as possible
out of the land, and the families will be regulated, by infanticide or
otherwise, to maintain a steady maximum population per unit area.
Near the periphery, of course, the families will tend to be greater, and
new families will be founded and new land gradually brought under
cultivation. In the interior, however, the population must be kept constant. Now suppose the rainfall increases. The same yield can be
obtained from the land with less work. The course of those families
which live near the edge of the community is simple; they find that
they can cultivate more land with the same effort, so they increase their
holding and expand and multiply. The number of these families whose
farms are bounded by unoccupied territory will be of the order $\pi\sqrt{n}$.
On the other hand, there is no room for the families in the interior to
found fresh farms; so that they must keep their numbers practically

---

[1] Huntington, Ellsworth: *Palestine and its Transformation* (London 1911, Constable),
pp. 400–1.

constant, whatever the climate. Hence an improvement in the climate will only cause an increase of the order $\pi\sqrt{n}$, i.e. a fraction $\pi\sqrt{n}$ of the normal n families.

'The results are very different when we consider the effect of an increased rainfall upon the population in a pastoral community. Here no efforts are made to cultivate the soil, and we have numerous families or tribes dotted about at a considerable distance from one another. Presumably here also the number of members of each tribe will be regulated so that they can just be supported by the produce of the maximum head of cattle which can be grazed on the land available. But there would seem to be an economic limit beyond which it would not pay to go on increasing the size of the flock or—what is proportional to this—the number of any one pastoral family. When the flocks become too large they are cumbrous to handle, a considerable organization becomes necessary, and in a primitive community the tribe will tend to break up into two smaller units.

'It is easy to predict what will happen in a community such as this if the climate changes, e.g. the rainfall increases. The ground will become more fertile and a larger number of animals, and consequently men, can be supported per unit area. Hence each flock will increase—not only those at the periphery, as in the agricultural community—and all the n families will increase. As pointed out above, this will probably result in an increase in the number of families rather than in the numbers of each tribe; but the important point is that a considerable increase will occur in the total number of human occupants of the unit area.

'If we contrast the two instances, we see that the essential difference lies in the rate of change in the population following a change in climate. In the agricultural community of n families, $\pi\sqrt{n}$ families will increase and multiply abnormally fast. In the pastoral community, all the n families or tribes will be augmented. Only the periphery will be affected in the agricultural community; the whole country will be affected in the pastoral community. Hence, if the climate improves, the population of the agricultural region is only increased very slowly, whereas the population of the Steppe increases with scarcely any lag.

'We can easily foresee what will happen if the climate becomes worse and the country less fertile. The agricultural peoples will experience times of famine and die off. They could not help themselves by enlarging their farms, even if there were room; for only those at the periphery can expand without infringing on their neighbours, and anyhow one family can only cultivate a given amount of land. The pastoral people, however, will not be in the same case. Each tribe will realize that it could exist quite well if only the grazing-ground were not in the possession of neighbouring tribes. It will try to oust the neighbouring tribes; and, since the whole Steppe is affected, there will be a simultaneous tendency to overflow into the surrounding territories.'[1]

[1] Communication to the writer from Professor F. A. Lindemann, Dr. Lee's Professor of Experimental Philosophy in the University of Oxford. The following observations, apropos of the hypothetical community of cultivators, are made by Mr. G. F. Hudson:

The ubiquitous effect of the climatic factor upon the whole of the Steppe and upon the whole muster-roll of the Nomad hordes that are in occupation of it is not only postulated *a priori* by the mathematical considerations which are set out in the passage just quoted, but is also demonstrated empirically by the frequency of the phenomenon of eruptions in successive waves, in which the first horde that breaks out of the fringe of the Desert into the fringe of the Sown turns out to be propelled from behind by a second horde, erupting out of the deeper interior of the Steppe and following in rapid succession at the first horde's heels. Thus, in all probability, the Aryas are propelled out of the Steppe by the Iranians, and certainly the Cimmerians by the Scythians, the Sakas by the Yuechi (and the Yuechi themselves by the Hiongnu), the Avars by the Khazars, the Magyars by the Pechenegs, the Ghuzz by the Cumans, the Shammar by the 'Anazah.[1] This phenomenon of a double wave is usually, though not invariably,[2] an indication that the force by which the particular eruption has been set in motion has been at work in the interior of the Steppe and not merely on the periphery; and this in turn points to the force in question being the climatic push of desiccation on the Steppe itself, and not the social pull of a vacuum in the sedentary region into which the particular eruption happens to discharge itself, since this latter force would only affect the Nomad hordes along the border.

Dr. Ellsworth Huntington's theory of a periodic oscillation of climatic zones implies, of course, that the resulting climatic pulsation is not only common to the whole area of the Steppe but is actually world-wide; and in his long-continued and widely extended investigation he has established some remarkable correlations between the findings of his physiographical researches in Asia

'In the marginal belt between arid and high-rainfall country, it surely makes all the difference whether the rainfall is ample or insufficient to raise crops. Thus, in the Middle Volga Black Earth Belt, which is extremely fertile but is liable to famine every now and then owing to the failure of rainfall (e.g. the famine of 1921, which caused peasants to emigrate wherever they could), a few inches more or less makes all the difference between dense population and complete uninhabitability; for, whereas an increase of aridity on the Steppe means that *fewer* Nomads can live on it, a decline of rainfall below the minimum necessary for dry cultivation means that *no* peasants can stay in the area affected (at least, none without relief, bank credits and what not). Professor Lindemann is apparently assuming that the settled land is universally made to give the maximum yield of which it is in any circumstances capable, so that no change of climate except a period of extreme drought can make any difference to it; but this is to make the problem highly abstract and hypothetical. I think he is right in saying that the same climatic change would make a greater increase of Nomads on the Steppe than of peasants in what would normally be a high-rainfall area; but in the marginal belt of fluctuation I think the fluctuations of population are likely to be the most violent of all.'

[1] The phenomenon of the double wave, as illustrated in the propulsion of the Cimmerians by the Scythians in the eruption of 825-725 B.C., made such an impression upon the first Hellenic student of Nomadism, Aristeas of Proconnesus, that he came to regard a chain of pressures as the normal relation between neighbouring Nomad hordes, whereas in reality this is only normal in the abnormal circumstances of an eruption. (For Aristeas' theory, see Herodotus, Bk. IV, ch. 13.)

[2] e.g. not in the case of the Magyars and the Pechenegs (see pp. 441-3, below).

and in North America. The result of this work is summed up graphically in a pair of curves—one derived from measurements of Californian tree-rings and the other from observations of the levels of Western and Central Asiatic lakes and inland seas—which register the respective fluctuations in the climates of these two widely separated regions (on the criterion of relative humidity or aridity) from 1300 B.C. to A.D. 1900.[1] The two curves manifestly correspond in a general way with one another. We have still to see whether they show any correspondence with the six-hundred-year cycle of Nomad explosions which we have surmised from the historical evidence as set out above in our table.

Dr. Huntington himself remarks[2] that his two curves 'have a length of centuries but do not show any regular periodicity'. We may add that the tree-ring curve, which is the better substantiated, is also the more highly irregular of the two. At the same time, Dr. Huntington's pair of physiographical curves do bear out, at a considerable number of points, our own historical six-hundred-year cycle with its alternation of three-hundred-year phases of relative effervescence and relative quiescence and with its maximum of effervescence in the first century of each effervescent tri-centennium. The first low level (denoting an access of aridity) that comes within Dr. Huntington's record falls in the thirteenth century B.C.: that is, a century later than our hypothetical century of maximum effervescence between 1425 and 1325.[3] At the same time, there are climatic low levels at 800 B.C., 200 B.C., and A.D. 400 (on the better substantiated tree-ring curve), which correspond to our ultra-effervescent centuries 825–725 B.C., 225–125 B.C., and A.D. 375–475. On the other hand, A.D. 1000, which falls within our next ultra-effervescent century running from A.D. 975 to A.D. 1075, is marked in both of Dr. Huntington's curves by a humid peak and not by an arid trough; and there is no trough, again, to correspond with our latest ultra-effervescent century, running from A.D. 1575 to A.D. 1675, which saw the simultaneous eruptions of the Zungar and Torgut Calmucks and the Shammar and 'Anazah Arabs. Of the three great eruptions which, on our pattern, are irregular, the Primitive Muslim Arab outbreak in the seventh century of the Christian Era and the Mongol outbreak in the thir-

---

[1] This graph will be found in Dr. Ellsworth Huntington's *The Climatic Factor as illustrated in Arid America* (Washington, D.C. 1914, Carnegie Institution of Washington), p. 172, and also in his *Civilisation and Climate*, 3rd ed. (New Haven 1924, Yale University Press), p. 319.

[2] *The Climatic Factor*, p. 173.

[3] It may be noted that, while the Aramaean eruption certainly, and the Libyan eruption probably, dates from the early part of the fourteenth century B.C., the Libyan eruption, at any rate, was still active in the thirteenth century. The Libyan Nomads invaded Egypt from the west *circa* 1221 B.C. and again, on perhaps two occasions, in the early years of the twelfth century.

teenth century of the Christian Era are both duly signalized, in
Dr. Huntington's pair of curves, by strongly pronounced troughs,
while on the other hand the outbreak of the [pseudo-]Avars and
the Turks in the middle of the sixth century of the Christian Era
is contradicted, in Dr. Huntington's pair of curves, by an Asiatic
maximum of humidity at A.D. 550 and a Californian maximum at
A.D. 610. Conversely, Dr. Huntington's curves show an arid trough
at or before A.D. 1500; and this offers a climatic explanation for the
Uzbeg irruption of that date into Transoxania and the backwash
of the Mongols from Outer into Inner Mongolia about a quarter
of a century later—two events which, on our chart, look like
exceptional disturbances in the middle of a phase of quiescence.

One of the most interesting facts in Dr. Huntington's physiographical evidence is the rapid and exuberant, though transitory,
access of humidity in the early decades of the fourteenth century
of the Christian Era, following upon the extreme access of aridity
by which the early decades of the thirteenth century had been
marked. This unusually violent swing of the climatic pendulum
is apparently well attested. For example, the Caspian rises rapidly
to a maximum in A.D. 1306 which is 37 feet higher than its level
at the present day; and the town of Aboskun, at the south-eastern
corner of the Caspian, is under water in A.D. 1325.[1] And, almost
simultaneously, between the years 1308 and 1311, the Lob Nor,
which receives the waters of the River Tarim, overflows its banks
and overwhelms 'the Dragon Town' (Lungshong).[2] We have
noticed already that the foregoing paroxysm of aridity coincides
in date with the demoniac eruption of the Mongols. And it will
now be seen that the physiographical recoil towards humidity likewise corresponds in date with the rapid ebb of the Mongols on
almost every coast of the Eurasian Steppe in the fourteenth century
of the Christian Era—an ebb which is signalized by the encroachments of the Wallachians and Moldavians and Lithuanians and
Dniepr Cossacks upon the ranges of the Golden Horde, and by
the conversion of the Khans of the Golden Horde and the Il-Khans
in Iran and the Chaghatayid Khans in the Oxus-Jaxartes Basin
and Zungaria to Islam, and by Timur's chastisement of the
Chaghatayids and the Jujids, and by the expulsion of the Great
Khans from China.

If we may fairly regard the increase of humidity at this time as
having been at least one of the causes of these social changes, we
can see two distinct ways in which this climatic cause would
operate. On the one hand, it would strengthen the inclination of

[1] Huntington, E.: *The Pulse of Asia* (London 1907, Constable), p. 344.
[2] Huntington, op. cit., pp. 287-8.

the neighbouring sedentary peoples to encroach upon the fringe of the Steppe at the Nomads' expense if the increase of humidity went so far towards correcting the previous excess of aridity on this fringe as to make the country suitable not only for Nomadic stock-breeding but also for sedentary agriculture. On the other hand, the same climatic change would weaken the resistance offered by the Nomads to their sedentary neighbours' pressure, because it would render the interior of the Steppe capable of supporting a larger stock of cattle, and therefore a larger population of Nomads, than before. The physiographical facts would thus go far towards answering the otherwise mysterious question why the Mongols erupted on all fronts with an unprecedented vehemence in the thirteenth century in order to recede with a bewildering tameness a century later. At the time when they went forth conquering and to conquer as far as Hungary in one direction and as Burma in another, the demons of drought and starvation were spurring the Mongols on. At the time when they abandoned the Ukraine and the Transoxanian oases and China, they knew that their native steppes could offer them an asylum because these steppes were now luxuriant once again with a heaven-sent vegetation.

In the present state of our knowledge, this is perhaps as far as we can carry our study of the part played by the climatic factor in the historically attested human fluctuations along the borders between the Desert and the Sown. We have seen that this climatic factor, in so far as its operation can be discerned, is apparently world-wide in its geographical range and is possibly also rhythmical in the Time-dimension. We have now to consider the human factor in the shape of the sedentary societies living round about the Nomad's domain; and it is evident *a priori* that the local operation of this human factor on one sector of the borderline will be quite independent of its local operation on other sectors, in consequence of the perpetual plurality of the sedentary societies by whose domains the Steppes have been encircled ever since the beginning of recorded history. It is also evident *a priori* that there will be no regular rhythm in the operation of this human factor in the Time-dimension, since we are confronted here with all the individuality and all the complexity of the histories of the sedentary civilizations, in place of the relatively simple and regular physical phenomenon of a periodic oscillation of climatic zones.

Indeed, in the operation of the human factor, any appearance of simultaneity or universality will prove, on inspection, to be the effect of a fortuitous coincidence. A case in point is the impressive synchronism of half a dozen far-flung movements of Nomad eruption round about the year A.D. 900. About A.D. 890, the Katāma

Berbers overrun the dominions of the 'Abbasid Caliphate in Ifriqīyah. In, or just before, A.D. 889, the Ghuzz break in from the
east upon the ranges of the Pechenegs between the Emba and
the Volga, with the result that the Pechenegs cross the Volga
and the Don and propel the Magyars—whom they find in occupation of the steppes west of the Don—right across the Carpathians
into the Hungarian Alföld. Again, some time before A.D. 900, the
Banu Hamdān Arabs make themselves masters of the 'Abbasid
Caliphate's dominions in the Jazīrah. In 914, the Carmathians
make a raid, out of eastern Arabia, upon the home province of the
Caliphate in 'Irāq. And far away, between the Khingan and Korea,
the Khitan trespass across the Pale and the Wall and occupy the
north-eastern fringes of intra-mural China in or after A.D. 927. At
first sight we seem here to be in the presence of a ubiquitous movement which must be explained by some universally operative cause
—presumably of the climatic order. Dr. Huntington's pair of
climatic curves, however, show a humid peak and not an arid
trough at this date; and, if we now look for explanations in the
human sphere, we shall find all that we need in the respective
political histories of the 'Abbasid, the Khazar, the Carolingian,
and the T'ang Empires.

The irruptions of the Katāma and the Banu Hamdān and the
Carmathians can all be traced to the attraction exerted by the social
vacuum which was already being created by the decline of the
'Abbasid Caliphate in the ninth century of the Christian Era—in
anticipation of the Caliphate's final break-up during the post-
Syriac interregnum of A.D. 975–1275. (Incidentally, the Katāma
were not Nomads of the Steppe, but highlanders,[1] and they were
led on their war-path by the Fātimids, who were—or claimed to
be—the 'Abbasids' hereditary rivals; the Banu Hamdān had been
long domiciled in the Jazīrah before they made themselves the
political masters there; and the Carmathians were a militant sect
which had first raised its horn in 'Irāq itself, with its head-quarters
at Wāsit, and had only retreated to Arabia and recruited a following
among the Badu after it had been momentarily suppressed in the
sedentary region which was its earliest field of action.)[2]

As for the successive impacts of the Ghuzz upon the Pechenegs
and the Pechenegs upon the Magyars, this local disturbance of
equilibrium was started by a deliberate but only partially success-

[1] See Gautier, E. F.: Les Siècles Obscurs du Maghreb (Paris 1927, Payot), pp. 314–17.
[2] The unsuccessful insurrections of the Carmathians in 'Irāq and Syria took place
between A.D. 890 and A.D. 906. The East Arabian Province of Hasā, which was the
Carmathians' base of operations in the second and more notorious chapter of their
history, was acquired in A.D. 899 thanks to the conversion of a local Badu horde, the
'Abd-al-Qays, by a Carmathian missionary who had been sent thither from the original
head-quarters of the movement in 'Irāq.

ful stroke of policy on the part of the Khaqan of the Khazars
(an ex-Nomad horde which had long since become a sedentary
commercial power). The Khazar, wishing to rid himself of his
troublesome neighbours the unreclaimed Nomad Pechenegs, who
occupied the steppe within sight of his own capital on the Lower
Volga, made a compact with the still wilder Nomad Ghuzz, who
were ranging at that time on the Pechenegs' opposite (i.e. eastern)
flank, for a simultaneous assault upon the Pechenegs which would
wipe these nuisances out of existence. The Ghuzz fulfilled their
part of the compact. About A.D. 889, they duly assailed the Pechenegs and successfully occupied the Pechenegs' ranges right up to
the east bank of the Volga. But the Pechenegs, instead of passively
allowing themselves to be annihilated, made their way across the
Volga, broke right through the Khazar lines, and seized the ranges
of the Magyars on the farther side of the Don. Driven westward,
the Magyars first responded to an invitation from the East Roman
Government to invade Bulgaria, with which the East Roman Empire was then at war; but this first quest for a new home turned
out unfortunately for the Magyars, since the Bulgars retorted by
calling in their turn upon the Pechenegs. The Magyars were
punished for their attack upon Bulgaria by a combined attack from
the Bulgars and the Pechenegs which resulted in a severe defeat
for the Magyars; and this second disaster, which seems to have
occurred in A.D. 895, might have been the end of the Magyar horde,
if the misfortunes which the Khazar Khaqan's high policy had
incidentally brought upon them had not been retrieved by an incidental consequence of the policy of the long-defunct Austrasian
Emperor Charlemagne. In A.D. 791, Charlemagne had crushed the
Avar Nomads, who had been masters of the Hungarian Alföld
since the middle of the sixth century, and the subsequent rapid
decline of the Carolingian Empire had left the Alföld a no-man's-
land which was now in process of occupation by the sedentary
barbarian Slovaks. For the Magyars, expelled from the western
bay of the Steppe and repulsed from Bulgaria, the line of least
resistance now was to cross the Carpathians and fill the opportune
vacuum in the derelict Alföld. For a horde which had been waging
war with the Pechenegs and the Bulgars, the eviction of the Slovaks
from the Alföld was child's-play; and the Magyar conquest of the
Alföld followed hard upon the Magyar defeat at the hands of
the Pechenegs and the Bulgars.[1] Thus the historic disturbance

---

[1] In the foregoing account of the movements of the Ghuzz, the Pechenegs and the
Magyars in the ninth century of the Christian Era, the writer follows Mr. C. A. Macartney, whose reconstruction of this chapter of history, in the light of an acute analysis of
the evidence, will be found in his *The Magyars in the Ninth Century* (Cambridge 1930,
University Press).

of equilibrium on the western bay of the Eurasian Steppe at the close of the ninth century of the Christian Era—a disturbance which produced a lasting effect upon the history of Western Christendom by giving birth to the Hungarian Kingdom and the Hungarian nation—can be accounted for as the combined effect of two local acts of statesmanship: an act of the Khazar Khaqan at the time, and an act of the Emperor Charlemagne about a hundred years earlier. There is no need here to postulate the operation of any ubiquitous or universal cause.

As for the intrusion of the Khitan into intra-mural China in or after A.D. 927, this can be accounted for likewise as the effect of a local event in the political history of the Far Eastern World: that is to say, the extinction of the T'ang Dynasty in A.D. 907 and the lapse of China into anarchy pending the foundation of the Sung Dynasty in A.D. 960.[1]

It will be seen that it is a sheer fortuitous coincidence, and not the operation of any universal cause, that accounts for the appearance, at the turn of the ninth and tenth centuries, of a general Nomad eruption extending from the Maghrib front to the Manchuria front and from the Lower Euphrates front to the Alföld.

It remains for us to survey, quite briefly, the outstanding instances in which a Nomad eruption out of the Steppe can be traced, at least in part, to the attraction exerted by some kind of social vacuum in the domain of some sedentary society adjacent to the Steppes on one or other of our fifteen sectors of frontier. It may be convenient to cite, separately, first, the instances in which the vacuum coincides in date, either wholly or partly, with one of those alternate 'effervescent' phases in the life of the Steppe which have come to light in our table, and, secondly, the instances in which the vacuum occurs during one of our 'quiescent' phases. On the hypothesis that the series of Nomad eruptions is to be explained in part as the result of a climatic pulsation with a six-hundred-year cycle, we shall be able to explain the first set of instances as combined effects of two convergent causes, the one climatic and the other social, while the second set of instances will suggest possible human causes for a number of eruptions which, *ex hypothesi*, the climatic factor does not account for.

We may begin our catalogue of instances in which the social vacuum partly or wholly coincides with a phase of effervescence on the Steppes by citing the partial overlap of the post-Sumeric social interregnum *circa* 1875–1575 B.C. with the effervescent phase on the Steppes *circa* 2025–1725 B.C. We may suppose that the two causes combined to bring the Aryas down upon South-Western

---

[1] See II. D (v), vol. ii, pp. 120–1, above.

Asia in a spate which carried their van-guard from the Northern
bank of the Lower Jaxartes to the Mediterranean coast of Syria.[1]
We may next observe that, after the arrival of these Aryan Hyksos
at the Syrian extremity of the Sumeric World, they were drawn
on into the Egyptiac World by the social vacuum resulting from
the break-down of the Egyptiac universal state ('the Middle Empire') at the turn of the eighteenth and seventeenth centuries B.C.[2]
Again, the post-Minoan interregnum *circa* 1425–1125 B.C. wholly
coincides with the effervescent phase on the Steppes which we
have defined by the same conventional pair of dates; and this coincidence partially explains how the Achaean sedentary barbarians
from the European hinterland of the Minoan World, who had been
drawn into the vacuum arising from the collapse of the Minoan
'thalassocracy', came to join forces with the Nomad Libyans in the
Delta of the Nile and to compete with the Nomad Aramaeans for
the inheritance of the Egyptian dominion in Syria. To complete
the explanation, we have to bear in mind that the social vacuum
in the Minoan World overlapped chronologically, from about 1375
B.C. onwards, with a fresh social vacuum in the Egyptiac World
arising from the political decay of 'the New Empire' of Egypt.
When all these factors are taken together, it will be seen that, in
the convergent attacks of the Libyans, Aramaeans, and Achaeans
upon 'the New Empire' at the turn of the thirteenth and twelfth
centuries B.C., each of the three assailants was acting under the
combined influence of two distinct forces. The Achaeans were
being drawn off their native continent on to the sea and across the
sea by the attractive force of two successive social vacua: the first
in Crete and the second in Egypt. The Libyans and Aramaeans
were being pulled from in front by the attraction of the same social
vacuum in Egypt, and at the same time they were both being
pushed from behind by the physical force of an access of aridity
on the Afrasian Steppe.

Again, we may observe that the Babylonic 'Time of Troubles'
(*circa* 975–575 B.C.) and the Syriac 'Time of Troubles' (*circa* 925–
525 B.C.) both overlap in time with the phase of effervescence on
the Steppes *circa* 825–525 B.C., so that we have a social as well as
a climatic cause to account for the simultaneous irruption of the
Cimmerians and Scythians out of the Eurasian Steppe and the
Arabs out of the Afrasian Steppe upon Iran and the Jazīrah. In
the same region, the decay of the Seleucid successor-state of the
Achaemenian Empire overlaps with the beginning of the effervescent phase on the Steppes *circa* 225 B.C.–A.D. 75. If the Sakas

---

[1] See I. C (i) (*b*), vol. i, pp. 104–7, above.
[2] See II. D (vii), vol. ii, pp. 388–91, above.

and the Yuechi had been confronted by a united Achaemenian or even by a united Seleucid Empire in 135 B.C., when the pressure of desiccation on the Eurasian Steppe impelled them to try their fortunes across the Jaxartes and the Oxus, they might either have preferred to remain on the Steppe and face the prospect of starvation rather than court certain destruction in a military forlorn hope; or else this certain destruction would have overtaken them if they had embarked upon that desperate venture. It was an auspicious political event in the Nomads' Promised Land—the disruption of the former Achaemenian dominions into the three mutually hostile powers of the Seleucidae, the Arsacidae, and the Greek princes of Bactria—that gave the Eurasian Nomads their opening between the Pamirs and the Caspian in the second century B.C. Still more clearly, it was the death-agonies of the Seleucid Monarchy that gave the Arabs their opening in the Jazīrah and in Syria round about the beginning of the last century B.C.

Similarly, the post-Hellenic interregnum *circa* A.D. 375–675 substantially coincides in date with the phase of effervescence on the Steppes *circa* A.D. 375–675; and thus the attraction of the vacuum arising from the break-up of the Roman Empire combines with the pressure of desiccation on the Steppes to account for the irruption of the Huns into the Alföld at the beginning of the fifth century of the Christian Era; for the irruption of the Avars into the same enclave of steppe-land, commanding the derelict European provinces of the Empire, a hundred and fifty years later; for the infiltration of the Berbers into the African provinces of the Empire and of the Arabs into Syria from the fifth century onwards; and for the tremendous explosion of the Primitive Muslim Arabs in the seventh century. This last shattering explosion struck the Roman and the Sasanian Empire at a moment when these two Powers were both prostrated by the devastating social effects of their two internecine wars of A.D. 572–91 and A.D. 603–28.

Finally, the post-Syriac interregnum *circa* A.D. 975–1275 substantially coincides in date with the phase of effervescence on the Steppes *circa* A.D. 975–1275; and thus the attraction of the vacuum arising from the break-up of the 'Abbasid Caliphate and the Andalusian Umayyad Caliphate combines with the pressure of desiccation on the Steppes to account for the successive irruptions of the Murābits and the Muwahhids into the Maghrib and Andalusia; for the irruption of the Katāma (as followers of the Fātimids) into Egypt and Syria; for the infiltration of Badu from the North Arabian Steppe (Banu 'Uqayl and Banu Mazyad and Mirdasids and the like) into the fringes of the Jazīrah and 'Irāq and Syria; for the more violent outbreak of other Arabian Badu (the Banu Hilāl and

the Banu Sulaym) across Syria and Egypt into the Maghrib; and
for the successive eruptions of the Saljūqs in the eleventh century
of the Christian Era and the Ghuzz in the twelfth and the Mongols
in the thirteenth century out of the Eurasian Steppe into the
adjoining dominions of the ʿAbbasid Caliphate in South-Western
Asia.

An isolated, but particularly conspicuous, case in which there is
not only a hypothetical climatic push but an incontestible political
pull to account for an eruption of Nomads out of the Desert into
the Sown is the aggression of the Berber people who were known
in the Hellenic World as 'the Nomads' *par excellence*[1] against the
continental dominions of the Carthaginian Republic in the second
century B.C. We may observe that this century falls within a phase
of effervescence on the Steppe, *circa* 225 B.C.–A.D. 75, which also
saw the infiltration of the Sarmatians into the Hungarian Alföld
and the irruption of the Sakas into India. But it is a more pertinent observation that the second century B.C. opened immediately
after the close of the Hannibalic War, in which Rome had dealt
Carthage a knock-out blow, and that a little more than half-way
through the century the destruction of the vanquished party was
consummated in a war of annihilation, in which the Carthaginian
Republic and the city of Carthage itself were literally blotted
out. In seeking to account for the aggression of the Numidians
against the Carthaginian dominions in these circumstances, we may
allow the climatic factor whatever credit we will; but it is manifest
that the governing factor here was not climatic but political. The
governing factor was the persistent and undisguised incitement
and encouragement and support which the Numidian aggressors
received from the Romans, who had found in these African Nomads
a convenient instrument for breaking the spirit and wearing down
the strength of Carthage in preparation for the Roman *coup de
grâce*.

Turning now to those eruptions of Nomads which cannot be
traced *ex hypothesi* to the pressure of a climatic push, we need not
revert to the half-dozen instances, dating from round about the
turn of the ninth and tenth centuries of the Christian Era, which
we have examined already and have succeeded in explaining in
political terms.[2] We have merely to complete the list. We may
observe, for example, that the continuing decadence of the Egyptiac
Society accounts for the continuing infiltration of Libyans into
Egypt after the close of the phase of effervescence on the Steppes
which began about 1425 and ended about 1125 B.C. Similarly, we

---

[1] The Berber Νομάδες (latinized as 'Numidae') in the Saharan hinterland of Ifrīqiyah.
[2] See pp. 440–3, above.

may observe that the decadence in which Babylonia languished after the petering out of the Kassite régime accounts for the infiltration of the Chaldaeans—a process which seems to have begun later and lasted longer than the irruption of the Chaldaeans' kinsmen and contemporaries the Aramaeans into the Jazīrah and Syria. Again, the incursions of the Blemmyes and Nubians into Egypt and of the Berbers into the Roman provinces in North-West Africa, and the conquest of all the eastern provinces of the Empire by the Palmyrenes at the head of their Badawī clients—a set of irruptions out of the Desert into the Sown which all occurred more or less simultaneously round about the year A.D. 270—can all be accounted for satisfactorily as consequences of the bout of anarchy from which the Roman Empire was suffering at the time. There is no need to postulate a climatic cause for these inroads of Nomads from the Steppe, any more than for the contemporary inroads of the Franks from the North European forest (where an access of aridity, if it had actually occurred at the time, would certainly not have impelled these sedentary barbarians to invade the Roman Empire but would rather have made life more comfortable for them in their sylvan homes). Similarly, the invasion of intra-mural China, round about the year 300 of the Christian Era, by the Eurasian Nomad hordes who founded the barbarian principalities of Pe Yen and Pe Han and Wei on Sinic ground, can be accounted for satisfactorily as a consequence of the anarchy into which the Sinic Society fell in its last agonies, upon the failure of the indigenous successor-state of the 'second' or 'united' Tsin to restore the structure of the Sinic universal state of Ts'in and Han. As for the conquest of the Oxus-Jaxartes Basin by the Uzbegs in and after A.D. 1500, it may possibly be explained in part by the access of aridity, about this date, which appears in Dr. Ellsworth Huntington's pair of curves. But the principal cause of the catastrophe was manifestly not climatic but political. The Uzbegs found their opportunity in the weakness of the Timurids. And the Timurids were weak because Timur Lenk himself had prematurely exhausted the energies of the Iranic World by his fratricidal militarism.[1] Finally, in the Western Sudan in the fifteenth century of the Christian Era, we can explain the occupation of Timbuktu by the Tuareg Nomads from the Sahara between 1434 and 1469 as a consequence of the political anarchy which intervened in the Sudan between the fall of the sedentary Empire of Malle and the rise of the sedentary Empire of Songhay.

If we now re-examine our table of Nomad eruptions from the Steppes, we shall see that we have found satisfactory human

[1] For the militarism of Timur Lenk, see IV. C (iii) (c) 3 (α), vol. iv, pp. 491–501, below.

explanations, in the political or social conditions of the sedentary regions round about, for almost every one of the eruptions that obtrude themselves exceptionally in the course of the alternate phases of relative quiescence on the Steppes. This fact perhaps increases the probability that these alternations of social 'quiescence' and social 'effervescence', which emerge from a tabulation of the recorded historical facts, may correspond to, and proceed from, a climatic cycle of alternate bouts of humidity and aridity. At any rate, if we eliminate all entries for which a satisfactory human explanation can be found, the regularity of the alternation and the sharpness of the contrast between our alternate three-hundred-year periods is considerably enhanced.

In any case, our survey of the evidence appears to confirm the view that all the recorded eruptions of the Nomads out of the Desert into the Sown can be traced to the operation of some external force, which may be either a climatic push or a social pull or a combination of the two.

Before we conclude our examination of the effects which the social and political conditions in the regions round about the Steppes may have upon the eruptions of the Nomads, we must take note of the fact that these effects are sometimes negative as well as positive. We have reviewed a number of instances in which the domain of some sedentary society adjoining the Steppes has invited an irruption of Nomads by offering the attraction of a social vacuum. But there are other instances in which a Nomad invasion that has been evoked by a social pull or been impelled by a climatic push had been brought to a halt and even, perhaps, been driven back pell mell by the opposition of some sedentary military power. In another connexion,[1] we have noticed how many times the hegemony or dominion over South-Western Asia has fallen to some power which has constituted itself an effective warden of the north-eastern marches of South-Western Asia, between the Pamirs and the Caspian, over against the Nomads of the Eurasian Steppe. This is only one signal instance of a play of political forces which, in all places and at all times, has profoundly affected the fortunes of those Nomad hordes that have ventured to trespass upon the preserves of their sedentary neighbours.

The Lydian Monarchy made its fortune by annihilating the Cimmerian marauders in Anatolia about the middle of the seventh century B.C.; and, before the end of the same century, the Medes justified their title to be the principal heirs of the Assyrians by annihilating the Scythian marauders in Iran. In the sixth century B.C. the Achaemenidae justified their universal empire by chastising

[1] In II. D (v), vol. ii, pp. 136–50, above.

the Massagetae. In the latter part of the second century B.C. the
Arsacidae won their spurs, and laid the foundations of their empire,
by preventing the Sakas and the Yuechi, who had just overwhelmed
the Greek principality in Bactria, from overrunning Western Iran
—with the result that the course of this Nomad irruption was
deflected south-eastward into Seistan and Sind and ultimately into
Maharashtra. In the fifth century of the Christian Era, the Sasanidae emulated the feat of their Arsacid predecessors by checking
the irruption of the Huns at the line of the Oxus and deflecting
its course into the Panjab and the Ganges Basin. This success of
the Sasanidae in keeping their north-eastern frontier almost invio-
late against the Huns is thrown into relief by the contemporary
failure of the Roman Power in Europe and the Gupta Power in
India to keep the same horde of Nomad invaders at bay. The
reason why the Huns failed to occupy Western Iran, when they
succeeded in overrunning the plains of Hindustan and forcing their
way into Gaul and Italy, is manifestly political and not climatic.
At the beginning of the sixteenth century of the Christian Era,
the Uzbegs had the same experience as the Sakas. Having easily
overwhelmed the Timurid Powers in the Oxus-Jaxartes Basin, as
the Sakas overwhelmed the Greek Power in the same region, the
Uzbegs were beaten back from Western Iran by Ismāʿīl Shāh
Safawī as valiantly as the Sakas were beaten back by Mithradates
the Arsacid. On the same front the Mongols, with their demoniac
drive, succeeded in overwhelming not only the Oxus-Jaxartes Basin
but Iran and ʿIrāq and the Jazīrah into the bargain; yet at the line
of the Euphrates their advance was brought to a halt—belatedly
but for ever—from A.D. 1261 onwards by the resistance of the
Egyptian Mamlūks.

On another front of the Eurasian Steppe, between the Khingan
Range and the Tien Shan, the Nomad confederacy of the Hiongnu
met more than its match in the Sinic universal state of the Han;
and in the seventh century of the Christian Era the Empire of the
T'ang, which was a reincarnation of the Empire of the Han, not
only repulsed and crushed, but momentarily even subjugated the
Nomad confederacy which had been organized in the sixth century
by the Turks. On the same front, in the eighteenth century of the
Christian Era, the Zungar Calmuck successors of these Central
Asian Nomad Turks met their match in the Manchu successors
of the T'ang and the Han; and simultaneously, in the gap between
the Caspian and the Urals—through which horde after horde of
Sarmatians and Huns and Avars and Magyars and Mongols had
poured irresistibly time and again—the Torgut kinsmen of the
Zungars met their match in the Empire of Muscovy.

Similar experiences have befallen the Nomads who have erupted out of the Afrasian Steppe. The Aramaean invaders of the Jazīrah were brought to a halt by the indomitable resistance of Assyria. The Primitive Muslim Arabs, who conquered the Sasanian Empire —lock, stock, and barrel—almost at one blow, were successfully brought to a halt by the Roman Empire at the line of the Taurus, while the Franks drove them back from the Loire in A.D. 732 and expelled them from Septimania in 755 and dislodged them from the southern foothills of the Pyrenees in 788. Finally, in the nineteenth and the twentieth century of the Christian Era, the Sanūsīs of the Libyan Desert and the Wahhābīs of the Arabian Desert have found, each time when they have attempted to break their bounds, that even the disciplined enthusiasm that can be infused into the spirit of the Afrasian Nomad by the inspiration of a religious faith is no match for the weapons of the modern Western World, whether these weapons are wielded by the French or English or Italian hands that made them or by the Egyptian peasant-conscripts of a Mehmed 'Alī.

There is one more form of interaction between the Nomads and the sedentary societies round about them which calls for consideration, and that is the effect upon the Nomads of conversion to the sedentary societies' religions. In glancing at the histories of the Khazars and of the three westernmost appanages of the Mongol Empire, we have seen the conversion of the Khazars to Judaism and the conversion of the Golden Horde and the Il-Khans and the Chaghatayids to Islam acting as a social solvent which apparently relaxes the moral fibre of the converts and precipitates their political downfall.[1] In these instances, however, we are dealing with a religious conversion which overtook a horde *after* it had erupted out of the interior of the Steppe and had settled down either on the outermost edge of the region in which Nomadism is at home or else actually on the farther side of the border, on positively alien ground. There are other instances in which the Nomad is converted or influenced by an alien religion while he is still leading his natural life in his native haunts; and in such instances the alien religious influence appears—on the showing of the historical evidence—to produce just the opposite moral effect. So far from acting as a laxative, it acts as a stimulant, and it is apt to precipitate an eruption instead of heralding a *débâcle*.

This stimulating effect of an alien religious influence is a conspicuous feature in the life of the Afrasian Nomads. The preaching of Islam by Muhammad, and the prodigious outbreak of the Primitive Muslim Arabs, were preceded by successive infiltrations

[1] See pp. 429–30, above.

of Judaism and Nestorianism and Monophysitism into Arabia. It was a Carmathian missionary who set the Badu of the Hasā in motion in the tenth century of the Christian Era; and the preaching of Muhammad 'Abd-al-Wahhāb in the eighteenth century set the Badu of the Najd in motion, to the same effect, in the nineteenth century and in the twentieth. In the African portion of the Afrasian Steppe there are also celebrated examples of the same phenomenon. It was under the leadership of a Shi'ite propagandist that the Katāma Berbers overran Ifriqīyah in A.D. 890 and Egypt and Syria in A.D. 969–70. As for the Murābits and the Muwahhids, their very titles testify that the Berbers who made their conquests under these names in the eleventh and in the twelfth century of the Christian Era respectively were stimulated by a religious enthusiasm and drawn on by a religious purpose. The Fulbe Nomads, who emulated in the nineteenth century those conquests in the Western Sudan that had been made in the eleventh century by the Murābits, were likewise inspired by a religious faith which in their case was the Wahhābī faith of their Arab contemporaries in the Najd. We have already touched upon the Sanūsī movement, which stimulated the Nomads of the Libyan Desert to establish an empire that extended, at one moment in the nineteenth century, from the Cyrenaica to Wadai.

These religious landmarks in the life of the Afrasian Nomads are well known, but it is worth noticing that there are certain Eurasian parallels. For example, the irruption of the Saljūqs into the Asiatic dominions of the 'Abbasid Caliphate and of the East Roman Empire alike, in the course of the eleventh century of the Christian Era, had been preceded by the conversion of the Saljūqs to Islam in A.D. 956; and the contemporary domination of the Ilek Khans over Transoxania and the Tarim Basin had been preceded by the conversion of their forefathers to Islam in A.D. 960. The prodigious outbreak of the Mongols in the thirteenth century of the Christian Era was preceded by a gradual infiltration of Mahayanian Buddhism and Manichaeism and Nestorianism into the north-eastern parts of Eurasia. The outbreak of the Calmucks in the seventeenth century of the Christian Era followed hard upon their conversion, at the turn of the sixteenth and seventeenth centuries, to the religion of the Yellow Sect of Lamaistic Mahayanian Buddhism which had taken shape in Tibet.[1]

This series of examples, taken together, seems to indicate that the religions of the sedentary societies are apt to stimulate the

---

[1] On the other hand, it must be recorded that the Mongols, who were converted to exactly the same form of Buddhism about one generation earlier than the Calmucks, remained quiescent in the seventeenth century when the Calmucks erupted.

Nomads into erupting out of the Desert into the Sown when these religious influences play upon the Nomad while he is still living his natural life upon his native ground. And the case of the Primitive Muslim Arabs seems to indicate further that this stimulus is strongest when the Nomads transmute these alien religious influences into some new religious creation of their own, instead of accepting them passively in the form in which they happen to come from their places of origin. Have we here stumbled at last upon one cause of Nomad eruptions which does not work externally and mechanically through the exertion of a climatic push or a social pull, but rather takes the spiritual form of Challenge-and-Response? If this is the fact, then we shall have to concede that, after all, the Nomads are not to be numbered without reserve among 'the peoples that have no history'. But second thoughts remind us that, in so far as the spiritual movement of Challenge-and-Response is discernible here, the souls that experience it are not the souls of the Nomads themselves but the souls of the oasis-dwellers who live in, but not of, the Steppe as outposts of the sedentary civilizations. Muhammad was not a Nomad herdsman but a commercial traveller; his Meccan kinsmen were business men; his Medinese helpers were tillers of the ground; and it was under the inspiration and leadership of these semi-aliens in their midst that the Arabian Nomads went forth conquering and to conquer in the seventh century of the Christian Era. The Carmathian Power in the Hasā and the Wahhābī Power in the Najd and the Sanūsī Power in the Libyan Desert have all been founded upon the oases, like the Primitive Muslim Power in the Hijāz which they have all consciously taken as their ensample. On the Eurasian Steppe, likewise, the religious influences which touched, and perhaps exhilarated, the Mongols in the thirteenth century of the Christian Era all emanated from the oases which were inhabited by the once Nomadic but long since domesticated Uighurs. And the Yellow Lamaism which converted the Calmucks and the Mongols some three, or three and a half, centuries ago has retained its hold upon these elusive converts by planting artificial oases among their grazing-grounds in the shape of Buddhist monasteries.

It seems, then, that the Nomads, in so far as they remain pure Nomads, are really 'a people without a history' after all. Their eruptions out of the Desert into the Sown, like the eruptions of a Vesuvius or an Etna, are the mechanical resolutions of vast but inanimate physical forces. They are not the agonies of an imprisoned Titan who is frantically struggling for liberty and light.

NOTE BY MR. G. F. HUDSON

With regard to the climatic theory in general, there are two difficulties which have to be overcome:

(1) As pointed out by Peisker in his criticisms of Huntington, the effect of an arid period on the Eurasian Steppe would be not only to increase the amount of desert but also to extend the grass-land northward at the expense of the Russo-Siberian forest belt; the summer would also be hotter, so that the main result would be simply that the Nomads' domain would shift northwards (that is, the portions of this domain which lie to the north of the Caspian-Gobi belt of deserts). The peasants, if there were any, on the fringe of the Steppe would be driven away by the increasing drought, quite apart from the Nomads' aggression. Of course, the shifting of the belts might not be exactly compensatory; but as regards the Eurasian Nomads dwelling between the desert belt and the Russo-Siberian forest belt, it does not seem clear why a period of aridity or south-to-north shift of climatic belts should actually have deprived the Nomads of any considerable amount of territory. The diagram below will show what I mean:

	Humid Period	Arid Period
1 2 3 4 5	🌲 🌲 🌲 Forest 🌲 🌲 🌲	🌲 🌲 Forest
6 7	‖‖‖‖‖‖‖‖‖‖ Good pasture	‖‖‖‖‖‖‖‖‖ Good pasture ⁄⁄⁄⁄⁄⁄⁄⁄⁄⁄ Poor pasture
8 9	⁄⁄⁄⁄⁄⁄⁄⁄⁄⁄⁄ Poor pasture	
10 11 12 13	~~~~~~~ Desert	~~~~~~~ Desert

Here we have in the arid phase less forest and more desert, but about the same quantity of steppe, which represents the degrees of humidity sufficient for grass but not enough for trees.

This objection does not apply in the same way to the Afrasian Steppe, but it does lie, I think, against the climatic theory for the Eurasian Nomads: Scythians, Huns, Avars, &c.

(2) I must admit that you have made out a very strong case for the six-hundred-year cycle, and the synchronizations between the Eurasian and Afrasian eruptions are most interesting. Nevertheless, as you point out, the eleventh and seventeenth centuries, for which you have shown such good evidence of general effervescence,

do not correspond to arid troughs in Huntington's curves. The Huntington curves, in so far as they can be relied on at all (and I am very doubtful about the lake-level curve, except where it can be verified, as it can be for the fourteenth-century levels of the Caspian and the Lob Nor), appear to give climatic changes that are quite irregular and have no fixed periodicity. I had a talk on the matter with [a distinguished expert], who is very sceptical about alleged periodicities; he pointed out to me that the great difficulty in explaining climatic changes or arriving at a general theory of them is the very delicate balance of forces which exists, so that a very insignificant cause may have effects on a vast scale. Again, the cycle should affect the Afrasian and Eurasian steppes equally; but, although you have given some remarkable synchronizations, there are other cases where they are lacking. There is no violent outbreak on the Afrasian Steppe corresponding to the Hun, Turk-Avar, or Mongol eruptions, while, conversely, the Eurasian Steppe is singularly quiescent in the seventh century of the Christian Era when the Primitive Muslim Arabs break out in the south.

There can be no doubt that there have been oscillations of climate in the last 4,000 years (the best attested is the humid peak in the fourteenth century of the Christian Era), and that they have been factors in the eruptions of Nomads; I would not, however, explain everything by the climatic push and the pull of sedentary breakdowns, because I think there is a measure of real development in Nomadic societies from their mixture with sedentaries, the growth of commerce, &c., and this factor gives them something of real history. It is true that the Nomad *qua* Nomad is unchanging, but so is the peasant *qua* peasant (until quite recently); it is in both cases a question of what sort of edifice can be built on these foundations, and clearly the peasant foundation gives more scope. As for the pull by the sedentary societies' vacua, I think this principle could be extended to all conquests of any kind: e.g., on this showing, the British conquest of India would be an automatic consequence of the break-up of the Mughal Empire, and so forth. The Nomad could not be 'pulled' off the Steppe but for his warlike and predatory disposition, which is a by-product of his mode of life, and which gives him always the will to raid his sedentary neighbour—a will which only the effective power of the latter restrains.

THE NUMERICAL RATIO BETWEEN SUBJECTS AND MASTERS IN THE OTTOMAN EMPIRE AND IN LACONIA

WE have seen that, including the slaves of slaves, the Pādishāh's slave-household mustered about 86,000 head all told; that some 56,000 of these were soldiers; and that, besides these 56,000 regular professional troops, the Ottoman Government disposed of a feudal cavalry, which aggregated 80,000 to 100,000 troopers all told; so that, in an extreme emergency, the Ottoman Power could mobilize perhaps as many as 100,000 men for a foreign campaign and rather more than 150,000 for the police-duty of keeping order among the 'human cattle' within the frontiers.[1] Reckoning in the women and children, the Pādishāh's household may have accounted for something like 200,000, and the feudal gentry for something like 400,000 souls out of the total population of the Ottoman Empire; and if we may hazard the conjecture that, even at the widest extension of the Empire in its most flourishing period, the total population can hardly have exceeded thirty millions, we may guess that the ratio of the Pādishāh's household to the total population was not lower than 1 in 150, while the ratio of the whole ruling element—including the feudal gentry, but excluding the Muslim 'human cattle' (e.g. the Muslim peasantry of the Arabic provinces) as well as the Christian 'human cattle'—would work out, on the same reckoning, at not lower than 1 in 50.

On the other hand, the Spartiate 'Peers', who were the ruling element in Laconia, evidently reckoned the ratio of their own numbers to the total population of Laconia as 1 in 100. This appears from the following account of an abortive conspiracy for the extermination of the Spartiate 'Peers' which was hatched by one Cinadon, who was a Spartiate 'Inferior', in the year 399 B.C.; that is, at a time when the territorial dominion of the Spartan city-state in the Peloponnesus still stood at its widest extent, and when Sparta and her allies had just won a great victory over Athens which had left Sparta the paramount Power in the whole Hellenic World. The account here quoted is given by Xenophon, an Athenian historian who knew Sparta, and the internal conditions of Laconia, from the inside. (The technical terms which occur in this passage have been explained in the relevant chapter, above.)

[1] See the second footnote on p. 45, above.

The conspiracy was betrayed to the Spartan Government by an informer; and

'the Overseers (οἱ ἔφοροι) asked the informer how he had thought that the movement would take place, whereupon he told them that Cinadon had taken him to the edge of the *piazza* (ἀγορά) and had asked him to count how many Spartiates were to be found there. "And so," said the informer, "I counted the King and the Overseers (τοὺς ἐφόρους) and the Privy Councillors (τοὺς γέροντας) and others, up to about forty, and then asked: 'Why ever did you tell me to count them, Cinadon?'— 'Because,' said Cinadon, 'you are to regard these as enemies and all the rest as allies'—amounting to more than 4000 persons who were in the *piazza* at the moment." He added that Cinadon pointed out to him in the streets one "enemy" here and two there as they passed them, while all the rest were "allies". When the Overseers (οἱ ἔφοροι) asked him what he believed the number of conspirators to be, the informer said that Cinadon had spoken with him on this point, too, and had told him that only a restricted number of trustworthy persons were in the confidence of the ring-leaders, but that the latter regarded themselves as being in virtual conspiracy with all the Serfs (εἵλωτες) and New Members (νεοδαμώδεις) and Inferiors (ὑπομείονες) and Dependents (περίοικοι); for wherever, among these classes, there was any mention of the Spartiates, there was not a man of them who could conceal the fact that he would be delighted to eat them alive.'[1]

The state of mind here described as prevailing among the subjects of the Spartiates, on the eve of Cinadon's abortive conspiracy to exterminate the Spartiates in 399 B.C., is remarkably reminiscent of the similar state of mind which our first-hand records of the Greek Revolutionary War of A.D. 1821–9 show to have prevailed, on the same spot, among the Christian ra'īyeh of the 'Osmanlis, who did succeed, when they rose in 1821, in wiping out the local representatives of the Ottoman ruling class—men, women, and children—in their Laconian citadel of Mistrà and throughout the Morea. The ruins of Mistrà, which remain down to this day as they were left on the morrow of the sack of the city in 1821, bear grim witness, for any visitor who seeks ocular testimony, to the virulence with which the 'Osmanlis were hated by their ra'īyeh— and the Spartans, before them, by their Helots.

The traditional ratio, assumed in the passage just quoted from Xenophon, of one Spartiate 'Peer' to every hundred inhabitants of Laconia is impossible to check, since we have no means of calculating the absolute figure of the total population. Even the absolute number of the Spartans themselves is a matter of conjecture. Such evidence as we possess seems to indicate that, after the enserfment of the inhabitants of the plain of Stenyclarus, in Messenia,

[1] Xenophon: *Hellenica*, Bk. III, ch. 3, paragraphs 4–11.

at the close of the second Messeno-Spartan War, and the redivision of these 'Helots' ' lands into allotments (κλῆροι) for maintaining Spartiate 'Peers', the maximum force of Spartiate heavy infantry (ὁπλῖται) that could be mobilized, when all the forty year-classes liable to active service were called out from the twenty-first to the sixtieth inclusive, was 3,200 men. In this period, the Spartan Government appears to have required the dependent but autonomous city-state communities in Laconia, the so-called Perioeci, to put one heavy infantryman into the field for every Spartiate, so that at this time the maximum total force of heavy infantry which Sparta could raise was 6,400. This (rather than Herodotus's round figure of 10,000) was probably the strength of the Lacedaemonian contingent of heavy infantry at the Battle of Plataea in 479 B.C. But at some date between 479 B.C. and 418 the Lacedaemonian military establishment appears to have been reorganized so as to put 6 Perioeci into the field for every 4 Spartiates, instead of 5 for 5. Under this new organization, the maximum strength of the Lacedaemonian heavy-infantry force seems to have been raised from 6,400 to 7,680, while the maximum strength of the Spartiate contingent was lowered from 3,200 to 3,072.[1]

[1] For these figures, see A. J. Toynbee: 'The Growth of Sparta', in *The Journal of Hellenic Studies*, vol. xxxiii (London 1913, Macmillan).

ANNEX TO III. C (i) (a)

SOME MAKE-WEIGHTS AGAINST SOCIAL RETARDATION IN THE GEOGRAPHICAL EXPANSION OF THE WESTERN WORLD

IN the relevant chapter we have reviewed certain pieces of evidence which apparently point to the conclusion that the social effect of geographical expansion in an outward direction from the geographical centre of a civilization towards the periphery is equivalent to a retardation of social progress in the Time-dimension; and a considerable part of this evidence has been drawn from the history of the geographical expansion of our own Western World.[1] In this connexion, it is interesting to observe that our Western Society has counteracted the operation of this social 'law' in its own case to a certain extent by perpetually discharging fresh currents of its social life-blood from the heart of the Western body social towards its ever-expanding extremities.

This enhancement and enrichment of the relatively low social vitality of Western Christendom in its fringes by replenishment and reinforcement from the centre has sometimes taken the direct form of a centrifugal migratory movement of population and sometimes the indirect form of a temporary political association of some country or community at the focus of our Western life with some other country or community in the penumbra. In this indirect or political form of cultural reinforcement the physical migration of persons has usually been on an infinitesimal scale. For the most part, it has been limited to a change—and this perhaps merely a seasonal change—of residence on the part of a sovereign or a dynasty or a court or an aristocracy or an army. In such cases, the reinforcement of the culture of the periphery by replenishment from the centre has chiefly consisted in a propagation of techniques and institutions and ideas: a propagation which is capable of being accomplished on the grand scale, both extensively and intensively, by a very small number of migrant individual *Kulturträger*, and this with cultural effects that could hardly have been outdone by a physical emigration *en masse*.

To consider the direct or physical form of cultural reinforcement first, we may take, as illustrations, the introduction of Lombard settlers into Sicily after this island had been incorporated into Western Christendom as a result of the Norman conquest in the

<hr />

[1] See III. C (i) (a), pp. 134-9, above.

eleventh century of the Christian Era;[1] the introduction of Flemish
settlers into England after the Norman conquest of this other island
on the opposite fringe of the Western World of the day; the introduction of Low Dutch settlers into the territories along the
southern shore of the Baltic, from the right bank of the Elbe to
the left bank of the Niemen, which were added to Western
Christendom by conquest, at the expense of Slavs and Prussians,
in the twelfth and thirteenth centuries; the introduction of German
miners into Slovakia, and of German peasants and burghers into
Transylvania, by the deliberate policy of the Hungarian Crown
after the conversion of Hungary to Western Christianity;[2] and the
introduction of other German settlers—for the most part from
Swabia—into the territories conquered, in the eighteenth century,
by the Hapsburg and Romanov Empires from the Ottoman Empire
and from the Eurasian Nomads (the descendants of these latter-day
German pioneers of Western Civilization along its south-eastern
land frontiers are scattered over a zone which stretches from the
Hungarian Alföld and Slavonia and the Banat of Temesvar through
the Bukovina and Southern Bessarabia and the *ci-devant* Nogay
Steppe to the great compact German settlement on the lower
Volga, just below Saratov).[3] In the same connexion we may also
mention two important waves of refugees: the French Huguenots,
who were dispersed abroad into England, South Africa, and the
Protestant states of Germany (particularly Prussia and Württem-
berg) after the Revocation of the Edict of Nantes in 1683;[4] and
the German Liberals who found asylum in the United States after
the failure of the Revolution of 1848 (these German political

[1] It was this Lombard immigration into Sicily that converted the Sicilians to the
Romance language which they speak at the present day, in place of the Greek which was
the native language of the Sicilians over a period of some fifteen or sixteen centuries
beginning at least as early as the fifth century B.C., when the language introduced by the
Greek colonists extinguished the languages previously spoken by the earlier inhabitants,
even where these pre-Greek layers of population survived physically in the interior. It is
remarkable that the Greek language in Sicily should have succumbed to the intrusive
Romance language of Lombardy under the Norman and Hohenstaufen régimes after
having survived the impact of Latin under the Roman Empire and the impact of Arabic
under the Aghlabid régime. The first Lombard colony in Sicily of which there is a
record dates from A.D. 1145. An examination of the Romance dialects of Sicily shows
that the colonists must have been drawn from Liguria and the Po Basin, as well as from
Apulia (Chalandon, F.: *Histoire de la Domination Normande en Italie et en Sicile* (Paris
1907, Picard, 2 vols.), vol. i, p. 349).
[2] The so-called Saxons whose descendants still survive in Transylvania down to this
day appear to have come, in reality, not from Saxony but from Luxemburg and the
Rhineland.
[3] For details of these German settlements see Grothe, H.: *Kleines Handwörterbuch des
Grenz- und Ausland-Deutschtums* (Munich and Berlin 1932, Oldenbourg). On the
administrative map of the Soviet Union, the territory of the Volga Germans constitutes
an autonomous community within the Russian Socialist Federal Soviet Republic, which
is itself one of the seven constituent members of the Union. According to Grothe, op.
cit., p. 305, the Volga German district had 663,996 inhabitants in 1920, of whom 442,362
were Germans.
[4] For this Huguenot diasporà, see II. D (vi), vol. ii, p. 213, above.

refugees were the van-guard of the great nineteenth-century German immigration into the United States which has done so much to counteract the deterioration of European culture under the adverse cultural conditions in 'the Middle West').

The indirect form of cultural reinforcement through a political link may be illustrated by the following table:

Point of the Compass	Countries politically associated		Dates of association
	Country in the focus of civilization	Country in the penumbra of civilization	
NW.	Normandy	England	1066–1204
NW.	Anjou	England	1154–1203
N.	Holstein	Denmark	1460–1864
NE.	Hohenzollern	Brandenburg	1415–
NE.	Cleves	Brandenburg	1614–
NE.	Brandenburg	Prussia	1618–
NE.	Meissen ('Saxony')	Poland	1697–1763
E.	Swabian Hapsburg dominions	Austria	1282–1801
E.	Luxemburg	Bohemia	1308–1437
E.	Anjou	Hungary	1310–82
E.	Luxemburg	Hungary	1387–1437
E.	Luxemburg + Flanders + Holland + Franche Comté	Austria	1482–1521
E.	Luxemburg + Flanders	Austria	1713–95
E.	Milan	Austria	1713–1859
E.	Austria	Hungary	1438–9 1453–7 1485–90 1526–1918 [1]
S.	Swabia	The Two Sicilies	1194–1266
S.	Anjou	Insular Sicily	1266–82
S.	Anjou	Continental Sicily	1266–1435
SW.	Franche Comté	Spain	1530–1674
SW.	Holland	Spain	1516–1609
SW.	Luxemburg + Flanders	Spain	1516–1713
SW.	Milan	Spain	1535–1713

Finally, we may remind ourselves of those signal cultural triumphs in which Western Christendom has succeeded in converting into propagandists of the Western Civilization those militant barbarians from beyond the pale who had previously threatened to cut the domain of the Western Christian Society short or even to extinguish Western Christendom altogether.

The English converts became instruments for propagating the Roman form of Christianity at the expense of Far Western Christendom in the Celtic fringe and of paganism in Central Germany.[2] The Scandinavian settlers in France who were converted into 'Normans' propagated the Western Christian culture at the expense of Orthodox Christendom and the Syriac World in Southern Italy and Sicily and Ifriqīyah and Syria.[3] The Scandinavians who were converted in their own homes propagated the

[1] See II. D (v), vol. ii, pp. 178–9, above.
[2] See II. D (vii), vol. ii, p. 336, with Annex II, above
[3] See II. D (v), vol. ii, p. 201, above.

same culture across the Baltic—the Danes into Wendland and Estland, and the Swedes into Finland.[1] The Magyars, who were converted from Nomadism to the sedentary civilization of Western Christendom after their settlement, at the gates of the Western World, in the Hungarian enclave of the Eurasian Steppe, served as a buffer to absorb the shock of their fellow Nomads—Pechenegs and Ghuzz and Cumans—who burst out of the Steppe during the next period of effervescence and broke into Hungary at the Magyars' heels. And the outpost which the Magyars—in their right-about-face as wardens of the Eurasian marches of Western Christendom against their own Nomadic kin and kind—once planted in Transylvania, in the extreme south-eastern angle of the Carpathians, survives down to this day in the isolated Magyar community who are known as the Széklers.

In these various ways, we see the 'law' that expansion in Space means retardation in social progress being counteracted perpetually, with some success, in the history of our Western Civilization.

[1] See II. D (v), vol. ii, p. 168, above.

THE CONCEPT OF THE SECOND COMING IN ITS PSYCHOLOGICAL SETTING

THE flash of intuition in which the concept of the Second Coming was first conceived must evidently have been a response to the particular challenge of the time and the place; and the critic who has not yet extricated himself from the modern error of supposing that things have nothing more in them than is to be found in their origins may make the mistake of depreciating the Christian doctrine of the Second Coming on the ground that it originated in a disappointment: the disappointment of the Primitive Christian community in the first generation when they realized that their Master had actually come and gone once without the looked-for effect. Here was a prophet in Israel who had boldly broken away from the Jewish Messianic tradition by adopting the unfamiliar and paradoxical principle of non-violence. He had been faithful to His principle, and the principle itself had apparently been confuted by the outcome; for He had allowed Himself to be put to death; and, as far as could be seen, His death had left His followers without prospects. If they were to find the heart to carry on their Master's mission, they must draw the sting of failure from their Master's career by projecting this career from the past into the future. If they were to preach Christ crucified—which was 'unto the Jews a stumblingblock and unto the Greeks foolishness'[1]—they must believe and proclaim that the career which had ended in the Crucifixion was only the First Coming of their Master, and that He was to come again in power and glory in order to prove that 'God hath chosen the foolish things of the World to confound the wise and God hath chosen the weak things of the World to confound the things which are mighty'.[2]

It is certainly true that the doctrine of the Second Coming was conceived in the Primitive Christian Church at a time when the Church was oppressed by a sense of weakness and failure, and when even its keenest minds had as yet no inkling of the tremendous victories which Christianity was to win in the fullness of time on the strength of the First Coming alone. It is also true that this doctrine of the Second Coming has since been adopted with the greatest enthusiasm by societies and sects and peoples that have been in this same disappointed or frustrated state of mind.

[1] 1 Corinthians i. 23. [2] 1 Corinthians i. 27.

In the myth of the Second Coming of Arthur, for example, the vanquished Britons have consoled themselves for the splendid failure of the historic Arthur to avert the ultimate victory of the English barbarian invaders.[1] In the myth of the Second Coming of Barbarossa, again, the Germans of the later Middle Ages have consoled themselves for their failure to maintain the hegemony over Western Christendom which their forefathers had held from the Völkerwanderung down to the age of the Hohenstaufen.

'To the south-west of the green plain that girdles in the rock of Salzburg, the gigantic mass of the Untersberg frowns over the road which winds up a long defile to the glen and lake of Berchtesgaden. There, far up among its limestone crags, in a spot scarcely accessible to human foot, the peasants of the valley point out to the traveller the black mouth of a cavern, and tell him that within Barbarossa lies amid his knights in an enchanted sleep, waiting the hour when the ravens shall cease to hover round the peak, and the pear-tree [shall] blossom in the valley, to descend with his Crusaders and bring back to Germany the golden age of peace and strength and unity. Often in the evil days that followed the fall of Frederick's house, often when tyranny seemed unendurable and anarchy endless, men thought on that cavern and sighed for the day when the long sleep of the just Emperor should be broken and his shield·be hung aloft again as of old in the camp's midst —a sign of help to the poor and the oppressed.'[2]

Barbarossa and his knights in their cave are re-sleeping the sleep of the Seven Sleepers of Ephesus, whose awaking is a sign that the persecution of the Christian Church by the Roman Empire is overpast.

The most striking of all the derivative versions of the Second Coming is that which reflects the disappointment of the Shī'ah.

'The Shi'ite Movement began in the first century of Islam as political propaganda against the Umayyad dynasty of Caliphs in favour of the house of 'Alī, the son-in-law and cousin of the Prophet. It was then hand in glove with the orthodox, and succeeded both in impressing its historical point of view on orthodox sentiment and in overthrowing the hated dynasty, only to be cheated of its political hopes by the establishment of the rival 'Abbāsid line, and to fall instead under a more methodical persecution than hitherto. Shi'ism now took to the catacombs, and soon became a separate heretical sect, distinguished by the doctrine of allegiance to a divinely appointed, sinless, and infallible spiritual leader, the Imām, instead of an elective lay head or Caliph. The Imāmate they held to be hereditary in the house of 'Alī, but the various sub-groups differed on the point at which the succession of Imāms was interrupted. The belief of the principal group, or "Twelvers", to which the Shi'ites of Persia and 'Irāq still belong, was

<hr />

[1] See Part II. D (vii), vol. ii, pp. 339–40, above.
[2] Bryce, James: *The Holy Roman Empire*, ch. xi, *ad fin.*

that the twelfth Imām of the line disappeared about the year 873 [of the Christian Era] into a cave at Hillah, but that he continues, through the heads of the religious organisation, to provide spiritual and temporal guidance for his people, and will reappear as the promised Mahdī to bring the long reign of tyranny to an end. This strange doctrine of a "Hidden Imām" or "Expected Imām", often referred to as "the Master of the Age", is recalled by the ceremony at Hillah of which Ibn Baṭṭūṭah gives a graphic description.'[1]

'The inhabitants of Hillah are all Shīʿites of the "Twelvers" Sect. . . . Near the principal market of this town there is a mosque, the door of which is covered with a silk curtain. They call this the Sanctuary of the Master of the Age. Every evening before sunset, a hundred of the townsmen, following their custom, go with arms and drawn swords to the governor of the city and receive from him a saddled and bridled horse or mule. With this they go in procession . . . to the Sanctuary of the Master of the Age. They halt at the door and call out: "In the name of God, O Master of the Age, in the name of God, come forth! Corruption is abroad and injustice is rife! This is the hour for thy advent, that by thee God may discover the true from the false." They continue to call out thus, sounding their drums and bugles and trumpets, until the hour of sunset prayer; for they hold that Muhammad the son of Al-Hasan al-ʿAskarī entered this mosque and disappeared from sight in it, and that he will emerge from it; for he, in their view, is "the Expected Imām".'[2]

If we now turn our attention again to the doctrine of the Second Coming in its classic Christian exposition, we shall see that it is really an example of 'etherealization'. For the angel's promise to the Apostles, on Olivet, after the Ascension, that 'this same Jesus, which is taken up from you into Heaven, shall so come in like manner as ye have seen him go into Heaven',[3] is manifestly a mythological projection into the future, in physical imagery, of the spiritual return in which the Apostles' vanished Master reasserts His presence in the Apostles' hearts when the Apostles take heart of grace to execute, in spite of the Master's physical departure, that audacious mission which the Master, when he was actually present in the flesh, had once laid upon them. This creative revival of the Apostles' courage and faith, after a moment of disillusionment and despair, is described in the Acts—again in mythological language—in the image of the descent of the Holy Ghost upon them on the Day of Pentecost.[4] In this connexion it is noteworthy that, in the account which is given, in the same book, of the last colloquy between the Apostles and Jesus, the Master makes and

---

[1] Gibb, H. A. R.: *Ibn Baṭṭúta: Travels in Asia and Africa, A.D. 1325–54, translated and selected* (London 1929, Routledge), Introduction, pp. 38–9. Compare Browne, E. G.: *A Literary History of Persia*, vol. i (London 1908, Fisher Unwin), chs. ix and xii.
[2] Ibn Baṭṭūtah, Gibb's translation, pp. 98–9.
[3] Acts i. 11. [4] Acts ii. 1–4.

reaffirms the explicit promise that they 'shall be baptized with the Holy Ghost not many days hence'[1] and that, in the power with which this baptism will endue them, they 'shall be witnesses unto' Jesus 'both in Jerusalem and in all Judaea and in Samaria, and unto the uttermost part of the Earth'.[2] At the same time, Jesus implicitly answers in the negative the naive question: 'Lord, wilt thou at this time restore again the Kingdom to Israel?'[3] in the answer: 'It is not for you to know the times or the seasons.'[4] And in this context the prophecy of His literal Second Coming in the flesh, which is put into the mouth of the angel after the Ascension has taken place, is not attributed to Jesus Himself.

[1] Acts i. 5.   [2] Acts i. 8.   [3] Acts i. 6.   [4] Acts i. 7.

THE POLITICAL CAREER OF MUHAMMAD

THE Empire which Muhammad founded on his return from Medina to Mecca can bear comparison with the empire which Caesar founded on his return from Gaul to Rome; for although, at Muhammad's death in A.D. 632, his political heritage was still no more than a barbarian principality in the no-man's-land beyond the Arabian frontier of the Roman Empire, the founder's companion and second successor 'Umar (*imperabat* A.D. 634–44), who survived Muhammad by a dozen years, lived to expand the Caliphate into a framework for a reintegrated Syriac universal state by conquering the Roman dominions in Syria and Egypt with one hand and the entire domain of the Sasanian Empire with the other.[1] Under the successive régimes of the Umayyads and the 'Abbasids, this great empire remained 'a going concern' for some three hundred years; and this immense political achievement was the outcome of Muhammad's political success during the second or politico-religious stage of his career.

Thus Muhammad's political activity is noteworthy as a factor of first-rate historical importance in the histories of civilizations; and it is also noteworthy as a phenomenon in Muhammad's own personal career, because it makes this particular career an exception to a rule which appears to hold good in the case of every other career that we have reviewed in our survey of the Withdrawal-and-Return *motif* in the lives of individuals.

This rule is the law of 'etherealization' which we have taken as our criterion of growth[2] and which is in fact obeyed in the growths of the other personalities whose careers we have cited as illustrations of the *motif* of Withdrawal-and-Return. In each of these other cases, the capacity in which the growing personality has returned to Society after his temporary withdrawal has been more ethereal than the same personality's social capacity in the first chapter of his career, before his withdrawal has taken place. David and Philopoemen withdraw as soldiers and return as statesmen; Solon withdraws as a merchant and returns as a statesman; Caesar withdraws as a politician and returns as a statesman; Loyola withdraws as a soldier and returns as a saint; and all these changes of capacity are in the direction of 'etherealization'. On the other hand,

[1] For the function of the Caliphate as a 'reintegration' or 'resumption' of the Syriac universal state which had originally been embodied in the Achaemenian Empire before the Hellenic intrusion upon the Syriac World, see I. C (i) (b), vol. i, pp. 73–7, above.
[2] See III. C (i) (c), above.

Muhammad's career, taken as a whole, appears to have been a movement in the opposite sense. For though in the first stage of his career he withdraws as a merchant and returns as a prophet, in the second stage he withdraws as a prophet and returns as a conqueror. In other words, the second stage of Muhammad's career, which is the conspicuously successful stage, is apparently the exact inverse of the career of Loyola; and if Loyola's career is a striking example of spiritual transfiguration, Muhammad's, by the same token, is an equally striking example of spiritual bathos. This exceptional feature in Muhammad's career calls for further examination.

Muhammad's overwhelming political success has undoubtedly made a deep impress upon Islam—the great institution of which Muhammad is the founder. This impress has lasted down to our own day; and it comes out clearly in the contrast between Islam and Christianity; for, broadly speaking, each of the two religions has tended, in its attitude towards politics, to follow the course which its founder indicated either by precept or by example. The Christian Churches have been guided, on the whole, by the injunction to 'render unto Caesar the things which are Caesar's and unto God the things that are God's';[1] and though the Orthodox and Protestant 'Established Churches' are important exceptions to this rule, the incorporation of these 'Established Churches' into the bodies politic of the secular states that have enslaved them has always remained imperfect and continued to appear unnatural. In Islam, on the other hand, the relation between the religious and the political elements of the institution is not that of a belated and artificial union. In Islam, the two elements cohere in an original and organic unity; so that, in Islamic sociology, such dichotomies as 'religious and secular', 'ecclesiastical and civil', 'clerical and lay' have no application. In the Islamic Society, Church and State are actually identical; and, in this undifferentiated social entity, the secular interest and the secular spirit have hitherto predominated over the religious in a fashion which makes even the most thoroughly enslaved of the Christian 'Established Churches' appear comparatively 'un-political' and 'other-worldly' by this Islamic standard of comparison.[2]

[1] Matt. xxii. 21.

[2] In the history of Christianity, perhaps the nearest approach to this identity of Church and State in Islam has been the ideal of the *Respublica Christiana* which, in Western Christendom, was entertained by the more ambitious of the Roman Pontiffs in the Middle Ages. The goal of this ideal was to eliminate the dichotomy between Church and State by incorporating the ramshackle and parochial states of medieval Western Christendom into the body social of an all-embracing Roman Church. But this ideal never came near to being realized; and, even if the goal had actually been achieved, the resulting Christian Commonwealth of the West would not have been altogether homologous with Islam; for, if Church and State had been fused together in Western Christendom in this fashion, the dominant interest and spirit in the resulting union would have been the religious and not the secular.

Thus the political, secular, mundane element has been exceptionally prominent not only in Muhammad's personal career, but in the subsequent history of the institution which is the monument of Muhammad's life-work. In quarters hostile to Islam and to its founder, this 'worldliness' has always been a popular object of denunciation; and, on impartial consideration, there is evidently much to be said for the view that Islam, as an institution, has suffered throughout its history from the note of secularity which has been characteristic of it hitherto. In so far as this note of secularity has been a social blemish in the history of Islam, it must also be regarded as having been a personal misfortune in the career of Muhammad. The monument of Muhammad's life-work might have been something more ethereal than Islam as Islam has been and is, if only the Prophet's career had not taken this decisively political turn in its last chapter. The hostile critics, however, go farther than this. They denounce Muhammad's unfortunate metamorphosis, after his *Hijrah*, from a prophet into a conqueror as a mark of moral turpitude. And this judgement cannot, in equity, be allowed to pass without taking into consideration the circumstances in which the metamorphosis occurred.

Was Muhammad a vulgar impostor, who posed as a prophet with his eye upon a throne from the outset? This calumny is conclusively refuted by the record of Muhammad's life during the thirteen years, or thereabouts, that intervened between his first announcement of his prophetic mission in Mecca *circa* A.D. 609 and his flight in A.D. 622 from Mecca to Medina. The announcement was first made secretly to an intimate circle which did not extend beyond his wife and family and a handful of personal friends; and this secrecy was justified by the sequel; for, when the propaganda came to public notice after the secret had been preserved for three years, the Meccan Prophet and his followers at once found themselves exposed to the vehement and active hostility of the ruling oligarchy, in whose belief the new doctrine was calculated to place the vital interests of Mecca in jeopardy.[1] Muhammad's life was only saved from death by violence because his uncle Abu Tālib, who was the head of his clan, would not consent to his being outlawed, so that it was impossible for the dominant conservative party to take Muhammad's life without precipitating a blood-feud; yet, in the fifth year of the mission, the persecution became so

[1] The point in Muhammad's message which incensed the Quraysh was the denunciation of idolatry, which was the corollary of the proclamation of the unity of God. The Quraysh feared that this impiety, if it prevailed, would not only bring down upon Mecca the wrath of the divinities whose existence was being denied by the blasphemer, but would also ruin the pilgrimage traffic, which was attracted to Mecca by the presence there of the shrines and cults of a number of other divinities, besides Allah, who enjoyed a Pan-Arabian prestige.

severe that a number of the Faithful had to take refuge overseas
in the Christian Kingdom of Abyssinia; and the persecutors then
retaliated by boycotting Muhammad and his clansmen and blockad-
ing them in their own quarter of Mecca, with the intention of
starving them into recantation in lieu of putting them to the sword
at the cost of civil war. Down to the thirteenth year of the mission,
when Muhammad finally withdrew from Mecca to Medina and
abandoned the purely prophetic for the politico-religious career,
Muhammad's preaching was manifestly, from the worldly point of
view, an utter failure. As the result of thirteen years of propaganda,
he had won no more than a handful of converts—most of whom
had been compelled to fly the country—and he had drawn upon
himself the implacable and apparently invincible hostility of the
dominant powers in his native community. A prophet who persisted in his mission in these circumstances for this number of
years can only have been animated by a deep and genuine religious
conviction; and he can only have supposed that he was sacrificing
his worldly prospects. He cannot have suspected that he was on
the road to making his worldly fortune.

Muhammad, therefore, must be acquitted of the charge of having
entertained ulterior political designs during the Meccan period of
his prophetic mission. But we have still to explain how it was that
he eventually took, nevertheless, to the political career in which he
was afterwards so triumphantly successful.

Perhaps the explanation is to be found in the nature of the social
milieu into which Muhammad happened to be born. If it is asked
why he did not 'render unto Caesar the things which are Caesar's'
the obvious answer is that, unlike Jesus, Muhammad did not
happen to live under Caesar's jurisdiction. Whereas Jesus was a
member of the internal proletariat of the Roman Empire, and, as
such, was at the Roman Government's mercy, Muhammad was a
member of the external proletariat whose home was in the no-man's-
land outside the Roman frontiers and beyond the reach of Caesar's
arm. This extreme difference of milieu explains, at least in part, the
extreme difference between the earthly fortunes of these two prophets who, in addressing themselves to their fellow men, each
'claimed to be the messenger of their God, bringing them a strange
message, wholly subversive of their former beliefs and practices:
claiming, in short, to be their dictator, though dictating not his own
words, but God's'.[1]

'There is no example in history of such a claim being at first favour-
ably received, unless by any chance it is made by one already sovereign.[2]

[1] Margoliouth, D. S.: *Mohammedanism* (Home University Library Series: London,
no date, Williams and Norgate), p. 51.
[2] For this rather rare situation and its usual outcome, see V. C (i) (d) 6 (δ) Annex,
in vol. v, below.—A. J. T.

In most communities it has meant death, or at best condign punishment, for the person who makes it. The better the order of the community, the less chance has a prophet. The execution of Socrates took place after a legal trial, in the most highly civilized and most tolerant state of Antiquity.'[1]

We may add that Jesus, in spite of His rendering unto Caesar the things that were Caesar's, and in spite of His refusal to allow His followers to resort to violence in order to save Him from arrest,[2] was nevertheless put to death by the Roman authorities. His mortal offence in Roman eyes was that 'he taught . . . as one having authority'[3]—an attitude which no Sovereign Power is willing, in the last resort, to tolerate in any of its subjects.

Muhammad's attitude, in proclaiming his prophetic message, was the same; and assuredly he would have met the same fate at the same early stage if he had been conducting his prophetic mission inside, instead of outside, the Roman frontiers, either in Jesus's day or in his own. In this situation, it would have made no difference to Muhammad's immediate personal fortunes whether, when the Roman authorities had sought his life, he had chosen the path of non-resistance or had turned at bay; for Jesus was not the only Jewish prophet of his age who met his death at Roman hands. The same fate overtook the Theudases and Judases who desperately resorted, within the ambit of the Roman imperium, to the militant tactics which the historical Muhammad was able to execute with brilliant success in the no-man's-land of Arabia. If Muhammad had been living under Roman rule, his mission would have resulted in his losing his life, whatever line he had taken in dealing with the Roman authorities; and we can only conjecture, on the historic analogy of Jesus and the Christian Church, that if Muhammad had lived in these circumstances and had died, as Jesus died, without offering resistance, then Islam might have become something different from, and spiritually higher than, what it has become in fact. The historic development of Islam is a consequence of the fact that Muhammad's career, in Muhammad's actual circumstances, developed quite differently. Instead of sealing his prophetic message with his blood by becoming Caesar's victim, it was Muhammad's ironic destiny to compromise and debase his prophetic message by becoming an Arabian Caesar himself.

'The problem . . . is . . .: How was it that he escaped death when once his mission had been proclaimed? And the reply is: Because there was no orderly government. . . . Justice, it would seem, could only be executed within the tribe, and . . . it was impossible to assail the Pro-

---

[1] Margoliouth, op. cit., pp. 51–2.
[2] Matt. xxvi. 51–4; John xviii. 11 and 36.   [3] Matt. vii. 29.

phet . . . for such an assault would have led to civil war between the Meccan tribes: a consequence which it was their common interest to avert.'[1]

We have seen how this political situation was brought about by Abu Tālib's refusal to withdraw his patriarchal protection from his nephew. The result was a political stalemate, which was not unlike the stalemate that followed the introduction of Christianity, some four centuries later, into the similarly constituted Scandinavian Society in Iceland.[2] The operation of the primitive social system of kin-group-solidarity and blood-feud in a political vacuum made it impossible for the new religion to be stamped out by violence and likewise impossible for it to prevail by peaceful propaganda; and there were only two possible issues from this impasse: either the negotiation of a *modus vivendi* between the pagans and the religious revolutionaries or the creation, by the one or the other party, of a body politic to fill the political vacuum and thus to pave the way for a solution by force. In this predicament, the Icelanders adopted the former alternative and Muhammad the latter. The Icelanders negotiated a *modus vivendi* which averted civil war and obviated the necessity for establishing an effective government in Iceland, at the price of a voluntary general acceptance of the new faith. Muhammad, on the other hand, embraced the opportunity, when it came his way, of arming himself in the panoply of political power and using this power as an instrument for imposing Islam upon Mecca by force.

No doubt, when he accepted the fateful invitation to organize a government in Medina, Muhammad assured his own conscience that he was acting as single-heartedly as ever in the cause of God. Had not God laid upon him the duty of conveying the revelation of God's truth to his fellow men? And would he not be executing this duty if he embraced this heaven-sent opportunity of providing the new religion, whose path had been obstructed for ten years by human *force majeure*, with a human political vehicle without which, as ten years' personal experience showed, Islam could make no further practical progress? No doubt, Muhammad reasoned with his conscience thus; and no doubt he was deceiving himself in yielding to his own arguments; for, in the event, the temporal power with which the Arabian Prophet endowed—or encumbered—his Islam at this crucial point in his career has proved to be not a vehicle but a prison-house, which has cribbed and cabined and confined the spirit of Islam ever since.

The truth, then, seems to be that, in the invitation to Medina,

---

[1] Margoliouth, op. cit., pp. 52–3.
[2] See II. D (vii), vol. ii, pp. 354–5, above.

Muhammad was confronted with a challenge to which his spirit failed to rise. In accepting the invitation, he was renouncing the sublime role of the nobly un-honoured prophet and contenting himself with the commonplace role of the magnificently successful statesman. The prospect of effective practical action which the call to Medina opened up for the Prophet's long repressed and thwarted practical genius blinded the Prophet's vision and warped his judgement. For even on the eve of the worldly call, in the second phase of his thirteen-years-long worldly failure in Mecca, Muhammad had been content with the faithful performance of a prophet's duty, as is shown by his apostrophe to the idolaters: 'Is aught else laid upon God's messengers but a plain delivery of the message?'[1] This simple understanding and acceptance of his prophetic mission were thrown to the winds by the Prophet when a new career was offered him in the alien political sphere; and, in the language of worldly wisdom, this *volte-face* was amply 'justified by success'. The Prophet's latent political genius was so transcendent that the modest office of 'honest broker' in an anarchy-ridden Arabian oasis[2] was transformed in his hands into the sovereignty of a state which was destined to eclipse the Empire of Rome and emulate the Empire of the Achaemenidae. This tragic worldly success of the founder of Islam—a success which was pernicious for the institution which he had founded—points the truth that, for a prophet, to be *felix opportunitate mortis*[3] is the highest good and to be *capax imperii*[4] the unkindest gift that the Gods can bestow upon him. The chance to prove his political mettle in action, which Fortune brought, was just as fatal to the prophet *manqué*, Muhammad, as it was to the Caesar *manqué*, Galba.

---

[1] Qur'ān, Surah xvi, verse 35: فَهَلْ عَلَى ٱلرُّسُلِ إِلَّا ٱلْبَلَاغُ ٱلْمُبِينُ

[2] The arbitral function which Muhammad was invited to perform at Medina in mediating between the local clans and factions who could not make peace unaided, was not unlike the function of an aesymnêtês in a Hellenic city-state or a podestà in a medieval Italian commune.

[3] Tacitus: *Agricola*, ch. 45.   [4] Tacitus: *Histories*, i. 49.

THE RELATIVITY OF IBN KHALDŪN'S HISTORICAL THOUGHT

A MODERN Western reader of Ibn Khaldūn will possibly be surprised to find 'asabīyah—the *esprit de corps* which expresses itself in effective social action—regarded by the Arabic social philosopher as a rare phenomenon which is hardly to be found except among the members of Nomad hordes. To a modern Western sociologist, the êthos of a modern Western national state, or the êthos of a Hellenic or a medieval Western city-state, will seem to afford at least as good an illustration of 'asabīyah as the êthos of a Nomad horde. In order to follow the course of Ibn Khaldūn's thought, we have to keep in mind the nature of his historical background and his personal experience; and it is evident that, in Ibn Khaldūn's mental picture of world-history, there were two great events of outstanding importance and significance. The first of these events was the reintegration of the Syriac universal state, in the form of the Caliphate, through the conquests of the Primitive Muslim Arabs; the second was the eventual devastation of the derelict domain of the Caliphate in the Maghrib by the Banu Hilāl after the Caliphate had broken up.

In both these historic transactions, there was a collision between an aggressive minority of Nomads and a passive majority of sedentary peasants and bourgeois; in both cases the majority allowed the minority to work its will upon them; and in both cases this happened because the majority lacked the dynamic social quality of 'asabīyah which the minority possessed. In the mental picture which Ibn Khaldūn constructs out of this historical evidence, the lack of 'asabīyah or deficiency in social vitality is taken to be the normal êthos of sedentary populations in all times and places (see the *Muqaddamāt*, Book I, section 2, in the chapters entitled: 'The inhabitants of the open country are less corrupt than the bourgeoisie'; 'The inhabitants of the open country are more courageous than the bourgeoisie'; 'The submission of the bourgeoisie to constituted authorities impairs their bravery and makes them strangers to the notion of self-help').[1] Conversely, in Ibn Khaldūn's mental picture, the possession of 'asabīyah is taken to be virtually a mono-

---

[1] For Ibn Khaldūn's own first-hand observation of this contrast as between the Arabs of Andalusia who have lost their 'asabīyah and the Berbers of the Maghrib who have retained theirs, see the *Muqaddamāt*, Introduction (de Slane's translation, vol. i, pp. 63 and 319 and 338–40).

poly of the Nomads ('The faculty of living in the desert is confined
to communities that are animated by a strong *esprit de corps*').
Since Ibn Khaldūn also takes it as an axiom that this *esprit de corps*
is the psychic protoplasm out of which all bodies politic and bodies
social are built up, he infers that 'semi-savage tribes are more
capable than other peoples of making conquests', and that 'the
extent of conquests is in inverse ratio to the degree of civilization
exhibited by the conquerors'.

This conclusion leaves him with one obvious unsolved conun-
drum. For, if the conquests of the Primitive Muslim Arabs in the
first century of the Hijrah and the conquests of the Banu Hilāl in
the fifth century of the Hijrah are both alike to be ascribed to the
potency of Nomadic *'asabīyah*, what is the differentiating factor
which accounts for the extreme difference in the outcome of the
two historic transactions? He supplies an answer to his riddle by
introducing (in the last chapters of section 2 and the first chapters
of section 3 of Book I) the suggestion that *'asabīyah* is not the only
kind of social protoplasm after all; an alternative—and superior—
kind exists in the shape of religion. ('In general, the Arabs are incapable of founding an empire *unless* they have received a tincture
of religion of a certain strength from some prophet or saint'; 'The
religious teaching of a prophet or a preacher of the truth is the only
basis on which a great and powerful empire can be founded'; and
'A dynasty which starts its career by placing itself on a religious
basis will thereby double the effectiveness of the *esprit de corps*
which is the means of its establishment'; though, at the same time,
'It is impossible to establish a domain or to found a dynasty without
possessing the support of a people animated by *esprit de corps*'; and
'An enterprise which aims at securing the triumph of the religious
principle can only succeed if it finds a strong party to support it'.)
Thus Ibn Khaldūn explains the success of the Primitive Muslim
Arabs in their empire-building by the fact that, in this case, the
two dynamic forces of religion and *'asabīyah* were working together;
and he explains the failure of the Banu Hilāl to accomplish anything but destruction by the fact that, in this other case, the force of
'asabīyah had no religious reinforcement. Again, he perceives that
the eventual decay of the Umayyad and 'Abbāsid Caliphates has
been due to the atrophy of the socially constructive êthos of the
conquering minority and the re-emergence of the socially uncon-
structive êthos of the conquered majority; and he infers that this
is the general explanation of the eventual decay which overtakes all
empires. ('When an empire has acquired its natural form through
the establishment of autocracy and the introduction of luxury, it
tends to decay'; 'Empires, like individual human beings, have their

specific life-span'; 'In empires, the habits of the Nomadic life are gradually replaced by those of the sedentary life.')

Every reader of Ibn Khaldūn's work will be filled with admiration for the vigour and the brilliance of the thought which has succeeded in making so much out of the amount of evidence that the thinker has had at his disposal; but a modern Western critic may feel that Ibn Khaldūn's empirical foundation is rather too narrow to bear the weight or to justify the range of his masterly generalizations. In the terms that we are employing in this Study of History, Ibn Khaldūn is ascribing to sedentary societies *sans phrase* a certain êthos (i.e. a deficiency in ʿasabīyah) which is really only characteristic of sedentary social life in the particular circumstances in which Ibn Khaldūn happens to be familiar with it: that is to say, in the circumstances exhibited by the internal proletariat of a declining civilization in the penultimate phase of its decline when it is passing through its universal state. Conversely, Ibn Khaldūn is ascribing to Nomadic societies *sans phrase* another êthos (i.e. the possession of ʿasabīyah), which is really no monopoly of Nomadism, but is equally characteristic of the non-Nomadic members of any external proletariat (i.e. the sedentary North-European as well as the Nomadic Arab and Berber and Eurasian members of the external proletariat of the Roman Empire). Thus, in our perspective, Ibn Khaldūn's equation of ʿasabīyah with the êthos of Nomadism and *lā ʿasabīyah* with the êthos of sedentary life seems much too sweeping. In our eyes, the equation only seems to hold good in the particular case in which the Nomadic horde happens to belong to the external proletariat and the sedentary population to the internal proletariat of a declining civilization. And we can think of other historic cases in which a sedentary population has displayed at least as vigorous an ʿasabīyah as any community of Nomads. Again, Ibn Khaldūn's explanation of the decay of empires is only applicable, in our eyes, to the particular case of an empire founded by Nomads (see the examination of this case in Part III. A, above[1]), which is, of course, the only case of empire-building that Ibn Khaldūn takes into account. This explanation will not seem adequate to a student of history for whom the classic instance of a universal state happens to be the Roman Empire or the Empire of Ts'in and Han, and not the Arab Caliphate.

In offering these criticisms, however, we must not forget that our ability to make them does not arise from any inherent superiority of our intellectual powers, but simply from the external accident that we happen to have at our disposal a wider field of historical evidence to work upon. If any political philosopher capable of

[1] In the present volume, on pp. 22–6.

comprehending Ibn Khaldūn's ideas had ever arisen in Western Christendom at any time during the first four centuries of our Western history, this imaginary genius would assuredly have found in Ibn Khaldūn's propositions a satisfactory philosophical explanation of all the historical evidence that was actually at the disposal of Western minds in that epoch. He would have found in the barbarians' apparent monopoly of ʿasabīyah, and in the absence of this quality among the derelict provincials of the defunct Roman Empire, the explanation of the later empires that were successively built, on Roman ruins, by the Merovingians and the Carolingians and the Ottos; and he would have explained the eventual decay of each of these barbarian empires by the Khaldunian generalization that the êthos of the conquering minority is inevitably diluted and contaminated and obliterated in process of time by contact with the êthos of the conquered majority.

In this context, we may remind ourselves of the axiom which we have taken as the starting-point of our present Study of History: the axiom that all historical thought is inevitably relative to the particular circumstances of the thinker's own time and place. This is a law of Human Nature from which no human genius can be exempt. Ibn Khaldūn points out the application of the law to the ideas of his predecessor Tartūshī;[1] and his critical mind would assuredly have been ready to admit that its own workings were subject to the same limitation.

[1] Ibn Khaldūn: *Muqaddamāt*, de Slane's translation, vol. i, p. 322.

THE VICTORY OF THE CITY-STATE RÉGIME OVER THE KINGDOM-STATE RÉGIME IN THE HELLENIC WORLD

THE partition of Western Christendom in the fourteenth century of the Christian Era into two incompatible worlds[1] has a parallel in the situation of the Hellenic Society in the fifth century B.C., when Hellas was likewise partitioned between a world of city-states and a world of cantons and kingdoms which were survivals of a pre-city-state phase of the Hellenic Civilization. But this superficial similarity between the two situations turns out, on inspection, to overlie two important differences. In the first place, the city-state was a much older institution in fifth-century Hellas than it was in the fourteenth-century Western World. It was as old an institution in Hellas as Feudalism was in Western Christendom; and it had been called into existence in Hellas to serve the primary purpose, which Feudalism served in the West, of preserving Society from Chaos in the first chapter of its history on the morrow of its birth. In the second place, the city-state régime had made relatively much greater progress in Hellas by the fifth century than it had made in Western Christendom by the fourteenth.

In fourteenth-century Western Christendom, as we have seen, the feudal régime was still the rule and the city-state régime the exception almost everywhere outside Northern Italy and Flanders. On the other hand, in fifth-century Hellas, the 'Classical' city-state régime had already become the rule, and the 'Homeric' kingdom-state régime the exception, throughout the Hellenic World of the age. In the Peloponnese, a fifth-century movement towards synoec-ism in Argos and Mantinea and Elis[2] left only one patch of Pelo-ponnesian territory, in the south-western corner of Arcadia, still living under the pre-city-state dispensation.[3] The whole of insular

[1] See the present volume, pp. 341–50, above.

[2] This movement seems to have taken place in the decade following the repulse of Xerxes' invasion of European Greece in 480–479 B.C. (For the original authorities, see Hill, G. F.: *Sources for Greek History between the Persian and Peloponnesian Wars* (Oxford 1907, Clarendon Press), pp. 291–6.) In Argos and Mantinea, at any rate, the movement seems to have been an imitation of Athens, who was at the height of her prestige owing to the leading part which she had played in the victorious Hellenic resistance to Xerxes. Compare the imitation of British political institutions abroad at the time when Great Britain was at the height of her prestige after the Napoleonic Wars.

[3] It is possible that the formation of city-states in this district was artificially pre-vented by the deliberate policy of the Lacedaemonian Government, which was interested in preventing the rise of any strong power in the neighbourhood of the most vulnerable section of its land-frontier. It is significant that the military débacle of the Spartans in 371 B.C. was immediately followed by the synoecism of the South-West Arcadian cantons into the new city-state of Megalopolis under the auspices of the victorious Thebans.

and transmarine Hellas was at this time already on a city-state basis; and indeed the Greek colonies in the Black Sea and the Cyrenaica and the West had never lived on any other basis, since they had been founded as city-states by communities in the homeland which had previously organized their own lives on the city-state pattern. Thus, by the time of the outbreak of the Peloponnesian War in 431 B.C., the only part of the Hellenic World, apart from one small district in the Peloponnese, which had not yet adopted the city-state régime was the culturally backward northern half of Continental European Greece outside an imaginary line running approximately from Naupactus at the mouth of the Gulf of Corinth to Thermopylae at the head of the Gulf of Malis. The Continental Greek peoples beyond this line were backwoodsmen who, in the fifth century, were regarded by the city-state Greeks as 'barbarians'.[1] Their very cultural backwardness made them impotent to resist the impact of the energetic and progressive city-state form of Hellenic culture; and this culture was being radiated into the interior of Northern Continental Greece at close quarters from the colonial city-states which had been planted by Chalcis and Eretria and Andros on the east coast and by Corinth on both coasts of the Greek Peninsula.[2]

On the west coast, the process of penetration was gradual and on the whole pacific. The two nations on the seaboard, the Thesproti and the Chaones, had already made the change from a monarchical to a republican constitution by the time of the Atheno-Peloponnesian War.[3] Thereafter, monarchy reasserted itself in this quarter when a growing local consciousness of pressure from the maritime city-states stimulated the several nations in Epirus to enter into a federation; for this federation was formed under the leadership of the Molossi, an inland people who were then still untouched by the anti-monarchical movement. In Epirus, however, this recrudescence of monarchy was accidental and temporary; and the monarchical régime did not long survive the career of King Pyrrhus (*regnabat circa* 307–272 B.C.), whose reckless expenditure of his people's blood and treasure for his own gratification was 'too much of a good thing' for Epirot public opinion to accept at royal hands with equanimity.[4] The Epirot monarchy did not outlast the reign

---

[1] e.g., by Thucydides in his account of military operations on the west side of Northern Greece in the years 430–429 B.C. (See Book II, chs. 68, 80, and 81.)

[2] For the reason why these colonies were planted on the outer edge of the Hellenic World, and not at points nearer home from the standpoint of the mother-cities, see I. C (i) (b), Annex II, vol. i, pp. 405–6, above.

[3] Thucydides, ii. 80.

[4] Compare the effect of the career of Pyrrhus's modern Western analogue Charles XII of Sweden, 'the Hero of the North', upon the subsequent course of Swedish constitutional history.

of Pyrrhus's grandson, and Epirus became a federal republic by a
peaceful revolution about the year 230 B.C.

On the east coast, the victory of the city-state over the canton
and the monarchy was not won so quickly or so easily; for, while
Thessaly made a pacific change-over from the canton régime to the
city-state régime in the fourth century B.C., Macedonia was the
theatre of a struggle between the traditional monarchical régime
and the intrusive city-state régime in which the city-state régime
was worsted. And although this decision was not definitive, it gave
the Macedonian Monarchy a two-centuries-longer lease of life
(379–168 B.C.) with momentous historical consequences.

As the Hellenic World expanded and the power began to pass
from the small states at the centre to new states of larger calibre on
the periphery,[1] it became evident that one of the new Hellenic
Great Powers would arise in the neighbourhood of the Thermaic
Gulf (the Gulf of Salonica) and the lower valley of the River Axius
(Vardar).[2] The open question was whether the nucleus of this new
Power would be the Macedonian Kingdom which had been established on the coastal plain west of the Gulf by Macedonian Greek
conquerors who had descended from the highlands of the interior;
or whether alternatively the new Power would spring from the
Chalcidian city-states which had been established on the peninsula
east of the Gulf by Euboean Greek colonists who had come in from
overseas as apostles of the new city-state dispensation on this outlying fringe of the Hellenic World. From about the time of Xerxes'
invasion of Continental European Greece (480–479 B.C.), both these
possible aspirants for the future role of Northern Great Power began
to qualify themselves for eventually assuming that position by
acquiring those qualifications which they did not yet possess. The
qualifications which either party already possessed and which either
had still to acquire were inverse to one another. In 480 B.C., the
Kingdom of Macedon already possessed the supra-city-state scale
of territory and population but lacked the city-state culture, while
at the same date the colonial city-states in Chalcidicê were abreast
of the general Hellenic city-state culture of their day but lacked the
supra-city-state scale. It was to be a race between the two com-

---

[1] For an analysis of this law of the Balance of Power, see III. C (ii) (b), pp. 301–6, above,
and also Part XI, below.
[2] A study of the Athenian tribute-lists shows that, in the fifth century B.C., the north
coast of the Aegean was increasing, and the east coast decreasing, in wealth and importance. The Greek city-states along the Anatolian seaboard suffered from being the
battle-field of the fifty years' war (499–449 B.C.) between Hellas and the Achaemenian
Power; and the peace-settlement which definitively liberated them from the Achaemenian yoke cut them off from their economic hinterland in Anatolia in order to fasten
upon them the heavier yoke of Athens. Meanwhile, the north coast of the Aegean was
going up in the world, partly owing to the exploitation of its mineral resources and
naval stores, and partly owing to the rise in civilization of the peoples in the interior.

petitors for power, to see which would be the first to make good its own particular defect and in consequence be the first to seize the coming political opportunity.

King Alexander I of Macedon, who was on the throne at the time of Xerxes' expedition, seems to have been the earliest Macedonian King to conceive the policy of increasing the efficiency of his kingdom by introducing the city-state culture without changing the traditional monarchical constitution; and in the sphere of military equipment and organization the Kingdom was brought up to the city-state standard of the time by Alexander's second successor Archelaus (*regnabat circa* 413–399 B.C.).[1] But between the death of King Archelaus in 399 B.C. and the beginning of the decisive reign of King Philip II in 359 B.C., the Kingdom of Macedon went through a bout of recurrent disorder and inefficiency, and this Macedonian relapse gave the Chalcidians an opening which they proceeded to take with an energy which carried them to the verge of success.

The descendants of the Euboean colonists who had founded the city-states of Chalcidicê displayed two political inclinations which were rare virtues in citizens of Greek city-states. They were inclined to combine politically with each other, and they were not averse from taking into partnership the more backward peoples of the hinterland. These two virtues told in favour of their adding to their territory and increasing their power. The Chalcidians' first territorial acquisition was the city of Olynthus,[2] which was handed over to them in 479 B.C. by a retreating Achaemenian general who had paused to take the city from its previous Bottiaean occupants as a punishment for their defection from the losing cause.[3] Thereafter, about 432 B.C., on the eve of the outbreak of the Atheno-Peloponnesian War, the reigning King of Macedon, Perdiccas II, who was anxious to weaken the power of Athens in his neighbourhood, raised up a formidable future rival to his own country at closer quarters by persuading the Chalcidians to evacuate and dismantle their original settlements on the coasts of the Peninsula, in which they had been living till that time; to migrate inland to Olynthus; and to establish in Olynthus a single strong Chalcidian city-state. In exchange for the agricultural land which they would be abandoning on the seaboard, Perdiccas offered the Chalcidians the usufruct of land in the interior, in the neighbourhood of Lake Bolbê (Beshik Göl) in Macedonian territory.[4] The Chalcidians accepted the offer and revolted against Athens. Their revolt, which

[1] For the military reforms of Archelaus, which included the building of forts and the cutting of roads, see Thucydides, ii. 100.
[2] See Gude, M.: *A History of Olynthus* (Baltimore 1933, Johns Hopkins University Press). [3] Herodotus, viii. 127. [4] Thucydides, i. 58.

was successful, was one of the strokes that eventually brought the Athenian Empire to the ground; and therewith the Chalcidians started on a new career as a unitary power.

The political unification which these Chalcidian communities achieved on this occasion was not just a 'synoecism' of the well-known Continental Greek type in which a number of small communities surrendered their separate political individuality altogether in order to merge themselves in a new body politic. The Chalcidian communities which united to establish a 'Greater Olynthus' *circa* 432 B.C. were no mere villages or groups of villages like the Arcadian communities which were brought together *circa* 370 B.C. to make Megalopolis. They were city-states—albeit small city-states—with about three centuries of independent political existence behind them since the time of their foundation in the eighth century B.C. Such communities could hardly have been persuaded to renounce their corporate identity completely. Even among the more backward and rudimentary communities of South-West Arcadia, the surrender of identity which was involved in the synoecism of Megalopolis, some sixty years later, aroused opposition which had to be overcome partly by force and partly by compromise.[1] The Chalcidians resolved this political crux by anticipating the Romans in the invention of 'dual citizenship': a constitutional device which offered a practical solution for the problem of creating a commonwealth that would combine the city-state structure with the supra-city-state scale.[2] The Chalcidian communities which united to establish 'Greater Olynthus' did not surrender their own respective identities. They continued to exist as city-states of which their members remained citizens. But every citizen of every participating state now became simultaneously a citizen of Greater Olynthus, and his Olynthian citizenship was henceforth of very much greater importance than his local citizenship, because the more important powers and functions of government were now invested in the comprehensive Olynthian body politic while the constituent city-states were reduced to the status of municipalities.

---

[1] See the illuminating account of the synoecism of Megalopolis in Pausanias: *Graeciae Descriptio*, Bk. VIII, ch. 27.

[2] In Hellenic constitutional history, this invention of 'dual citizenship' ($\sigma\upsilon\mu\pi\text{o}\lambda\iota\tau\epsilon\acute{\iota}\alpha$) is the analogue of the invention of 'representative government' in the constitutional history of our Western World. The Western feudal kingdom started life endowed with the political asset of magnitude; and the crucial political problem for Western statesmanship was to organize some method of self-government for a state on this large scale. On the other hand, the Hellenic city-state started life endowed with the asset of self-government; and the crucial political problem for Hellenic statesmanship was to devise some method of creating a state of supra-city-state scale out of a congeries of self-governing and self-conscious city-states. The solution of the Western problem has been to apply to the constitution of deliberative bodies the principle of election, on the analogy of the use of election as a method of appointing executive officials. The solution of the Hellenic problem was 'dual citizenship'.

This new political organization gave the Chalcidians such strength that within forty years, in about the year 392 B.C., they were able to take advantage of a change of rulers in Macedonia and an Illyrian invasion of the Kingdom from the interior in order to extract from a new occupant of the Macedonian throne, King Amyntas III, a treaty which gave the Chalcidian Commonwealth important commercial advantages in Macedonia as the price of a defensive alliance;[1] and this transaction was followed by a transfer of possession—whether in freehold or on lease or on loan—of a large slice of Macedonian territory.[2] A few years later, about 385 B.C., when Amyntas had established himself on his throne and —justifiably or unjustifiably—demanded the transferred territory back, the Chalcidians evidently decided that their hour had struck. They started a military and political offensive on all fronts, with the deliberate object of incorporating into their commonwealth, by persuasion or by coercion, not only the Kingdom of Macedonia but also the still independent non-Chalcidian colonial city-states along the coast. Their forward policy in these years (circa 385–383 B.C.) is vividly described in a speech which Xenophon puts into the mouth of the envoys from two of the threatened states—Acanthus[3] and Apollonia—who came to Sparta to ask for military assistance.[4]

'Gentlemen, we have come to tell you of a portentous political movement in Hellas which has, we fancy, escaped your attention. It is a matter of common knowledge that Olynthus is the most powerful state on the North Aegean Coast. It is a state which has induced other states to unite with it on the basis of a common law and a common citizenship; and on this basis the Olynthians have eventually obtained the adhesion of some states of larger calibre. They have now embarked on a policy of liberating the cities of Macedonia from their lawful sovereign King Amyntas; the nearest of the Macedonian cities have acquiesced, and they have forthwith turned their batteries upon the larger Macedonian cities at a greater distance. By the time when we left home, a large number of Macedonian cities were in the Chalcidians' hands; and the list included Pella, which is the biggest city of which Macedonia can boast. We stayed long enough to see Amyntas evacuating the cities and on the verge of being driven out of Macedonia altogether. The Olynthians have also sent a warning to the Governments of Acanthus and Apollonia that, unless we agree to supply them with a contingent of troops, we must expect them to take military measures against us. Now our own desire, gentlemen, is to go on living under our ancestral laws as citizens of our own city-states; but nevertheless

---

[1] A considerable part of the text of this treaty, including the commercial provisions, has been recovered by our modern Western archaeologists (text in Dittenberger, W.: Sylloge Inscriptionum Graecarum, 3rd ed., No. 135).

[2] For this transfer of territory, see Diodorus of Agyrium: A Library of Universal History, xiv. 92 and xv. 19.

[3] Acanthus was an Andrian colony.   [4] Xenophon: Hellenica, V. ii. 11–19.

we shall find ourselves compelled to join the Olynthians unless some
one comes to our rescue. . . . They already hold Potidaea[1] on the Isthmus
of Pallenê; and you must reckon that the cities on the Pallenê Peninsula[2]
are likely to share Potidaea's fate. In fact, we can give you a striking
piece of evidence of the terror in which those states already live; and
this is that they have not ventured to join us in our present embassy
to you although their hatred of Olynthus is extreme. . . .

'How can you be indifferent to the formation of this new Great Power
—a Power which will be equally strong on land and on sea? They
possess all the elements of sea-power in their abundant local supplies
of timber and in their ample revenues from harbour-dues and trading-
stations and in the great man-power for which they command the
necessary food-supply. Moreover, they have as their neighbours the
republican Thracians[3] who are already the Olynthians' satellites as it
is; and if they actually become their subjects, then Olynthus will gain
another important accession of strength from this quarter. Moreover,
if these Thracians accept Olynthian supremacy, the gold mines on
Mount Pangaeus will be positively inviting the Olynthians to come and
take them. In all that we have been saying to you, there is nothing that
is not being said openly, ten thousand times over, in the Public Assembly
of the Olynthian Commonwealth. Their self-confidence is beyond
description—and possibly it is one of the innate dispositions of Human
Nature that self-confidence should increase in the same ratio as power.

'Well, gentlemen, this is our report on the situation in the North;
and it is now for you to make up your minds whether such a situation
requires intervention on your part. We may perhaps add just this, that,
while we have represented the power of Olynthus as a great power, it
is not yet a power that it would be very difficult to overthrow. The
states that are unwilling partners in the Olynthian Commonwealth will
quickly secede if they see that Olynthus has met her match. But when
once they have been welded together by the mutual grant of reciprocal
civil rights[4] which they have already voted, and when once they have
realized the advantage of throwing in their lot with the paramount
Power, we fear that what the Olynthians have done may prove less easy
to undo.'

This speech would serve, *mutatis mutandis*, for the discourse of
some envoy from one of the Greek city-states in Campania whom
we might imagine arriving at Tarentum, perhaps half a century
later than this, in order to warn the Government of Sparta's
Italian daughter-city about the portentous political movement in
Italy which was gathering momentum in the victorious progress of

[1] A Corinthian colony.—A. J. T.
[2] The principal cities on the Pallenê Peninsula were Eretrian colonies.—A. J. T.
[3] These 'republican Thracians' (Θρᾷκες οἱ ἀβασίλευτοι) are probably the Thracian and
Paeonian communities in the Lower Basin of the River Strymon (Struma), who were
more civilized than the Thracians of the interior and who, for a century past, had felt
their independence to be threatened by the eastward expansion of Macedonia.—A. J. T.
[4] Literally, 'by arrangements for contracting marriages and holding property across
the frontiers'.—A. J. T.

Rome. For Olynthus, in the years 385–383 B.C., had embarked on
a course of political aggrandisement which might conceivably have
carried her to the height of power which Rome actually attained in
the momentous half-century which opened with her first intervention in Campania in 343 B.C. Had the historic appeal of Acanthus
and Apollonia to Sparta fallen on deaf ears, we can imagine, on this
Roman analogy, the successive stages by which Olynthus might
have risen to greatness in the next forty or fifty years. If the Macedonian Plain was her Campania and Pella her Capua in 383 B.C.,
then Upper Macedonia might have become her Samnium[1] and 'the
republican Thracians' her Sabines[2] and the wild Thracians her
Gauls. By one means and another—here using naked force and
there exerting the attraction of a superior culture—she might have
brought within the ambit of her expanding commonwealth the
whole of Northern Greece, with its rough and backward but
vigorous and receptive population.

Like Rome in Italy, Olynthus in Greece was a city-state which
found itself standing in the fourth century B.C. on the geographical
border-line between the modern cosmos of city-states and the old-
fashioned pre-city-state penumbra of the Hellenic World at a
moment when the peoples of the penumbra were being impelled
by the stimulus of their long irradiation with the intrusive city-
state culture to adopt the city-state régime and to participate in the
life of the city-state society. This was evidently a favourable
moment for some strong and far-sighted and ambitious city-state
on the border line to expand its own commonwealth to a supra-city-
state scale by incorporating the territory and man-power of an
awakening barbarian world which was still politically malleable because it was still free from any unforgettable political memories or
unalterable political habits.[3] And if Olynthian statesmanship had

[1] The Kingdom of Macedon in the Salonican Campania, whose capital city of Pella
was momentarily incorporated into the Olynthian Commonwealth *circa* 385–383 B.C.,
had been founded by Macedonian Greek conquerors from the highlands of the interior,
just as Capua and the other Oscan city-states of the Italian Campania had been founded
—or occupied—by Oscan conquerors from the highlands of Samnium (the Abruzzi).
In the early fourth century B.C., the three cantons of Upper Macedonia (Elimea, Orestis
and Lyncus) were in much the same stage of civilization as the cantons of Samnium
(Caraceni, Pentri, Caudini, Hirpini) half a century later. No doubt they would have
fought as hard to expel the Olynthians from the territory of their Macedonian kinsmen
in the lowlands as the Samnites actually fought to expel the Romans from Capua; and
no doubt, like the Samnites, they would have eventually succumbed to the superior
organization and superior culture of their city-state antagonist.

[2] Linguistically, these 'republican Thracians' may have had as close an affinity with
the Olynthians as the Sabines had with the Romans. At any rate, two of these particular
'Thracian' communities, namely the Odomanti and the Tynteni (the latter are known
only from their coins), were presumably kinsmen of their homonyms the Athamanes and
Atintanes in Epirus; and these two Epirot peoples were presumably Greek-speaking.
(The Odomanti appear to be identical with Herodotus's Siropaeones or Paeonians of Siris
(the modern Serrhes). Compare Herodotus, v. 15 and 115, with Livy, xlv. 4.)

[3] For the psychological plasticity of the inhabitants of 'new countries' see p. 303,
footnote 1, above.

been allowed the same free hand in Northern Greece as Roman
statesmanship was actually allowed in Central Italy, we can carry
our hypothetical analogy farther. We can imagine that when
Olynthus had consolidated in the North a commonwealth on an
overwhelmingly larger scale than any of the historic city-states of
Central Greece and the Peloponnese, she might have completed
her political mission by eventually incorporating into her commonwealth the southern half of the Greek Peninsula, as Rome eventually incorporated Magna Graecia and Sicily into hers. In Thessaly
Olynthus might have found her Apulia, in Aetolia her Lucania, in
Athens and Sparta her Tarentum and her Syracuse; and the Achaemenian Power might have met at Olynthian hands the fate which
Roman hands inflicted upon Carthage.

In the actual event, the fortunes of Olynthus and of Rome turned
out quite differently; for whereas Tarentum neglected to oppose
the aggrandisement of Rome till it was just too late to undo the
constructive work of Roman statesmanship,[1] the Spartan Government exerted itself at once to nip the political development of
Olynthus in the bud. A Lacedaemonian expeditionary force was
sent to the North in 382 B.C.; and within three years the ambitions
of Olynthus had been frustrated once and for all. In 379 B.C.
Olynthus had to capitulate to her Lacedaemonian besiegers; and
the principal point in the Lacedaemonian peace-terms was that the
Chalcidian Commonwealth should be dissolved into its original
constituents. In thus overthrowing Olynthus, Sparta was unwittingly working not for herself and not for Hellas but for the
Crown of Macedon. For it was Sparta's intervention between
Olynthus and Macedon in 382–379 B.C. that gave King Philip his
opportunity to make himself master of all Continental Greece
between 359 B.C. and 338. Thirty years after the time when Sparta
saved Macedon from Olynthus, another call for help against a rising
Power was heard from the North; and this time the roles were reversed. In 349 B.C., it was the city-state of Olynthus that was the
Northern victim and the Kingdom of Macedon that was the
Northern aggressor. The danger was just as real and just as urgent
as it had been on the earlier occasion. But in Southern Greece
times had changed; and not all the eloquence of a Demosthenes
could move the Athenians to intervene now in the effective manner
of Sparta in 382. Accordingly, in 349–348 B.C., the dissevered cities
of Chalcidicê fell one after another until the Macedonian triumph
was consummated by the fall of the *ci-devant* Chalcidian metropolis

[1] The Tarentines did their best by enlisting the services of the most destructive of the
Epigoni. Yet even Pyrrhus's sword, which worked such political havoc in Continental
Greece, was incapable of hewing in pieces the sinewy body politic which Roman
statesmanship had created in Italy.

Olynthus itself. And this time the Chalcidians received no mercy. Their lands were confiscated and their persons were either sold into slavery or deported into the interior. Therewith, the common-wealth that had aspired, a generation earlier, to become the new Northern Power was utterly blotted out. There had been no such act of barbarism in Hellenic history since the notorious destruction of Sybaris; and unhappily the fate of Olynthus in 348 B.C. was to become a precedent. In 335 B.C. the same fate was to overtake Thebes at the hands of Philip's son, and thereafter it was to over-take Syracuse and Tarentum and Corinth at the hands of the Romans.[1]

Thus, in the event, the new Northern Power that was to unify European Greece was established, not by the Olynthian Common-wealth, but by the Kingdom of Macedon; and in 338 B.C., when King Philip crowned his extraordinary achievement by routing the Athenians at Chaeronea and invading Laconia,[2] the Athenians assuredly regretted their lukewarmness and the Spartans their hostility towards Olynthus twelve years and forty years earlier. Between them, the two leading city-states of Southern Continental Greece had allowed the primitive institution of monarchy, which had been on the verge of extinction in the Hellenic World, to rise almost from the grave and to reassert its ascendancy over the cos-mos of city-states, not only in Northern Greece, but in the whole Hellenic World to the east of the Ionian Sea.

In the long run, no doubt, this anachronistic recrudescence of monarchy in the Hellenic World did not avail to deflect the course on which Hellenic history was already set. By the fourth century B.C., the city-state régime had become so thoroughly bred into the bone of the Hellenic Society that it could not be bred out again by anything short of the final dissolution of the Society itself; and, on a long view, the sensational triumph of monarchy in the careers of Philip and Alexander was ineffective and ephemeral. Though Hellenic monarchy in the person of Alexander accomplished one tremendous deed of destruction in the break-up of the Achaeme-nian Empire, the only constructive achievement of Alexander and his successors in Asia that had any enduring effect was the calling into existence, *in partibus Orientalium*, of a vast new world of Hel-lenic city-states. Moreover, in the Hellenic West, the aping of

---

[1] For the destruction of Greek communities by the Romans in the age of Polybius, see p. 312, above.
[2] For the transfer of the territory of Dentheliâtis from Spartan to Messenian sover-eignty on this occasion, see the passage quoted from Tacitus in Part III. A, on p. 78, above. On the same occasion, Philip cut Laconia short in other directions as well by putting Tegea and Megalopolis in possession of the debatable territories on the northern frontier, and Argos in possession of the Thyreâtis and Cynuria. (For details see Beloch, K. J.: *Griechische Geschichte*, iii (i), 2nd ed. (Berlin and Leipzig 1922, de Gruyter), pp. 574-5.)

Macedonian royalty by the latter-day despots of Syracuse was not imitated by the new non-Greek Great Powers that were rising on the periphery of the Hellenic World in this quarter. Both the Roman Commonwealth and the Carthaginian Empire were built up on a city-state basis; and this triumph of the city-state in the West secured the ultimate victory to the city-state throughout the Hellenic World, since it was the Roman Commonwealth that delivered 'the knock-out blow' in the internecine warfare between the new Hellenic Great Powers of the supra-city-state calibre. The last round of this struggle was fought between the Roman Commonwealth and the Macedonian Kingdom; and when Macedon suffered her final disaster in 168 B.C. the Macedonian Monarchy which had been reprieved by Spartan arms in 382–379 was deliberately abolished by Roman policy. In the peace settlement that followed the overthrow of King Perseus after the Battle of Pydna, the territory of his *ci-devant* kingdom was rearticulated by Roman commissioners into four confederacies of city-states, and therewith the political transformation of Macedonia, which Olynthian statesmanship had attempted two centuries earlier, was accomplished at last.

Thereafter, in the penultimate phase of Hellenic history, the Hellenic universal state that was established within the framework of the Roman Empire took the form of an immense confederacy of city-states encircling the Mediterranean. And thus the city-state asserted itself decisively, as the master-institution of the Hellenic Society, at the end of the story as well as at the beginning. Yet, even so, the historical consequences of the monarchical interlude were important enough.

One consequence was the forfeiture by Continental Greece of its political supremacy in the Hellenic World and the transfer of the sceptre into the hands of a non-Greek city-state in Italy. In an earlier passage in this Study,[1] we have observed that, in the deadly competition for an exclusive and permanent dominion over the Hellenic World, the two Powers that survived to encounter one another in the last round were the two Powers that were guarding the continental marches of the Hellenic World, against the European Barbarism, at the root of the Greek Peninsula and at the root of the Italian Peninsula respectively. As things turned out, it was the Greek Power that succumbed and the Italian Power that was victorious; but we may fairly speculate whether the outcome would have been the same if the warden of the Continental Greek marches in the second century B.C. had been not the Macedonian Kingdom but an Olynthian Commonwealth.

[1] In II. D (v), vol. ii, pp. 160–3, above.

The fatal weakness of the Macedonian Kingdom at the time
when it had to measure its strength against Rome lay in its failure
to weld the whole of Continental Greece together into a single
commonwealth as the Roman city-state had welded the whole of
Italy. This critical time found Continental Greece once more
divided against herself and therefore impotent to put forth the
political and military strength which would have been at her command if only she could have united her forces. And the apple
of discord was the principle of monarchy; for the city-states of
Southern Greece had never been able to reconcile themselves to
the Pan-Hellenic union under the presidency of the Macedonian
Crown which had been imposed upon them by King Philip II in
338 B.C. Philip's Pan-Hellenic Confederacy did not survive the
scramble for power among the successors of Alexander. From
the morrow of Alexander's death in 323 B.C. until the outbreak
of the last Romano-Macedonian War in 171, Continental Greece
was wasting her strength in an inconclusive and interminable
domestic conflict between Northern Monarchy and Southern Republicanism.[1] And it was this domestic conflict that rendered
Continental Greece impotent to intervene effectively in the Hannibalic War, when the destinies of the Hellenic World were being
finally decided. After the Battle of Cannae, King Philip V of
Macedon did indeed enter the arena on the side of the momentarily
victorious but fundamentally weaker of the two antagonists. His
action, however, was almost paralysed by a fear—which was to be
justified by the event—that Aetolia might take the opportunity to
attack him on the flank; and for this reason his intervention had
no decisive effect upon the issue of the struggle between Rome and
Carthage and simply served to implant in the Roman Government's minds a determination to make themselves secure in Greece
as soon as their hands were free in Italy.

If the North-Greek Great Power had been established in the
fourth century B.C. by the Chalcidian Commonwealth instead of
by the Macedonian Crown, the course of Greek history during the
next two hundred years might have been very different; for if a
commonwealth of city-states had succeeded in welding together

[1] We have touched upon some aspects of this conflict already in examining the social
milieu of Polybius. In the first stage, the city-states of Southern Greece won a partial and
fitful independence from the Crown of Macedon by allowing themselves to become the
pawns of the Crown of Egypt in the diplomatic game between the Great Powers of the
periphery. The policy of the Aetolian and Achaean Confederacies was to weld the
shrunken city-state cosmos of Southern Greece into a Central Power strong enough to
insist upon holding aloof from the combats between the surrounding monarchies.
(Compare the project, which was mooted in Germany between A.D. 1815 and 1866, for a
Confederation of German States from which Prussia as well as Austria was to be
excluded.) We have seen how the Aetolian and Achaean policy broke down in the last
three decades of the third century B.C.

all the territories and peoples that were actually united under the Macedonian Crown by King Philip II, this Power would have possessed a combination of qualities which was never possessed by either Macedon or Thebes or Sparta or Athens. A Chalcidian Commonwealth would have enjoyed the material advantage of the supra-city-state scale which was enjoyed by Macedonia, but was lacking to the three city-states that had tried and failed before her to achieve the political union of Greece, and at the same time a Chalcidian Commonwealth would have possessed a spiritual asset which was lacking to Macedonia. As a commonwealth of city-states, it would have been recognized to be a polity of the same species as the historic city-states of the South; and therefore Thebes and Athens and Sparta, when they bowed to the new Great Power's overwhelmingly superior strength, would not have been inwardly humiliated and alienated, as they actually were in 338 B.C., by a feeling that they were submitting themselves, under sheer *force majeure*, to a barbarous and reactionary régime which was the very negation of everything that the city-state had stood for since its first emergence.

The Roman historian Livy, in a celebrated passage,[1] has speculated upon what would have happened if, in the fourth century B.C., Alexander the Great had turned his arms against the Roman Commonwealth. On this distinguished precedent we may venture to put an imaginary question of our own. What would have been the course of history if the career of Alexander the Great and the career of his father Philip had been ruled out *a priori* by the previous incorporation of Macedonia into a vast Chalcidian Commonwealth of city-states? In that event might not Hannibal, on the morrow of Cannae, have found himself able to summon to his aid a politically united Greece which would have been a Power of the same calibre as Roman Italy? And in the face of such overwhelming odds as these, could Rome have avoided the fate which actually overtook Olynthus in 348 and Macedon in 168 and Carthage in 146 B.C?

[1] Titi Livi, *ab Urbe Condita*, Liber IX, caps. xvii–xix.

INDEX[1]

Ababdeh, the, i. 308.

Abāqā, Il-Khān, i. 358.

'Abbasid Caliphate, of Baghdad: as Syriac universal state, i. 67, 72, 76–7, 105, 155; ii. 141, 235; iii. 322; as warden of marches, i. 376; ii. 141 seqq.; break-up of, i. 67–8, 71 n., 105, 356, 357, 360, 364; ii. 76, 142, 165, 237, 244, 367; iii. 322, 441, 445, 473; Buwayhid domination of, i. 355, 356; ii. 142, 448; centre of gravity of, i. 74, 349; conquest of Umayyads, i. 58, 73 seqq., 107 n.; ii. 141, 142 n., 204 n.; decline of, i. 356, 359; ii. 448 n.; iii. 441, 474; foundation of, i. 73, 354; ii. 141; Jews, status of, ii. 243–4; range of, i. 105, 107; revolts against, i. 354–6; successor-states of, i. 68; ii. 78, 142, 144; iii. 29, 30; unification of territories under, i. 74 seqq. See also under INDUS VALLEY; SALJŪQS; SLAVERY.

'Abbasid Caliphate, of Cairo: as ghost of Baghdad Caliphate, i. 67 n., 70, 360, 396; ii. 75–6; extinction of, i. 72. See also under MAMLŪKS.

'Abd-al-'Azīz Āl Sa'ūd, see IBN SA'ŪD.

'Abdallāh b. Maymūn, i. 355.

'Abd-ar-Rahmān (invader of Gaul), ii. 361, 362, 379, 380, 427 seqq.

'Abd-ar-Rahmān ibn Muhammad ibn Khaldūn al-Hadramī, see IBN KHALDŪN.

Abu 'l-Ghāzi Khān Uzbeg, ii. 150.

Abu 'l-Khayr Khān Uzbeg, i. 373.

Abu Muslim, ii. 141.

Abu Sa'īd the Timurid, Sultan, ii. 149.

Abu Tālib, iii. 468, 471.

Abyssinia, i. 259; backwardness of, ii. 364–5, 367; conversion to Christianity, ii. 364 n., 366, 406; Coptic Monophysite Christians of, ii. 258, 270, 364–5, 403; iii. 137; culture of, ii. 365; Islam, impact of, ii. 365–6, 403; isolation of, i. 29; ii. 365, 366; Jews of (Falasha), ii. 257, 259, 270, 271, 312, 365, 403, 406–7; iii. 137; language of, ii. 365; physiography of, ii. 365, 367; political independence of, ii. 365; racial origin of people of, i. 215; stimulus, absence of, ii. 366–7, 384; Western nations, relations with, ii. 366–7. See also under ETHIOPIA; SLAVERY.

Acciajuoli, the, iii. 374 n.

Achaean Confederacy, the, iii. 274, 312 seqq., 339–41, 357 n., 365 n., 368, 488. See also under SPARTA.

Achaeans, the: as external proletariat of Minoan World, i. 333; ii. 316; as fathers of Hellenic Civilization, i. 100, 333; ii. 315–17, 320, 321, 360, 434, 436, 439, 442, 443; iii. 2 n., 113, 117; culture of, ii. 319, 355–6; irruption of, into Minoan World, i. 93, 96, 100, 101 n., 104, 116, 410; ii. 439; iii. 113, 444; language of, i. 101 n.; migration of, into Asia, i. 101–2, 114 n.; iii. 444; origin of, i. 217; settlements of, in Italy, i. 114 n.; ii. 85; — on Greek mainland, ii. 85. See also under AKHAIWOI.

Achaemenian Empire, the: as Syriac universal state, i. 78, 119; ii. 21, 76; iii. 141, 448; as warden of Syriac marches, i. 376, 380; ii. 138–9, 141, 143, 146, 147, 448–9; break-up of, i. 5, 59, 75, 76; ii. 21 n., 79, 139, 141 n., 142, 281, 285, 288; iii. 197, 445, 486; capital of, i. 119; ii. 124 n.; expansion of, i. 78 n.; ii. 76, 114, 116, 138–9, 203; iii. 138 n. (See also under EGYPT; OXUS-JAXARTES BASIN); Hellenic World, relations with, see under HELLENIC CIVILIZATION; genesis of, i. 78, 81; ii. 139; languages of, i. 81; physiography of, ii. 21, 139–40; range of, ii. 370; reintegration of, in 'Abbasid and Umayyad Caliphates, i. 58–9, 76–7, 86, 155; ii. 11 n., 76, 77 n., 140, 202, 203, 235, 288, 370, 411; iii. 276 n., 466, 473; successor-states of, i. 86; ii. 11 n., 79, 143, 281; iii. 310. See also under CAMBYSES; CARTHAGE; CYRUS; DARIUS; XERXES.

Achilles, myth of, iii. 117.

Açoka Maurya, Emperor, i. 85, 86, 87–8 n., 91 n.; ii. 352 n.; iii. 191.

Acre, fall of (1291), ii. 172, 451.

Action: fields of, iii. 223 seqq., 289; identity of, with life, iii. 235; source of, iii. 230 seqq. See also under INDIVIDUALS.

---

[1] In the cross-references in this index, references in small capitals (e.g. INDUS VALLEY, &c., at the end of the heading 'Abbasid Caliphate) are to other main headings, while references in ordinary type are to sub-divisions of the same main heading.

2¼.48

Printed in Great Britain by Jarrold & Sons, Ltd., Norwich